THE NATION TRANSFORMED

The Creation of an Industrial Society

THE NATION TRANSFORMED

The Creation of an Industrial Society

SELECTED AND EDITED WITH INTRODUCTION
AND NOTES BY

Sigmund Diamond

GEORGE BRAZILLER

NEW YORK 1963

ACKNOWLEDGMENTS

Selection from Mary Antin, *The Promised Land*, reprinted with the permission of the Houghton Mifflin Company, Boston. Copyright 1912.

Selections from Alan Conway, ed., *The Welsh in America: Letters from the Immigrants*, reprinted with the permission of the University of Minnesota Press, Minneapolis. Copyright 1961.

Selection from William Graham Sumner, "The Bequests of the Nineteenth Century to the Twentieth," in Albert G. Keller and Maurice R. Davie, eds., *Essays of W. G. Sumner*, reprinted with the permission of the Yale University Press, New Haven. Copyright 1934.

To
Arthur H. Cole
and
Frederick Merk
to whom everything is owed

Preface

The period Sigmund Diamond deals with in these pages has come to be known as "The Gilded Age." It was one of the most fascinating and frustrating eras in American history. The years between Reconstruction and the Progressive Era brought both prosperity and depression, unprecedented abundance and shocking poverty. Rapidly expanding production in factories and on farms created material wealth from which the large middle class did assuredly benefit. The wealth brought also a variety of cultural advances in the growing American cities: universities, medical schools, libraries, and museums. The advent of large-scale manufacturing led to a shift in political and economic hegemony from the agrarians to the industrialists, and with the shift came maladjustments that reformers as yet could do little to rectify. Never before or since in American history have the rich been so rich and the poor so poor.

It was these defects in the new society of abundance that earned it an ironic label. In 1873 when Mark Twain and Charles Dudley Warner published their novel, *The Gilded Age*, they apologized in satiric vein for not having been able to find examples in the United States of the society they were spoofing:

"In a state where there is no fever of speculation, no inflamed desire for sudden wealth, where the poor are all simpleminded and contented, and the rich are all honest and generous, where society is in a condition of primitive purity, and politics is the occupation of only the capable and patriotic, there are necessarily no materials for such a history as we have constructed."

These years were more distinguished for what was gilt than for what was golden, but they form a vital part of American historical development. Sigmund Diamond, through his analytic introductions and fresh, illuminating selections, recreates the age in all its raw youth, grandeur and misery, and promise of a better future. The pages that follow cover the sweep of social, economic, and intellectual history from the Philadelphia Exposition of 1876 to the St. Louis Exposition of 1904. It is a brilliant panorama.

FRANK FREIDEL

Contents

CONTENTS

CONTENTS xi

a man who has failed to yield to [the union's] argument and has
gone to work? . . . A. . . . it depends upon the temperament of the
man. We would go after him a hundred and one ways, if we can,
to drive him out of the community.
Q. You don't know of his offending the labor people in any
way? . . . A. I suppose he disobeyed the laws of the unions. They
say, "We will run you out of town." "Ain't you gone yet?" "Your
time will come." Well, not with the wife he has.

The Philosophy of Organized Labor—*Samuel Gompers, Witness* 206
Q. Do you not think it is true that the average legislator is very
anxious to please the working people and to promote their interests . . . ?—A. The average legislator is not a very courageous man.

The Sweat-Shops—*A Report* 218
In Chicago . . . the sweating system seems to be a direct outgrowth of the factory system; that is, the sweat-shops have gradually superseded the manufacturers' shops.

How the Other Half Lives—*Jacob A. Riis* 231
The endless panorama of the tenements, rows upon rows, between
stony streets, stretches to the north, to the south, and to the west
as far as the eye reaches.

Letters from Welsh Immigrants 254
The white man [of West Virginia] is about the most contemptible
person on the face of God's earth. He is unbearably ignorant and
does not know it. . . . These detestable cranks seem to think that
the poor niggar was made to receive their insults and brutality.

The *Padrone* System—*A Report* 268
The padrone system, or bossism, can be defined as the forced
tribute the newly arrived [Italian immigrant] pays to those who
are already acquainted with the ways and language of the
country.

Ward Politics and the Gangs—*Robert A. Woods* 276
Almost every boy in the tenement-house quarters of the district
is member of a gang. The boy who does not belong to one is not
only the exception, but the very rare exception.

The Public School: Maker of Americans—*Mary Antin* 285
The public school has done its best for us foreigners, and for the
country, when it has made us into good Americans.

The Newsboys of New York—*Helen Campbell* 295
They began as "street rats," . . . and pilfered and gnawed at all

our faith in this ultimate triumph of good over evil. Our survey began with pictures of horrid slaughter and desolation; it ends with the picture of a world covered with cheerful homesteads, blessed with a Sabbath of perpetual peace.

THE NATION TRANSFORMED

The Creation of an Industrial Society

Introduction

Sigmund Diamond

1

On May 10, 1876, a gigantic throng of more than one hundred thousand people—tired and hot, but eager with anticipation—swarmed into Fairmount Park, Philadelphia, in quest of the excitement that only a world's fair can offer. Fifteen bitter years had passed since the guns had boomed across the harbor at Charleston, South Carolina; and though peace had brought relief and gratitude, a nation still distracted and tormented by the problems of Reconstruction and caught fast in the grip of a relentless depression had had little cause for enthusiastic celebration. But on the morning of May 10, the season of celebration began. The great centennial exposition was being opened by the President of the United States; and in honoring those whose efforts had forged national unity in 1776, Americans of 1876 found at last what had so long eluded them—that pride in an accomplishment to which all had contributed might provide the basis for a new-found unity and hope. What at the beginning had been an untried form of government, a republic, had survived a century of the cruelest buffeting, of international wars and civil wars—and still it stood. It was reason enough for gratitude and for celebration.

But there were still other reasons, less weighty but perhaps even closer to the hearts and minds of the thousands who made their way to the exhibition hall that dwarfed the best that the expositions of Paris and Dresden had offered and that shamed even Queen Victoria's Crystal Palace. They came to gawk at the celebrities—at President Grant, at Dom Pedro, the Emperor of Brazil, at the ambassadors from the royal courts of exotic China and Austria-Hungary and the Tsar of all the Russias. They came to hear the President speak of "the specimens of their skill" that had been sent by "the enlightened agricultural, commercial, and manufacturing people of the world. . . ." Above all, they came to see the wonders that they and others had created. There were the exotic products of far-off places—porcelains and tapestries from France, teak and ivory from Siam,

3

sables from Russia, delicate china from Bavaria, Japanese toys which
seemed, to American eyes, only slightly more dainty than Japanese people. There were the innocent products that lent delight—miniature music-
boxes; a pretty black marble fountain "which sent up a constant jet of
cologne water, where the tired visitor might enjoy the delightful privilege
of bathing his forehead with the refreshing liquid"; the newest thing in
automatic soda fountains, the Minnehaha, made of Tennessee and Italian
marble and decorated with bronze dolphins and silver crowns and a lion's
head from which the bubbly liquid flowed. There were the less innocent
products—Gatling guns and Dahlgren torpedoes and Krupp cannon.
Above all, there were the miraculous inventions that were changing the
world—steel bridges, giant locomotives, and that amazing source of power,
the Corliss steam engine whose 1,500 horses provided all the power
needed for the Exposition.

Painting, music, and sculpture were pushed off into the wings; technology and industry held the center of the stage. "The farmer saw new
machines, seeds, and processes," the official handbook of the centennial
concluded; "the mechanic, ingenious inventions and tools, and products
of the finest workmanship . . . the man of science, the wonders of nature
and the results of the investigation of the best brains of all lands. Thus
each returned to his own home with a store of information available in
his own special trade or profession." There were some, a few, who
wondered at the absence of exhibits of some characteristics of American
life. When puzzled Columbia asked what she should display, James
Russell Lowell's Brother Jonathan answered tartly:

> Show 'em your Civil Service, and explain
> How all men's loss is everybody's gain;
> Show your new patents to increase your rents
> By paying quarters for collecting cents;
> Show your short cut to cure financial ills
> By making paper-collars current bills;
> Show your new bleaching process, cheap and brief,
> To wit: a jury chosen by the thief;
> Show your State Legislatures; show your Rings;
> And challenge Europe to produce such things
> As high officials sitting half in sight
> To share the plunder and to fix things right;
> If that don't fetch her, why, you only need
> To show your latest style in martyrs—Tweed . . .[1]

And there were even those who raised portentous questions about the
nature of a society which could produce such an exposition. Eugène
Pottier, author of *The Internationale,* living in exile in the United States,
caught a glimpse of a dark and bloody future in the midst of the gaiety:

. . . Let us get to the bottom of things.
Industry, is this, then, the spectacle for which you propose
                    That we judge you?
You clothe yourself in striking colors;
But we who know bloody rags,
                    We will exhibit them.
Yes, we will exhibit the hollow bellies of the masses,
Their wan poverty full of dark threats
                    To stability,
The poorest bowed down under the heaviest taxes,
In your topsy-turvy world revolving about the false axis
                    Of Property.
Exhibit your pride. These brick Bastilles,
Powerful prisons that you call factories,
                    And which we must tear down,
And the sad slaves, sealed in their cells,
Not knowing the sun and the clean country air,
Do you want to exhibit them? . . .[2]

But this was still the New World, for all that the country was a century
old, and most Americans were more likely to see promises than problems.
For them, it was Walt Whitman who saw in the exposition the true vision
of things to come.

Away with old romance!
Away with novels, plots and plays of foreign courts,
Away with love verses sugar'd in rhyme, the intrigues, amours of idlers . . .
I raise a voice for far superber things for poets and for art,
To exalt the present and the real,
To teach the average man the glory of his daily walk and trade,
To sing in song how exercise and chemical life are never to be baffled,
To manual work for each and all, to plough, hoe, dig,
To plant and tend the tree, the berry, vegetables, flowers,
For every man to see to it that he really do something, for every woman too;
To use the hammer and the saw, (rip, or cross-cut,)
To cultivate a turn for carpentering, plastering, painting,
To work as tailor, tailoress, nurse, hostler, porter,
To invent a little, something ingenious, to aid the washing, cooking, cleaning,
And hold it no disgrace to take a hand at them themselves. . . .

The American people were engaged in a great task of construction.
"Mightier than Egypt's tombs . . . fairer than Roma's temples," they
planned to raise a

                    great cathedral sacred industry, no tomb,
                    A keep for life for practical invention.[3]

And in the excitement of the task there was little concern for still un-
solved problems of the previous half century and but dim anticipation
of the new problems their own enterprise would create.

2

One day while floating along on the river, Huck Finn's raft encountered
a steamboat. "She was a big one, and she was coming in a hurry, too . . .
All of a sudden she bulged out, big and scary, with a long row of wide-
open furnace doors shining like red-hot teeth. . . ." For the American
people, the encounter with the last third of the nineteenth century must
have been like Huck's with the steamboat; strange, new forces were loose
that threatened to run over the old familiar, but flimsy, shelters. A new
society—an industrial society—was being created, and its creation involved
the uprooting and transplanting of millions of people, the raising of new
groups to power and the decline of the once-powerful, the learning of
new routines and habits and disciplines, the sloughing off of old ideas.
Nothing was left untouched—the state itself in its relation to citizens, the
churches, the family; all were altered because the circumstances of life
itself were being altered.

Behind these changes—beneficent to some, cataclysmic to others—lay
a new method of production, based on factory and machine, with an
increasingly refined technology that made use of ever-increasing supplies
of capital and specialized labor. Regional differences remained, though,
with the passage of time these tended to be more important to local-
colorist writers, exploiting a nostalgia for the past, than to men-of-affairs,
for whom it was the present reality of a great national market, welded
together by a network of railroads and communications, that was to be
exploited. And while the face of the land was itself being made over, so,
too, were the millions of men and women from rural America and from
Europe, who, pouring into the new industrial centers of the nation, were
subjected to the new discipline of factory labor. With startling speed, a
nation of farmers and small-town merchants began to learn, if not wholly
to master, the techniques of an industrial society.

During the two decades after 1870, industrial growth in the United
States reached a pace the world had not yet seen. In 1870, mining and
manufacturing contributed only 14 percent to the national income; farming, 20 percent. By the end of the century, the contribution of farming—
reduced now to 16 percent—was matched by that of finance, while the
contribution of mining and manufacturing rose to 21 percent. In that
year, the world's largest producer of food and raw materials had become
as well the world's largest manufacturer. Total population, benefiting
from both a high birth rate and immigration, rose rapidly, from 40 million in 1870 to 76 million in 1900, but the increase was not evenly
distributed throughout the country; some occupations and some sections

grew more rapidly than others. Just under 60 percent of the American labor force worked on farms in 1860, but only 37 percent in 1900; only 26 percent worked in industry and transportation in 1860, but 46 percent did so in 1900. If the small New England town and Middle Western river entrepôt were characteristic of an earlier landscape, they were being roughly shouldered aside towards the end of the century by mill towns, steel towns, coal towns that sprang up it seemed almost everywhere.

Most spectacular, of course, was the growth of the great city, that most characteristic institution of an industrial society. In 1860, one-sixth of the American people lived in urban areas; in 1900, one-third. During that stretch of four decades, the population of the great cities grew more than twice as fast as that of the country as a whole. By the end of the century New York, Chicago, and Philadelphia were all booming metropolises, each with well over one million people. Rural Massachusetts, having pretty much disappeared from the census returns, was to be found mainly in the poems of John Greenleaf Whittier; as early as 1890, four out of every five persons in that state were town dwellers.

Nor was the landscape of the mind unaffected. When once sturdy farmers had become rural hicks, when slick traders had become captains of industry, when the hub of affairs had shifted from countinghouse to banking house, standards which had once been settled became problematic. To swim with the new tide of affairs meant to choose a new career and a new place to live, to learn new skills and new ideas. And even those who fought to preserve the old had to contend with the forces that threatened to make their world obsolete. Whether one tried to swim with the tide or hold it back or change its course made little difference. It provided the environment in which life was lived and, sometimes subtly, sometimes ruthlessly, forced men to alter the ways in which they worked and thought.

Behind these changes lay a revolution that began in transportation and communication and spread quickly to the processes of production and distribution. Railroads had long since surpassed canals in importance, but their own expansion had been slowed by the Civil War. Between 1870, however, and 1893, when the depression again slowed the momentum of development, the mileage of railroads increased from 30,000 to 170,000; by 1900, it rose to 193,000. As early as 1887, nearly 33,000 towns were served by the railroad network. It was the hope that the development of cheap transportation would permit them to reach out to distant markets that spurred the merchants of Boston, Baltimore, New York, Philadelphia, and dozens of inland towns to mobilize the capital and skills necessary to lay down the railroad network. Sometimes these hopes proved illusory, sometimes realistic, but in any case the development of the railroad was the major economic stimulus of the post–Civil War period.

First of all, railroad construction itself provided a direct stimulus to industrial production. With a labor force that mushroomed to 200,000 by the 1880's, the railroads were an enormous market for the products of stone quarries, lumber mills, and iron factories and for the excess capital of domestic and, especially, foreign investors. Most important, of course, was the effect on the basic iron and steel industry. In 1874, Sir Lowthian Bell, a Middlesborough ironmaster, maintained that iron would never be produced more cheaply in the United States than in Britain because of the high cost of labor and of transporting iron ore to coal.[4] Even as he spoke his forecast was being disproved. By linking the sections of the country with each other, the railroad made it possible to bring together more efficiently and cheaply the elements of industrial production. The railroad not only created the demand for rails, locomotives, rolling stock, and bridges, but it provided the conditions for satisfying the demand—a fast, cheap, certain method for bringing iron ore to coal.

By 1875, railroads consumed more than half the iron produced in the United States, and their insatiable demands were producing far-reaching technological changes within the industry. Rolling mills and blast furnaces, using coke, could turn out iron at ten times the pace of the old charcoal-fueled ovens. No longer did scarce supplies of expensive charcoal provide a limiting factor on the size of the furnace; fed on unlimited supplies of cheap coal from western Pennsylvania and stimulated by the appetite of the railroads, the size of the furnaces increased steadily. Blast furnaces which before the Civil War were producing at an average daily rate of 40 tons were producing a daily average of more than 400 tons at the turn of the century. Not even the great depression of the 1870's could markedly delay the rapid growth of the steel industry. Steel production rose from 140,000 tons in 1873, to 500,000 in 1877, to 2,500,000 in 1886. By the end of the century, only twenty-five years after Sir Lowthian Bell had made his gloomy forecast of the prospects of the American steel industry, the Carnegie Steel Company alone was turning out about four-fifths as much steel as the entire British industry.

But the railroad stimulated the economy in yet another way, by creating the great national market that made mass production possible. Local producers who had dominated regional markets now faced the competition of products manufactured in distant factories and hauled to every section of the country by the railroad. The growth in size of markets encouraged businessmen to produce in larger quantities to take advantage of lower costs and to experiment in the development of low-cost mass-production methods. Andrew Carnegie's lieutenant, Charles M. Schwab, reported that Carnegie once tore down and rebuilt a new steel mill because they had learned, during its construction, how to save one dollar per ton rather than the fifty cents on the output of the first design. Spurred on to reduce costs to lower and lower levels so as to capture wider markets, the steel industry brought down the price of steel rails from $160 per ton in 1875 to $17 in 1898. Other industries felt the impact of the same forces. Textile manufacturing, meat packing, canning, and flour milling, for example, had long passed the pioneering stage of mass production when it was introduced into the automobile industry so dramatically by Henry Ford in 1914.

The rapid development of American industry depended not only upon changes in technology—as in the case of mass production—but also upon changes in organization. Standardization of parts, long practiced in the Connecticut gun industry, spread to other industries—sewing machines and clocks, for example—and eventually into the standardization of the final assembly of products. Nor was the drive for rationalization confined to the workshop. Office, accounting department, and sales division were subjected to increasingly rigorous supervision in an attempt to cut costs by providing standardized methods of procedure. Organization—as well as land, labor, and capital—was seen to be a variable influencing the level of costs and productivity, and fundamental changes were made in traditional modes of assigning tasks in shop and office, supervising the activities of the work force, determining the proper relation of supervisory to production personnel, and determining the locus of authority within the business enterprise. In these circumstances, when new products and new processes were being introduced of a complexity never before encountered, the nature of work itself changed.

There was room for the handyman in the village, but not in the factory. When production depended increasingly upon the performance of specified, even measured, tasks, the Jack-of-all-trades had to yield to the specialist. And specialization was not a characteristic of a specific industry, a specific region, a specific trade. What Professor Thomas C. Cochran has called the "general entrepreneur" of the pre–Civil War period—the man who shifted his interests easily between foreign trade, wholesaling, banking, and real estate, for example—made way for the man whose career was confined to a particular industry. Specialist workmen replaced general artisans; specialist retailers replaced the general store; the investment banking houses that specialized in the flotation of stocks and bonds were different from the bankers who gave short-term credit to business. Undirected and unplanned, a far-flung network of connections developed between individuals and groups whose relationships depended not on personal choice or face-to-face contact but on the particular position each occupied in the processes of production and exchange. For some, power and influence were the results; for others, apparent impotence; but so tightly woven were the relationships that few could act without affecting the lives of countless nameless others.

The problems of adjustment would have been great even if the rate of industrial progress had been steady and continuous. The fact is, however, that it was sporadic, and the combination of discontinuity in development and complexity in organization made for an increasingly unstable economy whose alternating cycles of expansion and contraction brought bewildering uncertainty. To compete successfully for markets required the application of the latest techniques of science and technology to reduce costs to competitive levels. The very costs of modernization were so great, however, that only when factories operated at or near capacity could economies of production be achieved. But to operate at that level would cause prices to fall. Every glimmer of hope for potential new markets—the establishment of a new railroad line, a new wave of immigration, the opening of new territory, the enactment of a new tariff —was desperately grasped and was followed by a frenzy of expansion, only to be followed in turn by idle plant and equipment when the markets had been saturated.

For much of the last third of the century, moreover, the headlong rush to capture new markets and to drive out competitors from old took place in an atmosphere of benign indifference to many of the methods of businessmen. Ebulliently optimistic, Americans of all ranks poured their money into ventures to build great cities where there were yet no people, to construct railroads where there were no passengers and no freight, to promote new enterprises that, at least on paper, promised to dwarf existing firms. Often it was the prospect of immediate profit from the promotion of these enterprises, not profit from the conduct of a business, that led to their creation. Often, too, insiders operating in the absence of law or in bland indifference to the law milked the treasuries and manipulated the stocks of their companies to line their own pockets. And in so doing they frequently had the acquiescence, sometimes tacit, sometimes active, of legislatures and courts at every level of government.

So powerful, indeed, had business become, so increasingly tenacious its hold on the imagination, so visible the activities of its more flamboyant practitioners, that in the period after the Civil War the businessman stepped out into the limelight as one of the prime makers of his age. The great fortunes of an earlier day—the wealth of a Girard, a Lorillard, even of the first John Jacob Astor—seemed puny compared to the new fortunes of the Fields, the Armours, the Pillsburys. What had there ever been to compare with the Vanderbilts, the Rockefellers, or with Andrew Carnegie's annual income of twenty-five million dollars? Some, to be sure, like Rockefeller, shunned notoriety, though not even he could escape the headline of the Hepburn Committee and other investigators of monopoly. Others courted it, like George Vanderbilt whose estate in Asheville, North Carolina, cost more than the congressional appropriation for the Department of Agriculture. In any case, whether they were held out as models to be emulated or examples to be scorned, how could they be ignored? They sat at the center of the web of influence which penetrated into every section of the country. Their decisions helped shape the environment in which all had to live and, increasingly, that environment began to rub hard against large numbers of people.

How would the American people react to that environment? What groups would emerge to new importance as a result of the strategic position they now occupied in an industrial society, and which would find only a slippery handhold? How would the first gain consciousness of their new-found importance and how would the others respond to their impotence? Would concentration of economic power be compatible with the traditional dispersion of political power? Could immigrants of all degrees of ethnic and social diversity accept the imposed discipline of industrial labor and the self-discipline of democratic society? Would life be enlarged in an industrial society—would there be a new and generous vision of what was humanly possible—or would life narrow down to a struggle to escape uncertainty? Conceivably the questions might not be answered; they could not be ignored.

Perhaps the most important lesson that was being learned as the century drew to a close was the recognition that the answers to these questions escaped individual solutions. Only as individuals formed organizations and hammered out joint programs could they attempt to impose their wills and mold the social environment to their own choosing. The first to learn this lesson, because technological change had given them the initiative, were the businessmen themselves. Heavy investments in plant and equipment were necessary to meet the competition of rivals in the search for markets, but so incredibly productive was the new technology that it tended constantly to outstrip the absorptive ability of the markets. Moreover, so great was the cost of the new technology that economies of production could be achieved only when plants operated at near capacity. But this, like the ruthless competition between industrial rivals, drove down prices and threatened the security of even the most efficient. How to escape from this cruel dilemma became an overriding concern of American businessmen towards the turn of the century, and led them into a search for "order" the major outcome of which was the discovery of the importance of organization.

First of all, of course, came changes within the scope of activities of the single firm. So efficient had Andrew Carnegie's operations become, for example, that he was already the dominant producer in the basic iron and steel industry when, in the 1880's, he began to reach out into all branches of the industry. Through his partnership with Henry Clay Frick he had access to coal, railroads, and coking plants. He bought into Michigan iron ore land and, finally, into the great Mesabi iron range. He built ore ships for the Great Lakes, a port at Conneaut to handle them, and a railroad to haul the ore to Pittsburgh. Even so, however, he could not free himself from the threat of combinations in the steel-consuming industries which were powerful enough to affect his prices. In 1900, he announced plans to carry combination a long step forward by entering directly into the manufacture of steel wire, tubes, and similar products himself. In the end, he was dissuaded from doing so by the offer of J. P. Morgan to buy him out for $450,000,000, and Morgan himself, once the way was cleared, proceeded to establish order in the industry through the organization of the world's first billion-dollar company, the United States Steel Corporation.

But organizational efforts to limit the effects of competition and create stability could not, in the nature of the case, be confined to the level of the single firm. The railroads pioneered in efforts to create intercompany agreements, because it was they that first experienced the chaotic results of excessive competition. Direct mergers carried out under the sponsorship of the banking houses that financed the consolidations, as well as "traffic associations" to fix rates and share traffic were attempted. Railroads, though, for a variety of reasons were more vulnerable than other industries, and the railroad entrepreneurs were not allowed a free hand in the efforts to achieve stability. Eventually, government regulation was invoked. Still, by 1900 the vast national railroad network had been so shaken down that only six large systems controlled 95 percent of the mileage. Other industries followed the same path.

As early as the 1870's, "pools" were organized to divide territorial markets, fix production quotas, and set prices, but these "gentlemen's agreements"—generally organized in the black despair of the bottom of a business depression—could not withstand the tendency of their own members to violate the rules during the corrosive optimism of a business upturn which gave promise of new killings to be made. John D. Rockefeller's Standard Oil Company provided the first spectacular example of a more effective form of industrial organization—the trust. The shareholders of a number of competing firms turned over their voting stock to "trustees" in return for nonvoting, interest-bearing certificates; in this way, general pricing and marketing policies could be established for all the companies in the trust. But the trust, too, proved to be only an interim form of organization. Held to be in violation of the law, it was soon replaced, with the aid of complaisant state legislatures who provided the necessary enabling acts, by the holding company, a single company which held a controlling interest in several subordinate ones.

Nearly everywhere the attainment of these new forms of organization depended upon the cooperation of or was carried out under the sponsorship of the great investment bankers. No less than industrial managers were they fearful of excessive competition, and with the leverage provided by their financial assistance they insinuated their own people into corporate boards of directors and attempted to bend corporate policy toward conservative programs. The effort to do so involved corporation executives in activities their forebears knew not of. Time was when the successful businessman had only to concern himself with costs and prices; other variables could be taken for granted. But this was no longer true, and even costs and prices depended upon such factors as the program of political parties, the attitude of labor, the quality and degree of its organization, the temper of the legislature, belligerent or pacific, the state of public opinion—all of them variables over which the business-man could exercise only limited authority. Yet, if he were to attain the environment needed to provide a climate of security in which to carry out his affairs, more and more had to be brought within his purview and made susceptible to his influence. Increasingly powerful, the businessman was also, by virtue of the way in which every area of the social environment bore in upon him, increasingly vulnerable as well. With greater power and greater vulnerability, small wonder that he became increasingly self-conscious.

If the process of industrialization elevated some, it depressed others. The same forces which locked industrial enterprises into a network of relations with others were working in the agricultural sector of the economy as well, reshaping the social environment and altering the position of the farmer. It had been only a few years since the passage of the Homestead Act, which both presupposed and presumably guaranteed the existence of the independent farmer. Yet the application of science to agriculture and transport and the increasing involvement of farmers in market relations undermined their traditional independence and forced even them, the most fiercely individualist of all sections of society, into experiments in new forms of social organization. The railroad which carried the farmer into the new territories of the Great Plains linked him to distant markets, where he could get cash for his crops, and to distant sources of supply, where he could satisfy his needs more cheaply than with household production. Whatever his degree of self-sufficiency before, he was now simply another specialist exchanging his products for those of others. Technology itself contributed to the change. With sickle and flail a man could reap only about 7½ acres, but with a mechanical reaper he could handle a hundred or more. Heavy steel plows, barbed wire for fencing, mechanical reapers and binders, and steam traction engines contributed to an amazing expansion of productivity. Though agriculture lost 3,500,000 workers between 1870 and 1900, efficiency rose by 86 percent during the same period.

Yet there was a debit side to the ledger. Technological aids were indispensable for survival, but not all could afford them. By the turn of the century, it has been estimated, the cost of establishing even a modest farm was in the neighborhood of $1000. The need for capital was becoming increasingly great, but not always was it possible to obtain. Some of the problems that bedeviled farmers—like winter blizzards and summer droughts and plagues of grasshoppers—they could not control. Nor, at least at the start, was there much that could be done to offset the social consequences of the very pattern of land settlement—the unbearable monotony and loneliness that resulted from the wide dispersion of homesteads and the absence of centers of social interaction. But some of the problems of the farmer were in the order of society, not in the order of nature; these, presumably, might be understood and solved.

The root of the problem lay in the relation of costs to prices. The farmer sold his cotton, his wheat, and his corn on a world market, and the prices he obtained—which he could do little to influence—seemed to bear little relation to his costs of production. He sold in an unprotected world market; he bought in a national market where tariffs and combinations seemed to single him out for victimization. The railroad, which controlled transportation to distant markets, imposed steep freight rates, partly because of the high cost of shipping bulky, seasonal freight one-way without compensating return freight, partly because of its tendency to charge what the traffic would bear in the absence of competing means of transportation. For every bushel of corn the farmer shipped from Nebraska to Chicago, it took another bushel to pay the freight charges. Freight rates west of the Missouri were double those from Chicago to the east. The farmer's conviction that railroad rates were excessive seemed confirmed by the spectacle of railroad rate wars and special low rates granted to favored customers who could guarantee large shipments over long hauls. The grain elevator company, too, seemed in the business of exploiting the farmer; it charged excessive rates and downgraded the quality of his grain. The prices of machinery, manufactured by companies organized in trusts or protected by tariffs, seemed exorbitant, and so did the cost of credit.

Most farmers, lacking adequate financial resources, carried on by buying machinery on credit and by mortgaging land, crops, buildings, and equipment. This was supportable as long as prices maintained a fairly stable level, but a series of crop failures in the late 1880's and the industrial depression of 1893 ushered in a prolonged period of agricultural instability and unrest. In western Kansas alone twenty towns were depopulated, and all over the Great Plains marginal lands were abandoned and farms were consolidated. Lands which had been mortgaged fell into the hands of banks and finance companies, and former proprietors—when they did not leave the land entirely—were reduced to the ranks of tenant farmers. In 1880, when the first national census of tenancy was taken, 25 percent of all American farms were tenant-operated; by 1900, somewhat over one-third were operated by tenants.

It was clear that for farmers, as well as businessmen, new forms of organization were needed to keep the jaws of the cost-price vise from closing. For some, escape could be found by organizing agricultural production on a vast scale—as on the great "bonanza farms" of Minnesota—so that full advantage could be taken of the economies of machine production; but few farmers had the capital necessary to buy the required land and equipment. Others might shift their production from staple crops to truck gardening or dairy farming, but this, too, required capital and technical knowledge. For the majority, escape seemed possible, as in the case of industry, only by interfarm organization, though the most appropriate form of organization and the decision as to whether economic or political action would be most effective took years to determine. The struggle of the farmers to organize and to work out their relationship to an industrial society provided some of the sharpest and most characteristic political controversies of the post–Civil War period.

The first of the great national farm movements to be organized was the Patrons of Husbandry, or the Grange, founded in 1867 by Oliver H. Kelley, a former clerk in the Department of Agriculture. Designed originally to help farmers break down the impoverished isolation of their lives and to provide social and intellectual nourishment, it was soon converted—out of the farmers' own interest in the problems that pressed most heavily upon them—into an organization that concerned itself with ameliorating the economic conditions of rural life. Cooperative enterprises came to occupy the center of their attention. Cooperative grain elevators, cooperative stores, cooperative schemes for purchasing supplies and marketing products, even cooperatives to manufacture farm machinery were organized, but these found tough sledding against the entrenched opposition of better organized, richer competitors. One factor in the farmer's cost of production proved not to be amenable to economic pressure—the railroad; and the farmers were forced, almost despite themselves, to organize politically. Working in some states through the existing political parties, in others through antimonopoly parties of their own, farmers succeeded in enacting "Granger laws" regulating railroad rates. These state acts were first held to be constitutional by the United States Supreme Court in 1876, then unconstitutional when the Court reversed itself in 1886, but the political momentum they generated lead eventually to federal regulation of railroads. By the 1870's the Grange had declined in effectiveness and in popular support, but its place was taken by more militant groups—the Farmers' Alliances of the West and South—which showed that they had not forgotten the importance of organization for economic and political action.

Demanding the nationalization of railroads and telegraph lines, recovery of unused railroad land grants, graduated income tax, an end to alien ownership of land, and currency inflation through the coinage of silver, the farmers' movement—organized politically as the Populist party—made rapid progress in the South and West in the depressed economic circumstances of the early 1890's. The Populist party won striking successes in the elections of 1890 and 1892, but in 1896 the combination of an upturn in business, the capture of the party by the Democrats, and an aggressive campaign by the Republicans led to their defeat. At the end of the century, the farmers—though they had influenced the character of much state and national legislation—had not yet succeeded in attaining the program or the degree of organizational strength that permitted them to achieve the position they wanted. But they had learned that without organization their case was hopeless, they had begun to redefine themselves in relation to other groups in their society, and increasingly they began to see their plight more in terms of present realities than outworn myths.

Industrialists and farmers were not alone in having to puzzle out their relationship to a new universe of national markets and rapid technological innovations. Industrial labor, too, had to work out its mode of accommodation and, of all groups, it was perhaps the one most directly under the gun of industrial pressures.

If organization was the prerequisite of survival, industrial workers began the struggle under special handicaps. There was, first of all, the question of definition: What did it mean to be a worker and what did it portend? Clearly the semiskilled tender of a machine in a factory was a very different person from the skilled artisan who worked by and for himself, but what conception did he have of his own role and what relation did this bear to the strategy he adopted to govern his relations with others? Different conceptions suggested different strategies, each with different implications for the kind of organization that was felt to be desirable and for whether organization was felt to be desirable at all. If, for example, the sewing-machine operator, the steel puddler, the carpenter felt himself forever tied to his position, he might have responded by developing a sense of common purpose and common destiny with others of his same rank. But where any industrial or clerical job was conceived as only a steppingstone to something higher, where, in fact, the worker was urged by both precept and example to identify himself not with his peers but with the successful in whose steps he or his children might one day stand, a powerful psychological solvent existed to destroy that self-conception which might result in unity of action with others.

There were, moreover, certain characteristics of late nineteenth-century industrial society itself which reinforced this psychology. The isolation of markets had once protected workers in one area from the competition of others in more remote areas, but the development of the transportation network brought even workers in the most distant places into competition. And when competition between trades and areas seemed to be correlated with ethnic differences, the problem of achieving organizational unity seemed almost insurmountable. Finally, that endemic feature of industrial civilization, the business cycle, served to compound the difficulties of achieving a viable organization. On the business upswing workers, like farmers, felt squeezed between relatively fixed wages and mounting living costs, and they might be moved to organize and to protest. But on the business downturn, the reverse occurred; loath to protest because of the fear of unemployment, they were reluctant to antagonize their employers and jeopardize their jobs by making new demands.

There were, then, both psychological and structural impediments to organization even had there been no opposition from employers and a clear-cut program on the part of labor itself. But of course there was employer opposition, as the widespread use of the strikebreaker, the lockout, the blacklist, and industrial espionage testifies. And there was no clear-cut program on the part of labor with respect either to organizational form or long-range goals.

The earliest of the labor organizations to appear after the Civil War, the National Labor Union and the Knights of Labor, were concerned more with devising methods to escape from industrialism than with coming to grips with it. Cooperation was to be the way. The trade unions had failed, Uriah Stephens, president of the Knights maintained, because they had concerned themselves too narrowly with the problems of workingmen. It was cooperation, his successor Terence V. Powderly argued, that would "eventually make every man his own master—every man his own employer. . . . There is no good reason why labor cannot, through cooperation, own and operate mines, factories and railroads."[5]

The Knights grew rapidly, especially after 1885 when they succeeded in forcing Jay Gould to negotiate a contract with the employees of his railroad; but the fact is that the leadership of the Knights, believing in the harmony of all social groups, was reluctant to follow a militant program in support of trade-union interests. Even their very organizational form militated against the use of economic pressures on employers. Their goal was the organization of all producers into a single irresistible coalition that would abolish the wage system and usher in a new society, and their structure—reflecting that goal—grouped all workers, regardless of craft, into a single territorial unit. It was a structure better adapted to agitation and political action than to bargaining with employers, and when Powderly himself expressed his disapproval of militant trade-union actions during the Chicago strikes of 1886, disillusioned members turned away by the thousands.

Even before the formation of the American Federation of Labor in 1886 it was apparent that fundamental differences in philosophy—and therefore in strategy and organization—existed within the Knights of

Labor. Aligned against the official leadership was a group of national
unions, organized on craft lines, which was less interested in the reform
of a social order than in the achievement of better conditions for workmen even while they remained workmen. It was the bargaining function
of labor that was to be preeminent, not its political function; hence its
organization on craft rather than territorial lines, its concern with immediate economic issues rather than general programs of reform, the importance of strikes and boycotts in the arsenal of labor's weapons. Industrial disputes did not end with the achievement of this new organizational
form; indeed they became even more bitter, as strikes on railroads and in
steel mills, packing houses, mines, and factories testified. But the importance of labor organization was not to be measured in terms of strikes
won or lost. It lay in the fact that behind the emerging form of organization was a definition of status and a strategy of action. The status—the
worker as indispensable member of an industrial order. The strategy—
collective action to improve the conditions of life.

To speak of the importance of organization as the mode of adjusting
to the conditions of industrial life, to speak of the new self-consciousness
of both groups thrust up into significance by the economic changes of
the late nineteenth century and of those cast down, is not only to speak
from the perspective of a later age but somehow to deprive the period
of the passion it possessed. For organizations were not created without
bitter struggles between men and in the minds of men and, once
achieved, they were involved in dramatic efforts to influence the shape
of the environment. The attempt of persons to understand the forces
remaking their world and, by organization, to control them, constitutes,
indeed, the major motif of the social history of the late nineteenth
century.

By the last decade of the century there seemed little enough to give
hope that an acceptable solution to the problems of industrialization
could be found. A later generation was to speak blithely of the "Gay
Nineties," but to most of those who were then alive it was more a period
of *fin de siècle* despair than of buoyant optimism. The American people
had long since developed elaborate explanations to account for their special place in human history, to explain why they were not condemned to
suffer the same history and the same destiny as the nations of Europe.
But there seemed much in the circumstances of the 1890's to belie this
optimistic version of the past and forecast of the future.

Poverty was one of these circumstances. Even in 1890, possibly the
peak year of prosperity before the First World War, one contemporary
estimated that of the 12,500,000 families in the United States, 11,000,000
had an average income of less than $380 a year. Andrew Carnegie defied
any man to show that there was pauperism in the United States, but

a few years after he spoke one out of every ten persons who died on the Island of Manhattan was being buried in Potter's Field. The gap between rich and poor—growing more visible every day—may have been the most glaring cleavage in American society, but it was not the only one. City people mocked country folk, who were at once envious and angry. Native Americans wondered at what was to be done with hundreds of thousands of Irish, German, Scandinavian, Italian, and Polish immigrants, and the latter found it no less difficult to make common cause with each other. Nor was the conflict only potential. Violent outbursts at the Haymarket riots of 1886 and the great strikes at Homestead and Pullman gave evidence of the savagery of industrial warfare and led many to conjure up visions of a new and bloodier Paris Commune on American soil.

No institution of the industrial age gave greater grounds for anxiety than its most characteristic product—the city; nowhere were its attractions greater, nowhere were its sins more apparent, nowhere its conflicts more violent. "The turbid air," wrote Henry James, describing New York, "the tramp, the whole quality and allure, the consummate monotonous commonness, of the pushing male crowd, moving in its dense mass—with the confusion carried to chaos for any intelligence, any perception; a welter of objects and sounds in which relief, detachment, dignity, meaning perished utterly and lost all rights. . . . All the signs of the heaped industrial battle-field, all the sounds and silences, grim, pushing, intruding silences too, of the universal will to move—to move, move, move as an end in itself, an appetite at any price."

It was in the city that the contrast between Fifth Avenue luxury and Bowery squalor was most apparent; it was in the city that national guard armories—great Gothic castles with crenellated walls—were built to protect the propertied from the imminent onslaught of the poor; it was in the city that teeming multitudes, alien and native, looked at each other with fear; and it was in the city that were to be found the beneficiaries and the derelicts of industrial society. Increasingly, too, the city came to make its weight felt in the political arena, but the way in which its power was organized served only to intensify the fears of an older generation. To the respectable, the urban political machine was a mechanism of graft and corruption. To the immigrant, it was Santa Claus wintertime and summertime—an avenue to power and influence, a helping hand in time of need, the purveyor of jobs and the provider of excitement. For such as had been reared in the tradition of the small town as a college of the virtuous, the industrial polyglot city was a center of infection.

As optimism was the temper of the start of the period, fear was the keynote of its close. The reality of overt strife could not be ignored; neither could the overwhelming evidence of brooding hostility between social classes and ethnic and racial groups. How was it all to be explained? By the will of God? But surely even the most pious Christian must feel a pang of guilt at the thought of millions condemned to misery. By the survival of the fittest? Perhaps, but did not a truer understanding of the theory of evolution suggest that man need not passively submit to the pressures of his environment, that intelligence might be used to control the course of his development? By the rigorous laws of competition? But private striving, the theorists had said, would lead to public welfare, and where, in the midst of rural poverty and urban squalor, could that be found? By the theories of Marxism? By the corrupting influence of materialism? Older explanations were clearly inadequate, but no new theory could win universal assent. The palpable facts of industrialization were in themselves disturbing; what made them frightening was that, in the absence of an adequate theory, it was difficult to read the future.

It was not, however, a record of failure. Even as their world was disintegrating, the American people at the turn of the century had begun the task of adjusting to the new order of things. Technology and urbanization were not to be wiped away, they were to be lived with; and already many had learned the lesson that if men do not organize they can not solve their social problems or achieve their social goals.

3

In 1904 the United States was host to another great international exposition. Coincident with the Universal Exposition of St. Louis, held to mark the centennial of the Louisiana Purchase, hundreds of the most renowned scientists and scholars of every country of the world met at an International Congress of Arts and Science to discuss the problem of the unity of knowledge. Yet not only scientific problems were discussed. No aspect of human activity was left untouched, and the roster of social problems touched upon by the scholars at St. Louis in 1904 makes the Philadelphia Exposition of 1876 seem almost arcadian. Race relations, the cooperative movement, the struggle of social classes, slums and settlement houses, government regulation of industry, imperialism and the quest for colonies —the problems that had not been foreseen by a more innocent generation were now high on the agenda.

The great German sociologist Max Weber, musing upon the future, saw a gradual convergence of American with European history. "For while it is correct to say that the burden of historical tradition does not overwhelm the United States," he said,

and that the problems originating from the power of tradition do not exist here, yet the effects of the power of capitalism are the stronger and will, sooner or later, further the development of land monopolies. When the land has become sufficiently dear so as to secure a certain rent, when the accumulation of large fortunes has reached a still-higher point than to-day, when, at the same time, the possibility of gaining proportionate profits by constant new investments in trade and industry has been diminished so far that the 'captains of industry,' as has occurred everywhere in the world, begin to strive for hereditary preservation of their possessions instead of new investments that bring both gain and danger, then, indeed, the desire of the capitalistic families to form a 'nobility' will arise. . . .

The equally eminent German economist Werner Sombart was even more apprehensive:

What capitalism has tossed together, in crowds, in great cities and centres of industry, is . . . an inarticulate mass of individuals who have completely broken with the past, who have cut themselves loose from all communal ties, from home, village, and kindred, beginning life anew with a complete destruction of their old ideals. The labourer's only support is the comrade of his fate. . . . Hence arises a host of confederates who are distinguished by one thing above all others, not by individuality, not by common tradition, but by their mass, their massiveness. . . . And if we would picture to ourselves the social movement of our day, it invariably appears to us as an inexhaustible stream of men hardly one of whom stands out clearly, flowing over the whole land as far as the eye can see, to the farthest horizon where the last of them roll away into darkness.

The two German scholars saw little future for representative democracy in the United States; it was to be swept away by the masses, hungering for power, or by the elite, determined to keep what it had.

They were answered by a less eminent, but perhaps more prescient, American scholar, the sociologist Edward Alsworth Ross. "How is the attitude of a man towards the rest of his class affected by the fact that socio-economic classes are in a hierarchy, and individuals are constantly escaping from one class into a higher?" he asked.

Does not the secret hope of rising prompt many a man to identify himself in imagination with the class he hopes to belong to rather than the class he actually belongs to? Are not the conflicts that, in view of their clear oppositions of interest, one would expect to break out . . . between working men and employees, frequently averted because the natural leaders and molders of opinion among the working men hope to become capitalists . . . ? In this epoch of democracy and deliquescence, society by no means falls apart into neat segments, as it did two centuries ago. Caste has had its day, and the compartment society, with thick bulkheads of privileges, prejudice, non-intercourse, and non-intermarriage separating the classes, is well-nigh extinct. To-day the imprint each manner of life tends to leave on those who lead it is continually effaced by such assimilating influences as church, school, press, party, voluntary association, and public opinion.

But not even for Ross was this the best of all possible worlds. In a world of increasing organization—

what will be the fate of personal individuality? Will there be more room for spontaneity and choice, or is the individual doomed to shrivel as social aggregates enlarge . . . ? As that cockle-shell, the individual soul, leaving the tranquil pool of tribal life, passes first into the sheltered lake of some city community, then into the perilous sea of national life, does it enjoy an ever-widening scope for free movement and self-direction, or does it, too frail to navigate the vaster expanses, become more and more the sport of irresistible waves and currents?[6]

We ponder his question—a legacy of the nineteenth century—even yet.

NOTES

1. James Russell Lowell, "The World's Fair, 1876," *The Nation*, XXI (August 5, 1875), 82.

2. Translated from "The Workingmen of America to the Workingmen of France," in Eugène Pottier, *Chants Révolutionnaires* (Paris, 1937), pp. 205–214.

3. "Song of the Exposition," in *The Complete Writings of Walt Whitman* (New York and London, 1902), I, 238–250.

4. Frank Thistlethwaite, *The Great Experiment* (Cambridge, England, 1955), pp. 210–211.

5. Terence V. Powderly, *The Path I Trod* (New York, 1940), pp. 266–270.

6. The quotations are from the speeches by Weber, Sombart, and Ross in Howard J. Rogers, ed., *Congress of Arts and Science, Universal Exposition, St. Louis, 1904* (Boston, 1906–1907), VII, 744, 796; V, 876, 882, 877.

PART I

THE TRANSFORMING
INFLUENCES

Speaking before the Congress of Arts and Science in St. Louis in 1904,
John Bates Clark, America's foremost academic economist, described the
difficulties that lay in the way of making accurate economic analyses.
Most of the work of the economists, he said, had consisted in searching
for standards of value, wages, interest, and rent, and in attaining "truths
so general that it is not dependent on the amount of progress which a
society has made." The trouble was that the tendency of values, wages,
and the like to conform to the theoretical standards of the economist was
obstructed by adverse influences; the price of a commodity, the wage of
a workman, the rent of a parcel of land was seldom exactly "natural." The
difference between actuality and theory was attributed to "friction and
obstruction rather than to anything more general and legitimate. It has
not been clearly perceived that it is organic change in society itself which
causes the abiding differences between the traditional standards of value,
wages, and rent, and the actual rates."

Professor Clark was not prepared to incorporate these organic changes
in a general body of economic theory, but at the time it was no small
accomplishment to point them out and to insist upon their relevance for
the understanding of economic change. "Population is increasing, capital
is accumulating, migrations are going on," he said;

revolutionary inventions are in progress, the languid Orient is suffering in-
vasions by the irrepressible Occident and is itself about to undergo a radical
transformation and also to act in a powerful way on the destinies of the West.
These movements do not go on so completely of themselves as to permit no
promoting or interfering by the State. Nations seek to control and guide them
in a conscious and purposeful way. Diplomacy, war, and experimental law-
making, not to mention more experimental platform-making, range themselves
among the forces with which the economist has to reckon. . . .

Of the forces transforming the economy at the end of the nineteenth
century, some were in the order of science and technology, others were
in the order of human organization. The factory was indeed a place
where, as one contemporary put it, "raw material can be converted into
finished goods by consecutive, harmonious processes carried along by a
central power . . ." but the factory was also a particular mode of human
organization, one which required the learning of new skills and the
imposition of a special discipline. To some extent changes in human
organization were forced by technology itself, but the process was by no
means automatic. Moreover, it became increasingly clear toward the end

of the century that if some forms of organization could release human energy and thereby encourage productivity, others would bottle it up and retard expansion.

In the selections that follow, changes in both technology and organization are discussed. David A. Wells, noted economist and former official of the United States Treasury, describes the vast expansion in American industrial and agricultural productivity. Carroll D. Wright, first United States Commissioner of Labor, and journalist Philip G. Hubert, Jr., see the factory as a center of technological and human resources and speculate upon its influence on human welfare. Marshall M. Kirkman, railroad executive, building upon the analogy with the army, discusses the problem of achieving efficiency and order within the railroad. The classic paper of Frederick W. Taylor, pioneer of "scientific management," demonstrates abundantly the inextricable connection between technological change and factory organization. Finally, the selections from the great Chicago Conference on Trusts reveal something of the range of attitudes that existed at the end of the century toward industrial combinations.

Economic Changes

David A. Wells

When the historian of the future writes the history of the nineteenth
century he will doubtless assign to the period embraced by the life of the
generation terminating in 1885, a place of importance, considered in its
relations to the interests of humanity, second to but very few, and perhaps to none, of the many similar epochs of time in any of the centuries
that have preceded it; inasmuch as all economists who have specially
studied this matter are substantially agreed that, within the period
named, man in general has attained to such a greater control over the
forces of Nature, and has so compassed their use, that he has been able
to do far more work in a given time, produce far more product, measured
by quantity in a ratio to a given amount of labor, and reduce the effort
necessary to insure a comfortable subsistence in a far greater measure
than it was possible for him to accomplish twenty or thirty years anterior
to the time of the present writing (1889). In the absence of sufficiently
complete data, it is not easy, and perhaps not possible, to estimate
accurately, and specifically state the average saving in time and labor in
the world's work of production and distribution that has been thus
achieved. In a few departments of industrial effort the saving in both of
these factors has certainly amounted to seventy or eighty per cent; in not
a few to more than fifty per cent.* . . .

The displacement of muscular labor in some of the cotton-mills of the
United States, within the last ten years, by improved machinery, has been
from thirty-three to fifty per cent, and the average work of one operative,

David A. Wells, *Recent Economic Changes* (New York: D. Appleton and Co.,
1899), pp. 27-28, 50-55, 57-61, 91-96, 98-102, 105-111.

* According to the United States Bureau of Labor (report for 1886), the gain in
the power of production in some of the leading industries of the United States "during
the past fifteen or twenty years," as measured by the displacement of the muscular
labor formerly employed to effect a given result (i. e., amount of product) has been
as follows: In the manufacture of agricultural implements, from fifty to seventy per
cent; in the manufacture of shoes, eighty per cent; in the manufacture of carriages,
sixty-five per cent; in the manufacture of machines and machinery, forty per cent;
in the silk-manufacture, fifty per cent, and so on.

working one year, in the best mills of the United States, will now, according to Mr. Atkinson, supply the annual wants of 1,600 fully clothed Chinese, or 3,000 partially clothed East Indians. In 1840 an operative in the cotton-mills of Rhode Island, working thirteen to fourteen hours a day, turned off 9,600 yards of standard sheeting in a year; in 1886 the operative in the same mill made about 30,000 yards, working ten hours a day. In 1840 the wages were $176 a year; in 1886 the wages were $285 a year.

The United States census returns for 1880 report a very large increase in the amount of coal and copper produced during the ten previous years in this country, with a very large comparative diminution in the number of hands employed in these two great mining industries; in anthracite coal the increase in the number of hands employed having been 33·2 per cent, as compared with an increase of product of 82·7; while in the case of copper the ratios were 15·8 and 70·8, respectively. For such results, the use of cheaper and more powerful blasting agents (dynamite), and of the steam-drill, furnish an explanation. And, in the way of further illustration, it may be stated that a car-load of coal, in the principal mining districts of the United States, can now (1889) be mined, hoisted, screened, cleaned, and loaded in one half the time that it required ten years previously.

The report of the United States Commissioner of Labor for 1886 furnishes the following additional illustrations:

"In the manufacture of agricultural implements, specific evidence is submitted showing that six hundred men now do the work that, fifteen or twenty years ago, would have required 2,145 men—a displacement of 1,545.

"The manufacture of boots and shoes offers some very wonderful facts in this connection. In one large and long-established manufactory the proprietors testify that it would require five hundred persons, working by hand processes, to make as many women's boots and shoes as a hundred persons now make with the aid of machinery—a displacement of eighty per cent.

"Another firm, engaged in the manufacture of children's shoes, states that the introduction of new machinery within the past thirty years has displaced about six times the amount of hand-labor required, and that the cost of the product has been reduced one half.

"On another grade of goods, the facts collected by the agents of the bureau show that one man can now do the work which twenty years ago required ten men.

"In the manufacture of flour there has been a displacement of nearly three fourths of the manual labor necessary to produce the same product. In the manufacture of furniture, from one half to three fourths only of the old number of persons is now required. In the manufacture of wallpaper, the best evidence puts the displacement in the proportion of one hundred to one. In the manufacture of metals and metallic goods, long-established firms testify that machinery has decreased manual labor 33⅓ percent."

In 1845 the boot and shoe makers of Massachusetts made an average production, under the then existing conditions of manufacturing, of 1·52 pairs of boots for each working day. In 1885 each employé in the State made on an average 4·2 pairs daily, while at the present time in Lynn and Haverhill the daily average of each person is seven pairs per day, "showing an increase in the power of production in forty years of four hundred per cent."

The business of making bottles has been arduous and unhealthy, with a waste of about thirty-three per cent of the "melting"; and, although this waste is used afterward, there is a deterioration in its quality from its employment a second time. For many years this specialty of industrial production experienced little improvement; but it finally commenced in the substitution in 1885 of the so-called Siemens "tank" furnace, in place of the old-fashioned "coal" furnace for the melting of glass; one of the former supplanting eight of the latter; requiring four men in place of twenty-eight to feed it, producing 1,000,000 square feet of glass per month, in place of a former product of 115,000 feet, and working continuously, while the coal-furnaces work on an average but eighteen days per month. Such an improvement in the methods of manufacture, as might be expected, revolutionized the former equilibrium, in this department of the glass industry as respects the supply and demand of both labor and product, and occasioned serious riots among the glass-workers of Charleroi, in Belgium, where it was first introduced. The process of producing the bottle by "blowing" was not, however, affected by the above noticed improvement; but within the last year (1888) a practical method of producing bottles is reported as having been invented and practically applied in England, which now bids fair to entirely do away with the process of "blowing," with an accompanying immense increase of daily product and a corresponding reduction in the former cost of labor. . . .

Nothing has had a greater influence in making possible the rapidity with which certain branches of retail business are now conducted, as compared with ten years ago—more especially the sale of groceries—than the cheap and rapid production of paper bags. At the outset, these bags were all made by hand-labor; but now machinery has crowded out the hand-workers, and factories are in existence in the United States which produce millions of paper bags per week, and not unfrequently fill single orders for three millions. Paper sacks for the transportation of flour are now (1889) used to the extent of about one hundred millions per annum; and to this same extent have superseded the use and requirement of cotton sacks and of barrels. With machinery have also come many improvements: square bags that stand up of themselves, and need only when filled from a measure to have the top edges turned over to make the package at once ready for delivery. A purchaser can now also take his butter or lard in paper trays that are brine and grease proof; his vinegar in paper jars that are warranted not to soak for one hour; a bottle of wine wrapped in a corrugated case that would not break if he dropped it on the pavement, and his oysters in paper pails that will hold water overnight. A few years ago, to have furnished gratuitously these packages, would have been deemed extravagance; but now it is found to pay as a matter of business.

The increase in the producing capacity of the United States in respect to the manufacture of paper during the years from 1880 to 1887 inclusive, was also very striking, namely: in number of mills, twenty-five per cent; in product, sixty-seven per cent; in value of product, twenty-seven per cent. The reduction in the prices of paper in the United States under such circumstances has been very great, and since 1872, for all qualities, full fifty per cent.

The *sobriquet* of an apothecary was formerly that of a pill-maker; but the modern apothecary no longer makes pills, except upon special pre-scriptions; inasmuch as scores of large manufactories now produce pills by machinery according to the standard or other formulas, and every apothecary keeps and sells them, because they are cheaper, better, and more attractive than any that he can make himself.

Certain branches of occupation formerly of considerable importance under the influence of recent improvements seem to be passing out of existence. Previous to 1872, nearly all the calicoes of the world were dyed or printed with a coloring principle extracted from the root known as *madder*; the cultivation and preparation of which involved the use of thousands of acres of land in Holland, Belgium, eastern France, Italy, and the Levant, and the employment of many hundreds of men, women, and children, and of large amounts of capital; the importation of madder into the United Kingdom for the year 1872 having been 28,731,600 pounds, and into the United States for the same year 7,786,000 pounds. To-day, two or three chemical establishments in Germany and England, employ-ing but few men and a comparatively small capital, manufacture from coal-tar, at a greatly reduced price, the same coloring principle; and the former great business of growing and preparing madder—with the land, labor, and capital involved—is gradually becoming extinct; the importa-tions into Great Britain for the year 1887 having declined to 1,934,700 pounds, and into the United States to 1,049,800 pounds.

The old-time business of making millstones—entitled to rank among the first of labor-saving inventions at the very dawn of civilization—is rapidly passing into oblivion, because millstones are no longer necessary or economical for grinding the cereals. The steel roller produces more and better flour in the same time at less cost, and as an inevitable consequence is rapidly taking the place of the millstone in all countries that know how to use machinery. And, as the art of skillfully grooving the surface of a hard, flinty rock for its conversion into a millstone is so laborious, so difficult of accomplishment (four or five years of service being required in France from an apprentice before he is allowed to touch a valuable stone), and to a certain extent so dangerous from the flying particles of steel and stone, humanity, apart from all economic considerations, may well rejoice at its desuetude. . . .

But in respect to no other one article has change in the conditions of production and distribution been productive of such momentous consequences as in the case of wheat. On the great wheat-fields of the State of Dakota, where machinery is applied to agriculture to such an extent that the requirement for manual labor has been reduced to a minimum, the annual product of one man's labor, working to the best advantage, is understood to be now equivalent to the production of 5,500 bushels of wheat. In the great mills of Minnesota, the labor of another one man for a year, under similar conditions as regards machinery, is in like manner equivalent to the conversion of this unit of 5,500 bushels of wheat into a thousand barrels of flour, leaving 500 bushels for seed-purposes; and, although the conditions for analysis of the next step in the way of results are more difficult, it is reasonably certain that the year's labor of one and a half men more—or, at the most, two men—employed in railroad transportation, is equivalent to putting this thousand barrels of flour on a dock in New York ready for exportation, where the addition of a fraction of a cent a pound to the price will further transport and deliver it at almost any port of Europe.

Here, then, we have the labor of three men for one year, working with machinery, resulting in the producing all the flour that a thousand other men ordinarily eat in a year, allowing one barrel of flour for the average consumption of each adult. Before such a result the question of wages paid in the different branches of flour production and transportation becomes an insignificant factor in determining a market; and, accordingly, American flour grown in Dakota, and ground in Minneapolis, from a thousand to fifteen hundred miles from the nearest seaboard, and under the auspices of men paid from a dollar and a half to two dollars and a half per day for their labor, is sold in European markets at rates which are determinative of the prices which Russian peasants, Egyptian "fellahs," and Indian "ryots," can obtain in the same markets for similar grain grown by them on equally good soil, and with from fifteen to twenty cents per day wages for their labor.

On the wheat-farms of the Northwestern United States it was claimed in 1887 that, with wages at twenty-five dollars per month and board for permanent employés, wheat could be produced for forty cents per bushel;

while in Rhenish Prussia, with wages at six dollars per month, the cost of production was reported to be eighty cents per bushel.

How much more significantly differences manifest themselves in the results of mechanical production, when long periods of time are taken for comparison, is illustrated by a statement made by Adam Smith in his "Wealth of Nations" (first published in 1776), respecting the manufacture of pins, and which then seemed to him as something extraordinary, and a statement of the present condition of this business, as set forth in an official report to the United States Department of State in the year 1888. . . . In the time of Adam Smith it was regarded as a wonderful achievement for ten men to make 48,000 pins a day, but now three men can make 7,500,000 pins of a vastly superior character in the same time.

A great number of other similar and equally remarkable experiences, derived from almost every department of industry except the handicrafts, might be presented; but it would seem that enough evidence has been offered to prove abundantly, that in the increased control which mankind has acquired over the forces of Nature, and in the increased utilization of such control—mainly through machinery—for the work of production and distribution, is to be found a cause sufficient to account for most if not all the economic disturbance which, since the year 1873, has been certainly universal in its influence over the domain of civilization; abnormal to the extent of justifying the claim of having been unprecedented in character, and which bids fair in a greater or less degree to indefinitely continue. Other causes may and doubtless have contributed to such a condition of affairs, but in this one cause alone (if the influences referred to can be properly considered as a unity) it would seem there has been sufficient of potentiality to account not only for all the economic phenomena that are under discussion, but to occasion a feeling of wonder that the world has accommodated itself so readily to the extent that it has to its new conditions, and that the disturbances have not been very much greater and more disastrous. . . .

CHANGES IN THE RELATIONS OF LABOR AND CAPITAL

Consider next how potent for economic disturbance have been the changes in recent years in the relations of labor and capital, and how clearly and unmistakably these changes are consequents or derivatives from a more potent and antecedent agency.

Machinery is now recognized as essential to cheap production. Nobody can produce effectively and economically without it, and what was formerly known as domestic manufacture is now almost obsolete. But machinery is one of the most expensive of all products, and its extensive purchase and use require an amount of capital far beyond the capacity of the ordinary individual to furnish. There are very few men in the world possessed of an amount of wealth sufficient to individually construct and own an extensive line of railway or telegraph, a first-class steamship, or a great factory. It is also to be remembered that for carrying on production by the most modern and effective methods large capital is needed, not only for machinery, but also for the purchasing and carrying of extensive stocks of crude material and finished products.

Sugar can now be, and generally is, refined at a profit of an eighth of a cent a pound, and sometimes as low as a sixteenth; or, in other words, from eight to sixteen pounds of raw sugar must now be treated in refining in order to make a cent; from eight hundred to sixteen hundred pounds to make a dollar; from eighty thousand to one hundred and sixty thousand pounds to make a hundred dollars, and so on. The mere capital requisite for providing and carrying the raw material necessary for the successful prosecution of this business, apart from all other conditions, places it, therefore, of necessity beyond the reach of any ordinary capitalist or producer. It has been before stated that, in the manufacture of jewelry by machinery, one boy can make up nine thousand sleeve-buttons per day; four girls also, working by modern methods, can put together in the same time eight thousand collar-buttons. But to run an establishment with such facilities the manufacturer must keep constantly in stock thirty thousand dollars' worth of cut ornamental stones, and a stock of cuff-buttons that represents nine thousand different designs and patterns. Hence from such conditions have grown up great corporations or stock companies, which are only forms of associated capital organized for effective use and protection. They are regarded to some extent as evils; but they are necessary, as there is apparently no other way in which the work of production and distribution, in accordance with the requirements of the age, can be prosecuted. The rapidity, however, with which such combinations of capital are organizing for the purpose of promoting industrial and commercial undertakings on a scale heretofore wholly unprecedented, and the tendency they have to crystallize into something far more complex than what has been familiar to the public as corporations, with the impressive names of syndicates, trusts, etc., also constitute one of the remarkable features of modern business methods. It must also be admitted that the whole tendency of recent economic development is in the direction of limiting the area within which the influence of competition is effective.

And when once a great association of capital has been effected, it becomes necessary to have a master-mind to manage it—a man who is competent to use and direct other men, who is fertile in expedient and quick to note and profit by any improvements in methods of production and variations in prices. Such a man is a general of industry, and corresponds in position and functions to the general of an army.

What, as a consequence, has happened to the employés? Coincident with and as a result of this change in the methods of production, the

modern manufacturing system has been brought into a condition analogous to that of a military organization, in which the individual no longer
works as independently as formerly, but as a private in the ranks, obeying
orders, keeping step, as it were, to the tap of the drum, and having nothing to say as to the plan of his work, of its final completion, or of its
ultimate use and distribution. In short, the people who work in the
modern factory are, as a rule, taught to do one thing—to perform one
and generally a simple operation; and when there is no more of that
kind of work to do, they are in a measure helpless. The result has been
that the individualism or independence of the producer in manufacturing
has been in a great degree destroyed, and with it has also in a great degree been destroyed the pride which the workman formerly took in his
work—that fertility of resource which formerly was a special characteristic of American workmen, and that element of skill that comes from long
and varied practice and reflection and responsibility. Not many years ago
every shoemaker was or could be his own employer. The boots and shoes
passed directly from an individual producer to the consumer. Now this
condition of things has passed away. Boots and shoes are made in large
factories; and machinery has been so utilized, and the division of labor
in connection with it has been carried to such an extent, that the process
of making a shoe is said to be divided into sixty-four parts, or the shoemaker of to-day is only the sixty-fourth part of what a shoemaker once
was. It is also asserted that "the constant employment at one sixty-fourth
part of a shoe not only offers no encouragement to mental activity, but
dulls by its monotony the brain of the employé to such an extent that
the power to think and reason is almost lost."

As the division of labor in manufacturing—more especially in the case
of textiles—is increased, the tendency is to supplement the employment
of men with the labor of women and children. The whole number of
employés in the cotton-mills of the United States, according to the census
of 1880, was 172,544; of this number, 59,685 were men, and 112,859
women and children. In Massachusetts, out of 61,246 employés in the
cotton-mills, 22,180 are males, 31,496 women, and 7,570 children. In the
latter State certain manufacturing towns, owing to the disparity in the
numbers of men and women employed, and in favor of the latter, are
coming to be known by the appellation of "*she-towns.*" During recent
years the increase in the employment of child-labor in Germany has been
so noticeable, that the factory inspectors of Saxony in their official report
for 1888 have suggested that such labor be altogether forbidden by the
State, and that the hours during which youths between the ages of fourteen to sixteen may be legally employed in factories should be limited
to six.

Another exceedingly interesting and developing feature of the new
situation is that, as machinery has destroyed the handicrafts, and asso-

ciated capital has placed individual capital at a disadvantage, so machinery and associated capital in turn, guided by the same common influences, now war upon machinery and other associated capital. Thus the now well-ascertained and accepted fact, based on long experience, that power is most economically applied when applied on the largest possible scale, is rapidly and inevitably leading to the concentration of manufacturing in the largest establishments, and the gradual extinction of those which are small. Such also has already been, and such will continue to be, the outcome of railroad, telegraph, and steamship development and experience; and another quarter of a century will not unlikely see all of the numerous companies that at present make up the vast railroad system of the United States consolidated, for sound economic reasons, under a comparatively few organizations or companies. . . .

Such changes in the direction of the concentration of production by machinery in large establishments are, moreover, in a certain and large sense, not voluntary on the part of the possessors and controllers of capital, but necessary or even compulsory. If an eighth or a sixteenth of a cent a pound is all the profit that competition and modern improvements will permit in the business of refining sugar, such business has got to be conducted on a large scale to admit of the realization of any profit. An establishment fitted up with all modern improvements, and refining the absolutely large but comparatively small quantity of a million pounds per annum, could realize, at a sixteenth of a cent a pound profit on its work, but $625. Accordingly, the successful refiner of sugars of to-day, in place of being as formerly a manufacturer exclusively, must now, as a condition of full success, be his own importer, do his own literage, own his own wharfs and warehouses, make his own barrels and boxes, prepare his own bone-black, and ever be ready to discard and replace his expensive machinery with every new improvement. But to do all this successfully requires not only the command of large capital, but of business qualifications of the very highest order—two conditions that but comparatively few can command. It is not, therefore, to be wondered at that, under the advent of these new conditions, one half of the sugar-refineries that were in operation in the seaboard cities of the United States in 1875 have since failed or discontinued operations.

In the great beef slaughtering and packing establishments at Chicago, which slaughter a thousand head of cattle and upward in a day, economies are effected which are not possible when this industry is carried on, as usual, upon a very small scale. Every part of the animal—hide, horns, hoofs, bones, blood, and hair—which in the hands of the ordinary butcher are of little value or a dead loss, are turned to a profit by the Chicago packers in the manufacture of glue, bone-dust, fertilizers, etc.; and accordingly the great packers can afford to and do pay more for cattle than would otherwise be possible—an advance estimated by the best authorities at two dollars a head. Nor does this increased price which Western stock-growers receive come out of the consumer of beef. It is made possible only by converting the portions of an ox that would otherwise be sheer waste into products of value.

The following statements have recently been made in California, on what is claimed to be good authority ("Overland Monthly"), of the comparative cost of growing wheat in that State on ranches, or farms of different sizes. On ranches of 1,000 acres, the average cost is reported at 92½ cents per 100 pounds; on 2,000 acres, 85 cents; on 6,000 acres, 75 cents; on 15,000 acres, 60 cents; on 30,000 acres, 50 cents; and on 50,000 acres, 40 cents. Accepting these estimates as correct, it follows that the inducements to grow wheat in California by agriculturists with limited capital and on a small scale are anything but encouraging. . . .

It was a matter of congratulation after the conclusion of the American war in 1865, that the large plantation system of cotton-raising would be broken up, and a system of smaller crops, by small and independent farmers or yeomanry, would take its place. Experience has not, however, verified this expectation; but, on the contrary, has shown that it is doubtful whether any profit can accrue to a cultivator of cotton whose annual crop is less than fifty bales.

"Cotton (at the South) is made an exclusive crop, because it can be sold for cash—for an actual and certain price in gold. It is a mere trifle to get eight or nine cents for a pound of cotton, but for a bale of 450 pounds it is $40. The bale of cotton is therefore a reward which the anxious farmer works for during an entire year, and for which he will spend half as much in money before the cotton is grown, besides all his labor and time. And the man who can not make eight or ten bales at least has almost no object in life, and nothing to live on."—*Bradstreet's Journal.*

About fifteen years ago the new and so-called "roller process" for crushing and separating wheat was discovered and brought into use. Its advantages over the old method of grinding by millstones were that it separated the flour more perfectly from the hull or bran of the berry of the wheat, gave more flour to a bushel of wheat, and raised both its color and strength (nutriment). As soon as these facts were demonstrated, the universal adoption of the roller mills and the total abolition of the stone mills became only a question of time, as the latter could not compete with the former. The cost of building mills to operate by the roller process is, however, much greater than that of the old stone mills. Formerly, from $25,000 to $50,000 was an ample capital with which to engage in flour-milling in the United States, where water-power only was employed; but at the present time from $100,000 to $150,000 is required to go into the business upon a basis with any promise of success, even with a small mill; while the great mills of Minneapolis, St. Louis, and Milwaukee cost from

$250,000 to $500,000 each, and include "steam" as well as water-power. The consequence of requiring so much more capital to participate in the flour business now than formerly is that the smaller flour-mills in the United States are being crushed, or forced into consolidation with the larger companies, the latter being able, from dealing in such immense quantities, to buy their wheat more economically, obtain lower rates of freight, and, by contracting ahead, keep constantly running.* At the same time there is a tendency to drive the milling industry from points in the country to the larger cities, and central grain and flour markets where cheap freights and large supplies of wheat are available. As might have been anticipated, therefore, the Milwaukee "Directory of American Millers," for 1886, shows a decrease in the number of flour-mills in the United States for that year, as compared with 1884, of 6,812, out of a total in the latter year of 25,079, but an increase at the same time in capacity for flour production. These new conditions of milling have been followed by a movement in England for the consolidation in great cities of the flour-mills and bakeries into single establishments, where the bread-making of the whole community may be done in immense ovens, under the most scientific conditions, and at a material saving in cost.

The improvements in recent years in the production of sugar from the beet, and the artificial encouragement of this industry in the continental states of Europe through the payment of large bounties, has in turn compelled the *large* producers of cane-sugars in the tropics to entirely abandon their old methods of working, and reorganize this industry on a most gigantic scale as a condition of continued existence. Thus, for example, although the business of cane-sugar production was commenced more than three hundred years ago on the island of Cuba, the grinding of the cane by animal or "wind" power, and the boiling and granulating by ancient, slow, and wasteful methods, was everywhere kept up until within a very recent period, as it still is by small planters in every tropical country. But at the present time, upon the great plantations of Cuba and some other countries, the cane is conveyed from the fields by a system of railroads to manufacturing centers, which are really huge factories, with all the characteristics of factory life about them, and with the former home or rural idea connected with this industry completely eliminated. In these factories, where the first cost of the machinery plant often represents as large a sum as $200,000 to $250,000, with an equally large annual outlay for labor and other expenses, all grades of sugar from the "crude" to the "partially refined" are manufactured at a cost that once would not have been deemed possible. In Dakota and Manitoba the employment on

* What has happened in this business in the United States is true also of Great Britain. In both countries the new system of milling and the concentration of the business in great establishments has led to over-production, undue competition, and minimized profits; and in both countries great milling syndicates or trusts have been formed to regulate production and prices.

single wheat estates of a hundred reapers and an aggregate of three hundred laborers for a season has been regarded as something unprecedented in agricultural industry; but on one sugar estate in Cuba—"El Balboa"— from fifteen hundred to two thousand hands, invariably negroes, are employed, who work under severe discipline, in watches or relays, during the grinding season, by day and night, the same as in the large iron-mills and furnaces of the United States. . . .

Attention is next asked to the economic—industrial, commercial, and financial—disturbances that have also resulted in recent years from changes, in the sense of improvements, in the details of the distribution of products; and as the best method of showing this, the recent course of trade in respect to the practical distribution and supply of one of the great articles of commerce, namely, tin-plate, is selected.

Before the days of the swift steamship and the telegraph, the business of distributing tin-plate for consumption in the United States was largely in the hands of one of the great mercantile firms of New York, who brought to it large enterprise and experience. At every place in the world where tin was produced and tin-plate manufactured they had their confidential correspondent or agent, and every foreign mail brought to them exclusive and prompt returns of the state of the market. Those who dealt with such a firm dealt with them under conditions which, while not discriminating unfavorably to any buyer, were certainly extraordinarily favorable to the seller, and great fortunes were amassed. But to-day how stands that business? There is no man, however obscure he may be, who wants to know any morning the state of the tin-plate market in any part of the world, but can find it in the mercantile journals. If he wants to know more in detail, he joins a little syndicate for news, and then he can be put in possession of every transaction of importance that took place the day previous in Cornwall, Liverpool, in the Strait of Sunda, in Australia, or South America. What has been the result? There are no longer great warehouses where tin in great quantities and of all sizes, waiting for customers, is stored. The business has passed into the hands of men who do not own or manage stores. They have simply desks in offices. They go round and find who is going to use tin in the next six months. They hear of a railroad-bridge which is to be constructed; of a certain number of cars which are to be covered; that the salmon-canneries on the Columbia River or Puget's Sound are likely to require seventy thousand boxes of tin to pack the catch of this year, as compared with a requirement of sixty thousand last year—a business, by the way, which a few years ago was not in existence—and they will go to the builders, contractors, or business-managers, and say to them: "You will want at such a time so much tin. I will buy it for you at the lowest market price, not of New York, but of the world, and I will put it in your possession, in any part of the continent, on a given day, and you shall cash the bill and pay me a percentage commission"—possibly a fraction of one per cent; thus bringing a former great and complicated business of importing, warehousing, selling at wholesale and retail, and employing many middle-men, clerks, book-keepers, and large capital, to a mere commission business, which dispenses to a great extent with the employment of intermediates, and does not necessarily require the possession or control of any capital.

Let us next go one step farther, and see what has happened at the same time to the man whose business it has been not to sell but to manufacture tin-plate into articles for domestic use, or for other consumption. Thirty or forty years ago the tinman, whose occupation was mainly one of handicraft, was recognized as one of the leading and most skillful mechanics in every village, town, and city. His occupation has, however, now well-nigh passed away. For example, a townsman and a farmer desires a supply of milk-cans. He never thinks of going to his corner tinman, because he knows that in New York and Chicago and Philadelphia, and other large towns and cities, there is a special establishment fitted up with special machinery, which will make his can better and fifty per cent cheaper than he can have it made by hand in his own town. And so in regard to almost all the other articles which the tinman formerly made. He simply keeps a stock of machine-made goods, as a small merchant, and his business has come down from that of a general, comprehensive mechanic to little other than a tinker and mender of pots and pans. Where great quantities of tin-plate are required for a particular use, as, for example, the canning of salmon or lobsters, of biscuit, or of fruit and vegetables, the plates come direct from the manufactory to the manufacturer of cans or boxes, in such previously agreed-upon sizes and shapes as will obviate any waste of material, and reduce to a minimum the time and labor necessary to adapt them to their respective uses. And by this arrangement alone, in one cracker (biscuit) bakery in the United States, consuming forty thousand tin boxes per month, forty men are now enabled to produce as large a product of boxes in a given time as formerly required fifty men; and, taken in connection with machinery, the labor of twenty-five men in the entire business has become equivalent to that of the fifty who until recently worked by other methods. And what has been thus affirmed of tin-plate might be equally affirmed of a great variety of other leading commodities; the blacksmith, for example, no longer making, but buying his horseshoes, nails, nuts, and bolts; the carpenter his doors, sash, blinds, and moldings; the wheelwright his spokes, hubs, and felloes; the harness-maker his straps, girths, and collars; the painter his paints ground and mixed, and so on; the change in methods of distribution and preparation for final consumption having been equally radical in almost every case, though varying somewhat in respect to particulars.

The same influences have also to a great degree revolutionized the nature of retail trade, which has been aptly described as, "until lately, the recourse of men whose character, skill, thrift, and ambition won credit, and enabled them to dispense with large capital." Experience has shown that, under a good organization of clerks, shopmen, porters, and distributors, it costs much less proportionally to sell a large amount of goods than a small amount, and that the buyer of large quantities can, without sacrifice of satisfactory profit, afford to offer to his retail customers such advantages in respect to prices and range of selection as almost to preclude competition on the part of dealers operating on a smaller scale, no matter how otherwise capable, honest, and diligent they may be. The various retail trades, in the cities and larger towns of all civilized countries, are accordingly being rapidly superseded by vast and skillfully organized establishments—and in Great Britain and Europe by co-operative associations—which can sell at little over wholesale prices a great variety of merchandise, dry-goods, manufactures of leather, books, stationery, furs, ready-made clothing, hats and caps, and sometimes groceries and hardware, and at the same time give their customers far greater conveniences than can be offered by the ordinary shop-keeper or tradesman. In London, the extension of the "tramway" or street-railroad system is even advocated on the single ground that the big stores need quicker access to their branch establishments, in order to still further promote the economy of goods distribution. . . .

Keeping economy in distribution constantly in view as an essential for material progress, the tendency is also everywhere to dispense to the greatest extent with the "middleman," and put the locomotive and the telegraph in his place. Retail grocers, as before shown, now buy their teas directly of the Chinaman, and dispense with the services of the East Indian merchant and his warehouses. Manufacturers deal more directly with retailers, with the result, it is claimed, of steadying supply and demand, and preventing the recurrence of business crises. The English cotton-spinner at Manchester buys his raw cotton by cable in the interior towns of the cotton-growing States of North America, and dispenses with the services of the American broker or commission-merchant. European manufacturers now send their agents with samples of merchandise to almost every locality in America, Asia, and the Pacific islands, where commerce is protected and transportation practicable, and offer supplies, even in comparatively small quantities, on better terms than dealers and consumers can obtain from the established wholesale or retail merchants of their vicinity. A woolen manufacturer, for example, prepares a set of patterns for an ensuing season, sends his agent around the world with them, and makes exactly as many pieces as his customers want, not weaving a single yard for chance sale. A great importing house will take orders for goods to be delivered two or three months afterward, and import exactly what is ordered and no more. Rent, insurance, handling, and profits are thus minimized. Before the days of railroad extension, country buyers used to have to come to the centers of trade in spring and fall to lay in their supplies; now they come every month, if they wish, to assort a stock which is on an average much less heavy than it used to be, and can be replenished by the dealer at very short notice by telegraph to the manufacturer, whether he resides at home or beyond an ocean. The great dry-goods houses of the large commercial cities are in turn reducing their storage and becoming mere sales-rooms, the merchandise marketed by them being forwarded directly from the point of manufacture to that of distribution. A commission house may, therefore, carry on a large business, and yet not appear to the public to be extensively occupied. One not inconsiderable gain from such a change in goods distribution accrues from a consequent reduction in the high rates and aggregates of city fire insurances.

From these specimen experiences it is clear that an almost total revolution has taken place, and is yet in progress, in every branch and in every relation of the world's industrial and commercial system. Some of these changes have been eminently destructive, and all of them have inevitably occasioned, and for a long time yet will continue to occasion, great disturbances in old methods, and entail losses of capital and changes of occupation on the part of individuals. And yet the world wonders, and commissions of great states inquire, without coming to definite conclusions, why trade and industry in recent years have been universally and abnormally disturbed and depressed.

The Factory in Civilization

Carroll D. Wright

One of the most attractive departments of human knowledge is what may be denominated the evolution of industrial forces. The progress of the systems of labor gives to science a field for the practical application of the doctrines of evolution, entirely relieved from the abstract philosophical distinctions, which, in greater or less degree, surround those doctrines when applied to growth in other departments. . . .

The factory system is of recent origin, and is entirely the creation of influences existing or coming into existence during the last half of the eighteenth century. These influences were both direct and subtle in their character, but all important in their place and in their combination. As a great fact, the system originated in no preconceived plan, nor did it spring from any spasmodic exercise of human wisdom; on the contrary, "it was formed and shaped by the irresistible force of circumstances, fortunately aided and guided by men who were able to profit by circumstances." [Taylor's Factory System, 1–11.] To borrow the expression of Cooke Taylor, . . . "Those who were called the fathers of the system were not such demons as they have sometimes been described, nor yet were they perfect angels; they were simply men of great intelligence, industry, and enterprise; they have bequeathed the system to this age with the imperfections incident to every human institution, and the task of harmonizing their innovation with existing institutions, and with the true spirit of righteousness belongs really to the great employers of labor rather than to the professed teachers of morality. It is too late to inquire whether the system ought, or ought not to have been established; for established it is, and established it will remain in spite of all the schemes of the socialists or the insane panaceas of quack economists."* . . .

A factory is an establishment where several workmen are collected together for the purpose of obtaining greater and cheaper conveniences

Carroll D. Wright, "The Factory as an Element in Civilization," *Journal of Social Science*, XVI (December, 1882), 101–126.
* Cf. Taylor's Dedication to "Factory System."

for labor than they could procure individually at their homes; for producing results by their combined efforts, which they could not accomplish separately; and for saving the loss of time which the carrying of an article from place to place, during the several processes necessary to complete its manufacture, would occasion.

The principle of a factory is, that each laborer, working separately, is controlled by some associating principle, which directs his producing powers to effect a common result, which it is the object of all collectively, to attain.

Factories are, therefore, the legitimate outgrowth of the universal tendency to association which is inherent in our nature, and by the development of which every advance in human improvement and human happiness has been gained.

The first force which tended to create this system was that of invention, and the stimulus to this grew out of the difficulty the weavers experienced in obtaining a sufficient supply of yarn to keep their looms in operation.

Invention, paradoxical as it may seem, had really aggravated the difficulty by a device for facilitating the process of weaving. I have reference to the fly shuttle, invented in 1738, by John Kay. By this device one man alone was enabled to weave the widest cloth, while prior to Kay's invention, two persons were required.

One can readily see how this increased the difficulty of obtaining a supply of yarn, for the one thread wheel, though turning from morning till night in thousands of cottages, could not keep pace either with the weaver's shuttle, or with the demand of the merchant. [Baines' History of the Cotton Manufacture, 117.]

In 1738, the very first gleams of the genius which was to remove the difficulties were discovered, and wings were given to a manufacture which had been creeping on the earth. An elementary mechanical contrivance was invented, whereby a single pair of hands could spin twenty, a hundred, or even one thousand threads. I need not carry you through the details of the various inventions which culminated in a grand constellation of mechanical devices, as perfect and as wonderful as any class of inventions, and which have influenced the world in a deeper sense than any other save printing. . . .

While the processes of production had become in England more efficient, through the invention of spinning machines, whereby the weavers were kept busy and allowed no rest, it was only where a stream gave force to turn a mill wheel that the spinner or the wool-worker could establish his factory, while if this difficulty even had not existed, the inefficiency of distribution would have rendered useless, to a large degree, a greatly augmented production. . . .

England at once seized on the discovery of the canal as the means by which to free herself from the bondage in which she had been held.

"From the year 1767, a net-work of water-roads was flung over the country; and before the movement had spent its force, Great Britain alone was traversed in every direction by three thousand miles of navigable canals." [Green, History of the English People, vol. 1, p. 279.]

The free and cheap distribution of coal and iron at once became an important factor, in fact the chief element in the development of the factory system; and now for the first time in the history of civilization, a new motive power became indispensable to growth, for "what was needed to turn England into a manufacturing country was some means of transforming the force" of the sun "stored up in coal into a labor force; and it was this transformation which was brought about through the agency of steam." [Green.]

The location of mills upon streams of water was no longer a physical necessity; they could be built and run near large towns, where they could be fed from the crowded population. The influence of this change of location has been the cause of most of the so-called factory evils.

The power loom closed the catalogue of machines essential for the inauguration of the era of mechanical supremacy; what inventions will come during the continuance of that era, cannot be predicted, for we are still at the beginning of the age of invention.

The wonderful results of its first twenty years of life are sufficient to indicate something of the future. . . .

In France, Germany, and Belgium, the [factory] system predominates, although the domestic system of labor in these countries has continued to exist to considerable extent.

The new system, which has found its most rapid extension in the United States, has enabled the manufacturers of this country, with our wonderful stores of raw materials at hand, to become the successful rivals in the mechanic arts of any country that desires to compete with them.

It has changed the conditions of masses of people; it has become an active element in the processes of civilization, and has changed the character of legislation and of National policy everywhere.

Is this great, powerful, and growing system a power for good or for evil? Does it mean the elevation of the race or its retrogression?

When we speak of civilization we have in mind the progress of society towards a more perfect state, as indicated by the growth of a long period of time; we do not simply contemplate specific reforms or especial evils, but the trend of all social influences.

When we speak of the factory system we are apt to let our thoughts dwell upon the evils that we know or imagine belong to it; this is certainly true when civilization and the factory system are suggested in the same sentence. This is wrong, for we should contemplate the factory system in its general influence upon society and especially upon that portion of society most intimately connected with the factory.

My position is that the system has been and is a most potent element in promoting civilization. I assume, of course, and the assumption is in entire harmony with my thoughts, that the civilization of the nineteenth century is better than that of the eighteenth. . . .

None of the systems of labor which existed prior to the present or factory system, were particularly conducive to a higher civilization. Wages have been paid for services rendered since the wants of men induced one to serve another, yet the wage-system is of recent origin as a system. It arose out of the feudal system of labor and was the first fruits of the efforts of men to free themselves from villeinage. The origin of the wage-system cannot be given a birth-day as can the factory system. It is true, however, that the wage-system rendered the factory system possible, and they have since grown together. The first may give way to some other method for dividing the profits of production, but the factory system perfected, must, whether under socialistic or whatever political system, remain, until disintegration is the rule in society.

The feudal and slave systems had nothing in them from which society could draw the forces necessary to growth; on the contrary, they reflected the most depressing influences, and were actually the allies of retro-gression.

The domestic system, which claims the 18th century almost entirely, was woven into the two systems which existed before and came after it; in fact, it has not yet disappeared.

It is simple fact, however, when we say that the factory system set aside the domestic system of industry; it is idyllic sentiment when we say that the domestic system surpassed the former, and nothing but sentiment.

There is something poetic in the idea of the weaver of old England, before the spinning machinery was invented, working at his loom in his cottage, with his family about him, some carding, others spinning the wool or the cotton for the weaver, and writers and speakers are constantly be-wailing the departure of such scenes.

I am well aware that I speak against popular impression, and largely against popular sentiment when I assert that the factory system in every respect is vastly superior as an element in civilization to the domestic system which preceded it; that the social and moral influences of the present outshine the social and moral influences of the old. The hue and cry against the prevailing system has not been entirely genuine on either side of the Atlantic. Abuses have existed, great and abominable enough, but not equal to those which have existed in the imagination of men who would have us believe that virtue is something of the past.

The condition of the workers of society has never been the ideal con-dition, and the worker is too often the victim of the contemptible selfish-ness which tempts a man to commit the crime of robbing the operative of his just share in the results of his toil. The evils of the factory system are sufficient to call out all the sentiments of justice, and philanthropy, which enable us to deal with wrong and oppression; all this I do not dispute, but I claim that with all its faults and attendant evils the factory system is a vast improvement upon the domestic system of industry in almost every respect, not only with reference to the individual and the family, but to society and the state.

The usual mistake is to consider the factory system as the creator of evils, and not only evils, but of evil disposed persons. This can hardly be shown to be true, although it is that the system may congregate evils or evil disposed persons, and thus give the appearance of creating that which already existed.

It is difficult, I know, to establish close comparisons of the conditions under the two systems, because they are not often found to be con-temporaneous; yet sufficient evidence will be adduced, I think, from a consideration of the features of the two, and which I am able to present, to establish the truth of my assertions.

Do not construe what I say against the domestic system of industry as in the least antagonistic to the family, for I am one of those who be-lieve that its integrity is the integrity of the nation; that the sacredness of its compacts is the sacredness and the preservation and the extension of the race; that the inviolability of its purity and its peace is the most emphatic source of anxiety of law-makers; and that any tendency, whether societary or political, towards its decay or even towards its dis-respect, deserves the immediate condemnation and active opposition of all citizens as the leading cause of irreligion, and of national dis-integration.

It should not be forgotten that "the term factory system, in technology, designates the combined operation of many orders of work-people . . . in tending with assiduous skill a series of productive machines continually propelled by a central power. This definition includes such organizations as cotton-mills, flax-mills, silk and woolen-mills, and many other works; but it excludes those in which the mechanisms do not form a connected series, nor are dependent on one prime mover." It involves in its strictest sense "the idea of a vast automatum, composed of various mechanical and intellectual organs, acting in uninterrupted concert for the production of a common object, all of them being subordinated to a self-regulated moving force." [Dr. Ure, Phil. of Mfgs., p. 13.]

So a factory becomes a scientific structure, its parts harmonious, the calculations requisite for their harmony involving the highest mathe-matical skill, and in the factory the operative is always the master of the machine and never the machine the master of the operative.

Under the domestic system of industry grew up that great pauper class in England, which was a disgrace to civilization. It was fed by the agricultural districts more than by those devoted to manufactures. It continued to grow until one-fourth of the annual budget was for the support of paupers. The evil became fixed upon the social life as one of its permanent phases. Legislation, philanthropy, charity, were utterly powerless in checking it, and it was not checked till the inventions in cotton manufactures came, since which events it has been on the decline, taking the decades together. The factory absorbed many who had been under public support; on the other hand it drew by the allurements of better wages, from the peasantry, and without any guaranties as to permanency or care as to moral responsibility, yet on the whole the state was benefited more than any class was injured.

The domestic laborers' home, instead of being the poetic one, was far from the character poetry has given it. Huddled together in what poetry calls a cottage, and history a hut, the weaver's family lived and worked, without comfort, conveniences, good food, good air, and without much intelligence. Drunkenness and theft of materials made each home the scene of crime and want and disorder. Superstition ruled and envy swayed the workers. If the members of a family endowed with more virtue and intelligence than the common herd, tried to so conduct themselves as to secure at least self-respect, they were either abused or ostracized by their neighbors. The ignorance under the old system added to the squalor of the homes under it, and what all these elements failed to produce in making the hut an actual den, was faithfully performed, in too many instances, by the swine of the family. . . .

Sentiment has done much, as I have said, to create false impressions as to the two systems of labor. Goldsmith's Auburn, and Crabbe's Village, hardly reflect the truest picture of their country's home life.

The reports of the Poor Laws Commissioners of England are truer exponents of conditions, and show whether the town was, during the first fifty years of the new system, staining the country or the country the town. . . . Agriculturists gave children and youth no more than half the wages paid them in factories, while they filled the workhouses with the unemployed. Under the operation of the miserable poor laws which the domestic system fathered, the peasantry were penned up in close parishes, where they increased beyond the demand for their labor, and where the children were allowed to grow up in laziness and ignorance which unfitted them from ever becoming industrious men and women.

But in the chief manufacturing districts, while the condition of the factory children became the subject of legislation for protection, their condition was one to be envied beside that of the children in mining and agricultural districts.

The spasmodic nature of work under the domestic system caused much disturbance, for hand working is always more or less discontinuous from the caprice of the operative, while much time must be lost in gathering and returning materials. For these and obvious reasons a hand-weaver could very seldom turn off in a week much more than one-half what his loom could produce if kept continuously in action during the working hours of the day, at the rate which the weaver in his working paroxysms impelled it. [Ure, 333.]

The regular order maintained in the factory cures this evil of the old system and enables the operative to know with reasonable certainty the wages he is to receive at the next pay day. His life and habits become more orderly, and he finds, too, that as he has left the closeness of his home shop for the usually clean and well lighted factory, he imbibes more freely of the health-giving tonic of the atmosphere. It is commonly supposed that cotton factories are crowded with operatives. From the nature of things the spinning and weaving rooms cannot be crowded. The spinning mules, in their advancing and retreating locomotion must have five or six times the space to work in that the actual bulk of the mechanism requires, and where the machinery stands the operative cannot. In the weaving rooms there can be no crowding of persons. . . .

Bad air is one of the surest influences to intemperance, and it is clearly susceptible of proof that intemperance does not exist, and has not existed to such alarming degrees, under the new as under the old system; certainly the influence of bad air has not been as potent.

The regularity required in mills is such as to render persons who are in the habit of getting intoxicated unfit to be employed there, and many manufacturers object to employing persons guilty of the vice; yet, notwithstanding all the efforts which have been made to stop the habit, the beer-drinking operatives of factory towns still constitute a most serious drawback to the success of industrial enterprises, but its effects are not so ruinous under the new as under the old system. . . .

Better morals, better sanitary conditions, better health, better wages, these are the practical results of the factory system, as compared with that which preceded it, and the results of all these have been a keener intelligence. Under the domestic system there existed no common centres of thought and action. Religious bigotry has fought against the new order, because it tends to destroy the power of the church. Association kills such power in time. One of the chief causes of trouble in Ireland, outside land difficulties, is its individual system of labor which predominates. Fill Ireland with factories and her elevation is assured; indeed, the north of Ireland, with its linen factories, is prosperous today.

The factory brings mental friction, contact, which could not exist under the old system. Take our own factories in New England, today, fed as they are by French Canadian operatives; when they go back to their own land, as many do, they carry with them the results, whatever they are, of contact with a new system, and the effects of such contact will tell upon their children if not upon themselves. The factory brings progress and intelligence; it establishes at the centres, the public hall for the lyceum and the concert; and even literary institutions have been the result of the direct influence of the system. . . .

While the factory system is superior in almost every respect to the individual system, the former is not free from positive evils because human nature is not perfect. These evils are few compared to the magnitude of the benefits of the system, but they should be kept constantly in mind, that public sentiment may be strong enough some day to remove them, in fact, it is removing them.

Whatever there was that was good, in the old household plan of labor, so far as keeping the family together at all times and working under the care of the head, was temporarily lost when the factory system took its place, in so far as the old workers entered the factories. This evil, like most others attendant upon the new order, has been greatly exaggerated. The workers under the old system, strenuously opposed the establishment of the new, and this led to the employment of great numbers of parish children, a feature of employment which was eagerly fostered by parish officers. Yet, while the working of young children in mills is something to be condemned in our own time, when it began it placed them in a far better condition than they had ever been in, or could have expected to be in, for it made them self-supporting.

The children have been excluded from the factories in all countries, gradually, till the laws of most States, European and American, prohibit their employment under fourteen years of age.

A great evil which even now attracts attention, and in our own country too, is the employment of married women. This occurs more generally with Irish and Canadian women, and too often is the result of the indolence or stupidity of the father. Employers have done much to check this evil, which is not so much an evil to the present as to the future generations. It is bad enough for the present. It robs the young of the care of their natural protectors, it demoralizes the older children, it makes home dreary, and robs it of its amenities. The factory mother's hours of labor in the mills are as long as those of others, and then comes the thousand and one duties of the home, in which although she may be aided by members of the family, there is little rest. No ten hour law can reach the overworked housewife in any walk of life, certainly not when she is a factory worker. Her employment in the mills is a crime to her offspring, and logically, a crime to the State, and the sooner law and sentiment make it impossible for her to stand at the loom, the sooner the character of mill operatives will be elevated. I count their employment with the consequent train of evils, the worst, and the very worst of the evils of a system which is the grandeur of the age, in an industrial point of view.

It is gratifying to know that in Massachusetts cotton mills only about eight per cent of the females employed are married women. This is equally true of English factories, and I believe that in both countries the number is gradually decreasing. So, too, the number of operatives who live in individual homes is increasing.

The employment of children is an evil which has been stimulated as much by the actions of parents as by mill owners.

These evils, however, have been the result of development rather than of inauguration, and thus will disappear as education, in its broad sense, takes the place of ignorance.

The evil effects of the kind of labor performed in mills, so far as health is concerned, have been considerable, while less than those attending the household system.

All employments have features not conducive to health. These features or conditions are incidental, and cannot be separated from the employment. In mining coal, for instance, the nature of the occupation is bad in nearly all respects; but coal must be had, and there is never any lack of miners. What, then, shall be done?

Operators are in duty bound, of course, to make all evils, whether incidental or artificial, as light as possible, and should introduce every improvement which will lighten the burden of any class who, by their mental incapacity or other causes, are content to seek employment in the lowest grades of labor. Machinery is constantly elevating the grades of labor, and the laborer. The working of mines, even, is today an easy task compared to what it was a few years ago.

The workers themselves have much responsibility on their own shoulders, so far as the healthfulness or unhealthfulness of an occupation is concerned.

Let the children of factory-workers everywhere be educated in the rudiments of sanitary science, and then let law say that bad air shall be prohibited, and I believe the vexed temperance question will not trouble us to the extent it has. Drunkenness and intemperance are not the necessary accompanying evils of the factory system, and never have been; but wherever corporations furnish unhealthy home surroundings, there the evils of intemperance will be more or less felt in all the directions in which the results of rum find their wonderful ramifications.

The domestic system of labor could not deal with machinery; machinery really initiated the factory system; that is, the latter is the result of machinery. But machinery has done something more,—it has brought with it new phases of civilization, for while it means the factory system in one sense, it is the type and representative of the civilization of this period, because it embodies, so far as mechanics are concerned, the concentrated, clearly wrought out thought of the age. While books represent thought, machinery is the embodiment of thought.

Industry and poverty are not hand-maidens, and as poverty is lessened good morals thrive. If labor, employment of the mind, is an essential to good morals, then the highest kind of employment, that requiring the most application and the best intellectual effort, means the best morals. This condition, I take courage to assert, is superinduced eventually by the factory system, for by it the operative is usually employed in a higher grade of labor than that which occupied him in his previous condition. For this reason the present system of productive industry is constantly narrowing the limits of the class that occupies the bottom step of social order.

One of the inevitable results of the factory is to enable men to secure a livelihood in less hours than of old; this is grand in itself, for as the time required to earn a living grows shorter, our civilization grows up.

That system which demands of a man all his time for the earning of mere subsistence is demoralizing in all respects.

"As to the abasement of intelligence which is said to follow in proportion as tasks are subdivided, it is a conjecture more than a truth shown by experience. This abasement is presumed, not proven. It would be necessary to prove, for example, that the hand weaver, who throws the shuttle and gives motion to the loom, is of a superior class to the machine weaver who assists, without coöperating, in this double movement. Those who really know the facts would have just the opposite opinion. Employing the muscles in several operations instead of one, has nothing in it to elevate the faculties,"* and this is all the opponents of machinery claim. In their "view, the most imperfect machines, those which require the most effort, are the ones which sharpen the intellectual faculties to the greatest degree. We can easily see where this argument would carry us if pushed to the end."* . . .

The fact that the lowest grade of operatives can now be employed in mills, does not signify more ignorance, but, as I have said, a raising of the lowest to higher employments, and as the world progresses in its refinement, the lowest, which is high comparatively, seems all the lower. Society will bring all up, unless society is compelled to take up what is called a simpler system of labor. We should not forget that growth in civilization means complication, not simplification, nor that the machine is the servant of the workman, and not his competitor.

It is obvious that the factory system has not affected society as badly as has been generally believed; and if it has, in its introduction, brought evils, it has done much to remove others. "The unheard of power it has given labor, the wealth that has sprung from it, are not the sole property of any class or body of men. They constitute a kind of common fund, which, though irregularly divided," as are all the gifts of nature to finite understandings, "ought at least to satisfy the material, and many of the moral wants of society." [Reybaud, Cotton, 22.]

* Cf. Reybaud, Cotton.

The softening of the misery caused by the change in systems has occurred, but in subtle ways. Transition stages are always harsh upon the
generation that experiences them; the great point is that they should be
productive of good results in the end.

The mind recoils at the contemplation of the conditions which the vast
increase of population would have imposed without the factory system.

"It is a sad law, perhaps, but it is an invariable law, that industry, in
its march, takes no account of the positions that it overturns, nor of the
destinies that it modifies. We must keep step with its progress, or be left
upon the road. It always accomplishes its work, which is to make better
goods at a lower price, to supply more wants and also those of a better
order, not with regard for any class, but having in view the whole human
race. Industry is this, or it is not industry; true to its instincts it has no
sentiment in it, unless it is for its own interest; and yet such is the harmony of things, when they are abandoned to their natural course, notwithstanding the selfishness of industry, directed to its own good, it turns
finally to secure the good of all, and while requiring service for itself, it
serves at the same time by virtue of its resources and its power." [Rey-
baud, Cotton, 13.]

Recent writers, notwithstanding all the facts of history, find a solution
for whatever difficulties result from the production of goods under the
factory system, in the dispersion of congregated labor, and a return to
simple methods when they would have the machines owned and manipulated as individual property, under individual enterprise; but it is safe
to assert that "a people who have once adopted the large system of production, are not likely to recede from it"; labor is more productive on the
system of large industrial enterprises; the produce is greater in proportion
to the labor employed; the same number of persons can be supported
equally well with less toil and greater leisure; and in the moral aspect of
the question, something better is aimed at as the good of industrial improvement, than to disperse the workers of society over the earth to be
employed in pent up houses, and the sin-breeding small shops of another
age, where there would be scarcely any community of interest, or necessary mental communion with other human beings. . . .

It is from such influences we discern the elevation of an increased proportion of working people from the position of unskilled to that of skilled
laborers, and the opening of an adequate field of remunerative employment to women, two of the most important improvements which could
be desired in the condition of the working classes. Since, therefore, the
extension of the factory system tends strongly towards both these results,
it may be considered as one of the features of the present age, which is
the most favorable to their more permanent advancement. [Cf. Morrison,
Lab. & Cap. 195.]

It is also true that the factory system has stamped itself most emphatically upon the written law of all countries where it has taken root, as well as upon the social and moral laws which lie at the bottom of the forces which make written law what it is. . . .

The social battles which men have fought have been among the severest for human rights, and they mark eras in social conditions as clearly as do field contests in which more human lives have been lost, perhaps, but in which no greater human interests have been involved.

At the time of the institution of the factory system, there were upon the statute books of England but few laws relating to master and man; those which did exist were largely of criminal bearing, establishing punishment for various short comings of the men, but with the coming of the new system, the evils of poor law abuses came into full view, and while pauper children were vastly better off in the factories than in the parish poorhouses, they attracted attention and became the subjects of parliamentary protection. For the first time, there appeared some of the consequences of congregated labor, or rather the effects of the congregation of one class of labor appeared. A whole generation of operatives were growing up under conditions of comparative physical degeneracy, of mental ignorance and moral corruption, all of which existed before, but which the factory system brought into strong light.

And now the great question began to be asked, "Has the nation any right to interfere? Shall society suffer that individuals may profit?" Shall the next and succeeding generations be weakened morally and intellectually that estates may be enlarged? . . .

The weal or woe of the operative population depends largely upon the temper in which the employers carry the responsibility entrusted to them. I know of no trust more sacred than that given into the hands of the Captains of Industry, for they deal with human beings in close relations; not through the media of speech or exhortation, but of positive association, and by this they can make or mar. Granted that the material is often poor, the intellects often dull; then all the more sacred the trust and all the greater the responsibility. The rich and powerful manufacturer with the adjuncts of education and good business training, holds in his hand something more than the means of subsistence for those he employs, he holds their moral well-being in his keeping, in so far as it is in his power to mould their morals. He is something more than a producer, he is an instrument of God for the upbuilding of the race.

This may sound like sentiment; I am willing to call it sentiment, but I know it means the best material prosperity, and that every employer who has been guided by such sentiments has been rewarded two fold, first, in witnessing the wonderful improvement of his people, and second, in seeing his dividends increase, and the wages of the operatives increase with his dividends.

The factory system of the future will be run on this basis. The instances of such are multiplying rapidly now, and whenever it occurs, the system outstrips the pulpit in the actual work of the gospel, that is, in the work of humanity. It needs no gift of prophecy to foretell the future of a system which has in it more possibilities for good for the masses who must work for day wages, than any scheme which has yet been devised by philanthropy alone.

To make the system what it will be, the factory itself must be rebuilt, and so ordered in all its appointments that the great question for the labor reformer shall be, how to get people out of their homes and into the factory. The agitation of such a novel proposition will bring all the responsibility for bad conditions directly home to the individual, and then the law can handle the difficulty. . . .

The Business of a Factory

Philip G. Hubert, Jr.

One hot evening in July last I stood on the brink of a little canal that skirts a row of noble buildings constituting the largest textile mill in New England and perhaps in the world, and watched hundreds and thousands of mill-hands pour over the bridge that connects the mills with the town of which they are the chief support and pride. As the great bell clanged forth its six peals, one could hear the cessation of toil for the day. The mighty turbines, fed by this canal from the Merrimac, ceased to revolve, the great Corliss engines that in recent years have come to the aid of water-power in all big mills, came to a stop; the three hundred thousand spindles, the eight thousand looms, and the thousands of other ponderous machines, ingenious and effective almost past belief, for picking, cleaning, roving, bleaching, printing, drying, and finishing the one hundred million yards of cotton and woolen goods turned out from these mills every year —all this vast mass of machinery, scattered over sixty acres of flooring, came to a stop. Bell-time, as six o'clock in the afternoon is called in all New England mill-towns, had come. In place of the hum and clatter of machinery, the patter of innumerable feet made itself heard. Then the first of the army of five thousand operatives began to come, first by driblets, comprising those who did not need to wash, or did not care to, then the larger streams as the doors of some great room were thrown open, each operative having to go and come by a special staircase in order to avoid the gorging of any particular exit in case of fire, and finally the dense stream of humanity, male and female, big and little, until the broad iron bridge was packed and shook under the strain. Browning's description of the rats as they came in answer to the three shrill notes of the Pied Piper came to my mind.

I hope that should any of the mill-hands of this particular mill ever read these lines they will take no offence at the comparison. The picture was not an unpleasant one; it had just the diversity suggested by the poet.

Philip G. Hubert, Jr., "The Business of a Factory," *Scribner's Magazine*, XXI (January-June, 1897), 306–331.

There were men and women, boys and girls, of all ages and colors—even green, and blue, and yellow, and striped—for the operatives in the printing and dyeing shops are as apt to be covered with color as the miller is powdered with flour; here were the fat and the lean, the tall and the short, pretty women and women—less pretty; dark and fair, neat and sloven. And it should be said here that no such squalid poverty saddens the visitor to these mills as can be seen in every manufacturing town in England. Every woman and girl wore shoes; the poor slattern, barefooted, and with a ragged shawl thrown over her head, that one finds by the thousand coming from the cotton-mills of England, was conspicuous by her absence. The women and girls of our manufacturing towns, especially where the native American stock still holds its own, retain a vivid appreciation of pretty things in dress and adornment. In some of the cotton towns, such as Fall River, where the French Canadian and the Irish have driven the Yankee girl from the spindles and the loom, there is less concern for personal appearance than in Lynn, for instance, with its American shoe operatives, or in Manchester with its American thread-makers. Among the more recent recruits to the mills are the Armenians and Polish Jews, of whom there are some in almost all the New England manufacturing towns.

Watching the privates of this army of workers pour forth from the mills where they have been at work since half past six in the morning, with an hour's rest at noon, and bearing in mind the fact that these mills have been in steady and profitable operation for nearly half a century, the management of this vast machine for turning out and selling one hundred million yards of goods a year will impress any one as possessing as much general interest, and far more human interest, than the processes of manufacture themselves. How is the business conducted, whether the product be cotton-yarn, printed calico, watches, shoes, or bicycles? What are the principles governing the art of making money by the manufacture and sale of articles requiring an army of operatives?

One feature of the manufacturing industries of a country that makes them of perhaps more interest than the agricultural industries, is the constant change in the character of the product, as well as in the methods of manufacture. The farmers' products seldom or never change. The wheat sealed up in Egyptian tombs fifteen hundred years before the birth of Christ is found to be identical with that grown in Egypt to-day, and upon being planted yields a similar crop to that now grown. Not only do manufactured objects change every few years, but the field is constantly enlarged by the appearance of new things to make—things not dreamed of a few years ago. Electricity now gives employment to hundreds of thousands of persons whose great-grandfathers never heard of a telegraph, a telephone, an electric light, or a motor. While new farms spring up every day in the wilderness, it is always the same old wheat or corn that results. But every day some new factory begins turning out a product the like of which was never seen before, and, in some cases, let us hope, may not be seen again. More than this, it is not reasonable to suppose that this stream of novelty which began to flow with the printing press, the steam-engine, and the electric spark, will ever cease. It would be strange if we happy possessors of these wonderful tools, unknown to our forefathers, should fail to profit by them, and turn out still more wonderful things in the future. The next century ought certainly to give the world gifts as valuable as steam and electricity. The factories of 1997 will make wonders, of which we have no conception. The field is, however, already so large that one branch of manufacture must be taken as a type of all, and I have selected the making of calicoes as offering the best illustrations of this business of manufacturing. The business problems met with by the man who undertakes to buy cotton, weave, print, and sell it as calico, are similar in kind with those of the man who makes shoes, or lamps, or watches. They involve accurate judgment not only of what the public is asking for, but—far more important—what it is going to ask for; the purchase of raw material, the hiring of labor, the judicious management of an army of people so as to avoid laxity on one hand and strikes on the other, the discovery of new and better processes, the choice of designs, the manufacture itself, finally the disposal of the product by a thousand channels, native and foreign.

Let me, therefore, take a big cotton-mill making and printing its own calicoes, as the type of an American manufacturing business. If a man wants to enter the business of making calicoes, the question of capital is the first consideration. Most of our cotton-mills and paper-mills are stock corporations, largely because of the vast capital needed. The larger the plant the cheaper the product, is an axiom in the cotton business, especially when staple goods, such as sheetings, are to be made. There is always a market here or abroad for American sheeting, and the sales are often made in such vast quantities that the danger of overstocking the market is as nothing compared with fancy dress-goods, shoes, or worsted cloths, the fashions of which change from one year to another. It is not unusual to hear of the sale of thousands of bales of sheetings in one operation. It follows, therefore, that the manufacturer must be ready to take advantage of these periods of profit, so to speak, and be ready with his tens of thousands of bales of goods, where the manufacturer of goods liable to depreciation through change of fashion, such as shoes, hats, fancy printed cloths, etc., does not dare to manufacture much beyond the current demand of the market, and is consequently debarred from manu-facture upon the vast scale seen in the mills at Fall River, Lowell, and Lawrence. The capital needed for cotton-mills being therefore very large —the mill I have selected as a type having a capital of three million dollars, and its property being assessed at nearly five millions—the ownership is commonly held by a stock company. Boston is said to depend for its cake upon the profits of the New England cotton-mills. When cotton goods sell at a loss, Commonwealth Avenue, metaphorically speaking, is reduced to bread. It speaks well for the business that in the last twenty-five years there have been no failures of importance among the New England cotton-mills. Some years ago, in times of wide-spread financial trouble, one of the big mills at Fall River was compelled to offer its creditors stock instead of money in payment of large obligations; within eight years this stock doubled in value, so that these creditors are not to be pitied. Boston, and a hundred New England towns, harbor thousands and thousands of people, often past middle life and out of business, whose sole dependence is upon the shares they hold in this or that mill, which they may never see, but from which they draw their incomes; they rely wholly upon the judgment and integrity of the officers of the corporation. Upon the other hand, these officers find their task made easy by the confidence of the stockholders, who, when poor times come, accept small dividends without grumbling. To invest savings in mill stock has been the custom for generations in hundreds of New England families, and it may be largely due to the stability of the New England mills that so many other big business properties throughout the country have found it possible within the last few years to reorganize as stock corporations. . . .

The necessary capital having been subscribed and the manufacture of cotton goods decided upon, the question of site is next to be settled. In the past good water-power has been of the chief importance in the selection of a mill site. The splendid water-power on the Merrimac, at Lowell, Nashua, Lawrence, and elsewhere explained the existence of gigantic mills at these places. Steam, however, is rapidly replacing water-power, notwithstanding the improvements made in turbine wheels. In most of the older mills of New England steam now shares about equally the work with water, while in the new mills it takes almost the whole burden. Of course in factories where the power needed is small, such as in making hats, clothing, shoes, etc., steam has entirely replaced water, the higher cost being of no importance when its greater reliability is considered. As yet electricity has not appeared as motive power, except in small industries. What the tremendous works at Niagara will do in this field remains to be seen. It is easier with electricity to adapt the power to the needs of the day whether they are great or small, than with steam. Mr. Atkinson foresees the ultimate dispersion of these mill armies to their homes, when electric power can be sent from place to place without loss; then, as before the introduction of steam-power, the weaver will work his loom and the spinner his spindles in his own cottage instead of in the big mill. Whether or not the change will be to the benefit of the operative is still a mooted question among experts. One of the agents of a big mill, a man who has studied the problem at close quarters for twenty years, tells me that the change would be a misfortune for the mill-hand. In the mill the worker has the law as his champion in providing good air and light, and in limiting the hours of labor; in his own cottage the hours of labor will be measured only by the endurance of the weaker members of the family, while the sanitary arrangements are apt to be defective as compared to those of a modern mill.

It is commonly admitted that while a man or woman who does some small thing in the manufacture of an article—whether it is piecing the broken yarns of a spinning machine, or cutting the eye of a needle, or gathering matches for boxing—may become marvellously expert, the operator runs the risk of becoming more or less of a machine. The girl who stands at the end of a frame of one hundred spindles and sees a broken thread, catches it with lightning-like rapidity and joins it with a touch; the one who cuts the eyes in needles can do the same thing with a human hair; and the girls who pack matches pick up the requisite number for the box, whether it is one hundred, more or less, without counting them, judging simply by touch whether or not the right number is there, and doing it as fast as the eye can follow the hand. Mr. Ruskin contends, probably with reason, that the minute division of labor that makes such wonders possible brutalizes the laborer, and that if the girl made the whole article instead of doing one operation out of fifty, she would gain in intelligence if not in expertness. From an economic, or rather an industrial point of view, however, manufacturing has to be carried on at present with the greatest subdivision of labor possible. Fierce competition and a small margin of profit demand it. Mr. Ruskin's dream of a manufacturing community in which the same person shall shear the sheep, clean the wool, dye it, card, spin, and weave it, doing all this in country homes made beautiful with flowers, working but six hours a day, and devoting the rest of the time to reading good books, raising flowers, and singing songs, is a very pretty dream to be made possible only when some philanthropist provides a market at good profit as well as the pleasant conditions for this labor. For the present steam-power is the only power suitable for the work of manufacturing, and this compels the work to be done at one spot. . . .

This minute subdivision of labor which threatens, according to some economists, to make the operative only a part of a machine, and needing to be little more intelligent than one of its wheels, may go on at one end of the industry to be counter-balanced at the other end by a process of aggrandizement. Just as in the large cities the department store is absorbing the smaller shops of its neighborhood, so the large factory of the future may absorb its smaller rivals, not only in the same branch of industry but in many others. There are great mills in New England to-day which not only spin and weave, but print, using wool and silk as well as cotton, something unheard of a few years ago. It is an interesting speculation among experts as to how long it will be before the same gigantic mill will turn out cotton goods, woollen goods, silks, shoes, umbrellas, hats and caps, and writing-paper. The very process that makes the operative merely the attendant upon a machine favors such a development. When there is no sale for cotton, the army of hands will start up the shoe machines, just as, in the department stores, when business is dull at the silk counter the clerks may be put at selling cigars. This may sound extremely fanciful, but there are indications of such a trend. It may be remembered that when, some thirty years ago, a Philadelphia clothier introduced umbrellas as a part of his stock the innovation was widely denounced as a sinful encroachment upon the rights of umbrella shops. Yet to-day it would be hard to say what the department store does not sell; it supplies or attempts to supply all that man needs from a cradle to a coffin. So the first cotton factory that adds shoes to its list of products may excite criticism, but if there is profit in the change it is sure to come. . . .

The business organization of most big factories is simple enough. Almost all cotton-mill properties are managed by a board of directors elected by the stockholders. These directors appoint officers, among whom the treasurer and the agent are the important personages, the first having charge of the finances, the buying of supplies, payment of expenses, and selling of goods; the second having the actual manufacture of the goods under his control, the hiring of labor, the management of the shops or mills. The treasurer of most New England manufacturing corporations lives in Boston, where the goods are sold, and the agent lives near the mills. Taking a big cotton-mill, the agent employs a head or superintendent for each of the important departments, such as the carding, roving, spinning, weaving, bleaching, printing, and packing. Under these superintendents there may be many or few foremen, according to the character of the work. In some departments where the work is all of the same character, each girl of the three hundred in a room doing precisely what her neighbor does, year in and year out, a few foremen suffice. In one room at the mill I have in mind, a room 800 feet long by 70 feet wide, the girls who tend the spindles need small advice, and being paid by the product turned out from their machines, they need small supervision. In other departments, the print works, for instance, there are a variety of operations requiring comparatively few men, but a high grade of intelligence and constant supervision by expert foremen. The transfer of the designs to the copper rolls used in printing, the mixing of the colors, the adjustment of elaborate machinery, all this delicate work requires vast experience. The discipline of such mills is by no means military. In visiting several of the largest of them I was impressed with the friendly relations between superintendents and men. "We never scold," said the agent of a big mill. "If a man or girl proves to be habitually careless or idle, a discharge follows; but for small infractions of rules we trust the various foremen to look after their own people. In the sixteen years I have been here we have had no strikes." At half-past six in the morning the bell rings for work to begin; there is an hour's intermission at noon, and then from one to six it goes on again. On Saturdays all work in most cotton-mills stops for the day at noon. The law limits factory work in Massachusetts to fifty-eight hours a week. In New York State there is no such limit. In some trades, the Lynn shoe shops, for instance, work begins at seven o'clock and there is only half an hour's stop at noon. In Connecticut, the hours at Waterbury and Ansonia are the same as in Lynn. In the paper-mills of Massachusetts and Connecticut work begins at half-past six, with an hour at noon.

Opinions differ as to whether or not the growth of the factory system is a blessing to a community, but, as a rule, it is conceded that the standard of intelligence and of living among the mill-hands of New England is not so high now as it was forty years ago. And this, notwithstanding higher wages and shorter hours. In 1850, the average mill-hand earned $175 a year, as against $300 at present, and worked thirteen hours a day as against ten hours to-day. The American farmer's daughter who worked in the cotton mills fifty years ago has been almost wholly displaced, first by women of Irish and English birth, and more recently by the French Canadian, all representing lower types. The very growth of the mills has tended to do away with certain features of factory life, that worked for good in smaller communities. In the old days, say in 1850, the American girls who made cotton cloth in Lowell, or shoes in Lynn, or thread in Manchester, had their own singing and reading societies, their benevolent clubs, and church sociables. The owner or agent of a small mill in a small town was able to exercise something of a paternal supervision over the few hundred girls or men who might work for him. With the immense increase in mill plants, the force now numbering thousands where it was hundreds fifty years ago, this is impossible. Yet, whether it be as a matter of self-interest or not, the visitor to Lowell, Manchester, Lawrence, Fall River, and other factory centres will find an attempt on the part of mill owners to help the hands after they leave the buildings. Saving societies, libraries, hospitals are common. In Lawrence there are no less than three flourishing co-operative stores patronized exclusively by mill-hands. The rise in power of the unions seems to have made the mill-hands suspicious of all interference with matters outside the mill. One is apt to find a dozen unions in a cotton-mill, and in the shoe shops there are unions for every one of the score or more of operations through which a shoe passes. The factory law of Massachusetts prescribes that wages shall be paid weekly. This rule has been found to work rather disadvantageously so far as saving by the mill-hand goes, for, receiving no large sum of money in a lump, he finds it difficult to spare from the comparatively small weekly wage. Efforts are made almost periodically by many mill corporations to render the homes of the hands more sanitary than they were in earlier years, and attractive with gardens and flowers. In some towns, notably in Manchester, where the mill operatives number many native Americans, some success in this direction has been met with; in other towns, notably the larger centres—Lowell, Nashua, Fall River, Lawrence—where the population is either foreign-born or but one generation removed from it, not much has been effected. The hands live mostly in tenements unadorned with gardens or even grass-plats. A large number of the hands in every factory are young people who have to board, necessitating the existence in all mill towns of large rows of tenements known as boarding-houses, as a rule dreary homes inside and out. The people who live in them, looking upon themselves as temporary inmates or tenants only, cannot be induced to better their surroundings, and will decline to care for the vines and flowers offered to them by their employers. . . .

As in most other trades, strikes are the bane of the factory owner's existence. With a plant worth perhaps a million dollars brought to a standstill, and perhaps half a million dollars' worth of raw material in process of manufacture, a strike coming at an awkward time of year means tremendous loss.

Next in importance, or perhaps even of more importance than the character of the hands, comes the character of the machinery in use. The entire machinery of a mill may be said to change every twenty years, just as the entire material of the human body is said to change every seven years, or eleven years—I forget which. I asked one mill superintendent, a veteran who has seen the inside of about every mill in the country, what he looked at most carefully upon entering a rival establishment. "First the machinery, then the hands." Nine-tenths of the machinery used in cotton and woollen manufacture, ninety-nine hundredths of that used in shoe making, and all of that used in paper-mills is made in this country. In cotton-mills we still use English carders, as the machines for cleaning the cotton from small imperfections are called. In return for their carders we have given the English the most important improvement made in cotton manufacture during this generation—the Rabbeth spindle, which makes ten thousand revolutions a minute, as against half that speed with the old-fashioned spindle. It has been estimated by General William F. Draper, an expert on the subject, that the Rabbeth spindle, invented in 1866 by Francis J. Rabbeth, of Ilion, N. Y., has effected a saving of $100,-000,000 to this country since its introduction about 1870. In equipping a new factory there is always a certain advantage over older establishments, thanks to changes and improvements in the machinery. What is done to-day in the new mills just finished at the South would astonish the mill-hands of twenty years ago. As a rule, these changes in cotton machinery have been introduced without opposition. The spinning and weaving, for instance, are paid for by the piece, so that the introduction of the Rabbeth spindle, doing twice the work and requiring actually less care and watchfulness on the part of the operator, found its champions as well as its detractors. In some trades, however, the spirit that led to the breaking-up of Arkwright's spinning frames because they did so much work survives. The shoe manufacturers of Lynn have not yet dared to introduce a certain lasting machine largely employed in Europe and in certain western cities of this country because the lasters' trades union forbids its use. According to the leading shoemakers of Lynn, this machine would revolutionize the business. One firm has very recently induced the Lynn lasters' union to consent to the introduction of two of these machines as experiments, the lasters themselves to try the machines and to fix the conditions under which they may be used if used at all. It is evident that in a big manufactory it is not everything to invent a labor-saving machine; endless tact must be used to induce the unions to allow its use.

That the purchase of raw material for a big factory requires the services of a dozen experts may well be imagined, when the vast sums of money involved are considered. In one cotton-mill of New England there was used last year 25,000 bales of cotton, worth about $1,000,000, 8,000,-000 pounds of wool, 50,000 tons of coal, and $100,000 worth of coloring matter and dyes. It is hardly necessary to say that an expert at a liberal salary the year round is essential for each of these purchases. The cotton buyer spends his whole time in the South watching the growing crops, purchasing sometimes a year before the crop is grown, keeping an eye on the stock on hand in different parts of the country and calculating to a nicety exactly what will be needed and when. All the cotton for a big mill is thus bought where it is grown. The same is true of the wool, and the coal buyer lives in the mining regions of Pennsylvania. The coloring matter used in printing a yard of calico that sells for ten cents costs less than the twentieth part of a cent, yet fortunes have been spent in recent years in efforts to reduce this cost. It is said that one mill-owner of Rhode Island spent $70,000 inside of three years in experiments to replace madder dyes, the experiments, by the way, leading to nothing valuable in the end. The chemist at one cotton-mill I have in mind, a modest man, who spends his time mixing colors and testing dyes in his laboratory, receives a salary of $5,000 a year. He has to know not only how to prepare the colors for the printers, but how to insure their permanency. "Will it wash?" is about the first question asked by every woman who examines a piece of calico on the dry-goods counter. The chemist is responsible for that. . . .

In all factory work it is essential to have as complete a system of checks upon defective work as possible, especially since the opposition of the unions to improved machinery has made payment by the piece obligatory. In cotton-mills to-day more than seventy per cent. of the hands are paid by the piece, in shoe factories ninety per cent., in brass-ware factories eighty per cent., and in paper-mills sixty per cent. The visitor to any big cotton-mill will notice that the spools of yarn from the spinners all bear a colored chalk mark, the finished roll of cloth from the looms a similar mark, and so on, from first to last, every piece of work bearing a mark, sometimes red, sometimes blue, all the colors and shades of the rainbow being used, and often two colors together. By this means each piece is traced back. The weaver who finds that the yarn furnished to her is defective in the spinning has only to examine the chalk-mark on the spool to find out who spun it, and so on through the whole operation till the finished piece of goods reaches the packer. . . .

A factory having been put up in a suitable spot, equipped with proper machinery, and a force of competent hands engaged, the important question arises: What kind of goods shall be made? This is a question to be decided by the persons who sell the product of the mill—the selling agents. Under the direction of these agents, the art director, so to speak, of the corporation seeks high and low for designs, takes suggestions where he can, employs designers and artists. We can surpass the world at machinery, but as yet we have to go to Paris for our designs. Each of the big mills where printed goods are made keeps its man in Paris watching the new designs and buying the best he can from the professional designers, of which there are a hundred in Paris, some of them earning as high as $20,000 a year. A designer of international reputation commands his own price, inasmuch as the design makes or mars the product; it sells or does not sell according to the favor the pattern meets with. The question is often asked: How do the men who make designs know what kind of goods the public is going to demand? The designs for next winter's goods are already finished. How does the artist know that the fickle public is not going to discard all that it has admired this year, and go wild over what it now ignores? This year the colors are faint and suggestive; next year they may be kaleidoscopic in brilliancy. This year ladies' shoes run to a point, next year they may be square-toed. Upon an accurate forecast of the public's whims in these matters depends success. Well, the truth seems to be that sudden or violent as these fluctuations appear, there is really an evolutionary process involved. Each style or fashion has in it the germs of what is to follow, perhaps visible only to experts, but to be discerned. The designer accents the peculiar attributes of a pattern that has found favor one year in order to create his design for the next season. The short life of a design is somewhat surprising. Out of the six or eight hundred patterns made during this last year by the largest calico-mill in the country it is not likely that ten will be called for two years hence. The designs (the word design covering the texture of the material as well as its ornamentation) for every class of goods have to be virtually new every year, and the explanation given for this is hardly flattering to the fair wearers of these pretty mousselines, lawns, organdies, cashmeres, serges, and brocades.

"Not only," said a mill agent, "do fashions change in a bewildering way, and a most expensive way to us manufacturers, but they have a way of changing so radically that new goods may be wholly unsalable if they bear any resemblance to the dress goods in demand last year. Why? Simply because a woman who buys a new dress wants a pattern and a color wholly different from that of her last year's frock, in order that there may be no question as to its being a new frock. She not only wants a different design, but a very different one, so that he, or more probably, she, who runs may see that it is a new dress." . . .

The element of chance thus enters more or less into any manufacture dependent upon changes of fashion. As the styles for summer have to be made in winter, and those for winter in summer, a manufacturer cannot wait to see what the public wants; he has to take his chances. What he has made may or may not meet with favor. If it does not, his whole product will have to be sold at cost or less, to be sent to the confines of civilization. Upon the other hand, fortunes are often made when fashion veers in favor of a particular style of goods. . . .

Some factories, usually very small ones, depend wholly upon novelties. Each year some new trifle comes up upon which the whole establishment is put to work. Holiday goods, the trifles sold by sidewalk pedlers, and many cheap toys are of this class where the ingenuity of the deviser or designer is everything. Of a curious character was a small factory near Philadelphia, devoted wholly at one time to the manufacture of hoaxes sold through advertisement. Among the notable successes of this precious establishment was a device warranted to kill the potato-bug. Thousands of farmers sent their half-dollars in exchange for two little slabs of wood with the directions: "Place the bug between these two blocks of wood and press hard." This seems scarcely worth noting as an industry, and yet incredible sums of money are made out of the manufacture of things hardly less trivial. Many readers may remember the vogue of a wooden ball fastened to a rubber string, so that the ball when thrown returned to the hand. It is said that the patentee and manufacturer of that toy made $80,000 in one season from it.

The demand for novelties, always novelties, imposes a constant expense and drain upon all manufacturing corporations, and yet it is the novelties that offer the greatest field for profit. Staple goods not affected by fashion must be sold almost at cost because every mill can make them, and the stocks of such goods on hand are always enormous. When orders are scarce and a mill agent hesitates about letting his hands go for fear that he may not be able to get the best of them back in time of need, the force may be used in turning out coarse staple goods, sure to find a market some day. But such work offers only a minimum margin of profit. One case of fancy goods that sell well brings in a larger profit than one hundred cases of some staple article that every mill in the country, North and South, can turn out. Novelty is the cry of all manufacturers. Give us something new to make. Every year the mills of this country turn out from three to five thousand new designs, of which perhaps one thousand find a profitable sale.

A factory having produced a stock of goods from the best designs to be obtained by its agents here and abroad, the next step is to sell at a profit. Twenty-five years ago the mill or factory sold all its goods to the jobbers, who in turn distributed them to the retailers throughout the country. Each mill had its selling agents who undertook to dispose of its product to the jobbers. A retailer could buy nothing directly from the agent of the mill. Within the last ten or fifteen years the small jobber has been eliminated. In 1850 there were half a hundred dry-goods jobbers in New York City and as many in Boston all doing a good business. To-day the number has dwindled to half a dozen in each city. The same thing is true of Philadelphia and Chicago. Only a few of the very largest jobbing houses have survived. The selling agents of the mills now go direct to the retailer, because the retailers have in many instances become buyers upon a much larger scale than the small jobber of former days. Go into the Boston or New York office of the agent of any important mill, and you will find plenty of samples and clerks, but almost no buyers. The agent now goes to the buyer. The agent of the largest cotton-mill in western Massachusetts told me that he sent his men to every large dry-goods shop in Boston every day, and his partner in New York did the same thing there. At certain seasons Boston and New York, twenty-five or thirty years ago, were overrun with the buyers of dry-goods houses from all parts of the country. There were hotels and even newspapers devoted to these buyers and their doings. Much of this business has passed away. To-day the travelling men, "drummers," of the mills and the few large jobbing houses that have survived, scour the country, taking their samples to the retailer. A few large jobbers, doing an immense business, still survive in all our large centres because they have the machinery for the distribution of goods in channels where it is not worth the while of the agent to enter—small shops in small towns. The small jobber who gave up business when he found the mills selling directly to the retail shops who could buy even more goods at a time than he could, had neither the capital nor the army of travelling men necessary to do business upon this scale. The jobber who could buy five thousand cases of goods at a time, and had the machinery and the means for disposing of it, survives because the mills sell cheapest to the largest buyer, and the jobber who buys on this scale is more important that even the largest retail store. But the small jobber, buying one hundred cases of the same goods, gets no better terms than the big retailer and has therefore no excuse for being. Some of the big department stores now obtain a monopoly of certain patterns or designs by taking the whole output of the mill, thus doing what was formerly in the power of only the greatest of jobbers.

The object of the country merchant in sending his buyer to New York or Boston every year was to get a more attractive stock than that obtained by his rival on the next block, and at better prices. The buyer comes no more to headquarters. A few big jobbers send their men to him, as I have said, and supplement these visits in the following way: The big jobber's travelling man, making a specialty, say of the eastern end of Long Island, and having a number of customers in that region, not only takes his samples over the route several times each season, but he promises his customer that when novelties of importance or goods at extraordinarily low prices appear in New York he will take care that some are sent out to this customer. The travelling man has an accurate knowledge of the selling capacity of his customer, and an agreement with him to the effect that the country merchant will take a certain amount of whatever goods the "drummer" may see fit to send him in an emergency. Much depends, as will be seen, upon the judgment of this latter. If he abuses his privilege, there will be trouble. If, on the contrary, he acts with good judgment, he will be invaluable.

Now suppose that one day a certain mill comes to the house in New York with the offer of a big stock of new and fashionable goods, or goods at a remarkably low price; the outside force is called together and an estimate is made of the quantity of such goods that can be distributed. The Long Island man puts down this customer of his for three cases, that one for one case, and some one else for half a case. The jobbing house may be able, by taking the whole country, to buy the whole stock of this pattern from the mill, thus getting exceptional terms and a monopoly of the pattern. The country merchant who gets the goods, of which his rival across the way can get none, will make money or lose it according to their desirability. He may receive too many goods in this way, in which case he can restrict the privilege of the New York house, or he may find that he could have sold five times as much of a cheap and popular style of goods as he received. I have been told of instances in which five thousand cases of printed calicoes, or about eight million yards, have been disposed of in this way in one morning by the largest jobbing house in this country.

The search for a foreign outlet for American manufacturers began more than half a century ago and still goes on. Every year some new market is discovered. Our old competitor, England, fights hard, but we can often beat her on her own ground. Everyone may know that we send our New England cotton-cloth to the British colonies by the thousand cases, but it may be news to many that 25,000 American ploughs went to the Argentine Republic last year, and that the thousands of watches distributed to the Japanese army as rewards of bravery were made in this country. . . .

"Taylorism"

Frederick W. Taylor

The ordinary, piece-work system involves a permanent antagonism between employers and men, and a certainty of punishment for each workman who reaches a high rate of efficiency. The demoralizing effect of this system is most serious. Under it, even the best workmen are forced continually to act the part of hypocrites, to hold their own in the struggle against the encroachments of their employers.

The system introduced by the writer, however, is directly the opposite, both in theory and in its results. It makes each workman's interests the same as that of his employer, pays a premium for high efficiency, and soon convinces each man that it is for his permanent advantage to turn out each day the best quality and maximum quantity of work.

The writer has endeavored in the following pages to describe the system of management introduced by him in the works of the Midvale Steel Company, of Philadelphia, which has been employed by them during the past ten years with the most satisfactory results.

The system consists of three principal elements:

(1) An elementary rate-fixing department.

(2) The differential rate system of piece-work.

(3) What he believes to be the best method of managing men who work by the day.

Elementary rate-fixing differs from other methods of making piece-work prices in that a careful study is made of the time required to do each of the many elementary operations into which the manufacturing of an establishment may be analyzed or divided. These elementary operations are then classified, recorded, and indexed, and when a piece-work price is wanted for work, the job is first divided into its elementary operations, the time required to do each elementary operation is found from the records, and the total time for the job is summed up from these data. While this method seems complicated at the first glance, it is, in fact, far

Frederick W. Taylor, "A Piece-Rate System," *Transactions of the American Society of Mechanical Engineers,* XVI (1895), 856–903.

simpler and more effective than the old method of recording the time required to do whole jobs of work, and then, after looking over the records of similar jobs, guessing at the time required for any new piece of work.

The differential rate system of piece-work consists briefly in offering two differential rates for the same job; a high price per piece, in case the work is finished in the shortest possible time and in perfect condition, and a low price, if it takes a longer time to do the job, or if there are any imperfections in the work. (The high rate should be such that the workman can earn more per day than is usually paid in similar establishments.) This is directly the opposite of the ordinary plan of piece-work, in which the wages of the workmen are reduced when they increase their productivity.

The system by which the writer proposes managing the men who are on day-work consists in paying *men* and not *positions*. Each man's wages, as far as possible, are fixed according to the skill and energy with which he performs his work, and not according to the position which he fills. Every endeavor is made to stimulate each man's personal ambition. This involves keeping systematic and careful records of the performance of each man, as to his punctuality, attendance, integrity, rapidity, skill, and accuracy, and a readjustment from time to time of the wages paid him, in accordance with this record.

The advantages of this system of management are:

First. That the manufactures are produced cheaper under it, while at the same time the workmen earn higher wages than are usually paid.

Second. Since the rate-fixing is done from accurate knowledge instead of more or less by guess-work, the motive for holding back on work, or "soldiering," and endeavoring to deceive the employers as to the time required to do work, is entirely removed, and with it the greatest cause for hard feelings and war between the management and the men.

Third. Since the basis from which piece-work as well as day rates are fixed is that of exact observation, instead of being founded upon accident or deception, as is too frequently the case under ordinary systems, the men are treated with greater uniformity and justice, and respond by doing more and better work.

Fourth. It is for the common interest of both the management and the men to cooperate in every way, so as to turn out each day the maximum quantity and best quality of work.

Fifth. The system is rapid, while other systems are slow, in attaining the maximum productivity of each machine and man; and when this maximum is once reached, it is automatically maintained by the differential rate.

Sixth. It automatically selects and attracts the best men for each class of work, and it develops many first-class men who would otherwise remain slow or inaccurate, while at the same time it discourages and sifts out men who are incurably lazy or inferior.

Finally. One of the chief advantages derived from the above effects of the system is, that it promotes a most friendly feeling between the men and their employers, and so renders labor unions and strikes unnecessary.

There has never been a strike under the differential rate system of piece-work, although it has been in operation for the past ten years in the steel business, which has been during this period more subject to strikes and labor troubles than almost any other industry.

It is not unusual for the manager of a manufacturing business to go most minutely into every detail of the buying and selling and financiering, and arrange every element of these branches in the most systematic manner, and according to principles that have been carefully planned to insure the business against almost any contingency which may arise, while the manufacturing is turned over to a superintendent or foreman, with little or no restrictions as to the principles and methods which he is to pursue, either in the management of his men or the care of the company's plant.

Such managers belong distinctly to the old school of manufacturers; and among them are to be found, in spite of their lack of system, many of the best and most successful men of the country. They believe in men, not in methods, in the management of their shops; and what they would call system in the office and sales departments, would be called red tape by them in the factory. Through their keen insight and knowledge of character they are able to select and train good superintendents, who in turn secure good workmen; and frequently the business prospers under this system (or rather, lack of system) for a term of years.

The modern manufacturer, however, seeks not only to secure the best superintendents and workmen, but to surround each department of his manufacture with the most carefully woven network of system and method, which should render the business, for a considerable period, at least, independent of the loss of any one man, and frequently of any combination of men.

It is the lack of this system and method which, in the judgment of the writer, constitutes the greatest risk in manufacturing; placing, as it frequently does, the success of the business at the hazard of the health or whims of a few employees.

Even after fully realizing the importance of adopting the best possible system and methods of management for securing a proper return from employees and as an insurance against strikes and the carelessness and laziness of men, there are difficulties in the problem of selecting methods of management which shall be adequate to the purpose, and yet be free from red tape, and inexpensive. . . .

Now, among the methods of management in common use there is certainly a great choice; and before describing the "differential rate" system it is desirable to briefly consider the more important of the other methods.

The simplest of all systems is the "day-work" plan, in which the employees are divided into certain classes, and a standard rate of wages is paid to each class of men; the laborers all receiving one rate of pay, the machinists all another rate, and the engineers all another, etc. The men are paid according to the position which they fill, and not according to their individual character, energy, skill, and reliability.

The effect of this system is distinctly demoralizing and levelling; even the ambitious men soon conclude that since there is no profit to them in working hard, the best thing for them to do is to work just as little as they can and still keep their position. And under these conditions the invariable tendency is to drag them all down even below the level of the medium.

The proper and legitimate answer to this herding of men together into classes, regardless of personal character and performance, is the formation of the labor union, and the strike, either to increase the rate of pay and improve conditions of employment, or to resist the lowering of wages and other encroachments on the part of employers.

The necessity for the labor union, however, disappears when *men* are paid, and not *positions;* that is, when the employers take pains to study the character and performance of each of their employees and pay them accordingly, when accurate records are kept of each man's attendance, punctuality, the amount and quality of work done by him, and his attitude towards his employers and fellow-workmen.

As soon as the men recognize that they have free scope for the exercise of their proper ambition, that as they work harder and better their wages are from time to time increased, and that they are given a better class of work to do—when they recognize this, the best of them have no use for the labor union.

Every manufacturer must from necessity employ a certain amount of day-labor which cannot come under the piece-work system; and yet how few employers are willing to go to the trouble and expense of the slight organization necessary to handle their men in this way? How few of them realize that, by the employment of an extra clerk and foreman, and a simple system of labor returns, to record the performance and readjust the wages of their men, so as to stimulate their personal ambition, the output of a gang of twenty or thirty men can be readily doubled in many cases, and at a comparatively slight increase of wages per capita!

The clerk in the factory is the particular horror of the old-style manufacturer. He realizes the expense each time that he looks at him, and fails to see any adequate return; yet by the plan here described the clerk becomes one of the most valuable agents of the company.

If the plan of grading labor and recording each man's performance is so much superior to the old day-work method of handling men, why is it not all that is required? Because no foreman can watch and study all of his men all of the time, and because any system of laying out and apportioning work, and of returns and records, which is sufficiently elaborate to keep proper account of the performance of each workman, is more complicated than piece-work. It is evident that that system is the best which, in attaining the desired result, presents in the long run the course of least resistance.

The inherent and most serious defect of even the best managed day-work lies in the fact that there is nothing about the system that is self-sustaining. When once the men are working at a rapid pace, there is nothing but the constant, unremitting watchfulness and energy of the management to keep them there; while with every form of piece-work each new rate that is fixed insures a given speed for another section of work, and to that extent relieves the foreman from worry.

From the best type of day-work to ordinary piece-work the step is a short one. With good day-work the various operations of manufacturing should have been divided into small sections or jobs, in order to properly gauge the efficiency of the men; and the quickest time should have been recorded in which each operation has been performed. The change from paying by the hour to paying by the job is then readily accomplished.

The theory upon which the ordinary system of piece-work operates to the benefit of the manufacturer is exceedingly simple. Each workman, with a definite price for each job before him, contrives a way of doing it in a shorter time, either by working harder or by improving his method; and he thus makes a larger profit. After the job has been repeated a number of times at the more rapid rate, the manufacturer thinks that he should also begin to share in the gain, and therefore reduces the price of the job to a figure at which the workman, although working harder, earns, perhaps, but little more than he originally did when on day-work.

The actual working of the system, however, is far different. Even the most stupid man, after receiving two or three piece-work "cuts" as a reward for his having worked harder, resents this treatment and seeks a remedy for it in the future. Thus begins a war, generally an amicable war, but none the less a war, between the workmen and the management. The latter endeavors by every means to induce the workmen to increase the output, and the men gauge the rapidity with which they work, so as never to earn over a certain rate of wages, knowing that if they exceed this amount the piece-work price will surely be cut, sooner or later.

But the war is by no means restricted to piece-work. Every intelligent workman realizes the importance, to his own interest, of starting in on each new job as slowly as possible. There are few foremen or superintendents who have anything but a general idea as to how long it should take to do a piece of work that is new to them. Therefore, before fixing a piece-work price, they prefer to have the job done for the first time by the day. They watch the progress of the work as closely as their other duties will permit, and make up their minds how quickly it can be done. It becomes the workman's interest then to go just as slowly as possible, and still convince his foreman that he is working well.

The extent to which, even in our largest and best-managed establishments, this plan of holding back on the work—"marking time," or "soldiering," as it is called—is carried on by the men, can scarcely be understood by one who has not worked among them. It is by no means uncommon for men to work at the rate of one-third, or even one-quarter, their maximum speed, and still preserve the appearance of working hard. And when a rate has once been fixed on such a false basis, it is easy for the men to nurse successfully "a soft snap" of this sort through a term of years, earning in the meanwhile just as much wages as they think they can without having the rate cut.

Thus arises a system of hypocrisy and deceit on the part of the men which is thoroughly demoralizing, and which has led many workmen to regard their employers as their natural enemies, to be opposed in whatever they want, believing that whatever is for the interest of the management must necessarily be to their detriment.

The effect of this system of piece-work on the character of the men is, in many cases, so serious as to make it doubtful whether, on the whole, well-managed day-work is not preferable.

There are several modifications of the ordinary method of piece-work which tend to lessen the evils of the system, but I know of none that can eradicate the fundamental causes for war, and enable the managers and the men to heartily coöperate in obtaining the maximum product from the establishment. It is the writer's opinion, however, that the differential rate system of piece-work, which will be described later, in most cases entirely harmonizes the interests of both parties. . . .

Coöperation, or profit sharing, has entered the mind of every student of the subject as one of the possible and most attractive solutions of the problem; and there have been certain instances, both in England and France, of at least a partial success of coöperative experiments.

So far as I know, however, these trials have been made either in small towns, remote from the manufacturing centres, or in industries which in many respects are not subject to ordinary manufacturing conditions.

Coöperative experiments have failed, and, I think, are generally destined to fail, for several reasons, the first and most important of which is, that no form of coöperation has yet been devised in which each individual is allowed free scope for his personal ambition. This always has been and will remain a more powerful incentive to exertion than a desire for the general welfare. The few misplaced drones, who do the loafing

and share equally in the profits with the rest, under coöperation are sure
to drag the better men down toward their level.

The second and almost equally strong reason for failure lies in the
remoteness of the reward. The average workman (I don't say all men)
cannot look forward to a profit which is six months or a year away. The
nice time which they are sure to have to-day, if they take things easily,
proves more attractive than hard work, with a possible reward to be
shared with others six months later.

Other and formidable difficulties in the path of coöperation are, the
equitable division of the profits, and the fact that, while workmen are
always ready to share the profits, they are neither able nor willing to
share the losses. Further than this, in many cases, it is neither right nor
just that they should share either in the profits or the losses, since these
may be due in great part to causes entirely beyond their influence or
control, and to which they do not contribute.

When we recognize the real antagonism that exists between the
interests of the men and their employers, under all of the systems of
piece-work in common use; and when we remember the apparently
irreconcilable conflict implied in the fundamental and perfectly legitimate aims of the two: namely, on the part of the men:

THE UNIVERSAL DESIRE TO RECEIVE THE LARGEST POSSIBLE WAGES FOR
THEIR TIME.

And on the part of the employers:

THE DESIRE TO RECEIVE THE LARGEST POSSIBLE RETURN FOR THE WAGES
PAID.

What wonder that most of us arrive at the conclusion that no system of
piece-work can be devised which shall enable the two to coöperate without antagonism, and to their mutual benefit?

Yet it is the opinion of the writer, that even if a system has not already
been found which harmonizes the interests of the two, still the basis for
harmonious coöperation lies in the two following facts:

*First. That the workmen in nearly every trade can and will materially
increase their present output per day, providing they are assured of a
permanent and larger return for their time than they have heretofore
received.*

*Second. That the employers can well afford to pay higher wages per
piece even permanently, providing each man and machine in the establishment turns out a proportionately larger amount of work.*

The truth of the latter statement arises from the well-recognized fact
that, in most lines of manufacture, the indirect expenses equal or exceed
the wages paid directly to the workmen, and that these expenses remain
approximately constant, whether the output of the establishment is great
or small.

From this it follows that it is always cheaper to pay higher wages to the workmen when the output is proportionately increased; the diminution in the indirect portion of the cost per piece being greater than the increase in wages. Many manufacturers, in considering the cost of production, fail to realize the effect that the *volume of output has on the cost.* They lose sight of the fact that taxes, insurance, depreciation, rent, interest, salaries, office expenses, miscellaneous labor, sales expenses, and frequently the cost of power (which in the aggregate amount to as much as wages paid to workmen), remain about the same whether the output of the establishment is great or small.

In our endeavor to solve the piece-work problem by the application of the two fundamental facts above referred to, let us consider the obstacles in the path of harmonious coöperation, and suggest a method for their removal.

The most formidable obstacle is the lack of knowledge on the part of both the men and the management (but chiefly the latter) of the quickest time in which each piece of work can be done; or, briefly, the lack of accurate time-tables for the work of the place.

The remedy for this trouble lies in the establishment in every factory of a proper rate-fixing department; a department which shall have equal dignity and command equal respect with the engineering and managing departments, and which shall be organized and conducted in an equally scientific and practical manner.

The rate-fixing, as at present conducted, even in our best-managed establishments, is very similar to the mechanical engineering of fifty or sixty years ago. Mechanical engineering at that time consisted in imitating machines which were in more or less successful use, or in guessing at the dimensions and strength of the parts of a new machine; and as the parts broke down or gave out, in replacing them with stronger ones. Thus each new machine presented a problem almost independent of former designs, and one which could only be solved by months or years of practical experience and a series of break-downs.

Modern engineering, however, has become a study, not of individual machines, but of the resistance of materials, the fundamental principles of mechanics, and of the elements of design.

On the other hand, the ordinary rate-fixing (even the best of it), like the old-style engineering, is done by a foreman or superintendent, who, with the aid of a clerk, looks over the record of the time in which a whole job was done as nearly like the new one as can be found, and then guesses at the time required to do the new job. No attempt is made to analyze and time each of the classes of work, or elements of which a job is composed; although it is a far simpler task to resolve each job into its elements, to make a careful study of the quickest time in which each of the elementary operations can be done, and then to properly classify, tabulate, and index this information, and use it when required for rate fixing, than it is to fix rates, with even an approximation to justice, under the common system of guessing.

In fact, it has never occurred to most superintendents that the work of their establishments consists of various combinations of elementary operations which can be timed in this way; and a suggestion that this is a practical way of dealing with the piece-work problem usually meets with derision, or, at the best, with the answer that "It might do for some simple business, but my work is entirely too complicated."

Yet this elementary system of fixing rates has been in successful operation for the past ten years, on work complicated in its nature, and covering almost as wide a range of variety as any manufacturing that the writer knows of. In 1883, while foreman of the machine shop of the Midvale Steel Company of Philadelphia, it occurred to the writer that it was simpler to time each of the elements of the various kinds of work done in the place, and then find the quickest time in which each job could be done, by summing up the total times of its component parts, than it was to search through the records of former jobs, and guess at the proper price. After practising this method of rate-fixing himself for about a year, as well as circumstances would permit, it became evident that the system was a success. The writer then established the rate-fixing department, which has given out piece-work prices in the place ever since.

This department far more than paid for itself from the very start; but it was several years before the full benefits of the system were felt, owing to the fact that the best methods of making and recording time observations of work done by the men, as well as of determining the maximum capacity of each of the machines in the place, and of making working-tables and time-tables, were not at first adopted.

Before the best results were finally attained in the case of work done by metal-cutting tools, such as lathes, planers, boring mills, etc., a long and expensive series of experiments was made, to determine, formulate, and finally practically apply to each machine the law governing the proper cutting speed of tools; namely, the effect on the cutting speed of altering any one of the following variables: the shape of the tool (*i.e.*, lip angle, clearance angle, and the line of the cutting edge), the duration of the cut, the quality or hardness of the metal being cut, the depth of the cut, and the thickness of the feed or shaving.

It is the writer's opinion that a more complicated and difficult piece of rate-fixing could not be found than that of determining the proper price for doing all kinds of machine work on miscellaneous steel and iron castings and forgings, which vary in their chemical composition from the softest iron to the hardest tool steel. Yet this problem was solved through the rate-fixing department and the "differential rate," with the final result of completely harmonizing the men and the management, in place of the constant war that existed under the old system. At the same time the quality of the work was improved, and the output of the machinery and the men was doubled, and, in many cases, trebled. At the start there was naturally great opposition to the rate-fixing department, particularly to the man who was taking time observations of the various elements of the work; but when the men found that rates were fixed without regard to the records of the quickest time in which they had actually done each job, and that the knowledge of the department was more accurate than their own, the motive for hanging back or "soldiering" on this work ceased, and with it the greatest cause for antagonism and war between the men and the management. . . .

Whether coöperation, the differential plan, or some other form of piece-work be chosen in connection with elementary rate-fixing, as the best method of working, there are certain fundamental facts and principles which must be recognized and incorporated in any system of management, before true and lasting success can be attained; and most of these facts and principles will be found to be not far removed from what the strictest moralists would call justice.

The most important of these facts is, that MEN WILL NOT DO AN EXTRA-ORDINARY DAY'S WORK FOR AN ORDINARY DAY'S PAY; and any attempt on the part of employers to get the best work out of their men and give them the standard wages paid by their neighbors will surely be, and ought to be, doomed to failure.

Justice, however, not only demands for the workman an increased reward for a large day's work, but should compel him to suffer an appropriate loss in case his work falls off either in quantity or quality. It is quite as important that the deductions for bad work should be just, and graded in proportion to the shortcomings of the workman, as that the reward should be proportional to the work done.

The fear of being discharged, which is practically the only penalty applied in many establishments, is entirely inadequate to producing the best quantity and quality of work; since the workmen find that they can take many liberties before the management makes up its mind to apply this extreme penalty.

It is clear that the differential rate satisfies automatically, as it were, the above conditions of properly graded rewards and deductions. Whenever a workman works for a day (or even a shorter period) at his maximum, he receives under this system unusually high wages; but when he falls off either in quantity or quality from the highest rate of efficiency his pay falls below even the ordinary.

The lower differential rate should be fixed at a figure which will allow the workman to earn scarcely an ordinary day's pay when he falls off from his maximum pace, so as to give him every inducement to work hard and well.

The exact percentage beyond the usual standard which must be paid to induce men to work to their maximum varies with different trades and with different sections of the country. And there are places in the United States where the men (generally speaking) are so lazy and demoralized that no sufficient inducement can be offered to make them do a full day's work.

It is not, however, sufficient that each workman's ambition should be aroused by the prospect of larger pay at the end of even a comparatively short period of time. The stimulus to maximum exertion should be a daily one.

This involves such vigorous and rapid inspection and returns as to enable each workman in most cases to know each day the exact result of his previous day's work—*i.e.*, whether he has succeeded in earning his maximum pay, and exactly what his losses are for careless or defective work. Two-thirds of the moral effect, either of a reward or penalty, is lost by even a short postponement.

It will again be noted that the differential rate system forces this condition both upon the management and the workmen, since the men, while working under it, are above all anxious to know at the earliest possible minute whether they have earned their high rate or not. And it is equally important for the management to know whether the work has been properly done.

As far as possible each man's work should be inspected and measured separately, and his pay and losses should depend upon his individual efforts alone. It is, of course, a necessity that much of the work of manufacturing—such, for instance, as running roll-trains, hammers, or paper machines—should be done by gangs of men who coöperate to turn out a common product, and that each gang of men should be paid a definite price for the work turned out, just as if they were a single man.

In the distribution of the earnings of a gang among its members, the percentage which each man receives should, however, depend not only upon the kind of work which each man performs, but upon the accuracy and energy with which he fills his position.

In this way the personal ambition of each of a gang of men may be given its proper scope.

Again, we find the differential rate acting as a most powerful lever to force each man in a gang of workmen to do his best; since if, through the carelessness or laziness of any one man, the gang fails to earn its high rate, the drone will surely be obliged by his companions to do his best the next time or else get out.

A great advantage of the differential rate system is that it quickly drives away all inferior workmen, and attracts the men best suited to the class of work to which it is applied; since none but really good men can work fast enough and accurately enough to earn the high rate; and the low rate should be made so small as to be unattractive even to an inferior man.

If for no other reason than it secures to an establishment a quick and active set of workmen, the differential rate is a valuable aid, since men are largely creatures of habit; and if the piece-workers of a place are forced to move quickly and work hard the day-workers soon get into the same way, and the whole shop takes on a more rapid pace.

The greatest advantage, however, of the differential rate for piece-work, in connection with a proper rate-fixing department, is that together they produce the proper mental attitude on the part of the men and the management toward each other. In place of the indolence and indifference which characterize the workmen of many day-work establishments, and to a considerable extent also their employers; and in place of the constant watchfulness, suspicion, and even antagonism with which too frequently the men and the management regard each other, under the ordinary piece-work plan, both sides soon appreciate the fact that with the differential rate it is their common interest to coöperate to the fullest extent, and to devote every energy to turning out daily the largest possible output. This common interest quickly replaces antagonism, and establishes a most friendly feeling.

Of the two devices for increasing the output of a shop, the differential rate and the scientific rate-fixing department, the latter is by far the more important. The differential rate is invaluable at the start, as a means of convincing men that the management is in earnest in its intention of paying a premium for hard work; and it at all times furnishes the best means of maintaining the top notch of production; but when, through its application, the men and the management have come to appreciate the mutual benefit of harmonious coöperation and respect for each other's rights, it ceases to be an absolute necessity. On the other hand, the rate-fixing department, for an establishment doing a large variety of work, becomes absolutely indispensable. The longer it is in operation the more necessary it becomes.

Practically, the greatest need felt in an establishment wishing to start a rate-fixing department is the lack of data as to the proper rate of speed at which work should be done.

There are hundreds of operations which are common to most large establishments; yet each concern studies the speed problem for itself, and days of labor are wasted in what should be settled once for all, and recorded in a form which is available to all manufacturers. . . .

How to Run a Railroad

Marshall M. Kirkman

The force that operates a railway is like an army. It is methodically organized and drilled. It has its commanders, its rank and file; its officers, sub-officers and privates. Its action is, however, peaceful and conciliatory. It strives at all times to preserve amicable relations with everyone.

The officers and employes of railroads are trained to obey in all matters relating to their business. In other things they are free. It is necessary that they should be obedient. The co-operation of a multitude can not otherwise be secured.

Insubordination among railway men is as great an offense as insubordination in an army. A country thus cursed is in a great danger as if its soldiers were traitorous. In the operations of railroads, the interest of the owner in the employe must be constant, intelligent and marked; upon the part of the employe, loyalty to the property must be sturdy, unswerving and apparent; the interests of the two are, in the main, identical, and it follows that differences between them must in every case be equitably solved if patiently borne. There is no other way.

Rules and regulations governing trains and the station and track forces of railroads must have the force and effectiveness of a criminal code. Disobedience endangers both life and property. It also prevents, here as elsewhere, effective and economical service.

All who enter the service of railroads do so on a perfect equality. They are at best merely experimental at first. But here equality ends. The energetic, capable, faithful and ambitious at once forge to the front. They do not need anyone to assist or favor them. Their merits are sufficient. It is a great mistake to suppose that anybody can get ahead or long keep ahead through influence. No one short of the owner of a property can maintain an unfit person in position. The natural law of

Marshall M. Kirkman, *The Science of Railways: Organization and Forces*, 5th ed. (New York and Chicago: The World Railway Publishing Company, 1896), I, 63–67, 69–70, 72–75, 79–83, 113–116, 170–175, 181–186.

selection operates in the railway service as it does everywhere else. It arranges and classifies the force and, sooner or later, assigns every person to his appropriate sphere of duty.

In railway practice each person must be adapted to the field he occupies. When he is not, the public and the owner suffer, because his deficiencies retard the efforts of others. Each must fit perfectly the place he fills, must be familiar with his duties, and able and willing to perform them effectively. Not only must he be physically and mentally capable, but he must be morally so. He must command the confidence and respect of his associates, his employers, and the public.

A railroad, to be effective, must be effectively governed.

Justice and wisdom must reign.

The highest as well as the lowest must be amenable to law and duty. The rights of the community, the interests of the owner and the welfare of the employe require this.

Opportunity to pursue private enmities and advantage must be minimized.

Everyone must be accorded his proper rights.

Investigation must precede judgment and wisdom and moderation must attend the execution of disciplinary practices.

These things require that there should at all times be intelligent supervision of the property; that those who labor, who evince wisdom, interest and faithfulness should be distinguished from those who do not; that those who pass judgment, who reward, or punish, should be dispassionate, resolute and wise. A company thus governed will never be made the pack-horse of private opportunity. A force thus ruled is invincible, no matter how tried. . . .

Subordination is a cardinal principle of organized labor—subordination to the employer, subordination to each other according to rank and natural precedence. It is based upon a just conception of the rights of men in their relation to property. All men, however, are entitled to justice and humane treatment.

The discipline of corporate forces is as absolute as that of a man of war. Obedience to superior authority is unqualified. It is, however, the privilege and duty of every subordinate in emergencies, when an order is given, to make such suggestions as the circumstances of the case demand. Here his responsibility ends, except in criminal cases.

An order once given, must be obeyed. Absolutism such as this involves grave responsibilities. It presupposes skill, accurate knowledge and appreciation.

In the administrative department of carriers lack of discipline breeds insubordination, idleness and extravagance. It engenders kindred evils in the operating department, with the added element of danger.

It is necessary that the forces of a railroad should possess *esprit de corps,* coupled with interest, intelligence, and courage that no event can deaden or divert.

While the discipline of corporate life is as absolute as that of an army, there is this difference between them: army life destroys the individuality of all below the rank of officer; corporate life intensifies the personality of subordinates by recognition and promotion. Everyone knows that promotion will follow intelligence, faithfulness and industry. The officers of railroads are drawn from the ranks. It is therefore for the interests of such corporations to build up the intelligence and morale of subordinates; to strengthen the force by careful selection and cultivation. Individuals should be taught to think and act for themselves in all cases where discretion can safely be allowed. They will thus be taught self reliance, and the exercise of prudence and good judgment. . . .

The work of those in the employ of railroads must be continuous, systematic and orderly. It is said that cleanliness is next to godliness. I think, however, orderliness comes next, because it is the most distinctive characteristic of the creator. Cleanliness is largely conventional. But systemization or orderliness lies at the foundation of every beneficent thing whether of nature or man.

The Greeks taught policy. We should add to it method. The latter must be practiced by those who lead, by those who hope to win favorable notice, who hope to achieve distinction. It is not a thing confined to any particular occupation or place. In railway employ it is as necessary in the general office as in the machine shop; at the station as on the train; as beneficent in the department buildings and bridges as in that of the track. There must be a place for everything and everything must be in its place. There is a time to do everything and a necessity that everything should be done at such time. Men in judging of the capabilities of others therefore must make no mistake in giving great weight to qualities of orderliness and systemization.

Slothfulness and inactivity indicate worthlessness and precede or attend decay of mental and physical faculties. They are evinced in a lack of method and system just as the effective exercise of these forces indicates life and growth: one anticipates work and seizes it at the right time and in the most effective way; the other makes no preparation and succumbs to difficulties instead of surmounting them.

In corporate life it is the unsystematic man whose cry is most importunate for more help, for additional assistance. The cause of his distress he does not surmise and can not be taught. It is an inherent, fundamental difficulty. There is, therefore, no cure for it. Such men are natural "hewers of wood and drawers of water." They are not equal to any kind of place or power no matter how restricted the field or how abundant the opportunity. . . .

Next to its traffic the most effective resource of a company is its officers

and employes. The first duty of a stranger coming into the service, therefore, whether as president or brakeman, is to familiarize himself with
those about him; to study their individual capabilities, virtues, rights
and desires.

Every service should afford abundant material for filling its higher
offices. It is better to promote an average man than to bring a better one
from abroad.

The best manager is he who can achieve the greatest results with the
material at hand. In railway practice the most important thing, from the
manager's point of view, is the character of the men he has about him.
The building up of his force is his constant aim; this he does by proper
recognition and promotion. When he has occasion to fill an office he does
not go elsewhere if there is a man that may properly be promoted or that
with schooling may be rendered competent. By such a course he builds
up and maintains the esprit de corps of the service. Any other course
quickly destroys the loyalty of the men and their effectiveness as a body.

The railway service is a miniature world. It is cosmopolitan. Every
nationality contributes its quota, while all degrees of taste, cultivation and
talent are represented in its ranks. Not all men are equal either in
interest, industry or intelligence. Men of different temperament or nationality work with different degrees of intensity and effectiveness. The
result, consequently, per unit of labor, is not the same. Rewards are,
therefore, relative. The quantity of labor required per unit of traffic
decreases with every improvement of the service. Every advance made
heightens effectiveness and decreases cost. The incentive to improvement is, therefore, boundless. Nor is opportunity restricted: no one can
say how far improvement may be carried. . . .

In considering the relations that exist between the officers and
employes of a railway and between the employer and those working for
him, much thought has been given to the adoption of some practicable
method whereby the interest of the employe may be increased. It is a
well recognized fact that work performed under the stimulus of self
interest is greater in quantity and of better quality than that of a
perfunctory nature.

Men work according to the measure of reward in store for them. Wages
are generally based on this. It is impossible, however, to distinguish
nicely between those who average very high and others. More or less
uniformity is unavoidable. Wherever this uniformity is not based on
actual performance it is unjust to the employe and operates to the disadvantage of the employer. While the subject has received much attention, no solution of it has yet been found. It is purely a practical one and
must be worked out little by little, like every other great advance. Of
particular experiments that have been made with a view to the discovery
of some method of inciting the efforts of employes outside of and in

addition to the incentive of pay and possible advancement, the experiment has been tried of offering special inducements to invest in the stock of the employer, thus giving employes a proprietary interest. In the case, however, of the low priced employe the interest thus acquired is so limited as not to sensibly overcome the natural disinclination of men to do more than is absolutely necessary, or at least more than is called for by the letter of the contract. Another plan is to divide a certain percentage of profit among employes upon the basis of wages. The defect of this method is that where such percentage is apportioned among all without regard to merit no special inducement is offered an employe to excel.

Another plan that meets with more favor is that of awarding premiums for economy and usefulness. There are, however, several things connected with awards for economy that require careful consideration. 1. As regards the classes of employes who shall be eligible for such awards and the scope of the award. Thus, while we might reward an engineer for economy in the use of the oil dealt out to him, the official who purchased it could not reasonably expect a share of the amount saved in the purchasing of the oil, even though such saving might be the result of his shrewdness and care in buying. 2. While a section foreman might receive a premium for economy in the use of material, the supervising engineer could not be allowed a share in any saving that might be effected through the introduction of an improved system of track laying, or the relocation of the line of a road. 3. It might be desirable to reward a conductor for bringing his train through on time and in safety, but the superintendent could not be rewarded for the proper arrangement of his time card. I say could not, but in this I may be mistaken. It may be desirable and practicable to carry the system of rewarding merit into every branch of the service, be it high or low.

It is apparent that no fixed rule can be laid down as to the standard or unit upon which to compute the saving effected by an employe. That which might be economy under one condition would be wastefulness under another. Each case must be considered by itself, and those whose duty it is to award premiums must be governed largely by their judgment and the particular circumstances of the case.

Moreover, in awarding premiums another difficulty arises, namely to discriminate against economy that in the long run increases cost or endangers life or property. Any temptation to lessen present cost at such expense must be carefully guarded against. Economy can not, especially, be exercised at the expense of safety and efficiency. An engineer, who, to save fuel, should incur risk by reducing the speed of his train on a level track or up grade, making up for lost time by increased speed on down grades, can not be rewarded therefor.

Similar difficulties are met with in awarding premiums for building up business. The amount of increased traffic that results from increased effort on the part of the agents of a company can never be exactly determined. Averages only can be taken, and these for a series of years. This requires elaborate and more or less fallacious statistics. All the circumstances affecting the traffic require to be carefully considered; it will not do to have one class of business increased at the expense of another in order to earn a premium; nor must privileges be extended to the detriment of the carrier, and so on. Every phase of the subject must be considered. The demoralization that would result from favoritism in granting awards requires also to be carefully guarded against. And, finally, it can not be admitted, even tacitly, that in granting awards, no matter what they may be, the company acknowledges that its employes are not expected to do their best under all circumstances. . . .

In general, that form of organization is best for corporate property that enforces the most minute responsibility and offers the greatest encouragement to those who work for it; that enables a company to know the measure of faithfulness and capacity of its servants; that rewards the trustworthy and takes cognizance of the derelict.

The growth of associations and unions among railway employes brings to the problem of operating corporations a quantity previously unknown. These influences it is impossible to forecast. If not wisely governed, such societies will deaden in the heart of the employe all interest in the affairs of the employer beyond those of a mercenary nature. This truth can not be learned too early by employers or be respected too implicitly. If it is not, the ultimate downfall of corporations is certain. Men who through extraneous agencies, seek to gain unjust advantages, can not too quickly learn that those who have money will not jeopardize it in properties thus threatened. Men will not put money into objects that exist at the mercy of those who have nothing in common with them.

It is probable that many labor associations have, at the bottom, a belief that the employer does not properly regard the interests of his employe. This belief is false. But in order to dispel it and in doing so break up such combinations as are subversive of the employe's interest, railways must actively interest themselves in the concerns of those who work for them. Their interests are jeopardized, not because they have been disregardful but because their employes believed they have. This erroneous impression the owner must correct if he would not have foreign and unfriendly agents meddling in his affairs. There are two ways in which corporations may and do manifest their interest in those who work for them. In America it is done by kindly treatment, the payment of high wages, continued service, promotion, and by making the employe self reliant and independent. In many countries wages are unavoidably low, and so corporations eke out their efforts by small annuities and distress funds, and by special interest in the sicknesses, discomforts and forebodings of those who work for them.

The vicissitudes of corporate service require a paternal form of government. The owner must be the father. Failure to recognize this will aggravate the growth of unfriendly labor associations.

No labor organization ever formed, no mattter how great the provocation, can prove beneficial unless those in charge are men of such exceptional wisdom and probity of character as to make their interest in everything they concern themselves about a blessing. No labor organization can ever be beneficial that qualifies the service or lessens the interest of the employe in the employer.

In general, employes are safer in the hands of the employer than in those of anyone else. His interest is permanent, material and fatherly.

The conception of the employer by those who work for him must be broad and charitable. Nothing is attainable without this. Employes must not be quick to believe they are treated unjustly, are overlooked or forgotten. They must be governed by reason. They must accept the conditions of life as they are. They must go ahead sturdily and cheerfully, believing that if they comprehend their business and are active in the discharge of it, their services will be recognized. They must also appreciate this truth, that those who are preferred are, on the whole, worthy of it. That while there are exceptions to the rule, they are unworthy of regard. Disappointed men, instead of repining, must seek by renewed zeal and attachment the recognition they desire. They must not seek, in such emergencies, through combinations, or otherwise, to force what they can not peaceably attain. Force may operate to their advantage for the moment, but will result in lowering their status and otherwise unfitting them to compete with their fellow men. He can never hope to attain eminence, to become a leader, to be independent, to be self sustaining, who seeks thus to bolster his fortunes.

Unflagging industry and continual study is the only road to preferment. All others are makeshift, temporary and incomplete. When men do not progress as fast as they think they should, let them work and study the harder; do more and better work. There is no other road to preferment. . . .

It was at one time thought to be practically impossible to manage a great railway effectively. This was true formerly. It is true now where organization commensurate with the property is not effected. It will continue to be true hereafter wherever individual responsibility is not provided for and co-operative effort maintained.

The same difficulty that is experienced in guarding an extended frontier, or military line, in time of war, is experienced in watching the interests of a long line of railroad. While the attention of the management is occupied in strengthening some weak point in the system, dangers more or less serious threaten it elsewhere. To guard against this it must be protected at every point by men disciplined and fitted to govern.

The extent of territory to be watched is so great upon a railroad that it is impossible for the central management to keep itself advised, except generally, of what is needed at remote points; an arrangement perfected and set in motion today will need revision tomorrow or the day following, but in the multiplicity of affairs the exigency will pass unnoticed if proper provision is not made to have it looked after on the spot by local officials. A great railroad can not long exist as an entity that does not provide for a suitable division of authority and responsibility. It may last for many years, but its ultimate downfall is sure. Why? Because only those clothed with the responsibility of management can appreciate the significance of its affairs, or can be induced to assume the responsibility of acting for it.

No one, except the manager of a railroad, can estimate the injury a property suffers from neglect to clothe its officials with necessary authority and discretion. In no other way can needed changes be made promptly and effectively from time to time. Wherever the local operating officers of a railroad are deficient in number, experience, talent, or discretion, opportunity will be lost and antique methods of business pursued. On the other hand, if the general staff is deficient in number and authority, its members will be so overworked as to be practically inaccessible to those who ought to go to them for advice and assistance; so that the probability of their attention being called by subordinates to matters that ought to have their action will grow less and less likely as intercourse becomes more and more difficult. Subordinates will quickly discover, where such a state of affairs exists, that the royal road to preferment does not lie so much in bringing needed matters to the attention of the management as in abstinence and complaisance. . . .

In the early history of railroads their management was personal and autocratic; the superintendent, a man gifted with energy and clearness of perception, moulded the property to his will; it teemed with projects emanating from him and of which he was a part. But as the properties grew, he found himself unable to give his personal attention to everything. This, however, did not daunt or discourage him. Able, ambitious, indefatigable, faithful, he sought to do everything and do it well. He ended by doing nothing. He was the victim of over ambition; he saw that by trusting his subordinates he lessened his own importance as the dispenser of details, while if he did not trust them they threw the burden of action and responsibility upon him. This was exactly what he desired. He was suspicious of everyone and impatient of everything that did not emanate in him. Like all tyrants, he was narrow and arbitrary. His methods and undue assumptions lessened the interest and pride of officers and employes in the enterprise, without building up anything to take its place except his own personality.

The remedy for this state of affairs was found in trusting men and in making their authority and responsibility commensurate with their duty and the necessities of the situation.

Much depends upon the organization and the talent of those in charge of a railroad. Men differ widely as to their ability to animate others. One officer will receive the maximum service of which men are capable. Another will be able to impress only such subordinates as labor in his immediate presence; still another, personally capable and faithful, will be surrounded by incompetent, dull and heavy witted operatives, who render only an indolent support. Manifestly only the first named has the capacity to manage. He alone possesses the ability essential to the operation of a railroad with its vast interests and multitudinous affairs. But what of the other two—the men who know how to work themselves, but are incapable of getting work out of others? Manifestly they are only fit to fill subordinate positions, to hew wood and draw water. But their own estimate will be far different from this. They will not recognize the incidents we describe. Nor will others in every case. Hence we shall oftentimes find them occupying positions of high responsibility or actively aspiring thereto. They are not unconscious of their failings, but believe them to be offset by compensating advantages. Vain delusion. They are the bane of the business world; the men who render the sagacity of investors fruitless; who tear down the edifices erected by others more gifted; who fritter away opportunities that would, in better hands, be seized and profited by. When such men are placed in charge of a railway, we may trace in advance its future. But however baneful, they are not so fatally destructive as the autocratic manager of earlier days. They are simply stupid; he blighted the men about him and in doing so ultimately blighted the property.

To obtain the highest results at the least cost, a road should be large enough to occupy the maximum attention of the minimum number of officials necessary to such enterprises.

The enormous number of details that press unceasingly for attention on a railroad is so much beyond the capacity of a single person that much of the work is neglected if the organization lacks comprehensiveness. Work will be carried on without adequate preparation or consultation, or will be allowed to lapse entirely.

Ability to act for others grows with its exercise. The spirit is one to be cultivated. Some one must be trusted. The danger is not in trusting subordinates, but in neglecting to educate them so that they may be trusted; in neglecting to instruct them and build up in them a sense of loyalty. . . .

There are many points of resemblance between the organization of the service of a government and that of a railway. The same spirit animates both. In neither is there any financial risk to the employe. The servants of each act for some one else. They have many things in common; are alike in many things.

The difference between efficiency and inefficiency in corporate service is not occasioned so much by inherent differences in men as by differences of method. If a service is wisely organized and governed, efficiency follows; if not wisely organized and governed, inefficiency follows. . . .

The railway service possesses for those connected with it the insidious charm that attaches to political life, without the attendant publicity and gross vilification of the latter. Its attachés, while striving zealously for the common good, are rarely embarrassed in their official life by any friendships except those of convenience. Weighing, with the precision of courtiers, the probabilities of this or that interest, they are ever ready to welcome the victor. The chief that has embarrassed his administration and alienated his supporters in efforts to surround himself with men personally devoted to his fortunes, sees eventually with apprehension and shame that their support is governed wholly by policy, and their friendship by self interest. An officer who is saluted on every hand with cordial recognition today, is passed by tomorrow with cold indifference. His star, as long as it is in the ascendant, excites attention and speculation; but a day is sufficient to destroy the prospects and blast the hopes of the most aspiring, and call from obscurity men without friends or prospects of advancement. These features of corporate life attend more particularly autocratic forms of government such as characterized the service of railroads in their early days; they are, however, still to be found, here and there, in a mild form, but are everywhere tempered and modified by the influence of the owner, who is as much concerned in building up competent men as he is in building up his property.

In every railway organization, underneath the surface the most active, albeit good natured, rivalry exists. The strife to which this gives birth renders the life of the railway man one of continual surprises and harrassing perplexities. This is unavoidable where so many men possessing substantially the same peculiarities of education, temper and object, are brought into active intercourse.

The finest administrative ability that can be found animates and controls our railways. Doing a colossal business, extending over immense areas of country and employing thousands of men in the prime of life, energetic and ambitious, moving in their places with the precision of soldiers, yet each animated by a determination to achieve personal success, their successful government demands abilities of the highest order.

How to control these myriads of men without destroying their individuality and pride; how to throw around them and the officers that control them the safeguards essential to the protection of a company's interests, are questions that occur to all who are interested in making the service efficient.

While the organization of different corporations appears, to a superficial observer, to be substantially the same, the widest diversity exists.

Thus, roads situated in the immediate vicinity of the proprietors are held under greater restraint by the owner, because of such proximity, than those more remote. No organization, however, is to be commended that does not conform to certain well known principles of civil service that experience has taught as being necessary to good government. Such matters are not open to argument. Properties remote from owners, if not properly organized, pass, by easy and imperceptible stages, from the control of their owners to that of their managers. This may be avoided by systematic organization. However, the danger of demoralizing a force by placing checks upon managers, in many cases, deters owners from attempting it. Now, while absolute authority is essential, it should be concurrent. Arbitrary power is prone to be unjust, to disregard common principles of good government; to govern through fear rather than justice. The remedy is simple. But we must look to see this remedy applied by those whom it is designed to hold in check. Nothing can be accomplished without their active sympathy and aid.

Methods of organization necessary to secure good government under all circumstances must originate with the manager; they dignify his office, ennoble his character and add to his fame. This is true of both public corporations and private enterprises. The task, while simple, demands thought and elaboration; it requires the enforcement of such safeguards as will secure the unity of the force as a whole without weakening the authority or lessening the responsibility of those entrusted with the management of affairs. In constructing such an organization the builder must be sincere; he must also be worldly wise. He must possess practical experience, coupled with a knowledge of the principles that underlie the control of men and the building up within them of those qualities that distinguish highly capable and faithful men from those who lack such characteristics. . . .

The Problem of the Trusts

AARON JONES

Grand Master National Grange Patrons of Husbandry

Every citizen of this republic should be free to use his labor as will best contribute to his benefit and happiness, not, however, infringing on the rights of any other citizen.

The right to acquire, own, control and enjoy the use and income of property, is an inalienable right, that should be enjoyed by each individual. Governments are organized and laws are enacted to better protect life, liberty and the ownership and use of property. It is the legitimate function of governments to protect its citizens in the full and free enjoyment of these rights. It is for this security of life and the ownership of property that people are willing to pay taxes for the support of state and national governments.

The tendency of the times is for conducting large business enterprises and concentration of business into the hands of a few. In the early history of this country, when individuals desired to do a more extended business than they had capital to control, partnerships were formed of two or more, and the business was conducted by them jointly. These partnerships gave them no additional powers or privileges beyond those enjoyed by the individual citizen.

As the demand [increased] for concentration and the conduct of business on a still greater scale, the laws provided for the formation of corporations to conduct certain lines of business, and the state granted them certificates of incorporation with certain defined privileges and the right to conduct business along certain lines, and in the case of canals and railroads they were granted the extraordinary power of condemning lands found necessary for the constructions of their roads or canals, and issue stock, limiting liability within certain limits defined by law, and granting absolute control of the minority of stock by the majority, and many other advantages and privileges not enjoyed by any individual citizen. These forms of corporation served a useful purpose, but within the past few years, the ambitions of men to acquire power and wealth rapidly, these corporations have been consolidating many separate corporations located

Chicago Conference on Trusts, 1899 (Chicago: The Civic Federation, 1900), pp. 218–221, 253–261, 329–338, 404–409, 569–576.

in one or several states, selling out their plants to a corporation organized for the purpose of buying up all these separate plants and conducting them under one management, and it has been found that the increased power possessed by these large consolidated corporations or trusts, as they are commonly known, have caused them to pursue a policy that has infringed on the rights of individuals, or have used their influences in restraint of trade, been detrimental to the rights of labor, destroyed the value of other property, and deprived other individuals of the use of their capital, and so far as this has been done, is clearly against public policy; and subversive of the best interests of the republic. The purpose of this conference, as I understand, is to consider this great question so vitally [a]ffecting the property rights of the citizens of the United States and make such recommendation to the Congress of the United States and the several legislatures as will secure such legislation as will in no wise cripple legitimate enterprise and the development of the resources of our country, and yet secure the passage of such laws as will restrain the abuses that have grown up in corporate management of the various corporations now doing business in the United States. This is one of the most important questions now confronting the American people and one that must be met, and wisely met, or the republic is drifting on very dangerous grounds, that sooner or later will subvert the liberties of the people. . . .

It occurs to me that the first step to be taken in remedial legislation is to pass a well-considered anti-trust law by the Congress of the United States, clearly defining what practices on the part of any corporation would be injurious to public policy, and cripple or injure individual enterprise, thrift, and the acquirement and use of the property of any citizen of the republic; and to supplement this law by equally well-considered anti-trust laws by each of the several state legislatures to reach and apply to such phases of the matter as could not be reached by the act of Congress of the United States. These laws should have such provisions for their enforcement and provide penalties for violations by fines or imprisonment or both as will insure the compliance and observance of the laws by all corporations and combinations. To make these laws effective, it is absolutely necessary to know what these trusts and combinations are doing; and as these trusts have assumed so far as appearances go, to be honest, legitimate corporations, it is difficult to ascertain which ones are operating in a way detrimental to public policy. It would therefore seem that these laws should provide for government and state inspection of their business, of their books, agreements, receipts and expenditures, and that the state may have full knowledge, the right to examine all vouchers and records of the meetings of directors and managers; in short, full and complete knowledge of all the business of affairs of the corporation. The individuals in seeking a corporation franchise have asked the state to help them to a privilege or advantage they did not possess as individuals, or they would not seek to be incorporated as a corporation; and on account of that advantage granted and to protect the public, this inspection should be rigid and full. . . .

If the corporations are conducting legitimate business, no injury will be done them by inspection. If they are using the power granted to them by the state, to crush out other enterprises and deprive other citizens of the use and value of their property in order to avoid competition; if they are using their power and influence in restraint of trade; if they are using large sums of money to illegitimately control political parties or to control legislation, as was testified before the Congressional investigation that the "Sugar trust made it a rule to make political contributions to the Republican party in Republican states and to the Democratic party in Democratic states." Mr. Havemeyer testified that, "We get a good deal of protection for our contributions," and when asked if his company had not endeavored to control legislation of Congress with a view of making money out of such legislation, he answered: "Undoubtedly. That is what I have been down here for," and many other cases might be cited. If they have agreements with railroad companies for rebates of freight, as has been shown to be the case in the Standard Oil trust and many others, these practices are most reprehensible and should be punished by such penalties as will effectually stop them. The agreements and conspiracies to depress the prices of raw material and staple products are equally against public policy.

In speaking for the agricultural interests of our country, that great basic industry that produces 70 per cent of the wealth of the country, and furnishes 60 per cent of the freight on all railroads, lake, river, and coastwise trade, and 69 per cent of all exports, and that make it possible for the other industrial interests of our country to prosper, I desire to say, these practices and conditions most seriously and injuriously affect it, and they demand of the legislatures of the several states and of the national Congress, well considered and effective legislation that will prevent the injurious practices of trusts and combinations.

I believe it to be the settled purpose of a majority of the people, to hold our representatives in Congress and in the several legislatures personally responsible for the enactment of such laws as will restrain and prevent the continuance of acts of trusts that are against public policy. I do not believe that the people hold any one party, as responsible for the present conditions, but I do believe that each individual member holding official position will be, and is, held for his voice and vote and action in the enactment of demanded remedial and protective legislation.

Our country is so vast, its interests so extended, and the constantly increasing wealth in its multiplied forms of the people need carefully considered laws governing the rights and uses of property, that corporations or individuals by agreements, may not be able to oppress or destroy any of the great industries of the nation. The demand of the times is for sound, sensible, good business men, with broad common sense, to frame the laws of our country, state and nation.

BENJAMIN R. TUCKER

Editor New York Liberty

Having to deal very briefly with the problem with which the so-called trusts confront us, I go at once to the heart of the subject, taking my stand on these propositions: That the right to co-operate is as unquestionable as the right to compete; that the right to compete involves the right to refrain from competition; that co-operation is often a method of competition, and that competition is always, in the larger view, a method of co-operation; that each is a legitimate, orderly, non-invasive exercise of the individual will under the social law of equal liberty; and that any man or institution attempting to prohibit or restrict either, by legislative enactment or by any form of invasive force, is, in so far as such man or institution may fairly be judged by such attempt, an enemy of liberty, an enemy of progress, an enemy of society, and an enemy of the human race.

Viewed in the light of these irrefutable propositions, the trust, then, like every other industrial combination endeavoring to do collectively nothing but what each member of the combination rightfully may endeavor to do individually, is, *per se*, an unimpeachable institution. To assail or control or deny this form of co-operation on the ground that it is itself a denial of competition is an absurdity. It is an absurdity, because it proves too much. The trust is a denial of competition in no other sense than that in which competition itself is a denial of competition. The trust denies competition only by producing and selling more cheaply than those outside of the trust can produce and sell; but in that sense every successful individual competitor also denies competition. And if the trust is to be suppressed by such denial of competition, then the very competition in the name of which the trust is to be suppressed must itself be suppressed also. I repeat: the argument proves too much. The fact is that there is one denial of competition which is the right of all, and that there is another denial of competition which is the right of none. All of us, whether out of a trust or in it, have a right to deny competition by competing, but none of us, whether in a trust or out of it, have a right to deny competition by arbitrary decree, by interference with voluntary effort, by forcible suppression of initiative.

Again: To claim that the trust should be abolished or controlled because the great resources and consequent power of endurance which it acquires by combination give it an undue advantage, and thereby enable it to crush competition, is equally an argument that proves too much. If John D. Rockefeller were to start a grocery store in his individual capacity, we should not think of suppressing or restricting or hampering his enterprise simply because, with his five hundred millions, he could afford to sell groceries at less than cost until the day when the accumulated ruins of all other grocery stores should afford him a sure foundation for a profitable business. But, if Rockefeller's possession of five hundred millions is not a good ground for the suppression of his grocery store, no better ground is the control of still greater wealth for the suppression of his oil trust. It is true that these vast accumulations under one control are abnormal and dangerous, but the reasons for them lie outside of and behind and beneath all trusts and industrial combinations—reasons which I shall come to presently—reasons which are all, in some form or other, an arbitrary denial of liberty: and but for these reasons, but for these denials of liberty, John D. Rockefeller never could have acquired five hundred millions, nor would any combination of men be able to control an aggregation of wealth that could not be easily and successfully met by some other combination of men.

Again: There is no warrant in reason for deriving a right to control trusts from the state grant of corporate privileges under which they are organized. In the first place, it being pure usurpation to presume to endow any body of men with rights and exemptions that are not theirs already under the social law of equal liberty, corporate privileges are in themselves a wrong; and one wrong is not to be undone by attempting to offset it with another. But, even admitting the justice of corporation charters, the avowed purpose in granting them is to encourage co-operation, and thus stimulate industrial and commercial development for the benefit of the community. Now, to make this encouragement an excuse for its own nullification by a proportionate restriction of co-operation would be to add one more to those interminable imitations of the task of Sisyphus for which that stupid institution which we call the state has ever been notorious.

Of somewhat the same nature, but rather more plausible at first blush, is the proposition to cripple the trusts by stripping them of those law-created privileges and monopolies which are conferred, not upon trusts as corporate bodies, but upon sundry individuals and interests, ostensibly for protection of the producer and inventor, but really for purposes of plunder, and which most trusts acquire in the process of merging the original capitals of their constituent members. I refer, of course, to tariffs, patents, and copyrights. Now, tariffs, patents, and copyrights either have their foundations in justice, or they have not their foundations in justice. If they have their foundations in justice, why should men guilty of nothing but a legitimate act of co-operation and partnership be punished therefor by having their just rights taken from them? If they have not their foundations in justice, why should men who refrain from co-operation be left in possession of unjust privileges that are denied to men who co-operate? If tariffs are unjust, they should not be levied at all. If patents and copyrights are unjust, they should not be granted to anyone whomsoever. But, if tariffs and patents and copyrights are just, they should be levied or granted in the interest of all who are entitled to their benefits from the viewpoint of the motives in which these privileges have their origin, and to make such levy or grant dependent upon any foreign motive, such, for instance, as willingness to refrain from co-operation, would be sheer impertinence.

Nevertheless, at this point in the hunt for the solution of the trust problem, the discerning student may begin to realize that he is hot on the trail. The thought arises that the trusts, instead of growing out of competition, as is so generally supposed, have been made possible only by the absence of competition, only by the difficulty of competition, only by the obstacles placed in the way of competition—only, in short, by those arbitrary limitations of competition which we find in those law-created privileges and monopolies of which I have just spoken, and in one or two others, less direct, but still more far-reaching and deadly in their destructive influence upon enterprise. And it is with this thought that anarchism, the doctrine that in all matters there should be the greatest amount of individual liberty compatible with equality of liberty, approaches the case in hand, and offers its diagnosis and its remedy.

The first and great fact to be noted in the case, I have already hinted at. It is the fact that the trusts owe their power to vast accumulation and concentration of wealth, unmatched, and, under present conditions, unmatchable, by any equal accumulation of wealth, and that this accumulation has been effected by the combination of separate accumulations only less vast and in themselves already gigantic, each of which owed its existence to one or more of the only means by which large fortunes can be rolled up, interest, rent, and monopolistic profit. But for interest, rent, and monopolistic profit, therefore, trusts would be impossible. Now, what causes interest, rent, and monopolistic profit? For all three there is but one cause—the denial of liberty, the suppression of restriction of competition, the legal creation of monopolies.

This single cause, however, takes various shapes.

Monopolistic profit is due to that denial of liberty which takes the shape of patent, copyright, and tariff legislation, patent and copyright laws directly forbidding competition, and tariff laws placing competition at a fatal disadvantage.

Rent is due to that denial of liberty which takes the shape of land monopoly, vesting titles to land in individuals and associations which do not use it, and thereby compelling the non-owning users to pay tribute to the non-using owners as a condition of admission to the competitive market.

Interest is due to that denial of liberty which takes the shape of money monopoly, depriving all individuals and associations, save such as hold a certain kind of property, of the right to issue promissory notes as currency, and thereby compelling all holders of property, other than the kind thus privileged, as well as all non-proprietors, to pay tribute to the holders of the privileged property for the use of a circulating medium and instrument of credit which, in the complex stage that industry and commerce have now reached, has become the chief essential of a competitive market.

Now, anarchism, which, as I have said, is the doctrine that in all matters, there should be the greatest amount of individual liberty compatible with equality of liberty, finds that none of these denials of liberty are necessary to the maintenance of equality of liberty, but that each and every one of them, on the contrary, is destructive of equality of liberty. Therefore it declares them unnecessary, arbitrary, oppressive, and unjust, and demands their immediate cessation. . . .

If, then, the four monopolies to which I have referred are unnecessary denials of liberty, and therefore unjust denials of liberty, and if they are the sustaining causes of interest, rent, and monopolistic profit, and if, in turn, this usurious trinity is the cause of all vast accumulations of wealth —for further proof of which propositions I must, because of the limitation of my time, refer you to the economic writings of the anarchistic school— it clearly follows that the adequate solution of the problem with which the trusts confront us is to be found only in abolition of these monopolies and the consequent guarantee of perfectly free competition.

The most serious of these four monopolies is unquestionably the money monopoly, and I believe that perfect freedom in finance alone would wipe out nearly all the trusts, or at least render them harmless, and perhaps helpful. Mr. Bryan told a very important truth when he declared that the destruction of the money trust would at the same time kill all the other trusts. Unhappily, Mr. Bryan does not propose to destroy the money trust. He wishes simply to transform it from a gold trust into a gold and silver trust. The money trust cannot be destroyed by the remonetization of silver. That would be only a mitigation of the monopoly, not the abolishment of it. It can be abolished only by monetizing all wealth that has a market value—that is, by giving to all wealth the right to circulate wherever it can on its own merits. And this is not only a solution of the trust question, but the first step that should be taken, and the greatest single step that can be taken, in economic and social reform.

I have tried, in the few minutes allotted to me, to state concisely the attitude of anarchism toward industrial combinations. It discountenances all direct attacks on them, all interference with them, all anti-trust legislation whatsoever. In fact, it regards industrial combinations as very useful whenever they spring into existence in response to demand created in a healthy social body. If at present they are baneful, it is because they are symptoms of a social disease originally caused and persistently aggravated by a regimen of tyranny and quackery. Anarchism wants to call off the quacks, and give liberty, nature's great cure-all, a chance to do its perfect work. . . .

SAMUEL GOMPERS

President American Federation of Labor

We are all conscious of the giant strides with which industry during the past decade has combined and concentrated into the modern trust. There is considerable difference of opinion, however, as to what is regarded by many as an intolerable evil.

Organized labor is deeply concerned regarding the "swift and intense concentration of the industries," and realizes that unless successfully confronted by an equal or superior power there is economic danger and political subjugation in store for all.

But organized labor looks with apprehension at the many panaceas and remedies offered by theorists to curb the growth and development or destroy the combinations of industry. We have seen those who know little of statecraft and less of economics urge the adoption of laws to "regulate" interstate commerce and laws to "prevent" combinations and trusts, and we have also seen that these measures, when enacted, have been the very instruments employed to deprive labor of the benefit of organized effort while at the same time they have simply proven incentives to more subtly and surely lubricate the wheels of capital's combination.

For our part, we are convinced that the state is not capable of preventing the legitimate development or natural concentration of industry. All the propositions to do so which have come under our observation would beyond doubt react with greater force and injury upon the working people of our country than upon the trusts.

The great wrongs attributable to the trusts are their corrupting influence on the politics of the country, but as the state has always been the representative of the wealth possessors we shall be compelled to endure this evil until the toilers are organized and educated to the degree when they shall know that the state is by rights theirs, and finally and justly come to their own while never relaxing in their efforts to secure the very best possible economic, social and material improvement in their condition.

There is no tenderer or more vulnerable spot in the anatomy of trusts than their dividend paying function, there is no power on earth other than the trade unions which wields so potent a weapon to penetrate, disrupt, and, if necessary, crumble the whole fabric. This, however, will not be necessary, nor will it occur, for the trade unions will go on organizing, agitating and educating, in order that material improvement may keep pace with industrial development, until the time when the workers, who will then form nearly the whole people, develop their ability to administer the functions of government in the interest of all.

There will be no cataclysm, but a transition so gentle that most men will wonder how it all happened.

In the early days of our modern capitalist system, when the individual employer was the rule under which industry was conducted, the individual workmen deemed themselves sufficiently capable to cope for their rights; when industry developed and employers formed companies, the workmen formed unions; when industry concentrated into great combinations, the workingmen formed their national and international unions, as employments became trustified, the toilers organized federations of all unions—local, national and international—such as the American Federation of Labor.

We shall continue to organize and federate the grand army of labor, and with our mottoes, lesser hours of labor, higher wages, and an elevated standard of life, we shall establish equal and exact justice to all. *"Labor Omnia Vincit."*

JOHN W. HAYES

General Secretary and Treasurer Order Knights of Labor

The question which we are invited here to discuss—"Trust and Combinations"—is fast pressing itself for solution before the highest tribunal in the nation, the court of final resort, for all questions of public policy, the court of public opinion. It is too vital, too important, to be confined to the narrow limits of commercial affairs, of mere business operation, or mercenary speculation. It touches the very foundations of our free institutions, involves the liberty of the people, the comfort, happiness and prosperity of millions of free men, and the stability of our governmental system, established by the fathers to defend and protect coming generations in their inherent rights, which rights were declared by them to be the gift of nature to all her children. . . .

I shall, therefore, discuss this question only as it bears upon the broad field of human rights, and deny at the outset the moral right of any individual, or combination of individuals, to so monopolize any natural field of industry to such an extent as to be able to dictate the conditions which govern the lives of that portion of society which gains its maintenance by the exercise of productive industry in that particular field. I assert that it is contrary to the best interests of society—indeed, that government has not the constitutional power to enact such legislation as will make it possible for any combination of individuals to so limit the volume of production in any natural field for its own particular advantage, or so create conditions that any individual or combination of individuals may have despotic power over the lives of any citizen or number of citizens.

I further assert and maintain that these great combinations are an assault upon the inherent and constitutional rights of the citizen, and that the real and vital advantage to be gained is the despotic control over labor. Virtually to own and command the labor engaged in any particular field, and consequently it is an assault upon that portion of the people. If one field may be invaded and reduced to despotic dictation, all may be, and the logical outcome must be the conquest of all fields of production, the establishment of a despotism in each, the enslavement of the people, the overthrow of our free institutions, and the erection of moneyed aristocracy. Thus would our boasted free institutions become a fraud and a pretense, our government perverted, and only used as a machine to enforce the wills of the dictators. . . .

The definition that a trust is an aggressive combination of private individuals leads naturally to the inquiry, against what or whom is this aggression or assault to be directed? Is it an organization of private individuals formed to attack some similar organization in a competitive rivalry, the result of which will affect the private interests of those immediately concerned, leaving the unsuccessful and unfortunate the ability to recover from any injuries they might suffer from the contest, with their social status unaffected and their capacity and ability to produce unimpaired? Or is it possible that this aggression is against society, against the established social and political conditions, which guarantees to every citizen the right and opportunity to labor in any field of industry he may find most favorable to his pursuit of happiness and the enjoyment of his liberty? What more nearly concerns the happiness of man than the enjoyment of the full return of his industry, or his liberty, more than the access to any field of industry nature has provided, from which he may gather the necessities and comforts which minister to his happiness and the happiness of those depending upon him? It is the duty of society and government to foster and encourage production, to guard every field of industry for the common good of society, and to develop the producing energy to the greatest extent possible.

There is no fear that a people can produce too much of anything that is serviceable and useful to the community; that the people can become too comfortable or too industrious. The good of society demands that the productive energy be developed to the greatest degree possible; that the fields of industry be not circumscribed, and that free access be guaranteed and preserved to all who require or desire to exercise their productive labor in such fields. The controlling of any field of industry by any individual or combination of individuals is contrary to the declared spirit of our institutions, for it recognizes the power of such individual or combinations to restrict production, even to absolutely close the field of opportunity against the citizen, if they consider their personal interests will be benefited thereby.

The great corporations, the trusts, with their capital, their machinery, special privileges, and other advantages, are overwhelming the individual, reducing him to the condition of a mere tool, to be used in their great undertakings for their individual profit, and of no more consequence than a piece of dumb machinery. Man is the slave of necessity, and he who controls the necessities has the power of a despot. The first and prime necessity is the opportunity to exercise his industry in some productive field where he can secure the means of existence. To close this field, to cut off this opportunity, is to sentence him to death. To restrict the exercise of his productive ability, or limit the terms of his access to the opportunity by the will of another, is to make him the slave of another. It is claimed by short-sighted, selfish, and mercenary men that if the opportunity is closed in one field there are others to which the individual may turn. This is too silly and childish an assertion to merit notice. First, because no such possibility should be allowed to exist under our free institutions; and next, because were it possible for one field to be monopolized, it is possible for all to be, and the individual would turn from the field closed against him to find all others in the same condition. Even were this not so, his skill, experience, and training in that field would be lost to him, and he would enter a new one at a disadvantage in the competition with trained minds and skilled hands already employed, and an injustice would be done on the one hand, and undue favor extended on the other. The trust, by monopolizing the field, becomes the dictator of the conditions which govern the life of every individual engaged in the field monopolized. By limiting the extent to which he may exercise his productive energy, limiting his wage, or the possible amount of his earnings, it dictates the quality and quantity of food the worker may eat, the kind of clothes he may wear, the kind of shelter he may provide for his family, the opportunity for education and improvement his children may have, and, by cutting his opportunity to labor, it denies him even the right to live. . . .

The legislation enacted by the government, if uninfluenced, naturally would be the expression of the popular will in the interests of individuals and society. This legislation it becomes the interest of the trust to influence and pervert to its own profit and advantage. This opens the door to corruption of the legislative branch of government and the oppression and overawing of the popular will. The representatives of the people are corrupted, and the class dependent on the trust for its employment and maintenance intimidated and practically disfranchised through fear of loss of employment and enforced idleness. They are compelled to support the methods of the trust or neglect to exercise their rights as citizens. In this way the independence of the citizen is destroyed, his manhood degraded, his right to give free expression to his opinions upon public affairs abridged. He becomes a sycophant, a moral coward, a helpless dependent upon the will of his master, and the will of the trusts become the only voice heard. Legislation in this way becomes merely the dictation of the trust, and the pretense that it is the emanation of popular will is false and fraudulent. In this way the power and machinery of government are gradually transferred from the people to the corporation, and that which was founded and intended to protect the citizen and defend his natural and civil rights becomes the means of his oppression. This is unquestionably treason, a conspiracy to usurp and pervert the government, to overthrow free institutions, and to establish a despotism and a favored and dominant class, practically autocratic in its use of power. That this is not only possible, but practically in operation at the present time, is proven by the history of our political campaigns for the past two decades, and a review of the legislation enacted in the interests of corporations, which constitute the great bulk of all legislation, municipal, state, and national. It is universally admitted that legislation emanates from the class benefited by it, and, looking over the mass of legislation, one is at no loss to decide what class is benefited. Therefore, there can be no doubt as to what influence brought about its enactment. The fraud, corruption, and bribery of legislatures, the open defiance of executive authority, the corruption of courts and their officials, the usurpation of power and the legal assumption of rights, the ready appeal to the military and arrogant overriding of the civil authority by this power in controversies between corporations and employes; the defiance of municipal authorities in questions between corporations and muncipalities, the employment of armed mercenaries to enforce their decrees, the constant and never-ceasing struggle of corporations to compel as many hours of labor and as low a rate of wages as is possible to enforce, are all clearly indicative of the character, desires and purposes, and show beyond any question such combinations to be the enemies of society and of any form of government which tends to abridge or control their power over the citizen, or the exercise of their will in any undertaking their greed and avarice may suggest, regardless of the rights, interest, liberties, or happiness of the people, or even the interests of the people's government. Their intents are unquestionably treasonable, and if carried to their ultimate results will certainly cause the overthrow of our institutions and government.

In this world all things work in a circle. So it will and must be with trusts if carried to their logical culmination. The inspiring motive which called them into being will prove their destruction, as well as the destruction of our government. They will end by destroying themselves, as well as the government which gave them birth. The very nature of the system proves this. . . .

I do not hesitate to proclaim that in recognizing it at all we are nourishing a serpent, fostering treason, giving aid and comfort to the enemies of society, welcoming an invader, assisting in the overthrow of free institutions and popular government, inviting a dictator, and laying the foundation of despotism. We are sowing the seed of revolution and may reap the harvest upon the bloody fields of civil strife or amid the groans and sighs of fettered slaves, bereft of manhood, wallowing in moral degradation, ignorance, and vice, degraded from the exalted dignity of citizenship in a free and mighty nation to a condition of sycophantic dependence upon the despotic decree of an autocrat. . . .

JOHN BATES CLARK

Columbia University

. . . I accept and use the loose definition of the term trust that is current in popular thought and speech. It is any corporation that is big enough to be menacing. There is, indeed, an intermediate form of the trust which allows the companies or firms that compose it to retain a separate existence, though they form a combination, or pool, for the purpose of limiting production and raising prices. Such forms of the trust can probably be crushed by law; but the result of this will be to cause many of them to take the shape of monster corporations; and it is in this form that you will finally have them to deal with.

I claim the immunities of a theoretical student when I enter the realm of prophecy, and, on the basis of laws and tendencies that are plainly discernible, make a somewhat confident assertion concerning the type of trust legislation that is likely to be permanent. Very unlike the sweeping prohibitions with which the statute books of many states have been supplied, is the law that will survive and will accomplish what we all have in view, the protection of the public from the extortions of monopolies. It will do in reality what the ordinary anti-trust law fails to do, for it will have on its side what the ordinary statute has against it, namely, the power of economic law.

Three distinct things are often confounded and indiscriminately attacked: The first is capital as such; the second is centralization, and the third is true monopoly. Popular attacks on monopoly often take the shape of attacks on capital itself. I am happy to say that this has not happened in the present conference: for we have heard again and again, in the utterance of speakers who have opposed trusts, expressions that show that they are not assailing capital. They are assailing aggregations of capital. They oppose centralization because of the element of monopoly that at present inheres in it. Poor as is the opinion that I entertain of many existing anti-trust laws, I must, in fairness, say that they also strike not at capital itself, but at the centralized form of it. The present effort of the people is to stop centralization in order to preclude monopoly, while their effort will ultimately be to crush the element of monopoly out of massed capital and let massing continue. The line of cleavage between what is good and will abide, and what is harmful and must go, is not between capital and centralization, but between centralization and monopoly.

If it were impossible to have capital in great masses without having true monopolies, I would favor a heroic effort to stem the current of natural progress and keep the general capital of each branch of business in the shape of separate smaller and competing capitals. Monopoly is evil, and almost wholly so; and if the massing of productive wealth necessarily means monopoly, farewell to centralization. We shall do our best to get rid of it, and shall suffer the loss of productive power that this entails, as the price that we are willing to pay for being rid of a great evil. The fact is that massed capital does not need to bring with it a regime of true monopoly. We shall soon see why this is true, and before doing so it is well worth while to notice how much will be gained if we can safely allow the natural and centralizing tendency to go on. It means the survival of the most productive forms of business. It is first and chiefly because it can give more for a dollar than little establishments can give that the great establishments supplant them. They out-do the small ones in serving the public, and this power of superior service is soon to have a new and unique field in which to display itself. We are entering on an era of world-wide industrial connection. Asia and Africa are incorporating themselves into the economic organism of which Europe and America are the center. There is coming a neck-and-neck contest between European countries and the United States for lucrative connections with the outlying regions. There is also coming a later and grander contest between both America and Europe, on the one hand, and Asia and Africa on the other, for the command of the traffic of the world. In this contest victory involves more than any hurried expressions of mine can indicate. It means a leading position in the permanent progress of the world. It means positive wealth, high wages, and intellectual gains that cannot be enjoyed by those who develop less power.

In the momentous struggle that is before us and that will yield to the successful the greatest of mundane prizes, I want my country to come uppermost. To that end I wish it to have every advantage that it can have in the way of productive power. I wish it to be able to meet the fiercest competition, not by accepting low pay for its labor, but by creating the largest possible product. Do you suppose that this is possible if it reverts to the plan of multiplying little shops, with the wastes that this system entails? Mechanical invention, on the one hand, and organization, on the other, can save us in the sharpest economic contests.

There is a competing power that comes from poverty. Pauper labor is a dangerous antagonist. We have perceived this at times, in the rivalries of America and Europe, and shall see it more plainly when the poorly paid dwellers in Asia shall enter the manufacturing field and try conclusions with us in an effort to command the largest markets. If they under-bid us it will be because they take less than we do for their labor; while if we under-bid them it will be because we produce more by our labor. Against the competing power that rests on poverty is to be arrayed the competing power that rests on economic strength, and this strength can come, in a decisive measure, only to that country that combines with inventive genius an organizing genius, and so adds to the power of the engine, the dynamos and the automatic machine, the power of centralized capital. I wish that successful country to be ours. I wish that our workmen may excel not in power to live on a little, but in power to create much, and to offer what they create for a correspondingly large reward.

Is this possible under a régime of great combinations? I firmly believe that it is so; though it will not be possible without the wisest laws, honestly enforced, and backed by all the moral energy that the present anti-trust campaign is developing.

Why is it that trusts have not raised the prices of their products to an undeniable and startling extent? Why has it, until lately, been almost a debatable question whether they raise them at all? Are their managers filled with an enthusiasm of humanity and a desire to scatter gifts among the people? Have they conscientious scruples against making undue profits? They do not raise prices very much because they cannot. Why they cannot do it the public does not altogether understand.

In the lucid intervals in which they tell the truth to the people, managers of trusts say that they cannot greatly raise prices without bringing new competitors into the field. As has been said, the foundation of a combination is liable to "build mills," and so to defeat the purpose for which the combination is formed. To keep the new mills from coming into existence a wise policy keeps prices at a moderate level. Within limits it is safe to raise them, but beyond such limits it is not safe. The competitor who is not now in the field, but who will enter it at once if prices are unduly raised, is the protector of the purchasing public against extortion. He is also the protector of the workmen, for the fact that he will begin his operations if too many of the old mills are closed, prevents the closing of them. In technical phrase it is potential competition that is the power that holds trusts in check. The competition that is now latent, but is ready to spring into activity if very high prices are exacted, is even now efficient in preventing high prices. It is to be the permanent policy of wise and successful peoples to utilize this natural economic force for all that it is worth.

At present it is not an adequate regulator. The potential competitor encounters unnecessary obstacles when he tries to become an active competitor. There are abnormal difficulties and dangers in his way, and the consequence of this is that he is often reluctant and tardy in his action; and the fear of him is a far less potent influence with the managers of trusts than it easily might be made to be.

The European competitor is usually a potential competitor because of the tariff which deters him from becoming an actual one. Shall we sweep away all duties on trust-made articles? That would make this latent competition active, and would do much to keep trusts in check. As a theoretical economist I am not prepared to favor so sweeping a measure; but where there are duties that are not at all necessary for the protection of an industry as such, but are necessary for the protection of a trust in an industry, these particular duties should go.

A domestic competitor is sometimes only a potential one because of patents. A trust often sustains itself by securing a monopoly of the kinds of machinery that are needed in an industry. Shall we abolish patents? Far from it; but we should reform our patent laws, and while making them afford a greater incentive than they now do to invention, should prevent patents from being instruments of extortion or oppression.

Railroads have the power to handicap the potential competitor, and it is an open secret that they are doing it. Discriminating rates for carrying freight are an intolerable evil, and they tend distinctly to build up real monopolies. If legal acuteness backed by popular energy can secure it, this evil must be suppressed.

These measures have already received attention in popular discussions and in the discussions of this conference. There is another type of law that, as I venture to affirm, is of even greater consequence than any that is before the public. The ability to make discriminating prices puts a terrible power into the hands of a trust. If in my small field it can sell goods at prices that are below the cost of making them, while it sustains itself by charging high prices in a score of other fields, it can crush me without itself sustaining any injury. If, on the other hand, it were obliged, in order to attack me, to lower the prices of all its goods, wherever they might be sold, it would be in danger of ruining itself in the pursuit of its hostile object. Its losses would be proportionate to the magnitude of its operations. Many a small competitor is in a position to beat a trust in a contest of cut-throat competition, if only the trust were compelled to make its low prices uniform for all customers. There is no saving power in a great capital, if a ruinous competition entails losses that are proportionate to the capital.

Akin to the power to make prices low in one locality and high in many others is the power to reduce the prices of one grade or variety of goods, and to sustain them on other varieties. My mill may make only one specialized product, and the mills of the trust may make that kind of goods and twenty others. If it is willing to lose money for a time on the goods that I produce, and to make money on all other kinds, it can ruin me if it will.

Akin to these resources for predatory warfare is the power to boycott customers who will not give their whole patronage to the trust, or to make special rebates to those wholesale or retail merchants who will refuse to buy any goods from independent producers. Such producers may find most markets closed against their goods, however cheap and excellent they may be.

The power to do all these things gives to the trust a great and abnormal advantage which the law can take away.

Predatory competition that is evil and that crushes producers who have a right to survive rests mainly in one of these three methods of discriminating and unfair treatment of customers. That power must be destroyed. With a fair field and no favor the independent producer is the protector of the public and of the wage-earner; but with an unfair field and much favor he is the first and most unfortunate victim. Save him, and you save the great interests of the public. You can do this if you find or make a way to success in that type of legislation that will prevent the single evil, discrimination in the treatment of customers. Put them all under what in diplomacy would be called a "most favored nation clause"; secure to all of them the benefit of the best treatment that the trust gives to any of its customers, and you may forego all other attempts to regulate their charges. Economic law that acts even now in a way that limits their exactions, will act far more efficiently. It will keep prices and wages at or near their natural levels and that, too, without sacrificing the prosperity that a high organization of industry insures. Carry that policy to success—conquer the difficulties that lie in the way of it—and you will secure for our country a happy union of productive power, that will give us the command of the markets of the world, and justice, that will develop the manhood and insure the contentment of our citizens.

LAURENCE GRONLUND

Socialist, Editorial Staff New York Journal

We mean legitimate, sound trusts, not fraudulent concerns, such, for instance, where smooth scoundrels sell to gullible people millions worth of worthless common stock, which they know will never produce a dividend. There are plenty of means and of laws to take care of this class. The legitimate trusts are either associations of capital—and to those, department stores belong—or unions of labor. We shall deal with both, though it is the former alone that creates difficulties for us.

Let us at the start understand that it is impossible to crush out either kind of trusts. The politicians who propose that remedy are either supremely ignorant or downright demagogues. In order to find out how to deal with trusts of capital, we must understand their origin.

They are not the outcome of "prohibitive" or other tariffs; neither are they the products of railroad discriminations, though they often are considerably assisted thereby. They are economic necessities, due to our complex civilization. Our commercial and industrial affairs have shown during the last hundred years an ever accelerating tendency to larger schemes, more elaborate organization, more intricate machinery. Our vast iron and steel industry comes down from the village blacksmith, our huge shoe factories from the village cobbler, our textile industry from the village hand-loom. At one time everyone worked for himself. Then came small, then large firms, followed by joint-stock companies and corporations. Finally, during the last generation, trusts, more and more extensive and intricate organizations, having for purpose to limit or abolish competition, since it was found to have become highly injurious and unprofitable.

Thus it cannot be too much emphasized that trusts are not due to any casual cause, not to wrong-headedness, not to vicious business principles, often even not to voluntary choice. A brewer in England declared, "We are compelled to take over the other breweries; we don't want to, but we are obliged to." It is an irresistible tendency, of late appalling in its rapidity, to be ascribed to increase of population, scientific discoveries and mechanical inventions.

Of course, it cannot be stopped. To try to crush the trusts would be like the attempt by a dam to stop the mighty Mississippi. The trust will go on; the various industries in each line will come under a central management. They will in our country develop in all directions, till finally— some time during the Twentieth Century—all considerable industries will be under the control of trusts, extending from the Atlantic to the Pacific. There is absolutely no help for it.

Still we say, the trust is not at all a monster; it is a phenomenon at which to look fearlessly, and to utilize for the public welfare. For this purpose we must fully understand wherein the dangers of the trust consist. It is generally supposed that the only interest the public has is how the trust affects wages and prices. We think this is a great error. We do not believe that trusts as yet have seriously lowered wages or raised prices. They surely need not do it. And we know that in many cases they have lowered prices and raised wages.

But there are two very serious dangers that threaten in the future. Let us assume that the time has come when every considerable industry has come under one head, one manager, whose sway will extend from ocean to ocean. What powers will such a chief not have, what power especially for mischief! Then the trust, indeed, will be capable of seriously affecting the public welfare; then indeed it may lower wages and raise prices, if it has a mind to. Can a democracy like ours stand such a state of things? Can it tolerate in its midst a handful of such autocrats, whose aim is simply private greed, and who do not need to care a particle for social need? Already we are now living under an absolutism of capital to which other nations are strangers—but what will it be then?

Again, in every trust, the owners virtually abdicate all their powers in favor of the manager. Hence, when all our industries have become trusts, capital will have had its character completely changed. Formerly capitalists performed a highly important function, that of directing production; capital had a social character, and was subject to noteworthy social obligations, which sometimes were splendidly discharged. But in the future our capitalholders will become industrially and economically useless, first superfluous, then harmful; they actually will become rudimentary organs in the social organism, and capital-holding will become a pure personal privilege, subject to no social obligation whatever. Can a democracy like ours stand this; will a democracy stand it? No. Such a state of affairs will be simply the last step but one.

Even before trusts arose, when we only had large enterprises that controlled matters of vital interest to the people, the public was forced to step in, in order merely to secure the rights of consumers. Public control has again and again been asserted. Grandmother always has had her way. So with still greater force it will be in the future. The organization of trusts is admirable; it knocks into the heads of all with sledge-hammer blows the patent truth that system is better than planlessness. The machinery of the trust is all ready to the hands of democracy—to public control. No one would think of socializing an industry that was divided into a hundred thousand businesses. But this is a national monopoly. That is why the trust movement is an irreversible step along the path to universal co-operation.

This, we say, is the first answer to the question, what to do with the trusts: Look forward to the future public ownership and management of their enterprises, but let this change proceed slowly. However, prepare for it, make it the ideal of the coming century, and treat the trusts accordingly.

The second thing to do, meanwhile, is to protect labor against the trusts. That they in the future may raise prices arbitrarily is bad enough, but that they arbitrarily may reduce wages is much worse. Oh, if the trusts would believe that it is to their advantage to include their employes in the benefits which they achieve, if they would conclude to revive the ancient guilds on a higher plane, then the future might be quite bright— but they are too selfish for that!

How, then, protect labor? For our laboring people to help our demagogues in attempting to crush the trust would be suicidal. They would be the first and only ones to feel the blows of such an enterprise. Undoubtedly our trades unions are trusts. Our work people generally do not know what they owe to trades unions, especially what they owe to the old English trades unionists, who kept up their unions in spite of parliamentary terrors. That they now enjoy higher wages and shorter hours is due to the unions. Though strikes often are disastrous to the participants, there never was one, either won or lost, that did not benefit the working people as a class.

It is well that work people are fast coming to look upon the workman as positively immoral who holds aloof from his fellows and refuses to enter the union of his trade. With the arrival of the trust, their ideal has become an organization, controlling the entire labor-force of the country, nothing less than a National Syndicate of Labor. They are right. Unless the labor trusts develop equally with trusts of capital, our civilization will soon come to a halt. . . .

These unions, of course, must be organized in a thorough democratic fashion, so that every workman will have a vote that counts as much as that of everyone else. Moreover, the State, as the representative of the whole community, will rectify the many serious blunders that trade unions in the past have committed, and which sometimes have made them absolutely anti-social institutions, such as the limitation of apprentices and forbidding able workmen to do the best they can.

This is the way to protect adult labor. But we must also protect our growing-up youths against the trusts—both of capital and labor. We must have a new education for our boys—a truly democratic education. Every phase of civilization has had its appropriate education. A good education under the ancient regime was different from a good education during the Middle Ages, and that again very different from a good education for the Twentieth Century. Our boys must be trained into being all-round men, fit to take their places in a perfect democracy. Next, our people now are being forced—especially by the trusts—to take their places according to their capacity, as portions of a great machinery. That is, we are fast becoming a nation of specialists. Specialization evidently is the law that will govern our future. No man will amount to anything unless he becomes a specialist in something useful, and just by becoming such a specialist will he become a valuable member of a perfect democracy. . . .

Lastly, we come to the third things we can do about the trusts. While public control of what is now strictly private business should be merely the ideal for the next century, and not be attempted until its close, there is some business that should immediately be entered upon. That is the so-called public utilities, such as municipal ownership and management of waterworks, of course, of street transportation in every form, of gas works, and electric power works. These may not yet be trusts—only large enterprises. But in Brooklyn we find surface and elevated roads already a trust, and in Manhattan they will soon be that. It would be highly desirable, and the best thing for itself, if the new democracy would in its next national platform incorporate a plank demanding municipal control. Nothing would so convince our people of the blessings of public control, and prove to them that government can do business as well and even better, than private parties, as such an object lesson. . . .

Then there are public utilities that come under the jurisdiction of the Nation which will furnish splendid opportunities for curbing the trusts. We should have a National express system, to which the late convention with Germany ought to give a great impulse, a National telegraph, National banks of deposit (postal savings banks) and National banks of loans from the funds thus accumulated, and finally National control of railroads. We do at present advocate National ownership and management of these latter; this might as yet be too big a mouthful to digest, but National control of railroad fares and freight-rates—this is perfectly practicable, and has been several times recommended to Congress. It would with one stroke abolish the unjust discrimination, both between localities and between shippers, which the interstate commission has been unable to effect. If trusts should ever dare to raise prices, such a National control of freight rates will immediately bring them to their senses. It is perfectly practicable, we contend. Through a committee of Congress it is just as easy to establish schedules of fares and freight rates on all our railroads, and to enforce them, as through the committee on ways and means to establish schedules of duties on imports and to enforce them, as is now done.

This is a practical way, and, we think, a far-seeing way to utilize the trusts for the public welfare, while to attempt to crush the trusts, we repeat, is simply the notion of the demagogues. . . .

CLEM STUDEBAKER

Manufacturer, South Bend, Ind.

Within certain reasonable limits the combination of agencies for the production of a given article decreases the cost of production. Such combinations enable the use of the latest improved machinery, and the adoption of general facilities to expedite the progress of work usually impossible if the manufacture is carried on with limited capital, or with small productive capacity. Further, it is well known that managerial assistance usually costs little more for a business of great magnitude than for one the output of which is small. On the other hand, however, whenever a business becomes so large that its oversight is impossible by one executive head, then it is often the case that economies are less likely to be successfully practiced. Such I imagine would be the case if it were undertaken to operate plants widely separated throughout the country. As to whether the decrease of cost of production ought to be beneficial to society, or the reverse, I think this answers itself in the asking. Morally considered, society ought to be benefited by every honest and proper improvement of conditions in the material world.

To what extent a decrease of the cost of production will profit the consumer will depend largely on the necessity which constrains the purchaser to share with him in the saving. If the combination in question were such as to utterly preclude competition, the benefit which would accrue to the consumer by a saving effected by the producer would quite possibly be inappreciable. Most producers under such circumstances would be quite likely to arrogate to themselves credit for the saving effected, and would consider that a division of the benefits under such circumstances would come under the head of philanthropy or benevolences rather than matter of fact business.

I would regard a general combination of all of the manufacturing plants for the production of any given article of manufacture as likely to be to some extent disadvantageous to the wage earner. The operation of some factories would perhaps be discontinued in favor of others more eligibly situated, and to the degree that concentration of forces would increase productiveness, there would be a correspondingly diminished demand for laborers. But this, of course, happens whenever improved machinery is introduced, or whenever there is a readjustment of production occasioned by a change in conditions affecting such production.

I do not imagine that combination among industrial enterprises will very seriously affect middlemen. In some cases commercial traveling men could be dispensed with, but the day when the public can be conveniently supplied without the intervention of the merchant, is a long ways off.

No true monopoly is possible in this country except that enjoyed by virtue of a patent granted by the United States. If those who undertake to inaugurate trusts had a monopoly of the trust business there would be cause for alarm. But any one can go into the trust or combination business who is able to find others who will join him. Herein is the safety of society. Combinations of capital build railroads and decrease the cost of travel and transportation. Some part of that saving they keep as profit, but whenever they undertake to keep so much of it from the public as to give them unusually large returns on their capital, a rival road springs up, and down goes the cost to the consumer. Trusts have undertaken to enfold producers so as to limit competition, but in vain. No sooner have they gathered into the fold all in sight than up springs another. And this will continue to be the case so long as there are profits made which allure outside capital, and outside capital is left free to take a hand in. Sugar refining, the manufacture of tobacco, etc., are cases in point. Whenever these great companies give evidence of making large profits, some powerful rival comes into the field, and competition proceeds to regulate prices on a lower plane. . . .

As manufacturers we feel no concern about combinations of capital in our line of business. It is the brain power of a competitor, rather than his capital in money, which makes him formidable in the struggle.

PART II

THE BUSINESSMAN:
FOR AND AGAINST

During the period following the Civil War, no status in American society was subjected to more ruthless criticism or defended with such zeal as that of the businessman. For one thing, the great men of business had become far more numerous. When, in 1845, Moses Yale Beach, owner of the New York Sun, compiled a roster of the richest merchants of New York, he listed only twenty-one as millionaires. By 1892, the New York Tribune found there were more than four thousand millionaires in the United States. The millionaire-businessman had also become far more visible to his fellow citizens; the great scale of his business activities, his forays into politics, his heroic appetites in the fields of entertainment and culture conspired to bring him into the limelight.

At the outset, criticism of the businessman was likely to focus upon an alleged failure in the businessman himself, his lack of both ethical and aesthetic standards. E. L. Godkin of the Nation, *certainly no enemy of the social order, did as much as any man to impeach the businessman for having the moral principles of a hawk and the aesthetic standards of a sot. The "Vanderbilt Memorial Bronze" on the Hudson River Railroad Depot, he wrote on November 18, 1869, "makes ridiculous what before was at worst only disagreeable." The symbolic bee-hives with which the bronze pediment was studded served only to "typify the industry and devotion to business of a man who never served the country at large, nor the State, nor the city, in any public office; nor ever spent the time which is money in advancing the cause of any charity; nor in promoting education, which the self-made man may despise; nor in fostering the arts, which can always wait." Was the great industrialist a public benefactor, or a latter-day version of the medieval robber baron, swooping down from his mountain lair to plunder the innocent? Godkin had no doubt:*

In short, there, in the glory of brass, are portrayed, in a fashion quite good enough, the trophies of a lineal successor of the mediaeval baron that we read about, who may have been illiterate indeed; and who was not humanitarian; and not finished in his morals; and not, for his manners, the delight of the re-fined society of his neighborhood; nor yet beloved by his dependents; but who knew how to take advantage of lines of travel; who had a keen eye for roads, and had the heart and hand to levy contribution on all who passed by his way.

With the passage of time, however, criticism of the businessman tended increasingly to become criticism of society, for the businessman was coming to be seen mainly as a symbol of a social order. Necessarily, therefore, defense of the businessman was forced to become defense of

117

the particular system which allowed him to operate as he wished. When Chauncey M. Depew, United States Senator and New York Central Railroad executive, spoke at the unveiling of the Vanderbilt memorial at Vanderbilt University in 1897, it was difficult to tell exactly what he was eulogizing, the man or the system:

The American Commonwealth is built upon the individual. It recognizes neither classes nor masses. We have thus become a nation of self-made men. We live under just and equal laws and all avenues for a career are open. Freedom of opportunity and preservation of the results of forecast, industry, thrift, and honesty have made the United States the most prosperous and wealthy country in the world. Commodore Vanderbilt is a conspicuous example of the productive possibilities of our free and elastic conditions. He neither gave nor asked quarter. The same country, the same laws, the same open avenues, the same opportunities which he had before him are equally before every other man.

In the selections that follow, Godkin discusses the businessman from the perspective of history; Henry Demarest Lloyd, the great antagonist of the Standard Oil Company, from the perspective of a critic of society. Edward Atkinson, New England textile manufacturer and business publicist, tells his audience of workingmen that the businessman is indispensable to their welfare.

The Expenditure of Rich Men

E. L. Godkin

From the earliest times of which we have any historical knowledge rich men have had to exercise a good deal of ingenuity in expending their income. The old notion that wealth is desired for the sake of power was never completely true. It has always been desired also, as a rule, for the sake of display. The cases have been rare in which rich men have been content to be secretly or unobtrusively rich. They have always wished people to know they were rich. It has, also, from the earliest times, been considered appropriate that display should accompany power. A powerful man who was not wealthy and made no display, has, in all ages, been considered a strange, exceptional person. As soon as a man became powerful, the world has always thought it becoming that he should also be rich, and should furnish evidences of his riches that would impress the popular imagination. . . . Of course, except in the case of rulers, he could not put his money into armies or fleets. Consequently, as a private man, he has put it into tangible, visible property, things which people could see and envy, or wonder over. . . . He, too, has been held bound to spend his money in ways in which the public in general expected him to spend it, and in which it had become usual for men of his kind to expend it. His expenditure was, therefore, in a certain sense, the product of the popular manners. If a man in England, for instance, expends money like a rich Turkish pasha, or Indian prince, he is frowned on or laughed at. But if he keeps a great racing stable, or turns large tracts of land into a grouse moor or a deer forest, in which to amuse himself by killing wild animals, it is thought natural and simple.

But one of the odd things about wealth is the small impression the preachers and moralists have ever made about it. From the very earliest times its deceitfulness, its inability to produce happiness, its fertility in temptation, its want of connection with virtue and purity, have been among the commonplaces of religion and morality. Hesiod declaims

E. L. Godkin, "The Expenditure of Rich Men," *Scribner's Magazine*, XX (1896), 495–501.

against it, and exposes its bad effects on the character of its possessors, and Christ makes it exceedingly hard for the rich man to get to heaven. The folly of winning wealth or caring for it has a prominent place in mediæval theology. Since the Reformation there has not been so much declamation against it, but the rich man's position has always been held, even among Protestants, to be exceedingly perilous. His temptations might not be so great as they used to be, but his responsibilities were quadrupled. The modern philanthropic movement, in particular, has laid heavy burdens on him. He is now allowed to have wealth, but the ethical writers and the clergy supervise his expenditure closely. If he does not give freely for charitable objects, or for the support of institutions of beneficence, he is severely criticised. His stewardship is insisted on. In the Middle Ages this was his own lookout. If he endowed monasteries, or bequeathed foundations for widows, or old men, or orphans, it was with the view of making provision for his own soul in the future world, and did not stand much higher in morals or religion than that old English legacy for the expenses of burning heretics. But in our times he is expected to endow for love of his kind or country, and gifts for his soul's sake would be considered an expression of selfishness.

In Europe, as I have said, the association of displays of wealth with political power has lasted since states were founded. It was largely made possible in the ancient world through slavery. From what we know through architectural remains, or historic record, there was no length, in that world, to which a great man could not go in the display of his possessions. What we hear or see of Hadrian's villa, or Diocletian's palace at Spalatro, makes Versailles seem a mere bauble. The stories told of the villas of Lucullus, or Mæcenas, even if half true, show that our modern rich men know but little of the possibilities of luxury. . . .

All this is now changed in Europe. As power has left the upper classes, display has ceased. To be quiet and unobserved is the mark of distinction. Women of Madame de Sevigné's rank travel in dark-colored little broughams. Peers in England are indistinguishable when they move about in public, from any one else. Distinction is sought in manners, in speech, in general simplicity of demeanor, rather than in show of any kind. An attempt to produce on anybody, high or low, any impression but one of envy, by sumptuousness of living or equipage, would prove a total failure. It may be said, without exaggeration, that the quietness of every description is now the "note" of the higher class in all countries in Europe—quietness of manner, of voice, of dress, of equipages, of, in short, nearly everything which brings them in contact with their fellow-men. Comfort is the quest of the "old nobility" generally. Ostentation is left to the newly enriched, but there can hardly be a doubt that this is largely due to loss of power. Wealth now means nothing but wealth. The European noble was, in fact, everywhere but in Venice, a great territorial lord. It was incumbent on him as a mark of his position, as soon as he came out of his mediæval "keep," to live in a great house, if only for purposes of entertainment. His retinue required large accommodation; his guests required more, and more still was added for the needs of the popular imagination. But the system of which he was the product, which made his château or mansion grow out of the soil like his crops, was never transferred to this country. The few large grants which marked our early history never brought forth large mansions or great retinues. The great houses of that period, such as those of the Van Rensselaers or Livingstons on the Hudson, or of the planters on the James River, are simply moderate sized mansions which, on most estates in England or France, would be considered small. Hospitality was in none of them exercised on anything like the European scale. None of them was ever occupied by anybody who exercised anything more than influence over his fellow-citizens. In fact most of them are to-day mainly interesting as showing the pains taken to put up comfortable abodes in what were then very out-of-the-way places.

All this amounts to saying that the building of great houses was, down to our own time, a really utilitarian mode of spending wealth. It was intended to maintain and support the influence of the ruling class by means which was sure to impress the popular mind, and which the popular mind called for. The great territorial owners had a recognized place in government and society which demanded, at first a strong, and later, an extensive, dwelling-place. It was, in short, the product and indication of the contemporary manners as dwelling-places generally are. If we travel through a country in which castles and fortified houses are numerous, as they used to be prior to the fourteenth century all over Europe, we conclude infallibly that the law is weak, and that neighbors make armed attacks on each other in the style described in the Paston Letters. If we find, coming down later, as in the Elizabethan period, strongholds abandoned for extensive and ornamental residences with plenty of unprotected windows, we conclude that the government is omnipotent and the great men live in peace. If we go through a democratic country like Switzerland, and find moderation in the size of houses and in the manner of living, the custom of the country, we conclude that the majority is in power, and that every man has his say in the management of the state. In short it may be truly said that dwelling-places, from the Indian's tepee up to the palace of the great noble, indicate, far more clearly than books or constitutions, the political and social condition of the country. . . .

American fortunes are now said to be greater than any of those of Europe, and nearly, if not quite, as numerous. But the rich American is face to face with a problem by which the European was not, and is not troubled. He has to decide for himself, what is decided for the European by tradition, by custom, by descent, if not by responsibilities, how to spend his money. The old rich class in Europe may be said to inherit their obligations of every kind. When a man comes of age, if he inherits wealth, and is of what is called "good family," he finds settled for him the kind of house he shall live in, the number of horses and servants he shall keep, the extent to which he shall entertain. His income is, in truth, already disposed of by will, or settlement, or custom. There are certain people he is expected to maintain in a certain way, a certain style in which he is to live. This has led to, what appears to the American, the curious reluctance of the Englishman "to lay down his carriage." To certain families, houses, and properties, to certain social positions, in short, is attached the obligation of "keeping a carriage." It is one of the outward and visible signs of the owner's place in the state. To the American it is generally a mere convenience, which some years he possesses and other years he does not, and the absence of which excites no remark among his neighbors. If an Englishman of a certain rank gives it up, it indicates the occurrence of a pecuniary catastrophe. It advertises misfortune to the world. It says that he has been vanquished in a struggle, that his position is in danger, and his friends sympathize with him accordingly, partly because the women of his family do not, as with us, use public conveyances in the cities.

From all these responsibilities and suggestions the American, when he "makes his pile," is free. He can say for himself how the owner of millions in a country like this ought to live. He may have one servant, eat in the basement, sup on Sunday evenings on scalloped oysters, and sit in his shirt-sleeves on his own stoop in a one hundred thousand dollar house, and nobody will make any remark. Or he may surround himself with lackeys, whom he treats as equals, and who teach him how the master of lackeys should behave, give gorgeous entertainments to other rich men like himself, at which his wife will eclipse in finery all other wives, and nobody will express interest or surprise except people who long for invitations from him. Or he may, after a period of such luxury, "burst up," sell everything out, and go live in Orange or Flushing. Or his wife may "tire of housekeeping," and they may retire to an expensive apartment in the Waldorf, or Savoy, after storing their furniture, or selling it at auction. What this indicates is simply that great wealth has not yet entered into our manners. No rules have yet been drawn to guide wealthy Americans in their manner of life. Englishmen, Frenchmen, Prussians, Austrians, Swiss, of rank and of fortune, have ways of spending their money, notions of their own of what their position and personal dignity require. But nothing of the kind is yet national in America. The result is that we constantly see wealthy Americans travelling in Europe, without the slightest idea of what they will or ought to do next, except get rid of their money as fast as possible, by the payment of monstrous prices and monstrous fees, or the committal of other acts which to Europeans are simply vulgar eccentricities, but which our countrymen try to cover up by calling them "American" when "irrational" would be a more fitting appellation. Some of this confusion of mind is due, as Matthew Arnold has suggested in one of his letters, to the absence among us of an aristocracy to set an example of behavior to our rich men. In European countries the newly enriched drop easily into the ranks of the aristocracy by a mere process of imitation. They try to dress and behave in the same way, and though a little fun may be made of them at first, they and their sons soon disappear in the crowd.

Ours do not enjoy such an advantage. They have to be, therefore, their own models, and there are finesses of manners and points of view in an aristocracy which are rarely got hold of except by long contact. By aristocracy I do not mean simply rich or well born people, but people who have studied and long practised the social art, which is simply another name for the art of being agreeable. The notion that it consists simply in being kindly, and doing pleasant things for people, and having plenty of money, is one of the American delusions. The social art, like all other arts, is only carried to perfection, or to high excellence, by people who carefully practise it, or pay great attention to it. It consists largely in what are called "minor morals," that is, in doing things in society which long custom has settled on as suitable for the set of people with whom one associates. . . . Like a large number of other things in civilized life, to be well practised it needs to be practised without thought, as something one is bred to. It is better obtained from books, or by study, than not at all, but it is most easily learned by observation. Ease of manner, taste in dress, tone of voice, insight into the ways of looking at small things of well mannered people, are most easily acquired by seeing them in others. The benefit of watching adepts in this art have been enjoyed by but few rich men in America, and the result is that the rich world with us can hardly be called a social world at all. There can hardly be said to be among us what is called in Europe a "world" or "monde," in which there is a stock of common traditional manners and topics and interests, which men and women have derived from their parents, and a common mode of behavior which has assumed an air of sanctity. Our very rich people are generally simply rich people with everything in the way of social life to learn, but with a desire to learn which is kept in check by the general belief in the community that they have nothing at all to learn, and that it is enough to be rich.

That, under these circumstances, they should, in somewhat slavish imitation of Europe, choose the most conspicuous European mode of asserting social supremacy, the building of great houses, is not surprising. But in this imitation they make two radical mistakes. They want the two principal reasons for European great houses. One is that great houses are in Europe signs either of great territorial possessions, or of the practice of hospitality on a scale unknown among us. . . . These are the excuses for great houses in England, France, or Austria. The owner is a great land-holder, and has in this way from time immemorial given notice of the fact. Or he is the centre of a large circle of men and women who have practised the social art, who know how to idle and have the means to idle, can talk to each other so as to entertain each other about sport, or art, or literature, or politics, are, in short, glad to meet each other in luxurious surroundings.

No such conditions exist in America. In the first place, we have no great landholders, and there is no popular recognition of the fact that a great landowner, or great man of any sort, needs a great house. In the second place, we have no capital to draw on for a large company of men and women who will amuse each other in a social way, even from Friday to Monday. The absence of anything we can call society, that is the union of wealth and culture in the same persons, in all the large American cities, except possibly Boston, is one of the marked and remarkable features of our time. It is, therefore, naturally what one might expect, that we rarely hear of Americans figuring in cultivated circles in England. Those who go there with social aspirations desire most to get into what is called "the Prince of Wales's set," in which their national peculiarities furnish great amusement among a class of people to whom amusement is the main thing. It would be easy enough to fill forty or fifty rooms from "Friday to Monday" in a house near New York or Boston. But what kind of company would it be? How many of the guests would have anything to say to each other? Suppose "stocks" to be ruled out, where would the topics of con-versation be found? Would there be much to talk about except the size of the host's fortune, and that of some other persons present? How many of the men would wish to sit with the ladies in the evening and participate with them in conversation? Would the host attempt two such gatherings, without abandoning his efforts in disgust, selling out the whole concern, and going to Europe?

One fatal difficulty in the way of such modes of hospitality with us is the difference of social culture between our men and women. As a rule in the European circle called "society" the men and women are interested in the same topics, and these topics are entirely outside what is called "business"; they are literary or artistic, or in some degree intellectual, or else sporting. With us such topics are left almost entirely to women. Whatever is done among us for real society is done by women. It is they, as a general rule, who have opinions about music, or the drama, or literature, or philosophy, or dress, or art. It is they who have reflected on these things, who know something and have something to say about them. It is a rare thing for husbands or sons to share in these interests. For the most part they care little about them; they go into no society but dinners, and at dinners they talk stocks and money. A meeting of women for discussion on such subjects would be a dreadful bore to them.

The husband feels better employed in making money for his wife and daughters to spend seeing the sights abroad. This difference in the culture of the sexes, and in the practice of the social art, is in fact so great in some parts of the country, as to make happy marriages rare or brief. It makes immense houses, with many chambers, in town or country, almost an absurdity in our present stage of progress.

Another, and the most serious reason against spending money in America in building great dwelling-houses, is, as I have already indicated, that the dwellings of leading men in every country should be in some sort of accord with the national manners. If there be what is called a "note" in American polity, it is equality of conditions, that there should neither be an immoderate display of wealth, nor of poverty, that no man should be raised so far above the generality in outward seeming as to excite either envy, hatred, or malice; that, above all things, wealth should not become an object of apprehension. We undoubtedly owe to suspicion and dislike of great wealth and displays of it, the Bryan platform, with its absurdities and its atrocities. The accumulation of great fortunes since the war, honestly it may be, but in ways mysterious or unknown to the plain man, has introduced among us the greatest of European curses—class hatred, the feeling among one large body of the community that they are being cheated or oppressed by another body. . . . We know that from the earliest times there has not been, and we know that there is not now, the smallest popular dislike to the successful man's "living like a gentleman," as the saying is, that is, with quiet comfort, and with a reasonable amount of personal attendance. But the popular gall rises when an American citizen appears, in the character of a Montmorenci, or a Noailles, or a Westminster, in a gorgeous palace, at the head of a large army of foreign lackeys. They ask themselves what does this mean? Whither are we tending? Is it possible we are about to renew on this soil, at the end of the nineteenth century, the extravagances and follies of the later Roman Empire and of the age of Louis XIV? What it does mean, in most cases, is simply that the citizen has more money than he finds it easy to dispose of. Consequently the only thing he can think of is building a residence for himself, which, like Versailles, shall astonish the world, if in no other way, by its cost.

All this may be said without denying in the least the great liberality of American millionaires. What colleges, schools, museums, and charities owe to them is something new in the history of the world. They have set Europe an example in this matter which is one of the glories of America. It is a pity to have them lessen its effect or turn attention away from it, by extravagance or frivolity, the more so because there is a mode still open to them of getting rid of cumbersome money, which is untried, and is full of honest fame and endless memory. We mean the beautifying of our cities with monuments and buildings. This should really be, and, I believe, will eventually become, the American way of *displaying* wealth. . . . We are enormously rich, but except one or two things, like the Boston Library and the Washington public buildings, what have we to show? Almost nothing. Ugliness from the artistic point of view is the mark of all our cities. The stranger looks through them in vain for anything but population and hotels. No arches, no great churches, no court houses, no city halls, no statues, no tombs, no municipal splendors of any description, nothing but huge inns.

I fear, too, of this poverty we are not likely soon to be rid, owing to the character of the government. It will always, under the régime of universal suffrage, be difficult in any city to get the average tax-payer to do much for art, or to allow art, as we see in the case of the Sherman Monument, to be made anything but the expression of his own admiration for somebody. It is almost impossible to prevent monuments or buildings being jobs or caricatures, through the play of popular politics on a subject which was no more meant for its treatment by majorities than the standard of value. Governments in all European countries do much for art. They erect fine public buildings under the best artistic conditions. They endow and maintain picture galleries and museums. In fact the cultivation of art is one of their accepted functions. Nothing of the kind is known among us. It would infuriate Populists and Bryanites to know that our Treasury was putting tens of thousands of dollars into books and paintings, or bric-à-brac, or even into art education. An École des Beaux Arts, or National Gallery, seems to be an impossibility for us. Whatever is done for beauty in America, must, it seems, at least for a long time to come, be done by private munificence. If we are to have noble arches, or gateways, or buildings, or monuments of any description, if our cities are to have other attractions than large hotels, it is evident our rich men must be induced to use for this purpose the wealth which it seems often to puzzle them to spend. Such works would be a far more striking evidence of the owner's opulence than any private palace, would give his name a perpetuity which can never be got from a private house, and would rid him completely from the imputation of selfishness. . . .

The Capitalist Finds a Champion

Edward Atkinson

. . . When you form your associations like the old guilds, and make the condition of membership that every man shall be master of his own art, as well as master of his own time, then you will benefit yourself and everybody else.

There is nothing like a club of men who are engaged in the same occupation, bringing them together, comparing notes, teaching them to find out the value of their own work and the price at which it ought to be sold. But they must find it out for themselves, and not take the word of another man who very likely knows nothing about the work, the conditions, or the relations of the men to their employers.

The object of association is to develop your *own* individuality, your *own* capacity, and thus enable you to get all that your work is worth *without* reducing you to the level of the most unskilful or the most incompetent man who is in the trade.

If there could be a method devised for creating and maintaining disparity between the rich and the poor, it would consist in able, skilful, and intelligent men parting with the control of their own time, and placing themselves on a level with the least skilful, the least capable, and the least industrious of those who engage in the same pursuit.

I do not say you do this. I leave it for you to find out whether you do or not; but let me tell you one thing,—if you put first-class spinners and weavers in the same place with second-class spinners and weavers, without discrimination, it will be just like packing first quality and second quality goods in the same bale; they will all be sold for just what the seconds are worth. If the goods are not inspected, they will all be sold at just what the mispicks or bad smashes are worth, and when they are sold at the price, the owner of the mill can only pay the best weaver what the work of the poorest weaver is worth who makes mispicks or bad smashes.

Edward Atkinson, "The Service Which Capital Renders When Employed by Labor," *Addresses upon the Labor Question* (Boston: Franklin Press: Rand, Avery and Company, 1886), pp. 13–26.

Another mistake which is constantly made is that the capitalist is getting a very big share of the product of almost every thing. This is not so, especially in the arts in which capital is most freely used.

Now, what are the facts? If a man could build a cotton-mill to-day, at the prices of materials and machinery, to make heavy sheetings, spending one million dollars on it, he would make in that factory goods worth about one and one-quarter million dollars every year, at six cents a yard. If he could get one-third to one-quarter of a cent a yard, he could keep up his factory and earn six per cent on his investment.

What would become of the other five and three-quarters?

It would be spent for materials, for labor, and for the salary of a superintendent competent to put the materials and the labor together, unless the owner were his own boss.

Some of you know what it is to work in a mill under an incompetent manager or an incompetent owner, who cannot put the materials and the labor together in a proper way.

When such a fellow as that takes hold, the workman loses his wages, and the owner loses his profit and generally loses his mill.

The cheapest man is the one who *knows how to do it*, no matter what his price is. Just as the cheapest workman is the best workman, no matter what *his* price is. The more he knows *how*, the higher his price will be, and the cheaper he will make the goods. The price of the goods will be the only limit on the price of his work. . . .

Take a shoe factory. If you put sixty thousand dollars into a shoe factory, you will turn out three hundred thousand to four hundred thousand dollars' worth of shoes a year, worth from one dollar to three dollars per pair. If the owner can get from three to ten cents a pair, according to the price, he is satisfied.

What becomes of the rest,—ninety-seven cents in each one dollar, two dollars and ninety cents in each three dollar pair? Is it not all paid out for leather, for shoe thread, and for labor? . . .

Now, we will take up a bigger enterprise than any which I have yet named. About one-fifth part of all the capital in the United States, of every name and nature, is to-day invested in railroads. There is more fuss made about the big fortunes of the railroad capitalists than of any other; but there are only one or two of them who have stolen their share or cheated other people out of it. There is no defence for such men.

But there are other men who have not cheated anybody,—men of the most honorable character, who build railroads, operate them honestly and fairly, and who have made big fortunes out of them. How did they do it?

Some of you live out at Olneyville very likely, or about that distance away from Providence. If an expressman owning a car would carry a barrel of flour for you, from a store in Providence out to your house, you would give him the empty barrel for his profit, wouldn't you, provided you could not do any better? and you would feel very well satisfied with the bargain.

Very well. Vanderbilt ran a cart from Chicago to Providence, with a steam-engine instead of a horse, over the Lake Shore and New York Central railroads. He carted, or some other man did, who ran another railroad alongside of his, all the flour that you ate last year, from Chicago to Providence, about one thousand miles, for sixty-eight cents a barrel, or less; very often less.

What profit did he make? Fourteen cents a barrel; no more; sometimes less. Not so much as the value of the empty barrel.

What if he did make two hundred millions of dollars or more by the job, he and his father working together twenty-five or thirty years? Wasn't he a cheap man for you to employ as a teamster? Didn't he cart flour cheaply enough? Do you grudge him the fourteen cents? . . .

In 1865 the New York Central, Vanderbilt line, charged three dollars forty-five cents for moving a barrel of flour one thousand miles. Last year they charged sixty-eight cents, sometimes less.

The difference between these two prices on the flour consumed by the people of the United States last year was one hundred thirty-eight million, five hundred thousand dollars. Your share of the saving, each of you (for you each need one barrel of flour per year, for each adult member of your family), was two dollars seventy-seven cents a barrel.

Vanderbilt made his two hundred million dollars by cheapening the cost of carrying the flour, and saving each of us two dollars seventy-seven cents, last year, on our flour. How many barrels do you use in a year, at one barrel a head,—count your two children of ten, or under, as one grown person? For every family of four, Vanderbilt saved ten dollars last year, as compared to 1865; while he made fifty-six cents profit. . . .

What do we work for? Money? or what money will buy? Obviously for what money will buy.

Working people who support their families on from four hundred to one thousand dollars a year, spend one-half of their money for food, even now. What would it have cost them for the same supply of food, if Vanderbilt, and other men of the same character, had *not* put their capital into railroads? . . .

Now, when there is a strike on a railroad, what happens? It stops your supply of food, doesn't it, and stops my supply of food. Who gets any thing out of it?

When work stops, production stops, and somebody loses. Who makes?

There is a better way to get higher wages; that is, for each man to keep the control of his own time, his own hands, and his own brain, and to do the best work in his power. Then he is sure to be paid for it, and the goods will be made at lower cost, or the flour will be moved at the lowest price. . . .

In order to get at the root of this question and learn what are the bottom facts, let us get as far away from our own pursuits as we can, so as to obtain a view of the matter from the outside.

Bread is the staff of life. And, although man does not live by bread alone, we must each have one barrel of flour a year. Now, one man, working one year (or what is the same thing, three men each working one hundred days in the season) can raise wheat enough in Dakota to supply one thousand men with flour for one year.

Of what use would this wheat be to us, if we could not get it? How could we get it from a place two thousand miles away, except by way of a railroad? Some people say labor does all the work, and ought therefore to have all the product. True: let labor go to Dakota, and bring the flour two thousand miles to Providence on a wheelbarrow, and it may have all the profit. I prefer to hire a capitalist to bring my barrel.

There is a big strike on what is called the "Gould" system of railroads. It is, or was, alleged that the strike will extend until it covers the whole railroad system between the East and West.

Well, suppose this should happen. Who will be struck hardest, and who will pay the costs? Capitalists who own the railroads? Not a bit of it. *You will.* The wages of the men who are employed upon the railroads are never paid out of the capital invested in them. It would not be possible. They would eat up the railroads, if they ate up the capital. Then what? The wages of the men who operate the railroads are paid out of the current receipts for moving food and fuel, timber and dry goods, which you use or eat. You pay them. How many of railroad men are there? About five men to a mile,—625,000 in the whole United States.

There are now twenty million men and women at work in the United States; and those who work for wages, earn small salaries, or run small farms by hard labor, count nearly nineteen million out of the twenty million, and consume nineteen-twentieths of all that is produced or moved over all the railroads.

This body of the railroad men is one of the largest single divisions, and they are among the best paid. You pay them, each one your share.

Last year the New York Central Railroad earned its part of a profit of fourteen cents a barrel, for moving a barrel of flour a thousand miles. In their part of the work, this corporation employed 15,309 men and boys, and I suppose a few women as clerks. They paid them an average of $544.60 a year each for their work. That is to say, you paid your share to the railroad, and the railroad paid the men at this rate. This railroad business is the most wonderful thing in the world. Some of you think labor does all the work, and ought to have all the pay; and some of these shallow fellows, tonguey chaps, get up and talk about the tyranny of capital, and say that these great corporations rule the country. Well, perhaps they do. I will give you some figures. Last year the railroads of the

United States moved a little over four hundred million tons an average distance of a hundred and ten miles. You can't comprehend such big figures, unless you are used to them. What did they move? What was all the fuss about? Why couldn't they let it alone? Why couldn't they let labor do all the work, and take all the pay?

They moved cotton and corn, wool and mutton, beef and pork, timber and coal, iron and groceries, what for? Only that you and I might have breakfast, dinner, and supper, a roof over our heads, some clothes to wear, some fuel to burn, and some tools to work with. What else? Well, just for that, over seven tons were moved a hundred and ten miles for every one of us, and for every one of our families. As much for you as for me. Just as much for Terry Gallagher as for Cornelius Vanderbilt,—hardly any difference.

Think of it a minute—seven tons; seventy barrels of flour, or twenty-eight bales of cotton, or a hundred cases of sixteen-ounce cassimere, or fourteen big casks of sugar. Think of any other lot of food or dry goods, and how much work it would be to move each lot a hundred and ten miles, just to give each of us and each of our children breakfast, dinner, and supper, clothes, fuel, and shelter. What will you take to do the job, and how long will it take you? Labor does all the work, and ought to have all the pay—does it? Bid for it, then—who will do it at a dollar and twenty-five cents a ton? eight dollars and seventy-five cents for the job? That is what the great railway corporations got for it—no more. Shall I say nine dollars? Who bids ten dollars? Going, going, gone to the railroad every time; because the railroad saves you just so much work every year, as it would take to move that seven tons apiece a hundred and ten miles. If they didn't do this, how would you live, and where would you live? Do you grudge the New York Central its profit of fourteen cents a barrel for moving your barrel of flour a thousand miles? . . .

I tell you, my friends, you must get the bottom facts; don't let shysters throw dust in your eyes; it's devil's dust, poor shoddy, it won't wash. . . .

Suppose all these railroad-men strike, and get all the profit, out of which the interest on the debts and the dividends on the stock are paid, the corporation would then be unable to earn fourteen cents a barrel for moving a barrel of flour a thousand miles.

That would put the road into bankruptcy. Who would then take it up and run it? Of course this won't happen. But suppose the men strike on all the railroads, and the price of freight is put up. Who pays it? You pay it on every barrel of flour, every ton of coal, every pound of beef which you use, or every yard of cloth which you make.

Suppose *you* strike back when there is no profit on cotton manufacturing or on woollen manufacturing. What happens then? Either the price of the goods must be put up, or the mill must stop. Who pays for that? The capitalist who owns the mill? Not a bit of it. He waits.

The men who run the railroads, the carpenters, masons, mechanics all over the country, pay for it in a higher price for goods.

Now, suppose we all strike. The measure of enough is a little more. I should like to strike, and get a little more. You would like to strike, and get a little more. The next man would like to strike, and get a little more. And when we have all struck, and all have got a little more, what have we accomplished and where are we?

For the time being we have had an interruption of business, a decrease of product, a temporary scarcity; and then the same kind of a distribution goes on—only at high prices, as it went on before at low prices. In the meantime, middle-men who happened to have a big stock of goods when the strike began will take the rise in price, and the rest of us will pay it.

What else can you make of it? None of us work for money, although we think we do. We work for what we can buy with our money. The important point is, that there should be the biggest product for the least amount of work. Large product, low prices, high wages,—that is what we all want.

Small rates of profit on capital come from big production, hard work for the capitalist (and perhaps he will get rich), but easier work for the laborer, lower prices, and higher wages.

That is the natural course of events,—just what has happened in the last fifty years. There never was a time in the history of this country when the general rate of wages was as high as it is now, the general product so large, the cost of living so low, and the proportionate profit of capital so small. . . .

The old saying is a very true one: "Three generations from shirt-sleeves to shirt-sleeves." Perhaps, in these modern times, it may be four, possibly five; but that is about the end of it.

Now it sounds like a very selfish and malignant principle, to hold up for approval the rule of each man for himself. But I omit the rest of the adage,—"The Devil take the hindmost;" because it isn't true, unless the hindmost is a fool himself, and is willing to let the Devil take him.

Here is a man—well, we will take the late A. T. Stewart as an example. He set up a big shop, and everybody went to it to buy something, and Stewart made a big fortune, which is rapidly disappearing. How did he do it? Exactly in the way in which Vanderbilt ran a railroad. He hired the best men, distributed the goods at the lowest prices, at a small profit on each sale, but he made a big fortune out of very large sales.

Why did everybody go to his shop? In order to help make Stewart's fortune? Not a bit of it. Each one went there because he benefited himself, or thought he did, which is the same thing. He got the best goods for cash, at the lowest price.

If you could only find out a way to establish a big public market here in Providence, and systemize the distribution of food, meat, vegetables, or fruit, in the way in which Stewart organized and distributed dry goods, every man of you could save ten or fifteen, and perhaps twenty to twenty-five, per cent on the price that you now pay for a comparatively poor supply of the same food.

If you can't get the market in any other way, better hire an A. T. Stewart to do it, if you can find one.

The biggest problem waiting to be solved is how to distribute meat, fish, bread, beans, potatoes, and milk, etc., at the lowest cost.

There is a man named Samuel Howe in New York, who has a large capital, with which he has built a big bakery. He sells the best bread over the counter to any one who will come and carry it away, at three cents a pound. I cannot find any bread in Boston so good at five cents a pound.

It costs more to distribute bakers' bread after it is finished, and taken out of the oven, than it does to raise the wheat, or to grind it, or to move it fifteen hundred miles, or to bake it. All these elements of cost could be covered here in Providence with a profit, to the capitalist who works on a large scale, at three cents a pound. I venture to say, that, if you weigh the loaves of bread that you buy, you will find that you pay from five to eight cents a pound.

What are you going to do about it? Strike? or pass a law regulating the baking of bread, which will put up the price instead of putting it down?

Each man serves the other; and every man is a working man, except the drones: they are few in number,—relatively unimportant.

The capitalist does the largest service, and gets the best price per man at the smallest rate for each service.

The skilled workman comes next, and gets a good price because he does good work.

The common laborer does the least, and gets the least for it.

What are you going to do about it? Put the common laborer on top? That is what they tried to do with the carpet-bag government down in South Carolina, when they nearly ruined the State, and reduced almost every one to poverty. When the whole thing broke down, they changed their method. . . .

The labor question will be solved when every man and boy is given good opportunity to get good instruction, mental and manual, and an even chance in the use of the only thing that we all have in common, whether we be rich or poor,—the use of his own time.

The man who comprehends the use of time, and who keeps the control of his own time, his hands, and his brain, will come out on top every time.

A good way to bring these things about is to form clubs, associations, societies, or any other way of bringing men together; that is to say, bringing them into a position in which they teach themselves how to serve other people, by doing for them something that they want to have done and are willing to pay for.

In all honest work, the dollar of the man's earnings, whether measured at five hundred dollars a year, or five hundred thousand dollars, is the measure of the service which he has rendered, and for which he is paid. And it is because no man can live for himself alone, that no man can make profitable use of his capital without giving employment to some other man by such use. Capital is used in the service of labor, just as truly as labor is employed in the service of capital.

There is no Devil to take the hindmost, except the Devil has a fair claim upon him; and that is the hindmost man's own lookout, rather than yours or mine. We will do all we can to help him; but, after all, no other man can help a man who cannot help himself.

There is always plenty of room on the front seats in every profession, every trade, every art, every industry. There are men in this audience who will fill some of those seats, but they won't be boosted into them from behind; they will get there by using their own brains and their own hands. Do they keep other men out of those seats, or do they hold other men down in order to get them?

Did Vanderbilt keep any of you down, by saving you two dollars and seventy-five cents on a barrel of flour, while he was making fourteen cents?

Service for service. Product for product. In these words all the great laws of commerce are condensed, and no commerce can be permanent except it be conducted under these rules. . . .

The Political Economy of
$73,000,000

Henry Demarest Lloyd

I

Four years ago it was proposed to expel political economy from its place in the course of the British Association for the Advancement of Science, on the ground that it had failed to make good its scientific pretensions. In the speeches at the dinner given, in 1876, by the Cobden Club, to celebrate the centenary of the Wealth of Nations, and in the eager discussion about political economy which followed in the English reviews, there was unmistakable despondency in the tone of the economists. Bagehot owns that political economy lies rather dead in the public mind, and confesses that it deals not with real men, but imaginary ones. Jevons sees signs of the disruption of the orthodox school. Bonamy Price, of Oxford, declares its scientific method to be a mistake. To Cairnes one feature is prominent in all debate for the settlement of the Irish land question—"a profound distrust of political economy." Harriet Martineau won no small part of her fame by popularizing the truths of political economy in her celebrated tales; but later in life, in her Autobiography, she tells the world that had so eagerly swallowed her sweetened doses of supply and demand that what she had at first taken to be a science she had come to regard as no science at all. A great school of Continental students of the welfare of man in society has long rejected the dominant ideas and methods of what in England and America is called orthodox political economy; orthodox, probably, because no two of its expounders agree. The most philosophic mind that England has produced in this generation, capable of a few great generalizations, and capable of not making little ones,— Sir Henry Maine,—calls for a new political economy, which shall use the methods that have been so fruitful in the historical study of early human

Henry D. Lloyd, "The Political Economy of Seventy-three Million Dollars," *Atlantic Monthly*, L (1882), 69–81.

institutions. In these studies, price, rent, the market, property, competition, and freedom of contract are shown to have arisen in places and ways never even dreamed of by the deductive economist. Comte strenuously denied that political economy was a science, and he and his followers thought it immoral to waste good lives in elaborating hypotheses assuming the supremacy of self-interest and competition, when the crying want of mankind is to destroy that supremacy. The study makes little headway in our colleges. . . . And Professor Dunbar, of the chair of political economy of Harvard, said, in 1876, that for one hundred years the United States had done nothing toward developing its theory. Our high thinkers, like Ruskin, Carlyle, and Emerson, have refused from the first to acknowledge its authority. According to Ruskin, nothing has ever been so disgraceful to human intellect as the acceptance among us of the common doctrines of political economy as a science. He holds that the economic principles taught to our multitudes, so far as accepted, lead straight to national destruction; that they are like a science of gymnastics which assumes that the human being is all skeleton, and that they found an ossifiant theory of human progress on the negation of a soul. Emerson says, nobly and simply, The best political economy is the care and culture of men. Our great statesmen do not look on this science, which is supposed to be specially theirs, with more favor than the moralists. Gladstone said, at the Adam Smith dinner, that not much remained for political economy to do, except in regard to the currency; and yet so much has this science done to prevent man from understanding what man invented, that Gladstone has elsewhere declared that of all studies the currency question is most provocative of insanity. Bismarck told an American member of Congress, in 1879, speaking of the German monetary reform of 1873, "We listened to an eminent economist, and we now see that we have put only plain water into our soup-boiler." No one has more happily anticipated the drift of recent criticism than Daniel Webster, who wrote to a friend in a letter lately published,—

"For my part, though I like the investigation of particular questions, I give up what is called the science of political economy. There is no such science. There are no rules on these subjects so fixed and invariable that their aggregate constitutes a science. I have recently run over twenty volumes from Adam Smith to Professor Dew, and if from the whole I were to pick out with one hand all mere truisms, and with the other all doubtful propositions, little would be left." . . .

Never more than now have we needed such a help as this political economy has pretended to be. The reaction against it comes at a time when the body of the people are growing uneasy at the peril of a position between workingmen who combine and capitalists who consolidate. Rings and bosses are rising to the top in the evolution of industry as in that of politics. New facts, like the union in one person of the common carrier and the owner of the highway, are baffling our statesmen. A few individuals are becoming rich enough to control almost all the great markets, including the legislatures. We feel ourselves caught in the whirl of new forces, and flung forward every day a step farther into a future dim with the portents of struggle between Titans reared on steam, electricity, and credit. It is an unfortunate moment for the break-down of the science that claimed to be able to reconcile self-interest with the harmony of interests.

Adam Smith modestly termed his great book An Enquiry into the Nature and Causes of the Wealth of Nations. The political economy of his successors is taught, in the universities of England and most of the colleges of this country, not as an investigation to be pursued in the laboratory of facts, but as a body of settled truths, revealed by teachers, and to be applied as a universal solvent. It is what nothing can be,—an apostolic science. Mill's language shows that he regards history as an arsenal from which to draw facts to reinforce his economic theories, not as a record in which the development of society may be observed, and its laws discovered by the methods that have given such practical and brilliant results in the hands of Maine, Von Maurer, Roscher, Nasse, De Laveleye, and Leslie. . . . Senior, of Oxford, states that it depends more on reasoning than on observation, and that its principal difficulty consists not in the ascertainment of its facts, but the use of its terms. Its facts according to him may be stated in a very few sentences, and indeed in a very few words. Precisely the same view is taken by Professor Sumner, of Yale College. In a recent address in Brooklyn, on Revenue Reform, he said, "Unfortunately the economist can't create facts, and history furnishes him but few. Consequently, hypotheses have to be used."

In abstract political economy, wealth is the subject, desire of wealth the motive, competition the regulator, supply and demand the law, freedom of contract the condition, and equalization of rent, wages, other prices, and profits the result. If the critic looks with distrust on a science of human conduct founded on assumptions, and doubts the stability of a structure reared with syllogistic brick on imaginary foundations, to what a dead stop must he come before the unscientific vagueness of this term "wealth." Mill says wealth consists of all useful and agreeable objects which have exchangeable value. Accept this definition, and how vast the territory it covers. It reaches from the individual to the nation, from the family to the stock exchange, where the economist most nearly finds his ideal. What man wants of man varies with countless contingencies, from those of sympathy down. Adam Smith, the greatest expositor of the virtue of self-interest that ever lived, his editor, Thorold Rogers, tells us, impaired his fortune by his benevolence. His greatest disciple, Cobden, spent his life and his private means to give the poor cheap bread. Ideals of life determine whether iron shall be turned into artillery to teach

Hindoos free trade at the cannon's mouth, or into plowshares for American homesteads. The buccaneer looked for gold, and is poor; the Puritan
sought freedom, and is rich. Fashion kills the manufacture of lustrous
woolen dress stuffs. Government fixes whether land shall descend by the
land law of the people, as in France, or by the land law of the nobles, as
in England. Custom says that grocers may, but that doctors and plumbers
shall not, undersell each other. According to the age, society will build
cathedrals or railroads. Sex hedges one half the world with the gravest
physiological and social limitations. If you are a Calvinist, free will must
have something to say about your desire of wealth. This science of wealth
is the science of man—and woman. Every note of the human voice,
whether of preacher or pirate, mother or Magdalen, must be heard in
the formulas of wealth. The world of wealth is the world of soul, over-
soul, and under-soul; and yet its philosophers attempt to lay down its
facts and terms in one sentence, or, as Senior says, in a very few words,
and Sumner has to make hypotheses. . . .

All the machinery of the abstract political economist is driven by the
force of competition. "Only through competition," says Mill, "has political
economy any pretensions to the character of a science. . . . Assume competition to be the exclusive regulator of rents, wages, profits, and prices,
and principles of broad generality and scientific precision may be laid
down, according to which they will be regulated. . . . As an abstract or
hypothetical science, political economy cannot do anything more." The
critic of this method wants a political economy that will disclose the
actual, not the hypothetical, regulator of prices, wages, rents, and profits.
By excluding all forces but those of competition, these economists shut
themselves out from the consideration of the gravest problems of the day,
which are questions of combination, and not of competition. On the other
hand, their principle of competition does not fit the questions which they
choose to attack. Their competition equalizes values with the cost of production, leveling the wages of laborers down to the cost of subsistence,
and leveling the rent of landlords up to all the produce of the farm above
the maintenance of the tenant. As to the facts of the theory, take an extensive view. The death of Babylon, the decay of Venice, the maturity of
London, the growth of New York, and the rise of Chicago are not phenomena of equalization, but of inequalization—tide-marks of a westward
flood and ebb. Take a narrower range. McCulloch says that the principles
of political economy and the forces of modern industry have obliterated
the differences in the wages of British labor noticed by Adam Smith.
Cliffe Leslie shows by the logic of facts that steam, new gold, and railroads have created new centres of wealth and industry, and have made
the modern disparities of English wages greater than they were in the
time of Adam Smith. The same forces that are inequalizing wages are inequalizing profits. He would be a bold man who could assert that there

had been a process of equalization in the political economy of New England since the days when the Pilgrim Fathers, unconsciously reproducing the earliest idea of the race, founded a society on the principle of the ancient village community. Competition shifts taxation, theoretically, upon consumers, but one of the strongest lobbies in Washington, during the recent session, was kept there by the proprietors of patent medicines, to procure the repeal of the stamp tax they pay. At a time when a hundred wedding-rings were pawned in one town in a single week for money to buy bread with, as Cobden tells us, English landlords were proving by Ricardo's theory of competition that a tax on corn could not fall on the laborer. By the same theory Mill taught the laborers that to have large families was as wicked as to be guilty of habitual drunkenness, because wages would go down if population went up. But, as a matter of fact, population and wages have been rising together in England, for many years. Their theory of rent is the achievement of which the English economists are most proud. It justifies the landlord in taking all the produce of the soil above the cost of subsistence. If the farmer tried to keep more for his share, competition, the force which, according to Mill, equalizes the profits of occupations, would take it away from him. The landlords of England, in the words of the editor of the Pall Mall Gazette, are starving the workers of their country to have their rents. Our faith that the theories of competition explain the facts of this kind of rent is shaken by the discovery that it appeared in East Indian political economy, where competition is unknown. The Mohammedan emperors of Delhi, the Mahratta princes, the Sikhs of the Punjab, different in many other things, were alike, Maine says, in this, that they took so much of the produce of the soil as to leave the cultivators little more than the means of bare subsistence. . . . The Irish land courts have reduced rents by an average of eighteen to thirty per cent. Even Ricardo would have to admit that a sovereignty was working through the land courts that overtopped competition. American rent is generally fixed by custom at one third the produce of the farm. Belgian rent and French rent, where they exist, have their peculiarities. English rent is an historical product, whose determining forces have been all kinds, from conquest to American competition. Among these forces are such legislation and lack of legislation in the interest of a dominant class as permit the landlords to continue paying taxes on land on the valuation of 1692, while their tenants and laborers are taxed on the value to-day of what they consume. Among these forces, too, must be counted the predisposition against change which keeps the British farmer growing wheat in the very shadow of London smoke, while the Belgian and French farmers supply the metropolis with its fresh vegetables. Rent, Mill asserts, is the result of a monopoly; but rent is paid in Dakota in the same counties in which the best government land can be had upon payment of a few dollars in fees to the land office. The theory of rent reduces the share of the tenant in the produce of the soil to the cost of subsistence, but in the Mississippi Valley a very large proportion of the tenant farmers grow well-to-do, and those who begin as renters usually end as land-owners. . . .

The competitive political economists ignore the natural history of their subject, its economic news. The differences of character and circumstances that make the English and French disposed to stay at home, while the Irish and Germans emigrate freely, are not to be explained by competition. The abstract economists dismiss as aberrations and exceptions to their cosmopolitan equilibrium those mysterious storms, which burst with something like periodicity over the world of credit, scattering ruin within the areas of high tariff and low tariff, free trade and protection, specie payments and "flat" money, and the single and double standard. Political economy of the competitive school is dumb before the railroad question, for it is one of combination. A parliamentary commission reports that it has become more and more evident that competition must fail to do for railroads what it does for ordinary trade, and that no means have yet been devised by which competition between them can be maintained. Equally beyond the reach of this competitive science is the socialistic drift of modern government, which forbids self-interest to commit murder by the sale of adulterated food, which taxes property by a majority vote for the education of the masses and the regulation of their plumbing, and which in Great Britain offers to pay at the national expense the arrears of hundreds of thousands of Irish tenants. The labor question is the appearance among workingmen of the same spirit of combination that has given us railroad pools, the telegraph consolidation, the oil monopoly, and countless smaller "corners," and it cannot be solved by a science of competition. The professors assume that competition is the exclusive regulator of wages, but we see workingmen kill a workingman for competing with them. Rumors are in the air of a general strike this summer. It will include the telegraph operators and the railroad men. Communication by wire is to be cut as well as communication by rail. Civilization, at the lifting of the finger of some Knight of Labor, is to be disintegrated. . . . A new organization of workingmen, the Knights of Labor, has sprung into existence within a year or two, and already numbers two hundred thousand members. Its principle is the unification of labor. Its motto, finer than the formulas of the economists, is, Injustice to one is injustice to all. Its purpose is to settle the differences between employers and employed, without strikes, if possible, but if a strike must be made, to back it up with the strength of the whole body. Twenty-five years' experience has taught these men that individual trades-unions can be crushed out. They are going to "pool," like the railroads. Such a great fact as that in France the French Revolution was a turning point in the welfare of the laboring classes, whose condition, as Mill shows, has risen, and risen permanently, since then, is not on speaking terms with the theory of exclusive regulation of wages by competition. *Laissez-faire* theories of politics and political economy are useless in the treatment of the labor question, in the regulation of railroads, sanitary and educational government, and a multitude of similar questions. It is not to be denied that competition is an industrial force, and a mighty one, but it is only one. By neglecting the other forces, from sympathy to monopoly, the abstract political economist deduces principles which fit no realities, and has to neglect those realities for which we need principles most. When combination comes in at the door, this political economy of competition flies out of the window. It is a political economy of persons, not of people.

II

There is not, says Comte, any purely industrial human being. But occasionally there flourish, outside the jails, persons who are almost ideal exemplifications of the principles of the competitive political economy. America has produced the most successful of these practical political economists. His career illustrates what may be accomplished by a scientific devotion to the principles of competition, laissez-faire, desire of wealth, and self-interest, if not the harmony of interests.

While the Crystal Palace exhibition of 1853 was open in New York, there came to seek his fortune in the city a slender, black-eyed, black-haired boy, from the interior of the State. He brought with him a very handsome mahogany box. In the box was an invention: "a little thing," he once said, "I had brought from my country home, and thought was going to make my fortune and revolutionize the world. It was a mouse-trap." The unsophisticated boy left his treasure on the seat of a Sixth Avenue car, while he stood on the platform to stare at the crowd, and it was stolen. But he pursued and caught the thief, who was an old offender, for whom the police of New York were looking at that moment. The Herald of the next day, under the heading How a Mouse-Trap caught a Thief, gave his first taste of publicity to the youth who for the next thirty years was to be continually before the public, and, by a singular coincidence, always in connection with some kind of trap. The genius that had divined from afar that the great city was full of mice, and had contrived a trap to catch them, could not be stolen. Its first impulse grew to be a passion. Brains and strict attention to the laws of supply and demand have made the country boy the greatest mouse-catcher of America, and his traps have become the envy of every man of feline aspirations.

Four of his inventions were masterpieces. In the first of them he gained the confidence of his simple prey by assuming a position of trust as director, and afterwards as president, of the largest railroad but one in his native State. At once there began to turn before the eyes of the stockholders and the public a kaleidoscope of ruin: shower after shower of

stocks and bonds issued to run the road, while the trustee and his pals—
pal is old English for fellow trustee—drank dry the stream of earnings; a
devil's dance of lawyers, judges, legislators, governors, and Tammany
politicians, flinging themselves into every attitude of betrayal of trust,—
an orgy of fiduciary harlotry, led by a great law reformer; a tangled web
of injunctions and counter-injunctions, and more injunctions, contradic-
tory orders of courts, perjured affidavits,—every thread spun by its poison-
ous spinner around and around a trust; a phantasmagoria of prosperity of
busy trains and steamers, crowded ferries, marble opera-houses, bursting
warehouses, glowing mills, precious franchises, and rich contracts,—a fair
but hollow scene, where all the expenses go to the owner, and all the
receipts to the trustee.

Our economist, having been charged with a fraud upon his road, at
once procured from one of his courts the place of receiver, with a fund of
$8,000,000, to protect his trust against himself. In one of his stock-
exchange campaigns he locked up $12,500,000 of money,—other people's
money. New York rocked in the preliminary throes of panic, and there
would have been a crash had not Secretary McCulloch interposed with
the announcement that he would issue $50,000,000 of legal tenders, if
this hand were not taken off the throat of business. An honest editor,
Samuel Bowles, who denounced the alliance of Tammany and Erie, was
abducted and illegally jailed. Assassination was attempted upon Dorman
B. Eaton, another fearless denunciator, who was left for dead on the
streets of New York, for having dared to act out the courageous words of
Emerson: "Good nature is plentiful, but we want justice, with heart of
steel to fight down the proud."

When this student of the science of abstraction became trustee, his
trust was in debt $51,065,943. Under his administration of the laws of
competition, this became $115,449,211, while the mileage increased but
186 miles. In four months the increase was $23,500,000. The moral bank-
ruptcy that festooned this ruin could not be expressed in figures. These
surprising achievements in the pursuit of wealth led the New York legislature to order an investigation. The political economist of the mouse-
trap was charmingly frank in his answers to the committee:—

I was first elected president of the Erie Railroad in 1868, and I was
president in 1869, 1870, and 1871. I do not remember whether I approved
payment to William M. Tweed of money for legal services, while he was
senator. I do not know whether he is a lawyer. He was a director of Erie
and member of its executive committee. I would not have allowed
pecuniary transactions with Mr. Tweed to be put in the shape of legal
services, if my attention had been called to them. I do not contemplate
going to Europe to-morrow. I should say that paper was in my handwriting. The name William M. Tweed is in my handwriting. The words in
my handwriting are, William M. Tweed, legal disbursements as per order

J. G., $35,000, April 25, 1871. The approval of voucher, April 5, 1869, name of William M. Tweed, legal expenses, $15,000, looks like my handwriting. Mr. Tweed's name at the top is my handwriting, and I should say his name at the foot of the receipt is my handwriting. He was senator in 1869; also in 1871 and 1872. The "legal account" was of an india-rubber character. I gave large amounts for elections in 1869, 1870, 1871, and 1872 in the senatorial and assembly districts. It was what they said would be necessary to carry the day in addition to the amount forwarded by the committee. I contributed more or less to all the districts along the line of the road. We had to look after four States, New York, New Jersey, Pennsylvania, and Ohio. It was the custom, when men received nominations, to come to me for contributions, and I made them, and considered them good paying investments for the company. In a republican district, I was a strong republican; in a democratic district, I was democratic; and in doubtful districts, I was doubtful. In politics, I was an Erie railroad man, every time. We had friends who were on both sides,—friends in a business way. The amounts contributed for the elections were large, but I could not give any definite estimate. No names occur to me at the moment. I am a poor hand to remember names. I had relations in several States. I did not keep separate what I paid out in New Jersey from what I paid out in New York. We had the same ground to go over there, *and there has been so much of it.* It has been so extensive that I have no details now to refresh my mind. You might as well go back and ask me how many cars of freight were moved on a particular day. . . .*

It was no ordinary trap in which Wall Street and the whole country were caught on that darkest day of all our financial history,—Black Friday, September 21, 1869. On one side, it was supported by the New York Sub-Treasury, whose chief held his position for the purposes of the Gold Conspiracy. On another side, it rested in the coffers of the Erie Railroad, whose president was the boy of the mouse-trap. At a third point, it had, apparently, a personal connection with the President of the United States. Through the Tenth National Bank, whose president was the president of the Erie, it had the facilities of the National Banking Association. The Stock Exchange was the pitfall. Black panic, which this conjurer of the irresistible laws of trade had before called to his aid, came, bringing ruin to thousands, madness and death to more than one. In the Stock Exchange, the wires melted under the fire of dispatches. There are to-day men proud to tell you that in that moment of frenzy and horror they hunted, rope in hand, for this disciple of self-interest, and if they could have caught him would have hanged the maker of the

* Report of the Select Committee, appointed by the Assembly of the State of New York, May 11, 1873, to investigate Alleged Mismanagement on the part of the Erie Railway Company, together with the Testimony taken before said Committee, page 545, *et seq.*

mouse-trap that caught a thief only sixteen years before. But the president of the Erie road fled to his arsenal on Twenty-Third Street, and was secure. He saved his millions, for while his partners, by his advice, were buying, he was selling, selling, selling. He was promoted from investigation by a committee of the New York legislature to investigation by a committee of Congress. He told them, "I had my own views about the market, and my own fish to fry." He saved the millions of his magnetic lieutenant Fisk, by teaching him to repudiate the orders given to his brokers. Before their victims could crawl out from under the ruins of Black Friday they were served, as Charles Francis Adams, Jr., in his Chapters of Erie tell us, with injunctions prepared in batches, by David Dudley Field, forbidding them "from pressing their pretended claims . . . by any proceedings." A law reformer devised a scheme, and a judge supported it, by which the men who had been knocked down and robbed were prohibited, in the name of justice, from seeking justice. Physicians, licensed by the state to heal, preparing poisons for the use of assassins!

In December, 1880, what may be accomplished by steadfast faithfulness to the principles of competition was shown by a statement, made by the most trustworthy financial paper in the United States, that our political economist was in control of ten thousand miles of railroad, or more than one ninth the entire mileage of the country.

It was during the same month that the conflict between the Western Union and American Union telegraph companies was raging at its worst. The American Union had been started in 1879, by our hero, with an investment of less than five million dollars. Western Union stock tumbled to seventy-seven and one half in the last month of 1880. So little interest did he take in the stock market at this time that he did not visit Wall Street, but when not at home spent his time at the Windsor, across the street. Swinging his legs from a back-tilted chair, he would tell his friends that Western Union was a worthless bundle of expiring patents, uncertain contracts, and old wire, and that he should not buy a share above sixty. February 5, 1881, Western Union and the American Union and the Atlantic and Pacific telegraph companies were consolidated, and the telegraph capital of the three, which was then sixty million dollars against four hundred thousand in 1856, was increased to eighty millions. The stock had never gone below seventy-seven and one half, but the inventor of the American Union snare was the owner of most of it. The price advanced to one hundred and thirty-seven and seven eighths, and the public found that the ex-trustee of Erie, the ally of the Tammany ring, the corrupter of justice, and the artificer of panic was master of the rapid transit of news and confidence within the United States, and between them and the rest of the world.

Hardly had the details of the telegraph consolidation been announced, February, 1881, when a flutter in the New York Stock Exchange followed the publication of a letter from the president of the Manhattan Elevated Railroad Company, begging the State to remit the taxes due from the company. It was a piteous plea for escape from ruin, and the stock began to fall. Next rose into view the highest judicial officer of the State, who declared with great indignation that Manhattan had forfeited its charter by insolvency, by failure to build roads, as stipulated by its charter, and by its shameless watering of stock. He began suit to wipe it out of existence. The public applauded with a thrill of satisfaction, and more stockholders sold. The hidden hand pulled another wire, and the editor of the New York World began to launch forth through its columns startling exhibits of the financial rottenness of the company, and editorial, that is virtuous, indignation at its abuse of the public and its franchises. Then came another *can-can* in the courts, led by lawyers, who danced long and well, according to the New York code of legal ethics that if a lawyer is not a judge he need not be a gentleman, and if he is a judge he need not be investigated. Receivers were appointed, more stock-watering was authorized by the courts, and affidavits poured forth from insiders that the company was hopelessly and irretrievably bankrupt, and its stock worthless. Manhattan stockholders flung their certificates away for what they could get. The price sank to fifteen and one fourth. Suddenly what had seemed a mass of ruin crystallized into the symmetrical structure of a monopoly, and on its peak, but a few days after he had sworn that Manhattan was hopelessly and irretrievably insolvent, sat the manufacturer of mouse-traps, master of the rapid transit of the greatest city of America. The prentice hand that had fashioned the Erie trap had become the perfect instrument of an artist in the science of exchange. A suit, begun in the name of the people by the highest officer of justice, was set up as a rack on the floor of the Stock Exchange, and used there for six months as an instrument of torture. A judge of the supreme court sat in the manipulators' rooms, and turned the screw by which the victims were forced to surrender their property. Receivers were appointed and dismissed, injunctions given and denied, orders issued and rescinded, and stock exchange arguments made in the guise of decisions: all this was done just as was demanded by our expert in the theory of the value of judicial honor. He bought his law in the courts where it was cheapest, and sold it in the Stock Exchange where it was dearest. Ninety thousand shares of Manhattan stock were shaken out in eight days, at an average price of twenty. The same judge did this who appointed his relatives to places among the wreckers of Continental Life Insurance Company of New York. Judge Barnard signed an Erie order in the rooms of a wanton; Judge Westbrook has repeatedly held court in a worse place,—the private office of this dealer in judicial virtue.

When receivers were appointed for Manhattan, they were two hired men in the employ of him who was known to the court to be suing the company privately, and their bonds, signed by his associates, were ready in advance of the action of the court. The lawyer who was conducting the private suit against Manhattan was retained as assistant in the people's suit by the attorney-general, and the company he was suing was compelled to pay his fees. The attorney-general began his public suit on the same day the wrecker of Manhattan began his private suit. When the attorney-general dismissed his action, not a single day had been given to the people for the trial of their case against the company on its merits. In July, 1881, suits were pending against the three elevated railroad companies in all the courts in New York in which they could be brought. Every appeal for relief to the courts by those whose property was being forced out of them was met by rebuff, and by the victory of the men in whose private offices the court sat to decide a public action, brought in the public name by a public officer. One of the reasons given by the attorney-general for discontinuing his suit was that arrangements had been made for the payment of the taxes in dispute. The latest incident in this extraordinary history is the appearance at Albany of a powerful lobby to procure from the legislature release from these taxes. This lobby is described by the New York Times—which has attacked the Manhattan iniquity with a brilliant intrepidity equal to that with which it overthrew the Tammany ring—as the most dangerous which has appeared in Albany for many years.

Procuring one hundred shares of Metropolitan Elevated Railroad stock, the manipulator of Manhattan solicited the position of director of Metropolitan, and, under promises that he would build this company up, obtained for himself and his associates the control of the Metropolitan board of direction. Then, owning in all but one sixty-fifth of the property, they deliberately proceeded to rob it. Owners of Manhattan and trustees of Metropolitan, they stripped the latter company of the ten per cent annual dividend guaranteed by Manhattan, and substituted for it a contingent dividend of four per cent, which may or may not be paid. This they did against the protests of the Metropolitan stockholders whose agents they were. In all this work a prominent part was taken by a great philanthropist, who, having sworn that the New York elevated railroad company of which he was president was earning ten per cent net a year, accepted for its stockholders a six per cent annual dividend guaranteed by Manhattan, which he had sworn to be bankrupt; and after he had sworn Manhattan to be bankrupt, allowed it an annual dividend of four per cent. The same willingness to call up the spirit of panic showed itself as in the gold conspiracy. To make certain stockholders of Metropolitan surrender their property, attacks were made in The World on the credit of the Shoe and Leather Bank and the Tradesmen's Bank, behind which they were supposed to have found financial refuge. When a property owner of New York remonstrated with Vice-President Galloway of the Manhattan about some encroachments by the elevated roads, he received this reply, which embodied the whole of one of the latter-day theories of wealth: "We have the legislature on our side, the courts on our side, and we hire our law by the year."

A man who braves the heart-broken rage of fifty millions of men, and in daylight shoots their President, we call an assassin. George Washington hanged as a spy a man who traveled the high-road as an instrument in Benedict Arnold's treachery. We teach our children to execrate as traitors the men who stood up in a fair fight to divide the Union. What shall we call the man and the men who seduce, but do not assassinate,—Guiteaus of political economy who would overcome, not one, but all departments of our government; who travel by night and under-ground to betray trusts they have invited; who, living among us as fellow-men and neighbors, loyal to the covenants of society, are traitors to all the ties of honor, justice, and mercy that make the American community possible, and the want of which makes the Paris commune? By what title do these men hold their acquisitions? Private property is sacred, but plunder must not be private. A philosopher of the commune said, "Property is theft." American self-government must have a philosophy to say, Theft shall not be property.

It is March 13, 1882. The boy who brought his mahogany box and his mouse-trap to New York in 1853 sits in an office rich with plate-glass and precious woods. He opens his box, which like him has grown, and shows a group of friends twenty-three million dollars of Western Union stock, twelve millions of Missouri Pacific stock, eight millions of elevated railroad stocks and bonds, ten millions of Wabash common and preferred, and other stock. "Morosini," he says, "can bring you down twenty millions more, or so, in bonds and other things." This, like the Erie restitution, was a "partial list." Seventy-three millions, and more, accumulated by an enthusiast in competition in twenty-nine years of office work! Never before in the history of the desire of wealth had such a sight been seen. The mouse-trap man's wires told the news to the people of two continents, and the world held its breath.

On the same day, while the president of the Wabash road, which had appropriated for dividends to stockholders the wages due its men, was thus spreading out his millions, a day laborer, in the employ of the Wabash at St. Louis, said to a reporter:—

The delay in the payment of my wages has reduced me almost to beggary. Had not the grocer helped me with credit in January and February, my children would have starved.

An engineer said:—

My family were sick in January. They had no doctor and no medicines. I could not get the money due me from the Wabash road.

An old man, who watched a crossing,—an infirm old man, with a family,—said:—

My rent is six dollars a month; my groceries are eighteen dollars. This leaves us one dollar a month for clothing, medicine, and other necessaries. My pay is twenty-five dollars a month, and I have to wait two months for that. We are on the edge of starvation.

It is a solemn truth, that of Ruskin's, that every man has to choose in this world whether he will be a laborer or an assassin. There are men who murder for money, but there must be no science of assassination.

PART III

THE CITY AND THE FACTORY

At the beginning of the twentieth century Professor G. Stanley Hall pleaded with his fellow psychologists to break the grip of past dogmas and to let themselves be strangers to no phase of human life. The older thinkers, he said, instead of laying bare the constitution of the universe were only documenting their own souls with unusual fullness for the benefit of the future generalizer. But their work, though suggestive, was premature, and in any case life itself was incomparably fuller and richer than their pallid descriptions:

. . . our watchword must be not merely back to Kant or even Aristotle, but back to a reëxamination of the primitive events of secular life, gathered by the most systematic outer and inner observation, and even from history, literature, experience, and wherever psychic life is most voluminous and intense; pain, misery, famine, war, revolutions, shame, revivals, every passionate state in which Despine says all vice and crime originate; love, fervid as Dante knew it, crowds, the struggle of the individual soul with besetting sin . . . the anemic thinker, who can realize in his own person so little of the stormy life of man, must seek every possible contact with it. He must live where he can among animals, children, defectives, the insane, criminals, paupers, saints, sinners, the sick, the well; must know grief and joy. . . . Psychology lives not merely in the study, but where doubt and belief, sanity and inherited insanity, struggle together; where temptation and conscience wage their wars, in the mob, the cloister; where rage, terror, and pity became convulsive and sweep all before them, and where love of the lie usurps that of the truth.

Nowhere could the welter of contradictions which Hall pleaded to be studied more easily be found than in the growing industrial city. Here were grinding poverty and luxurious ease, the squalor of the tenement and the Fifth Avenue château, the confusion of many tongues. And here, too, was the battleground of old standards and new ideas.

Immigration, the factory system, poverty, the increasing tempo of life are, of course, analytically distinct, but they all came to a focus in the industrial city and to separate them does violence to historical reality as it presented itself to the people of the period. In the selections that follow, no attempt has been made to separate them. The voices that speak in these documents are, for the most part, those of relatively obscure men and women who were caught up in events or of slightly less obscure persons who tried to describe and understand them.

In the voice of Lucy Larcom, onetime leader of the Lowell mill girls, we have an echo from an earlier age and are given an impression of the impact of industrialization on a mind formed at a time when a factory was looked upon as a school for moral uplift. The report on the working girls of Boston was written at a time when the reverse had become true, when people looked upon the shop and factory as breeders of prostitution. In the testimony of the witnesses before the Senate Committee on Labor and Capital and the United States Industrial Commission, a variety of opinions on the problems of industrial labor is expressed. Some of the witnesses, like Conrad Carl, the New York tailor, speak of the effects of technological change on their security of employment; others, militant rank-and-file unionists like Abraham Bisno and teamster Thomas McGuire, take no nonsense from the congressmen and talk tough. Mrs. J. S. Robb, "an American lady" and wife of a nonunion painter, won't be intimidated by congressmen or union men. Samuel Gompers, president of the American Federation of Labor, uses the occasion to discuss his philosophy of organization.

With the report of the Illinois Bureau of Labor Statistics on the sweat-shops of Chicago begins a series on immigrants and their role in indus-trialization. Jacob A. Riis, reforming journalist, describes the ethnic and racial ghettos of New York. A series of letters from Welsh immigrants, workers in the coal mines and steel mills of Pennsylvania and West Vir-ginia, show the immigrant at work in still another range of occupations and tell of his troubles with employers and Irish strikebreakers. The report of the United States Industrial Commission on the padrone *system analyzes one method of mobilizing immigrants into an industrial labor force, a method which has had lasting consequences for both urban poli-tics and urban crime. Robert A. Woods, founder of Andover House, the first settlement house in Boston, tells of the connection between the street-corner society of the immigrant and the organization of the urban politi-cal machine. With great poignancy, Mary Antin's reminiscences suggest that it was the ability of the public school to get the immigrant to accept a common version of American history—to accept new heroes and new myths in the place of those of Old World tradition—that helped create a sense of common nationality.*

The concluding group of selections presents one of the most obvious contrasts of urban life—the poverty and aimlessness described by Helen Campbell, and the wealth and frivolity so seriously presented by Mrs. John Sherwood and so lovingly portrayed by the famous Ward McAllister, who may have been one of the few things gilded in the misnamed Gilded Age. Finally, Dr. George Miller Beard, inventor of the word "neurasthe-nia," discusses a problem that at least since his day has come to be a stock in trade of every observer of the American scene—the relation be-tween the circumstances of American life and the apparent high incidence of emotional disorders.

The selections may not be as disparate as they seem. Permeating them all is an awareness of the effects of industrialization and city life. And in most of them is a perception that the tendency of the time had been from individual independence to the interdependence of man upon man, of craft upon craft, from individualism to solidarity.

American Factory Life

Lucy Larcom

The past has an interest of its own, but its chief value to us lies in its relation to the future. Progress being the natural order, every good thing makes us hope for a better. The history of American cotton manufactures has certainly been a record of external prosperity. Fortunes have been made, machinery has been improved, and employment has been given to vast numbers of people. Can progress also be traced in the condition and character of the toilers at factory labor? The material elements of civilization are not so important as the state of the human beings who make up a nationality. Persons are more than things. It is not impossible that much of our boasted advancement may be that of a railway train with its passengers left behind. If the painful pictures which have been given us of the tendencies observable in some of our large manufacturing cities are to be regarded as realities, another too familiar comparison suggests itself, that of the Juggernaut car. Mammon is an idol still worshipped; and he is heedless now as in any former age, of the victims of whose souls he crushes. But there must be a brighter view for us, and better possibilities.

In comparing the past with the present, we may sum up what was best in the earlier life at Lowell, for so many years the representative manufacturing city of the United States. First, and last too, in importance, was the character of the toilers themselves. They were almost all New England women of an average much above mediocrity; intelligent, industrious, and conscientious. They were such young women as grow up everywhere around our country firesides, and in our village schools and academies. They were the daughters of the land, who have since become its mothers and teachers. Is there any large proportion of such women in our cotton mills now? And if not, why not?

The answer to these questions must follow a brief consideration of

Lucy Larcom, "American Factory Life—Past, Present and Future," Journal of Social Science, XVI (December 1882), 141–146.

manufacturing life in its general traits, and in its earlier characteristics at Lowell.

A feature of the social life there, which must not be overlooked, was the great care for the morals of those employed, as shown by certain restrictions and regulations which grew, to a great extent, out of the moral sentiment of the community itself. All the previous associations of the Lowell mill-girl required a high standard of personal character among the people where she lived and worked. Employers and employed sympathized entirely in this matter. The same may be said of the churches. While their influence for good cannot be overstated, while it is true that the city was fortunate in her first ministers, it is also true that because these girls were what they were, the Christian idea as to purity and rightness of life was a controlling power among the people. The churches were not only filled, but often almost entirely supported by those who worked in the mills. However tinged with doctrinal peculiarities, the various Christian organizations were in harmony as to deeper spiritual principles, and practical rules of living; and they formed centres around which these young girls grouped themselves for companionship and for general helpfulness. Intellectual tastes formed also a common ground on which they met, so that, for many years, Lowell was looked upon much in the light of a school for mental and moral development. In this way the gathering of so many young strangers together was an advantage, rather than the injury which might have been feared.

They were nearly all, as we have seen, girls who had grown up under the wholesome strictness of New England family ties, who naturally kept fresh around them the spirit of the homes from which they were only temporarily absent. The comparatively small number then employed in the mills must also be considered as a favorable circumstance. True, there were thousands at work, but there are tens of thousands now, and these larger numbers complicate the question as to the civilizing influence of factory labor.

The congregating of very great numbers of people at any occupation cannot be considered as altogether favorable to personal development. Even the public school has its questionable aspect, although the purpose of the institution, and the surveillance of committees and teachers are a protection. We instinctively feel that we were not made for a gregarious life; that something is lost by attrition with crowds. The necessity of mingling with a promiscuous throng was felt to be an evil, even in the days when one was sure of many pleasant companionships; an evil which was to be conquered, or turned into good by the resolute will of the individual. To hold faithfully to one's own distinct thought and purpose amid the confusions of a mixed multitude, is no easy thing. And self respect by no means implies lack of sympathy; by the value we attach to our own separate personality, the worth of other lives may fairly be measured. Emerson bids us think of every human being as an island; and the island-nature of which we are all conscious in ourselves is to be respected. Men and women cannot regard other men and women, whatever their condition, merely as "the masses," without doing themselves also a great wrong.

In the old times the girl of studious tastes felt most keenly the impossibility of secluding herself among her books during the few hours she could call her own; but the difficulty was sometimes obviated by associating herself with girls of similar tastes. The chances were often against her being able to do this; yet if she found herself, as she not unfrequently did, one of three or four very dissimilar occupants of a room, she could, perhaps, manage to keep one little corner by the window sacred to her own chair and table and small pile of books; for room-mates were, in the main, considerate of one another's wishes. But, alas for her when the spirit of re-arrangement, which is one of woman's household weaknesses, took possession of her companions, and she came in, some evening, to find a revolution in the furniture of their common sleeping apartment, by which her one nook of refuge had been obliterated, and herself left to the condition of an ejected tenant on the highway without a shelter for what she held most precious!

A petty trouble this may seem, but it was no less a trouble for being a little ludicrous. If she could laugh her annoyance away, so much the better for her! Yet it is a somewhat serious matter when one cannot find seclusion for thought, or reading, or study, at any hour of any day. The Lowell mill-girl, in her boarding-house, and at her work, we know, did find ways of conquering circumstances, either by ignoring them, or accommodating herself to them; but to do so must always have required force of character. A little space around us, a door that we can sometimes shut between ourselves and the world, is what stronger and weaker alike require for self-development.

The necessity for close and indiscriminate contact must, perhaps, always be one of the unmanageable difficulties in the way of factory toilers. In other respects, things are certainly easier for them now than in earlier times. There is more leisure, ten hours a day instead of thirteen or fourteen; wages are higher than formerly; and we hear of libraries and reading-rooms established purposely for mill-people in some places. Judging the present by the past, and measuring improvement by opportunity, we should look for more cultivation among them, but the general report is, that the reverse is true. And the evident reason of the change is in the different sort of persons employed at that kind of labor now. They are mostly foreigners, from the lower stratifications of European society, without the tastes and aspirations which have always characterized our New Englanders.

We go back to the question, how it was that this change came about, and we find that it was inevitable. We do not like to say that it was inevitable from the very nature of factory labor, yet sometimes it seems so. A mill-girl among her spindles or shuttles, thirty or forty years ago, had not the slightest idea of always remaining there. When she went back to her country life and saw her daughters growing up around her in homes of their own, she did not expect them to go and toil in a mill as she had done. She had higher ambitions for them. She expected them to teach, or to take some other useful position in society; and she used the money she had earned in the factory to give them an education; or, if she was a woman of humbler desires, she laid it by for their dowry, against the time when they also should be mistress of their own households.

It would have been as unreasonable to think of New England women spending their whole lives at factory labor, as it would be to expect the students in a college to stay there always. Their work was not its own end; it was pursued for a purpose beyond itself; for an opening into freer life. It is true that some mill-girls have continued many years at Lowell, but usually those who have remained have taken some more responsible situation than that of daily labor; the care of a boarding-house, for instance. And it is also true that American girls still go to work in the mills, and are respectable and respected there; but the associations are far from agreeable and other employments are preferred. Most of the work in factories is too mechanical to be really enjoyed by an intelligent person. And the stolid nature is in danger of becoming more stolid in tending machinery which requires little thought, and of which the operator comes to be regarded, and to regard himself, merely as an adjunct. So employed, the toiler's only hope of elevation is in keeping his mind above his work.

As we have seen, the bright New England mill-girls of a former generation did not undertake their toil for its own sake, or with the intention of continuing at it for any long time. It was for the interest of employers to introduce laborers who would be more permanent. In this way a distinct manufacturing population has appeared in our larger cities; and it is from what these are and will be, that the influence of factories is hereafter to be judged. We have now not so much our own people as the undeveloped populations of Europe to deal with. We cannot expect of them the intellect, the morals, and the Christianity that pervaded our first manufacturing towns, and that made the atmosphere there as pure and sweet as a summer day among the White Hills; it is the factory people of the Old World who now fill our mills; it is, in effect, Great Britain's unanswered labor problem that is handed over to us to be solved.

No better standard of civilization than that of our forefathers has yet been set up; namely, the intelligence, the morals and humanity of the people themselves, of whatsoever sex, station, or occupation. And it follows that our foreign mill-laborers must be educated up to the idea of American citizenship, must learn to hold themselves responsible members of the nation which has adopted them, or that our manufacturing cities will eventually become as great a disgrace to us as England's are to her. Until these laborers see this for themselves, those who invite them hither must largely be responsible for them. The most ignorant must be dealt with patiently and steadily, as if they were children; and every opportunity for mental and moral cultivation must be placed within reach of all. Never, for a moment, can we allow in ourselves a feeling of contempt for them, as "the lower classes." Whether we will or not, they are to control, to a vast extent, the destinies of our country; they are to stand beside us, equal members of a Republic we love. One indispensable element of true civilization is a common regard for the interests of every person composing the community. If factory labor makes a person less manly or less womanly, it is not a civilized occupation. But it has been proved not to have that effect, necessarily; and it may nobly be made a life-occupation when he who pursues it sees it to be his best way of supporting himself and those dependent on him.

With the introduction of foreign laborers a new phase of life in our manufacturing towns has appeared; the tendency is to the employment of whole families in the mills. Here may be an advantage for the future. Families must have homes; and if they are so cared for as to be true homes, those who grow up in them may find better opportunities for self-improvement than in boarding-houses. In its best days, the factory boarding-house was but a tent in the wilderness to the sojourning mill-girl, whence she looked with moist eyes to the home that awaited her in some rural Canaan beyond, her type of Heaven.

Whether in families or in boarding-houses, moral safeguards will always be necessary to the welfare of a floating population; and not least for the larger liberty of those who do not need them. Work, the mere use of the hands, as we all know, has in it no moral or progressive quality. Work is only great through the impulse that guides it, the motive in the worker's mind. The laborer must be greater than his occupation, or it will crush him. Work and money both find their only real value in lending power to manhood and womanhood, in strengthening the forces of humanity for good. The factory is a prison, if the toilers therein cannot find their way out of it, whenever that is their desire. Education is the laborer's right, and it is a key that opens many doors.

A modern writer has well said, with regard to liberal advantages of education for all: "It is obvious that the more any man knows of a great subject, the less likelihood there is of his continuing in the position of a weaver or a carpenter. Intellectual vitality signifies social elevation; and though some may be disposed to ask the grave question, 'How could society dispense with its weavers or carpenters?' yet our business relates primarily to the higher considerations, forasmuch as the *man* is of more importance than the *weaver*. When manhood rises, the industrial arts will feel the benefit of the elevation." It is persons who make a people; and if we are a humanely civilized people we shall so guard the occupations we offer our citizens, that, if we cannot make them intrinsically elevating, they shall, at least, not be de-humanizing. If any form of labor needful for the general comfort becomes so, it must be through the selfishness or neglect of those who control affairs. And we have no better lesson for the future than that which the past grew to vigorous health in learning; that a free nation can grow up only through free opportunities of self-development for its individual members; that high personal character only can ennoble labor; but that character can and does elevate labor of any kind; and that it is not so much by industries and products, as by the men and women who make their work honorable, that we are to estimate the value of our American civilization, and find our true place among the nations.

The Working Girls of Boston

The population of the city of Boston, according to the Tenth United States Census, in 1880, was 362,839; of this number 172,268 were males and 190,571 were females. The whole number of persons engaged in that year in all occupations was 149,194, the males numbering 110,313 and the females 38,881; out of this latter number of females employed in all occupations, there were, in round numbers, 20,000 employed in occupations other than domestic service, and these constitute the body of the working girls of Boston.

To ascertain all the conditions surrounding this large and important class has been the desire of the bureau for some years, but other lines of investigation have prevented the special study of this matter until last year, when a very thorough and searching investigation was commenced. The bureau undertook to ascertain the moral, sanitary, physical, and economical conditions of the working girls of Boston. Of course it was not possible to get a complete personal history of every one of the 20,000 involved, nor was it necessary, but if such personal history for 1,000 at least could be obtained accurately, it would scientifically indicate the condition of the whole, and would answer every purpose of the investigation. To this end, discreet agents were employed to secure by personal application at the homes of the working girls the information desired; the names of girls in various employments were obtained during the daytime, lists were prepared and given to the agents, whose duty it was to call in the evening at the places of residence of those designated.

The average weekly income from all sources whatever for 544 girls was $5 per week or less, while 435 received a total average weekly income of from $5 to $10, there being only 53 receiving a total average weekly income of over $10 per week. *Brought into specific averages, we find that the average weekly income for the year was in personal service $5.25, in trade $4.81, in manufactures $5.22, or the general average for all involved for the whole year was $5.17 per week. This latter figure must stand as the total average weekly income from all sources, earnings, assistance, and*

Fifteenth Annual Report, Bureau of Statistics of Labor, Massachusetts (Boston, 1884), pp. 92–126.

other work, of the working girls of Boston. It should be remembered that the average weekly earnings from occupation only, distributed over the whole year, was but $4.91; the total average yearly income from all sources was $269.07; for the different departments, $273.02 in personal service, $250.63 in trade, and $271.41 in manufactures. . . .

A good deal of complaint is made in regard to the low wages quite generally paid to working girls in all the various occupations in which they were found employed. The cause of complaint, especially under "Trade," is ascribed to the fact that girls living "at home," with little or no board to pay, work for very low wages. This is considered a great hardship to the lone working girl who is entirely dependent upon her own resources. The mothers in some cases have said that it takes more than the girls earn to feed and clothe them, and some of the girls have been taken from their work and are now idle on that account. In the large stores, employés are reported as hired at the lowest figures possible, and it is said, that wages in the future are likely to be even less.

In the manufacture of men's clothing, considerable complaint is made by the girls as to the very small wages now made in the business. Almost invariably, when anything was said by them concerning wages, the cry was "pay is too small"; in these cases, the pay ranges from $3 to $6 generally, a baster on canvas (13½ years old), reporting only $1.25. It is said that many of the girls get discouraged, as they hardly earn enough to pay running expenses, and are obliged to practise the most rigid economy. One girl says she "turns her clothes upside down, inside out, and outside in, not being able to make enough over living expenses to buy new clothes." A certain class of piece masters are said to be responsible for low wages; they take work from firms and do it much lower than they need to—"at any rate," as one girl puts it, "girls used to make better pay before they came."

Shirt, dress, and cloak makers, earning $4, $5, $6, and $7 a week, complain very much of the small pay, while in other occupations, where the pay ranges from $2 to $5 a week, the same state of affairs is reported. In paper box making, one girl receiving $8 a week says girls work harder than the men, and are paid much less—unjustly, she thinks. The wages in this occupation are reported as falling off. Another girl, who formerly worked as saleswoman at $4.50 a week, says it was not sufficient to pay for room and board, provide suitable clothing to make a decent appearance in the store, and meet other ordinary expenses.

In some cases girls testify that their work is worth more than they receive for it, and think they ought to have better wages. But as others always stand ready to take their places at even less pay, they have to be satisfied with what they get. . . .

In several instances, girls report increase or expected increase, of wages, and for this reason, they seem to be quite well pleased at their prospects.

In many places, it appears to be the custom to engage help at small rates of pay, and gradually increase wages until the maximum is reached. Many girls also serve a certain length of time for nothing, until they become familiar with the business and are then placed on piece work, the same as the rest of the employés. Table girls in restaurants often have their weekly earnings increased by small fees received from regular customers, and in the holiday season by small presents, the fees amounting in some cases to 50 cents or $1.00, and even $2 to $3 a week.

Directly connected with the question of wages received, are the prices paid to piece workers, the graded prices paid to employés working by the week, and the prices paid for overtime during the busy seasons. . . .

MEN's CLOTHING.—A *tailoress* on boy's suits, gets from 85 cents to $3.50 a suit; she does not get a $3.50 suit very often, and can not make eight "85 cent" suits a week; present wages are reported as $6.

A *tailoress* (40 years old) says five years ago she used to get $10 a week and had received the same wages for years; she is now getting $9 (as reported).

Five *custom tailoresses* are reported as getting $12 to $13, 2 at $9, $7.50, and $5 respectively. One other reports that custom work pays well, and she makes in the busy season $9 a week; in dull times, much less.

A *coat maker* says she gets 75 cents for making a frock coat, and 60 cents for a sack coat. In good times, she can make 16 coats a week; the week for which wages were returned ($7), she made 12 coats, but had to take work home nights and worked until 10 o'clock. Another coat maker reports that in Montreal, she could make but $2.75 a week; in Boston, at former place of employment, she made $7 in summer and $6 in winter, and at present place, she earns $4 in winter and $5.50 in summer. Another coat maker says she has to work overtime at home to average $6 per week.

Coat basters report pay much less now than formerly; one girl formerly earning $7 a week has been cut down to $6.

A *pantaloon stitcher* says wages on piece work have been so cut down that girls who formerly earned $9 cannot possibly make now more than $5 per week. Pantaloon finishers take pantaloons which have been sewed up on machine, turn up and put in canvas in the bottoms, tack pockets, put in all the waistband linings and sew on the buttons, for 12½ cents, formerly 15 to 20 cents; they can finish 16 pairs a week by working from 8 A.M. till dark in summer, and till 7 or 8 P.M. in winter.

Bushelwomen getting $4, $5.50, and $7 respectively, say their employers pay as much if not more than others, and when working after hours, one girl says they get 20 cents per hour.

A *machine presser* says she used to get $7 a week for what she now receives $5; and now has to work harder.

Machine button-hole makers receive 20 cents per hundred. . . . One other girl says she is paid 25 cents per 100, and can do 800 button-holes per day, while some girls can make 900. The work is very unsteady, and a good deal of time is lost.

Shirt makers, on the best grades, and on custom work, can make good wages when work is brisk, $9, $10, $11, and $12 being made on piece-work; one price reported being 50 cents a shirt, except button-holes. On cheaper grades of work, the prices paid are 77 cents, $1.12, $1.18, to $1.95 per dozen. For thick flannnel shirts, except button-holes, 75 cents per dozen is paid; it takes two days to make a dozen. The nicest flannel shirts have much work in them, and $2 per dozen is paid, it taking the *best* workers two days to make a dozen.

Overall makers receive 5 cents a pair when made at home, and 50 cents per dozen when made in the shop.

WOMEN'S CLOTHING.—*Dressmakers* are paid $1.25 to $1.75 for making a suit; a suit made for the first-named price sells for $12, and can be made in a day by working in the evening. When paid $1.75, if any extra work not done by self is added, as plaiting, the cost is deducted, the maker actually receiving $1.35; the prices of suits are graded according to the quality of goods, as high as $5 being allowed. It takes two days to make a suit. Another dressmaker has been working at home for two months making suits for $5 apiece, her weekly wage being reported as $5; for overtime in one instance, 12½ cents an hour was paid.

Dressmakers, for themselves, get from $2 to $3 per day, with meals; when on a long job, one reports that she gets $10 a week.

Milliners can earn from $15 to $25 a week in busy seasons; at other times, not near so much.

Seamstresses on dresses are paid 75 cents to $1 per day; in private families, $1 a day and board; and when going out by the day, $1.50 per day. A seamstress on buttons gets 10 cents a set for sewing buttons on wrappers, a set being 18 wrappers.

A *sewing machine operator* on fine "white goods," can make from $11 to $15 a week.

A *button-hole maker* on ladies' dresses gets 3 cents apiece; a good price, it is said, and good wages can be made.

Cloak and sack makers say they have to work very hard to average $6 a week the year round, prices being low; one girl gives her weekly earn-ings for the year, as follows:—8 weeks at $9; 8 at $2.50; 13 at $9; 13 at $2.50; 5 at $9; and 5 weeks idle; average $6.09. The prices paid in some places are 15 cents for an entire cloak, raised, however, on protest to 25 cents; and 22 cents for making a short walking coat, running two rows of stitching around the entire edge and sewing on 30 buttons. It takes 3½ hours to make a cloak for 25 cents. In making Jersey sacks, one girl says she got 90 cents for making a sack by hand, which took three days to finish; she was obliged to take the work home and sit up until 11 at night to make $2.50 a week. Another girl says she has to baste, stitch, and face with crinoline, and finish seven seams, for 25 cents.

For making boys' waists, 30 cents a dozen is paid, button-holes included. It took one girl one whole day to make the sleeves for 2 dozen boys' waists.

For hemming linen handkerchiefs, 2⅛ cents a dozen is paid for large ones, and 1¾ cents for small ones; one girl hemmed 75 dozen a day (machine work) when the work was good.

Hoopskirt makers get 82 cents a dozen.

Bustle makers used to get 65, 75, and 85 cents a dozen, but the price has been recently cut down 15 cents; the bustles are now made for 50, 60, and 70 cents per dozen. They can do 1½ dozen a day by working from 8.30 A.M. to 6 P.M., with half an hour for dinner. The work is often slack and they are now making a bustle which pays but 25 cents a dozen, and a girl can make a dozen only per day.

A *book folder*, working by the piece, gets from 3½ to 7 cents per 100 sheets, according to the number of folds. At one place, little girls are hired at 6 and 7 cents an hour, the highest price paid being 12 cents an hour. It is not possible to make more than $5 a week on an average; the girls formerly received a percentage of 10 cents on the dollar earned and it was a great incentive to hard work; it has since been taken off. One girl once made $7.50 a week, but it nearly killed her, and she has since limited herself to $1 a day. A book-sewer reports a percentage of 10 cents on every dollar made as being now given to sewers, to equal pay of folders.

In *Boots and Shoes*, there have been 7 or 8 cut-downs in 8 years; the girls have to work very hard to make $8 a week, and then only in the busy season (for about 2 months).

In *Rubber Goods*, there have been constant cut-downs, and but little work. Circulars are now made for 6 cents apiece, for which girls were formerly paid 15 cents, since cut to 10, 8, and 6 cents successively. Girls used to make $12 to $14 a week, but now only from $3 to $6; the factories were reported as running on short time and at low rates, one factory reducing from 600 to 100 hands, those being retained who most needed work. A button-hole maker on gossamers says she left for the reason that the work was put out on new machines because it could be done cheaper. The girls in the shop could not work at same figures and make anything. The employer pays $75 for the use of the machine, the girls get 4 cents per 100, and the employer pays 5 cents royalty per 100; it was claimed that 4000 button-holes could be made in a day. In sewing waterproof hats, girls get paid at the rate of $1 for *six* dozen, the price formerly paid being 30 cents *a dozen;* they can sew from 7 to 9 an hour. . . .

One table girl in restaurant says she is required to pay for all crockery broken. In stores, one girl says they are obliged to pay one half of the selling price for broken crockery or ware; one other girl who accidentally broke a show-case, left because the price was to be taken from her pay; she was working at the time on 3 per cent commission sales (with no other pay), and one stormy day she made 5 cents. Two machine operators on cloaks were required to pay 25 and 35 cents respectively for the use of machines; two operators on gossamers were required to pay for needles and thread, in one case 25 cents for a spool of thread and 15 cents a half-dozen for machine needles; they were forbidden to buy them outside; the wages in both cases were reported as $5 a week. . . .

The moral condition of the working girls cannot be stated with that statistical accuracy which belongs to the other conditions we have discussed, and yet in certain directions we have the most positive information and of such a character that it possesses all the value of a statistical statement.

It has often been said that the shop girls are an immoral class, that it is largely from their ranks that prostitution is recruited, and the vile charge has often been made that in great stores where many girls are employed, an engagement often depends upon the willingness of the saleswoman or shop girl to become the intimate friend of either the proprietor or head of a department. The assertion is often very flippantly bandied about that when a girl seeks employment and the wages offered are very low and she objects to such low wages, she is coolly informed that she must seek some gentleman to help her to support herself. In addition to our desire to ascertain the general moral condition which surrounds the working girls of Boston, we have had a very strong desire to ascertain the truth or falsity of these damaging assertions and charges, and first, we will consider the girls in their homes and employments. Under social condition, we dealt very fully with the condition of the girls in their homes.

It was seen that a very large proportion of them were living at home with parents and friends. In addition to this we found that in nearly all the cases where a girl was called upon in the evening and found to be out, her parents or the friends with whom she was living, knew of her whereabouts, and would oftentimes send for her to come home and give the information sought by the agents. This evidence in itself is very emphatic in establishing the moral surroundings at least of the girls involved. A few of the girls testify to ill treatment by friends or relatives, but as a rule, they were surrounded by such home influences that it is entirely unreasonable to believe them to be guilty of walking in evil ways. Some of them have spoken very frankly about ill treatment by their employers; some of these say that the employers or the men placed in charge are in the habit of speaking very roughly to employés and oftentimes while they do not swear at the girls, they use violent and sometimes bad langauge before them; others are said to curse and swear at the girls and treat them very shabbily. One girl says she has been subjected to rough words and harsh treatment from the foreman in charge of the department; his general demeanor is bad. She says he is a good tool for employers, who are all right themselves apparently, but that they do not know of many things which otherwise might be remedied; they place implicit confidence in him and having little or no knowledge of their help, they do not know but what their employés are well treated.

Another girl says her employer is good natured according to his mood; if he does not like the way the work is done, he is apt to take it rudely from her hands and tell her to leave; on the other hand, he might feel good natured enough to pay her in advance if he thought she needed money.

In some places, during working hours, no one is allowed to call upon the girls employed; even on the occasion of the death of a friend who was killed, the girl was notified after much trouble, and then only through a speaking tube. This girl says she was absent two and three-quarter hours, and her employer, although knowing the circumstances, would not allow her the time; he also fails to pay for overwork when done. Other girls speak of the bad language used by employers, and in some cases say they had left for this reason.

Only five girls were found of the whole number interviewed who gave any specific reasons why their surroundings in the shops and places of employment were not of a moral character. In almost every case, the answer was that, so far as known, there were no immoral influences exerted over the girls at their work, but rather that the moral atmosphere of the places where employed was very good and as pleasant as could be wished. In fact, it is reasonable to suppose that employers are as anxious to have good moral conditions exist in their places as any other class of men.

The working girls seen by the agents were well appearing generally, frank and honest in their statements, and gave every indication that they were leading orderly, upright lives. Certainly, there was little or no evidence to the contrary, nor has there been anything adduced in support of the rumors to which we have referred. They were mentioned frequently to the agents, both by the working girls and by women of bad repute, but, as already remarked, in only five instances could these rumors be traced to anything tangible whatever, and these instances were of such a trivial nature that they are hardly entitled to a place in this Report.

We do not hesitate to assert that the working girls of Boston are, as a rule, living in a moral atmosphere so far as their homes are concerned, and that they are not corrupted by their employers, and that employers do not seek to corrupt them. All such statements originate in the idea that girls cannot dress well with the small wages they receive, unless they lead immoral lives in which they receive pecuniary assistance.

The testimony of capable and honest women, of the heads of departments in dry goods stores, millinery establishments, of forewomen in shops, matrons of homes, and of all those best informed and in the best position to give testimony on this point, is that the working girls are as respectable, as moral, and as virtuous as any class of women in our community; that they are making as heroic a struggle for existence as any class is a fact which all the statistics prove.

The idea that well dressed girls receiving low wages must live disreputable lives is a very common one, but, as has been shown under economic condition and other chapters of this Report, a large number of these girls live in comfortable homes with parents in comparatively easy circumstances and well able and willing to support their children, who pay little or no board and spend their earnings as they please, chiefly for dress. Many are graduates from the High School, and large numbers are employed for months in making out commercial lists and addressing envelopes for the pittance of two or three dollars per week; at the end of such service they leave and their places are filled by others recently graduated from school; the supply of this labor always exceeds the demand.

Other well dressed girls, who live at home, turn their earnings into the common family fund and their clothes are provided for by their parents and these are generally made during the evening by themselves, and by skill and ingenuity a good appearance is made at little cost. It is only the few who are well dressed and helped by their friends who attract attention, and of these the question is often asked, how can they dress well when they earn so little? Such questions led to the idea that they take up prostitution, but the fact that the girl works hard all day for three or four dollars a week is sufficient proof that she is not living in prostitution; girls cannot work hard all day and be prostitutes too.

There is another class of working women who live in the city among strangers, whose home is the boarding house or lodging room and who are away from home influence, but our conclusion from the facts gathered is that their number is much less than is generally supposed; but many of this class have good homes in the country, or friends living there, to which they return when sick or out of work, and they are often supplied with clothing by their friends at a distance. There are others however who have no home but the boarding house, and no friends to depend upon for aid, sympathy, or moral encouragement, and it is among this class of shop girls chiefly, that the aid and assistance of the benevolent and charitably inclined people of our city should be directed. It is among these that Boffin's Bower exerts a great influence, and with whom the name of Jennie Collins is a household word; but none of these girls can by any possible stretch of the imagination be charged with being dissolute. Our agents have visited them in their rooms and held free and frank converse with them; they have spoken frankly about themselves as to how they were circumstanced, and our agents have come away impressed with the heroic struggle they are making to lead a proper life. The weakest and least competent go to Boffin's Bower and to some other establishments, where, if they are in need of a meal or dinner, they can get it without lowering themselves by begging. . . .

Interviews upon this subject with prostitutes on the streets and with night policemen on their beats, all tend to show one thing, that all such statements as those referred to are utterly false and without foundation.

A captain of police expressed the matter well when he said that people, who charge the working women with walking the streets at night for evil purposes, do not know what they are talking about; night walkers are all of them hardened convicts or prostitutes; some of them may have been hard working women, but no working woman ever walks the streets as a prostitute. This captain said that when a girl falls from virtue, she has first to graduate as a "parlor girl," and then serves some time in a still lower house before she is hardened enough to take to the streets. All the officers with whom our agents conversed on the subject gave similar testimony.

We have been thus explicit upon this particular point of our investigation because men have come to this office with the assertion that the streets were crowded with working girls in the evening, who were in the habit of soliciting men to accompany them home, and these gentlemen have expressed themselves as greatly astonished that in a city as well regulated as Boston, girls should come out of stores and shops and ply their vocation as night walkers on the streets in the evening.

The only remark we can make in this matter, after having given, as we have, positive testimony that such charges are absolutely untrue, is, that if gentlemen have had such experiences on our streets it does not speak well for them and indicates to our mind that the first offence was on their part and that they were again mistaken in supposing the girls they were approaching were working girls.

Let us now consider how far the ranks of prostitution are fed by girls from our shops. From 170 inmates of houses of ill-repute, known to the police, we have gathered some very valuable information; the causes given for their taking up the life they follow is of interest. Of these 170, 22 declined to give any cause, 17 entered their present life on account of ill-treatment at home, 59 from choice, most of them on account of love of easy life and love of dress, 26 testify that they were driven into the life by poor pay and hard work, while 46 were led into the life through seduction. It is important to know just the course so far as given through which these women have passed before entering their present life. . . .

To summarize the previous occupation, or that immediately preceding their entry upon the life of shame, we reach the following results: 60 came directly from housework, table or hotel work; 32 from textile factories; 6 from shoe factories; 19 were dressmakers, seamstresses, or tailoresses; 5 were saleswomen; 18 had been in various occupations, while 30 had had no previous occupation.

The foregoing statements do not prove unfavorable to the working girls. These 170 women are leading lives of shame it is true, many of them leading lives of sorrow, also. Often during this investigation when considering this class of women, and the temptation to which girls are exposed, we have wished that public condemnation could fall as severely upon the seducer, and upon the tempter, as it has in the past upon his victim. This punishment would be quite severe enough.

In conclusion, so far as this part on moral condition is concerned, we can most freely and positively assert that the working girls of Boston are making an heroic, an honest, and a virtuous struggle to earn an honorable livelihood, and that it is rare that one of them can be found following a life other than one of integrity. We can also assert, to the credit of the merchants and employers of Boston, that they do not make the honor of the girls they employ the price of a position.

If, in our future investigations, we find this is not true, we assure the guilty ones that their infamous business shall be exposed.

We, of course, do not wish to be understood as asserting that the working girls are any better than the same number of girls in any other calling, for the amount of private immorality in any community or among any class cannot be traced, yet they come out of this investigation with as good a name as that which can attach to any class.

We only wish it were possible to investigate and expose the conduct of men who help women into fallen lives, and then see these men meet the punishment which justly belongs to them.

The fact that here and there a girl forsakes the path of virtue and lives a sinful life should not be used to the detriment of the class to which she belongs, especially when her life is peculiarly exposed to temptation, as is the case with girls struggling along on five dollars or less per week. It is easy to be good on a sure and generous income; it requires the strongest character to enable one to be good and respectable on an unstable income of five dollars per week. . . .

The Workingman's View of
His Situation

*The following testimony was given by Conrad Carl, tailor, and Thomas B.
McGuire, truck driver, before the Committee of the Senate on the Relations
Between Labor and Capital, meeting in New York on August 20 and 28, 1883.*

TESTIMONY OF CONRAD CARL

CONRAD CARL sworn and examined.

By Mr. PUGH:

Question. How long have you resided in this city?—Answer. Nearly
thirty years.

Q. What has been your profession or occupation?—A. I have been a
tailor since boyhood.

Q. Are you an employé or an employer?—A. An employé.

Q. Have you been an employé during the whole time you have been
in the business?—A. The whole time.

Q. Please give us any information that you may have as to the relation
existing between the employers and the employés in the tailoring business in this city, as to wages, as to treatment of the one by the other class,
as to the feeling that exists between the employers and the employed
generally, and all that you know in regard to the subject that we are
authorized to inquire into?

A. During the time I have been here the tailoring business is altered
in three different ways. Before we had sewing-machines we worked
piece-work with our wives, and very often our children. We had no trouble then with our neighbors, nor with the landlord, because it was a very
still business, very quiet; but in 1854 or 1855, and later, the sewing-machine was invented and introduced, and it stitched very nicely, nicer than
the tailor could do; and the bosses said: "We want you to use the sewing-
machine; you have to buy one." Many of the tailors had a few dollars in

Testimony of the Senate Committee on the Relations Between Labor and Capital
(Washington, D.C.: Government Printing Office, 1885), Vol. I, pp. 413–421,
771–783.

the bank, and they took the money and bought machines. Many others had no money, but must help themselves; so they brought their stitching, the coat or vest, to the other tailors who had sewing-machines, and paid them a few cents for the stitching. Later, when the money was given out for the work, we found out that we could earn no more than we could without the machine; but the money for the machine was gone now, and we found that the machine was only for the profit of the bosses; that they got their work quicker, and it was done nicer.

Q. How about the average wages?—A. The average wages before the war (that marks an epoch, you know) was from $8 to $10 a week for a man working with his wife.

Q. Is the work graded in any way? Do certain employés do certain kinds of work? Is the work classified in the shop?—A. At that time it was divided among vest-makers, pants-makers, and coat-makers.

Q. You have cutters, I suppose?—A. The cutter was in the shop, in the boss's shop. We worked at home in our rooms. We had to buy fuel to heat the irons for pressing, and light in the winter; and we worked very deep in the night. The hours of working at that time were about fifteen to twenty hours a day.

Q. You worked by the day then, and not by the piece?—A. Piece-work, only piece-work, in our own rooms.

Q. Was working that length of time voluntary, or was it required by the employer?—A. He had no place to put us in. He would not pay out the money to hire a large room or hall to put his tailors in to make the coats or vests, and the tailor himself had to give his room for the business and had to buy coal and furnish the light to do the work for the boss.

Q. And then the tailors bought sewing-machines to do the work?— A. Yes.

Q. You say they worked from fifteen to eighteen hours a day before the war; how is it now?—A. Now they have to work quicker, because they cannot work so long. The machine makes too much noise in the place, and the neighbors want to sleep, and we have to stop sewing earlier; so we have to work faster. We work now in excitement—in a hurry. It is hunting; it is not work at all; it is a hunt.

Q. You turn out two or three times as much work per day now as you did in prior times before the war?—A. Yes, sir; two or three times as much; and we have to do it, because the wages are two-thirds lower than they were five or ten years back. . . .

Q. How much wages were paid a day after the war?—A. From 1864 to 1873, in the paper time, they ran from $20 to $25 a week for a tailor and his wife. A tailor is nothing without a wife, and very often a child. If the child is old enough, about twelve or fourteen years, it is employed in the tailor's business; but the children often go out into the factories to earn something.

Q. How much did you make after the war, from 1864 to 1873?—A. I made boys' fine fancy jackets and could get from $2 to $3.50 or $4 apiece for them.

Q. Was that for the jacket, or for the making of it?—A. For the making of it.

Q. How much are you paid for making a vest of the same sort now?—A. The highest is $1.

Q. For what sort of a vest?—A. Not vests—jackets.

Q. How much were you paid for pants from 1864 to 1873?—A. From five shillings to a dollar or nine shillings apiece.

Q. Now how much is paid?—A. It is from 15 to 28 cents.

Q. On what sort of material do you work?—A. All wool.

Q. What was paid for making a coat, from 1864 to 1873?—A. From 12 shillings to three or four dollars.

Q. How much is paid now?—A. From 40 cents to a dollar.

Q. You state, then, that there has been a reduction of two-thirds in the pay for some kinds of work?—A. Yes, sir.

By Mr. George:

Q. Is that owing to the change from hand work to machine work, or is it a reduction from the prices paid for machine work before the war?—A. From machine work to machine work. Hand work was before the war.

By the Chairman:

Q. Are the machines on which the work is done now the same as those that were used formerly?—A. They have better machines now—quicker.

Q. Did you do that fast work of which you have told us from 1864 to 1873?—A. No, sir; the fast work began about five or six years ago, when the wages lowered.

Q. You, of course, make more pieces in a given time than you did by hand; what is the difference between the amount of work that you can turn out with a machine and the amount you could turn out by hand?—A. I have to make now four jackets a day, with my wife and daughter's assistance.

Q. You do that with the machine?—A. All machine work.

Q. Working by hand, how many could you turn out?—A. Oh, with the hand I could make only one.

Q. Have you any idea of the number of tailors, men and women, who are engaged in that work in this city?—A. You mean in the clothing business—in the custom trade? That is another part of the business.

Q. I understand that. How many do you think there are?—A. I don't know; eighteen or twenty thousand.

Q. What proportion of them are women and what proportion men, according to your best judgment?—A. I guess there are many more women than men.

Q. The pay of the women is the same as the pay of the men for the same quantity of work, I suppose?—A. Yes; in cases where a manufacturer—that is, a middleman—gets work from the shop and brings it into his store and employs hands to make it, women get paid by the piece also. If the manufacturer gets 25 cents for a piece, he pays for the machine work on that piece so many cents to the machine-worker, he pays so many cents to the presser, so many cents to the finisher, and so many to the button-sewer—so much to each one—and what remains is to pay his rent and to pay for the machinery.

Q. What is your knowledge as to the amount that workers of that class are able to save from their wages?—A. I don't know any one that does save except those manufacturers.

Q. As a class, then, the workers save nothing?—A. No.

Q. What sort of house-room do they have? What is the character, in general, of the food and clothing which they are able to purchase with what they can make by their labor?—A. They live in tenement houses four or five stories high, and have two or three rooms.

Q. What is the character of their clothing?—A. They buy the clothing that they make—the cheapest of it.

Q. What about the character of food that they are able to provide for themselves?—A. Food? They have no time to eat dinner. They have a sandwich in the middle of the day, and in the evening when they go away from work it is the same, and they drink lager or anything they can get.

Q. They are kept busy all the time and have but little opportunity for rest?—A. Yes.

Q. What is the state of feeling between the employers and their employés in that business? How do you workingmen feel towards the people who employ you and pay you?—A. Well, I must say the workingmen are discouraged. If I speak with them they go back and don't like to speak much about the business and the pay. They fear that if they say how it is they will get sent out of the shop. They hate the bosses and the foremen more than the bosses, and that feeling is deep.

Q. Why do they feel so towards the foremen?—A. They know that they do a wrong onto them; they know that.

Q. Do not the foremen act under the instruction of the bosses?—A. Well, it seems so.

Q. Could not the boss correct the wrong that the foreman does, if it is a wrong?—A. Well, when we complain that the foreman is so and so, the boss says, "Oh, I have nothing to do with it; I don't know; go to the foreman; it is the foreman's business." Then when we go to the foreman he says, "Oh, I can't pay more; these are my rules; if you don't like it, go to the boss."

Q. And when you do go to the boss he sends you back to the foreman? —A. Yes; he says, "I have nothing to do with this; that is my foreman's business; go to him." Therefore the workmen hate them both.

Q. But can you explain why they hate the foremen, as you say they do, more than the bosses, when the bosses keep the foremen there and could discharge them and get better ones in the places if they desired?—A. Gentlemen, if I say all this here—if it is made public I come out of work.

By Mr. PUGH:

Q. Then you are testifying here under the apprehension of punishment for what you have stated?—A. Well, I have no fear for any one, you know, and if you think it is better that I say it, I do so.

Q. What is your feeling of restraint in testifying? What injury would you be subjected to for telling the truth? Would the workingmen in your business testify under a fear of being punished by their employers for telling the truth?—A. Yes. It is nothing but fear.

By Mr. GEORGE:

Q. Can you state the average wages per diem of the tailors in this city at the present time? How much do they make per day on an average, working as you say they do work, by the piece?—A. A man may earn from eight to nine dollars a week.

Q. How much can the best hands earn?—A. It will not be more than that. I think there is not much difference between the best and the worst. If a piece comes from the machine to the presser it has to be done just as quick as the other ones. One has to work as quick as the other. They all are good workers and have to work together; one wheel goes onto the other wheel and they have all to run together.

Q. How much can the women earn? About the same as the men?— A. No. A machine-girl gets from eight to nine dollars a week—just as much and sometimes more as a presser; and one who sews or finishes, puts the buttons on jackets, pants or vests, makes from three to four dollars.

Q. Then a woman who works the machine can make as much as a man can, but a woman who sews, who does the work that cannot be done by the machine, makes only three or four dollars a week?—A. Yes.

Q. How much did the average tailor make per week before the invention of machines?—A. They made from eight to ten dollars a week. But at that time I could buy for $10 more provisions and clothes than I can buy now for $20.

Q. You get about the same wages, then, about the same amount of money, but it was worth twice as much to you then because it had double the purchasing power of your present wages. Is that the idea?—A. Yes, sir.

Q. How many hours do you work to make eight or nine dollars a week?—A. From sunrise to sunset; and my wife works also. I can't say that I earn that amount of money; my wife earns part of it.

Q. What do you say are the average earnings?—A. Well, a family of three (we are three at home) will make from sixteen to eighteen dollars a week.

Q. How many hours do the tailors generally work now?—A. From sunrise to sunset.

Q. That produces them eight or nine dollars a week?—A. Yes.

By the CHAIRMAN:

Q. What are the hours of work in winter?—A. They make a light in the morning and they have a light burning until 9 or 10 o'clock in the evening.

Q. Have you any objection to giving us the names of some of the bosses and foremen that you know, who control a large number of laborers of the class to which you belong? This committee desires to obtain such information as you can give in regard to the condition of those engaged in your trade, and if there is any attempt to punish you for giving such information I think you can find protection from the country, or from some source. We cannot compel you to give the information, but we desire you to state, if you will, the names of some of these bosses and foremen, so that if they do not think proper to come here and speak for themselves the country will understand that you have told us the truth.—A. Now, sir, if I lose my work who can give me another work? I am an old man now, you know, and the young ones, they get the work and they say, "He is an old man; what can he do?" I was in one business for twenty-two years, and now since two years I am in another business, because this business is slower. I was a member of our union for eight or nine years, and a committee was appointed to get statistics about the house-workers, to find out their situation, but we have no funds and we must leave that. We found that it was necessary that something should be done against the house-workers, but we could not carry it out because we had no funds to send people around to get this information. Here are some of the questions that we put in our circular: "Do you work at home? How many hours a day? How many hours a day does your wife help? Do any of your children work, and how many? How large is your family? Have you any help besides your wife and children? Do your children go to school? What is the cost of the work at home (for fuel and light)? What is the average earnings a week and how much a year? How many days have you been at work during the last year? In how many rooms do you live? What rent do you pay? Are you compelled to work on Sunday to support your family? Do you go to church on Sunday? Have you got time and means to visit Central Park or any other place of pleasure? Does your family or you go to hear public lectures? What sickness did you or your family have during the last year? Of what kind were they? How many deaths in the family? What were the ages of the deceased? What was your doctor's bill during the last year? What was your expense for medicine during the last year?"

Q. That circular, you say, was designed to collect information about the tailoring business especially?—A. Yes.

Q. Are not the tailors the hardest-worked and poorest-paid class of laborers in the city?—A. The hardest worked, the longest hours, and the poorest paid.

Q. What proportion of them belong to labor unions? Do all or most of them belong to the unions?—A. No. They are all dispersed—they are all discouraged; they have no union at all.

Q. To what do you attribute that? What is the reason of it?—A. Well, they have not had success in getting higher wages. As often as they came together or went on a strike, they lost, always.

Q. And their wages, you say, have been gradually reduced?—A. Yes, and some of them that have houses, they are hungrier than the others; they corrupt the foremen, give them money, and get more work for themselves, and take it home and employ poor men and women.

Q. You say there is no separate union of the tailors?—A. No. It was, but it is not now.

Q. There are, you say, between eighteen and twenty thousand working tailors in this city?—A. Yes. I was very glad when the act of the legislature came that cigar-making in tenement houses is forbidden.

Q. What is your idea of the value of strikes as a means of remedying your troubles?—A. It is not always of great value, but it is a necessity. It springs from necessity, and the sooner the workingman will go on strike when he cannot remain on the work—so poor as the workingmen are, they cannot carry that on—the burden is too great. . . .

Q. But is it not the same necessity which drives them to strike that also makes the strike a failure, namely, the want of means to support themselves while the strike continues?—A. Yes. They have no funds, and they are discouraged. We wanted to get up agitation to get this house-worker system done away with. We wanted to rent a little hall and get together there, ten or twelve tailors with their machines, and then go to the bosses and say, "Here, we are a company; give us the work and we will give you a guarantee that we will make it right." But we can't afford to pay for the fuel and light, and the rent of the hall, and then we were going to say to the bosses, "Now you see you pay too little for the expenses which we have for your work." But I could not bring the men out; they remained at home; they are discouraged. Therefore the legislature, in my opinion, will have to take this matter up and forbid house-work in all branches. . . .

Q. You think labor is the pack-horse that carries all the burden?—A.

Yes. If anybody is to help that, legislation must do it. Who shall do it? Shall the workingmen make a revolution or a rebellion? The workingman is the peacefulest man in the world when he can have his living, but if he goes on strike the whole world cries out that they are a dangerous class; but the workingmen are glad when they can be home by their wives and children making a living. I have my arguments here against indirect taxes, and I will read them: "So long as legislation is unjust to the poor, to tax the poor who have nothing but their daily earnings, to tax them by indirect taxes, there is no way to better the condition of the workingmen. The foundation of all society is based upon injustice, to make the rich richer and the poor poorer. The rich receive donations from the State by legislation; from the laboring men will be taken the last cent, by high rents and high-priced provisions. No wonder the rich become proud and brutal and say, 'Damn the public.' The indirect taxes are a fraud and a crime against the workingmen, and society will have its punishment sooner or later for it. Such legislation creates dangerous men. The millionaire corrupts the courts and legislation. He does not care for the law nor the Constitution. He has neither a duty nor a love for the country; he is proud for himself; a State in the State opposed to the State. The dangerous classes are not to be found in the tenement houses and filthy districts, but in mansions and villas. To make rich people as we have to-day, means to make them superior to their fellow-citizens; to give them power to dictate to their fellow-citizens their own will. They deprive the laboring men of their right to protect themselves. When there lies so great a wrong on the bottom of society as to tax the laboring man by indirect taxes, there grows wrong after wrong, and it will grow as high as Babylon's tower if we do not go against it in time. Does not history show what may arise from unjust taxation? Did not the Flemish taxation imposed by the Spanish ruler in Holland create an eighty years' war? Did not England lose his American colonies by unjust taxation? Let those pay the taxes who reap out of the nation more than they need. This is just and natural. The nation is the great fountain out of which the riches flow. Tributary to her are those who reap the fruits. Begin in time to remedy this wrong. There might come a time in which a compromise is too late, and in my opinion a compromise in time is cheaper than a war."

Q. What do you mean by "indirect taxes" which the poor people pay? Just specify the indirect taxes that you complain of.—A. The landlord says: "My rent is from this day higher." And when I ask him why, he says: "The taxes grow higher; I have to pay more taxes." That is the answer the landlord gives me. When I go to buy meat and vegetables all is so dear, and the groceryman says: "I have to pay $10 more rent." A lot 25 by 100 feet pays $400 taxes in New York, and when the landlord has to pay more taxes he charges more rent; and at last it comes on the workingman.

Q. Then one of the indirect taxes to which you refer is the tax on real estate which the landlord collects of you in the form of rent?—A. Yes.

Q. Is there any other indirect tax that occurs to you; or is rent the only great oppressive tax of which you complain?—A. Well, rent touches all.

Q. That is the particular tax which most oppresses you, is it?—A. Yes, sir.

Q. You spoke a little while ago of the corruption of the bosses and foreman in giving more work to some men than to others; is that the reason why you hate the foreman worse than the boss?—A. It is not only I who hate him; they all hate him.

Q. I do not mean you personally, but the tailors as a class, who, as you say, complain more of the foreman than of the boss.—A. Yes; they do.

Q. The foreman is likely to have his favorite; he does not distribute the work fairly; is that it?—A. That is what does it.

Q. Now the class of workers to which you belong seems to be very severely oppressed, and it is much better for you to state all the facts as you know them and as they exist, because the employers will hate you more if you leave the idea here that there is something worse behind that you do not dare to tell than they will if you just frankly expose this skeleton in the closet and let the worst be known. I think you had better, therefore, tell the whole truth, under compulsion by the committee.—A. I guess I have no right to name persons here.

Q. I do not ask you to give names, but simply to state any abuses that you know to exist—A. I am no informer or complainer; I am here as a witness. Those persons did not do anything wrong to me, and they could go before the court, and I cannot come and say I know it certainly if they go before the court and make a complaint against me. It is all mystery. Everybody knows it, but it is a mystery.

Q. Nobody can hurt you for telling the truth.—A. Well, I can't state the fact that such things are in existence.

Q. What sort of things do you refer to?—A. That such tailors which have a house or a pile of money get more work in the shops than the others.

Q. Is this the point: that men with families, who live in houses and have their families to support, get more work than men who are without families?—A. No; the point is this, that those who employ other hands besides their own families, ten or twelve or fifty hands, that they have more power. They make 1,000 coats in a week, some of them.

Q. They make for other bosses who are above them?—A. Yes; they make for the clothing bosses. They are tailors, and they employ other tailors to make the work and get something out of them. . . .

Q. Are you a man of family yourself?—A. I have five children, and two are dead.

Q. How old is your oldest child?—A. Twenty-eight years.

Q. Does he work at the same business as yourself?—A. No.

Q. Does he live with you, or is he married?—A. He is married.

Q. And your next child is how old?—A. Twenty-five. She is married.

Q. And the next?—A. She is 23. She is not married. She works with me. I have another girl of 17, who helps around the house. My youngest is a son, who is sick since he was twelve years old with epilepsy.

Q. What wages do you average from week to week?—A. Fifteen and twenty dollars.

Q. You are an unusually good workman, I suppose?—A. I make the samples in the shops—the best work.

Q. Do your wife and daughter also work?—A. Yes.

Q. Do the figures you have stated include the wages of your wife and daughter as well as your own wages?—A. Sure; the whole family.

Q. Then it is not you alone, but it is you three, who earn this amount? —A. Yes, sir.

Q. What rent do you pay?—A. $9.50 now, for three rooms.

Q. What part of the city do you live in?—A. In the Tenth ward, in Christie street, in a tenement house, on the top floor.

Q. How many stories high is the house?—A. Five.

Q. Describe your rooms to us as well as you can.—A. There are six rooms in the half floor, and I have three in front, and my daughter and her husband have the other three, in the back. They are all lighted. There is no house in the rear. I have lived there now eleven years. When I moved in I paid $15.

Q. And you pay only $9.50 now; to what do you attribute the fall in the rent?—A. At that time I paid $15 I earned $25 or $28 a week, and I could pay $15 rent.

Q. Then rents have come down somewhat with the wages?—A. Well, they pay all more now; but I have a good landlord, who don't raise on me.

Q. Is it easier or harder for you to get a living for yourself and family now than it was ten years ago?—A. It was easier ten years ago. . . .

TESTIMONY OF THOMAS B. McGUIRE

Thomas B. McGuire sworn and examined.

By Mr. Call:

Question. Where do you live?—Answer. In New York.

Q. What is your occupation?—A. At present I am a truck-driver. I was formerly an expressman.

Q. How long have you been in those respective employments?

A. I have been in the express business about five years. I embarked something like $300 in the business, thinking that I might become something of a capitalist eventually, but I found competition so great that it was impossible for me to do so; I found that the railroad companies had their regular wagons and their collectors on the trains previous to their reaching the city asking for the privilege of carrying the people's baggage, and by that means they were enabled to get any business of that kind that was to be had. I found also that another company had taken the furniture moving into their hands. A case in point: A gentleman in New street asked me one time what I would charge him to bring two truck-loads from a certain station in Jersey. I told him $75. It was 23 miles out there; the truck was a four-horse truck, and I was to handle everything. He went to the Metropolitan Van Company and had the work done for $60. Now, my profit on that job at the price I asked, had I received the work, would have been somewhere in the neighborhood of $20; but that company did the work with better appliances than I could have furnished and made a great deal more money than I could have made out of it. A man in the express business today owning one or two horses and a wagon cannot even eke out an existence from the business. The competition is too great; that is, the competition from these monopolies. For instance, the Adams Express Company and all those other express companies do local express work also, and by that means they prevent people who go into the business in New York City from ever getting any higher up than barely existing—not, living but barely existing. That is my experience. I found that when I lost a horse I was not able to replace him; that is, I could not accumulate enough out of my earnings to do so. I found, more-over, that I was not able to buy feed for my horses even at low prices. Some two years ago I paid $2.10 for 80 pounds of oats, while these cor-porations could buy the same quantity for $1.60 or $1.80; I paid from $2.50 to $3 a set for horse shoeing, while they had theirs done by contract at a price which would not amount to $1.25 or $1.50 for each horse. So that everything is against a man going into the express business in a small way.

Q. Is it or is it not better for a man to loan whatever little capital he may have at 3 per cent. and to hire for wages, than to buy an express wagon and horses and go into business for himself?—A. It is certainly bet-ter; because he is then certain of some little return per week and his 3 per cent. is all right too, that is, provided the banks do not fail. There is great danger they say now of the banks failing, and they are going to ask the Senate to help them I believe.

Q. We have nothing to do with the savings banks. They are State in-stitutions.—A. Well, the national banks I know do not pay 3 per cent. But the stock of the national banks is a very good investment. I would like to invest in that way myself if I could.

Q. You think that an investment in a savings bank at 3 per cent. is better than an investment in a horse and wagon to carry on the express business?—A. Yes, sir.

Q. So far as your observation goes, it is better than trucking or any other of those employments?—A. It is, undoubtedly. For instance, I worked for a firm as a truckman, and I was paid so much per week. Previous to my going there a man had been doing that business for $100 a month, furnishing his own truck and helper. Out of that $100 he had to pay $25 a month for his stabling in the Knickerbocker stables; he paid his boy on the truck something like $7 a week, and he had to be on hand all the time, and he was responsible for all losses. For instance, he lost a package of jewelry which was valued at $600, and he had to pay that $600, and he was forced to give the business up through that loss.

Q. What capital would be required to begin an express business here with a reasonable prospect of success?—A. Ten thousand dollars would give a man a fair opportunity to compete with these large companies, I think.

Q. How was it fifteen or twenty years ago in regard to that?—A. This competition did not exist at that time. Then a man embarking $300 in the business had an excellent chance of becoming a successful expressman and accumulating some money and probably some property.

Q. How is it as to trucking in that respect?—A. Men who embarked in trucking twenty years ago have become wealthy, to my own knowledge, have become the owners of houses and other property, and are doing a vast business, some of them having from fifteen to twenty trucks. They have got employment from different large dry-goods dealers, importers, and others, and they have got into the good graces of some of our custom house officers and got the run of the public stores. Those men who have the custom-house licenses are the only ones that are permitted to do the carting from those public establishments, and in that way they have a monopoly of the business. As a rule you will find them to be active members of one of the "grand old" parties, and of course through that means they have a great deal of influence that other men cannot reach to.

Q. What capital would now be required to begin that business with a fair prospect of success?—A. At the present time, to be able to go into that business with any chance of success, you would have to be somewhat of a ward politician. If you were that, probably with $25,000 you might be able to compete with these other people with a fair chance of success.

Q. You think it would be necessary to be a ward politician and also to have $25,000?—A. Yes, sir. Then also you would have to be able to manage the primaries, and, if it was necessary, to be one of the judges at the primary, so as to make your man "the candidate of the people" at the next election.

Q. Do you mean that that is a sort of a Government position, but that a man must have the money besides?—A. It is not exactly a Government position, but it is a position where bribery is necessary to keep the people under the control of a certain class of politicians. If a man can do those things he will get a good living.

Q. How is it about the hack business?—A. Well, individual ownership of hacks is becoming obsolete. Large stables are taking up the business entirely. Corporations usually take that business to themselves. For instance, a man who can afford to lease a large stable, and can manage to get men at starvation wages, and put them on a hack, and put a livery on them, with a gold band and brass buttons, to show that they are slaves —I beg pardon; I did not intend to use the word slaves; there are no slaves in this country now—to show that they are merely servants, that class of stable-keepers can secure the patronage of what are called the moneyed classes, who pay a dollar an hour for the use of these cabs, with these men dressed up in that fashion to drive them, and of course they monopolize the business.

Q. What amount of money do you think would be required to engage in that business with a fair prospect of success?—A. Fifty thousand dollars would set up a very nice establishment; or probably if the uniforms could be had cheap a little less might do. A good supply of uniforms is the principal thing.

Q. What else do they give those men besides?—A. They give them permission to exist, and if they own tenement houses they give these men leave to live in them, raising the rent on them every year. They give them enough wages to secure a bare existence, and if the men are found taking 25 cents from a passenger they are immediately discharged and sent adrift to go and compete with somebody else in some other business.

By Mr. GEORGE:

Q. Do you mean if they are found taking a donation from a passenger they are discharged?—A. Yes, sir.

By Mr. CALL:

Q. Why don't those men who are so fond of the gold bands and brass buttons go into some other employment?—A. Well, merely because the unskilled labor market is overstocked, and will be while men work ten hours a day. If the hours of labor were shorter the surplus of labor would disappear, and therefore workingmen could command better wages.

Q. A man who can drive a hack can drive horses. Now, do you understand that in all this great country there is no demand for the services of a man who knows how to drive horses?—A. I have not the slightest doubt that there is a great demand for me in Cincinnati probably, or some other place, if I could get enough money to pay my railroad fare, or to live there till I found employment.

Q. Then the difficulty, I understand, is in getting from here to that place?—A. There is no difficulty in getting from here to there, provided you have the wherewithal to pay your fare.

Q. The difficulty is in finding means to pay for the transportation?—A. Undoubtedly.

Q. Then you think that if the means of transportation were provided, and you knew of a situation in Cincinnati or some place else which you could get that would be the remedy?—A. It would; provided a man had not to be discharged to make a place for me. But, if a man had to be discharged, it would simply be taking from the surplus labor here and adding to the surplus there. There are something like 10,000 drivers in the city of New York. . . .

Q. Well, here, is my suggestion. This is a great country and there is a vast amount of labor required all over it, and a great demand for labor in many parts of the country; now if some means were provided by which these men who are tempted to stay here (as you say) by the gold bands and brass buttons, could go to such places where they could get a good comfortable living in the country at cheap rates and receive $20 or $30 a month compensation, would not that be a very good exchange for them?—A. If you have any influence to get me a position just like that, I would like you to use it, and to get me also transportation for myself and family. If you can do that, I shall be most willing to accept that magnificent salary. In the last two weeks I have answered several advertisements from persons in the city of New York and two from the country. One of the city advertisers, a wholesale house, offered me $6 a week to drive a truck. From the country people I received no answer at all; I suppose because I stated the wages I wanted.

Q. What wages did you name?—A. I told them I would take $12 a week, and feed my family as best I could. . . .

By the CHAIRMAN:

Q. What are you going to do?—A. Well, I suppose I have got to keep on until I find some place where I can put some other fellow out and take his place. I need not care whether he starves or not, so long as I am all right myself. I believe that is the system now, and, of course, I have got to follow it out. . . .

By Mr. CALL:

Q. Suppose you could make a contract with some person on a farm in Illinois, or Ohio, or Iowa, or Minnesota, or anywhere in the West or Northwest, by which you could have a comfortable and abundant subsistence for yourself and family, with a house to live in, and, say, $20 a month wages; could you not make a very good start on that?—A. I would be willing to do better than that. If they will guarantee me food, clothing, and shelter for myself and family for twenty years, I will give them my services for nothing. . . .

Q. Are you in pretty good health?—A. Well, yes. I suppose all the damage I have ever suffered to my health has been in handling those heavy cases that I spoke of. I can't get anything to do, but at the same time they give me permission to be taxed to pay Vanderbilt $40 a minute on his Government bonds.

Q. What tax do you pay?—A. Let me see. The tax is $28 for every man, woman, and child.

Q. Does the National Government take that tax direct from you?—A. The city of New York pays it to the State government, I believe, the State to the National Government, and so on.

Q. Can you tell us what tax the State pays to the National Government?—A. Well, I have never made that a study, but I know that the taxes are very heavy.

Q. I think you are mistaken in regard to the State paying any tax to the National Government.—A. Does not the State help to pay the expenses of the National Government?

Q. Not directly. The National Government has its customs laws and its internal-revenue system. If you buy a cigar you pay something in that way to the National Government; but the cost of food and of the other necessaries of life is not increased by national taxation that I am aware of.—A. Well, I use a pipe of tobacco occasionally, and I have to pay a tax on that to the National Government, and I used to have to pay a tax whenever I bought a box of matches, but this good Government of ours took that stamp tax off. Then there is a tariff on all foreign goods, and if I buy them I have to pay my quota of that taxation.

Q. Yes; but do you have to buy any foreign goods?—A. All the purchases that are made in my establishment are made by my wife, and, like all the rest of the fair sex, she *is very fond* of that which is imported. If she was not, I suppose she would not have married me, for I was imported myself. I noticed, recently, that two little handkerchiefs that she bought for the children, were marked "imported." Now, I believe I was taxed something even on those little articles, for I believe there is a tariff of 40 per cent., or something like that, on cotton and linen. But, of course, that does not make any difference to me, for I recognize the fact that it makes no difference with the workingmen whether there is a tariff or no tariff. The poor unfortunate laborer is just like the kernel of wheat between the upper and the lower millstone; in any case he is certain to be ground. He *produces* all the wealth while the men who produce nothing *have* all the wealth.

By Mr. CALL:

Q. How does the man who produces nothing get the wealth?—A. Well, let me see—class legislation, national banks, railroad monopolies, telegraph monopolies, Wall street gambling, horse racing, keeping gin-mills, and all the etceteras, and there is one thing more that I had very nearly forgotten, groundrent. . . .

By Mr. GEORGE:

Q. Did you ever know of a bank lending money to a truckman?—A. I was going to mention that, but I was going to put my answer in another way to make it lucid. The banks never lend money to the truckmen or anybody else without collateral, and I never had very much of that. But when this money is loaned, it must be loaned at a rate of interest. Now, when there is only $13 per capita for each individual in the United States, and the interest foots up $20 per capita, where are they going to get the other $7? There is the injustice. The moment the money is loaned, that recognizes the fact that there is a debt, and the moment that debt is there, the man is no longer producing for himself but for the other man, the one who lends the money.

By Mr. CALL:

Q. I understand that theory very well, but——A. [Interrupting.] It is not a theory, it is a bare fact. That is how the banks are favored by this class legislation, and while they have their representatives in Congress to make laws for us, and while our Senators get so well paid at the rate of $8,000 a year——

Q. [Interposing.] Are you certain that a Senator gets $8,000 a year?—A. I beg pardon. I take that back. I don't know how much they get, but I know it is said that they are bought up very often.

Q. Are you quite sure that you are giving correct testimony?—A. I think I have read in a book called the Star Almanac (I am very fond of reading), that a Senator's salary is in the neighborhood of $8,000 a year. If I am mistaken about that it is an error of the head and not of the heart.

Q. Why not have a little more charity?—A. I have given over having any charity for politicians. I saw them to-day in one of our civil courts dispossessing a poor woman, and the man who did it——

Q. [Interposing.] You don't condemn us for that, I hope?—A. No; but is it not part of the system of government under which we are living?

Q. Well, we are not responsible for that. We do not make the Government.—A. No; but you are a part of it.

Q. What have you to suggest to us by way of a remedy for these evils?—A. Well, I would have you to look into all these things in place of spending your time making magnificent speeches. For instance, I live in a tenement house, three stories up, where the water comes in through the roof, and I cannot better myself. My little children will have to go to work before they are able to work. Why? Simply because this present system under which we are living is all for self, all for the privileged classes, nothing for the man who produces all the wealth.

Q. Let us see about that. You arraign me here as one of the representatives of this corrupt and oppressive system. Now, I have taken my two hands and gone out into the woods and built a house for myself to live in, and I have seen the rain come through and fall on my people, and I have gone into the fields day after day and worked with my own hands to make something to eat for myself and my family. Now it would be the height of folly for me on that account to utter a tirade against you because you had happened to get $10,000 in some way and I had not. There are two sides to this question. You talk about the "politicians" without knowing whether we are politicians or not. You have no knowledge whether I have sought political life or not. However, without indulging in any recriminations (for false accusations never do any good), let us see how the evils that do exist can be remedied. You say that you would have us to look into the social condition of the people. That is all very well; but what power have we to change existing conditions? We are sworn legislators under a constitutional form of government, sworn to exercise no powers but those which that Constitution gives us. You arraign us here because of the case of some poor woman who has been turned out, you say, by some politician in this city. Now, what power have we to prevent that under our form of government?—A. You have got the power to see that every man gets what the Constitution guarantees to him—an opportunity to enjoy life, liberty, and the pursuit of happiness.

Q. Do you understand it to be a fact that we have that power?—A. Yes; the Constitution reads that way.

Q. Is that all there is in the Constitution?—A. That is about as far as I want to go.

By the CHAIRMAN:

Q. That is in the Declaration of Independence, it is not?—A. Well, have it the Declaration. When I was thirteen years old I was in the Army of the United States, so I have had but little opportunity for education or study. I merely give you that point because I generally hear it on election day from the gentlemen who say they are "glad to see the horny-handed sons of toil gathering around the banner" under which they vote, and all that sort of thing.

By Mr. CALL:

Q. Why do not "the horny-handed sons of toil" send men of their own choosing to make laws for them?—A. Simply because the entire political system from top to bottom is a system of bribery and corruption.

Q. Then you distrust popular government?—A. I do under the present arrangement. The moment an alderman is elected, some railroad corporation will write to him, saying, "Mr. Reilley, we are glad to see that you have been elected alderman; call upon us immediately, and we will see that you have two or three conductors appointed upon our line."

Q. Are not those very often taken from among the sons of toil?—A. Yes, sir; but the latter is entirely arranged by the idlers who never do any labor. A man who works for his living has to work too long and too hard to be able to find time and opportunity to educate himself in "politics."

Q. You seem to be pretty well educated?—A. Oh, no; I have listened to the politicians somewhat, and being of rather an inquiring turn of mind, I have followed them up a little closer than some of the others do. I heard what they said to the people about election times, and then I tried to see if it would work in practice, but I found it wouldn't.

Q. Don't you think anybody else in the country has done that besides you?—A. Oh, undoubtedly. I am only a drop in the bucket.

Q. Then, how is it that, with so many people looking out for their interests, the workingmen do not get better representative men to make laws for them?—A. Simply because the system of bribery is so complete that it is impossible, and if anybody believes in independent political action and tries to carry it out, he will have the papers of the city of New York hounding him as a "socialist" or a "communist." Whenever a man undertakes to advocate the cause of the working people, the papers come out and denounce what he says as the "ravings of a demagogue," and so on, and for that reason our poor unfortunate, untutored, workingmen are deceived, and are simple enough to believe in the party who promise them that they will do away with the system of convict labor and make the reforms for them.

Q. Do you think you are giving a proper description of the workingmen of this country?—A. I know I am giving a proper description of the workingmen of New York.

Q. What do you call a workingman?—A. Every man that works for a living, every man who produces anything useful. . . .

Q. And you would consider a priest, who worked faithfully to comfort his parishioners, a workingman, I suppose?—A. Yes; provided he had cushioned pews in the front of the church for the working classes, and hard boards for the idlers——

Q. [Interposing.] Oh, well, he might be very superstitious and fanatical and all that, but still, if he came to your family when they were sick and did all he could do to relieve and comfort them, he would be a useful man, no matter what he thought or did about pews. But suppose that the workingmen, according to your definition, that is the men who work with their hands, the cigar-makers, the truck-men, the blacksmiths, the carpenters, and so on, were able to elect a candidate of their own for mayor of this city, would not the probability be that that representative of theirs would not be a corrupt man who might be bought up to betray their interests? I have a better opinion of the workingmen and of humanity generally than you seem to have.—A. Well, I suppose that is because you mingle with the decent classes. I don't.

Q. No; I don't know of any decenter classes than the working people. I have mingled with them all my life, and I do not understand why you should say that the candidate of the workingmen would be corrupt.—A. Well, you put me questions that I would have to know the minds of men in order to answer. I say this, however, if you will take your legislators from the class you belong to, and not from among the whisky class, who produce nothing but headache and delirium tremens——

Q. [Interposing.] Who takes them from that class now?—A. The politicians who control the caucus.

Q. How can that class of politicians control the caucus if you working people attend there and vote?—A. Oh, yes; and if we do attend there they will have three men appointed who won't count our votes.

Q. You need not tell me that the class of men to which you belong will let any three men cheat them out of their votes?—A. Well, I would like to have you ask every witness that comes here and that knows anything about it, whether men are not appointed here in that way to count the votes, and allowed to count them to suit themselves.

Q. Don't you know how to remedy that? Cannot you workingmen vote that the caucus shall not appoint the three men who count the votes, but that the appointment shall be made in public meeting by the people?—A. According to the law we cannot appoint an inspector of election; he has got to be appointed by the dominant party at the police headquarters.

Q. Then your idea is that popular government is a failure?—A. Under these conditions.

Q. Well, according to your theory, we have arrived at the conclusion that the people are not sensible enough to keep themselves from being cheated. Now, what remedy have you to propose for that?—A. In the first place, let me say that I have got no theory. I am speaking of actual facts. In the next place, the only way to remedy this evil is, instead of these party preferences, to let the primary be an open one just the same as our election is, and let an inspector of election be taken from each party, and if there is a third party, as for instance a workingmen's party, let them also be entitled to have one of the inspectors. In that way we would have some chance of having a fair election.

Q. That is what I understand to be the law and the practice now?—A. It is not so in our primaries here. . . .

By Mr. CALL:

. . . Q. I guess you are mistaken.—A. No, I am positive of it. In the city of Brooklyn there is an entirely different law from that which we have in the city of New York; so you see the State does control it. Again, speaking of counting votes, or rather of seeing the ballots deposited, for the primary is one thing and casting the ballot another thing. For instance, if we had a labor party in the field we would have no man present to see the votes being counted.

Q. Why not?—A. Because the recognized parties are the Republicans, the Democrats, the Tammany Hall Democrats, and the Irving Hall Democrats.

Q. If there is any such law as that it is not worth a snap of your finger. It is entirely contrary to the Constitution of the United States.—A. To give you an example of the way these things are done, I went some time ago to get up a meeting at the corner of Fifteenth street and First avenue. I went to Captain Walling, and he sent me to the captain of the precinct, and the captain of the precinct sent me to the sergeant, and the sergeant sent me to a policeman, and the policeman told me he had no authority.

Q. What did you want permission to do?—A. To go out on the street and talk politics.

Q. You don't mean to tell me that there is any law here that compels you to get permission to go out on the street to talk politics?—A. Yes, I do.

Q. You mean that you must have permission to hold a public meeting on the streets, not permission for an individual to talk politics on the streets?—A. Yes; a public meeting. But, if an individual begins to talk and gathers a crowd around him, then he is violating a corporation ordinance.

Q. Of course every municipal government has control of its streets. Would you change that?—A. No, sir; but I would want that there should be no such thing as class legislation.

Q. That is right; but the city of New York has control of its streets, and it may say where a public meeting shall be held on the streets or where it shall not; now, how would you change that?—A. I would simply ask that the people should be allowed at all times to have the same rights here that they have in Europe under monarchical forms of government.

Q. You ought not to have any city government that would do what you complain of—that would make class legislation.—A. How can we prevent it when these cliques control the whole thing through a system of appointments—I call it bribery. All the appointments, from the street-cleaning department down, are made in that way here.

By Mr. GEORGE:

Q. Do you mean that all those classes you have mentioned who have political influence are required to do certain political work in order to retain their places?—A. That is what I mean. You have got it correctly.

By Mr. CALL:

Q. They do not appoint hackmen, though. What you mean is that that is an incidental effect?—A. I say that wherever a political position is held it is held for the purpose of retaining the party in office, and if I had my way I would prevent any man who held an office in the gift of the people from voting, because he will vote to keep his bread and butter, and his vote will count just as much as mine or any other man's.

By Mr. GEORGE:

Q. That is one practical idea, to prevent any person holding an office under the Government from voting. Is there anything else that you would do?—A. Well, I would also prevent them from having a hand in the primaries.

Q. What else?—A. I guess that after that we could manage our own affairs.

Q. You think that would stop the bribery of which you speak, so that things generally would be improved?—A. Yes, sir; I think that if that was stopped we would have a fair chance of getting representative men from the people instead of from the politicians.

Q. Do you think that would bring about relief in the matter of insufficient wages and competition in the different employments of life?—A. It would prevent class legislation; it would probably make our railroads and our telegraphs the property of the Government the same as the Post-Office is now; and that would do something for us.

Q. But supposing that the fellows who got the Government then should do just as the other fellows do now, and use its patronage for their own friends and for their own party purposes, what would you do?—A. I have stated to you that I would not allow any man in the employ of the Government to vote.

Q. Then you would take the right of suffrage away from all who were connected with the Government?—A. Yes; just the same as you take it away from the soldier.

Q. But supposing you did that, would not those men still be able to use their influence?—A. They might, with money, but we would find a way to deal with that.

Q. Would they not have the same motive to use their influence that they have now?—A. Most undoubtedly; but the man who did it would be a criminal in the eye of the law. Anybody who does anything to subvert the liberties of the people is a criminal.

The CHAIRMAN. I don't care to listen to accusations of this kind much longer. This witness evidently looks upon the legislative bodies of this country as made up of a set of rascals, and he cannot expect anything from a committee which is a part of such a body.

The WITNESS. I did not think that Senator Blair would take the matter that way.

The CHAIRMAN. No, you don't understand me. I feel like this, my friend, that on an average we human beings are all very much alike. I have never known a single instance of bribery in the House of Representatives or in the Senate of the United States; never a single instance of the kind, and I have been there eight years; and I don't believe that either of the other Senators here present have ever known of an instance. There is a very general and wide-spread misconception as to the personal character of the legislators of this country. I don't believe that, man for man, the church in the United States, or any other organization in the United States, averages any better in the matter of personal moral character than do the members of Congress, and you labor under a very serious mistake, and approach the subject from a wrong direction when you come to it with the idea that anybody is here or anybody is there to deal with these great public questions dishonestly. I speak now of the members of Congress generally, and I say that the great majority in either party is composed of honest men. These problems of life are very serious, and I can see how a man in your position, having capacity and ability which, with proper opportunity, would enable you to fill any situation in the country—I can see how you, crowded by circumstances, may come to feel and think as you do, and what I say to you now I do not say reprovingly at all—God knows I do not. But, my friend, you are wrong in your estimate of men. The majority of men are honest men throughout the length and breadth of the world. I do not care to believe in the doctrine of total depravity, for that includes myself, and I don't choose to hold or to admit that I am only fit to be an exemplification hereafter of eternal punishment by fire. I don't believe that men are totally depraved. I believe that men on the whole are good, and that you can safely appeal to their better nature.

The WITNESS. I did not bring out this discussion myself. It was brought out by the questions of a member of the committee.

The CHAIRMAN. That is all true. I am not finding fault with you; I am only speaking of the evident condition of your mind on this subject, and I do wish, if I can, to disabuse you and others who feel and think as you do because life has been hard with them, of the idea that knaves are the rule rather than honest men. It is not so, and you are entirely mistaken and very unjust if you think that the legislators of this country, as a class, are the knaves that you represent them to be.

The WITNESS. Well, if you lived in New York as long as I have lived here, and had lived in the neighborhoods that I have lived in, and if you had looked around you and seen the practices that are going on there among the poorer classes; if you had seen them having to vote themselves slaves every year, I believe you would think as I do. They are trades unionists eleven months in the year and the other month they are worked up by political heat and they go and vote right against their convictions. If you saw these things and if you saw those people send their wives out to scrub other people's floors, and their little children to work as cash-boys and cash-girls in other people's stores, you would have just the same sentiments that I have.

The CHAIRMAN. I have seen some of the things you speak of, and I believe it is because you have seen so much of them that you feel and think as you do, but you are, nevertheless, in error as to the facts.

The Workingman's View of Labor Organization

The following testimony was given by Abraham Bisno, fare collector on the Chicago Elevated Railway, and Mrs. J. S. Robb, wife of a non-union painter, before a subcommittee of the (U.S.) Industrial Commission on the Chicago Labor Disputes of 1900, meeting in Chicago on March 21, 1900.

TESTIMONY OF ABRAHAM BISNO

Mr. Abraham Bisno, of Chicago, collector of fares for the Union Elevated Railway Company, was introduced as a witness, and, being duly sworn, testified as follows:

Q. (By Mr. CLARKE.) Please give your name.—A. A. Bisno.

Q. Post-office address.—A. 523 Evergreen avenue, Chicago.

Q. Present occupation.—A. Collecting fares on the loop here for the Union Elevated Railway Company.

Q. Former occupation.—A. I am a cloak maker by trade—made cloaks for some years—and I have had several occupations within the last few years. I have been the walking delegate for our union.

Q. What union is that?—A. The Chicago Cloak Makers' Union, and I have also been inspecting factories for the State.

Q. Under what administration?—A. Under Governor Altgeld's administration.

Q. (By Mr. KENNEDY.) You can not speak in a representative capacity now for the workingmen of Chicago who are affected by these strikes that are going on at this time?—A. I do not know; no, I think not.

Q. You think not?—A. No; I stated that to Mr. Clarke yesterday in speaking about it; that I should not represent anybody except some experience in the matter that I should like to submit.

Q. (By Mr. CLARKE.) Is the union to which you belong still in existence?—A. It is lately organized again; it was broken up after the defeat of the strike 2 years ago.

Q. Have you made a considerable study of labor problems?—A. Yes;

Report of the (U.S.) Industrial Commission on the Chicago Labor Disputes of 1900 (Washington, D.C.: Government Printing Office, 1901), Vol. VIII, pp. 53–58, 79–82.

within the last 16 years I have belonged to several labor organizations and to 2 educational societies, and have read a good deal on the labor problem, and have participated personally in various ways in the effort to effect what I thought would redress the grievances that we have by making an effort to get into the organized union.

Q. How long have you lived in this country?—A. Ever since 1881.

Q. What country did you come from?—A. Russia. I am a Russian Jew.

Q. What part of Russia?—A. Kiev, in the southern part of Russia.

Q. Are you a believer in the union of labor?—A. Yes. . . .

Q. (By Mr. CLARKE.) Do you understand that these strikes in Chicago have been on account of the refusal of employers to accede to the demands of labor for an increase in wages?—A. No; I understand that they are all pretending they don't want to have anything to do with the walking delegate and recognizing the union. The first demand of the machinists is that none but members of the union be employed.

I should like to say something in connection with this. Unless a firm recognizes the union and agrees to employ nobody except members of the union the union can not exist. In my own trade, when our union was weak, our best men were victimized, and were out of a job the most of the time; I mean our most intelligent men—men who did not want to put up with abuse easily. It was only when our union got so strong that we could protect our intelligent members that we were in a position to have a union at all. Two years ago, after we had lost a quarrel with a big firm which was very bitterly contested, and threw us on our knees, so to speak, I made a motion in our union to give up the organization, because if we were not able to protect every individual member of the organization all it was good for was to benefit scabs, to make hirelings and lickspittles, etc., in the trade—to make them foremen and contractors, etc. The bosses always supported those fellows and victimized our intelligent members— you may not call them intelligent. The fact was that we could not have an organization at all unless we had an organization that was competent to protect the individual member from being thrown out of employment for being a union man. We have never had anything to say when any of our men were thrown out of employment, except when they were thrown out of employment evidently for generating union thought. So when these men demand that the union be recognized to the extent of not employing other people except members of their union, this is essential to the very existence of their organization. It is a life-and-death question with them.

My experience is also that it is not the walking delegate that is creating trouble. In fact, so far as my holding my job in the union was concerned, it would have paid for me that there should be no trouble. I got my wages regularly when there was no trouble. The organization needs a man to collect dues, to find work for men who have no work, to find who needs men. There are a thousand and one things to be done by a walking delegate in an organization. If there is an organization at all the man is quite safe with his job; but when there is a strike the very existence of the organization is endangered, and consequently the job of the fellow is endangered; so it is better for the walking delegate that there should be no quarrel and no strike, and the walking delegate is generally against a strike, because his information is more extensive.

Q. (By Mr. CLARKE.) Suppose a walking delegate gets into politics?— A. I should like to discuss this trade-union feature before I get to politics. I have something to say on that, too. My experience is that the rank and file of the men in the union hall—I mean that are most radical in the union hall, are not so when they go to talk to the boss. I do not think it is true that a manufacturer himself can get the real sentiment of his men speaking to them individually. If a big manufacturer—that is, a rich fellow— takes a poor man, with whom the job is an extremely precious article, into his office and talks to him, he is not likely to get the real sentiments. The man will be afraid to tell him about the truth of it. The real sentiments are usually expressed in the union hall. There he votes and talks and works and voices his opinion and it is this opinion of the rank and file of the men that is being expressed when the walking delegate appears in a given factory and asks for a certain thing.

A gentleman testified here yesterday that the national officers are much more reasonable to talk to than the local officers. That is simply because the rank and file of the men have not such a hold on the national officers and can not throw national officers out of their jobs so easily for failing to carry out the wishes of the men who are suffering the abuses, and therefore a national officer can afford to be somewhat more lenient in dealing with the people. But if I work directly for a union and am told to go to a firm and make certain demands, I must report every word I said to the men there working in that factory. They insist on every abuse being remedied, and I must therefore submit to the manufacturer the abuse and the remedy; the rank and file of the men are directly controlling me. It is a hard job to be a walking delegate; it is a hard job to work for a big body of men. So far as I know, all so-called walking delegates—every one of them—would be able to make a better living in different callings. They do that work at a sacrifice, in a way, simply because they feel that the workingmen's interests are being abused; that they are the sufferers, and in the interest of humanity and civilization—interest as a man. Generally a man acquires principles; he falls in line with their interests, and shares his ability and interests with them so as to get redress for their troubles. It is a wrong on the part of intelligent men to throw on the walking delegate all the blame for creating the trouble.

Q. (By Mr. KENNEDY.) You heard something yesterday about a suspicion that certain business agents or walking delegates were corrupt?— A. Yes. Bosses would only be too willing that there should be such walking delegates, and they would not make such insinuations if that were true. If it were true they would keep still about it, but it is not true. A man becomes a walking delegate generally after he has been tried a long time—been fighting in the trade and had his sufferings; and the men are so alive, the interests that are being touched are so dear and near to the very life of the men, that they are alive to any suspicion in a matter like that where a man is not faithful. I know of one single case, where a man named Alberg, in the cutters' union—he was a member of the executive board, and finally sold out to the boss and became an assistant superintendent during a strike. I have not met during all this time a single workman in that trade who would shake hands with him. They would spit on him. They would go a considerable distance in order to avoid him. They can not think of any reptile, of anything born, that lives, that is meaner than treachery of that kind. The movements these men are engaged in are of vital importance to them; they consider them sacred to their lives and to those of their families, and they consider that treachery of that kind is the meanest that a human being can commit. A burglar, a murderer, a man that commits rape—any crime I could think of, is not half as mean as to endanger the lives and interests of the poor people who are in a quarrel against people that have so much more power than they have. So I do not think there is anything in this.

I should like to say something about politics. You have heard testimony here yesterday and to-day—the proposition made was to use the Government to appoint judges or some high officials that are not amenable to electors to crush out unions. Now, all these manufacturers want to use the Government in their effort to defeat the trade-union men. That same idea is expressed among the trade-union men.

Q. (By Mr. A. L. HARRIS.) The witness did not state it was for the purpose of crushing out trade unionism. It was to get justice, was it not?—A. He was not in favor of trade unions. He was not in favor of dealing with his men in an organized form in any shape or form. He said they were a lot of children; they were not safe outside on the streets by themselves unless they were under his guidance. And yet, in order to save himself from these children, he wants to use the Federal Government, where the judges would not be amenable to the votes of the people, to crush out these people.

Q. It is the State government and not the Federal. The Federal Government already appoints its judges.—A. That same thing expresses itself in an effort on the part of the workmen to see that their side is somewhat represented. I remember a time when it was not quite safe to do picket duty.

Q. (By Mr. CLARKE.) Why not?—A. Because the police were against us. Simply walking within a number of blocks of the factory was not permitted. That was in 1886. The picket to-day is essential to the good conduct of a strike. In our trade the employers have imported men from other States, and they have told these men that they wanted workmen, but did not tell them anything about the strike; simply told them they wanted workmen to come to their place. They offered them work for the year with an agreement at very good wages, so as to break up our strike. Now some of those men, when they come to the city, and we can approach them, we can persuade them that it is not right on their part to cut our throats. That is what we consider they are doing when we are engaged in a struggle at great sacrifice to ourselves and our families—the man that takes our job is actually cutting our throats. I should much prefer being hit over the head with a sandbag to being reduced to the mercy of my boss after I have lost a quarrel. The man that takes my job is inflicting on me a severe damage; and if I can approach a man and submit the conditions to him, and tell him how I was treated—this is what I was paid, this is the character of the suit, this is the price for labor, that is what has been the price for labor, this is how the work was cut down—there are ten chances to one I can persuade him not to take my job. I remember times when I was not permitted to stand on the sidewalk within 4 blocks of my boss's place. Now the police have got orders to interfere only when there is actual violence, and they let me go on the corner and meet the man who asks for the job and talk to him; and this is what the manufacturers call the city authorities being in favor of the strikers. There is not a single case where the city authorities have neglected to arrest and prosecute men that have actually violated the law; but because they have not made all the policemen arrest and prosecute strikers, the manufacturers, every one of them, complain that the city is not dealing justly with them. Now, I should like to say, in the first place, that picketing is essential to the conduct of a strike: that is, being permitted to go around a factory and see who goes in and comes out, and argue with the nonunion man or with the scab, because the workmen are the under dog, so to say, in the quarrel, and they have those chances.

Q. (By Mr. A. L. HARRIS.) Suppose that goes so far as to use insulting remarks.—A. The man against whom the insulting remarks are being used has recourse to law. There is a statute prohibiting a man from calling another bad names; there is another prohibiting a man from assaulting, and the law ought to be carried out to the letter. The community can not live unless the law is enforced.

Q. (By Mr. CLARKE.) Now that you speak of law, I want to ask you right there whether you consider yourself in any way in the employment of the concern after you have left its employment.—A. I am consulting all the time my own interests and the support of my family, and when I am working for a firm that I have helped to maintain and which has grown partially because of my labor, I consider that I have some moral right to the job.

Q. What right do you claim to have under the law to interfere with the conduct of any man's business when you sustain no contract relation whatever to that concern?—A. Simply the right of persuasion; the right of submitting my interests to my fellowmen; the right to talk to a scab and tell him the damages he is inflicting on me and what work we are trying to accomplish, and the fact that if we accomplish it his interest is going to be benefited; the right of common and joint agreement between me and another man to abstain from working when our employers are abusing us in one form or another.

Q. Then you must do this with reference to the hope of being reemployed by that same concern?—A. Yes.

Q. That is all the interest you have in it, then—the hope of being reemployed?—A. Yes; and that hope is generally verified, because every man that testified here yesterday—I mean at least both the shoe man and the other man—testified that they would much rather have their own employees, even after the strike, than to put in new ones; that their plants are adapted to the same class of employees.

Q. You recognize that the strike is a coercive measure—an act of war?—A. Partially; yes.

Q. Then you recognize that picketing is an act of war?—A. Partially; yes. It is to prevent the boss from getting employees so that he may be forced to reemploy us on the terms submitted in the proposition that may be under consideration.

Q. You recognize, then, that an act of war is an interference with the civil rights of a concern?—A. Yes; but then the reduction in wages, or failing to raise the wages when conditions warrant, are acts of war and interference with my civil rights in a time of peace. It is the same thing. I really earn my support in working in the factory. This man that testified here yesterday—he said, in my own case, the work is so specialized that my men are only adapted to do this particular class of work, and this particular job is the only means of his support; and if his wages are reduced, and if a foreman is put on and abuses him, and if his wages are not increased as the cost of living is increased, or if his boss does not share with him, the boss is to that extent making war on this man's interest; and that is war, in the nature of things, you see.

Q. If you and your employer do not get on harmoniously together, do not agree as to wages or hours of labor, or any other condition of employment, you have the option to leave and get employment elsewhere.—A. Not very well; not according to the statement of the man yesterday; there were not any people engaged in the business that use this particular class of skill. Let me cite to you one case that seems to me to cover a large class: A little while ago, about 3 months ago, I worked at the Western Electric Company. While there I went through one of the floors, and there I saw a man feeding a buzz saw with rubber plates. There was a big stack of rubber plates, and he took one of the pieces of plate to put it in that buzz saw and run it through. I asked him how long he had worked there. He said 10 years. He gets $1.50 a day. He had worked at that buzz saw for 3 years. He has a big stack of rubber plates he must feed into that buzz saw every day, that is, 10 hours. When he talked to me he had to move his hand in this way [indicating], what he is used to, as though he would take a piece of rubber plate and put it under this buzz saw. He is a part of this machine. It is not hard work. He has not developed his muscle and has not become hardy enough to apply himself to common labor anywhere, so that he could go out and take a pick and shovel and earn his living. He has become a part of that machine. That machine is the means of his subsistence and that of his family.

Q. Do you claim, as a matter of law and civil right—— A. (Interrupting.) He ought to have some civil rights, and his interest should be protected by law. When the facts are so plain, so evident, and the interests are so vital, so extensive, I claim it ought to be recognized and dealt with according to the necessities of the case.

Q. Your contention is, then, if I understand you, that he has a continuing interest in the employment, even after he leaves it voluntarily?— A. Yes, through the process of strike, and the organization; through the process that we have been discussing.

Q. Now, I would like to have you describe what you consider is legitimate as a means of persuasion.—A. I have partially described that. I can do that further.

Q. I wish you would.—A. I simply tell a man, if he is imported—take the case like that—I tell him partially the history of our trade, what we have succeeded in doing, what the organization has done, that if the organization is broken up the trade will go back to a certain condition in which we have existed before, the abuses that we have been suffering, and the redress we are trying to effect; also offering, in a majority of cases, to provide his support and a ticket for him to go back. Most organizations spend in every strike a very large proportion of their funds for tickets for people who have been imported to go back, or for the maintenance of the men—three or four dollars a week, whatever the average striker gets. If a man shows he understands the trade, and has been brought here by the cunning of the boss, we generally offer to pay him his subsistence the same as any other striker. So these are the inducements offered by the organization—partial payment for subsistence, etc.

Q. Supposing these arguments and inducements do not prevail upon him and he goes into the shop and goes to work, what is the next step?— A. That a good deal depends upon the temper of the men that argue. There are some men that will quietly submit if an injury is inflicted on them, and others will take the next best means to get redress. All the trade unions find violence against their interests.

Q. What are the steps of persuasion brought into use to influence a man who has failed to yield to argument and has gone to work?—A. Well, several. For instance, in one case we have alienated a man from the affections of his co-church members.

Q. That you call persuasion?—A. Yes; we went into the church and denounced the fellow as a traitor to our interests, cutting our throats, sort of sinning against the religious laws, inflicting damage on so many families.

Q. That is one step?—A. That was one of the means; called him a scab.

Q. Called him a scab?—A. Yes; on the streets.

Q. To his face?—A. Yes. As I told you, it depends upon the temperament of the man. We would go after him in a hundred and one ways, if we can, to drive him out of the community.

Q. That you call persuasion?—A. Within the law; and I think under certain conditions it is right for a person to violate the law and take the consequences. Supposing I am fined for calling a man a scab. I am put into a fine, say, of $10 and have to go to jail for 20 days. The abuse that I am suffering may be so great that I would take my medicine. I would tell a man he was a scab, and take my medicine for it and go to jail. . . .

TESTIMONY OF MRS. J. S. ROBB

At 4.55 p. m. Mrs. J. S. Robb requested to be heard as a witness and, being duly sworn, testified as follows:

Q. (By Mr. CLARKE.) Please give your name?—A. Well, there is only one reason that I care—I should not like to have my name published, on account of my husband.

Q. We can not take your testimony without your name.—A. My husband's name is J. S. Robb. We have suffered so much a little more won't hurt.

Q. Will you please give your post-office address?—A. No. 655 Bloomingdale avenue, Chicago.

Q. And your occupation?—A. I am a dressmaker, family seamstress. My husband is a painter.

Q. Do you carry on your work at your home?—A. No; at private families.

Q. You go out, then?—A. Yes; I go out.

Q. Now, we shall be glad to hear your statement.—A. The statement is just this: My husband has been for years contending with the powers that be; he has incurred the enmity of the house painters' union, simply by protecting the interests of his employers.

Q. (By Mr. KENNEDY.) He is a nonunion man?—A. He is a nonunion man at the present time. He has belonged to the painters' union two different times. He has been brought home to me beaten and maimed by the business agents, the entertainment committee—compulsory education.

I have gone to the front as an American woman. We are brought up that way. We are taught it is our duty, if adversity comes, for us to go to the front, if possible. Thank God I owe no man a cent. That has been going on ever since 1886. My husband has earned at his trade $7 since the 1st of last October. He is not allowed to work. There are bosses in the town, the city of Chicago, who are told if that man is given employment they will call strikes, sympathetic strikes; throw out—every building in Chicago can be tied up. . . .

Q. Has he ever sought entrance into the union?—A. He has sought entrance into the union. There was a fine entered against him of $100. He had been a member of the union twice.

Q. What was the offense?—A. The offense was going one Sunday and putting in a skylight over some $7,000 worth of fine electrical machinery while the work was on a strike. There was a star-chamber meeting called and a fine was entered against him of $100. He refused to pay it, consequently a vote of expulsion was taken. The contractors were Angus & Gindele, general contractors.

Q. Had he violated the rule?—A. That was the law. He worked, while there was a strike, in protecting the interests of his employer while putting in that skylight to prevent the destruction of thousands of dollars worth of fine electrical machinery at the power house of the West Side Union Traction Building. That was his offense.

Q. Has his employer not taken care of him since then?—A. Employers don't do those things—not Chicago employers. They laid for him, as they say, some six or seven men, in the halls of that power house, and beat him into insensibility. The policeman (turning her back to the commissioners) never saw it; very conveniently turned his back—policeman on the corner; I have forgotten now his name. Two men coming through the hall saved his life. They beat and kicked him into insensibility.

Q. (By Mr. CLARKE.) Did he know who did it?—A. Entertainment committee; that is all.

Q. Did he ever institute any prosecution?—A. The man was frightened out of his life. He would not allow me to see a lawyer to enter suit. I must have my living taken away from me. I am an American woman. I am not disposed to be thrown on charity. I have had to have coal brought to my house because I had none. I considered I was taking work from some woman that had no protector, when I have a husband who is able and willing to support me, and who has always had, when he has been at work, the very highest rate of wages, regardless of unions or any other corporation, because his employers considered him worthy of it.

Q. Do you wish us to understand that he was intimidated?—A. Certainly. The man is afraid of his life. Now, if he knew I was here this afternoon he would want to leave town to-night, if he had to walk.

Q. (By Mr. KENNEDY.) He will read it in the papers in the morning.—

A. Let him read it; I will stand for it. I went to the painter's union at one time and I told them I wanted them to allow my husband to work and support me; that he was able and willing to work, and I did not propose to be turned on charity by such people; that I was an American woman and as an American woman wanted my support in its proper channel.

Q. (By Mr. CLARKE.) What answer did you get?—A. They let him alone for a few months.

Q. Let him work?—A. Let him work.

Q. (By Mr. KENNEDY.) Did they call him a scab?—A. They called him a scab.

Q. Have you any children?—A. No.

Q. Does the fact that they call him a scab affect you socially?—A. Doesn't affect me socially, because I consider it is an honor to be independent. I am the one that has had to suffer, instead of having the comforts that I should have as an American woman. As my husband is a citizen and a voter and has had honorary service through the civil war and 5 years in the regular army—George Washington's Own—if that does not entitle him to protection under the Constitution of these United States in supporting me, is there any place in the world where there is protection?

Q. (By Mr. CLARKE.) Are you acquainted with the wives of working people?—A. I haven't the time. Every day is occupied that I possibly have. I have my regular customers, my private dressmaking. I have very ordinary prices. I do not get the pay my work should give me, simply because I feel—our expenses are very small; if you were to see the place we live in and the conditions under which I live, and my grocery bills, and the old soft coal I burn and all of that—of course I get two bushels of soft coal for a quarter, where hard coal is $7 a ton, you know.

Q. Do you know whether the wives of other working men consider it an honor to have their husbands called scabs?—A. You don't understand. I don't mean it exactly that way. I consider the word scab should be eliminated from the English language.

Q. You regard it as a term of reproach?—A. I regard it as a term of reproach. It is the vilest, to my mind, most contemptible word than can be applied. The word demands all the corruption, the low vileness that is in a man's character—to call another a scab.

Q. (By Mr. KENNEDY.) What synonym would you suggest to be used in the place of the word scab?—A. Well, I don't know that there is any word in the English language that can take the place of that word scab.

Q. (By Mr. CLARKE.) You think it is generally regarded as such a word of reproach that the use of it is practically intimidation?—A. I do. I think the word scab—as I have expressed my opinion freely and fully, there is nothing more I could say on the word scab. I don't think there is a word in the English language or that can be coined that would express the filth, contempt, and corruption of the word. It is a word I never allow used in the house. I have had a little adopted boy, and I have never allowed him to use the word.

Q. What remedy would you suggest?—A. My remedy lies in the governor of the State. Any corporation that is not for the benefit—is not conducted for the benefit of a community, its charter should be annulled. As long as they conduct themselves in a way that is beneficial, organization is all right. I belong to several myself. I find great benefit from them, in one way or another.

Q. (By Mr. KENNEDY.) What organizations do you belong to?—A. I am an officer of the National Blue and Gray organization, and I am a member of the relief corps.

Q. Do you belong to any secret societies?—A. I do not believe in secret societies; no.

Q. Do you have in any of these societies rules for the government and discipline of the members?—A. We have never had any occasion to use them.

Q. Have you such rules?—A. We have; very light.

Q. Provide punishment?—A. Don't know that there is any punishment.

Q. Do you provide for expulsion in case of nonpayment of dues?—A. No, not any of the organizations; there is no provision for expulsion. We are supposed to do our duty by one another and go on humanitarian principles. If my husband goes out to his work, or to look for work, I don't see that it is the right of any man or men to prevent him—the Constitution of the United States guarantees life, liberty, and the pursuit of happiness; and if the support and care of the ones that belong to a man—if that is not the pursuit of happiness I can not understand what is.

Q. (By Mr. CLARKE.) Do you feel that adequate police protection is afforded in case of these labor difficulties?—A. Adequate police protection is an unknown quantity, in a measure. Different minds have different opinions as to what adequate police protection is. During the Debs strike I saw policemen wearing white ribbons.

Q. What did that mean?—A. That was the American Railway Union emblem; it was also the Christian Temperance emblem. They were wearing the white ribbon in sympathy for the Debs organization. If the police and union labor leaders were taken out of politics, I think that it would be a great deal better. My husband is a voter; he is a citizen; what taxes we have to pay, we pay; and I think every man that is a taxpayer should have protection.

Q. (By Mr. A. L. HARRIS.) How long was your husband in the Army? —A. Four years in the volunteers, civil war, and 5 years in George Washington's Own First Infantry; and it seems to me that a man who has given 9 years of his life to his country's service is entitled to some protection under the laws. My husband is of Scotch birth, not American born. He is an American to all intents and purposes.

Q. How old is your husband?—A. Fifty-six years old.

Q. (By Mr. CLARKE.) You think your husband would not have any objection to belonging to the union?—A. My husband has never refused to belong to the union, but the conditions were such in the unions that no honorable man could belong to them and keep his respect. When a man belongs to a labor union once he ceases to be a free agent; he loses his individuality; it is what the president or the secretary wishes to do. In the city of Chicago to-day there are hundreds of families suffering for the necessities of life. Is the secretary or the business agent—are their cellars empty? The business agent draws $3 or whatever the standard rate of pay is. Gompers drawing his $9,000 a year——

Q. (By Mr. KENNEDY.) Who?—A. Gompers. What is his salary?

Mr. KENNEDY. Mr. Gompers' salary is $1,500.

The WITNESS. Mr. Gompers—I give him credit for a great deal of executive ability. To have to work at his trade as a cigar maker, his average at $15 a week, he would not be receiving $1,500 a year. He would not be going to Cuba for his health. His cellars are not empty. His children are not staying home from school for the need of proper clothing.

Mr. KENNEDY. From what I know of Mr. Gompers, and I have been at his house in Washington, he lives as ordinarily as any $12 a week man.

The WITNESS. What does he do with his family?

Mr. KENNEDY. He has a very large family, and lives very simply.

The WITNESS. They have all the comforts of life. Who is O'Connell?

Mr. KENNEDY. I do not know him.

The WITNESS. He is one of them; patent leather shoes and fine clothes. There are hundreds of them. I could mention them by name—officers of different unions; they are not suffering.

Q. (By Mr. CLARKE.) Don't you think the families of some of the strikers are suffering very much?—A. Most assuredly they are. I know a grocer who has refused them credit, and they are absolutely suffering. Unions and labor organizations are all right in their place. They are like everything else; they want to be used properly; and every law that is passed—well, of course, I am not a lawmaker, but I keep well read as to the laws that are passed, try to, according to my limited time.

Q. Have you any further statement to make on any phase of this question?—A. No, not exactly; only that I think there should be something done by the Government, either State or national, or some way, to make it possible for a man that is willing to work and support his family to be allowed to do it. My husband is a citizen; and, as I say, we pay our taxes, what little we have to pay. A few years ago I had 7 rooms, all carpeted and nicely furnished. Now I have 4 little old holes of rooms that I would be ashamed for anybody to see. I haven't a carpet on my floor. I have some little curtains up to the windows. I have an old cook stove that you would not get 2 cents for from an iron man. When a man earns $7—not because he is not willing. My husband never drinks a drop—a sober, industrious, honest man. His people were painters and grainers, the very best in Scotland, before him, for generations. He has been at nothing but the trade all his life, except the time he was in the Army, and why is it that I must keep to the front, as I consider I am taking the bread from some woman's mouth that has no protector?

Q. You don't know of his offending the labor people in any way except—— —A. (Interrupting.) I suppose he disobeyed the laws of the unions. They say, "We will run you out of town." "Ain't you gone yet?" "Your time will come." Well, not with the wife he has.

The Philosophy of Organized Labor

The following testimony was given by Samuel Gompers, President, American Federation of Labor, before the (U.S.) Industrial Commission on Capital and Labor, meeting in Washington, April 18, 1890.

TESTIMONY OF SAMUEL GOMPERS

Mr. Samuel Gompers was introduced as a witness, and, being duly sworn, testified as follows:

Mr. GOMPERS. With your permission I would say I would like my testimony to be general, where it will be of greater advantage, and specific and in detail, where the same purposes can be accomplished. My only desire is to give as clear testimony to the commission as I may be able to give.

Q. (By Mr. C. J. HARRIS.) What is your name and residence, and official position?—A. Samuel Gompers, president of the American Federation of Labor. My residence is No. 44 East One hundred and tenth street, New York City. The headquarters of the organization is at 423 and 425 G street NW., Washington, D. C.

Q. (By Mr. FARQUHAR.) Is the American Federation of Labor an organization that grew from its own genesis, or was it the successor of any other organization in the United States?—A. It was the successor of the National Labor Union, which went out of existence in 1868; rather, that was the last convention of that organization that was ever held; and from that day until 1881 there did not exist a general organization of labor in the United States, not at least on the trade union basis of organization. In 1881 a conference was held at Terre Haute, Ind., where the subject of the formation of a new national labor movement—ought to be inaugurated, or called into existence; and a call was issued for a congress to take place at Pittsburg, Pa., in November, 1881. It was there that the organization then known as the Federation of Organized Trades and Labor Unions of the United States and Canada was formed. It continued in existence from then under that name until 1886, when the convention, in-

Report on the (U.S.) Industrial Commission on Capital and Labor (Washington, D.C., Government Printing Office, 1901), Vol. VIII, pp. 606–657.

stead of being held at St. Louis, as the previous convention determined it should be held, a general vote of the members of the organization was taken, and Columbus, Ohio, was substituted for the place to hold the convention; and this change was made in order that the various national unions unaffiliated with the old organization might have an opportunity of meeting with the affiliated organizations and forming an amalgamation under some new name and greater activity and opportunity. The amalgamation was effected, and the name American Federation of Labor adopted. . . .

Q. (By Mr. FARQUHAR.) What is the result in the last 10 years? Have strikes decreased or increased—that is, compared with the increase of organized labor?—A. During the first year of organizations, as a rule, there are strikes. When workmen remain organized for any considerable length of time, strikes are reduced in number. It is a peculiar fact that when workmen are unorganized they imagine their employers are almighty and themselves absolutely impotent. When workmen organize for the first time, this transformation takes place: they imagine their employers absolutely impotent and themselves almighty, and the result of it is there is conflict. The employer, so far as strikes begun in his establishment are concerned, resents immediately the assumption of the workmen to appear by committee. He has been accustomed to look upon himself, as to his factory or his establishment, as "monarch of all he surveys" with undisputed sway, and the fact that his employees have an entity as an organization, to be represented by a committee, is something unheard of by him and absolutely intolerable. He imagines immediately that it is a question as to his right to his property; imagines immediately that his property is threatened, and surrounds himself with such safeguards—as the lamented Gladstone once said, "The entire resources of civilization had not yet been exhausted"—arms everybody who swears loyalty to the company, and often surrounds himself with a mercenary armed force, and all the wiles and devices that the acumen of our legal friends can suggest are always employed to overcome, overawe these "mutineers" against his authority.

Q. (By Mr. RATCHFORD.) To what extent, if any, is the employer, in your judgment, responsible for that condition of affairs?—A. To the same extent that the bourgeois of France, the royalists of France, were responsible in cowing the people of France, which resulted in the revolution and the brutality manifested by the people when they got power. The employers have simply cut wages whenever they thought it convenient. They looked upon their employees as part of the machinery; to exhibit, perhaps, some little sympathy when one was very critically injured or suffering, and then expected the worship of them all; the cutting of wages time and again, in season and out of season; the discharge of a man who proposed to exercise his right as a man, whether it was as a workman or as a citizen; and so on, driving practically the courage and heart out of the man; and when, through some incident, of which there are thousands, the men are organized of their own volition, quite frequently they touch shoulders for the first time outside of the shop—they touch shoulders, and the thrill simply enthuses them and intoxicates them with new-found power. It is only after the organization has administered a very costly lesson to the employer, and it is only after the workmen themselves have felt the pangs of hunger, perhaps, or other sacrifices resultant from strikes they suffer when unprepared, unorganized, that they are more careful of each other—both sides. They organize and try to meet each other and discuss with each other, and the better the workmen are organized the more able are they to convince the employer that there is an ethical side to the demands of labor. It required 40,000 people in the city of New York in my own trade in 1877 to demonstrate to the employers that we had a right to be heard in our own defense of our trade, and an opportunity to be heard in our own interests. It cost the miners of the country, in 1897, 16 weeks of suffering to secure a national conference and a national agreement. It cost the railroad brotherhoods long months of suffering, many of them sacrificing their positions, in the railroad strike of 1877, and in the Chicago, Burlington and Quincy strike, of the same year, to secure from the employers the right to be heard through committees, their representatives—that is, their committees of the organization to secure these rights. Workmen have had to stand the brunt of the suffering. The American Republic was not established without some suffering, without some sacrifice, and no tangible right has yet been achieved in the interest of the people unless it has been secured by sacrifices and persistency. After a while we become a little more tolerant to each other and recognize all have rights; get around the table and chaff each other; all recognize that they were not so reasonable in the beginning. Now we propose to meet and discuss our interests, and if we can not agree we propose in a more reasonable way to conduct our contests, each to decide how to hold out and bring the other one to terms. A strike, too, is to industry as the right that the British people contended for in placing in the House of Commons the power to close the purse strings to the Government. The rights of the British people were secured in two centuries— between 1500 and 1600—more than ever before, by the securing of that power to withhold the supplies; tied up the purse strings and compelled the Crown to yield. A strike on the part of workmen is to close production and compel better terms and more rights to be acceded to the producers. The economic results of strikes to workers have been advantageous. Without strikes their rights would not have been considered. It is not that workmen or organized labor desires the strike, but it will tenaciously hold to the right to strike. We recognize that peaceful industry is necessary to successful civilized life, but the right to strike and the preparation to strike is the greatest preventive to strikes. If the workmen were to make up their minds to-morrow that they would under no circumstances strike, the employers would do all the striking for them in the way of lesser wages and longer hours of labor.

Q. (By Representative GARDNER.) The whole philosophy is contest and conquest?—A. Except when there be like power on both sides; then it becomes reason, by the power on both sides; it then comes to reason rather than contest and conquest. It becomes a matter then of reason; and, as I tried to say in the earlier part of my testimony, no matter how just a cause is, unless that cause is backed up with power to enforce it, it is going to be crushed and annihilated. I tried to illustrate some time ago this proposition by the fact that when England has a dispute with the Afghanistans she immediately proceeds to bombard them unless they acquiesce in her demands; and she would have done the same thing in Venezuela; but when England has a dispute with the United States, she says, "Let us arbitrate" this question; and I think the United States in this regard, or any other nation, is not any different in that regard at all; and the employers are practically in the same position. When the strike occurred at Pullman, Mr. Pullman said he had nothing to arbitrate. His people were unorganized, but he met the committees; not now; he don't meet anyone now; but he used to meet the committees of his unorganized workmen; and the railroad managers—they simply throw their unorganized workmen into the streets if they have any grievances or supposed grievances, but when it comes to organized engineers, firemen, or conductors, or trainmen, who have fairly well organized unions, why, they meet them in conference, pat them on the back sometimes, and say they are jolly good fellows. The economic results to the workers have been invariably beneficial. Even strikes which have been lost have had their good, beneficial results upon the workers. For after all the question must be looked upon in a comprehensive, in a broad way. If the workers, say, have struck for an increase in wages, and the employers refuse to concede them, and finally defeat the workmen, yet as a matter of fact it is almost invariably the case that those who have taken the places of the men who went on strike were themselves receiving less wages before doing so. It is seldom, if ever, that a workman will go from a position where he receives higher wages to take the place of a striker at lower wages. It therefore shows that those who take the places of the strikers improve their material position in the matter of wages. It is asserted that those who strike are compelled to look out for other positions, which is naturally true; but in only isolated cases do they accept positions which pay them less than those they struck against; so that in the sum total of it there is an economic and social advantage. Strikes have convinced the employers of the economic advantage of reduced hours of labor; strikes have rid many a trade of the "jerry builder;" of the fraudulent employer who won't pay wages; strikes have enforced lien laws for wages, where laws have been previously unable to secure the payment; strikes have organized employers as well as employees; strikes have made strong and independent men who were for a long period of years cowards; strikes have made a more independent citizenship of men who often voted simply because it pleased the boss; strikes have given men greater lease of life; strikes have resulted in higher wages, better homes, and demand for better things; strikes have organized wage-earners, too. The strike has taken the place of the barbarous weapons of the dirk and bludgeon. Strikes in the modern sense can occur only in civilized countries.

Q. (By Mr. C. J. HARRIS.) Does the community at large suffer from strikes?—A. Seldom, if any, except temporarily. It is alleged by some that strikes diminish the wealth of a community and do irreparable injury. If a strike takes place and is not adjusted, it is the very best evidence, of itself, that the community is not suffering for the want of that article. If the community would begin to suffer for that article, employers would immediately concede the demand of the strikers, and the time which is lost in the strike is always made up in a greater continuity of industry after the strike is closed. It is seldom, if ever, workmen are continually employed throughout the entire year. A strike is simply a transferring of the time when idleness shall occur from the advantage of the employer to the advantage of the employees.

Q. (By Mr. KENNEDY.) A distinguished witness who was before this commission several weeks ago said that no strike was ever lost; if the men didn't gain the point in the matter of wages, they gained more in bringing their grievances before the public. Is that the view you take of it?—A. I have tried to make the same point in another way; yes. The social results and the economic advantages are beyond measure; and yet, I say that it is the constant effort of our organization to prevent strikes. We want to secure the same beneficent results without cessation of industry or interruption of commerce, and that can only be done when the workers are organized and the employers are organized, and the effect of the possession of machinery, of labor machinery, on production and distribution is in itself power, is in itself organization. I do not pretend to say—nor do I wish any wrong inference to be drawn from any statement I might make—that, by the organization of labor, strikes will be entirely eliminated from our system of society, from industry and commerce. I do not believe that that is at all possible so long as men's interests are absolutely diverse. . . .

Q. What are the effects of new and improved machinery on labor?—A. With the introduction of machinery, of new tools, and the division of labor and its subdivision trades become eliminated, or I should say that the different branches of one trade become differentiated or specialized. The trades which usually are annihilated are those which are subject to division more than any other. The trades that become differentiated and classified into various branches do not become extinguished; there are simply a larger number that go to make up the one finished product.

Q. So that your opinion is that specialization in a trade itself does not decrease the number of operatives?—A. Not necessarily. It would if a status would be created, but fortunately for humanity it would be a most difficult thing to establish a status from which there can be no departure either one way or another, and with the opportunities for education in our time I have little fear. Any attempt to establish status would be a failure, and a departure from status would be improvement. The fact is that with the division or subdivision of labor occasioned by the introduction of new tools and machinery the production of wealth or the necessaries and luxuries of life is carried on with greater velocity and speed than ever before. It tends to the cheapening of the selling price; it tends to the cheapening of the cost of production; and the movement on the part of labor for less hours of daily toil increases the demands, wants, and desires of the great body of consumers and gives an additional impetus to production again, and each in turn causes a still greater cheapening in the methods of production and gives an opportunity to the shorter-hour workers to gratify more desires and wants and be greater consumers of the wealth produced; so that there is not by any means a lessening of production. It does not mean the annihilation of the industry. It is true that under the present economic conditions during the process of the introduction and the period immediately after the introduction of new machinery and the specialization of different branches of industry it disarranges that industry, and as a consequence large numbers are thrown out of employment. It rearranges itself in the course of time, but unless the workers avail themselves of the opportunity to get still less hours of labor and increase their consuming power numbers of men are rendered what is popularly known as useless and superfluous, and the lack of a sufficient power of consumption on the part of the people, or rather the lack of opportunity for the widening and broadening of their consuming power, is the fact which contracts seasons of employment and throws workers out of employment. The productivity of labor is so great that unless the hours of labor are reduced those who are employed as producers have little leisure; then again, as consumers, if they do not increase their consuming power of necessity plants close down because labor with machinery has produced so much and the people have not consumed the production commensurately with the increased amount produced.

Q. So that you would say that the introduction of new machinery does not make a permanent displacement of labor?—A. It would, were it not for the extent of the movement of the wage earners to reduce the hours of labor. When the wage earners do not reduce their hours of labor in proportion to the progress made in the introduction of machinery, new

212 THE CITY AND THE FACTORY

tools, and the division and subdivision of labor, then there is a greater number who are unemployed.

Q. Would you say that new machinery, bringing in more rapid processes of production, has lightened the toil of the operatives?—A. No. The organizations of labor have lightened the toil of the workingman, if the toil has been lightened. As a matter of fact, the velocity with which machinery is now run calls forth the expenditure of nearly all the physical and mental force which the wage-earner can give to industry. In substantiation of my negative answer to your question, I would call attention to the fact that after the introduction of machinery, machinery propelled by the motive power of steam, the hours of labor of the working people were from sunup to sundown, and the machinery, which was costly, was not of advantage to the possessor unless it could be operated for a longer period than from sunup to sundown, and it was in that case as perhaps in all, that necessity, being the mother of invention, that which was absent was forthcoming; that was, artificial light to take the place of the rays of the sun after it had set for the day, and with the introduction of artificial light, gas, came the lengthening of the hours of labor of the working people both of the United States and continental Europe. Wherever machinery was at all introduced the object was to have the machinery operated as long as possible, and with the aid of gas the opportunity came. The organizations of the working people were very fragmentary, and few and weak. The hours of labor were lengthened until lives were destroyed by the thousands; and then came the introduction of woman and child labor. There was no restrictive legislation for them; and then came the efforts of the organizations of labor that called forth a yearning and cry of the whole human family against the slaughter of innocents in the factories of Great Britain particularly, and subsequently in the United States. And it was the power of organized labor—first in feeling that its cause was right, that men and women were being cut down in their manhood and womanhood and childhood, dwarfed or killed, that in a few generations the working people were bound to deteriorate physically, mentally, and morally; that they were deteriorating physically, mentally, and morally; and their ability as producers of wealth would have been destroyed in a few generations had the possessors of machines at that time continued in full sway—it was the efforts of the trade unions of Great Britain, first in their protests, second, in their strikes, and third in their appeals to the public conscience, which called forth the factory legislation which limited the hours of labor of women and children in certain industries. . . .

Q. (By Mr. CLARKE.) You believe in the wage system then, rather than in partnership?—A. I can not assent to that. I know that we are operating under the wage system. As to what system will ever come to take its place I am not prepared to say. I have given this subject much thought; I have read the works of the most advanced economists, competent economists in all schools of thought—the trade unionist, the socialist, the anarchist, the single taxer, the cooperationist, etc. I am not prepared to say, after having read, and with an honest endeavor to arrive at a conclusion—I am not prepared to say that either of their propositions are logical, scientific, or natural. I know that we are living under the wage system, and so long as that lasts, it is our purpose to secure a continually larger share for labor, for the wealth producers. Whether the time shall come, as this constantly increasing share to labor goes on, when profits shall be entirely eliminated, and the full product of labor, the net result of production, go to the laborer, thus abolishing the wage system; or whether, on the other hand, through the theory of the anarchist, there should be an abolition of all title in land other than its occupation and use, the abolition of the monopoly of the private issuance of money, the abolition of the patent system—whether we will return to the first principles; or whether, under the single tax, taxing the land to the full value of it—I am perfectly willing that the future shall determine and work out. I know that as the workers more thoroughly organize, and continually become larger sharers in the product of their toil, they will have the better opportunities of their physical and mental cultivation instilled into them, higher hopes and aspirations, and they will be the better prepared to meet the problems that will then confront them. For the present it is our purpose to secure better conditions and instill a larger amount of manhood and independence into the hearts and minds of the workers, and to broaden their mental sphere and the sphere of their affections.

Q. Is it not true that for many years, the tendency to improved condition of the working people of this country has been very marked, and that to-day they are larger sharers in their product than ever before?—A. That is true; yes, and it is wholly due to the efforts of their own organization.

Q. (By Senator KYLE.) You would not agree to the statement sometimes made that the conditions of the working man are growing worse and worse?—A. Oh, that is perfectly absurd.

Q. Of course you lay the improved conditions to the organization of labor?—A. Yes. That can be easily proven, for, as a matter of fact, where the workers remain unorganized, as a rule they have not shared in the great improvements that the working people have who have been organized, and, judging from cause and effect, one can easily determine that that for which I contend is a fact. During the entire industrial revival of industry of 1884 to 1886 and 1887, the textile workers in Cohoes, N. Y., I think, were the only body of working people in the country who suffered a reduction of wages, despite the revival of industry. They were unorganized. But, of course, I want to say this in connection with this matter: In our present economic condition of society we have with a very great degree of regularity a period of these industrial panics that the student can determine almost with the exactness that an astronomer does of the comets, the coming of these periods of industrial crises. Quite a number do not observe this economic phenomena. The worker knows that during these industrial panics he is out of a job; and you might have all the philosophy in the world, all the facts in the world to demonstrate the truthfulness of your position, but he is out of a job, and he can not understand that there has been any social improvement, not even that he has improved beyond the condition of his forefathers 10 centuries ago; he knows he is out of a job, and he is hungry, and the prospects of something in the future are very remote, and to him the world has been growing worse all the time; the world is in an awful condition, and it is in an awful condition truly, and we must remember this, when we consider the social progress; we must not compare this year with the last, or last year with the year before, but compare it for a century by decades, then the marvelous progress can be easily observed. One, of course, can not—unless he is as old as my friend, Major Farquhar—go back a century, but most of us young men can go back 20 or 30 years; we can mark the condition, and that which we do not know of our own knowledge we can ascertain of truthful recorders.

Q. To what do you attribute the vastly superior condition of the American workingmen over the European; the social condition; the advanced, you might say, scale of wages paid in America over the European condition?—A. First, the working people of Europe have emerged from a condition of slavery and serfdom to that of wage laborers. The workingmen of America have not had this hereditary condition of slavery and serfdom. There has been no special status for them as slaves or serfs, and in theory, at least, they were supposed to be equals to all others.

Another reason is the climatic conditions that obtain in our country. The changes from extreme heat to extreme cold make the people more active, more nervous; accelerates their motion, accelerates their thought; again, the vast domain of land, rich soil, that even to-day is beyond speculation, much less the knowledge of our own people—all these things have contributed to a better material condition for the working people of our country. I should add, I think, that the climate conditions, requiring better food, more nutritious food, better clothing, more comfortable clothing, better houses, better homes, have all been contributing factors for the workers to insist upon receiving—to secure these things in the shape of higher wages.

Q. He demands higher wages and gets them?—A. Yes.

Q. Comparatively higher wages?—A. He gets higher wages; comparatively higher wages.

Then again I will say that the productivity of the American laborer is far greater than that of his brother workman in any part of the world.

Q. How do you rate that?—A. I can not begin to tell you. I can say, however, that in every mechanical trade, when European workmen come over to this country and stand beside their American fellow workingmen it simply dazes them—the velocity of motion, the deftness, the quickness, the constant strain. The European bricklayer, the European carpenter, the European compositor—printer, the European tailor comes over here and works in the shop, or factory, or office, and he is simply intoxicated by the rapidity of the movements of the American workingman, and it is some months, with the greatest endeavor, before he can at all come near the production of the American workingman. He must do it in time or he will go without a job. . . .

Q. (By Senator KYLE.) I would like to ask you one more question, just in a word, if you can state to the commission your view of the outlook of the aggregations of capital in what are called trusts to-day upon the products as delivered to the consumer.—A. What, in price or quality?

Q. In price and quality; in the way the things are going on at the present time.—A. They have been increased; whether increased as a result of the trust or not I am not prepared to say. Some time to-day I referred to a number of causes which contributed to the enhancement of prices. I have called attention, too, to the fact that the constant tendency of prices is downward.

Q. You can not say, then, in the language of the platform gentlemen, "that we view with alarm," etc.?—A. No; I am not at all alarmed.

Q. With the present condition of things?—A. No; not at all. I am not a cheap man, anyway.

Q. You can give better prices to the laboring men, even if it has enhanced prices to the consumer a little bit?—A. The tendency of prices is downward. For a brief period there may be a fluctuation due to many causes; some I have already enumerated—I do not care to repeat them— by which prices are enhanced, but they soon fall back by reason of the labor-saving processes; the processes by which production is cheapened compels a lower selling price.

Q. If you were going to write a political platform to-day, then, to put the question straight, you would not begin by inveighing against trusts in the strongest language?—A. I have not been and am not likely to write platforms of political parties. That is something I am rather safe from. I have not caught the fever yet, and trust to continue to live free from it.

Q. (By Mr. A. L. HARRIS.) Then I take it that you do not believe that the rich are getting richer in this country and the poor constantly getting poorer?—A. I do not believe that the poor are getting poorer; those who are rich are becoming richer.

Q. I put it all together in order to give the quotation.—A. Yes; it seems to become a catch phrase, you know, but I do not think that they necessarily go together. There is a greater productivity in the world to-day, and the wage-earners are getting a larger share of the product of labor. They are not getting the share which, in my judgment, they are entitled to by any means.

Q. (By Mr. CLARKE.) Several times you have alluded to the antagonism between labor and capital?—A. I think that I did not say any antagonism between labor and capital.

Q. Perhaps you said between labor and its employers?—A. No; laborers and their employers.

Q. Yes; very well. Now is it not true that there is a very large identity of interests between them; that the influence of trades unionism is to promote that community of interest?—A. Wherever there is community of interest the trade union is willing to promote it.

Q. Is it not true that a great many working people of this country are themselves small capitalists?—A. Working people?

Q. Yes.—A. To a very limited extent they are—unless I do not comprehend the technical meaning of the term as you express it—the working people.

Q. For example, they are very large depositors in savings institutions? —A. That is not capital. A man having money in the bank would in itself not make him a capitalist.

Q. Is it not true those deposits are loaned very largely to the business affairs—in many cases to the employer of this labor?—A. Certainly.

Q. In that case which is the capitalist, the borrower or the lender?— A. Neither. The capitalist is the one having wealth, money, which is used for the purpose of creating additional wealth. That which is held as wealth and not used in production, for the creation of additional wealth, is not capital.

Q. Well, is it not true that there is capital and capital; there is productive capital and there is capital which is not engaged, not embarked in any industry which employs labor?—A. Then it is not capital; it is wealth, but not capital.

Q. I see your distinction; but the capital that is employed in productive industry sustains very close relation with labor, so there ought to be a very great harmony of interests between the owners of that capital and the owners of labor?—A. There has never yet existed identity of interests between buyer and seller of an article. If you have anything to sell and I want to buy it your interest and mine are not identical.

Q. (By Mr. A. L. HARRIS.) Is there not a possibility that the day will come when they will be substantially identical, when they recognize each other's rights?—A. I should regard that upon the same plan as I would the panaceas that are offered by our populists, socialists, anarchists, and single tax friends, as very remote and very far removed, if that time should ever come. I am perfectly satisfied to fight the battles of to-day, of those here, and those that come to-morrow, so their conditions may be improved, and they may be better prepared to fight in the contests or solve the problems that may be presented to them. The hope for a perfect millennium—well, it don't come every night; it don't come with the twinkling of the eye; it is a matter which we have got to work out, and every step that the workers make or take, every vantage point gained, is a solution in itself. I have often inquired of men who have ready-made patent solutions of this social problem, and I want to say to you, sir, that I have them offered to me on an average of two or three a week, and they are all equally unsatisfactory. I maintain that we are solving the problem every day; we are solving the problems as they confront us. One would imagine by what is often considered as the solution of the problem that it is going to fall among us, that a world cataclysm is going to take place; that there is going to be a social revolution; that we will go to bed one night under the present system and the morrow morning wake up with a revolution in full blast, and the next day organize a Heaven on earth. That is not the way that progress is made; that is not the way the social evolution is brought about; that is not the way the human family are going to have interests advanced. We are solving the problem day after day. As we get an hour's more leisure every day it means millions of golden hours, of opportunities, to the human family. As we get 25 cents a day wages increase it means another solution, another problem solved, and brings us nearer the time when a greater degree of justice and fair dealing will obtain among men. . . .

Q. There was some expression in what you read last there about wealth having the control of a State or two. Now, is it not a fact that popular government prevails in most of the States of this Union, and the people, irrespective of their means, vote without intimidation, and that their votes are honestly counted?—A. Yes; theoretically.

Q. Then how can it be true that wealth controls the State?—A. That is, practically.

Q. Well, how does wealth control the State?—A. It controls the political parties; it controls the avenues for advancement; it controls the State.

Q. Well, then, it must do it through somebody's weakness or corruption, since the people vote and their votes are counted?—A. A people who are economically dependent are not politically independent. . . .

Q. (By Mr. CLARKE.) Do you not think it is true that the average legislator is very anxious to please the working people of the country and to promote their interests, so far as he possibly can, without injuring the industries of his State?—A. The average legislator is not a very courageous man. I have spoken with a very large number of legislators, and found them individually to be intelligent men as a rule; and I have found them, when it came to a question of their collective action for the purpose of advancing a practical thought that they would privately advocate, I found them either unwilling or incapable to do it.

The Sweat Shops

The "sweating system" is one of respectable antiquity and is a surviving remnant of the industrial system which preceded the factory system, when industry was chiefly conducted on the piece-price plan in small shops or the homes of the workers. Machinery developed the modern factory and concentrated labor, but in the tailoring trades, the practice of sending out garments, ready-cut, to be made by journeymen at their homes and at a price per garment, has survived and is still maintained in custom work, in which the journeyman is still a skilled tailor who makes the whole garment. The modern demand for ready-made clothing in great quantities and of the cheaper grades, has, however, led to much subdivision of the labor on garments, and with it to the substitution of the contractor or sweater, with groups of employés in separate processes, for the individual tailor, skilled in all of them.

The odious but expressive name, "sweating," has been attached to the business because of its evil nature and consequences. In its worst form, and there are doubtless degrees in its development, it is simply extortion practiced upon people whose environment prevents their escape from it; in other words, it is a deliberate preying upon the necessities of the poor. In its economical aspect it is the culmination and final fruit of the competitive system in industry.

In practice, sweating consists of the farming out by competing manufacturers to competing contractors the material for garments, which, in turn, is distributed among competing men and women to be made up. The middle-man, or contractor, is the sweater, (though he also may be himself subjected to pressure from above) and his employés are the sweated or oppressed. He contracts to make up certain garments, at a given price per piece and then hires other people to do the work at a less price. His profit lies in the difference between the two prices. In the process he will furnish shop-room and machines to some, and allow others, usually the finishers, to take the work to their living and lodging-rooms in tenements.

The sweater may be compelled to under-bid his fellow contractor in order to get work, but he can count with a degree of certainty, on the

Bureau of Labor Statistics of Illinois, *Seventh Biennial Report* (Springfield, Ill., 1893), pp. 357–399.

eagerness of the people who work for him to also under-bid each other, so as to leave his margin of profit but little impaired. The system thrives upon the increasing demand for cheap, ready-made clothing, cheap cloaks, and cheap suits for children, which demand springs in turn from the rivalry of competing dealers and producers. Thus each class preys upon the other, and all of them upon the last and weakest.

Such is the logic and the operation of the process called sweating; it is practiced somewhat in other industries, but finds its fullest scope in the garment trade, because the articles can readily, and with comparative safety, be distributed to the shops and abodes of the workers. But the system is not new, except in new countries and new cities, and it is now hardly new in Chicago. . . .

IN CHICAGO

In Chicago, where it dates back scarcely a generation, the sweating system seems to be a direct outgrowth of the factory system; that is, the sweat-shops have gradually superseded the manufacturers' shops. It increases, with the demand for cheap clothing, the influx of cheap labor, and the consequent subdivision of the processes of manufacture. In the clothing trades in Chicago, three different sorts of shops have been developed, known among the employés as the "inside shops," or those conducted on the factory system by the manufacturers themselves; the "outside shops," or those conducted by the contractors; and the "home shops" or family groups.

Inside, or Manufacturers' Shops

In the inside shops the manufacturer deals with his employés through foremen and forewomen instead of contractors. These shops are in large buildings, steam is provided for motive power, the sanitary ordinances are, in a measure, observed, and the establishments, being large and permanent, are known to the munipical authorities and are subject to inspection. Even these shops, in which there is, strictly, no sub-letting, are pervaded and dominated by the influence of the sweating system. There is but little uniformity of hours, wages, rules, length of season or proportion of men to women and children. The competition of the outside contractors renders the position of employés constantly more precarious, and the inside shops which thrive are those which approximate most closely to the organization of the sweaters' shops, substituting many subdivisions of labor for the skilled workmen.

Formerly these shops employed cutters, button-holers and tailors or cloakmakers who did the whole work, taking the garment from the cutter and completing it, doing both machine and hand work. To increase their speed these skilled hands now have "hand-girls" who do the simple sewing, put on buttons, draw basting threads, etc. Formerly the skilled tailors or cloakmakers constituted a large majority of the employés, but with the growth of the sweating system the cutters alone increase in number and their speed is multiplied by the use of steam machinery. All goods not needed to fill urgent orders are now given direct from the cutters to the sweaters' shops. Some manufacturers have modified their own shops to mere cutters' shops and send all their garments to the contractors; others have found it unprofitable to manufacture for themselves and have resorted to the sweaters entirely. Thus the sweating system strengthens itself and eliminates the clothing factory proper. Very few of these remain, and those which were found are not enumerated as sweating shops.

Outside, or Contractors' Shops

Substantially all manufacturers employ a number of sweaters who conduct small shops on their own account. These underbid each other to obtain work. They do not make common cause against the manufacturers, either by combining among themselves or by uniting with their employés. On the contrary, they exploit their employés to the utmost to compensate themselves for the exactions of the manufacturers and the competition among themselves.

The economic position of the sweater is anomalous. He has no commercial risks; he gives the manufacturer no considerable security for the goods entrusted to his care, and rarely has more than a wagon load of them in his possession; he pays one week's rent in advance for his shop (which may also be his dwelling) and buys his sewing machines on the installment plan, paying for them 75 cents a week each; or, he may still further reduce his investment by requiring his operators to furnish their own machines. Finally, he does not pay his employés until he receives his money for the finished lot.

In the small shops the characteristics of the sweating system are accentuated, and the most marked of these are disorder and instability. The latter results from the irresponsibility of the sweater and the facility with which he may either establish himself or change his location. This has very much embarrassed the process of enumeration. A man may work in his bedroom to-day, in another man's shop to-morrow, in his own shop in a month, and before the end of the season abandon that for a place in a factory. If an inspector orders sanitary changes to be made within a week, the sweater may prefer to disappear before the close of the week and open another shop in another place. Such easy evasion of the authorities places the sweater almost beyond official control, and many of them overcrowd their shops, overwork their employés, hire small children, keep their shops unclean, and their sanitary arrangements foul and inadequate.

The provisional nature of the small shops also accounts largely for the absence of steam motive power for the sewing machines, though it is also explained by the statement that "leg power is cheaper than steam." The increasing employment of girls aged from 12 to 16 years as machine operators is making this motive power still cheaper, and at the same time more destructive of health and life.

The minute subdivision of the work in the sweaters' shops reduces the skill required to the lowest point. The whole number of employés, therefore, in all the outside shops, includes, besides a few of the skilled, who would, under the old system, be employed in the inside shops, a majority of unskilled hands of both sexes, earning low wages, easily replaced, and wholly at the mercy of the sweater. Subdivision thus reaches its highest development; operators stitch, pressers press, basters baste, button girls sew on buttons, others draw basting threads, and finishers finish. Sometimes one girl, with a button-hole machine, makes a specialty of the inside bands of knee-pants, making button holes by the thousand gross. On the other hand, coats requiring button holes made in cloth, and with more skill, are sent by the contractor to a button-hole shop, where two or three young men work machines, and where small boys or girls smear the holes in preparation for them.

Tenement Workers, or Finishers

In nearly every small shop there are some finishers, but in the case of knee-pants, trousers, cloaks and vests, the garments, after being cut, basted, stitched and button-holed, are given out to have all that remains, the felling and hand-stitching, done at home before the garment is pressed and sent to the factory.

These tenement workers are known as "finishers." They are generally associated with some one of the shops, but will take work from any of them. Hundreds of women and girls compete among themselves, keeping their names on the contractors' lists, as the contractors compete among themselves for work from the manufacturers.

These women sew in the intervals of their housework and the garments lie about the living rooms, across greasy chairs and tables, upon filthy floors and vermin-infested beds. Soils upon garments are so common that the presser in the shops is also a cleaner, provided with benzine, alcohol, etc., for the removal of grease and stains. The competition of the home finishers constantly presses upon the wages of the shop hands. In some localities nearly every house contains some of these home finishers; our enumerators have located a total of 1,836 of them in the several districts, and they increase as the shops increase and as immigration increases.

Typical Shops and Working Places

Many of the Bohemians and Scandinavians have acquired their own homes and their own shops, which are usually built upon the same premises, and are properly lighted and ventilated. Very few of the Scandinavians have shops in their dwellings. They prefer to combine, in groups of from three to eight, and rent a large building, which is then partitioned off according to their needs. There are of course exceptions even among these people, and some of them set up shops in places wholly unfit for such uses; but the baser localities and shops are usually occupied by Russian Jews, Poles and Italians. In the regions occupied by these, unclean and offensive conditions are not confined to the shops; they are equally features of the dwellings and persons and habits of the people. In these districts the worst of the shops are found located often in basements, and on alleys, or in wholly inadequate and unsanitary rooms in the dilapidated structures of these neighborhoods.

A few examples may be cited illustrating what some of these places are like: In one case several men were found at work pressing knee-pants in a low basement room poorly lighted and ventilated by two small windows. There was no floor in this room, and the people were living on the bare earth, which was damp and littered with every sort of rubbish. In another case seven persons were at work in a room 12 by 15 feet in dimensions and with but two windows. These people with the sewing machines of operators and the tables used by the pressers, so filled this meagre space that it was impossible to move about. Charcoal was used for heating the pressers' irons, and the air was offensive and prostrating to a degree. Separated from this shop-room by a frail partition which did not reach to the ceiling was a bedroom about 7 by 15 feet in size, containing two beds, for the use of the family of the sweater. In another instance, in a small basement room which measured only 7 feet 10 inches by 6 feet 6 inches, and without door or window opening to the outer air, a man was at work pressing knee-pants by the light of a very poor gasoline lamp and using a gasoline stove for heating his irons.

One of the principal aims of the sweater is the avoidance of rent. Hence the only requirement for a sweaters' shop is that the structure must be strong enough to sustain the jar of the machines. This condition being filled, any tenement-room is available, whether in loft, or basement, or stable. Fire-escapes in such buildings are unknown; water for flushing closets is rarely found, and the employés are equally at the mercy of fire and disease. Frequently the sweater's home is his shop, with a bed among the machines; or, the family sleeps on cots, which are removed during the day to make room for employés. Sometimes two or three employés are also boarders or lodgers, and the tenement dwelling is the shop; and cooking, sleeping, sewing and the nursing of the sick are going on simultaneously.

A shop was found in which 12 persons lived in 6 rooms, of which two were used as a shop. Knee-pants in all stages of completion filled the shop, the bed-rooms and kitchen. Nine men were employed at machines in a room 12 by 14, and there knee-pants were being manufactured by the thousand gross. This is in the rear of a swarming tenement in a wretched street. Sometimes the landlord is the sweater, using his own basement or outhouse for a shop and renting his rooms to his employés for dwellings. Only one case was found in which a tailor, not a sweater, had acquired a house. He is a skilled tailor, still doing "the whole work" at home, assisted by his wife. For nineteen years he has lived and worked in two wretched rear tenement rooms, paying by instalments for his house, which is still incumbered. All others in the trade who owned houses were found to be either sweaters or women finishers, whose able-bodied husbands follow other occupations, such as teaming, peddling, ditching, street cleaning, etc.

But the worst conditions of all prevail among the families who finish garments at home. Here the greatest squalor and filth abounds and the garments are of necessity exposed to it and a part of it during the process of finishing. A single room frequently serves as kitchen, bed-room, living-room and working-room. In the Italian quarter four families were found occupying one four-room flat, using one cook stove, and all the women and children sewing in the bed-rooms. For this flat they pay $10 a month, each family contributing $2.50 a month. Another group was found consisting of 13 persons, of whom 4 were fathers of families, and 5 were women and girls sewing on cloaks at home. These 13 people pay $8 per month rent, each family contributing $2. . . .

Proportions of Men, Women and Children

There are about three times as many women as there are men connected with the sweat shops. There were in all 10,933 persons enumerated as employés of the 666 shops visited. Of these, 2,669, or about one-fourth, were men and boys; the remainder, women and girls. Of the former, 221 were scheduled as boys, not as youths nor young men, but simply as boys. It was useless to inquire about ages, but the distinction between the boy and man is always sufficiently patent. Boys, proper, are employed as messengers or errand boys to carry goods to the button-holer, or to the finisher, or to fetch beer, and they usually receive about $1 a week. From this stage of usefulness they emerge, after a year or two, into regular shop hands, if they have not improved their opportunities to run away.

In the absence of an age classification the distinction between women, young women and girls is more difficult, but there were listed in all 8,264 of the sex, 1,939 of whom were recorded as women and 6,325 as young women and girls. Of the former, 1,836 were reported as home finishers by the several sweaters who furnished them work, that is, they were on the shop lists as outside workers; they are also mostly married women. This leaves 103 of the older women and 6,326 girls at work in shops. In fact the young and unmarried women constitute pretty much the entire female force in the shops. Judging from appearances the most of these girls are from 16 to 20 years of age, but there is a contingent in every shop of any importance, or in every dozen girls, who belong in the ranks of childhood and who may be anywhere from 10 to 14 years of age. They correspond in years with the boys before mentioned, and they are employed as button girls, that is, to sew buttons on, or to pull out basting threads, or to smear button-holes before they are worked. Whatever they do, however, they must do industriously and continuously, under a system of task service, and exposed to all the evil conditions and oppressions of the sweat shops. In number they are more than the boys of similar ages, and their lot is a harder one, by reason of their helplessness and confinement within the shop. From their primitive labors these little ones soon develop into hand-sewers with bodies forever bent by their work, or into machine operators driving machines at unseemly speed and at unseemly hours. There are probably five or six hundred of these children employed in the sweat shops in Chicago, who should be at home, at school or at play. There are as many thousand young girls in the shops, and several thousand other women in the service of sweaters, who overwork in overcrowded rooms and tenements for a part of the year, and go hungry and needy for want of work during the remainder. To these should be added from three to five thousand men who baste and stitch and press and swelter in the dreary environment of the sweat shop, hopeless of better things.

In the coat shops 30 per cent of the employés are men and no women are employed except in the shops; in the trousers shops only 13 per cent are men and half the women work outside the shops; in making vests 16 per cent of the people are men, and much the larger portion of the women work in shops; 40 per cent of the cloak-makers are men and a third of the women work at home; of the 1,690 in other kinds of shops 25 per cent are men, and practically none of the women work out of the shop.

In the tenement houses, among the finishers, the proportion of very young children who work is greater than in the shops, for every member of the family group must contribute in some degree to the family earnings. Children, consequently, learn to work next after they learn to walk. . . .

Observation among sweated people confirms the opinion that a direct consequence of their occupation is a general impairment of health in both sexes; in men the debility takes the form of consumption, either of the lungs or intestines, and of complete exhaustion and premature old age; the girls become victims of consumption, dyspepsia, and life-long pelvic disorders. These are the results of the overexertion, bad housing, undernourishment and noxious surroundings common to their calling and condition in life. But in addition to these disabilities they are constantly exposed to the inroads of typhoid and scarlet fevers, and other zymotic diseases. Cases of this kind develop in the tenements and too often have but scant medical or other attendance. At the same time and in the same apartments quantities of cloaks, clothing, or children's garments may be present in various stages of finishing. It is hardly necessary to establish the fact that children's clothing is sometimes thus exposed and thus infected with the most fatal maladies of childhood, for it is apparent that under the given conditions entire immunity from infection could not be possible; yet the following instances of disease in the presence or proximity of garment-making, are cited as those which came under the observation of the bureau:

A grandmother was found dying of cancer without medical attendance in the same room with a man and his wife and three children. The man and wife were at work finishing men's coats, many of which were lying about the room.

In a tenement house a man was found just recovering from malignant diphtheria, while in the room adjoining, on the same floor, and in the room above, knee-pants were being finished, and the work had not been suspended during any stage of the disease.

Two children, with a loathsome skin disease, were sewing buttons on knee-pants. The mother, to show how bad the case was, passed her hand over their faces, brushing the scales upon the clothing. . . .

Nationalities

The people engaged in this business are all of foreign birth or parentage, principally of foreign birth, and those of the same origin naturally gravitate to the same localities and the same shops. There are quarters of the city in which nearly every inhabitant is a Bohemian; another where Poles have settled; another occupied by Scandinavians, and others still by foreign Hebrews and Italians. Different nationalities also incline to group themselves on the manufacture of certain kinds of garments. Thus the Bohemians are mostly given to making coats; the Scandinavians are the largest contractors for vests, while the Jews turn their attention chiefly to cloaks. Germans and Poles are found contracting about equally for coats and trousers. Divisions on this line are not, however, very strongly defined, and in fact some of each race may be found in every branch of the business. The gravitation of newly arrived foreigners to the specific localities in which their race is congregated is common and natural. This attracts the sweater of the same nationality, who is thus enabled to recruit his employés from those who can speak no other language but his. It thus occurs that the race characteristics of shops are very marked, and an approximation can be made as to the nationality of the sweaters' victims based on the race and location of the sweater. . . .

It will be observed that this business is chiefly in the hands of the

Bohemians and Scandinavians so far as the number of shops is concerned. It is with these people, however, that the best shops are found, while the evils of the system are most conspicuous in the Russian, Polish, and Italian settlements. The exceptions to this rule of conformity between employers and employed are the one American and three Irish sweaters, who really employ whomsoever they can; and there are also two Jewish sweaters whose shops are filled with Polish vest-makers. The employés here characterized are only those at work in the shops. Presumably the 1,836 or more tenement house workers connected with the various shops also partake largely of the nationalities of their employers, but observations on this point indicate that a great many of the home finishers are Italian women. Italian men do not seek the sweat shop service, nor do they often become sweaters; they employ themselves in other ways; but their women do a great deal of home and shop sewing for the sweaters. . . .

In the inside, or manufacturer's shops, the employés are chiefly English-speaking people, such as German-American or Irish-American girls and Bohemian or Russian men who have aquired a speaking acquaintance with English. In the sweater's shops an English-speaking adult is rarely found. Russian-Hebrews, Poles, Bohemians, Swedes, Norwegians, Germans and Italians, usually of recent importation, have sole possession of these shops.

Newly arrived immigrants of these classes seem to be drawn to this city and into this occupation by chance rather than by design. It is not because of the attractions or allurements offered by the trade in Chicago, that immigrants are found in such numbers in the sweat shops, nor because these people are tailors or cloak-makers by trade in their native countries. Those who possess these trades in the old country will find places among the skilled workers in the factories or custom shops, or become contractors and start shops of their own when they come here. The raw immigrants who fill the sweat shops are the ignorant and unskilled, usually peasants or very poor towns people in their own countries, and they come to Chicago because they are induced to buy through tickets by some local agent who extols the western metropolis and profits by the longer journey. When they arrive they find their fellow countrymen peddling rags or junk, or petty wares, or washing bottles at $3 a week, or running a machine in a sweat shop, and they proceed to do likewise. In the last, a man's family can almost at once assist him, his wife as a finisher and his children in minor functions, for the reason that so little skill is required in the many separate processes. For ordinary efficiency in a sweaters' shop a fortnight's experience is ample. It is not skill nor intelligence that the sweater seeks; he thrives most with ignorance and poverty. The sweaters themselves are usually those who have been in this country for a number of years and have learned how to find and apply cheap labor to the execution of low-priced contracts, and to profit by it; consequently, the less the bewildered immigrant knows of the ways and wages in this country and the greater his need, the more readily can the contractor make terms with him to suit himself.

In all shops the pay of employés is controlled by the contractors, who are governed in turn by the terms of their contracts, or the necessities of their work-people. In the worst shops this principle is carried to an extreme which amounts to extortion, and illustrates sweating in its most cruel form. In these, beginners are frequently induced to work for nothing on the pretense of learning a trade; the very needy are employed at the lowest rates, or at indefinite or unspecified rates to be fixed when payment is made; advantage is taken of the ignorant, and work is given out to the tenement house workers always at the lowest figures which the individuals will accept regardless of the prices paid to others or of the value of the work.

Piece-work prices to home finishers range from 5 cents per dozen for finishing knee-pants and 2 cents a piece for cloaks, up to 12 cents a dozen for knee-pants and 16 cents a piece for cloaks. Within these limits the rates vary with the intelligence and independence of the worker. Women were found in three houses in the same block finishing knee-pants of the same size, grade and number for 5 cents, 8 cents, 6 cents and 12 cents per dozen; and finishing cloaks of the same lot for 5 cents, 8 cents, 10 cents and sixteen cents a piece. Those who were working for the least were new-comers who knew no English and were abjectly poor; the woman who received the most had been in this country 11 years, could speak the language, owned a tenement house and was not obliged to take work unless the prices suited her.

An Italian woman walked a mile each way to the shop throughout July, August and September to get cloaks to finish at 5 cents apiece, which she sub-let to her neighbors at 4 cents apiece. The standard price for finishing vests at home is 1 cent each; for trousers from 6 to 8 cents a pair; but every change in the style of a garment of any kind creates a new opportunity for bargaining about the price for the work on it. Sometimes a new name or number is given to an old style for the purpose of re-adjusting the price of making or finishing it; but as the varieties and changes in styles are many and often, the haggling and under-bidding is constant and the opportunities for imposition very great.

At all seasons the reserve army of labor presses heavily upon the regularly employed and this enables the sweater to dole out work in such small quantities that his employés are all eager to get as much as possible and will accept whatever price the sweater offers. This is true of all departments of the work, but especially of the home finishers who combine with their sewing the care of their children and the discharge of household duties. Very many of these finishers are married women, having able-bodied husbands who support their families. The women work when they can and for whatever they can get, and thus keep prices down for the women who are wholly dependent upon themselves for a living. Two Italian widows, with children, came under observation, who were dependent upon their earnings as finishers. The two children of one were fed daily at a charity nursery; coal and fuel were furnished by the county in winter; she paid $3 a month rent for a single room in a dark and damp basement; in 13 weeks she earned $9.37 finishing cloaks for a sweater. The other has a daughter 10 and a baby 3 years old, with whom she occupies two rooms in a rear tenement; she does all the work she can get finishing cloaks at from 2 to 8 cents apiece for a sweater, but receives so little for it that she can barely earn enough for her rent, and subsists upon charity. . . .

Characteristics of Sweat-Shop Communities

The people who are found in sweat-shops are rarely illiterate in their own languages, with perhaps the exception of the Italian peasants. Every Hebrew is taught to read his own literature in childhood, though very few of them can write, and still fewer can keep books of account. Almost none of them can read or write in the English language. The Scandinavians and Germans are all educated in excellent schools in their own countries, and read, write and keep accounts in their own language. Wholly illiterate are the Italians. Women finishers are found by scores who cannot count the pennies due them. None of them can read or write in any language.

The ability and desire to learn English varies with the nationality. Bohemians and many Poles send their children to parochial schools, but they learn neither to speak nor read English. Hebrew children go to the public schools, but, like many others, get only half time instruction for want of school accommodations. Italian parents gladly avail themselves of this excuse, and do not attempt to send their children to school at all. Italians do not learn English in the first generation, and in the second their children learn only what can be picked up in the streets. The boys are newsboys, rag pickers and shoe blacks; the girls are rag pickers or button girls, and even begin to sew on cloaks at a very early age.

In the matter of religion the sweaters' employés are either Catholics, Hebrews or Lutherans, the latter both Scandinavian and German, and principally women. The Hebrews are usually strictly orthodox, and are held together in swarming colonies by the need of having their own butchers. Sweaters' victims all keep the church holidays, except during the busy season, when work is frequently continued through seven days in the week. At other times the Italians, particularly, are punctilious about the observance of their *festas*, and the Hebrews in the observance

of their holy days. To many of them amusement is almost unknown. They
sleep late on Sundays and holidays, and sit listlessly about the rest of the
day, except when in church. Young men and girls are disposed to attend
night schools, or other free or cheap classes, when out of work or the
opportunity is afforded.

There are a number of organizations among the more intelligent and
self-helpful in the garment trades, among which are unions of the cutters,
the custom tailors, the ladies'-garment tailors, the cloak makers, the
women cloak makers, cloak cutters, and cloak pressers. The differences of
race, language and religion prove an obstacle to the growth of organization.

The food and clothing of these communities is necessarily simple and
meager. Among the Italians bread and maccaroni, with stale fruit and
vegetables, constitute the diet almost to the exclusion of meat. Among the
Hebrews the Mosaic prescription is some protection against the sale and
use of improper meats, but in general the groceries and meat shops in
these districts deal only in goods of defective and consequently cheap
quality. There is nothing fresh and good offered for sale. Milk is con-
spicuously absent even from the diet of little children, and every winter
there are long periods of rye bread and water in hundreds of families,
where the father is an operator without work in the shop or credit at the
store.

In the matter of clothing, all sorts of make-shifts are resorted to except
the appropriation of the garments they make. Italian women wear the
peasant costumes with which they come to this country as long as possible, which is usually very long, and buy second-hand clothing for their
children. Shoes are a very heavy item of expense among these people,
especially if they have far to walk to their work, or run sewing machines
after they get there. In many small shops men dispense with all clothing
except trousers and short-sleeved gauze undershirts, even in the presence
of women, and work in their bare feet. Girls who are thrown upon their
own resources were found still wearing the clothing brought from the old
country, and with small prospect of buying any other, as the earnings
of the busy season are otherwise absorbed during the dull season.

Very few sweaters' victims accumulate any savings. When they do they
become sweaters themselves. So far as observation extended no disposition was discovered among them to return to the countries whence they
came, even when they became able to do so. On the other hand they
manifest great desire to see their children attain some degree of prosperity greater than their own. Unfortunately their eagerness in this particular frequently defeats itself, for they send their young children to the
shop instead of to the school. Here their health is undermined; their
presence in the shop reduces the wages of adults, and both parents and
children become involved in a common struggle for existence. The result

is that discontent is universal. The sweater complains of increased competition and reduced prices and profits; the victims complain of low wages, of poor pay, of the long dull season, of the heat and overcrowding in the busy season, and of the poverty and toil from which they cannot escape. . . .

How the Other Half Lives

Jacob A. Riis

THE MIXED CROWD

When once I asked the agent of a notorious Fourth Ward alley how many people might be living in it I was told: One hundred and forty families, one hundred Irish, thirty-eight Italian, and two that spoke the German tongue. Barring the agent herself, there was not a native-born individual in the court. The answer was characteristic of the cosmopolitan character of lower New York, very nearly so of the whole of it, wherever it runs to alleys and courts. One may find for the asking an Italian, a German, a French, African, Spanish, Bohemian, Russian, Scandinavian, Jewish, and Chinese colony. Even the Arab, who peddles "holy earth" from the Battery as a direct importation from Jerusalem, has his exclusive preserves at the lower end of Washington Street. The one thing you shall vainly ask for in the chief city of America is a distinctively American community. There is none; certainly not among the tenements. Where have they gone to, the old inhabitants? I put the question to one who might fairly be presumed to be of the number, since I had found him sighing for the "good old days" when the legend "no Irish need apply" was familiar in the advertising columns of the newspapers. He looked at me with a puzzled air. "I don't know," he said. "I wish I did. Some went to California in '49, some to the war and never came back. The rest, I expect, have gone to heaven, or somewhere. I don't see them 'round here."

Whatever the merit of the good man's conjectures, his eyes did not deceive him. They are not here. In their place has come this queer conglomerate mass of heterogeneous elements, ever striving and working like whiskey and water in one glass, and with the like result: final union and a prevailing taint of whiskey. The once unwelcome Irishman has been followed in his turn by the Italian, the Russian Jew, and the Chinaman,

Jacob A. Riis, *How the Other Half Lives* (New York: Charles Scribner's Sons, 1890), pp. 21–27, 48–52, 104–119, 136–158.

and has himself taken a hand at opposition, quite as bitter and quite as ineffectual, against these later hordes. Wherever these have gone they have crowded him out, possessing the block, the street, the ward with their denser swarms. But the Irishman's revenge is complete. Victorious in defeat over his recent as over his more ancient foe, the one who opposed his coming no less than the one who drove him out, he dictates to both their politics, and, secure in possession of the offices, returns the native his greeting with interest, while collecting the rents of the Italian whose house he has bought with the profits of his saloon. As a landlord he is picturesquely autocratic. An amusing instance of his methods came under my notice while writing these lines. An inspector of the Health Department found an Italian family paying a man with a Celtic name twenty-five dollars a month for three small rooms in a ramshackle rear tenement—more than twice what they were worth—and expressed his astonishment to the tenant, an ignorant Sicilian laborer. He replied that he had once asked the landlord to reduce the rent, but he would not do it.

"Well! What did he say?" asked the inspector.

" 'Damma, man!' he said: 'if you speaka thata way to me, I fira you and your things in the streeta.' " And the frightened Italian paid the rent.

In justice to the Irish landlord it must be said that like an apt pupil he was merely showing forth the result of the schooling he had received, re-enacting, in his own way, the scheme of the tenements. It is only his frankness that shocks. The Irishman does not naturally take kindly to tenement life, though with characteristic versatility he adapts himself to its conditions at once. It does violence, nevertheless, to the best that is in him, and for that very reason of all who come within its sphere soonest corrupts him. The result is a sediment, the product of more than a generation in the city's slums, that, as distinguished from the larger body of his class, justly ranks at the foot of tenement dwellers, the so-called "low Irish."

It is not to be assumed, of course, that the whole body of the population living in the tenements, of which New Yorkers are in the habit of speaking vaguely as "the poor," or even the larger part of it, is to be classed as vicious or as poor in the sense of verging on beggary.

New York's wage-earners have no other place to live, more is the pity. They are truly poor for having no better homes; waxing poorer in purse as the exorbitant rents to which they are tied, as ever was serf to soil, keep rising. The wonder is that they are not all corrupted, and speedily, by their surroundings. If, on the contrary, there be a steady working up, if not out of the slough, the fact is a powerful argument for the optimist's belief that the world is, after all, growing better, not worse, and would go far toward disarming apprehension, were it not for the steadier growth of the sediment of the slums and its constant menace. Such an impulse toward better things there certainly is. The German rag-picker of thirty years ago, quite as low in the scale as his Italian successor, is the thrifty tradesman or prosperous farmer of to-day.*

The Italian scavenger of our time is fast graduating into exclusive control of the corner fruit-stands, while his black-eyed boy monopolizes the boot-blacking industry in which a few years ago he was an intruder. The Irish hod-carrier in the second generation has become a bricklayer, if not the Alderman of his ward, while the Chinese coolie is in almost exclusive possession of the laundry business. The reason is obvious. The poorest immigrant comes here with the purpose and ambition to better himself and, given half a chance, might be reasonably expected to make the most of it. To the false plea that he prefers the squalid homes in which his kind are housed there could be no better answer. The truth is, his half chance has too long been wanting, and for the bad result he has been unjustly blamed.

As emigration from east to west follows the latitude, so does the foreign influx in New York distribute itself along certain well-defined lines that waver and break only under the stronger pressure of a more gregarious race or the encroachments of inexorable business. A feeling of dependence upon mutual effort, natural to strangers in a strange land, unacquainted with its language and customs, sufficiently accounts for this.

The Irishman is the true cosmopolitan immigrant. All-pervading, he shares his lodging with perfect impartiality with the Italian, the Greek, and the "Dutchman," yielding only to sheer force of numbers, and objects equally to them all. A map of the city, colored to designate nationalities, would show more stripes than on the skin of a zebra, and more colors than any rainbow. The city on such a map would fall into two great halves, green for the Irish prevailing in the West Side tenement districts, and blue for the Germans on the East Side. But intermingled with these ground colors would be an odd variety of tints that would give the whole the appearance of an extraordinary crazy-quilt. From down in the Sixth Ward, upon the site of the old Collect Pond that in the days of the fathers drained the hills which are no more, the red of the Italian would be seen forcing its way northward along the line of Mulberry Street to the quarter of the French purple on Bleecker Street and South Fifth Avenue, to lose itself and reappear, after a lapse of miles, in the "Little Italy" of Harlem, east of Second Avenue. Dashes of red, sharply defined, would be seen strung through the Annexed District, northward to the city line. On the West Side the red would be seen overrunning the old Africa of Thompson Street, pushing the black of the negro rapidly uptown, against querulous

* The Sheriff Street Colony of rag-pickers, long since gone, is an instance in point. The thrifty Germans saved up money during years of hard work in squalor and apparently wretched poverty to buy a township in a Western State, and the whole colony moved out there in a body. There need be no doubt about their thriving there.

but unavailing protests, occupying his home, his church, his trade and all, with merciless impartiality. There is a church in Mulberry Street that has stood for two generations as a sort of milestone of these migrations. Built originally for the worship of staid New Yorkers of the "old stock," it was engulfed by the colored tide, when the draft-riots drove the negroes out of reach of Cherry Street and the Five Points. Within the past decade the advance wave of the Italian onset reached it, and to-day the arms of United Italy adorn its front. The negroes have made a stand at several points along Seventh and Eighth Avenues; but their main body, still pursued by the Italian foe, is on the march yet, and the black mark will be found overshadowing to-day many blocks on the East Side, with One Hundredth Street as the center, where colonies of them have settled recently.

Hardly less aggressive than the Italian, the Russian and Polish Jew, having overrun the district between Rivington and Division Streets, east of the Bowery, to the point of suffocation, is filling the tenements of the old Seventh Ward to the river front, and disputing with the Italian every foot of available space in the back alleys of Mulberry Street. The two races, differing hopelessly in much, have this in common: they carry their slums with them wherever they go, if allowed to do it. Little Italy already rivals its parent, the "Bend," in foulness. Other nationalities that begin at the bottom make a fresh start when crowded up the ladder. Happily both are manageable, the one by rabbinical, the other by the civil law. Between the dull gray of the Jew, his favorite color, and the Italian red, would be seen squeezed in on the map a sharp streak of yellow, marking the narrow boundaries of Chinatown. Dovetailed in with the German population, the poor but thrifty Bohemian might be picked out by the sombre hue of his life as of his philosophy, struggling against heavy odds in the big human bee-hives of the East Side. Colonies of his people extend northward, with long lapses of space, from below the Cooper Institute more than three miles. The Bohemian is the only foreigner with any considerable representation in the city who counts no wealthy man of his race, none who has not to work hard for a living, or has got beyond the reach of the tenement.

Down near the Battery the West Side emerald would be soiled by a dirty stain, spreading rapidly like a splash of ink on a sheet of blotting paper, headquarters of the Arab tribe, that in a single year has swelled from the original dozen to twelve hundred, intent, every mother's son, on trade and barter. Dots and dashes of color here and there would show where the Finnish sailors worship their djumala (God), the Greek pedlars the ancient name of their race, and the Swiss the goddess of thrift. And so on to the end of the long register, all toiling together in the galling fetters of the tenement. Were the question raised who makes the most of life thus mortgaged, who resists most stubbornly its levelling tendency—

knows how to drag even the barracks upward a part of the way at least toward the ideal plane of the home—the palm must be unhesitatingly awarded the Teuton. The Italian and the poor Jew rise only by compulsion. The Chinaman does not rise at all; here, as at home, he simply remains stationary. The Irishman's genius runs to public affairs rather than domestic life; wherever he is mustered in force the saloon is the gorgeous centre of political activity. The German struggles vainly to learn his trick; his Teutonic wit is too heavy, and the political ladder he raises from his saloon usually too short or too clumsy to reach the desired goal. The best part of his life is lived at home, and he makes himself a home independent of the surroundings, giving the lie to the saying, unhappily become a maxim of social truth, that pauperism and drunkenness naturally grow in the tenements. He makes the most of his tenement, and it should be added that whenever and as soon as he can save up money enough, he gets out and never crosses the threshold of one again.

THE ITALIAN IN NEW YORK

Certainly a picturesque, if not very tidy, element has been added to the population in the "assisted" Italian immigrant who claims so large a share of public attention, partly because he keeps coming at such a tremendous rate, but chiefly because he elects to stay in New York, or near enough for it to serve as his base of operations, and here promptly reproduces conditions of destitution and disorder which, set in the frame-work of Mediterranean exuberance, are the delight of the artist, but in a matter-of-fact American community become its danger and reproach. The reproduction is made easier in New York because he finds the material ready to hand in the worst of the slum tenements; but even where it is not he soon reduces what he does find to his own level, if allowed to follow his natural bent.* The Italian comes in at the bottom, and in the generation that came over the sea he stays there. In the slums he is welcomed as a tenant who "makes less trouble" than the contentious Irishman or the order-loving German, that is to say: is content to live in a pig-sty and submits to robbery at the hands of the rent-collector without murmur. Yet this very tractability makes of him in good hands, when firmly and intelligently managed, a really desirable tenant. But it is not his good fortune often to fall in with other hospitality upon his coming than that which brought him here for its own profit, and has no idea of letting go its grip upon him as long as there is a cent to be made out of him.

Recent Congressional inquiries have shown the nature of the "assistance" he receives from greedy steamship agents and "bankers," who per-

---

* The process can be observed in the Italian tenements in Harlem (Little Italy), which, since their occupation by these people, have been gradually sinking to the slum level.

suade him by false promises to mortgage his home, his few belongings, and his wages for months to come for a ticket to the land where plenty of work is to be had at princely wages. The padrone—the "banker" is nothing else—having made his ten per cent. out of him en route, receives him at the landing and turns him to double account as a wage-earner and a rent-payer. In each of these rôles he is made to yield a profit to his unscrupulous countryman, whom he trusts implicitly with the instinct of utter helplessness. The man is so ignorant that, as one of the sharpers who prey upon him put it once, it "would be downright sinful not to take him in." His ignorance and unconquerable suspicion of strangers dig the pit into which he falls. He not only knows no word of English, but he does not know enough to learn. Rarely only can he write his own language. Unlike the German, who begins learning English the day he lands as a matter of duty, or the Polish Jew, who takes it up as soon as he is able as an investment, the Italian learns slowly, if at all. Even his boy, born here, often speaks his native tongue indifferently. He is forced, therefore, to have constant recourse to the middle-man, who makes him pay handsomely at every turn. He hires him out to the railroad contractor, receiving a commission from the employer as well as from the laborer, and repeats the performance monthly, or as often as he can have him dismissed. In the city he contracts for his lodging, subletting to him space in the vilest tenements at extortionate rents, and sets an example that does not lack imitators. The "princely wages" have vanished with his coming, and in their place hardships and a dollar a day, beheft with the padrone's merciless mortgage, confront him. Bred to even worse fare, he takes both as a matter of course, and, applying the maxim that it is not what one makes but what he saves that makes him rich, manages to turn the very dirt of the streets into a hoard of gold, with which he either returns to his Southern home, or brings over his family to join in his work and in his fortunes the next season.

The discovery was made by earlier explorers that there is money in New York's ash-barrel, but it was left to the genius of the padrone to develop the full resources of the mine that has become the exclusive preserve of the Italian immigrant. Only a few years ago, when rag-picking was carried on in a desultory and irresponsible sort of way, the city hired gangs of men to trim the ash-scows before they were sent out to sea. The trimming consisted in levelling out the dirt as it was dumped from the carts, so that the scow might be evenly loaded. The men were paid a dollar and a half a day, kept what they found that was worth having, and allowed the swarms of Italians who hung about the dumps to do the heavy work for them, letting them have their pick of the loads for their trouble. To-day Italians contract for the work, paying large sums to be permitted to do it. The city received not less than $80,000 last year for the sale of this privilege to the contractors, who in addition have to pay gangs of their countrymen for sorting out the bones, rags, tin cans and other waste that are found in the ashes and form the staples of their trade and their sources of revenue. The effect has been vastly to increase the power of the padrone, or his ally, the contractor, by giving him exclusive control of the one industry in which the Italian was formerly an independent "dealer," and reducing him literally to the plane of the dump. Whenever the back of the sanitary police is turned, he will make his home in the filthy burrows where he works by day, sleeping and eating his meals under the dump, on the edge of slimy depths and amid surroundings full of unutterable horror. The city did not bargain to house, though it is content to board, him so long as he can make the ash-barrels yield the food to keep him alive, and a vigorous campaign is carried on at intervals against these unlicensed dump settlements; but the temptation of having to pay no rent is too strong, and they are driven from one dump only to find lodgement under another a few blocks farther up or down the river. The fiercest warfare is waged over the patronage of the dumps by rival factions represented by opposing contractors, and it has happened that the defeated party has endeavored to capture by strategy what he failed to carry by assault. It augurs unsuspected adaptability in the Italian to our system of self-government that these rivalries have more than once been suspected of being behind the sharpening of city ordinances, that were apparently made in good faith to prevent meddling with the refuse in the ash-barrels or in transit. . . .

JEWTOWN

The tenements grow taller, and the gaps in their ranks close up rapidly as we cross the Bowery and, leaving Chinatown and the Italians behind, invade the Hebrew quarter. Baxter Street, with its interminable rows of old clothes shops and its brigades of pullers-in—nicknamed "the Bay" in honor, perhaps, of the tars who lay to there after a cruise to stock up their togs, or maybe after the "schooners" of beer plentifully bespoke in that latitude—Bayard Street, with its synagogues and its crowds, gave us a foretaste of it. No need of asking here where we are. The jargon of the street, the signs of the sidewalk, the manner and dress of the people, their unmistakable physiognomy, betray their race at every step. Men with queer skull-caps, venerable beard, and the outlandish long-skirted kaftan of the Russian Jew, elbow the ugliest and the handsomest women in the land. The contrast is startling. The old women are hags; the young, houris. Wives and mothers at sixteen, at thirty they are old. So thoroughly has the chosen people crowded out the Gentiles in the Tenth Ward that, when the great Jewish holidays come around every year, the public schools in the district have practically to close up. Of their thousands of pupils scarce a handful come to school. Nor is there any suspicion that the rest are playing hookey. They stay honestly home to celebrate. There is no mistaking it: we are in Jewtown.

It is said that nowhere in the world are so many people crowded together on a square mile as here. The average five-story tenement adds a story or two to its stature in Ludlow Street and an extra building on the rear lot, and yet the sign "To Let" is the rarest of all there. Here is one seven stories high. The sanitary policeman whose beat this is will tell you that it contains thirty-six families, but the term has a widely different meaning here and on the avenues. In this house, where a case of small-pox was reported, there were fifty-eight babies and thirty-eight children that were over five years of age. In Essex Street two small rooms in a six-story tenement were made to hold a "family" of father and mother, twelve children and six boarders. The boarder plays as important a part in the domestic economy of Jewtown as the lodger in the Mulberry Street Bend. These are samples of the packing of the population that has run up the record here to the rate of three hundred and thirty thousand per square mile. The densest crowding of Old London, I pointed out before, never got beyond a hundred and seventy-five thousand. Even the alley is crowded out. Through dark hallways and filthy cellars, crowded, as is every foot of the street, with dirty children, the settlements in the rear are reached. Thieves know how to find them when pursued by the police, and the tramps that sneak in on chilly nights to fight for the warm spot in the yard over some baker's oven. They are out of place in this hive of busy industry, and they know it. It has nothing in common with them or with their philosophy of life, that the world owes the idler a living. Life here means the hardest kind of work almost from the cradle. The world as a debtor has no credit in Jewtown. Its promise to pay wouldn't buy one of the old hats that are hawked about Hester Street, unless backed by security representing labor done at lowest market rates. But this army of workers must have bread. It is cheap and filling, and bakeries abound. Wherever they are in the tenements the tramp will skulk in, if he can. There is such a tramps' roost in the rear of a tenement near the lower end of Ludlow Street, that is never without its tenants in winter. By a judicious practice of flopping over on the stone pavement at intervals and thus warming one side at a time, and with an empty box to put the feet in, it is possible to keep reasonably comfortable there even on a rainy night. In summer the yard is the only one in the neighborhood that does not do duty as a public dormitory.

Thrift is the watchword of Jewtown, as of its people the world over. It is at once its strength and its fatal weakness, its cardinal virtue and its foul disgrace. Become an over-mastering passion with these people who come here in droves from Eastern Europe to escape persecution, from which freedom could be bought only with gold, it has enslaved them in bondage worse than that from which they fled. Money is their God. Life itself is of little value compared with even the leanest bank account. In no other spot does life wear so intensely bald and materialistic an aspect as in Ludlow Street. Over and over again I have met with instances of these Polish or Russian Jews deliberately starving themselves to the point of physical exhaustion, while working night and day at a tremendous pressure to save a little money. An avenging Nemesis pursues this headlong hunt for wealth; there is no worse paid class anywhere. I once put the question to one of their own people, who, being a pawnbroker, and an unusually intelligent and charitable one, certainly enjoyed the advantage of a practical view of the situation: "Whence the many wretchedly poor people in such a colony of workers, where poverty, from a misfortune, has become a reproach, dreaded as the plague?"

"Immigration," he said, "brings us a lot. In five years it has averaged twenty-five thousand a year, of which more than seventy per cent. have stayed in New York. Half of them require and receive aid from the Hebrew Charities from the very start, lest they starve. That is one explanation. There is another class than the one that cannot get work: those who have had too much of it; who have worked and hoarded and lived, crowded together like pigs, on the scantiest fare and the worst to be got, bound to save whatever their earnings, until, worn out, they could work no longer. Then their hoards were soon exhausted. That is their story." And I knew that what he said was true.

Penury and poverty are wedded everywhere to dirt and disease, and Jewtown is no exception. It could not well be otherwise in such crowds, considering especially their low intellectual status. The managers of the Eastern Dispensary, which is in the very heart of their district, told the whole story when they said: "The diseases these people suffer from are not due to intemperance or immorality, but to ignorance, want of suitable food, and the foul air in which they live and work." The homes of the Hebrew quarter are its workshops also. . . . You are made fully aware of [economic conditions] before you have travelled the length of a single block in any of these East Side streets, by the whir of a thousand sewing-machines, worked at high pressure from earliest dawn till mind and muscle give out together. Every member of the family, from the youngest to the oldest, bears a hand, shut in the qualmy rooms, where meals are cooked and clothing washed and dried besides, the livelong day. It is not unusual to find a dozen persons—men, women, and children—at work in a single small room. The fact accounts for the contrast that strikes with wonder the observer who comes across from the Bend. Over there the entire population seems possessed of an uncontrollable impulse to get out into the street; here all its energies appear to be bent upon keeping in and away from it. Not that the streets are deserted. The overflow from these tenements is enough to make a crowd anywhere. The children alone would do it. Not old enough to work and no room for play, that is their story. In the home the child's place is usurped by the lodger, who performs the service of the Irishman's pig—pays the rent. In the street the army of hucksters crowd him out. Typhus fever and small-pox are bred here, and help solve the question what to do with him. Filth diseases both, they sprout naturally among the hordes that bring the germs with them from across the sea, and whose first instinct is to hide their sick lest the authorities carry them off to the hospital to be slaughtered, as they firmly believe. The health officers are on constant and sharp lookout for hidden fever-nests. Considering that half of the ready-made clothes that are sold in the big stores, if not a good deal more than half, are made in these tenement rooms, this is not excessive caution. It has happened more than once that a child recovering from small-pox, and in the most contagious stage of the disease, has been found crawling among heaps of half-finished clothing that the next day would be offered for sale on the counter of a Broadway store; or that a typhus fever patient has been discovered in a room whence perhaps a hundred coats had been sent home that week, each one with the wearer's death warrant, unseen and unsuspected, basted in the lining.

The health officers call the Tenth the typhus ward; in the office where deaths are registered it passes as the "suicide ward," for reasons not hard to understand; and among the police as the "crooked ward," on account of the number of "crooks," petty thieves and their allies, the "fences," receivers of stolen goods, who find the dense crowds congenial. The nearness of the Bowery, the great "thieves' highway," helps to keep up the supply of these, but Jewtown does not support its dives. Its troubles with the police are the characteristic crop of its intense business rivalries. Oppression, persecution, have not shorn the Jew of his native combativeness one whit. He is as ready to fight for his rights, or what he considers his rights, in a business transaction—synonymous generally with his advantage—as if he had not been robbed of them for eighteen hundred years. One strong impression survives with him from his days of bondage: the power of the law. On the slightest provocation he rushes off to invoke it for his protection. Doubtless the sensation is novel to him, and therefore pleasing. The police at the Eldridge Street station are in a constant turmoil over these everlasting fights. Somebody is always denouncing somebody else, and getting his enemy or himself locked up; frequently both, for the prisoner, when brought in, has generally as plausible a story to tell as his accuser, and as hot a charge to make. The day closes on a wild conflict of rival interests. Another dawns with the prisoner in court, but no complainant. Over night the case has been settled on a business basis, and the police dismiss their prisoner in deep disgust. . . .

Bitter as are his private feuds, it is not until his religious life is invaded that a real inside view is obtained of this Jew, whom the history of Christian civilization has taught nothing but fear and hatred. There are two or three missions in the district conducting a hopeless propagandism for the Messiah whom the Tenth Ward rejects, and they attract occasional crowds, who come to hear the Christian preacher as the Jews of old gathered to hear the apostles expound the new doctrine. The result is often strikingly similar. "For once," said a certain well-known minister of an uptown church to me, after such an experience, "I felt justified in comparing myself to Paul preaching salvation to the Jews. They kept still until I spoke of Jesus Christ as the Son of God. Then they got up and fell to arguing among themselves and to threatening me, until it looked as if they meant to take me out in Hester Street and stone me." As at Jerusalem, the Chief Captain was happily at hand with his centurions, in the person of a sergeant and three policemen, and the preacher was rescued. So, in all matters pertaining to their religious life that tinges all their customs, they stand, these East Side Jews, where the new day that dawned on Calvary left them standing, stubbornly refusing to see the light. A visit to a Jewish house of mourning is like bridging the gap of two thousand years. The inexpressibly sad and sorrowful wail for the dead, as it swells and rises in the hush of all sounds of life, comes back from the ages like a mournful echo of the voice of Rachel "weeping for her children and refusing to be comforted, because they are not."

Attached to many of the synagogues, which among the poorest Jews frequently consist of a scantily furnished room in a rear tenement, with a few wooden stools or benches for the congregation, are Talmudic schools that absorb a share of the growing youth. The school-master is not rarely a man of some attainments who has been stranded there, his native instinct for money-making having been smothered in the process that has made of him a learned man. It was of such a school in Eldridge Street that the wicked Isaac Iacob, who killed his enemy, his wife, and himself in one day, was janitor. But the majority of the children seek the public schools, where they are received sometimes with some misgivings on the part of the teachers, who find it necessary to inculcate lessons of cleanliness in the worst cases by practical demonstration with wash-bowl and soap. "He took hold of the soap as if it were some animal," said one of these teachers to me after such an experiment upon a new pupil, "and wiped three fingers across his face. He called that washing." In the Allen Street public school the experienced principal has embodied among the elementary lessons, to keep constantly before the children the duty that clearly lies next to their hands, a characteristic exercise. The question is asked daily from the teacher's desk: "What must I do to be healthy?" and the whole school responds:

> "I must keep my skin clean,
> Wear clean clothes,
> Breathe pure air,
> And live in the sunlight."

It seems little less than biting sarcasm to hear them say it, for to not a few of them all these things are known only by name. In their everyday life there is nothing even to suggest any of them. Only the demand of religious custom has power to make their parents clean up at stated intervals, and the young naturally are no better. As scholars, the children of the most ignorant Polish Jew keep fairly abreast of their more favored playmates, until it comes to mental arithmetic, when they leave them behind with a bound. It is surprising to see how strong the instinct of dollars and cents is in them. They can count, and correctly, almost before they can talk. . . .

Thursday night and Friday morning are bargain days in the "Pig-market." Then is the time to study the ways of this peculiar people to the best advantage. A common pulse beats in the quarters of the Polish Jews and in the Mulberry Bend, though they have little else in common. Life over yonder in fine weather is a perpetual holiday, here a veritable treadmill of industry. Friday brings out all the latent color and picturesqueness of the Italians, as of these Semites. The crowds and the common poverty are the bonds of sympathy between them. The Pig-market is in Hester Street, extending either way from Ludlow Street, and up and down the side streets two or three blocks, as the state of trade demands. The name was given to it probably in derision, for pork is the one ware that is not on sale in the Pig-market. There is scarcely anything else that can be hawked from a wagon that is not to be found, and at ridiculously low prices. Bandannas and tin cups at two cents, peaches at a cent a quart, "damaged" eggs for a song, hats for a quarter, and spectacles, warranted to suit the eye, at the optician's who has opened shop on a Hester Street door-step, for thirty five cents; frowsy-looking chickens and half-plucked geese, hung by the neck and protesting with wildly strutting feet even in death against the outrage, are the great staple of the market. Half or a quarter of a chicken can be bought here by those who cannot afford a whole. It took more than ten years of persistent effort on the part of the sanitary authorities to drive the trade in live fowl from the streets to the fowl-market on Gouverneur Slip, where the killing is now done according to Jewish rite by priests detailed for the purpose by the chief rabbi. Since then they have had a characteristic rumpus, that involved the entire Jewish community, over the fees for killing and the mode of collecting them. Here is a woman churning horse-radish on a machine she has chained and padlocked to a tree on the sidewalk, lest someone steal it. Beside her a butcher's stand with cuts at prices the avenues never dreamed of. Old coats are hawked for fifty cents, "as good as new," and "pants"—there are no trousers in Jewtown, only pants—at anything that can be got. There is a knot of half a dozen "pants" pedlars in the middle of the street, twice as many men of their own race fingering their wares and plucking at the seams with the anxious scrutiny of would-be buyers, though none of them has the least idea of investing in a pair. Yes, stop! This baker, fresh from his trough, bare-headed and with bare arms, has made an offer: for this pair thirty cents; a dollar and forty was the price asked. The pedlar shrugs his shoulders, and turns up his hands with a half pitying, wholly indignant air. What does the baker take him for? Such pants —. The baker has turned to go. With a jump like a panther's, the man with the pants has him by the sleeve. Will he give eighty cents? Sixty? Fifty? So help him, they are dirt cheap at that. Lose, will he, on the trade, lose all the profit of his day's pedling. The baker goes on unmoved. Forty then? What, not forty? Take them then for thirty, and wreck the life of a poor man. And the baker takes them and goes, well knowing that at least twenty cents of the thirty, two hundred per cent., were clear profit, if indeed the "pants" cost the pedlar anything.

The suspender pedlar is the mystery of the Pig-market, omnipresent and unfathomable. He is met at every step with his wares dangling over his shoulder, down his back, and in front. Millions of suspenders thus perambulate Jewtown all day on a sort of dress parade. Why suspenders, is the puzzle, and where do they all go to? The "pants" of Jewtown hang down with a common accord, as if they had never known the support of suspenders. It appears to be as characteristic a trait of the race as the long beard and the Sabbath silk hat of ancient pedigree. I have asked again and again. No one has ever been able to tell me what becomes of the suspenders of Jewtown. Perhaps they are hung up as bric-à-brac in its homes, or laid away and saved up as the equivalent of cash. I cannot tell. I only know that more suspenders are hawked about the Pig-market every day than would supply the whole of New York for a year, were they all bought and turned to use. . . .

THE BOHEMIANS—TENEMENT-HOUSE CIGARMAKING

Evil as the part is which the tenement plays in Jewtown as the pretext for circumventing the law that was made to benefit and relieve the tenant, we have not far to go to find it in even a worse rôle. If the tenement is here continually dragged into the eye of public condemnation and scorn, it is because in one way or another it is found directly responsible for, or intimately associated with, three-fourths of the miseries of the poor. In the Bohemian quarter it is made the vehicle for enforcing upon a proud race a slavery as real as any that ever disgraced the South. Not content with simply robbing the tenant, the owner, in the dual capacity of landlord and employer, reduces him to virtual serfdom by making his becoming *his* tenant, on such terms as he sees fit to make, the condition of employment at wages likewise of his own making. It does not help the case that this landlord employer, almost always a Jew, is frequently of the thrifty Polish race just described.

Perhaps the Bohemian quarter is hardly the proper name to give to the colony, for though it has distinct boundaries it is scattered over a wide area on the East Side, in wedge-like streaks that relieve the monotony of the solid German population by their strong contrasts. The two races mingle no more on this side of the Atlantic than on the rugged slopes of the Bohemian mountains; the echoes of the thirty years' war ring in New York, after two centuries and a half, with as fierce a hatred as the gigantic combat bred among the vanquished Czechs. A chief reason for this is doubtless the complete isolation of the Bohemian immigrant. Several causes operate to bring this about: his singularly harsh and unattractive language, which he can neither easily himself unlearn nor impart to others, his stubborn pride of race, and a popular prejudice which has forced upon him the unjust stigma of a disturber of the public peace and an enemy of organized labor. I greatly mistrust that the Bohemian on our shores is a much-abused man. To his traducer, who casts up anarchism against him, he replies that the last census (1880) shows his people to have the fewest criminals of all in proportion to numbers. In New York a Bohemian criminal is such a rarity that the case of two firebugs of several years ago is remembered with damaging distinctness. The accusation that he lives like the "rat" he is, cutting down wages by his underpaid labor, he throws back in the teeth of the trades unions with the counter-charge that they are the first cause of his attitude to the labor question.

A little way above Houston Street the first of his colonies is encountered, in Fifth Street and thereabouts. Then for a mile and a half scarce a Bohemian is to be found, until Thirty-eighth Street is reached. Fifty-fourth and Seventy-third Streets in their turn are the centres of populous Bohemian settlements. The location of the cigar factories, upon which he depends for a living, determines his choice of home, though there is less choice about it than with any other class in the community, save perhaps the colored people. Probably more than half of all the Bohemians in this city are cigarmakers, and it is the herding of these in great numbers in the so-called tenement factories, where the cheapest grade of work is done at the lowest wages, that constitutes at once their greatest hardship and the chief grudge of other workmen against them. The manufacturer who owns, say, from three or four to a dozen or more tenements contiguous to his shop, fills them up with these people, charging them outrageous rents, and demanding often even a preliminary deposit of five dollars "key money;" deals them out tobacco by the week, and devotes the rest of his energies to the paring down of wages to within a peg or two of the point where the tenant rebels in desperation. When he does rebel, he is given the alternative of submission, or eviction with entire loss of employment. His needs determine the issue. Usually he is not in a position to hesitate long. Unlike the Polish Jew, whose example of untiring industry he emulates, he has seldom much laid up against a rainy day. He is fond of a glass of beer, and likes to live as well as his means will permit. The shop triumphs, and fetters more galling than ever are forged for the tenant. In the opposite case, the newspapers have to record the throwing upon the street of a small army of people, with pitiful cases of destitution and family misery.

Men, women and children work together seven days in the week in these cheerless tenements to make a living for the family, from the break of day till far into the night. Often the wife is the original cigarmaker from the old home, the husband having adopted her trade here as a matter of necessity, because, knowing no word of English, he could get no other work. As they state the cause of the bitter hostility of the trades unions, she was the primary bone of contention in the day of the early Bohemian immigration. The unions refused to admit the women, and, as the support of the family depended upon her to a large extent, such terms as were offered had to be accepted. The manufacturer has ever since industriously fanned the antagonism between the unions and his hands, for his own advantage. The victory rests with him, since the Court of Appeals decided that the law, passed a few years ago, to prohibit cigarmaking in tenements was unconstitutional, and thus put an end to the struggle. While it lasted, all sorts of frightful stories were told of the shocking conditions under which people lived and worked in these tenements, from a sanitary point of view especially, and a general impression survives to this day that they are particularly desperate. The Board of Health, after a careful canvass, did not find them so then. I am satisfied from personal inspection, at a much later day, guided in a number of instances by the union cigarmakers themselves to the tenements which they considered the worst, that the accounts were greatly exaggerated. Doubtless the people are poor, in many cases very poor; but they are not uncleanly, rather the reverse; they live much better than the clothing-makers in the Tenth Ward, and in spite of their sallow look, that may be due to the all-pervading smell of tobacco, they do not appear to be less healthy than other in-door workers. I found on my tours of investigation several cases of consumption, of which one at least was said by the doctor to be due to the constant inhalation of tobacco fumes. But an examination of the death records in the Health Department does not support the claim that the Bohemian cigarmakers are peculiarly prone to that disease. On the contrary, the Bohemian percentage of deaths from consumption appears quite low. This, however, is a line of scientific inquiry which I leave to others to pursue, along with the more involved problem whether the falling off in the number of children, sometimes quite noticeable in the Bohemian settlements, is, as has been suggested, dependent upon the character of the parents' work. The sore grievances I found were the miserable wages and the enormous rents exacted for the minimum of accommodation. And surely these stand for enough of suffering.

Take a row of houses in East Tenth Street as an instance. They contained thirty-five families of cigarmakers, with probably not half a dozen persons in the whole lot of them, outside of the children, who could speak a word of English, though many had been in the country half a lifetime. This room with two windows giving on the street, and a rear attachment without windows, called a bedroom by courtesy, is rented at $12.25 a month. In the front room man and wife work at the bench from six in the morning till nine at night. They make a team, stripping the tobacco leaves together; then he makes the filler, and she rolls the wrapper on and finishes the cigar. For a thousand they receive $3.75, and can turn out together three thousand cigars a week. The point has been reached where the rebellion comes in, and the workers in these tenements are just now on a strike, demanding $5.00 and $5.50 for their work. The manufacturer having refused, they are expecting hourly to be served with notice to quit their homes, and the going of a stranger among them excites their resentment, until his errand is explained. While we are in the house, the ultimatum of the "boss" is received. He will give $3.75 a thousand, not another cent. Our host is a man of seeming intelligence, yet he has been nine years in New York and knows neither English nor German. Three bright little children play about the floor. . . .

A man with venerable beard and keen eyes answers our questions through an interpreter, in the next house. Very few brighter faces would be met in a day's walk among American mechanics, yet he has in nine years learned no syllable of English. German he probably does not want to learn. His story supplies the explanation, as did the stories of the others. In all that time he has been at work grubbing to earn bread. Wife and he by constant labor make three thousand cigars a week, earning $11.25 when there is no lack of material; when in winter they receive from the manufacturer tobacco for only two thousand, the rent of $10 for two rooms, practically one with a dark alcove, has nevertheless to be paid in full, and six mouths to be fed. He was a blacksmith in the old country, but cannot work at his trade here because he does not understand "Engliska." If he could, he says, with a bright look, he could do better work than he sees done here. It would seem happiness to him to knock off at 6 o'clock instead of working, as he now often has to do, till midnight. But how? He knows of no Bohemian blacksmith who can understand him; he should starve. Here, with his wife, he can make a living at least. "Aye," says she, turning, from listening, to her household duties, "it would be nice for sure to have father work at his trade." Then what a home she could make for them, and how happy they would be. Here is an unattainable ideal, indeed, of a workman in the most prosperous city in the world! There is genuine, if unspoken, pathos in the soft tap she gives her husband's hand as she goes about her work with a half-suppressed little sigh.

The very ash-barrels that stand in front of the big rows of tenements in Seventy-first and Seventy-third Streets advertise the business that is carried on within. They are filled to the brim with the stems of stripped tobacco leaves. The rank smell that waited for us on the corner of the block follows us into the hallways, penetrates every nook and cranny of the houses. As in the settlement farther down town, every room here has its work-bench with its stumpy knife and queer pouch of bed-tick, worn brown and greasy, fastened in front the whole length of the bench to receive the scraps of waste. This landlord-employer at all events gives three rooms for $12.50, if two be dark, one wholly and the other getting some light from the front room. The mother of the three bare-footed little children we met on the stairs was taken to the hospital the other day when she could no longer work. She will never come out alive. There is no waste in these tenements. Lives, like clothes, are worn through and out before put aside. Her place at the bench is taken already by another who divides with the head of the household his earnings of $15.50 a week. He has just come out successful of a strike that brought the pay of these tenements up to $4.50 per thousand cigars. Notice to quit had already been served on them, when the employer decided to give in, frightened by the prospective loss of rent. Asked how long he works, the man says: "from they can see till bed-time." Bed-time proves to be eleven o'clock. Seventeen hours a day, seven days in the week, at thirteen cents an hour for the two, six cents and a half for each! Good average earnings for a tenement-house cigarmaker in summer. In winter it is at least one-fourth less. In spite of it all, the rooms are cleanly kept. From the bed-room farthest back the woman brings out a pile of moist tobacco-leaves to be stripped. They are kept there, under cover lest they dry and crack, from Friday to Friday, when an accounting is made and fresh supplies given out. The people sleep there too, but the smell, offensive to the unfamiliar nose, does not bother them. They are used to it. . . .

But what of his being an Anarchist, this Bohemian—an infidel—I hear somebody say. Almost one might be persuaded by such facts as these—and they are everyday facts, not fancy—to retort: what more natural? With every hand raised against him in the old land and the new, in the land of his hoped-for freedom, what more logical than that his should be turned against society that seems to exist only for his oppression? But the charge is not half true. Naturally the Bohemian loves peace, as he loves music and song. As someone has said: He does not seek war, but when attacked knows better how to die than how to surrender. The Czech is the Irishman of Central Europe, with all his genius and his strong passions, with the same bitter traditions of landlord-robbery, perpetuated here where he thought to forget them; like him ever and on principle in the opposition, "agin the government" wherever he goes. Among such a people, ground by poverty until their songs have died in curses upon their oppressors, hopelessly isolated and ignorant of our language and our laws, it would not be hard for bad men at any time to lead a few astray. And this is what has been done. Yet, even with the occasional noise made by the few, the criminal statistics already alluded to quite dispose of the charge that they incline to turbulence and riot. So it is with the infidel propaganda, the legacy perhaps of the fierce contention through hundreds of years between Catholics and Protestants on Bohemia's soil, of bad faith and savage persecutions in the name of the Christians' God that disgrace its history. The Bohemian clergyman, who spoke for his people at the Christian Conference held in Chickering Hall two years ago, took even stronger ground. "They are Roman Catholics by birth, infidels by necessity, and Protestants by history and inclination," he said. Yet he added his testimony in the same breath to the fact that, though the Freethinkers had started two schools in the immediate neighborhood of his church to counteract its influence, his flock had grown in a few years from a mere handful at the start to proportions far beyond his hopes, gathering in both Anarchists and Freethinkers, and making good church members of them.

Thus the whole matter resolves itself once more into a question of education, all the more urgent because these people are poor, miserably poor almost to a man. "There is not," said one of them, who knew thoroughly what he was speaking of, "there is not one of them all, who, if he were to sell all he was worth to-morrow, would have money enough to buy a house and lot in the country."

THE COLOR LINE IN NEW YORK

The color line must be drawn through the tenements to give the picture its proper shading. The landlord does the drawing, does it with an absence of pretence, a frankness of despotism, that is nothing if not brutal. The Czar of all the Russias is not more absolute upon his own soil than the New York landlord in his dealings with colored tenants. Where he permits them to live, they go; where he shuts the door, stay out. By his grace they exist at all in certain localities; his ukase banishes them from others. He accepts the responsibility, when laid at his door, with unruffled complacency. It is business, he will tell you. And it is. He makes the prejudice in which he traffics pay him well, and that, as he thinks it quite superfluous to tell you, is what he is there for.

That his pencil does not make quite as black a mark as it did, that the hand that wields it does not bear down as hard as only a short half dozen years ago, is the hopeful sign of an awakening public conscience under the stress of which the line shows signs of wavering. But for this the landlord deserves no credit. It has come, is coming about despite him.

The line may not be wholly effaced while the name of the negro, alone among the world's races, is spelled with a small n. Natural selection will have more or less to do beyond a doubt in every age with dividing the races; only so, it may be, can they work out together their highest destiny. But with the despotism that deliberately assigns to the defenceless Black the lowest level for the purpose of robbing him there that has nothing to do. Of such slavery, different only in degree from the other kind that held him as a chattel, to be sold or bartered at the will of his master, this century, if signs fail not, will see the end in New York.

Ever since the war New York has been receiving the overflow of colored population from the Southern cities. In the last decade this migration has grown to such proportions that it is estimated that our Blacks have quite doubled in number since the Tenth Census. Whether the exchange has been of advantage to the negro may well be questioned. Trades of which he had practical control in his Southern home are not open to him here. I know that it may be answered that there is no industrial proscription of color; that it is a matter of choice. Perhaps so. At all events he does not choose then. How many colored carpenters or masons has anyone seen at work in New York? In the South there are enough of them and, if the testimony of the most intelligent of their people is worth anything, plenty of them have come here. As a matter of fact the colored man takes in New York, without a struggle, the lower level of menial service for which his past traditions and natural love of ease perhaps as yet fit him best. Even the colored barber is rapidly getting to be a thing of the past. Along shore, at any unskilled labor, he works unmolested; but he does not appear to prefer the job. His sphere thus defined, he naturally takes his stand among the poor, and in the homes of the poor. Until very recent times—the years since a change was wrought can be counted on the fingers of one hand—he was practically restricted in the choice of a home to a narrow section on the West Side, that nevertheless had a social top and bottom to it—the top in the tenements on the line of Seventh Avenue as far north as Thirty-second Street, where he was allowed to occupy the houses of unsavory reputation which the police had cleared and for which decent white tenants could not be found; the bottom in the vile rookeries of Thompson Street and South Fifth Avenue, the old "Africa" that is now fast becoming a modern Italy. To-day there are black colonies in Yorkville and Morrisania. The encroachment of business and the Italian below, and the swelling of the population above, have been the chief agents in working out his second emancipation, a very real one, for with his cutting loose from the old tenements there has come a distinct and gratifying improvement in the tenant, that argues louder than theories or speeches the influence of vile surroundings in debasing the man. The colored citizen whom this year's census man found in his Ninety-ninth Street "flat" is a very different individual from the "nigger" his predecessor counted in the black-and-tan slums of Thompson and Sullivan Streets. There is no more clean and orderly community in New York than the new settlement of colored people that is growing up on the East Side from Yorkville to Harlem.

Cleanliness is the characteristic of the negro in his new surroundings, as it was his virtue in the old. In this respect he is immensely the superior of the lowest of the whites, the Italians and the Polish Jews, below whom he has been classed in the past in the tenant scale. Nevertheless, he has always had to pay higher rents than even these for the poorest and most stinted rooms. The exceptions I have come across, in which the rents, though high, have seemed more nearly on a level with what was asked for the same number and size of rooms in the average tenement, were in the case of tumble-down rookeries in which no one else would live, and were always coupled with the condition that the landlord should "make no repairs." It can readily be seen that his profits were scarcely curtailed by his "humanity." The reason advanced for this systematic robbery is that white people will not live in the same house with colored tenants, or even in a house recently occupied by negroes, and that consequently its selling value is injured. The prejudice undoubtedly exists, but it is not lessened by the house agents, who have set up the maxim "once a colored house, always a colored house."

There is method in the maxim, as shown by an inquiry made last year by the *Real Estate Record*. It proved agents to be practically unanimous in the endorsement of the negro as a clean, orderly, and "profitable" tenant. Here is the testimony of one of the largest real estate firms in the city: "We would rather have negro tenants in our poorest class of tenements than the lower grades of foreign white people. We find the former cleaner than the latter, and they do not destroy the property so much. We also get higher prices. We have a tenement on Nineteenth Street, where we get $10 for two rooms which we could not get more than $7.50 for from white tenants previously. We have a four-story tenement on our books on Thirty-third Street, between Sixth and Seventh Avenues, with four rooms per floor—a parlor, two bedrooms, and a kitchen. We get $20 for the first floor, $24 for the second, $23 for the third and $20 for the fourth, in all $87 or $1,044 per annum. The size of the building is only 21+55." Another firm declared that in a specified instance they had saved fifteen to twenty per cent. on the gross rentals since they changed from white to colored tenants. Still another gave the following case of a front and rear tenement that had formerly been occupied by tenants of a "low European type," who had been turned out on account of filthy habits and poor pay. The negroes proved cleaner, better, and steadier tenants. Instead, however, of having their rents reduced in consequence, [there was] an increased rental of $17 per month, or $204 a year, and an advance of nearly thirteen and one-half per cent. on the gross rental "in favor" of the colored tenant. Profitable, surely! . . .

Poverty, abuse, and injustice alike the negro accepts with imperturbable cheerfulness. His philosophy is of the kind that has no room for repining. Whether he lives in an Eighth Ward barrack or in a tenement with a brown-stone front and pretensions to the title of "flat," he looks at the sunny side of life and enjoys it. He loves fine clothes and good living a good deal more than he does a bank account. The proverbial rainy day it would be rank ingratitude, from his point of view, to look for when the sun shines unclouded in a clear sky. His home surroundings, except when he is utterly depraved, reflect his blithesome temper. The poorest negro housekeeper's room in New York is bright with gaily-colored prints of his beloved "Abe Linkum," General Grant, President Garfield, Mrs. Cleveland, and other national celebrities, and cheery with flowers and singing birds. In the art of putting the best foot foremost, of disguising his poverty by making a little go a long way, our negro has no equal. When a fair share of prosperity is his, he knows how to make life and home very pleasant to those about him. Pianos and parlor furniture abound in the uptown homes of colored tenants and give them a very prosperous air. But even where the wolf howls at the door, he makes a bold and gorgeous front. The amount of "style" displayed on fine Sundays on Sixth and Seventh Avenues by colored holiday-makers would turn a pessimist black with wrath. The negro's great ambition is to rise in the social scale to which his color has made him a stranger and an outsider, and he is quite willing to accept the shadow for the substance where that is the best he can get. The claw-hammer coat and white tie of a waiter in a first-class summer hotel, with the chance of taking his ease in six months of winter, are to him the next best thing to mingling with the white quality he serves, on equal terms. His festive gatherings, pre-eminently his cake-walks, at which a sugared and frosted cake is the proud prize of the couple with the most aristocratic step and carriage, are comic mixtures of elaborate ceremonial and the joyous abandon of the natural man. With all his ludicrous incongruities, his sensuality and his lack of moral accountability, his superstition and other faults that are the effect of temperament and of centuries of slavery, he has his eminently good points. He is loyal to the backbone, proud of being an American and of his new-found citizenship. He is at least as easily moulded for good as for evil. His churches are crowded to the doors on Sunday nights when the colored colony turns out to worship. His people own church property in this city upon which they have paid half a million dollars out of the depth of their poverty, with comparatively little assistance from their white brethren. He is both willing and anxious to learn, and his intellectual status is distinctly improving. If his emotions are not very deeply rooted, they are at least sincere while they last, and until the tempter gets the upper hand again.

Of all the temptations that beset him, the one that troubles him and the police most is his passion for gambling. The game of policy is a kind of unlawful penny lottery specially adapted to his means, but patronized extensively by poor white players as well. It is the meanest of swindles, but reaps for its backers rich fortunes wherever colored people congregate. Between the fortune-teller and the policy shop, closely allied frauds always, the wages of many a hard day's work are wasted by the negro; but the loss causes him few regrets. Penniless, but with undaunted faith in his ultimate "luck," he looks forward to the time when he shall once more be able to take a hand at "beating policy." When periodically the negro's lucky numbers, 4–11–44, come out on the slips of the alleged daily drawings, that are supposed to be held in some far-off Western town, intense excitement reigns in Thompson Street and along the Avenue, where someone is always the winner. An immense impetus is given then to the bogus business that has no existence outside of the cigar stores and candy shops where it hides from the law, save in some cunning Bowery "broker's" back office, where the slips are printed and the "winnings" apportioned daily with due regard to the backer's interests.

It is a question whether "Africa" has been improved by the advent of the Italian, with the tramp from the Mulberry Street Bend in his train. The moral turpitude of Thompson Street has been notorious for years, and the mingling of the three elements does not seem to have wrought any change for the better. The border-land where the white and black races meet in common debauch, the aptly-named black-and-tan saloon, has never been debatable ground from a moral stand-point. It has always been the worst of the desperately bad. Than this commingling of the utterly depraved of both sexes, white and black, on such ground, there can be no greater abomination. Usually it is some foul cellar dive, perhaps run by the political "leader" of the district, who is "in with" the police. In any event it gathers to itself all the lawbreakers and all the human wrecks within reach. When a fight breaks out during the dance a dozen razors are handy in as many boot-legs, and there is always a job for the surgeon and the ambulance. The black "tough" is as handy with the razor in a fight as his peaceably inclined brother is with it in pursuit of his honest trade. As the Chinaman hides his knife in his sleeve and the Italian his stiletto in the bosom, so the negro goes to the ball with a razor in his boot-leg, and on occasion does as much execution with it as both of the others together. More than three-fourths of the business the police have with the colored people in New York arises in the black-and-tan district, now no longer fairly representative of their color.

I have touched briefly upon such facts in the negro's life as may serve to throw light on the social condition of his people in New York. If, when the account is made up between the races, it shall be claimed that he falls short of the result to be expected from twenty-five years of freedom, it may be well to turn to the other side of the ledger and see how much of the blame is borne by the prejudice and greed that have kept him from rising under a burden of responsibility to which he could hardly be equal. And in this view he may be seen to have advanced much farther and faster than before suspected, and to promise, after all, with fair treatment, quite as well as the rest of us, his white-skinned fellow-citizens, had any right to expect.

Letters from Welsh Immigrants

FROM JOHN POWELL IN HYDE PARK, LUZERNE COUNTY, PENNSYLVANIA

June 20, 1871

The strike which lasted for six months all but nine days has finished. An excellent strike in length, wasn't it? It is true that many families had to suffer great hardship, such as those newly come over to this country together with those who had wasted their earnings while the works were in operation rather than prepare for a time of this kind. But however great the need, nobody starved here and we believe that that fact in itself, that so many workmen could stay out for so long without starving, is ample proof that this country is excellent for the workmen of Old Britain. We had a terrible struggle here and the chief object of the company was to destroy our union because they knew that if they could succeed in this they could easily defeat us, but they failed and the union is stronger than ever. The company swore that they would not give us more than eighty-six cents a car even if they had to keep their works shut for two years but they had to give way on everything and to give ninety-three and a half cents a car. A car carries a ton and a half of clean coal. It is true that they got a number of old, spineless Irish to be blacklegs (turn-coats) at one of the pits and succeeded in getting hundreds of soldiers here to guard them going to work, coming from work, at work during the day and in their houses during the night, but they failed to defeat us. Had it not been for those old Irish we would have won a complete victory two months sooner had they been as united as the Welsh. But as other Irish, weak in faith, tended to give way with their brothers to the turn-coats it was judged that it would be better to compromise and so it was done and the struggle was brought to an end. Two Welshmen lost their lives at the end of the strike. You had the story of their murder in the papers that I sent to you.

FROM SAMUEL AB THOMAS IN ARNOT, TIOGA COUNTY, PENNSYLVANIA [1874]

There are four large coal works in Tioga County by the names of Morris

Alan Conway (ed.), *The Welsh in America: Letters from the Immigrants* (Minneapolis: University of Minnesota Press, 1961), pp. 191–192, 194–196, 200–210, 222–224, 228–230.

Run, Fallbrook, Antrim, and Arnot. You all know about the bankers' debts a few months ago which caused the new railroads to be stopped, mills and furnaces to be blown out, and the coal works to be stopped, etc. so that thousands of craftsmen, puddlers, and laborers have been thrown out of work to live or die as best as they can. We in this country have had to bend to the ground under the burdens placed on us by the avaricious, tyrannical masters. We were forced throughout the years to work for low wages which were hardly enough to keep body and soul together, to accept those wages in script which was worthless outside the local trading circle of the company and to buy all our goods from their store and pay twenty-five per cent more than we could get in other places together with robbing us of half of our coal, taxed for what we knew not, without any receipt. Also to show us their power, they forced us to sign the contract law which was against the law of the state government, that is that if any misunderstanding occurred between master and workman, the latter had to leave his house with ten days notice according to the contract law, whereas the state government allowed three months.

But although we suffered the above without grumbling throughout the years it was not enough to satisfy the greed of our masters, for early this winter they rushed on us with the fierceness of a lion on its prey lowering us to twenty per cent and also threatening us with ten per cent and forcing us to bind ourselves not to accept money for our labor until 20 May 1874. In the face of such tyranny and oppression, we called a meeting of the workmen for the purpose of drawing up some plan to withstand the continuance of such tyranny and oppression. We resolved to form a branch of the National Miners and Laborers Benevolent Association of Pennsylvania which was backed by the government a few years ago and gave it a charter. As I understand it this same union pays well throughout the country and we hope it will be the same here.

But when the company heard that we had formed a union, they stopped the works to kill it in its infancy and so it has been for two months. They put a notice on the wall containing the conditions under which we could restart working. (1) Are you a member of the union of miners in the County of Tioga or of any like society? (2) If you are not a member will you undertake not to join such a society in the future? (3) If you are a member will you undertake to break your connection with that society and not to join such a thing again?

When they understood that one and all we refused the above terms they put the screw to work, that is warning us to leave our houses within ten days and when the time came and we had not left our houses, they summoned us before the judge to demand why we refused to obey the warnings. The cruel judge would not listen to us as he had been bought body and soul by the company and gave judgment against us together with having to pay all costs. So hundreds and hundreds of families were forced to leave their houses and to look for fresh houses amid the snow and ice. What a terrible sight it was to see hundreds of innocent men, women, and children having to break up their comfortable homes without knowing where to go. But Providence worked for us, opening up the hearts of the farmers and tradesmen to take pity on us by opening their doors and taking us in together with helping with our keep. Also the union has played its part wonderfully and the country generally feels for us and sends contributions; to crown it all Providence has given us a milder winter than they have had in these parts. All the costs charged to us have been returned as costs cannot be charged unless the person is worth three hundred dollars.

P.S. In the circumstances I thought it better to send my family back to Wales. I heard that the ship had left but nothing more and if anyone reads these lines, news of them would be welcome whether they are dead or alive.

FROM RICHARD EDWARDS IN POTTSVILLE, PENNSYLVANIA [1888]

I am thankful that the strike in the coal works here ended in February. The workmen, poor things, had to go back to work for less money than was offered to them in January. They had been standing out in Lehigh Co. since the beginning of September and in Schuylkill, Carbon, and Northumberland for two months, all of which threw fifty to sixty thousand into idleness. It is difficult to imagine the tragedy and the trouble endured by thousands. Many were urging them to stand firm against oppression and to demand the same wages as paid before but as the price of coal had gone down, the companies refused to pay this, causing the most pitiful consequences. Besides the workmen's losses, the companies lost hundreds and thousands of dollars to keep the water out of the works, etc. Many of the best breakers were smashed by unknown people as revenge on the masters and hundreds of special police were employed to keep the peace and to prevent rioting. It appears that many of the colliers and miners in America were unwilling to accept decreases but one cannot avoid this when trade gets worse.

It is the same here in the iron and steel works. Strikes and suspensions are frequent everywhere. Competition is strong and the companies are taking advantage of this to employ Poles, Hungarians, Negroes, and foreigners unused to that kind of work and in this way making the old workmen idle. It is a good thing that Welshmen understand every kind of work better than they do, so that the Welsh get the jobs of foremen because they must have some experienced men whom they can trust as many accidents have taken place because some workman was not careful enough or did not know enough to avoid such occurrences. Hundreds of lives were lost because of this.

January 11, 1892

Coal Creek and Briceville are two famous coal villages in the eastern part of the above state about three miles from each other. There is a bed of excellent steam coal here, about four feet thick. At the end of the war in 1865, they started working coal here. Two Welsh brothers, Joseph and David Richards, opened the first coalmine and built log houses. Three of the coalmines were opened by other companies soon afterwards. A large community of Welsh settled in the place and chapels were built to hold religious services in Welsh. There are very few of the old settlers left here now. Within a few years Messrs. Richards sold their interests to the Knoxville Iron Company. The wages for cutting coal at that time were four cents a bushel. The wages for cutting coal now is fifty cents a ton. At the beginning of 1877 the owners demanded a lowering in wages. The colliers stood firm and the strike lasted for a long time. In the end, the Knoxville Iron Company made an agreement with the governor of the state to get convicts to work in their mines and this agreement was to last for six or seven years. The agreement was carried out and about 140 to 160 criminals sentenced to hard labor for their wicked deeds, such as thieves, housebreakers, murderers, etc. came to work in the valley. This strange migration forced the first settlers to sell their houses and land and to go elsewhere. There was bitter strife in the district, when the end of the first agreement came. The state government was approached and a number of major accusations about the barbaric cruelty used towards the prisoners were brought forward. A commission was appointed and a great number of witnesses were questioned, but the end was to legalize the institution of putting convicts to work in the coalmines. Consequently the convicts were kept working there until last summer.

In 1888, the railroad was extended for three miles to the south of Coal Creek and three additional collieries were opened in the valley. A village called Briceville was built containing many hundreds of houses and a great number of them together with the plots on which they stood belonged to the inhabitants. One of the chief shareholders and a governor of the colliery at the end of the railroad is a Welshman, raised in America. At the beginning of 1890 there was a series of complaints and misunderstandings between the employers and employees of this colliery and sometime last summer a stockade was built and about 120 to 140 convicts were put to work in the mine with two or three armed guards of the state of Tennessee to watch over them. This caused bitterness and uneasiness among the inhabitants of Briceville and in the district for twenty miles around because of the loss in the trading sense and the notoriety in the social sense.

At last, at the end of July, the colliers and their supporters gathered together in a band of about twenty-five hundred. They surrounded the stockade of the Tennessee mines and sent a deputation to the officer of the guards ordering him to leave and to take the convicts in orderly fashion with him to the state prison. If he refused to obey, the men would attack and let every convict go where he wished and the stockade would be smashed to pieces. The officer of the guards saw that it would be foolish to stand out against such a daring band and left in peace for the railroad station in Coal Creek, keeping watch on the prisoners. The collier army followed them shouting victoriously.

After going three miles and coming by the Knoxville Iron Company coalmine, the miners split into two parts, one half to follow the Briceville convicts to the station and the other to order the convicts at Coal Creek and their guard to follow their fellow convicts. Those in charge at this settlement also obeyed without opposition and soon two groups of convicts and guards could be seen on the railroad coalcars and the engine taking them safely to the prison in Knoxville.

After that the colliers met in council and twenty were put to guard the Knoxville Iron Company property so that there should be no damage done to it. Everyone else went home without firing a shot. No drinking was permitted and no one lost a pennyworth of his possessions. The governor called out the state militia and headed for Coal Creek but fortunately he left the soldiers in Knoxville and boldly went among the citizens whom he considered mob leaders and rebels against the government. He came to Coal Creek and a crowd gathered to meet him. His reception was polite but not enthusiastic. It was decided to have arbitration on the matter and within a week it was decided that the arbitration should last sixty days on condition that the governor should summon the legislature immediately to discuss the matter. In the meantime the convicts should return to the coalmines. The legislature met and sat for four weeks in September. A deputation of colliers went to Nashville to plead the injustice of the convict law but the members, two thirds of whom were farmers, would not give them a hearing. The state senators encouraged the governor to use every means to compel obedience to the law although the press throughout all the states demanded that the complaints of the colliers should be heard.

When the deputation returned from Nashville it was obvious that loyalty to the government had declined rapidly but to stop the trouble, the colliers raised the legal issue that the present agreement on convict labor was contrary to the laws of the United States and they won their case in the county court; but an appeal was lodged with a higher court in the state and judgment was given against the colliers. The Supreme Court's decision was published in the last week of October. On Thursday night of the same week, armed bands gathered around the two prisons in Coal Creek and Briceville firing sticks of dynamite and holes were blown in the stout wooden walls. The guards were frightened and the convicts were allowed to go where they wanted and Briceville prison was burned to the ground. It is said that the reason why the Knoxville Iron Company's prison was saved and not burned was that the works manager's house was attached to the prison and the convicts that were released pleaded that the kind wife of the manager should not be frightened or put in danger. She is a gentle and kind Welsh woman.

The following Sunday they attacked in the same fashion the Olive Springs prison, a coal village about fifteen miles south of Briceville. The convicts were set free and the prison burned. By the beginning of spring, Briceville was again free of convicts. After these disturbances, the governor offered large rewards for evidence against anyone who took part in the disturbances but not one accuser has come forward yet. The coalmines were run excellently in the last two months of the year by employing free labor. Everyone was fully and regularly employed. The only uneasy people were the owners of the two collieries and the government officers. The week before Christmas it was judged that harsher measures were being prepared by the government and on the morning of the last day of the year, twenty-two fully armed soldiers, one cannon, one Gatling gun and tons of equipment together with balls and powder arrived on a special train at Coal Creek station. Nobody knew of their coming. They went quickly into camp on top of the hill near the convict prison of the Knoxville Iron Company coalmine. On Saturday morning the second day of the year, a band of 125 convicts together with twenty-five armed guards were moved in railroad carriages near to the coalworks. The colliers and their supporters were angry and threatening. The following letter was distributed among the people of the neighborhood: "The convicts shall not stay here again. We pray for blessing on our people, destruction on the convicts, destruction on the instigators, destruction on the militia. We must attack. It makes no difference what the consequences may be, death, destruction, anarchy! One hundred and sixty-seven people think they can frighten us! Will we put up with this? No! never! The time has come to rush to the defense of our families and our homes!"

FROM JOHN R. WILLIAMS (A NATIVE OF ABERDARE) AT THE ALGOMA COAL AND COKE COMPANY, ALGOMA, MCDOWELL COUNTY, WEST VIRGINIA, TO WILLIAM THOMAS, BRYNAWEL, ABERDARE

November 10, 1895

You will I am sure be surprised to find I am in the wilds of West Virginia; well, I came down here in the middle of June last and I like to be here very much and I am getting on all right.

Up at Wilkes-Barre, I failed to get a show anyhow, the mining homes there block an Englishman; a foreigner has no chance in that state unless he is a citizen of the U.S.A. and that means residence in the country five years.

I worked for months at the Lehigh and Wilkes-Barre coal company's

Stanton colliery with a timberman and repairers gang. We were three in the gang and had the main engine planes to keep in repair. It was very hard work as the timbering had to be very heavy, not a stick allowed under 18 inches in diameter, the arms averaging 9 feet long with 12-foot collars, the seam we worked in being the celebrated Baltimore Vein, which is 18 feet in thickness in all. I never saw such splendid timbering in my life as is done in America. All the notching and dressing of the timber is done with the crosscut saw and adze, and must fit to a nicety, and that is the only good thing I have seen in American mining. As for everything else, they are as ancient as Adam. The head of the gang was getting $2.50 but my partner and I were only getting $1.88 (per day). The collieries of this company got to run so badly that I left and went to work in the No. 4 shaft of the Kingstone collieries. There again 2 worked with a timberman and earned more money, inasmuch that the miners were kept working more regular than Stanton.

The coal trade in the anthracite districts has been extremely dull all through the year, the production overwhelmingly overbalancing the demand. Labor is so plentiful that operators can do just what they please. Pennsylvania is swarming with foreigners—Poles, Hungarians, Slavish, Swedes, and Italians, etc.—who are fast driving the English, Welsh, and Scotch miners out of competition. Noticeably, the Poles and Hungarians are a harder-working people and physically stronger men than the English and Welsh. They live much harder and at about half the cost and can stand more and harder work than our countrymen.

Before the influx of the foreigners I have named into this country, the Welsh had the best show in the mines here, but in consequence of their foolhardy and unreasonable impositions in pretty well everything, they at length became perfectly unmanageable and the operators had no alternative but to send and get whole cargoes of the foreigners I have named, who now practically monopolize the business, and no longer will America hold out a friendly hand to the British miner who must stay at home and do the best he can there or come here and starve. There are in America today and especially in the west, thousands upon thousands of our countrymen who would gladly return to England and Wales if they could only do so, but they cannot find the money.

Our mines are situated in the Elkhorn about 18 miles up from Pocahontas, the latter place being about 650 miles from Norfolk on the Atlantic coast. The only railway communication for this coalfield is the Norfolk and Western Railroad.

We are on what is called the Pocahontas Flat Top Coalfield which comprises a very large area. The major part of this coalfield belongs to a company called the Flat Top Coal Land Association, who own something like two hundred thousand acres and upwards.

The coal is let at 10 cents per ton, with all timber free for mining purposes. As the name implies, the seam is nearly dead level in all directions and crops out to the surface nearly all over the field. The average thickness of the seam is seven and a half feet of clean coal in one block. It is the prettiest seam of coal I have ever seen. This coalfield is mixed up with a number of zig-zag valleys all over the shop and the slopes all covered with beautiful timber in great abundance, being pine, maple, oak, hickory, and ash. The climate of this state is different to that of Pennsylvania. In the summer the heat is very great during the day but beautifully cool in the mornings and evenings. In Pennsylvania it is unbearably hot at nights and a fellow can't sleep anyhow. I was jolly glad to clear out of it, if only for that very reason alone.

All over this Flat Top coalfield the various companies work the same seam of coal which is called the Pocahontas No. 3 Seam. The quality of this seam of coal is excellent, smokeless steam coal of remarkably fine quality. The various English analysts who have analyzed it one and all pronounce it to be equal to the very best Cardiff steam coal. There is not a particle of gas in this seam—that is, gas given off in working—and that is the salvation of the place. Had it been otherwise they could not compete in the market, as the coal in that event could not be blasted and another mode of working would be too expensive.

We work the coal on the pillar and stall system, drawing the pillars back, the headings being narrow, twelve feet wide, and the stalls six yards wide, with pillars fourteen yards wide. The miners hole under the coal about six feet and then blast it down, sending all out. The miners are paid 60 cents per car for all stall coal and 75 cents per car for all adze coal. The cars hold three tons. No yardage is paid on anything. The miners find all lights, tools and explosives and stand their own props.

Usually, two men work together in every place and fill out on an average six to eight cars per day. All other class of labor is day work. The average cost of production including everything is 40 to 48 cents per ton free on truck at colliery.

The company I am with hold nearly three thousand acres of coal, all leased from the Flat Top Association.

We have three openings on the coal and are now working on an average eight hundred tons per day but in six months time we can turn out two thousand tons per day if trade will allow it. We have two hundred coke ovens and turn out an excellent article. Our haulage from the main double partings underground is done by steam locomotives which do the work splendidly and there is no unpleasant effect from fumes, etc. as the coal is practically smokeless.

Unfortunately, we have about four feet of fine clay on top of our coal, the clay being in three beds. This clay roof is full of kettle bottoms as they are called here (bells at home) and we have also an abundance of the fossil remains of huge trees in this roof. It is a most dangerous roof and we have to watch it for our lives. Those bells are often eight feet in diameter and don't give the slightest warning but simply drop out without any warning whatever. We can't bring our props nearer than ten or twelve feet of the face, on account of blasting the coal.

We have three gangs of men under the charge of slatemen doing nothing but clearing falls, etc.

In America they work ten hours per day exclusive of the one-hour dinner time. We commence working coal at 7 A.M. and knock off at 6 P.M.

All our face haulage is done by mules and it is truly wonderful the hard work they stand. No horse can stand the same amount of work. All our cars (trams) have brakes, so it is all pulling or chain work and no shafting. They could not stand shafting on account of the great weight of the loads.

Now let me tell you something about the people we have in this country. About two thirds are niggars [sic] and practically all our miners are niggars. There are a few white ones among them.

Before I came here I was told the niggars were a most treacherous devilish lot of people to deal with and the only way to manage them was to knock them down with anything at hand, at any slight offense on their part. This was told me by several people in Pennsylvania who had had a great deal of experience with them, so when I came here I expected to have a jabbering semi-wild lot of people to deal with.

I started from Wilkes-Barre on a Monday and came by the Pennsylvania Railroad who booked me through for $17 and came via Harrisburgh, Hagerstown, and Roanoak [sic] and got into Pocahontas at noon on Wednesday. We had four hours to wait there to get up to Algoma. Being beastly tired of the train, I got into a large dining saloon. Presently two niggar young women came to me: they were about eighteen years old and they had delightfully melodious sweet voices and spoke in most guarded and beautiful English. "By jove," says I to myself, "if all the niggars are like these girls, I am jolly glad I came down here." Talking about modest and respectful behavior, why every other place I have ever been to both at home and America, were not in it. I came in contact with several of them, men this time, while waiting at Poco and found them all extremely well behaved and enlightened people. I am extremely fond of them and have not had the slightest trouble with them since I have been here. And I would rather manage five hundred of them than half a dozen of the white people of this country. In dealing with a niggar, you have to be very firm with them and insist upon having your instructions carried out to the letter. I treat them very respectfully and show them that I respect their race and they appreciate that more than words can tell, for most white people treat them otherwise, which is the greatest mistake.

I had not been at the mine a week before I found they were telling one another that the new colonel likes niggars, he don't say you damned black son of a bitch but he say kind things to us. There is not a niggar on the job who won't try to jump out of his skin if I ask him to.

The poor niggar has been shamefully abused and ill treated by white men, more the shame to them. Even the niggar children when you meet them on the road are different to white children, the former are polite and thoroughly well behaved, with no coarse language, the white children, quite the reverse, a filthy low set.

The niggar though is not without his faults. By nature he is an awful thief especially in the eatable line, chickens and turkeys a specialty, but if you catch him in the act, he is not a vicious thief, he will only turn round and make up some cock and bull story to account for it.

He is an awful liar but not a mean one. He lies for fun, bravado, because it's natural to him.

He is outrageously lazy too and like the boa constrictor will not work while his belly is full; consequently we are obliged to keep about double the number we require about the mines, to enable us to have a decent working force at any one time. They live in huts, shacks they are called here, around the mines and the highest standard of morality is not very strictly observed by them. They eat, cook, and sleep all through and through, men, women, girls and boys, makes no difference to them. Few of them go through the form of legal marriage but the greater number live in adultery and when they get tired of one another they change partners. In America, living in adultery is punishable by law, and every now and then lots of them get indicted, just to show that there is just such a law in existence. The penalty is that they must at once marry or go to jail.

The white man of this state and adjoining states is about the most contemptible person on the face of God's earth. He is unbearably ignorant and does not know it. He has generally been brought up on the mountains, hog fashion, and when they come to the mines and earn a lot of money, they swell out and don't know themselves. He is a small ferrety-eyed fellow, with hollow lanky cheeks, a thin pointed nose with about seventeen hairs on his chin and thirteen hairs on his upper lip, which he insultingly calls a moustache. That is the best description I can give you of the native white man of the South.

These detestable cranks seem to think that the poor niggar was made to receive their insults and brutality; so when they meet at those saloons where they sell poison for whisky and vitriol for brandy, those fearful rows begin.

The white men start by clubbing the niggar on the head with a revolver, for everybody is obliged to carry his shooting iron here, and then business is busy and the shooting becomes general, everyone firing away regardless of object, friend or foe. It is nothing unsual here to find four

or five fellows shot dead, and it is quite unusual if this is not the case
on pay nights which, thank God, only comes but once a month. After
doing the fiendish work they clear out to some other place and there is
an end to it unless the authorities come across the villain accidentally.
Such is life in West Virginia. I have seen about a score of fellows shot;
fellows at home dread a hammering with the fists more than those fellows dread a pistol shot. A short time ago, one of our fellows got shot
through the neck for cheating at cards and when the doctor told him
"this was a pretty narrow shave, Sam," he just grinned and said "Yes,
Doc, dis was powerful close, de devil nearly kissed me dis time." It is
forbidden by law to carry concealed firearms in the state, but in the face
of it everybody carries one and indeed would not be safe to go without
one. When I came here they told me I must buy a good revolver and
always carry it with me, so I got one and planted it in my hip pocket
and I did not like the feeling of this thing at all; I felt as if I carried a
gallows in my pocket all the time but like everything else I got accustomed to it and the thing comes as natural to me now as putting my
hat on.

All over the Union the election of public officials is now going on and
the Republicans are going in wholesale, the Democrats making a very
bad show and when the presidential election takes place in about two
years time the Americans will be happy again, for they will then have
a Republican president and not a Democrat.

FROM T. PUNTAN IN NEWPORT, KENTUCKY, TO ROBERT ROBERTS, EBBW VALE

November 7, 1881

I am sorry to say that I and Oakley, my son-in-law, have not had work
of any kind since last June because of the general strike in the Cincinnati
region. The reason for the present strike is as follows. It has always been
the custom for the masters at the mills at Cincinnati, Covington, Newport, Aurora, Terre Haute, Zanesville, and Portsmouth to pay their
workmen in each branch, especially those in the chief branches, ten
per cent more than the masters of the mills in Pittsburgh pay their
workmen because it is hotter here in the South and the material is not
the same as in Pittsburgh.

It seems that the chief purpose of the masters is to break the union
among the workmen here as did the masters of the Welsh works years
ago. There is the same tyrannical, oppressive, and overbearing spirit in
the masters on this side of the Atlantic as on the other. At the beginning
of the strike they gave warning that only nonunion men would in
future be employed by them. These nonunionists are called black sheep
and the unionists are called white sheep. Agents are sent to recruit black
sheep from various parts of this country and even from Europe, Wales
and England. I saw an account of about twenty-three who had come

from some part of Wales under the flattering influence of a man called John Price but I am glad to say that these Welshmen, when they understood that they had been misled, behaved worthy of the courage of the Welsh nation, opposing this traitor and his fellow traitors. They refused to work, joined the union, and went to earn their living in places where there was no enmity between labor and capital.

Most of the black sheep throughout the country are Germans. On Wednesday of last week, a number of black sheep from Reading, Pennsylvania, came to Newport under the care of Colonel Dayton, the owner of the Anchor Mill. But when the old settlers of the place heard of this, they gathered in a large crowd around the mill and the strangers and argued with the colonel and his sheep. After they had somehow finished one shift, they decided that if they could free themselves, they would not work another shift but leave at once and so it was. If they had been stubborn and refused to go, undoubtedly, it would have ended in a fight, how serious I do not know. Newport and Covington on the borders of Kentucky are dangerous neighborhoods for characters of that kind at such a time. Such characters are safer on the other side of the Ohio. The black sheep have worked some weeks in some of the mills in Cincinnati under protection and if this crowd had kept away, the disagreement would have ended weeks if not months ago.

Some confess that they could not work half the time last summer because of the heat. I heard from many old settlers who had been here thirty-eight years that last winter and summer were the coldest and the hottest they had ever known. It is said that two thousand workmen in these mills are now idle and have been idle for five months or twenty-two weeks. But I am glad to say that as I write these lines that I have heard that the strike has been settled with a victory for the men. After the aforementioned disturbances the masters and the workmen decided to have a meeting to argue the thing out fairly. So representatives of each branch of the workmen were elected and met the masters in one of the offices in Cincinnati and argued furiously for six days. The masters agreed to the same prices as when the men came out and signed the scale until the first of June so the mills are starting work again on 2 November.

Newport is a fine town with two ironmills, the Swift and the Anchor. The Swift mill is on the banks of the small river Licking which divides Newport and Covington. The Anchor mill is on the banks of the Ohio. Its owner is Colonel Dayton of Cincinnati. Its overseer is Mr. John Phillips, a man from Ebbw Vale. There is also a rod and bolt factory near the ironmill belonging to the above gentleman. About fifty yards away and lower down there is a building and machinery placed there by Welshmen from Ebbw Vale to make patent fuel, but the venture has turned out to be a failure because the machinery is too light. The chief builder and overseer of this machinery was one Rosewell of Ebbw Vale, brother of Thomas Rosewell, secretary to Mr. T. Henry, the house agent, Ebbw Vale. I am sorry to say that the above company has lost thousands of dollars after having earned them with much hard work. Below the above, there is a pipe foundry where scores of black men are working and some white men too. This is a very dangerous place to work because accidents are occurring all the time and the white men are most often the sufferers. On the other side of the street is a stove factory and about a hundred yards below, a great bridge crossing from Newport to Cincinnati. There are two large buildings belonging to one gentleman which is a watchcase factory employing some hundreds of people.

Most of the merchants are Germans but there are some old Welsh settlers who are quite wealthy and influential. Trade is beginning to look up with the beginning of the working year.

FROM H. J. THOMAS IN PITTSBURGH, PENNSYLVANIA

June 27, 1882

As yet there is no expectation that the strike wounds will be healed and there is little change in the situation. It is true that some mills are working, one in Cleveland, Ohio, one in Apollo, Armstrong County, Pennsylvania, and another near the city of Allegheny. These mills are worked by nonunion and unskilled labor, the sweepings of foreign countries, Swedes and Bohemians whom, it seems, were brought here to make good the shortage by the aristocratic elements for the purpose of bringing down the American workman to the low level in the European countries. No doubt much of this rubbish left their own lands for the good of those countries. Who knows but that the transporting of unskilled foreigners to this country, who undermine the rights of our workmen and help their oppressors to rob them of their just wages for their work and lower the dignity of the American workman, may provide the opportunity for someone in the federal government to put forward a law that will be second to the Chinese bill to prevent foreigners from emigrating to this country for ten or fifteen years.

Let the masters remember that the balance of power is in the hands of the sons of toil by the ballot box. It is a pity that someone does not whisper in the ears of the masters that there are breakers ahead. But this strike is not confined to the iron and steel workers but also to a large number of the coalminers. Two thousand of them have been on strike since the 1st of last April. They are trying to get four cents a bushel for mining coal. On the Monongahela River and the surrounding districts there are about 140 coalmines with thirteen thousand miners digging on an average fifteen million tons of the black diamonds (bituminous coal). Of this number of works referred to, twenty-one are on strike with two thousand workers. Every worker within the union is taxed $1 a week towards maintaining those on strike for the four cents.

Many of these miners are camping out in harmony like the Apostles long ago. They have two aims for adopting the gypsy life, thrift and to prepare tents if the masters throw them out of their cottages. Remember that the dignity of the workman in the United States is higher than on the Continent of Europe as the division between the rich John and the poor David is lower and perhaps this can be explained by one of the chief elements in the composition of the state and that is that quality and blue blood count for little. The rich are multiplying here quickly and an aristocracy is taking root in the land. The fact proving this is that the division is getting greater as the manual workers increase on the roads. It is certain that if the miner had four cents for every bushel he dug out, the voice of the country would not be against them saying that he was asking too much for his labor. But it is not so. When the coal comes from the pit it is riddled through screens and the bars of this instrument are one and a half inches from each other and all that falls through it is all profit for the master and a loss to the miner because he gets nothing for it.

On Saturday, 17th of this month, there was a majestic procession by different branches of industry. There were about thirty thousand in the procession but the rain fell in a flood and half of them fell out. Their banners were many and their mottoes showed their spirit. On one there was the outline of a male skeleton with the following words: "This is all of the man that works for nothing all day. All we ask is enough to make some stuffing." And another was "Competence obtained by honest labor is a blessing. Genius is gold in the mines. Talent is a miner who works and brings it out." Another was "Capital without labor like faith without works is dead."

P.S. Warn our nation from emigrating at this time for the strike is spreading rapidly. It would be too much to forecast what is in store for the sons of toil.

The *Padrone* System

In the period of industrial recovery following the civil war there was a pressing demand for labor. Special legislation was even invoked to aid in supplying this demand. Thus the act of 1864, for the encouragement of immigration, gave manufacturers and contractors the right to import foreign laborers under contract. Speculation in cheap labor ensued; agents were sent to foreign countries in search for workmen. The unenlightened peasants of Italy were the easiest victims of this speculation. Their coming, in fact, was not of their own accord, as was the case with the people of northern Europe, but they came usually under contract.

This difference between the Italian immigrant and the northern people, and the reason for their having been so easily exploited, is brought out by their illiteracy and ignorance of the English language.

The great bulk of Italian immigration has come from southern Italy, the provinces, Abruzzi, Auelbino, Basilicata, Sicily, Calabria, and Naples. Almost the whole number from these provinces are of the peasant class, accustomed to hard work and meager fare. Their illiteracy is high. In 1899 the illiteracy for all races of immigrants was 22.9 per cent, while for the immigrants from southern Italy it was 57.3 per cent and for northern Italy the illiteracy was only 11.4 per cent, showing clearly the contrast between this ignorant peasant class of unskilled laborers and the skilled workmen from the manufacturing centers of northern Italy. In 1900 the percentage of illiteracy for these immigrants was 54.5 in contrast to 24.2 for all races and 11.8 for the northern Italians. . . .

Some form of contract was then necessary to induce these people to leave their country, for by temperament they were not the self-reliant people of the north who came of their own volition. The dread of change, the fear of coming to a strange and unknown land, had to be counteracted by material inducements. It was thus that they came not in search of work, but under contract for several years, and thus were assured in advance of permanent work at what seemed to them high wages.

At this earliest stage in the Italian immigration the padrone was the agent of the contractor or manufacturer. Laborers were demanded, and

Reports of the (U.S.) Industrial Commission on Immigration and Education (Washington, D.C.: Government Printing Office, 1901), Vol. XV, pp. 430–436.

he acted simply as the agent in supplying specific demands. The manufacturer or contractor was of another nationality, but in looking for cheap labor he had recourse to an Italian already in this country. This Italian, undertaking to supply the number of laborers called for, went or sent to Italy for the number, who entered upon a contract binding themselves to service for from 1 to 3 years, and in rare instances even for 7 years. At the same time he furnished transportation and took care of them upon landing here until they were sent to the work for which they were contracted. It was thus that the padrone was merely a middleman, the man who stood between the contractor and the men. He was looked upon by the men as their representative, not as their employer, and upon him they depended.

Under this early system there were numerous ways in which the padrone could make money. In the first place, he had a commission from the men as well as from the contractor for furnishing the men, and commission on their passage. Upon getting them here he had a profit from boarding them until they went to work. This was deducted from their prospective earnings. After that the padrone usually furnished food and shelter for them while at work. This privilege was usually given free by the contractor who furnished shelter and for which the padrone charged rent. Then there was also the commission from sending money back to Italy, and finally the commission on the return passage after the contract had been completed.

But the padrone par excellence was not an agent and did not act for the contractor. He acted primarily upon his own initiative and for himself. Instead of waiting for a call for men, he would upon his own responsibility engage Italians to come, and contract for their labor for a certain number of years. After having brought them here he would farm them out to anyone who wanted them. He boarded them, received their wages, and paid them what he saw fit. Sometimes a laborer would receive $40 a year and as often only $40 for 2 years. Under this system the padrone occasionally would buy outright a minor from his or her parents. Men, women, and children were thus brought into the country, the boys to become bootblacks, newsboys, or strolling musicians. In this stage the padrone system most closely resembled the system as it existed in Italy, which meant in general the employment of children, or minors, in the "roving professions," such as strolling musicians, performers on the harp or hand organ, and street acrobats. These persons were under the direction of a master or padrone more or less inhuman, to whom belonged all the earnings of these persons. This system flourished most widely during the decade 1870–1880, and under its influence Italian immigration was stimulated to such an extent that the flow soon equaled the demand. The sphere of the padrone then changed. His work of inducing immigration was no longer necessary: immigrants came without having previously made contracts and governmental action was aimed at preventing the importation of contract labor. Under these two influences—the great increase in immigration and governmental opposition—the character of the padrone has changed.

As a result of this demand for laborers and the activities of the padroni, the Italian immigrants have been largely males, and until recent years have not come by families, as have the other nationalities, notably the German and Scandinavian people. . . .

Under [present] conditions it is probable that the padrone has very little to do with bringing Italians into the country, since it is no longer necessary to have a contract to bring them in, and because it is even unsafe according to Federal statutes. The padrone is now nothing more than an employment agent, and exists only because of the immigrants and their illiteracy and ignorance of American institutions. He procures his subjects at the port, upon their landing, by promising them steady work at high wages. If the immigrant does not get under the control of the padrone by this means, the immigrant need only go to the colony of his race in any of the large cities, where he will readily be picked up by one of the padroni and promised employment. By this means the newcomers are attached to the padrone, who is able to fulfill his promises, because he "stands in" with the contractors, he knows officials and bosses of the railroads, and he is thus in a way to furnish employment for his fellow-countrymen who can not speak English and have no other way of finding employment. It may then be said that the padrone system no longer exists, and that the padrone is an employment agency, which collects the labor only after it has already arrived in this country, and makes its profit through commissions and keeping boarders.

As Dr. Egisto Rossi, of the Italian Immigration Bureau, has summed up the situation, "The padrone system, or bossism, can be defined as the forced tribute which the newly arrived pays to those who are already acquainted with the ways and language of the country."

Though the character of the padrone is now that of an employment agent, it is undoubtedly true that no Italian has an employment agency license. But it is also true that in nine years there has never been a prosecution of an Italian for carrying on an employment agency without a license. His mode of operation is to go to the regular licensed agencies or to the contractors and furnish the men desired. The padrone also has no office of his own.

But the padrone does not employ the men alone and upon his own responsibility. He works together with the Italian banker, who is a somewhat more responsible party than the padrone; at least the men have more faith in him, because it is through him that they send money back to Italy, and with whom they keep their small savings. It is through the banker that the call is made for the number of men who are wanted, and it is his office where the arrangements with the men are made. He may advance the money for transportation, and even the commission if the men do not have the money. The padrone takes charge of the men in the capacity of a boss, takes them to the place of work, runs the boarding house or shanty store at the place of work, and acts as interpreter for the contractor.

The padroni may be divided into several classes. The first class is the small boss who furnishes many odd jobs for individuals. The next class is the boss who regularly supplies contractors and others with laborers in large numbers. This is the largest class and really stands for the padrone as he at present exists. Finally, there are bosses who at the same time are independent contractors. But this is the exception, for the padrone, it may be said, is never a foreman and just as rarely an independent contractor. His work is to act as an interpreter for the foreman and run the boarding house or shanty store.

For furnishing employment he receives a commission from the laborer. This commission depends upon the (1) length of the period of employment, (2) the wages to be received, and (3) whether they board themselves. If they board themselves, the commission is higher and varies from $1 to $10 a head. For a job of 5 or 6 months the commission may even rise to $10. In some cases the wages are paid to the padrone, but this is only when the contractor is dishonest and receives a share from the padrone. But if the contractor is honest, he knows that the people are generally cheated, and so he pays the men direct, deducting, however, the board and other charges as shown by the padrone.

Under this system the padrone is in combination with the Italian banker, who furnishes the money to pay for transportation, for the erection of shanties when they are not provided by the contractor, and to buy provisions. All this money is then deducted from the earnings of the men. The profits derived from the venture are finally shared by the padrone with the banker, who, however, finds his chief source of gain in holding the savings of the laborers, sending their money to Italy, and changing the money from American to Italian, in which process great shrinkage usually takes place.

The padrone has a further hold upon these people as a result of irregular employment. During the winter there is almost no employment at all. This means that during the greater part of 5 months these people are without work. When work is plentiful, the laborer who boards with his boss is said to be fortunate if he can save more than one-half of his earnings. Some of these earnings are sent to Italy or frequently squandered, so that the laborer often finds himself in winter without resources of his own. In such cases he finds it convenient to go to the boarding house of the boss or banker, where he remains until spring, when it is understood that he shall enter the employ of the boss. In New York there are large tenements owned by Italian bankers which serve as winter quarters for these laborers. Here the men are crowded together, a dozen or more in one room, under the worst sanitary conditions. It is frequently said that the padrone encourages the men in extravagance in order to have a firmer hold on their future earnings. The employment is even made irregular by the padrone, who furnishes employment for several weeks at a time and then keeps them idle, claiming that the work is not regular.

In the Ninth Special Report of the Commissioner of Labor, on the condition of Italians in Chicago, it was found that 21.67 per cent of persons of whom the question was asked answered that they worked for a padrone. Of this number 5.96 per cent reported that they paid no commission to the padrone for securing the job, while 94.04 per cent reported that they paid a commission. It was found that an average of $4.84 per individual, of the number reporting, was paid for the last job at which they worked, and the average time worked on this job was 11 weeks and 4 days per individual. The average amount paid per week to padrones for employment was thus 42 cents.

The Immigration Investigation Commission of 1895 found that from 500 to 600 laborers employed on sewers and waterworks padroni had deducted from their wages 10 cents and 15 cents each day for procuring employment.

The padrone provides transportation for the men. But in the rates he overcharges the men, charging for first-class transportation or regular ticket rates, and securing greatly reduced rates because of the large number. If the work is some distance from the city, the padrone often boards the men, and usually buys the privilege from the contractor at a fixed rate per head per month. In some cases the privilege is given by the contractor free, because the padrone saves him trouble in employing men, and is convenient to have around in managing the men. But usually the contractor sells the privilege of furnishing the laborers with board and lodging and wearing apparel, the cost of which is generally deducted from their wages. In consideration of the many advantages which the padroni have in this transaction, they generally have to pay pretty high prices for the privilege, which naturally comes out of the pockets of the immigrants. If the men board themselves, their food must be bought at the shanty store which is operated by the padrone. Notices are posted to this effect, and fines are imposed for disobedience. Even dismissal is often the penalty. Occasionally a fixed daily amount of purchases is required by the padrone, but only at the padrone store. For example, in 1894 Italian laborers were shipped from New York to Brunswick, Ga., for work on a sewerage contract. Each man paid the padrone $1 for finding the employment. The passage money, $7 per head, was paid by the banker with the understanding that this was to be deducted from their wages. The agent of the banker paid $25 a month rent for 10 huts, but charged each laborer $1 a month, which for 215 men was $215 a month. All supplies had to be bought at the shanty store, the penalty for disobedience being a fine of $5.

The quality of the food is as a rule very low even for Italians, and the prices are extortionate. The investigation of the United States Department of Labor (Ninth Annual Report) of the Italians in Chicago showed, among other things, that "the prices charged by padroni are frequently double those charged in Chicago markets for similar articles of food of the same quality." . . .

The prices paid at the shanty store of the padrone are from 2 to 3½ times those of the market prices, while in the case of vegetables the shanty price was 30 times the New York market price.

Besides the profit from supplying food to the men, the padrone charges from $1 to $3 a head for the shanties in which the men sleep. These shanties are often furnished without charge by the contractor, but the padrone nevertheless charges the men a rent to pay for his boarding privilege. Sometimes he even charges regular fees for medical service, though a regular physician is called in only in very serious cases.

As to the wages, it is seldom in Eastern States that only $1.25 per day is paid, though in 1894, 1895, and 1897 wages were $1, with very little work to be had even at that price. At present they vary from $1.35 to $1.75 per day. In the investigation of the Department of Labor (Ninth Annual Report, Italians in Chicago) it was shown that the average weekly earnings for Italian males were $6.41, and the average hours of work per week were 59.4. The highest average weekly wage was $8.25½ in manufactures and mechanical industries, and the next highest was $7.64½ in agriculture, fisheries, and mining. But this throws no direct light upon the wages or earnings received under the padrone. Under the earlier padrone system the padrone would import laborers under contract for 75 cents per day for two years' work. But the padrone could get $1.25 per day from railroads and contractors, and this difference would go to him. At present he is only an employment agent, and the wages are usually paid direct to the men, though only after the deductions have been made in favor of the padrone.

In the investigation of the New York Bureau of Labor Statistics into the alien labor employed on State contract work on the Erie Canal (Report 1898, p. 1153) it is stated that there were 15,000 common laborers employed, of whom 1,000 were American citizens, 13,500 were Italian aliens, 350 Poles, and 150 Hungarians. The highest wages paid these laborers was $1.75, and the lowest $1.20 per day. Of this number 600, or 4 per cent, received $1.20; 4,420, or 30 per cent, received $1.25, and 9,794, or 65 per cent, received $1.50, which shows that the rate for this labor, of which Italian aliens made up 90 per cent, was from $1.20 to $1.50 per day.

As to the amount of the employment the investigation of the Department of Labor shows that out of 2,663 persons employed in remunerative occupations 1,517, or 56.97 per cent, were unemployed some part of the year. The average time unemployed for these 1,517 persons was 7.1 months; for the 109 females in the number it was 6.4 months, and for the 1,408 males 7.2 months.

The nominally small earnings of these people thus becomes really very small when it is kept in mind that they are unemployed on an average from 5 to 7 months during the year, and must live during this time on the small savings which they may perhaps have been able to put aside from their earnings.

As to the kind of labor, it may be said that the padrone undertakes to furnish only unskilled labor in the large cities, though the Immigration Investigation Commission of 1895 reported "that padroni in New York not only guarantee to supply unskilled labor for sewer, railroad, and water-works construction, but also skilled labor for building trades, and will, furthermore, arrange for their transportation to a remote point if a small percentage of the passage money is advanced or guaranteed."

But in the country and small towns the padroni stand ready to furnish skilled workmen, masons, carpenters, stone cutters, and machinists. Occasionally Italians are employed through padroni in the endeavor to break a strike. For example, in the lockout in 1892–93 of the granite cutters Mr. Duncan testified before the commission that Italians were employed to take the place of the union men. But he said that they were inefficient and had to drift out of the work because of the minimum wage rate established by the union and the desire of the employer to have only the most profitable men. The general secretary-treasurer of the Granite Cutters' National Union describes a padrone system in New York City which was prepared to supply men to employers in the granite-cutting trade. The union has an 8-hour day with $4 in New York. The padrone gathers the Italians, who comply with the State law by declaring their intentions for citizenship. These men pay the padrone $12 commission, $6 remaining on deposit as a guaranty that at the end of the week the man supplied with work shall return $6 to the padrone; if not, his employment ceases. These $6 per man per week are paid by the padrone to the contractor, who has thus employed men at $3 under a $4 law in New York, which provides that mechanics employed in the State upon municipal, county, or State work shall be paid the prevailing rate of wages and work the prevailing hours. This is one of the very rare instances where skilled labor is furnished in New York by the padrone system, and it can not be taken as representative of the system.

The Italian immigrant, however, does not always limit himself to becoming a common laborer on railroad work and other excavations, but often becomes an artisan. In so far as he becomes an artisan he comes in conflict with American workmen, but the conflict is less sharp than formerly, because the American unions are organizing Italian labor. The Italians themselves are coming to understand the importance of organized labor. This is noticeable especially among the Italian hod carriers, masons, and stone cutters, and where this feeling and sense of organization has developed there is no opportunity for the padrone system.

Ward Politics and the Gangs

Robert A. Woods

It is not the purpose of this chapter to discuss methods of political reform, but to show the play of personal and social forces beneath the surface of boss rule and ward politics. To do this, it is necessary at the very
beginning to understand the prevalence and power of gangs, and their
methods of organization. The importance of the gang as a social factor
which the politician manipulates has never been fully appreciated except
by the politician. It is a sufficiently commonplace trait of human nature
for people to associate themselves together in groups and cliques, according to the attractions of congeniality. This force, however, seems to work
with great intensity in the tenement-house districts. Without pausing to
inquire the reasons, I shall describe the structure of the gang, and later
show its relation to ward politics.

The tendency begins among the children. Almost every boy in the
tenement-house quarters of the district is member of a gang. The boy
who does not belong to one is not only the exception, but the very rare
exception. There are certain characteristics in the make-up and life of all
gangs. To begin with, every gang has a "corner" where its members meet.
This "hang out," as it is sometimes called, may be in the centre of a block,
but still the gang speak of it as the "corner." The size of a gang varies: it
may number five or forty. As a rule, all the boys composing it come from
the immediate vicinity of the corner. Every gang has one or more leaders;
and of course its character depends very much upon the leaders, for as
one of the boys expressed it the leader says " 'Come,' and the push move."
As a matter of fact, a gang if at all large has two leaders and sometimes
three. In order to show the different kinds of leadership, let me describe
the qualities possessed by the three types in a large gang. First of all,
there is the gang's "bully." He is the best "scrapper" in the gang. Many
a hard-won battle has paved the way to this enviable position; but the

Robert A. Woods (ed.), *The City Wilderness: A Settlement Study . . . South End,
Boston* (Boston: Houghton, Mifflin, 1898), pp. 114–116, 118–120, 122–127, 129–130,
133–142.

position, often attained with so much difficulty, is not a sinecure. The bully not only has to defend the honor of the gang, but may have to defend his title at any time against the ambition of some "growing" member of the gang. Next there is the gang's "judge;" all matters in dispute are finally submitted to him if no agreement is reached. The boy who enjoys this honor has gained it not by election but by selection. The boys have gradually found out that he does not take sides, but is fair minded. Finally there is the gang's "counselor,"—the boy whom the gang looks to for its schemes both of pleasure and of mischief. In small gangs the bully may also be the judge and counselor, and even in large gangs it frequently happens that one boy dispenses both the latter functions. Here is the ward boss in embryo. . . .

It is interesting to know what becomes of these various gangs when the boys get to be seventeen or eighteen years old. The more respectable gangs, as a rule, club together and hire a room. The more vicious gangs prefer to use what little money they have in carousing. If by any chance they get a room, their rowdyism will cause their ejection either by the landlord or by the police. Consequently they have to fall back on the corner or some saloon, as their meeting-place. They nearly always seek a back street or the wharves, unfrequented by the police.

Not infrequently these gang connections are tenacious in the case of older men, who sometimes meet in the back of some store to play "forty-five," but more often would be found in a favorite saloon. In numerous cases a saloon serves as a club room for one or more gangs of these older men, who are loyally devoted to it. Many of them will walk by saloon after saloon thirsty, in order to reach a particular drinking place with enough money to secure the proprietor's welcome.

At this point, it is necessary to give some account of the young men's clubs, in order that the important part that these clubs play in ward politics may be seen; for all this network of social life is taken in hand by the politician. As I said before, the gangs which coalesce and form these clubs are the most respectable ones. They are led to do this partly through a desire to have a warm room, and partly because they are tired of standing on the corner and meeting the rebuffs of the policeman. Then such a club opens up the freedom of the district, socially, to them. The first month or two is a trying time for every new club. Each gang composing it is likely to have a candidate for the principal offices; and frequently the first election is the occasion for a quarrel between the rival gangs, which breaks up the club before it is well begun. There are about eight of these clubs in the particular section which I know best. The dues range from twenty-five to fifty cents per week, and the club pays usually from $25 to $35 per month for its room.

Nearly all of the clubs have a common programme. In the first place, each club, without any exception, gives a ball each winter in some large hall. The tickets invariably sell for fifty cents. These balls are important social functions in the district. As a rule, they are well managed financially, one club clearing $165 last winter. Then besides this annual ball, each club has a "social" once a week. This is a dance of a lower type than the balls, being interspersed with comic songs, humorous recitations, and buck dancing. About the same class of girls attend all the socials; they go from one club to the other. Almost without exception they are factory girls, and nearly all of them are bold and vulgar. It is a curious fact that the members do not want their sisters to attend these dances; and their custom is to leave the girls with whom they have danced before they reach the street. If you should enter the room of one of these clubs on the night of a social, about ten o'clock, you would have to push your way through a crowd of fellows blocking the entrance and massed against one side of the room, nearly all smoking, with hats on, and making "cracks" and "breaks," as they express it, at every newcomer. . . .

The worst dance halls are very nearly allied to the clubs, for all the halls have their special clientage. This clientage, like the club, is made up, though not so distinctly, of gangs. Consequently at nearly all the halls, the dancers are known to one another, and have more or less loyalty for the hall. At one hall a large group of fellows attend, nearly all of whom have stylish light coats and dudish attire, even if they do not know where the next meal is coming from. In winter their mistresses support them. In summer these men are fakirs and go to Nantasket and the beaches, and in the fall they take their gambling outfits to fairs at Brockton and elsewhere.

The description thus far of the gang, the social club, and the dance hall, shows that the politician does not need to deal with individuals. Ready at hand are these various social centres for him to make use of.

In addition to these social groups which take on a political character at election time, there are usually in the tenement-house sections several distinctly political clubs. Standing at the head of these clubs is the "machine club." It is now quite the custom of those in control of the party, and known as the "machine," to have such an organization. All the men in the ward having good political jobs are members. In one local club it is estimated that the City employees belonging to it draw salaries to the amount of $30,000 per year; in another club, outside the district, $80,000. It is natural that all the men in these clubs are anxious to maintain the machine. It is a question of bread and butter with them. In addition to City employees the various machine workers are enrolled. The room of the club is ordinarily very pleasant. There are, of course, in these clubs the usual social attractions, among other things poker and drinking. At the head of the club stands the boss of the ward.

So much for the organizations which are manipulated for political ends. The various typical actors in ward politics must now be described; first, the boss, his lieutenants, and "heelers." One of the bosses whom the writer knows is fairly typical. He is considered the "prince of jolliers," on account of his alluring ways. He has for many years been in public office of one kind or another. His early opportunities were small. His native abilities, however, enable him to fulfill his official duties with real effectiveness,—when political business does not interfere. As he not infrequently plays the rôle of Warwick in politics, he gets a glimpse of larger worlds to conquer. These, however, can exist for him only as tantalizing dreams, for the lack of that education possessed by many whom he brushes aside and scorns. He does not reap the rich harvest which comes to the members of his craft in other cities. He does not carry with him any of the obvious signs of marked prosperity. He would probably not refuse greater spoils, however. The possibilities in that direction in Boston are limited mainly to deals in connection with contracts for City works and supplies. The great corporations can only be nettled; they cannot be leeched. Their larger privileges are decided upon by the legislature. Even the licensing and police powers are retained by the State. It is to some extent the love of authority that urges the boss on. He knows his power, his mastery over men. There is one quality which this typical boss has that gives him a sort of moral leadership. He makes many general promises which he never intends to fulfill, but a specific promise he usually keeps. He is distinguished among the politicians of the city as being a man of his word. This is honesty or sagacity, as you choose to look upon it. There must be a certain degree of honor in dividing the spoils of politics, and the politician must provide something with which to feed his hungry followers. The jobs that he tries to get for his followers, however, are not secured as the private employer seeks men,—for efficiency. The motive of the boss in seeking favors from the City government is to satisfy claims against him and to maintain himself. In this, forsooth, he considers himself as merely going the way of the world. He is to a large extent justified in so thinking. The highly respectable contractor or corporation man, for instance, who directly or indirectly makes corrupt deals with him, does so because "business is business." The boss enters into these deals, and goes through the rest of his programme, not because he likes to, but because "it's politics." Both are caught in the toils of an evil system.

The boss has reduced to a science the knack of dominating men. If a "jolly" or the "glad hand" will not carry his point, he can quickly frown. The frown of the boss is supposed to carry terror to the hearts of those to whom he has rendered favors, or who expect jobs. This is easily accounted for, as without his approval no one in the ward can get a City job.

On the whole, partly for the love of position and power, and partly from a good heart, the boss enjoys doing good turns for men. Stories are

told by his admirers of his generous deeds. For instance, he has been
known to pay the funeral expenses of poor people who have no insurance.
At Christmas time and Thanksgiving he gives turkeys to certain needy
families. Dance tickets, baseball passes, tickets to the theatre, railway
passes, and so forth,—which cost him nothing, being simply incidental
results of his tools in the common council or the legislature voting "right,"
—are distributed with wise discrimination. He is always ready to treat.
Some go so far as to say that if he died to-morrow his friends would have
to pay his funeral expenses. This all sounds very generous; but the chief
admirers of the boss cannot deny that when the supremacy in the ward is
at all endangered, he makes capital of all his good deeds. In other words,
every man to whom he has granted a favor is made to feel that the boss
expects a vote.

I do not see how any man in his position, however good his character
to begin with, could do otherwise than use men as checkers on a board.
His ambition to boss the party in his ward necessitates his looking upon
men continually from the point of view of votes. The logic of the boss
system demands this. Votes are his business,—they mean money, power.
The boss can never be a disinterested member of society. He is forced
to make men act and vote with him,—the weaker their wills, the fewer
their convictions, the better for him. He gives another drink to the drunkard: he has a vote. The only morality he seeks in men is loyalty to him.
The merit system he regards always with a horror and indignation which
would be amusing if it were not so serious. . . .

There are certain lesser figures characteristic of ward politics known
as "heelers." They do the dirty work. As a rule, they prefer to serve the
well-established boss, as he can best protect them if they are found out
and prosecuted in the execution of their villainy. As a rule, a "heeler" is
a broken-down "bum," afraid of work, fond of his cups, in touch with
loafers and the semi-criminal class, more of a fox than they, energetic
enough in a campaign, possessed of a strong dramatic sense, loving the
excitement of ward politics with its dark plots and wire pulling, glad to
be lifted into temporary importance by having money to spend on the
"boys."

Some personal touches may make the heeler a little more real. One
whom I know wears eye-glasses, which are in picturesque contrast to the
unshaven face, filthy white shirt partly hidden by a frayed necktie, and
more filthy clothes sadly in need of repair. Once, on the eve of election,
—when therefore he had some money in his pocket,—I remember he had
on a clean collar and a new tie, but the shirt was still dirty. Perhaps his
ambition stopped short of a clean shirt—it meant just so much drink. He
lives with a "policy writer" and occasionally helps him in his work. In
reality a bar-room loafer, he knows the semi-criminal class and "bums"
better than any one else in the ward. He is just as fond of loafing as the

idlest one of the lot. Consequently he is known to them as "their kind," but his intelligence and "gift of the gab" make him a leader. He has a "frog in the throat" voice, which becomes barely a croak by caucus night. His method of buttonholing and poking out his head at a man, in very earnestness, is well calculated to be convincing. He really has considerable managing ability; and if he were clean for once and had a new suit, you might easily place him as a factory manager or a captain in a regiment. . . .

Besides the boss, his lieutenants, and his heelers, there are usually in all tenement-house wards a large number of aspirants for some elective office; together with the incumbents of such positions and some retired politicians. They all have their clientage. Occasionally one will find a man who is honest, and really wants to see an honest caucus, honest legislators, and civil service reform. Such men are few in number, however; and while a candidate of that kind will always be lauded in the campaign circulars by his followers for his honesty, his best friends will secretly wonder and shake their heads at his eccentricity. It is impossible to convince the knowing ones that any candidate is not "out for the stuff."

Men with a trade, or small contractors, will tell their friends openly that they want office because it will help them in their business. Apparently no thought enters their minds that they are seeking office for wrong ends. Furthermore, such an argument is forceful with numbers of the rank and file of voters. The painter expects a City contract; the young man desiring a liquor license not infrequently seeks to go to the common council for a "character recommendation," in order that he may the more readily secure a license. The point of view of the majority of candidates and voters, too, is that the municipal government is theirs to use. Of course, all these men have their following. Some are friendly to the boss, others not.

In analyzing ward politics, it is necessary to understand something of the morale of the various groups of voters. As to race complexion, in the local wards the Irish voters prevail. Next in number are the Jews. There is a good sprinkling of "Yankees," a term which for political purposes includes the British element. Foreigners other than those mentioned do not cut much of a figure in politics. It goes without saying that the greatest degree of political activity is found among the Irish. The Jews, however, are commencing to take considerable interest in politics. The most earnest and unselfish of them are Socialists, but some of them are quite as keenly after the main chance as the Irish politician. In one of the wards of the district there are five hundred Jewish voters. In justice to them it must be said that it is as yet early to prophesy what their position in politics will be. The social relations of the Irish and the Jews are not very cordial. There seems to be a special antipathy ordinarily on the part of the Irish for the Jews. Not so with the Irish politician. He solves the race problem in short order. He fraternizes with the Jew, eats with the Jew, drinks with the Jew, and dickers with him in politics. . . .

In noting the various classes of voters in these wards, it is also necessary to keep steadily in mind the large number of unemployed men. In the study of ward politics this factor has not been sufficiently appreciated. I do not refer now to the loafers, but to the honest unemployed. The number of men who are almost ready to fawn upon one for a job is simply appalling. Ask those in the settlements, at the charity headquarters, the mission churches, or the workingmen's resorts, and they will tell you the same story. Some of these men are looking for political jobs. Consider the hold the boss can gain upon them. The few secure a job; the many get promises. Those who get jobs are the slaves of the boss. He does not make the work, and there is no credit in what he does, but you cannot blame them for their slavery. What is the honest use of their suffrage compared with bread? According to the ethics of the district, a man who receives a job is under the most sacred obligations to the politician who bestowed it. The lack of employment, therefore, is one of the most important factors working in the interest of the boss and boss rule.

There is still another group that must be mentioned. There is in these wards a considerable number of young men who regard politics as El Dorado. They are poor but ambitious. Many of them have received a fairly good education. It more and more requires a "friendly pull" in order to secure a good position in business. In business, too, they have to meet strong prejudices of race and religion. Politics, therefore, is for them apparently the easiest way to success in life. In every ward such as we are describing, there are a few conspicuous examples of men living in comfort, who are reported rich, and have made their money in politics. It is told you, for instance, that the mother of one of these men lived in a garret and went barefoot out of sheer poverty. Thus the clever young fellow is encouraged to try his hand. Politics means business. Moral scruples are brushed aside. Victory at the caucus is the gateway of fortune.

The saloon in its relation to politics has already been referred to somewhat, and one need only touch upon it here in order to give it the proper place in this picture of ward politics. In each ward of such a section as this, it is safe to say that there are five or six hundred men who are more or less influenced by the political talk of the saloon. As has already been shown, gangs often use particular saloons as club-rooms. The men who frequent the saloons are, almost without exception, the men who attend the caucus. They are naturally influenced a great deal by the saloon keeper, whom they see almost daily. Drinking makes men sociable; and if a barkeeper is given money with which to treat the boys, even the fairly respectable men who are at the bar, after a round of drinks, look with favor upon the saloon keeper's candidate. The saloon is thus the place where political opinion is formed very quickly, and the opinions formed there are soon circulated through the community by the "saloon gossips." No man who wishes to become elected in these wards disregards the saloon. Other things being at all equal, the man who has the greater number of saloon keepers on his side will surely be elected.

In nearly all tenement-house wards, one party is strongly in the majority. Such being the case, a nomination at the caucus usually means an election at the polls. The caucus is therefore the place where the real contest occurs. There is no single event in the ward that can equal the caucus for interest. It is a scene where the various gangs meet, as so many tribes, and fight for supremacy; where ambitious young men strive together for a "start" in life; where fortunes are made and lost; where sensational attempts are made to "down" the boss; it is a scene where a strong, rough, "jollying" personality tells as in the good old days of the fighting barons. Again, it is a busy mart where men are bought and sold, a place where the drunkard can get the price of another drink, a place full of surprises, of unsuspected combinations, of damaging circulars sprung too late for answer, of small leaders fighting under new banners. It is besides the great social event for the men of the ward, when they gather in crowds and push and jostle and "jolly" and joke, and yell for their favorite, and bet on him as they might bet on horses. It is, moreover, a leveling event; an event in which the "thug" feels, not as good, but better than his more respectable neighbor. Finally the caucus is a place of action. It is the great ward drama—full of strong human touches, too often potent in tragedy to free institutions and the common welfare.

In case a boss is likely to be strongly opposed at a caucus for the election of ward officers, he can afford to spend a large sum of money in his campaign. How much he can afford to spend is in the main simply a question of business—of addition and subtraction. He stands, aside from the ambition to rule men, to get as much as possible out of politics for himself and the "gang." It is not necessary, usually, to spend much money direct for votes. Beer in the saloons, "beer parties" at the social clubs, and "house parties," getting work for the leaders of doubtful gangs, bailing a member of a tough gang out, employment of heelers to assess and register men falsely, and "circulars," are some of the common methods employed both by the boss and by his opponents, the "mongrels." Beer parties and house parties are time-honored institutions. The beer parties are conducted in much the same way as the smoke talks already described. Tickets are issued, and sometimes two or three hundred attend. A beer party is held for the purpose of making the friends of the candidate "solid," and of gaining recruits. There are certain heelers and local leaders who figure largely at such times, and are known as "beer party orators." The speaking of the candidate and his friends amidst smoke, sandwiches, and beer, is always personal. The fact that the candidate is a "good fellow" is the chief theme. Issues are not referred to. The house

party is a smaller gathering held at the home of the candidate early in
the campaign. Those invited are principally his lieutenants. Invitations
are issued, however, very seductively to the certain small leaders who are
not "fixed" as yet. The strong camaraderie induced by the beer, sandwiches, and other refreshments, makes the planning which is done at
such parties much more eager and effective. This social feeling creates
temporarily a new gang with all its loyalties; for the sentiment is quite
strong in these wards that those who attend such parties shall vote and
work for the candidate giving them. . . .

The Public School: Maker of Americans

Mary Antin

The public school has done its best for us foreigners, and for the country, when it has made us into good Americans. I am glad it is mine to tell how the miracle was wrought in one case. You should be glad to hear of it, you born Americans; for it is the story of the growth of your country; of the flocking of your brothers and sisters from the far ends of the earth to the flag you love; of the recruiting of your armies of workers, thinkers, and leaders. And you will be glad to hear of it, my comrades in adoption; for it is a rehearsal of your own experience, the thrill and wonder of which your own hearts have felt.

How long would you say, wise reader, it takes to make an American? By the middle of my second year in school I had reached the sixth grade. When, after the Christmas holidays, we began to study the life of Washington, running through a summary of the Revolution, and the early days of the Republic, it seemed to me that all my reading and study had been idle until then. The reader, the arithmetic, the song book, that had so fascinated me until now, became suddenly sober exercise books, tools wherewith to hew a way to the source of inspiration. When the teacher read to us out of a big book with many bookmarks in it, I sat rigid with attention in my little chair, my hands tightly clasped on the edge of my desk; and I painfully held my breath, to prevent sighs of disappointment escaping, as I saw the teacher skip the parts between bookmarks. When the class read, and it came my turn, my voice shook and the book trembled in my hands. I could not pronounce the name of George Washington without a pause. Never had I prayed, never had I chanted the songs of David, never had I called upon the Most Holy, in such utter reverence and worship as I repeated the simple sentences of my child's story of the patriot. I gazed with adoration at the portraits of George and Martha Washington, till I could see them with my eyes shut. And

Mary Antin, *The Promised Land* (Boston: Houghton, Mifflin, 1912), pp. 222–238.

whereas formerly my self-consciousness had bordered on conceit, and I thought myself an uncommon person, parading my schoolbooks through the streets, and swelling with pride when a teacher detained me in conversation, now I grew humble all at once, seeing how insignificant I was beside the Great.

As I read about the noble boy who could not tell a lie to save himself from punishment, I was for the first time truly repentant of my sins. Formerly I had fasted and prayed and made sacrifice on the Day of Atonement, but it was more than half play, in mimicry of my elders. I had no real horror of sin, and I knew so many ways of escaping punishment. I am sure my family, my neighbors, my teachers in Polotzk—all my world, in fact—strove together, by example and precept, to teach me goodness. Saintliness had a new incarnation in about every third person I knew. I did respect the saints, but I could not help seeing that most of them were a little bit stupid, and that mischief was much more fun than piety. Goodness, as I had known it, was respectable, but not necessarily admirable. The people I really admired, like my Uncle Solomon, and Cousin Rachel, were those who preached the least and laughed the most. My sister Frieda was perfectly good, but she did not think the less of me because I played tricks. What I loved in my friends was not inimitable. One could be downright good if one really wanted to. One could be learned if one had books and teachers. One could sing funny songs and tell anecdotes if one travelled about and picked up such things, like one's uncles and cousins. But a human being strictly good, perfectly wise, and unfailingly valiant, all at the same time, I had never heard or dreamed of. This wonderful George Washington was as inimitable as he was irreproachable. Even if I had never, never told a lie, I could not compare myself to George Washington; for I was not brave—I was afraid to go out when snowballs whizzed—and I could never be the First President of the United States.

So I was forced to revise my own estimate of myself. But the twin of my new-born humility, paradoxical as it may seem, was a sense of dignity I had never known before. For if I found that I was a person of small consequence, I discovered at the same time that I was more nobly related than I had ever supposed. I had relatives and friends who were notable people by the old standards,—I had never been ashamed of my family,—but this George Washington, who died long before I was born, was like a king in greatness, and he and I were Fellow Citizens. There was a great deal about Fellow Citizens in the patriotic literature we read at this time; and I knew from my father how he was a Citizen, through the process of naturalization, and how I also was a citizen, by virtue of my relation to him. Undoubtedly I was a Fellow Citizen, and George Washington was another. It thrilled me to realize what sudden greatness had fallen on me; and at the same time it sobered me, as with a sense of responsibility. I strove to conduct myself as befitted a Fellow Citizen.

Before books came into my life, I was given to star-gazing and day-dreaming. When books were given me, I fell upon them as a glutton pounces on his meat after a period of enforced starvation. I lived with my nose in a book, and took no notice of the alternations of the sun and stars. But now, after the advent of George Washington and the American Revolution, I began to dream again. I strayed on the common after school instead of hurrying home to read. I hung on fence rails, my pet book forgotten under my arm, and gazed off to the yellow-streaked February sunset, and beyond, and beyond. I was no longer the central figure of my dreams; the dry weeds in the lane crackled beneath the tread of Heroes.

What more could America give a child? Ah, much more! As I read how the patriots planned the Revolution, and the women gave their sons to die in battle, and the heroes led to victory, and the rejoicing people set up the Republic, it dawned on me gradually what was meant by *my country*. The people all desiring noble things, and striving for them together, defying their oppressors, giving their lives for each other—all this it was that made *my country*. It was not a thing that I *understood*; I could not go home and tell Frieda about it, as I told her other things I learned at school. But I knew one could say "my country" and *feel* it, as one felt "God" or "myself." My teacher, my schoolmates, Miss Dillingham, George Washington himself could not mean more than I when they said "my country," after I had once felt it. For the Country was for all the Citizens, and *I was a Citizen*. And when we stood up to sing "America," I shouted the words with all my might. I was in very earnest proclaiming to the world my love for my new-found country.

> "I love thy rocks and rills,
> Thy woods and templed hills."

Boston Harbor, Crescent Beach, Chelsea Square—all was hallowed ground to me. As the day approached when the school was to hold exercises in honor of Washington's Birthday, the halls resounded at all hours with the strains of patriotic songs; and I, who was a model of the attentive pupil, more than once lost my place in the lesson as I strained to hear, through closed doors, some neighboring class rehearsing "The Star-Spangled Banner." If the doors happened to open, and the chorus broke out unveiled—

> "O! say, does that Star-Spangled Banner yet wave
> O'er the land of the free, and the home of the brave?"—

delicious tremors ran up and down my spine, and I was faint with suppressed enthusiasm.

Where had been my country until now? What flag had I loved? What heroes had I worshipped? The very names of these things had been unknown to me. Well I knew that Polotzk was not my country. It was *goluth*—exile. On many occasions in the year we prayed to God to lead us out of exile. The beautiful Passover service closed with the words, "Next year, may we be in Jerusalem." On childish lips, indeed, those words were no conscious aspiration; we repeated the Hebrew syllables after our elders, but without their hope and longing. Still not a child among us was too young to feel in his own flesh the lash of the oppressor. We knew what it was to be Jews in exile, from the spiteful treatment we suffered at the hands of the smallest urchin who crossed himself; and thence we knew that Israel had good reason to pray for deliverance. But the story of the Exodus was not history to me in the sense that the story of the American Revolution was. It was more like a glorious myth, a belief in which had the effect of cutting me off from the actual world, by linking me with a world of phantoms. Those moments of exaltation which the contemplation of the Biblical past afforded us, allowing us to call ourselves the children of princes, served but to tinge with a more poignant sense of disinheritance the long humdrum stretches of our life. In very truth we were a people without a country. Surrounded by mocking foes and detractors, it was difficult for me to realize the persons of my people's heroes or the events in which they moved. Except in moments of abstraction from the world around me, I scarcely understood that Jerusalem was an actual spot on the earth, where once the Kings of the Bible, real people, like my neighbors in Polotzk, ruled in puissant majesty. For the conditions of our civil life did not permit us to cultivate a spirit of nationalism. The freedom of worship that was grudgingly granted within the narrow limits of the Pale by no means included the right to set up openly any ideal of a Hebrew State, any hero other than the Czar. What we children picked up of our ancient political history was confused with the miraculous story of the Creation, with the supernatural legends and hazy associations of Bible lore. As to our future, we Jews in Polotzk had no national expectations; only a life-worn dreamer here and there hoped to die in Palestine. If Fetchke and I sang, with my father, first making sure of our audience, "Zion, Zion, Holy Zion, not forever is it lost," we did not really picture to ourselves Judæa restored.

So it came to pass that we did not know what *my country* could mean to a man. And as we had no country, so we had no flag to love. It was by no far-fetched symbolism that the banner of the House of Romanoff became the emblem of our latter-day bondage in our eyes. Even a child would know how to hate the flag that we were forced, on pain of severe penalties, to hoist above our housetops, in celebration of the advent of one of our oppressors. And as it was with country and flag, so it was with heroes of war. We hated the uniform of the soldier, to the last brass button. On the person of a Gentile, it was the symbol of tyranny; on the person of a Jew, it was the emblem of shame.

So a little Jewish girl in Polotzk was apt to grow up hungry-minded and empty-hearted; and if, still in her outreaching youth, she was set down in a land of outspoken patriotism, she was likely to love her new country with a great love, and to embrace its heroes in a great worship. Naturalization, with us Russian Jews, may mean more than the adoption of the immigrant by America. It may mean the adoption of America by the immigrant.

On the day of the Washington celebration I recited a poem that I had composed in my enthusiasm. But "composed" is not the word. The process of putting on paper the sentiments that seethed in my soul was really very discomposing. I dug the words out of my heart, squeezed the rhymes out of my brain, forced the missing syllables out of their hiding-places in the dictionary. May I never again know such travail of the spirit as I endured during the fevered days when I was engaged on the poem. It was not as if I wanted to say that snow was white or grass was green. I could do that without a dictionary. It was a question now of the loftiest sentiments, of the most abstract truths, the names of which were very new in my vocabulary. It was necessary to use polysyllables, and plenty of them; and where to find rhymes for such words as "tyranny," "freedom," and "justice," when you had less than two years' acquaintance with English! The name I wished to celebrate was the most difficult of all. Nothing but "Washington" rhymed with "Washington." It was a most ambitious undertaking, but my heart could find no rest till it had proclaimed itself to the world; so I wrestled with my difficulties, and spared not ink, till inspiration perched on my penpoint, and my soul gave up its best.

When I had done, I was myself impressed with the length, gravity, and nobility of my poem. My father was overcome with emotion as he read it. His hands trembled as he held the paper to the light, and the mist gathered in his eyes. My teacher, Miss Dwight, was plainly astonished at my performance, and said many kind things, and asked many questions; all of which I took very solemnly, like one who had been in the clouds and returned to earth with a sign upon him. When Miss Dwight asked me to read my poem to the class on the day of celebration, I readily consented. It was not in me to refuse a chance to tell my schoolmates what I thought of George Washington.

I was not a heroic figure when I stood up in front of the class to pronounce the praises of the Father of his Country. Thin, pale, and hollow, with a shadow of short black curls on my brow, and the staring look of prominent eyes, I must have looked more frightened than imposing. My dress added no grace to my appearance. "Plaids" were in fashion, and my frock was of a red-and-green "plaid" that had a ghastly effect on my complexion. I hated it when I thought of it, but on the great day I did not know I had any dress on. Heels clapped together, and hands glued to my sides, I lifted up my voice in praise of George Washington. It was not much of a voice; like my hollow cheeks, it suggested consumption. My pronunciation was faulty, my declamation flat. But I had the courage of my convictions. I was face to face with twoscore Fellow Citizens, in clean blouses and extra frills. I must tell them what George Washington had done for their country—for *our* country—for me.

I can laugh now at the impossible metres, the grandiose phrases, the verbose repetitions of my poem. Years ago I must have laughed at it, when I threw my only copy into the wastebasket. The copy I am now turning over was loaned me by Miss Dwight, who faithfully preserved it all these years, for the sake, no doubt, of what I strove to express when I laboriously hitched together those dozen and more ungraceful stanzas. But to the forty Fellow Citizens sitting in rows in front of me it was no laughing matter. Even the bad boys sat in attitudes of attention, hypnotized by the solemnity of my demeanor. If they got any inkling of what the hail of big words was about, it must have been through occult suggestion. I fixed their eighty eyes with my single stare, and gave it to them, stanza after stanza, with such emphasis as the lameness of the lines permitted.

> He whose courage, will, amazing bravery,
>   Did free his land from a despot's rule,
> From man's greatest evil, almost slavery,
>   And all that's taught in tyranny's school,
> Who gave his land its liberty,
>   Who was he?
>
> 'T was he who e'er will be our pride,
>   Immortal Washington,
> Who always did in truth confide.
>   We hail our Washington!

The best of the verses were no better than these, but the children listened. They had to. Presently I gave them news, declaring that Washington

> Wrote the famous Constitution; sacred's the hand
> That this blessed guide to man had given, which says, "One
> And all of mankind are alike, excepting none."

This was received in respectful silence, possibly because the other Fellow Citizens were as hazy about historical facts as I at this point. "Hurrah for Washington!" they understood, and "Three cheers for the Red, White, and Blue!" was only to be expected on that occasion. But there ran a special note through my poem—a thought that only Israel Rubinstein or Beckie Aronovitch could have fully understood, besides myself. For I made myself the spokesman of the "luckless sons of Abraham," saying—

Then we weary Hebrew children at last found rest
In the land where reigned Freedom, and like a nest
To homeless birds your land proved to us, and therefore
Will we gratefully sing your praise evermore.

The boys and girls who had never been turned away from any door because of their father's religion sat as if fascinated in their places. But they woke up and applauded heartily when I was done, following the example of Miss Dwight, who wore the happy face which meant that one of her pupils had done well.

The recitation was repeated, by request, before several other classes, and the applause was equally prolonged at each repetition. After the exercises I was surrounded, praised, questioned, and made much of, by teachers as well as pupils. Plainly I had not poured my praise of George Washington into deaf ears. The teachers asked me if anybody had helped me with the poem. The girls invariably asked, "Mary Antin, how could you think of all those words?" None of them thought of the dictionary!

If I had been satisfied with my poem in the first place, the applause with which it was received by my teachers and schoolmates convinced me that I had produced a very fine thing indeed. So the person, whoever it was,—perhaps my father—who suggested that my tribute to Washington ought to be printed, did not find me difficult to persuade. When I had achieved an absolutely perfect copy of my verses, at the expense of a dozen sheets of blue-ruled note paper, I crossed the Mystic River to Boston and boldly invaded Newspaper Row.

It never occurred to me to send my manuscript by mail. In fact, it has never been my way to send a delegate where I could go myself. Consciously or unconsciously, I have always acted on the motto of a wise man who was one of the dearest friends that Boston kept for me until I came. "Personal presence moves the world," said the great Dr. Hale; and I went in person to beard the editor in his armchair.

From the ferry slip to the offices of the "Boston Transcript" the way was long, strange, and full of perils; but I kept resolutely on up Hanover Street, being familiar with that part of my route, till I came to a puzzling corner. There I stopped, utterly bewildered by the tangle of streets, the roar of traffic, the giddy swarm of pedestrians. With the precious manuscript tightly clasped, I balanced myself on the curbstone, afraid to plunge into the boiling vortex of the crossing. Every time I made a start, a clanging street car snatched up the way. I could not even pick out my street; the unobtrusive street signs were lost to my unpractised sight, in the glaring confusion of store signs and advertisements. If I accosted a pedestrian to ask the way, I had to speak several times before I was heard. Jews, hurrying by with bearded chins on their bosoms and eyes intent, shrugged their shoulders at the name "Transcript," and shrugged till they were out of sight. Italians sauntering behind their fruit carts answered by inquiry with a lift of the head that made their earrings gleam, and a wave of the hand that referred me to all four points of the compass at once. . . .

I found the "Transcript" building a waste of corridors tunnelled by a maze of staircases. On the glazed-glass doors were many signs with the names or nicknames of many persons: "City Editor"; "Beggars and Peddlers not Allowed." The nameless world not included in these categories was warned off, forbidden to be or do: "Private—No Admittance"; "Don't Knock." And the various inhospitable legends on the doors and walls were punctuated by frequent cuspidors on the floor. There was no sign anywhere of the welcome which I, as an author, expected to find in the home of a newspaper.

I was descending from the top story to the street for the seventh time, trying to decide what kind of editor a patriotic poem belonged to, when an untidy boy carrying broad paper streamers and whistling shrilly, in defiance of an express prohibition on the wall, bustled through the corridor and left a door ajar. I slipped in behind him, and found myself in a room full of editors. . . .

The room was noisy with typewriters, and nobody heard my "Please, can you tell me." At last one of the machines stopped, and the operator thought he heard something in the pause. He looked up through his own smoke. I guess he thought he saw something, for he stared. It troubled me a little to have him stare so. I realized suddenly that the hand in which I carried my manuscript was moist, and I was afraid it would make marks on the paper. I held out the mauscript to the editor, explaining that it was a poem about George Washington, and would he please print it in the "Transcript."

There was something queer about that particular editor. The way he stared and smiled made me feel about eleven inches high, and my voice kept growing smaller and smaller as I neared the end of my speech.

At last he spoke, laying down his pipe, and sitting back at his ease.

"So you have brought us a poem, my child?"

"It's about George Washington," I repeated impressively. "Don't you want to read it?"

"I should be delighted, my dear, but the fact is—"

He did not take my paper. He stood up and called across the room.

"Say, Jack! here is a young lady who has brought us a poem—about George Washington.—Wrote it yourself, my dear?—Wrote it all herself. What shall we do with her?"

Mr. Jack came over, and another man. My editor made me repeat my business, and they all looked interested, but nobody took my paper from me. They put their hands into their pockets, and my hand kept growing clammier all the time. The three seemed to be consulting, but I could not understand what they said, or why Mr. Jack laughed.

A fourth man, who had been writing busily at a desk near by, broke in on the consultation.

"That's enough, boys," he said, "that's enough. Take the young lady to Mr. Hurd."

Mr. Hurd, it was found, was away on a vacation, and of several other editors in several offices, to whom I was referred, none proved to be the proper editor to take charge of a poem about George Washington. At last an elderly editor suggested that as Mr. Hurd would be away for some time, I would do well to give up the "Transcript" and try the "Herald," across the way.

A little tired by my wanderings, and bewildered by the complexity of the editorial system, but still confident about my mission, I picked my way across Washington Street and found the "Herald" offices. Here I had instant good luck. The first editor I addressed took my paper and invited me to a seat. He read my poem much more quickly than I could myself, and said it was very nice, and asked me some questions, and made notes on a slip of paper which he pinned to my manuscript. He said he would have my piece printed very soon, and would send me a copy of the issue in which it appeared. As I was going, I could not help giving the editor my hand, although I had not experienced any handshaking in Newspaper Row. I felt that as author and editor we were on a very pleasant footing, and I gave him my hand in token of comradeship. . . .

When the paper with my poem in it arrived, the whole house pounced upon it at once. I was surprised to find that my verses were not all over the front page. The poem was a little hard to find, if anything, being tucked away in the middle of the voluminous sheet. But when we found it, it looked wonderful, just like real poetry, not at all as if somebody we knew had written it. It occupied a gratifying amount of space, and was introduced by a flattering biographical sketch of the author—the *author!* —the material for which the friendly editor had artfully drawn from me during that happy interview. And my name, as I had prophesied, was at the bottom!

When the excitement in the house had subsided, my father took all the change out of the cash drawer and went to buy up the "Herald." He did not count the pennies. He just bought "Heralds," all he could lay his hands on, and distributed them gratis to all our friends, relatives, and acquaintances; to all who could read, and to some who could not. For weeks he carried a clipping from the "Herald" in his breast pocket, and few were the occasions when he did not manage to introduce it into the conversation. He treasured that clipping as for years he had treasured the letters I wrote him from Polotzk.

Although my father bought up most of the issue containing my poem, a few hundred copies were left to circulate among the general public, enough to spread the flame of my patriotic ardor and to enkindle a thousand sluggish hearts. Really, there was something more solemn than vanity in my satisfaction. Pleased as I was with my notoriety—and nobody but I knew how exceedingly pleased—I had a sober feeling about it all. I enjoyed being praised and admired and envied; but what gave a divine flavor to my happiness was the idea that I had publicly borne testimony to the goodness of my exalted hero, to the greatness of my adopted country. I did not discount the homage of Arlington Street, because I did not properly rate the intelligence of its population. I took the admiration of my schoolmates without a grain of salt; it was just so much honey to me. I could not know that what made me great in the eyes of my neighbors was that "there was a piece about me in the paper"; it mattered very little to them what the "piece" was about. I thought they really admired my sentiments. On the street, in the schoolyard, I was pointed out. The people said, "That's Mary Antin. She had her name in the paper." I thought they said, "This is she who loves her country and worships George Washington." . . .

The Newsboys of New York

Helen Campbell

. . . Most of us have never bothered ourselves about how the newsboy lives. We know that he exists. We are too apt to regard him only as a necessary evil. What is his daily life? What becomes of him? Does he ever grow up to man's estate, or are his inches never increased?

Though it is by no means true that all newsboys are wanderers, yet most of those seen in New York streets have no homes. Out from the alleys and by-ways of the slums pours this stream of child humanity, an army of happy barbarians, for they are happy in spite of privations that seem enough to crush the spirit of the bravest. Comparatively few in number before the war, they increased manyfold with the demand of that period, and swarm now at every point where a sale is probable. Naturally only the brightest among them prospered. They began as "street rats"—the old name of the police for them,—and pilfered and gnawed at all social foundations with the recklessness and energy of their prototypes. Their life was of the hardest. Driven out from the dens in tenement districts, where most of them were born, to beg or steal as need might be, they slept in boxes, or under stairways, and sometimes in hay barges in coldest nights of winter. Two of them were known to have slept for an entire winter in the iron tube of a bridge, and two others in a burned-out safe in Wall Street. Sometimes they slipped into the cabin of a ferry-boat. Old boilers were a favorite refuge, but first and chief, then and now, came the steam gratings, where at any time of night or day in winter one may find a crowd of shivering urchins warming half-frozen fingers and toes, or curled up in a heap snatching such sleep as is to be had under adverse circumstances.

Watch a group of this nature. Their faces are old from constant exposure as well as from the struggle for existence. Their thin clothes fluttering in the wind afford small protection against winter's cold, and are made up of contributions from all sources, often rescued from the

Helen Campbell, *Darkness and Daylight; or, Lights and Shadows of New York Life* (Hartford: A. D. Worthington and Co., 1892), pp. 112–118, 121–124, 127–138.

ragpicker and cut down to meet requirements. Shoes are of the same order, but worn only in winter, the toes even then looking stockingless, from gaping holes stopped sometimes by rags wound about the feet. Kicked and cuffed by every ruffian they meet, ordered about by the police, creeping into doorways as winter storms rage, they lose no atom of cheer, and shame the prosperous passer-by who gives them small thought save as a nuisance to be tolerated. They are the pertinacious little chaps who spring up at every crossing, almost at every hour of the day and night, and thrust a paper under your nose. They run to every fire, and are present wherever a horse falls down, or a street car gets into trouble, or a brawl is in progress. They are the boys who play toss-penny in the sun in the City Hall Park, who play baseball by electric light, who rob the push-cart of the Italian banana-seller, who can scent a "copper" a block away, and who always have a plentiful supply of crocodile tears when caught in *flagrante delicto*.

The tiny fellow who flies across your path with a bundle of papers under his arm found out, almost before he ceased to be a baby, that life is very earnest, and he knows that upon his success in disposing of his stock in trade depends his supper and a warm bed for the night. Though so young he has had as many knocks as are crowded into the lives of a good many folk twice his age. He is every inch a philosopher, too, for he accepts bad fortune with stoical indifference.

Homeless boys may be divided into two classes,—the street arab and the gutter-snipe. The newsboy may be found in both these classes. As a street arab he is strong, sturdy, self-reliant, full of fight, always ready to take his own part, as well as that of the gutter-snipe, who naturally looks to him for protection.

Gutter-snipe is the name which has been given to the more weakly street arab, the little fellow who, though scarcely more than a baby, is frequently left by brutalized parents at the mercy of any fate, no matter what. This little chap generally roams around until he finds some courageous street arab, scarcely bigger than himself, perhaps, to fight his battles and put him in the way of making a living, which is generally done by selling papers. In time the gutter-snipe becomes himself a full-fledged arab with a large *clientèle*, two hard and ready fists, and a horde of dependent and grateful snipes.

This is the evolution of the newsboy wherever he be found. Some of them bring up in penal institutions and reformatories, and no wonder. Their mornings are too apt to be spent in pitching pennies or frequenting policy-shops. They are passionately devoted to the theatre, and they will cheerfully give up a prospect of a warm bed for the night for an evening in some cheap playhouse. Their applause is always discriminating. They despise humbug, whether in real life or on the mimic stage. The cheap morality current in Bowery plays, where the villain always meets his just deserts, gives them a certain standard which is as high as can well be when one lives among fighters, stealers, gamblers, and swearers. After squandering his earnings for an evening's entertainment of this sort, a convenient doorway or a sidewalk grating, through whose bars an occasional breath of warm air is wafted from underground furnaces in winter, are often the only places he has to sleep. This is the boy who is the veritable street arab, the newsboy pure and simple. You can see him early any morning hugging some warm corner or huddled into some dark passage, waiting for the moment when the papers shall be ready for dis- tribution.

Their light-heartedness is a miracle. Merry as clowns, flashing back repartee to any joker, keen and quick to take points, they manage their small affairs with a wisdom one would believe impossible. Their views of life have come from association with "flash-men" of every order, with pugilists, pickpockets, cockfighters, and all the habitués of pot-houses or bucket-shops. . . .

Almost forty years ago these were the conditions for hundreds as they are to-day for thousands, though philanthropy has fought every step of the way, as industrial schools, lodging-houses, and Homes bear witness. Chief among these rank the Newsboys' Lodging-Houses, in many respects the most unique sight to be seen in New York.

A thousand difficulties hedged about the way of those who first sought to make life easier for this class, not the least of which were how not to assail too roughly their established opinions and habits, nor to touch their sturdy independence. They had a terror of Sunday-schools, believing them only a sort of trap to let them suddenly into the House of Refuge or some equally detested place. Even when the right sort of superin- tendent had been found, and a loft had been secured in the old "Sun" building and fitted up as a lodging-room, the small skeptics regarded the movement with great suspicion and contempt. . . .

In 1869 and 1870 8,835 different boys were entered. Many of them found good homes through the agency of the Children's Aid Society; some found places for themselves; and some drifted away no one knows where, too deeply tainted with the vices of street life for reclamation. In this same year the lads themselves paid $3,349 toward expenses.

What sort of home is it that their money helps to provide? The present one, with its familiar sign, "NEWSBOYS' LODGING HOUSE," on the corner of Duane and Chambers Street, is planned like the old one on Park Place. The cleanliness is perfect, for in all the years since its founding no case of contagious disease has occurred among the boys. The first story is rented for use as shops. The next has a large dining-room where nearly two hundred boys can sit down at table; a kitchen, laundry, store-room, servant's room, and rooms for the family of the superintendent. The next story is partitioned off into a school-room, gymnasium, and bath and washrooms, all fully supplied with cold and hot water, a steam-boiler below providing both the latter and the means of heating the rooms. The two upper stories are large and roomy dormitories, each furnished with from fifty to one hundred beds or berths, arranged like a ship's bunks, over each other. The beds have spring mattresses of wire and are supplied with white cotton sheets and plenty of comforters. For these beds the boys pay six cents a night each, including supper. For ten cents a boy may hire a "private room," which consists of a square space curtained off from the vulgar gaze and supplied with a bed and locker. The private rooms are always full, no matter what the population of the dormitories may be, showing that the newsboy shares the weakness of his more fortunate brothers.

Up to midnight the little lodgers are welcome to enter the house, but later than that they are not admitted. Once in, he is expected after supper to attend the night school and remain until the end of the session; and once outside the door after the hour of closing he must make the best of a night in the streets.

Confident of his ability to take care of himself, he resents the slightest encroachment upon his freedom. The discipline of the lodging-house, therefore, does not seek to impose any more restraints upon him than those which are absolutely necessary. He goes and comes as he pleases, except that if he accepts the hospitality of the lodging-house he must abide by the rules and regulations.

Supper is served at seven o'clock and is usually well patronized, especially on Mondays and Thursdays, which are pork-and-beans days. Every boy has his bed-number, which corresponds with the number of the locker in which he keeps his clothes. When he is ready to retire he applies to the superintendent's assistant, who sits beside the keyboard. The lodger gives his number and is handed the key of his locker, in which he bestows all his clothing but his shirt and trousers. He then mounts to the dormitory, and after carefully secreting his shirt and trousers under his mattress is ready for the sleep of childhood.

The boys are wakened at different hours. Some of them rise as early as two o'clock and go down town to the newspaper offices for their stock in trade. Others rise between that hour and five o'clock. All hands, however, are routed out at seven. The boys may enjoy instruction in the rudimentary branches every night from half-past seven until nine o'clock, with the exception of Sundays, when devotional services are held and addresses made by well-known citizens.

A large majority of the boys who frequent the lodging-houses are waifs pure and simple. They have never known a mother's or a father's care, and have no sense of identity. Generally they have no name, or if they ever had one have preferred to convert it into something short and practically descriptive. As a rule they are known by nicknames and nothing else, and in speaking of one another they generally do so by these names. As a rule these names indicate some personal peculiarity or characteristic. On a recent visit to a Newsboys' Lodging House pains were taken to learn the names of a group of boys who were holding an animated conversation. It was a representative group. A very thin little fellow was called "Skinny"; another boy with light hair and complexion, being nearly as blonde as an albino, was known only as "Whitey." When "Slobbery Jack" was asked how he came by his name, "Bumlets," who appeared to be chief spokesman of the party, exclaimed, "When he eats he scatters all down hisself." "Yaller" was the name given to an Italian boy of soft brown complexion. Near him stood "Kelly the Rake," who owned but one sleeve to his jacket. In newsboy parlance a "rake" is a boy who will appropriate to his own use anything he can lay his hands on. No one could give an explanation of "Snoddy's" name nor what it meant,—it was a thorough mystery to even the savants in newsboy parlance. In the crowd was "The Snitcher,"—"a fellow w'at tattles," said Bumlets, contemptuously, and near by stood the "King of Crapshooters." "A crapshooter," said Bumlets, "is a fellow w'ats fond of playin' toss-penny, throwin' dice, an' goin' to policy shops." The "King of Bums" was a tall and rather good-looking lad, who, no doubt, had come honestly by his name. The "Snipe-Shooter" was guilty of smoking cigar-stubs picked out of the gutter, a habit known among the boys as "snipe-shooting." "Hoppy," a little lame boy; "Dutchy," a German lad; "Smoke," a colored boy; "Pie-eater," a boy very fond of pie; "Sheeney," "Skittery," "Bag of Bones," "One Lung Pete," and "Scotty" were in the same group; and so also was "Jake the Oyster," a tender-hearted boy who was spoken of by the others as "a reg'lar soft puddin'.". . .

Since the foundation of the first Newsboys' Lodging House in 1854, the various homes have sheltered nearly two hundred and fifty thousand different boys at a total expense of about four hundred and fifty thousand dollars. The amount contributed by the lads themselves during these years is nearly one hundred and seventy-five thousand dollars. Multitudes have been sent to good homes in the West.

To awaken the demand for these children, thousands of circulars were sent out, through the city weeklies and the rural newspapers, to the country districts. Hundreds of applications poured in at once from the farmers, especially from the West. At first an effort was made to meet individual applications by sending just the kind of boy wanted. Each applicant wanted a "perfect boy," without any of the taints of earthly depravity. He must be well made, of good stock, never disposed to steal apples or pelt cattle, using language of perfect propriety, fond of making fires at daylight, and delighting in family-worship and prayer-meetings more than in fishing or skating.

The defects of the first plan of emigration were speedily developed, and another and more practicable one inaugurated which has since been followed. Companies of boys are formed, and after thoroughly cleaning and clothing them they are put under a competent agent and distributed among the farmers, the utmost care being taken to select good homes for all. The parties are usually made up from the brightest and most deserving, though often one picked up in the street tells a story so pitiful and so true that he is included. . . .

An average of three thousand a year is sent to the West, many of whom are formally adopted. A volume would not suffice for the letters that come back, or the strange experiences of many a boy who under the new influences grows into an honored citizen. . . .

The stranger in New York can hardly find a more interesting sight than the gymnasium or schoolroom through the week, or the crowded Sunday night meeting, where the singing is always a fascinating part of the programme. Thanksgiving Day, with its dinner, is no less amusing and suggestive. The boys watch all visitors and know by instinct how far they are in sympathy with them. They call loudly for talk from any one whose face appeals to them. Often they make speeches on their own account. Here is a specimen taken down by a stenographer who had been given a dark corner at the end of the room and thus was not suspected by the boys.

Mr. Brace, whose appearance always called out applause, had brought down some friends, and after one or two of them had spoken, he said,

"Boys, I want my friends to see that you have some talkers amongst yourselves. Whom do you choose for your speaker?"

"Paddy, Paddy!" they shouted. "Come out, Paddy, an' show yerself."

Paddy came forward and mounted a stool; a youngster not more than twelve, with little round eyes, a short nose profusely freckled, and a lithe form full of fun.

"Bummers," he began, "Snoozers, and citizens, I've come down here among yer to talk to yer a little. Me an' me friend Brace have come to see how ye're gittin' along an' to advise yer. You fellers w'at stands at the shops with yer noses over the railin', a smellin' of the roast beef an' hash,—you fellers who's got no home,—think of it, how are we to encourage yer. [Derisive laughter, and various ironical kinds of applause.] I say bummers, for ye're all bummers, [in a tone of kind patronage,] I was a bummer once meself. [Great laughter.] I hate to see yer spending yer money for penny ice-creams an' bad cigars. Why don't yer save yer money? You feller without no boots over there, how would you like a new pair, eh? [Laughter from all the boys but the one addressed.] Well, I hope you may get 'em. Rayther think you won't. I have hopes for yer all. I want yer to grow up to be rich men,—citizens, gover'ment men, lawyers, ginerals, an' inflooence men. Well, boys, I'll tell yer a story. Me dad was a hard un. One beautiful day he went on a spree, an' he come home an' told me, where's yer mother? an' I axed him I didn't know, an' he clipped me over the head with an iron pot an' knocked me down, an' me mother drapped in on him an' at it they wint. [Hi-hi's and demonstrative applause.] An' at it they wint agin, an' at it they kept; ye should have seen 'em, an' whilst they were a fightin' I slipped meself out o' the back dure an' away I wint like a scart dog. Well, boys, I wint on till I come to a Home; [great laughter among the boys] an' they tuk me in, [renewed laughter] an' thin I ran away, an' here I am. Now, boys, be good, mind yer manners, copy me, an' see what ye'll become."

A boy who wished to advocate the claims of the West, to which he was soon to go with a party sent out from the Children's Aid Society, made a long speech, a paragraph of which will show the sense of humor which seems to be the common property of all.

"Do ye want to be newsboys always, an' shoeblacks, an' timber merchants in a small way sellin' matches? If ye do, ye'll stay in New York; but if ye don't, ye'll go out West an' begin to be farmers, for the beginning of a farmer, me boys, is the makin' of a Congressman an' a President. Do ye want to be rowdies an' loafers an' shoulder-hitters? If ye do, why, thin, ye can keep around these diggins. Do ye want to be gintlemin an' indepindent citizens? Ye do? Thin make tracks fer the West. If ye want to be snoozers, an' bummers, an' policy-players, an' Peter-Funk min, why ye'll hang up yer caps an' stay round the groggeries; but if ye want to be min to make your mark in the country ye'll get up steam an' go ahead, an' there's lots on the prairies waiting for the likes o' ye. Well, I'll now come off the stump. I'm booked for the West in the next company from the Lodging-House. I hear they have big school-houses there, an' a place for me in the winter time. I've made up me mind to be somebody, an' you'll find me on a farm in the West an' I hope yees will come to see me soon. I thank ye, boys, for yer patient attintion. I can't say no more at present, boys. Good bye."

The newsboys' lodging-houses are like the ancient cities of refuge to these little fellows, and yet there are cases which the lodging-houses never reach.

"Recently," said a gentleman, "I found a tiny fellow playing a solitary game of marbles in a remote corner of the City Hall corridors. His little legs were very thin, and dark circles under his big gray eyes intensified the chalk-like pallor of his cheeks. He looked up when he became aware that some one was watching him, but resumed his game of solitaire as soon as he saw he had nothing to fear from the intruder.

"What are you doing here, my little fellow?" I asked.

The mite hastily gathered up all his marbles and stowed them very carefully away in his capacious trousers pocket. Then he backed up against the wall and surveyed me doubtfully. I repeated my question,— this time more gently, so as to reassure him.

"I'm waitin' fur Jack de Robber," he piped, and then, as he began to gain confidence, seeing no signs of "swipes" about me, he added, "him as brings me de Telies (Dailies) every day."

"And you sell the papers?"

"I sells 'em for Jack," he promptly answered.

I was glad, when I looked at the lad's attire, that he was protected for the time being by the comparative warmth of the corridor. Outdoors it was cold and blustering. Still I resolved to wait and see "Jack de Robber." Shortly after three o'clock a short chunky boy with a shock of black hair hustled through the door and made in the direction of my pale little friend. He was struggling with a big mass of papers and was issuing orders in a rather peremptory tone to his diminutive lieutenant.

"Do you know this little boy?" I asked.

"Jack de Robber" gave me a look which was not reassuring. "Does I naw him? Of corse I naws him. What de——!"

"Why don't you send him home to his mother; he's neither big enough nor strong enough to sell papers?"

At this Jack gave utterance to an oath too utterly original for reproduction; then he said, "Dat ere kid ain't got no mammy; I looks after dat kid meself."

I slipped a coin into Jack's hand and urged him to tell me the whole story. He dropped his heap of papers, tested the coin with his teeth, slid it into his pocket, and began:—

"Blokes is allus axin' 'bout dat ere kid, but you is de fust one what ever raised de ante. Dat ere kid don't naw no more 'bout his mammy'n me. Cause why? Cause he ain't never had no mammy."

Here Jack paused, as if determined to go no further, but another coin gave wings to his words.

"Dat ere kid," he resumed, "ain't got no more sand'n a John Chinee. He'd be kilt ony fur me. He can't come along de Row or up de alley widout gitin' his face broke. So I gives him papers to sell and looks arter him meself."

I asked Jack where the "Kid" and himself slept. "I ain't givin' dat away," said he, "ony taint no lodgin'-house where you has to git up early in the mawnin'. De 'Kid' and me likes to sleep late."

The "Kid," however, was now eager to be off with his papers, and without another word the protector and protégé sped into the street, filling the air with their shrill cries. . . .

Instances of this class of newsboys could be multiplied indefinitely. These are the absolute Bohemians of their kind, who prefer a doorway to a warm bed, and the sights of the streets any time and all the time to the simple restraints imposed by the lodging-houses.

The newsboy's life is filled with the hardest sort of work. His gains are not always in proportion, for he must begin often before light, huddling over the steam gratings at the printing-offices, and waiting for his share of the morning papers. He scurries to work these off before the hour for taking the evening editions, and sometimes cannot with his utmost diligence take in more than fifty cents a day, though it ranges from this to a dollar and a quarter. The period of elections is the harvest-time. A boy has been known to sell six hundred papers in two hours, at a profit of between eleven and twelve dollars.

Among over twenty-one thousand children who in the early years of the work were sent West, but twelve became criminals, and not more than six annually return to New York. No work done for children compares with this in importance, and whoever studies the record of the Children's Aid Society will be amazed at the good already accomplished. Twenty-one industrial schools, twelve night-schools, two free reading-rooms, six lodging-houses for girls and boys, four summer homes, and the Crippled Boys' Brush Shop, are the record plain to all; but who shall count the good that no man has recorded, but which has rescued thousands from the streets and given them the chance which is the right of every human soul.

The Small Talk of Society

Mrs. John Sherwood

One of the cleverest questions asked lately is, "What shall I talk about at a dinner-party?" Now if there is a woman in the world who does not know what to talk about, is it not a very difficult thing to tell her? One can almost as well answer such a question as, "What shall I see out of my eyes?"

Yet our young lady is not the first person who has dilated of late years upon the "decay of conversation," nor the only one who has sometimes felt the heaviness of silence descend upon her at a modern dinner. No doubt this same great and unanswerable question has been asked by many a traveller who, for the first time, has sat next an Englishman of good family (perhaps even with a handle to his name), who has answered all remarks by the proverbial but unsympathetic "Oh!" Indeed, it is to be feared that it is a fashion of young men nowadays to appear listless, to conceal what ideas they may happen to have, to try to appear stupid, if they are not so, throwing all the burden of the conversation on the lively, vivacious, good-humored girl, or the more accomplished married woman, who may be the next neighbor. Women's wits are proverbially quick, they talk readily, they read and think more than the average young man of fashion is prone to do; the result is a quick and a ready tongue. Yet the art of keeping up a flow of agreeable and incessant small-talk, not too heavy, not pretentious or egotistical, not scandalous, and not commonplace, is an art that is rare, and hardly to be prized too highly. . . .

It is a good plan for a shy young person, who has no confidence in her own powers of conversation, to fortify herelf with several topics of general interest, such as the last new novel, the last opera, the best and newest gallery of pictures, or the flower in fashion; and to invent a formula, if words are wanting in her organization, as to how these subjects should be introduced and handled. Many ideas will occur to her, and she can silently arrange them. Then she may keep these as a reserve force, using

Mrs. John Sherwood, *Manners and Social Uses* (New York: Harper and Brothers, 1897), pp. 320–327.

them only when the conversation drops, or she is unexpectedly brought to the necessity of keeping up the ball alone. Some people use this power rather unfairly, leading the conversation up to the point where they wish to enter; but these are not the people who need help—they can take care of themselves. After talking awhile in a perfunctory manner, many a shy young person has been astonished by a sudden rush of brilliant ideas, and finds herself talking naturally and well without effort. It is like the launching of a ship; certain blocks of shyness and habits of mental reserve are knocked away, and the brave frigate *Small-Talk* takes the water like a thing of life.

It demands much tact and cleverness to touch upon the ordinary events of the day at a mixed dinner, because, in the first place, nothing should be said which can hurt any one's feelings—politics, religion, and the stock market being generally ruled out; nor should one talk about that which everybody knows, for such small-talk is impertinent and irritating. No one wishes to be told that which he already understands better, perhaps, than we do. Nor are matters of too private a nature, such as one's health, or one's servants, or one's disappointments, still less one's good deeds, to be talked about.

Commonplace people also sometimes try society very much by their own inane and wholly useless criticisms. Supposing we take up music, it is far more agreeable to hear a person say, "How do you like Nilsson?" than to hear him say, "I like Nilsson, and I have these reasons for liking her." Let that come afterwards. When a person really qualified to discuss artists, or literary people, or artistic points, talks sensibly and in a chatty, easy way about them, it is the perfection of conversation; but when one wholly and utterly incompetent to do so lays down the law on such subjects he or she becomes a bore. But if the young person who does not know how to talk treats these questions interrogatively, ten chances to one, unless she is seated next an imbecile, she will get some very good and light small-talk out of her next neighbor. She may give a modest personal opinion, or narrate her own sensations at the opera, if she can do so without egotism, and she should always show a desire to be answered. If music and literature fail, let her try the subjects of dancing, polo-playing, and lawn-tennis. A very good story was told of a bright New York girl and a very haw—haw—stupid Englishman at a Newport dinner. The Englishman had said "Oh," and "Really," and "Quite so," to everything which this bright girl had asked him, when finally, very tired and very angry, she said, "Were you ever thrown in the hunting-field, and was your head hurt?" The man turned and gazed admiringly. "Now you've got me," was the reply. And he talked all the rest of the dinner of his croppers. Perhaps it may not be necessary or useful often to unlock so rich a *répertoire* as this; but it was a very welcome relief to this young lady not to do all the talking during three hours.

After a first introduction there is, no doubt, some difficulty in starting a conversation. The weather, the newspaper, the last accident, the little dog, the bric-à-brac, the love of horses, etc., are good and unfailing resources, except that very few people have the readiness to remember this wealth of subjects at once. To recollect a thing apropos of the moment is the gift of ready-witted people alone, and how many remember, hours after, a circumstance which would have told at that particular moment of embarrassment when one stood twiddling his hat, and another twisted her handkerchief. The French call *"l'esprit d'escalier"*—the "wit of the staircase"—the gift of remembering the good thing you might have said in the drawing-room, just too late, as you go up-stairs. However, two new people generally overcome this moment of embarrassment, and then some simple offer of service, such as, "Can I get you a chair?" "Is that window too cold?" "Can I bring you some tea?" occurs, and then the small-talk follows. . . .

Gossip may promote small-talk among those who are very intimate and who live in a narrow circle. But how profoundly uninteresting is it to an outsider!—how useless to the real man or woman of the world! That is, unless it is literary, musical, artistic gossip. Scandal ruins conversation, and should never be included even in a definition of small-talk. Polite, humorous, vivacious, speculative, dry, sarcastic, epigrammatic, intellectual, and practical people all meet around a dinner-table, and much agreeable small-talk should be the result. It is unfortunately true that there is sometimes a failure in this respect. Let a hostess remember one thing: there is no chance for vivacity of intellect if her room is too warm; her flowers and her guests will wilt together. There are those also who prefer her good dishes to talking, and the old gentleman in *Punch* who rebuked his lively neighbor for talking while there were "such *entrées* coming in" has his counterparts among ourselves.

Some shy talkers have a sort of empirical way of starting a subject with a question like this: "Do you know the meaning and derivation of the term 'bric-à-brac?' " "Do you believe in ghosts?" "What do you think of a ladies' club?" "Do you believe in chance?" "Is there more talent displayed in learning the violin than in playing a first-rate game of chess?" etc.

These are intellectual conundrums, and may be repeated indefinitely where the person questioned is disposed to answer. With a flow of good spirits and the feeling of ease which comes from a knowledge of society, such questions often bring out what Margaret Fuller called "good talk."

But if your neighbor says "Oh," "Really," "Indeed," 'I don't know," then the best way is to be purely practical, and talk of the chairs and tables, and the existing order of things, the length of trains, or the shortness of the dresses of the young ladies at the last ball, the prevailing idea that "ice-water is unhealthy," and other such extremely easy ideas. The sound of one's own voice is generally very sweet in one's own ears; let every lady try to cultivate a pleasant voice for those of other people, and also an agreeable and accurate pronunciation. The veriest nothings sound well when thus spoken. The best way to learn how to talk is, of course, to learn how to think: from full wells one brings up buckets full of clear water, but there can be small-talk without much thought. The fact remains that brilliant thinkers and scholars are not always good talkers, and there is no harm in the cultivation of the art of conversation, no harm in a little "cramming," if a person is afraid that language is not his strong point. The merest trifle generally suffices to start the flow of small-talk, and the person who can use this agreeable weapon of society is always popular and very much courted.

A Glimpse of High Society

Ward McAllister

ENTERING SOCIETY

I would now make some suggestions as to the proper way of introducing a young girl into New York society, particularly if she is not well supported by an old family connection. It is cruel to take a girl to a ball where she knows no one,

> "And to subject her to
> The fashionable stare of twenty score
> Of well-bred persons, called 'the world.' "

Had I charged a fee for every consultation with anxious mothers on this subject, I would be a rich man. I well remember a near relative of mine once writing me from Paris, as follows: "I consign my wife and daughter to your care. They will spend the winter in New York; at once give them a ball at Delmonico's, and draw on me for the outlay." I replied, "My dear fellow, how many people do you know in this city whom you could invite to a ball? The funds you send me will be used, but not in giving a ball." The girl being a beauty, all the rest was easy enough. I gave her theatre party after theatre party, followed by charming little suppers, asked to them the *jeunesse dorée* of the day; took her repeatedly to the opera, and saw that she was there always surrounded by admirers; incessantly talked of her fascinations; assured my young friends that she was endowed with a fortune equal to the mines of Ophir, that she danced like a dream, and possessed all the graces, a sunbeam across one's path; then saw to it that she had a prominent place in every cotillion, and a fitting partner; showed her whom to smile upon, and on whom to frown; gave her the *entrée* to all the nice houses; criticised severely her toilet until it became perfect; daily met her on the Avenue with the most charming man in town, who by one pretext or another I turned over to her; made her the constant subject of conversation; insisted upon it that

Ward McAllister, *Society as I Have Found It* (New York: Cassell, 1890), pp. 239–246, 248–252, 255–264.

she was to be the belle of the coming winter; advised her parents that she should have her first season at Bar Harbor, where she could learn to flirt to her heart's content, and vie with other girls. Her second summer, when she was older, I suggested her passing at Newport, where she should have a pair of ponies, a pretty trap, with a well-gotten-up groom, and Worth to dress her. Here I hinted that much must depend on her father's purse, as to her wardrobe. As a friend of mine once said to me, "Your pace is charming, but can you keep it up?" I also advised keeping the young girl well in hand and not letting her give offense to the powers that be; to see to it that she was not the first to arrive and the last to leave a ball, and further, that nothing was more winning in a girl than a pleasant bow and a gracious smile given to either young or old. The fashion now for women is to hold themselves erect. The modern manner of shaking hands I do not like, but yet it is adopted. Being interested in the girl's success, I further impressed upon her the importance of making herself agreeable to older people, remembering that much of her enjoyment would be derived from them. If asked to dance a cotillion, let it be conditional that no bouquet be sent her; to be cautious how she refused the first offers of marriage made her, as they were generally the best.

A word, just here, to the newly married. It works well to have the man more in love with you than you are with him. My advice to all young married women is to keep up flirting with their husbands as much after marriage as before; to make themselves as attractive to their husbands after their marriage as they were when they captivated them; not to neglect their toilet, but rather improve it; to be as coquettish and coy after they are bound together as before, when no ties held them. The more they are appreciated by the world, the more will their husbands value them. In fashionable life, conspicuous jealousy is a mistake. A woman is bound to take and hold a high social position. In this way she advances and strengthens her husband. How many women we see who have benefited their husbands, and secured for them these advantages. . . .

The launching of a beautiful young girl into society is one thing; it is another to place her family on a good, sound social footing. You can launch them into the social sea, but can they float? "Manners maketh man," is an old proverb. These they certainly must possess. There is no society in the world as generous as New York society is; "friend, parent, neighbor, all it will embrace," but once embraced they must have the power of sustaining themselves. The best quality for them to possess is modesty in asserting their claims; letting people seek them rather than attempting to rush too quickly to the front. The Prince of Wales, on a charming American young woman expressing her surprise at the cordial reception given her by London society, replied, "My dear lady, there are certain people who are bound to come to the front and stay there; you are one of them." It requires not only money, but brains, and, above all, infinite tact; possessing the three, your success is assured. If taken by the hand by a person in society you are at once led into the charmed circle, and then your own correct perceptions of what should or should not be done must do the rest. As a philosophical friend once said to me, "A gentleman can always walk, but he cannot afford to have a shabby equipage." Another philosopher soliloquized as follows: "The first evidence of wealth is your equipage." By the way, his definition of aristocracy in America was, the possession of hereditary wealth.

If you want to be fashionable, be always in the company of fashionable people. As an old beau suggested to me, If you see a fossil of a man, shabbily dressed, relying solely on his pedigree, dating back to time immemorial, who has the aspirations of a duke and the fortunes of a footman, do not cut him; it is better to cross the street and avoid meeting him. It is well to be in with the nobs who are born to their position, but the support of the swells is more advantageous, for society is sustained and carried on by the swells, the nobs looking quietly on and accepting the position, feeling they are there by divine right; but they do not make fashionable society, or carry it on. A nob can be a swell if he chooses, i.e. if he will spend the money; but for his social existence this is unnecessary. A nob is like a poet,—*nascitur non fit;* not so a swell,—he creates himself. . . .

Here, all men are more or less in business. We hardly have a class who are not. They are, of necessity, daily brought in contact with all sorts and conditions of men, and in self-defense oftentimes have to acquire and adopt an abrupt, a brusque manner of address, which, as a rule, they generally leave in their offices when they quit them. If they do not, they certainly should. When such rough manners become by practice a second nature, they unfit one to go into society. It pays well for young and old to cultivate politeness and courtesy. Nothing is gained by trying roughly to elbow yourself into society, and push your way through into the inner circle; for when such a one has reached it, he will find its atmosphere uncongenial and be only too glad to escape from it. . . .

I think the great secret of life is to be contented with the position to which it has pleased God to call you. Living myself in a modest, though comfortable little house in Twenty-first Street in this city, a Wall Street banker honored me with a visit, and exclaimed against my surroundings.

"What!" said he, "are you contented to live in this modest little house? Why, man, this will never do! The first thing you must have is a fine house. I will see that you get it. All that you have to do is to let me buy ten thousand shares of stock for you at the opening of the Board; by three I can sell it, and I will then send you a check for the profit of the transaction, which will not be less than ten thousand dollars! Do it for you? Of course I will, with pleasure. You will run no risk; if there is a loss I will bear it."

I thanked my friend, assured him I was wholly and absolutely contented, and must respectfully decline his offer. A similar offer was made to me by my old friend, Commodore Vanderbilt, in his house in Washington Place. I was a great admirer of this grand old man, and he was very fond of me. He had taken me over his stables, and was then showing me his parlors and statuary, and kept all the time calling me "his boy." I turned to him and said, "Commodore, you will be as great a railroad king, as you were once an ocean king, and as you call me your boy, why don't you make my fortune?" He thought a moment, and then said, slapping me on the back, "Mc, sell everything you have and put it in Harlem stock; it is now twenty-four; you will make more money than you will know how to take care of." If I had followed his advice, I would now have been indeed a millionaire.

One word more here about the Commodore. He then turned to me and said, "Mc, look at that bust,"—a bust of himself, by Powers. "What do you think Powers said of that head?"

"What did he say?" I replied.

"He said, 'It is a finer head than Webster's!' "

SUCCESS IN ENTERTAINING

The first object to be aimed at is to make your dinners so charming and agreeable that invitations to them are eagerly sought for, and to let all feel that it is a great privilege to dine at your house, where they are sure they will meet only those whom they wish to meet. You cannot instruct people by a book how to entertain, though Aristotle is said to have applied *his* talents to a compilation of a code of laws for the table. Success in entertaining is accomplished by magnetism and tact, which combined constitute social genius. It is the ladder to social success. If successfully done, it naturally creates jealousy. I have known a family who for years outdid every one in giving exquisite dinners—(this was when this city was a small community)—driven to Europe and passing the rest of their days there on finding a neighbor outdoing them. I myself once lost a charming friend by giving a better soup than he did. His wife rushed home from my house, and in despair, throwing up her hands to her husband, exclaimed, "Oh! what a soup!" I related this to my cousin, the distinguished *gourmet*, who laughingly said: "Why did you not at once invite them to pork and beans?"

The highest cultivation in social manners enables a person to conceal from the world his real feelings. He can go through any annoyance as if it were a pleasure; go to a rival's house as if to a dear friend's; "Smile and smile, yet murder while he smiles." A great compliment once paid me in Newport was the speech of an old public waiter, who had grown gray in the service, when to a *confrère* he exclaimed: "In this house, my friend, you meet none but quality."

In planning a dinner the question is not to whom you owe dinners, but who is most desirable. The success of the dinner depends as much upon the company as the cook. Discordant elements—people invited alphabetically, or to pay off debts—are fatal. Of course, I speak of ladies' dinners. And here, great tact must be used in bringing together young womanhood and the dowagers. A dinner wholly made up of young people is generally stupid. You require the experienced woman of the world, who has at her fingers' ends the history of past, present, and future. Critical, scandalous, with keen and ready wit, appreciating the dinner and wine at their worth. Ladies in beautiful toilets are necessary to the elegance of a dinner, as a most exquisitely arranged table is only a solemn affair surrounded by black coats. I make it a rule never to attend such dismal feasts, listening to prepared witticisms and "twice-told tales." So much for your guests.

The next step is an interview with your *chef*, if you have one, or *cordon bleu*, whom you must arouse to fever heat by working on his ambition and vanity. You must impress upon him that this particular dinner will give him fame and lead to fortune. My distinguished cousin, who enjoyed the reputation of being one of the most finished *gourmets* in this country, when he reached this point, would bury his head in his hands and (seemingly to the *chef*) rack his brain seeking inspiration, fearing lest the fatal mistake should occur of letting two white or brown sauces follow each other in succession; or truffles appear twice in that dinner. The distress that his countenance wore as he repeatedly looked up at the *chef*, as if for advice and assistance, would have its intended effect on the culinary artist, and *his* brain would at once act in sympathy.

The first battle is over the soup, and here there is a vast difference of opinion. In this country, where our servants are oftentimes unskilled, and have a charming habit of occasionally giving ladies a soup shower bath, I invariably discard two soups, and insist to the protesting *chef* that there shall be but one. Of course, if there are two, the one is light, the other heavy. Fortunately for the period in which we live, our great French artists have invented the *Tortue claire*, which takes the place of our forefathers' Mock Turtle soup, with forcemeat balls, well spiced, requiring an ostrich's digestion to survive it. We have this, then, as our soup. The *chef* here exclaims, "Monsieur must know that all *petites bouchées* must, of necessity, be made of chicken." We ask for a novelty, and his great genius suggests, under pressure, *mousse aux jambon*, which is attractive to the eye, and, if well made, at once establishes the reputation of the artist, satisfies the guests that they are in able hands, and allays their fears for their dinner.

There is but one season of the year when salmon should be served hot at a choice repast; that is in the spring and early summer, and even then it is too satisfying, not sufficiently delicate. The man who gives salmon

during the winter, I care not what sauce he serves with it, does an injury
to himself and his guests. Terrapin is with us as national a dish as canvas-
back, and at the choicest dinners is often a substitute for fish. It is a shell-
fish, and an admirable change from the oft repeated *filet de sole* or *filet de
bass*. At the South, terrapin soup, with plenty of eggs in it, was a dish for
the gods, and a standard dinner party dish in days when a Charleston and
Savannah dinner was an event to live for. But no Frenchman ever made
this soup. It requires the native born culinary genius of the African. . . .

And now, leaving the fish, we come to the *pièce de resistance* of the
dinner, called the *relévé*. No Frenchman will ever willingly cook a ladies'
dinner and give anything coarser or heavier than a *filet de bœuf*. He will
do it, if he has to, of course, but he will think you a barbarian if you order
him to do it. I eschew the mushroom and confine myself to the truffle in
the treatment of the *filet*. I oftentimes have a *filet à la mœlle de bœuf*, or
à la jardinière. In the fall of the year, turkey *poules à la Bordelaise, or à
la Toulouse*, or a saddle of Southdown mutton or lamb, are a good substitute. Let me here say that the American turkey, as found on Newport
Island, all its feathers being jet black and its diet grasshoppers, is exceptionally fine.

Now for the *entrées*. In a dinner of twelve or fourteen, one or two hot
entrées and one cold is sufficient. If you use the truffle with the *filet*, making a black sauce, you must follow it with a white souce, as a *riz de veau
à la Toulouse*, or a *suprême de volaille;* then a *chaud-froid*, say of *pâté de
foie gras en Bellevue*, which simply means *pâté de foie gras* incased in
jelly. Then a hot vegetable, as artichokes, sauce *Barigoule*, or *Italienne*, or
asparagus, sauce *Hollandaise*. Then your *sorbet*, known in France as *la
surprise*, as it is an ice, and produces on the mind the effect that the dinner is finished, when the grandest dish of the dinner makes its appearance
in the shape of the roast canvasbacks, woodcock, snipe, or truffled capons,
with salad.

I must be permitted a few words of and about this *sorbet*. It should
never be flavored with rum. A true Parisian *sorbet* is simply "*punch à la
Toscane*," flavored with *Maraschino* or bitter almonds; in other words, a
homœopathic dose of prussic acid. Then the *sorbet* is a digestive, and is
intended as such. *Granit*, or water ice, flavored with rum, is universally
given here. Instead of aiding digestion, it impedes it, and may be dangerous.

A Russian salad is a pleasing novelty at times, and is more attractive if
it comes in the shape of a *Macedoine de legumes*, Camembert cheese,
with a biscuit, with which you serve your Burgundy, your old Port, or
your Johannisberg, the only place in the dinner where you can introduce
this latter wine. A genuine Johannisberg, I may say here, by way of paren-
thesis, is rare in this country, for if obtained at the Chateau, it is comparatively a dry wine; if it is, as I have often seen it, still lusciously sweet after

having been here twenty years or more, you may be sure it is not a genuine Chateau wine.

The French always give a hot pudding, as pudding *suedoise*, or a *croute au Madère*, or *ananas*, but I always omit this dish to shorten the dinner. Then come your ices. The fashion now is to make them very ornamental, a *cornucopia* for instance, but I prefer a *pouding Nesselrode*, the best of all the ices if good cream is used.

American Life and "Modern Nervousness"

George M. Beard

The causes of American nervousness are complicated, but are not beyond analysis: First of all modern civilization. The phrase modern civilization is used with emphasis, for civilization alone does not cause nervousness. The Greeks were certainly civilized, but they were not nervous, and in the Greek language there is no word for that term. The ancient Romans were civilized, as judged by any standard. Civilization is therefore a relative term, and as such is employed throughout this treatise. The modern differ from the ancient civilizations mainly in these five elements—steam power, the periodical press, the telegraph, the sciences, and the mental activity of women. When civilization, plus these five factors, invades any nation, it must carry nervousness and nervous diseases along with it.

CIVILIZATION VERY LIMITED IN EXTENT

All that is said here of American nervousness refers only to a fraction of American society; for in America, as in all lands, the majority of the people are muscle-workers rather than brain-workers; have little education, and are not striving for honor, or expecting eminence or wealth. All our civilization hangs by a thread; the activity and force of the very few make us what we are as a nation; and if, through degeneracy, the descendants of these few revert to the condition of their not very remote ancestors, all our haughty civilization would be wiped away. With all our numerous colleges, such as they are, it is a rarity and surprise to meet in business relations with a college-educated man. . . .

In the lower orders, the classes that support our dispensaries and hospitals, in the tenements of our crowded cities, and even on farms in the country, by the mountain side—among the healthiest regions, we find, now and then, here and there cases of special varieties of nervous disease,

George M. Beard, *American Nervousness* (New York: G. P. Putnam's Sons, 1881), pp. 96–99, 101–107, 112–123, 125–126, 128–130, 293–298.

such as hay-fever, neurasthenia, etc.; but the proportion of diseases of this kind among these people is much smaller than among the in-door-living and brain-working classes, although insanity of the incurable kind is more common among the lower or the middle than in the very highest classes. . . .

The nervous system of man is the centre of the nerve-force supplying all the organs of the body. Like the steam engine, its force is limited, although it cannot be mathematically measured—and, unlike the steam engine, varies in amount of force with the food, the state of health and external conditions, varies with age, nutrition, occupation, and numberless factors. The force in this nervous system can, therefore, be increased or diminished by good or evil influences, medical or hygienic, or by the natural evolutions—growth, disease and decline; but none the less it is limited; and when new functions are interposed in the circuit, as modern civilization is constantly requiring us to do, there comes a period, sooner or later, varying in different individuals, and at different times of life, when the amount of force is insufficient to keep all the lamps actively burning; those that are weakest go out entirely, or, as more frequently happens, burn faint and feebly—they do not expire, but give an insufficient and unstable light—this is the philosophy of modern nervousness. . . .

NECESSARY EVILS OF SPECIALIZATION

One evil, and hardly looked for effect of the introduction of steam, together with the improved methods of manufacturing of recent times, has been the training in special departments or duties—so that artisans, instead of doing or preparing to do, all the varieties of the manipulations needed in the making of any article, are restricted to a few simple exiguous movements, to which they give their whole lives—in the making of a rifle, or a watch, each part is constructed by experts on that part. The effect of this exclusive concentration of mind and muscle to one mode of action, through months and years, is both negatively and positively pernicious, and notably so, when re-enforced, as it almost universally is, by the bad air of overheated and ill-ventilated establishments. Herein is one unanticipated cause of the increase of insanity and other diseases of the nervous system among the laboring and poorer classes. The steam engine, which would relieve work, as it was hoped, and allow us to be idle, has increased the amount of work done a thousand fold; and with that increase in quantity there has been a differentiation of quality and specialization of function which, so far forth, is depressing both to mind and body. In the professions—the constringing power of specialization is neutralized very successfully by general culture and observation, out of which specialties spring, and by which they are supported; but for the artisan there is no time, or chance, or hope, for such redeeming and antidotal influences.

CLOCKS AND WATCHES—NECESSITY OF PUNCTUALITY

The perfection of clocks and the invention of watches have something to do with modern nervousness, since they compel us to be on time, and excite the habit of looking to see the exact moment, so as not to be late for trains or appointments. Before the general use of these instruments of precision in time, there was a wider margin for all appointments; a longer period was required and prepared for, especially in travelling—coaches of the olden period were not expected to start like steamers or trains, on the instant—men judged of the time by probabilities, by looking at the sun, and needed not, as a rule, to be nervous about the loss of a moment, and had incomparably fewer experiences wherein a delay of a few moments might destroy the hopes of a lifetime. A nervous man cannot take out his watch and look at it when the time for an appointment or train is near, without affecting his pulse, and the effect on that pulse, if we could but measure and weigh it, would be found to be correlated to a loss to the nervous system. Punctuality is a greater thief of nervous force than is procrastination of time. We are under constant strain, mostly unconscious, oftentimes in sleeping as well as in waking hours, to get somewhere or do something at some definite moment. . . . There are those who prefer, or fancy they prefer, the sensations of movement and activity to the sensations of repose; but from the standpoint only of economy of nerve-force all our civilization is a mistake; every mile of advance into the domain of ideas, brings a conflict that knows no rest, and all conquests are to be paid for, before delivery often, in blood and nerve and life. . . .

THE TELEGRAPH

The telegraph is a cause of nervousness the potency of which is little understood. Before the days of Morse and his rivals, merchants were far less worried than now, and less business was transacted in a given time; prices fluctuated far less rapidly, and the fluctuations which now are transmitted instantaneously over the world were only known then by the slow communication of sailing vessels or steamships; hence we might wait for weeks or months for a cargo of tea from China, trusting for profit to prices that should follow their arrival; whereas, now, prices at each port are known at once all over the globe. This continual fluctuation of values, and the constant knowledge of those fluctuations in every part of the world, are the scourges of business men, the tyrants of trade—every cut in prices in wholesale lines in the smallest of any of the Western cities, becomes known in less than an hour all over the Union; thus competition is both diffused and intensified. . . .

EFFECT OF NOISE ON THE NERVES

. . . The noises that nature is constantly producing—the moans and roar of the wind, the rustling and trembling of the leaves and swaying of the branches, the roar of the sea and of waterfalls, the singing of birds, and even the cries of some wild animals—are mostly rhythmical to a greater or less degree, and always varying if not intermittent; to a savage or to a refined ear, on cultured or uncultured brains, they are rarely distressing, often pleasing, sometimes delightful and inspiring. Even the loudest sounds in nature, the roll of thunder, the howling of storms, and the roar of a cataract like Niagara—save in the exceptional cases of idiosyncrasy—are the occasions not of pain but of pleasure, and to observe them at their best men will compass the globe.

Many of the appliances and accompaniments of civilization, on the other hand, are the causes of noises that are unrhythmical, unmelodious and therefore annoying, if not injurious; manufactures, locomotion, travel, housekeeping even, are noise-producing factors, and when all these elements are concentred, as in great cities, they maintain through all the waking and some of the sleeping hours, an unintermittent vibration in the air that is more or less disagreeable to all, and in the case of an idiosyncrasy or severe illness may be unbearable and harmful. Rhythmical, melodious, musical sounds are not only agreeable, but when not too long maintained are beneficial, and may be ranked among our therapeutical agencies.

Unrhythmical, harsh, jarring sounds, to which we apply the term noise, are, on the contrary, to a greater or less degree, harmful or liable to be harmful; they cause severe molecular disturbance. . . .

RAILWAY TRAVELLING AND NERVOUSNESS

Whether railway travelling is directly the cause of nervous disease is a question of not a little interest. Reasoning deductively, without any special facts, it would seem that the molecular disturbance caused by travelling long distances, or living on trains as an employé, would have an unfavorable influence on the nervous system.

In practice this seems to be found; that in some cases—probably a minority of those who live on the road—functional nervous symptoms are excited, and there are some who are compelled to give up this mode of life. . . .

That railway travel, though beneficial to some, is sometimes injurious to the nerve system of the nervous, is demonstrable all the time in my patients; many while travelling by rail suffer from the symptoms of sea-sickness and with increase of nervousness.

RAPID DEVELOPMENT AND ACCEPTANCE OF NEW IDEAS

The rapidity with which new truths are discovered, accepted and popularized in modern times is a proof and result of the extravagance of our civilization.

Philosophies and discoveries as well as inventions which in the Middle

Ages would have been passed by or dismissed with the murder of the author, are in our time—and notably in our country—taken up and adopted, in innumerable ways made practical—modified, developed, actively opposed, possibly overthrown and displaced within a few years, and all of necessity at a great expenditure of force.

The experiments, inventions, and discoveries of Edison alone have made and are now making constant and exhausting draughts on the nervous forces of America and Europe, and have multiplied in very many ways, and made more complex and extensive, the tasks and agonies not only of practical men, but of professors and teachers and students everywhere; the simple attempt to master the multitudinous directions and details of the labors of this one young man with all his thousands and thousands of experiments and hundreds of patents and with all the soluble and insoluble physical problems suggested by his discoveries would itself be a sufficient task for even a genius in science; and any high school or college in which his labors were not recognized and the results of his labors were not taught would be patronized only for those who prefer the eighteenth century to the twentieth.

On the mercantile or practical side the promised discoveries and inventions of this one man have kept millions of capital and thousand of capitalists in suspense and distress on both sides of the sea. In contrast with the gradualness of thought movement in the Middle Ages, consider the dazzling swiftness with which the theory of evolution and the agnostic philosophy have extended and solidified their conquests until the whole world of thought seems hopelessly subjected to their autocracy. I once met in society a young man just entering the silver decade, but whose hair was white enough for one of sixty, and he said that the color changed in a single day, as a sign and result of a mental conflict in giving up his religion for science. . . .

INCREASE IN AMOUNT OF BUSINESS IN MODERN TIMES

The increase in the amount of business of nearly all kinds in modern times, especially in the last half century, is a fact that comes right before us when we ask the question, Why nervousness is so much on the increase? . . .

Manufacturers, under the impulses of steam-power and invention, have multiplied the burdens of mankind; and railways, telegraphs, canals, steamships, and the utilization of steam-power in agriculture, and in handling and preparing materials for transportation, have made it possible to transact a hundred-fold more business in a limited time than even in the eighteenth century; but with an increase rather than a decrease in business transactions. Increased facilities for agriculture, manufactures, and trades have developed sources of anxiety and of loss as well as profit, and have enhanced the risks of business; machinery has been increased in quantity and complexity, some parts, it is true, being lubricated by late inventions, others having the friction still more increased. . . .

INCREASED CAPACITY FOR SORROW—LOVE AND PHILANTHROPY

Capacity for disappointment and sorrow has increased with the advance of civilization. Fineness of organization, which is essential to the development of the civilization of modern times, is accompanied by intensified mental susceptibility.

In savagery, life is mostly sensual, with much mental force held in reserve, as with North American Indians, while the intellect has but slight strength; in a highly civilized people, some of the senses and all the emotions are quickly excited, and are attended with higher, sweeter, and more complex and rapturous pleasure than in savagery, and but for the controlling and inhibiting force of a better trained reason, would make progress, and even existence, in civilization, impossible. Relatively to the intellect, the savage has more emotion than the civilized man, but in absolute quantity and quality of emotion, the civilized man very far surpasses the savage; although, as the civilized man is constantly kept in check by the inhibitory power of the intellect, he appears to be far less emotional than the savage, who, as a rule, with some exceptions, acts out his feelings with comparatively little restraint. . . .

Of the poetry of love, as distinct from the physical type, the lower savages know nothing—their friendships, their married life, their home life with their offspring, show but fugitive traces of that enormous and tyrannous emotion out of which all our novels, romances, and dramas are builded. This potency of loving, including not only sexual, but filial, brotherly and sisterly affection, in all its ranges and ramifications, is a later evolution of human nature; like all other emotions, it is matched by a capacity for sorrow corresponding to its capacity for joy. Love, even when gratified, is a costly emotion; when disappointed, as it is so often likely to be, it costs still more, drawing largely, in the growing years of both sexes, on the margin of nerve-force, and thus becomes the channel through which not a few are carried on to neurasthenia, hysteria, epilepsy, or insanity. . . .

Organized philanthropy is wholly modern, and is the offspring of a higher evolved sympathy wedded to a form of poverty that could only arise out of the inequalities of civilization. Philanthropy that is sincere suffers more than those it hopes to save; for while "charity creates much of the misery that it relieves, it does not relieve all the misery that it creates."

REPRESSION OF EMOTION

One cause of the increase of nervous diseases is that the conventionalities of society require the emotions to be repressed, while the activity of our civilization gives an unprecedented freedom and opportunity for the expression of the intellect; the more we feel the more we must restrain our feelings. This expression of emotion and expression of reason, when carried to a high degree, as in the most active nations, tend to exhaustion, the one by excessive toil and friction, the other by restraining and shutting up within the mind those feelings which are best relieved by expression. Laughter and tears are safety-valves; the savage and the child laugh or cry when they feel like it—and it takes but little to make them feel like it; in a high civilization like the present, it is not polite either to laugh or to cry in public; the emotions which would lead us to do either the one or the other, thus turn in on the brain and expend themselves on its substance; the relief which should come from the movements of muscles in laughter and from the escape of tears in crying is denied us; nature will not, however, be robbed; her loss must be paid and the force which might be expended in muscular actions of the face in laughter and on the whole body in various movements reverberates on the brain and dies away in the cerebral cells.

Constant inhibition, restraining normal feelings, keeping back, covering, holding in check atomic forces of the mind and body, is an exhausting process, and to this process all civilization is constantly subjected. . . .

DOMESTIC AND FINANCIAL TROUBLE

Family and financial sorrows, and secret griefs of various kinds, are very commonly indeed the exciting cause of neurasthenia. In very many cases where overwork is the assigned cause—and where it is brought prominently into notice, the true cause, philosophically, is to be found in family broils or disappointments, business failures or mishaps, or some grief that comes very near to one, and, rightly or wrongly, is felt to be very serious.

The savage has no property and cannot fail; he has so little to win of wealth or possessions, that he has no need to be anxious. If his wife does not suit he divorces or murders her; and if all things seem to go wrong he kills himself. . . .

LIBERTY AS A CAUSE OF NERVOUSNESS

A factor in producing American nervousness is, beyond dispute, the liberty allowed, and the stimulus given, to Americans to rise out of the position in which they were born, whatever that may be, and to aspire to the highest possibilities of fortune and glory. In the older countries, the existence of classes and of nobility, and the general contexture and mechanism of society, make necessary so much strenuous effort to rise from poverty and paltriness and obscurity, that the majority do not attempt or even think of doing anything that their fathers did not do: thus trades, employments, and professions become the inheritance of families, save where great ambition is combined with great powers. There is a spirit of routine and spontaneous contentment and repose, which in America is only found among the extremely unambitious. In travelling in Europe one is often amazed to find individuals serving in menial, or at least most undignified positions, whose appearance and conversation show that they are capable of nobler things than they will ever accomplish. In this land, men of that order, their ambition once aroused, are far more likely to ascend in the social scale. Thus it is that in all classes there is a constant friction and unrest—a painful striving to see who shall be highest; and, as those who are at the bottom may soon be at the very top, there is almost as much stress and agony and excitement among some of the lowest orders as among the very highest. . . .

Protestantism, with the subdivision into sects which has sprung from it, is an element in the causation of the nervous diseases of our time.

No Catholic country is very nervous, and partly for this—that in a Catholic nation the burden of religion is carried by the church. In Protestant countries this burden is borne by each individual for himself; hence the doubts, bickerings, and antagonisms between individuals of the same sect and between churches, most noticeable in this land, where millions of excellent people are in constant disagreement about the way to heaven.

The difference between Canadians and Americans is observed as soon as we cross the border, the Catholic church and a limited monarchy acting as antidotes to neurasthenia and allied affections. Protestant England has imitated Catholicism, in a measure, by concentrating the machinery of religion and taking away the burden from the people. It is stated—although it is supposed that this kind of statistics are unreliable—that in Italy insanity has been on the increase during these few years in which there has been civil and religious liberty in that country. . . .

HABIT OF FORETHOUGHT

Much of the exhaustion connected with civilization is the direct product of the forethought and foreworry that makes civilization possible. In coming out of barbarism and advancing in the direction of enlightenment the first need is care for the future.

There is a story of an American who, on going to an Italian bootmaker to have some slight job performed, was met with a refusal to do the work required. On being asked why he refused, he replied that he had enough money to last him that day, and that he did not care to work. "Yes," said the American, "but how about to-morrow?" "Who ever saw to-morrow?" was the Italian's response.

Those who live on the philosophy suggested by that question, can never be very nervous. This forecasting, this forethinking, discounting the future, bearing constantly with us not only the real but imagined or possible sorrows and distresses, and not only of our own lives but those of our families and of our descendants, which is the very essence of civilization as distinguished from barbarism, involves a constant and exhausting expenditure of force. Without this forecasting, this sacrifice of the present to the future, this living for our posterity, there can be no high civilization and no great achievement; but it is, perhaps, the chief element of expense in all the ambitious classes, in all except the more degraded orders of modern society. We are exhorted, and on hygienic grounds very wisely, not to borrow trouble—but were there no discounting of disappointment, there would be no progress. The barbarian borrows no trouble; stationary people, like the Chinese, do so but to a slight degree; they keep both their nerve-force and their possibilities of progress in reserve. Those who have acquired or have inherited wealth, are saved an important percentage of this forecasting and fore-worry; like Christian, they throw off the burden at the golden gate, but unlike Christian, part of it they must retain; for they have still the fear that is ever with them of losing their wealth, and they have still all the ambitions and possible disappointments for themselves and for their children. . . .

RELATION OF HEALTH TO WEALTH AND POVERTY

Accumulated and transmitted wealth is to be in this, as in other countries, one of the safeguards of national health. Health is the offspring of relative wealth. In civilization, abject and oppressed poverty is sickly, or liable to sickness, and on the average is short-lived; febrile and inflammatory disorders, plagues, epidemics, great accidents and catastrophes even, visit first and last and remain longest with those who have no money. The anxiety that is almost always born of poverty; the fear of still greater poverty, of distressing want, of sickness that is sure to come; the positive deprivation of food that is convenient, of clothing that is comfortable, of dwellings that are sightly and healthful; the constant and hopeless association with misery, discomfort, and despair; the lack of education through books, schools, or travel; the absence of all but forced vacations—the result, and one of the worst results, of poverty—added to the corroding force of envy, and the friction of useless struggle,—all these factors that make up or attend upon simple want of money, are in every feature antagonistic to health and longevity. Only when the poor become absolute paupers, and the burden of life is taken from them and put upon the State or public charity, are they in a condition of assured health and long life. For the majority of the poor, and for many of the rich, the one dread is to come upon the town; but as compared with many a home the poorhouse is a sanitarium. . . . Here, in a sanitary point of view, the extremes of wealth and poverty meet; both conditions being similar in this —that they remove the friction which is the main cause of ill-health and short life. . . .

The augmenting wealth of the American people during the last quarter of a century is already making its impress on the national constitution, and in a variety of ways. A fat bank account tends to make a fat man; in all countries, amid all stages of civilization and semi-barbarism, the wealthy classes have been larger and heavier than the poor. Wealth, indeed, if it be abundant and permanent, supplies all the external conditions possible to humanity that are friendly to those qualities of the physique—plumpness, roundness, size—that are rightly believed to indicate well-balanced health: providing in liberal variety agreeable and nourishing food and drink, tasteful and commodious homes, and comfortable clothing; bringing within ready and tempting access, education, and the nameless and powerful diversions for muscle and mind, that only a reasonable degree of enlightenment can obtain or appreciate; inviting and fortifying calmness, steadiness, repose in thought and action; inspiring and maintaining in all the relations of existence, a spirit of self-confidence, independence, and self-esteem, which, from a psychological point of view, are, in the fight for life, qualities of the highest sanitary importance; in a word, minifying, along all the line of the physical functions, the processes of waste and magnifying the processes of repair. . . .

Poverty has, it is true, its good side from a hygienic as well as from other points of view; for, practically, good and evil are but relative terms, the upper and nether sides of the same substance, and constantly tending to change places. The chief advantage of poverty as a sanitary or hygienic force is that, in some exceptional natures, it inspires the wish and supplies the capacity to escape from it, and in the long struggle for liberty we acquire the power and the ambition for something higher and nobler than wealth; the impulse of the rebound sends us farther than we had dreamed; stung by early deprivation to the painful search for gold, we often find treasures that gold cannot buy. But for one whom poverty stimulates and strengthens, there are thousands whom it subjugates and destroys, entailing disease and an early death from generation to generation. . . .

In the centuries to come there will probably be found in America, not only in our large cities, but in every town and village, orders of financial nobility, above the need but not above the capacity or the disposition to work: strong at once in inherited wealth and inherited character; using their vast and easy resources for the upbuilding of manhood, physical and mental; and maintaining a just pride in transmitting these high ideals, and the means for realizing them, to their descendants. Families thus favored can live without physical discomfort, and work without worrying. Their healthy and well-adjusted forces can be concentrated at will, and in the beginning of life, on those objects best adapted to their tastes and talents; thus economizing and utilizing so much that those who are born poor and sickly and ignorant are compelled to waste in oftentimes fruitless struggle. The moral influence of such a class scattered through our society must be, on the whole, with various and obvious exceptions and qualifications, salutary and beneficent. By keeping constantly before the public high ideals of culture, for which wealth affords the means; by elevating the now dishonored qualities of serenity and placidity to the rank of virtues, where they justly belong, and by discriminatingly co-operating with those who are less favored in their toils and conflicts, they cannot help diffusing, by the laws of psychical contagion, a reverence for those same ideals in those who are able but most imperfectly to live according to them. Thus they may help to bring about that state of society where men shall no more boast of being overworked than of any other misfortune, and shall no longer be ashamed to admit that they have both the leisure and the desire for thought; and the throne of honor so long held by the practical man shall be filled, for the first time in the history of this nation, by the man of ideas. The germs of such a class have even now begun to appear, and already their power is clearly perceptible on American society. The essence of barbarism is equality, as the essence of civilization is inequality; but the increasing inequality of civilization may be in a degree corrected by scientific philanthropy.

PART IV

FARMERS IN AN INDUSTRIAL SOCIETY

PART IV

FARMERS IN AN
INDUSTRIAL SOCIETY

It has been the political side of the farmers' movement that has attracted most attention, but, like all complex social movements, it had its economic and social dimensions as well. The legislative demands of the farmer were almost obsessively economic, but they arose not only from consideration of the actual situation of the farmer but from comparison as well. There was, first, comparison with the situation that had once been his, a comparison that could not but yield the conclusion that the farmer was not one of the main beneficiaries of post–Civil War American society. There was, second, comparison with other segments of society, a comparison which served only to confirm the farmer's belief that he had been slighted in the distribution of the good things of life. A cure for the ills of the farmer based solely upon technological considerations was not, even then, too difficult to find, but it seemed incompatible with both historical tradition and humane public policy.

Speaking in St. Louis in 1904, the president of the Rhode Island College of Agricultural and Mechanic Arts, Kenyon Leech Butterfield, discussed the manner in which past history, present reality, and future policy complicated efforts to secure a solution to the farm problem. "Is the farm problem one of technique, plus business skill, plus . . . broad economic considerations?" he asked.

Is it not perfectly possible that agriculture as an industry may remain in a fairly satisfactory condition, and yet the farming class failed to maintain its status in the general social order? Is it not, for instance, quite within the bounds of probability to imagine a good degree of economic strength in the agricultural industry existing side-by-side with either a peasant régime or a landlord-and-tenant system? Yet would we expect from either system the same social fruitage that has been harvested from our American yeomanry? We conclude, then, that the farm problem consists in maintaining upon our farms a class of people who have succeeded in procuring for themselves the highest possible class status, not only in the industrial, but in the political and the social order—a relative status, moreover, that is measured by the demands of American ideals.

Exactly how this status—absolute and relative—was to be achieved, President Butterfield could not say, except, significantly, that it would be attained only through organization, that most sensitive "test of class efficiency."

Many of the dimensions of the farm problem are discussed in the documents below. For journalist E. V. Smalley, it was the impoverished social isolation of rural life that was the evil, and his recommended cure would

329

have required a wholesale reorganization of rural ecology. Ironically, the result he hoped for was soon to be achieved not by social innovation but by a technological invention—the automobile. The first important publication of the famous political scientist A. F. Bentley is a meticulously detailed case study of rural economy in a Nebraska township; it is as noteworthy for its methodology as for its substantive conclusions. Frank Basil Tracy and Populist Senator William Alfred Peffer discuss the political organization of the farmer.

Life on the Prairie Farms

E. V. Smalley

In no civilized country have the cultivators of the soil adapted their home life so badly to the conditions of nature as have the people of our great Northwestern prairies. This is a strong statement, but I am led to the conclusion by ten years of observation in our plains region. The European farmer lives in a village, where considerable social enjoyment is possible. The women gossip at the village well, and visit frequently at one another's houses; the children find playmates close at hand; there is a school, and, if the village be not a very small one, a church. The post wagon, with its uniformed postilion merrily blowing his horn, rattles through the street every day, and makes an event that draws people to the doors and windows. The old men gather of summer evenings to smoke their pipes and talk of the crops; the young men pitch quoits and play ball on the village green. Now and then a detachment of soldiers from some garrison town halts to rest. A peddler makes his rounds. A black-frocked priest tarries to join in the chat of the elder people, and to ask after the health of the children. In a word, something takes place to break the monotony of daily life. The dwellings, if small and meagerly furnished, have thick walls of brick or stone that keep out the summer's heat and the winter's chill.

Now contrast this life of the European peasant, to which there is a joyous side that lightens labor and privation, with the life of a poor settler on a homestead claim in one of the Dakotas or Nebraska. Every homesteader must live upon his claim for five years to perfect his title and get his patent; so that if there were not the universal American custom of isolated farm life to stand in the way, no farm villages would be possible in the first occupancy of a new region in the West without a change in our land laws. If the country were so thickly settled that every quarter-section of land (160 acres) had a family upon it, each family would be half a mile from any neighbor, supposing the houses to stand in

E. V. Smalley, "The Isolation of Life on Prairie Farms," *Atlantic Monthly*, LXXII (1893), 378–382.

the centre of the farms; and in any case the average distance between them could not be less. But many settlers own 320 acres, and a few have a square mile of land, 640 acres. Then there are school sections, belonging to the State, and not occupied at all, and everywhere you find vacant tracts owned by Eastern speculators or by mortgage companies, to which former settlers have abandoned their claims, going to newer regions, and leaving their debts and their land behind. Thus the average space separating the farmsteads is, in fact, always more than half a mile, and many settlers must go a mile or two to reach a neighbor's house. This condition obtains not on the frontiers alone, but in fairly well peopled agricultural districts.

If there be any region in the world where the natural gregarious instincts of mankind should assert itself, that region is our Northwestern prairies, where a short hot summer is followed by a long cold winter, and where there is little in the aspect of nature to furnish food for thought. On every hand the treeless plain stretches away to the horizon line. In summer, it is checkered with grain fields or carpeted with grass and flowers, and it is inspiring in its color and vastness; but one mile of it is almost exactly like another, save where some watercourse nurtures a fringe of willows and cottonwoods. When the snow covers the ground the prospect is bleak and dispiriting. No brooks babble under icy armor. There is no bird life after the wild geese and ducks have passed on their way south. The silence of death rests on the vast landscape, save when it is swept by cruel winds that search out every chink and cranny of the buildings, and drive through each unguarded aperture the dry, powdery snow. In such a region, you would expect the dwellings to be of substantial construction, but they are not. The new settler is too poor to build of brick or stone. He hauls a few loads of lumber from the nearest railway station, and puts up a frail little house of two, three or four rooms that looks as though the prairie winds would blow it away. Were it not for the invention of tarred building-paper, the flimsy walls would not keep out the wind and snow. With this paper the walls are sheathed under the weather-boards. The barn is often a nondescript affair of sod walls and straw roof. Lumber is much too dear to be used for dooryard fences, and there is no inclosure about the house. A barbed-wire fence surrounds the barnyard. Rarely are there any trees, for on the prairies trees grow very slowly, and must be nursed with care to get a start. There is a saying that you must first get the Indian out of the soil before a tree will grow at all; which means that some savage quality must be taken from the ground by cultivation.

In this cramped abode, from the windows of which there is nothing more cheerful in sight than the distant houses of other settlers, just as ugly and lonely, and stacks of straw and unthreshed grain, the farmer's family must live. In the summer there is a school for the children, one, two, or three miles away; but in the winter the distances across the snow-covered plains are too great for them to travel in severe weather; the schoolhouse is closed, and there is nothing for them to do but to house themselves and long for spring. Each family must live mainly to itself, and life, shut up in the little wooden farmhouses, cannot well be very cheerful. A drive to the nearest town is almost the only diversion. There the farmers and their wives gather in the stores and manage to enjoy a little sociability. The big coal stove gives out a grateful warmth, and there is a pleasant odor of dried codfish, groceries, and ready-made clothing. The women look at the display of thick cloths and garments, and wish the crop had been better, so that they could buy some of the things of which they are badly in need. The men smoke corncob pipes and talk politics. It is a cold drive home across the wind-swept prairies, but at least they have had a glimpse of a little broader and more comfortable life than that of the isolated farm.

There are few social events in the life of these prairie farmers to enliven the monotony of the long winter evenings; no singing-schools, spelling-schools, debating clubs, or church gatherings. Neighborly calls are infrequent, because of the long distances which separate the farmhouses, and because, too, of the lack of homogeneity of the people. They have no common past to talk about. They were strangers to one another when they arrived in this new land, and their work and ways have not thrown them much together. Often the strangeness is intensified by the differences of national origin. There are Swedes, Norwegians, Germans, French Canadians, and perhaps even such peculiar people as Finns and Icelanders, among the settlers, and the Americans come from many different States. It is hard to establish any social bond in such a mixed population, yet one and all need social intercourse, as the thing most essential to pleasant living, after food, fuel, shelter, and clothing. An alarming amount of insanity occurs in the new prairie States among farmers and their wives. In proportion to their numbers, the Scandinavian settlers furnish the largest contingent to the asylums. The reason is not far to seek. These people came from cheery little farm villages. Life in the fatherland was hard and toilsome, but it was not lonesome. Think for a moment how great the change must be from the white-walled, red-roofed village of a Norway fiord, with its church and schoolhouse, its fishing-boats on the blue inlet, and its green mountain walls towering aloft to snow fields, to an isolated cabin on a Dakota prairie, and say if it is any wonder that so many Scandinavians lose their mental balance.

There is but one remedy for the dreariness of farm life on the prairies: the isolated farmhouse must be abandoned, and the people must draw together in villages. The peasants of the Russian steppes did this centuries ago, and so did the dwellers on the great Danubian plain. In the older parts of our prairie States, in western Minnesota, eastern Nebraska and

Kansas, and the eastern parts of North and South Dakota, titles to homestead claims are now nearly all perfected by the required five years' occupancy of the land. Thus, there is no longer a necessity that the farmers should live upon the particular tracts which they cultivate. They might go out with their teams to till the fields, and return at evening to village homes. It would be entirely feasible to redivide the land in regions where it is all of nearly uniform fertility and value. Let us suppose that the owners of sixteen quarter-section farms, lying in a body and forming four full sections, should agree to remove their homes to the centre of the tract and run new dividing lines radiating to the outer boundaries. Each settler would still have 160 acres, and no one would live more than a mile from the remotest limit of his farm. The nearest fields could be used for stock, and the distant ones for grain. The homes of the sixteen families would surround a village green, where the schoolhouse would stand. This could be used for church services on Sunday, and for various social purposes on week-day evenings. Such a nucleus of population would, however, soon possess a church in common with other farmers in the neighborhood who might still cling to the old mode of isolated living, and there would probably be a store and a post office. An active social life would soon be developed in such a community. The school would go on winters as well as summers. Friendly attachments would be formed, and mutual helpfulness in farm and household work would soon develop into a habit. There would be nursing in illness and consolation for those mourning for their dead. If the plains people were thus brought together into hamlets, some home industries might be established that would add to family incomes, or at least save outlay. The economic weakness of farming in the North is the enforced idleness of the farmer and his work animals during the long winter. After threshing and fall ploughing are finished there is nothing to do but to feed the stock. Four or five months are unproductive, and all this time the people and the animals are consuming the fruits of the working season. Even the women are not fully occupied in the care of their little houses and the cooking of the simple meals; for the stockings are no longer knit at home, there is no hum of the spinning-wheel, and the clothing is bought ready-made at the stores. If it were possible to restore to the farm some of the minor handicrafts that were carried on in the country thirty or forty years ago, there would be great gain in comfort, intelligence, and contentment. Now and then, while traveling over the Dakota prairies, I hear of a family that sends to market some kind of delicate cheese, or makes sausages of superior quality that find ready sale in the neighboring towns, or preserves small fruits. These little industries might be much extended if the farmers lived in communities, where extra labor could be had when needed, and where there would be mental attrition to wear off the rust of the winter's indolence and stimulate effort on new lines.

The early French colonists who settled along the shores of the Red River of the North in Manitoba, divided the land into long, narrow strips running back from the river banks, and thus formed a continuous village many miles long. In this they followed the example of their ancestors who first occupied the shores of the St. Lawrence. It was adherence to this custom, and resistance to the division of the land into checkerboard squares, that brought on the rebellion of Riel and his half-breeds on the Saskatchewan. The Mennonites, who occupy the western side of the Red River just north of the American boundary, live in villages. With the exception of a few peculiar religious communities in Iowa and Kansas, I know of no other instances where farmers have established their homes in compact settlements. In all our prairie towns, however, one finds in winter many farmers' families who have left their houses and stock to the care of hired men, and are living in rooms over stores, or in parts of dwellings rented for temporary occupancy, in order to give their children opportunity for education and to escape the dreary monotony of isolation. The gregarious instinct thus asserts itself, in spite of habit, and of the inherited American idea that a farmer must live upon the land he tills, and must have no near neighbors. This habit will be hard to break, but I believe it must yield some time to the evident advantages of closer association. I have known instances, however, where efforts at more neighborly ways of living have been made on a small scale, and have failed. In the early settlement of Dakota, it sometimes happened that four families, taking each a quarter-section homestead, built their temporary dwellings on the adjacent corners, so as to be near together; but a few years later, when they were able to put up better buildings, they removed to the opposite sides of their claims, giving as a reason that their chickens got mixed up with their neighbors' fowls. In these instances, I should add, the people were Americans. There is a crusty individuality about the average American farmer, the inheritance of generations of isolated living, that does not take kindly to the familiarities of close association.

I am aware that nothing changes so slowly as the customs of a people. It will take a long time to modify the settled American habit of isolated farmsteads. If it is ever changed, the new system will have to be introduced near the top of the rural social scale, and work down gradually to the masses. A group of farmers of superior intelligence and of rather more than average means must set an example and establish a model farm village; or perhaps this could be done by the owner of one of the so-called bonanza farms, who might subdivide four sections of his land, as I have described, and invite purchasers to build their homes around a central village green; or, still better, he might himself put up the farmhouse and barns, and then offer the farms for sale. The experiment would be widely discussed by the newspapers, and this extensive free advertising could hardly fail to attract as purchasers a class of people with faith

in the idea, and possessed of such a sociable, neighborly disposition as
would open the way to harmonious living and to considerable practical
cooperation in field work and the care of animals. One successful community would soon lead to the formation of others, and the new system
would steadily spread. . . .

The Condition of the Western Farmer

Arthur F. Bentley

The study on which this paper is based was suggested by the desire of the writer to obtain some actual knowledge of the true economic condition of the farmers in the western states. The farmers' movement, culminating in its attempt to change the policy of the government in many important particulars, had for its *raison d'être* the depressed financial condition of the agricultural classes. Against this position, the other political parties urged that the financial depression affected all classes alike, and that in no way did farmers have greater difficulty in attaining prosperity than persons in other lines of activity. Realizing the worthlessness of the isolated examples cited for proof, as well by one side as by the other, the author undertook the present investigation. . . .

ECONOMIC HISTORY OF HARRISON TOWNSHIP

The boundaries of Harrison Township (or Precinct, as it was called before the county adopted township organization) coincide exactly with those of the congressional township known as township eleven, range eleven, west of the sixth principal meridian, and thus it contains very nearly thirty-six square miles. Its southeast corner is, as nearly as may be, the geographical center of Hall county. The main channel of the Platte river lies, at its nearest point, about five miles distant, while the northwestern corner of the township, is some thirteen or fourteen miles distant from the river. The lands are what we have designated in this paper as "second bottom" lands. The surface is very slightly undulating, so slightly indeed that one who was not a close observer might call it an almost perfect level. Through the northwestern quarter of the town runs a small stream, Prairie Creek, and there is one other streamlet which

Arthur F. Bentley, *The Condition of Western Farmer as Illustrated by the Economic History of a Nebraska Township* (Baltimore: Johns Hopkins University Studies in Historical and Political Science, 1893), Eleventh Series, Vols. VII–VIII.

contains running water only at certain times of the year. The fertility of the land is, on the whole, of a very high grade; this matter, however, will receive more careful attention hereafter.

The first settlement in Hall county, on that part of the "second bottom" lands which is drained by Prairie Creek, had been made in the year 1871, but it was not until 1872 that a claim of any sort was taken within the limits of Harrison township. By the end of that year, however, entries of some kind had been made on all of the government land therein. The first entry was in the latter part of March, when two pre-emptions were filed on quarter sections in the southeastern part of the township. In April nine entries were made, most of them homesteads, near the two claims taken in March; two, however, were pre-emptions, placed in the western part of the town by ranchers who hoped, while controlling under their own claims but a few hundred acres, to be able to have the use of many thousands of acres of unclaimed land around them for grazing their cattle. Needless to say, the rapidity of settlement surprised these men so greatly that they gave up their claims in disgust and moved farther away. In May there were six entries; in June, eleven; in July, six; in August, twelve; in September, nineteen; in October, three; and in November, two. This includes, it must be remembered, only the first entry on each tract of ground, the total number of such entries being seventy; and as the government land originally available for entry consisted of sixty-four quarter-sections, the average number of acres taken on each entry was 146.3.

Of these original entries, fourteen were pre-emptions, forty-seven were homesteads, and nine were soldiers' homestead declaratory statements, intended to mature in due time into homesteads proper,—all but four, in fact, doing so. It is proper, then, to say that there were fourteen pre-emptions as against fifty-six homesteads; that is, four-fifths of all entries were homesteads. This shows, at least, the relative estimation in which the two ways of taking land were held. It might at first sight seem that the taking of a homestead indicated that the settler came with the intention of residing permanently, but did not have sufficient means necessary for pre-emption. But such a conclusion must be looked at with caution, for in considering the individual cases we find that here and there a well-to-do "speculator" took a homestead, while on the contrary a pre-emption was occasionally taken by one whose possessions were as nearly nil as they well could be, and whose hopes of paying up on a pre-emption must have been based entirely on some wild notion of fabulous crops in the first years. Of the fourteen pre-emptions mentioned above, only one was paid up, that one being one of the two taken by the ranchmen whom we have spoken of before. Three men relinquished their pre-emptions to take homesteads on the same land, and four relinquished in order to take timber-claims on the same land; the remaining four gave up their holdings in the township altogether and moved away. This relinquishment of pre-emptions occurred almost entirely in the fall of '74, when the time given by law for "proving up" had expired, and the holders found themselves unable to pay the amounts required to complete their title under the pre-emption laws. It must be remembered that this land being within the Union Pacific ten-mile limit, pre-emptors were obliged to pay the government the double minimum price, $2.50 per acre. . . .

The last entry made on government land in the township was in February, 1884. In all 159 entries had been made, of which ninety-seven were homesteads, fourteen soldiers' homestead declaratory statements, twenty-five pre-emptions, and twenty-three timber claims. . . .

Those not familiar with the subject sometimes think of the conditions of colonization under our present land laws as having been of such a character that the empty-handed settler could, through the mediation of the government, soon become the possessor of a well-equipped farm. But a very little reflection shows us that the gift of the soil is by no means all that is needed as the foundation for a farm. To convert the raw prairie into a habitable and income-producing farm is not an easy task, and quite a little capital is needed to do it satisfactorily. Prof. Rodney Welch makes the following estimate of the necessary expenses.

Registering, etc.	$50.00	
Horses and implements	500.00	
Furniture, small stock, etc.	200.00	
House (sod), stables and seed	150.00	
Breaking forty acres sod	100.00	$1000.00

To this must be added the cost of sustenance for self and family during the year, or perhaps two years, which intervened before regular crops could be raised. The country being new, little work could be found by which the income could be helped out. It would be perfectly safe to say that the ordinary immigrant had very much less means than the amount mentioned, and was much hindered in his work by his lack of sufficient capital. Those who came out to their claims with practically no capital were usually forced to leave before much time had passed, though here and there a prosperous farmer is to be found who started out with not even a team with which to plow his land.

There were several things which tended to lighten the burdens of the settlers. One of these which helped them in many cases was their previous service in the army, for a very large proportion of the settlers had taken part in the Civil War. The amount of time spent in the army is deducted from the five years' residence on the land which is otherwise required of the "homesteader" before he can acquire title to his "claim." Besides this advantage, a pension gave to many the wherewithal on which to live until they could raise their first good crops. Much trouble and some expense was saved the settlers of Harrison township by the fact that they were located so near the government land office. The fact, too, that they were within a few miles' distance of lands that had been under cultivation for ten or fifteen years had a very important influence; for the new settlers could, in consequence, find near at hand the grain and other supplies which he needed during his first year's residence until he could raise crops for himself; and as the cost of transportation of such commodities was avoided, the amount which he would have to expend for support in these years was much less than would otherwise have been the case.

Another thing of very great importance, in many cases, was the simultaneous settlement of former neighbors of acquaintances in one locality, for they could render many mutual services which the lone settler was precluded, to a great extent, from receiving. Especially was this true when several brothers or a father and his sons came together and took "claims" side by side; and where the father had well-grown minor sons whose continuous services he could require, his possibility for prosperity was still more enhanced.

There were certain hardships to which the first settlers on the prairies were peculiarly liable, one of the most dreaded being the prairie fires, which, during some seasons of the year, frequently threatened certain destruction of house and home as well as crops. Another thing which caused much suffering and loss in the early times—one that has repeatedly been brought to the writer's notice—was the fact of residence at long distance from a physician. The disadvantage in this was twofold: first, the inability to get medical attendance promptly, and secondly, the great cost of it when obtained; a heavy bill was speedily incurred and bore a discouragingly large proportion to the scanty cash income during the first years of settlement.

But by all means the greatest hindrance during the early years and one that affected all settlers alike, was the grasshopper pest. . . . The *calopteni spreti*, or "mountain locusts," were first seen in small numbers in 1862; again in '64 and '65, and in '66 and '68 they were seen, but did little harm. In '69 in certain sections, as in Hall county, they destroyed the whole crop. The habit of the insects is to soar high in the air in immense swarms, and from time to time to pounce down on a field, often stripping it bare of all vegetation before continuing their flight. The grain most commonly devoured was corn. After '69 the pests were not seen in central Nebraska, till '73, and though in this year many families suffered very severe losses, yet the average crop for the whole state was fair, and prices of grain were not greatly raised. Hall county was fortunate enough to escape them almost entirely at this time. In the last days of July and the first of August, '74, they succeeded in devouring almost all the growing corn, and those settlers on the frontier whose "sod corn" had been their sole crop, and those farther east who had concentrated almost all their labor on that one crop, were sometimes reduced to a condition of absolute want. The years '75 and '76 saw the return of the "hoppers," as the settlers familiarly called them, but in neither year was the destruction so great as before.

It will be well to discuss in this place the standard of living of the early settler and its relation to his possibility of financial progress. It is true the early settler possessed very little property, but on the other hand his needs were few. A sod house gave him shelter and after the first year his farm furnished him most of the food he required. The standard of living was practically the same for all the settlers, so that with the purchase of a little clothing and a few groceries, one could live comfortably, as the times went, on a very small outlay of cash. True, it was a hard life to live, but as a better was well-nigh impossible, and as there was always bright hope of improvement in the future, the settler was content. Rivalry being so largely lacking, the forces which would tend to raise the standard of living were very weak, and all the incentives were for the farmer to invest upon his farm any surplus he might have, instead of consuming it in a less directly productive manner. The great difficulty of getting credit at the time furthered such investment, for capital was sorely needed upon the farms, and practically the only way for the farmer to put it there was by carefully avoiding all expenditures for living that were not absolutely necessary, and so saving the necessary amount, or what part of it he could. This form of investment, in turn, gave a certain degree of prosperity; and it may well be that the man who could maintain his footing under the circumstances which we have described, would not be able to prevent loss at the present day, when the conditions are so different; for a much higher standard of living must to-day be maintained, and it is now comparatively easy to fall into the habit of borrowing until all hope of retrieving one's fortunes is gone. This difference may to some extent account for the fact, which we shall see later, that fewer of the farmers were ruined in the early years by what we may call the prevalent agricultural conditions, than have, in recent years, failed in a similar manner.

The matters that we have mentioned present some of the salient features of the economic conditions that surrounded the first settlers. Bearing these facts in mind, let us now proceed to consider with more or less detail the financial condition of the farmers during the first few years after the settlement of the township was begun; and from that we can pass to a more hasty sketch of the changes from year to year until the present time.

The number who took claims or bought railroad land during 1872, and who followed up the taking of their claims by actual residence, was sixty-one; but probably many of these were only nominally residents until the following year. In 1873 the number of residents increased to seventy-three, thirteen new men coming in and one man leaving. Of the newcomers nine entered government land; three contracted for the purchase of railroad land, and one purchased his land of a non-resident holder of railroad contracts. The assessment rolls for '73 show no one in this township taxed as the owner of land, but twenty-two persons were assessed as the owners of personal property. During this year none but "sod crops" were raised, and, fortunately, the grasshoppers, so bad throughout the state as a whole, did scarcely any damage to the crops in Harrison township, so that the farmers were permitted to gather in whatever grain the newly opened soil could furnish. The one man who left during this year is said to have been a gambler and speculator who had come to the country with some vague idea of making a fortune in the immediate future, but who soon tired of even his nominal residence on a farm and sought more agreeable fields.

Though the grasshoppers did considerable damage in the state as a whole during 1873, as we have seen, yet their ravages were not so great as to cause very high prices for grain in the spring of the following year; nor was immigration to the part of the state which we are considering materially hindered thereby. In fact, in 1874 the number of arrivals in the township was larger than in 1873. Seventeen new settlers came, of whom nine entered upon government land, five on railroad land, and three purchased of older settlers. In this year we find taxes levied for the first time on real property; while thirty-eight persons were taxed on personal property. Owing to the grasshoppers and severe hot winds, the crops this year were very much damaged, the corn being wholly lost, and the small grains yielding less than one-half of an average crop. In consequence many persons were left entirely without means of support except such as they could obtain from the relief associations.

During 1874, five men gave up their holdings in Harrison township. Two of these were speculators; one lost his farm through legal complications consequent on mortgaging his personal property too often; a fourth, having no capital, had made no improvements on the land on which he was nominally resident, and had gained his support by working for neighbors, and, although he left as poor as he well could be, he cannot be said to have failed in farming. The fifth had completed his title to a homestead before selling, having been able to do this by taking advantage of the special privileges in time, etc., that the law gave to former soldiers. He had poor health and lacked in energy; the bad crops quickly discouraged him, so that he lost confidence in the country and its resources. Having an opportunity to do so, he willingly sold his farm and returned to his native state of Michigan to work in the more healthful pineries. Thus far, therefore, we find only one man whose departure can in any sense be said to have been caused, or even accelerated, by unfavorable conditions of soil or climate.

During 1875 prices of grain went higher than ever, owing to the crop failure of the preceding year, corn being sold at over $1 a bushel; and this affected the new settler in that in most cases he was compelled to buy grain for his own use. The bad years seem finally to have had their effect on immigration, for in 1875 no new settlers entered the township, while five either sold out or abandoned their claims and left the country. More than this, if we can place any dependence on the tax lists, there were this year but twenty-two persons in the township owning taxable personal property; although the number of persons to whom real estate was assessed had increased from one to thirteen. . . .

The number of such owners increased rapidly until '74, at which time there were more owners in residence than there are now; . . . it then decreased almost as rapidly, owing to the successive crop failures, until '77. With '78 began a new rise in the number of such inhabitants, which progressed steadily, though with a slight break in '81, until '85, when the number of resident owners reached its highest point. For three years longer the number remained almost stationary, but by '89 it had begun to fall again, until now there are hardly more owners in residence than in '73.

We are able to trace a very close connection between the number of resident owners in the various years and the climatic and crop conditions. The number of such owners increased on the wave of immigration until 1875, but a complete cessation of settlement was caused in that year by the grasshopper pest of the preceding seasons, and, in fact, the same cause was at the basis of the continued decrease in the number of resident owners, which lasted through '77. The crop of 1876, wherever it was not destroyed by grasshoppers, and the crop of '77 throughout the whole state were exceptionally good; and with the good crops came a renewed immigration to the state. Moreover, by 1878 the chances to take government land were pretty thoroughly exhausted, except in those parts of the state in which the sandy soil or the roughness of the land was a drawback, or in which it seemed that without irrigation success in agriculture would be very doubtful. This indicates another reason why the number of settlers in the township should so greatly increase at this time, the immigrants often turning back from the frontier and preferring to purchase railroad lands in tried parts of the state near the means of transportation, rather than to take from the government free land the value of which was very uncertain. We must here remember the fact, indicated in another place, that the settler who took government land really needed almost the same amount of capital in order to bring his "claim" well under cultivation as was required by the purchaser of railroad land on long time. In 1878 the crops throughout the state were very good, but hail caused almost total destruction of grain over at least half of Harrison township; and here we can observe the effect of unfavorable *local* conditions; for the number of newcomers in '79 was not at all affected by the losses of the previous year, being in fact greater than in any other year since 1872; but the number of removals was affected, being in 1879 much greater than the average. The temporary cessation of immigration during 1881 must be laid to the severe drouth of 1880 and the consequent crop failure. During the next five or six years crops were heavy and prices were good, and in connection with this we notice the steady increase in the number of resident owners. The decrease in the number of such owners in the late years must partly be attributed to the removal of prosperous farmers and partly to the removal of those who had met with failure—just in what proportion will better be seen at a later stage of this paper when we have more data before our consideration. . . .

Let us now briefly consider the various causes for selling or surrendering claims. [In the table on page 345] can be seen in the first column the number of owners who left owing to causes which can be classed together as "Prevalent agricultural conditions." All who left the country after unsuccessful attempts at farming, and whose troubles cannot be traced to some definite cause which would have affected them in like manner if occurring in one of the older states, are put in this column. We have already seen that by 1874 there had been only one man to be so classified. In the other columns are put those who left owing, as nearly as can be ascertained, to the causes enumerated. It has been a matter of the greatest difficulty to ascertain with exactness what were the reasons in each case which caused the individuals to leave, and often there is a plurality of causes, preventing easy classification. But each case has been considered carefully and the results are approximately correct.

Column I. [Table]—In regard to those in the first column, it will be noticed first that the great majority of the cases occur in comparatively late years. This is something of a surprise, as one would naturally expect to find the conditions of the early settlement less favorable for permanence of residence than those prevailing later. One thing which may have had its influence on this fact is the low standard of living which prevailed during the early years and which we have discussed above.

The first man here listed leaving in '74 would probably have stayed had his health been better and his energy consequently greater. The next one, in '76, was a hard worker, though with very small capital; after repeated crop failures he became so discouraged that he gave up his land and moved away. The case occurring the following year is almost exactly similar, except that a general tendency toward shiftlessness plays quite a large part in the failure to raise a good crop. Of those leaving in '82, one had really left his claim a few years before under circumstances similar to the second case named above, but did not sell until this year; the other had come in '79 with a small capital of, say $500, and had begun

CAUSES FOR SELLING OR SURRENDERING CLAIMS

	I.—Owing to prevalent agricultural conditions.	II.—Sales by those who had bought in hopes of an advance.	III.—Failure to improve or cultivate the land.	IV.—Involved in other troubles.	V.—Died.	VI.—To move to better farms.	VII.—To move to cheaper farms.	VIII.—To move to towns or villages.	TOTAL
1872									
3		1							1
4	1	2		1					5
5			2	1	2				5
1876	1	4	1	1		1			8
7	1	2	1	1		2			7
8				1	1	1		1	4
9			3			3		4	10
80		1	1	1	1	1			5
1881		1		1		1			3
2	2	1		1			1	1	6
3							1		1
4	1	2		1		2	2	1	9
5				1		2			3
1886		2		1				2	5
7				1			1	3	5
8	2					1			3
9				1	1	1	2	2	7
90	2	1				1			4
1901	3			2	2			2	9
2	1	2		1				2	6
	14	19	9	16	7	16	7	18	106

to open up a piece of railroad land, but finding that he could not meet his payments, he moved back to his old home to resume work at his trade and allowed his contracts to be canceled. The case of '84 was similar to the first one of '82. Of the two who thus lost their farms in '88, one was an original settler on government land, who kept steadily running behind till he was forced to sell his farm to pay his debts: the other had settled on railroad land in '78, and what with poor management and bad crops got into such a financial condition that he was forced to sell and had practically nothing left. The six cases remaining in this column, who left during '90, '91, and '92, were, with one exception, all purchasers from other individuals. No doubt the serious drouth of 1890 had much to do with accelerating their ruin. One of them had too little capital to enable him to pay up for his farm, and so had to give it up; he is now a renter in the same precinct; the second and third were at start moderately well off, but ran through everything and are now renters; the fourth was still better off at the start, but got into debt to everybody and so lost his land; the fifth, after twelve years' residence on and cultivation of an eighty-acre farm, found himself considerably behind-hand and sold out to move farther west, where free government land was to be had; the sixth and last started with a comparatively large capital, say $4000, and in six years had gotten rid of it all.

We note, then, that the settlers leaving in this general condition of improvement in the early years did so mainly because their continual loss of crops had thoroughly discouraged them with the prospects of the country, if, indeed, it had not made their further attempts at farming absolutely impossible; that there then follow several who had to give up because of unwise attempts to bring under cultivation railroad or other land with too small capital; and that lastly we have a class of men, mainly later purchasers, who fail and lose their farms owing to economic conditions, the cause of which is not apparent on the surface.

Column II.—This column includes all speculators. . . . We see that about half of the men whose prime purpose in farm residence was speculative, and who have since sold, had sold within the first five years. Of those who entered government land with this object in early years, most sold their land quickly; two or three have only recently sold, while a few still own. The remainder of those listed as selling in recent years belong to the class of comparatively late purchasers, as previously described.

Column III.—Those who did little or nothing on their land. These men came with the intention of farming, but owing to lack of capital, or attracted by opportunities to make good wages at other trades or occupations, they left after short residences. It is seen that all such cases occurred in the early years of settlement.

Column IV.—Those who left owing to complications other than those arising from their attempts at farming. Among such troubles may be mentioned becoming entangled in civil lawsuits; becoming surety for and having to pay the debts of another; speculating in cattle; committing crimes or misdemeanors, etc. Such cases occurred with great regularity, and it is evident were not dependent, to any extent, upon the characteristics of the special year or period.

Column V.—Here are included all those who died while resident owners of land within the township.

Column VI.—Those who, after a more or less successful career in Harrison, moved to better farms, or farms that suited them better. Most of these went to other parts of the country or to other counties in Nebraska where they could get larger tracts of land, or could be near relatives or friends; often the wife's desire to be near relatives was the cause of moving. A few moved back to their old homes further east, mainly Ohio or Iowa.

Column VII.—Those who moved to cheaper farms. Part of them left because they recognized that their original capital was insufficient to initiate and carry on the farming of the land which they had; part of them because of failing fortunes which they hoped to retrieve by a fresh start somewhere else. Some of these went further west and took homestead from the government.

Column VIII.—Those who have removed to towns or villages. Under this head are included the few whose capital was such that they could live comfortably on the income to be derived from its judicious investment; also those who have entered upon business as small merchants or saloon-keepers; or who have preferred the opportunities offered them by residence in towns to pursue trades with which they were conversant, where they could at the same time find pleasant social life and better education for their children. In all cases they are men who can be ranked as having been fairly successful farmers. As would be expected, they are almost all found toward the close of the period we are now considering.

What we learn from the facts in these latter columns simply confirms our former ideas of the condition prevailing in the various years. We need only add to the summary given above the remark that farming in this township seems to have been at its best in the middle part of the period that has elapsed since colonization began. After the drawbacks attending the first settlement were past, the prosperity of the settlers was at its highest point, and in the later years, while the older settlers have in the main increased their wealth, but at a much slower rate than before, yet those who have come in as purchasers from the older settlers have, almost without exception, fallen behind rather than gained in their net wealth.

LAND VALUES

When Harrison township was first settled, land in limited quantities could be purchased from the government by actual settlers for $2.50 an acre. At the same time the Union Pacific Railroad was asking $4 an acre for its lands. As the government land was all so quickly taken, and as sales were made by the railroad company at its own price we can consider the actual value of the lands from 1872 to 1874 to have been about $4 an acre. During the two or three years following 1874 there was absolutely no sale for farming land, but after immigration began again in 1878, the railroad price may be considered as indicative of the actual marketable value of the lands. In '78 and '79, $5 and $6 per acre were the current prices. From 1880 to 1884 land of the average quality brought from $6 to $8 per acre. These were the prices, of course, for unimproved land sold on long time and easy terms. A settler who wished to sell for cash would get very much less, unless the improvements represented a substantial sum. With the exception of two or three years prior to 1891 or '92, land has, since 1880, steadily increased in value, though usually it has been of rather slow sale, because owners have habitually asked prices for it above what purchasers were willing to pay. At the present time, land with average improvements will sell with comparative readiness for about $25 an acre, though owners often claim that they would refuse any offer of less than $30 to $35 an acre.

RENTING OF FARMING LANDS

Until quite recently the usual rent of farming land has been one-third of the produce, and there has always been plenty of land to be obtained upon such terms. But within the last two or three years the demand for farms has very greatly increased, and there has been a corresponding increase in the rent. Owners are beginning to ask for their farms either two-fifths of the produce, or a cash rent of from $1.50 to $2.25 for each acre of plow-land. In 1892 about four-fifths of the rented land was rented on shares, and the remainder for cash. In the same year, of the farms rented, about two-thirds were rented to tenants who resided on the lands; while the remaining one-third was rented to neighbors.

CREDIT

There are in general four ways in which the farmers have made use of the capital of others. These are, first, by obtaining credit with the retail dealers with whom they trade; second, by borrowing with real estate security; third, by borrowing with chattel security (and this includes most of the debt on agricultural implements, for the part of the price of such implements which is not paid in cash is usually secured by mortgage on the machinery itself); and fourth, by borrowing with unsecured promissory notes or with personal security. The first method is relatively unimportant, as the total amount of credit so obtained has necessarily been quite small. Let us then pass to the consideration of the three other forms.

When the township was settled, money could only be borrowed on chattel security, and was very difficult to obtain even at the high rates then offered and demanded; for capitalists were few, and the condition of the borrower was such as to warrant only the smallest line of credit. Moreover, the insecurity of the loan made the interest required very high. But in time real estate became of importance as security. The agent of the first company that loaned money upon real estate in this part of Nebraska appeared about 1875, and twelve per cent was the rate of interest demanded, with a bonus of from ten per cent to twenty-five per cent for commission. The rates have gradually lowered; in 1880 they were eight per cent interest and two per cent commission; then seven and two; later, seven and one; and now the current rate is six and one, while a certain large life insurance company will make all good loans of over $2000 that are desired at six per cent without commission. But for a long time the chattel mortgage held its own and was the form of security regularly in use for borrowing money; even the most well-to-do did not hesitate to allow such mortgages to appear on record against them. This has changed to a certain extent, however, and real estate or personal security is coming to be given in preference by the more prosperous farmers. Chattel mortgages are still frequently given by cattle-feeders as security for their extra purchases of stock for winter feeding, but even in this line of business they are less common than formerly. The amount of money now borrowed on personal security, or simply on individual note, is not large, for only the more prosperous can so borrow, and they are just those who want to and who do borrow the least. I was allowed to examine the books of a bank that does perhaps the greater part of the business of this township, and found only an insignificant amount of this last variety of paper.

Those few settlers who were able to borrow of a father or of other relatives in the eastern states had a very great advantage, especially in the first years of residence, as in trying times they could count on aid without having to pay the exorbitant interest charged by local lenders. Many were the occasions for borrowing in the early days; but most of the debt was incurred either to provide sustenance during a year of lost crops, or to make improvements, or to settle an unpaid balance of purchase money.

It will be necessary later to discuss in detail the use of credit in its relation to agricultural prosperity; but two general incentives to mortgaging may be here mentioned, the influence of which has been felt throughout a great part of the history of the township, but especially during the earlier days. The first incentive grew out of the appreciation in the price of land, the farmer being led into realizing this in advance by means of mortgaging; as fast as he could increase his loan he would do so, and use the sum obtained sometimes to make good deficiencies and losses, or for current expenditure, and sometimes for investment, whether legitimate or speculative, upon his farm. The second incentive lay in the fact of the relatively large returns of crop in proportion to the cost of the land. In the early days the farmer's profits were very high in proportion to the amount of capital employed, whenever his crops were at all good; and this often led him to purchase and cultivate more land than he was able to manage; then if bad crops, which he had not counted on, came, he would become hopelessly involved in debt. It is true the farmer may often have suffered from excessive interest and grasping creditors; but it was less frequently the avarice of the lender that got him into trouble than the fact that he was too sanguine and too prone to believe that he could safely go in debt, on the assumption that crops and prices in the future would equal those in the present. . . .

MARKETS, PRICES, AND FREIGHT RATES

During the years 1872 and '73 all the agricultural produce of Hall county could be readily sold to the new settlers, at prices so high as to make shipments to outside markets unprofitable. During the three following years it was necessary to bring grain into the country rather than ship it out, on account of the successive crop failures caused by grasshoppers and drouth; but with '77 a period of fairly good crops began, and during most of the time from then until '84 the markets in the western part of Nebraska, and in the Black Hills and other near regions in which settlement was just beginning gave better prices for corn and oats than could be realized by shipping them to eastern grain centers. Between '85 and '87 the activity in railroad building in states to the west gave rise to good markets for corn, and quite high prices prevailed. From 1877 to 1883, Chicago was by far the best market for wheat, but since 1883 the local mills have competed with it and absorbed a good share of the crop. Since 1887 it has been necessary to ship most of the grain to eastern markets, or sometimes to the South, and this is especially the case when crops are heavy. While therefore during a great part of the period we are considering the prices obtained for grain have been somewhat better than could be obtained by shipments to the eastern markets, yet since 1877 the price of wheat has been to a great extent affected by the net price to be obtained by shipping to Chicago and since 1887 the Chicago prices have had a by no means inconsiderable effect on the selling price of all grains. It is unfortunately impossible to obtain records showing the prices which grains have brought in the local markets, but [the table on page 351] gives the average prices for corn and wheat and oats in Chicago for each year since 1872.

In attempting to estimate, on the basis of the table of prices [on page 351], the profits which the farmer has been able to make on his grain, we should next have to take into account the cost of raising the grain and the cost of transporting it to market; and though we shall be unable to discuss this matter in detail here, a few facts bearing on the subject may not be out of place.

The cost of raising corn in Nebraska has been investigated by the Nebraska Bureau of Labor and Industrial Statistics, and in its report for 1891-92 the estimates of some six or seven hundred farmers are given, which make the average cost of the production of corn per acre to be $6.40, and therefore, figuring forty bushels of corn to the acre, the cost per bushel would be 16 cents. The method of this estimate is, however, faulty, in that the cost of husking and cribbing is estimated by the acre and not by the bushel, as it should be, and thus the size of the crop is entangled from the start with the cost per acre. Leaving out these items of husking and cribbing, the average cost per acre shown by the report is $4.90. From this latter figure, the cost per bushel should be estimated

AVERAGE CHICAGO PRICES OF CORN, WHEAT, AND OATS

	Corn "No. 2" cts. per bushel.	Wheat "No. 2" Spring cts. per bushel.	Oats "No. 2" cts. per bushel.
1872	34.3	111.5	26.1
3	32.3	102.9	25.6
4	59.3	97.6	41.7
5	54.8	88.9	41.
1876	40.	92.6	28.3
7	42.7	121.5	29.5
8	36.9	95.2	22.3
9	35.6	99.6	26.8
80	37.7	105.7	29.8
1881	50.	114.8	37.8
2	67.5	116.6	43.6
3	53.8	101.7	34.5
4	51.6	83.	29.1
5	43.	83.9	29.
1886	37.	76.6	27.6
7	39.5	75.6	26.
8	46.8	90.	28.6
9	34.	85.5	22.2
90	39.3	89.2	30.9
1	58.4	96.6	39.1

according to the size of the crop, and then an addition made to cover cost of husking and cribbing. Moreover, the figures given in the report do not include cost of hauling to market, which is for the farmers of Harrison township from one to two cents a bushel. The cost to the farmers we are considering of corn delivered by them at the marketplace cannot be estimated under from eighteen to twenty cents per bushel for a fairly good year, that is when the crop averages from thirty-five to forty bushels to the acre.

The report of the Bureau indicates that the cost of raising corn in the eastern counties is greater than in the western counties of the state. The reasons suggested for this are that the item of interest on the investment in the land in the newer counties is less than in the older ones, as is also the amount of cultivating which it is found necessary to give the land. Analogy with this conclusion would suggest that the cost of raising corn in Harrison was less in earlier days than now, and therefore, though the freight rates were much higher then than at present, yet the price which the farmer had to realize for his corn in order to make a profit from it was less than now.

As to freight rates on grain, [the table on page 352] will show all the changes since 1880-83 in the rates between Grand Island and Omaha, and between Grand Island and Chicago. A comparison made between the figures in the table itself will show how large the local rates have been as compared with through rates.* A comparison** of the rates here given with the Chicago prices of grain as seen in the table [on page 351] will show how much of the value of the product is absorbed in finding a market for it. If further deduction is made from the Chicago price for the commissions of two middlemen, we will begin to appreciate the position and feelings of the farmers who said that when he bought his

FREIGHT RATES
(in cts. per cwt.)

Grand Island to Omaha (150 miles).				Grand Island to Chicago (650 miles).			
Date effective	Corn	Wheat	Oats	Date effective	Corn	Wheat	Oats
Jan. 1, 1883	18	19½	18	Jan. 7, 1880	32	45	32
Apr. 16, '83	15	16½	15	Sept. 15, '82	38	43	38
Jan. 10, '84	18	19½	18	Apr. 5, '87	34	39	34
Mch. 1, '84	17	19½	18	Nov. 1, '87	25	30	25
Aug. 25, '84	20	20	20	Mch. 21, '90	22½	30	25
Apr. 5, '87	10	16	10	Oct. 22, '90	22	26	22
Nov. 1, '87	10	12	10	Jan. 15, '91	23	28	25
Mch. 7, '88	9½	11¾	9½				
Dec. 15, '88	10	12	10				

farm he thought he was really going to own the land, but that he soon discovered that he only held it on an uncertain tenure from the railroad companies. It will be noticed that the proportion of the market price will be paid for freight is much higher for corn and oats than for wheat, and in the former grains often runs over one-third of the total price. . . .

REAL ESTATE MORTGAGES

The bulk of the debt owed by farmers is secured by mortgages upon their farms, given in the main to resident agents of the large eastern loaning companies, and it is due to the size of this debt, and the debtor's consequent liability of losing his homestead if poor management or bad luck prevent him from meeting his payments as they fall due, that much of the recent wide-spread discontent has arisen.

[The table on page 353] shows the number and per cent of the farms mortgaged, and also the number and per cent of acres mortgaged. It then gives the face value of the mortgages as they stand in the office of the county clerk; but in order to allow for partial payments which have undoubtedly to some extent been made, and which it was not possible to investigate directly, a deduction of 5.21 per cent is made, since

* It must, however, be remembered that the through rates are not strictly to be found by adding the local Nebraska rates to the Omaha-Chicago rates, there being usually some deduction for through traffic.
** In making comparisons with the preceding table, figure wheat at 60 lbs. per bushel, oats at 32 lbs., and corn (shelled) at 56 lbs.

it has been shown by the census of 1890 that that per cent is the average proportion of partial payments on real estate mortgages for the State of Nebraska. With the total amount of debt thus calculated, we find the average indebtedness on each acre mortgaged to be $8.78, and the average debt per farm to be $1517.32. Now it would not be safe to estimate the average value of these farms, even when well improved, above, say, $25 an acre, so we can see what a large proportion on the average the debt on the mortgaged farms bears to their total value, being in fact considerably over one-third. With interest to pay on such a sum, and with the final payment to provide for, it is no wonder that the years of partial failure, always liable to occur in agriculture, become doubly discouraging to any but the most energetic farmer. . . .

REAL ESTATE MORTGAGES

Total number of farms mortgaged,	91.
Per cent. of farms mortgaged,	67.41
Total number of acres mortgaged,	15,720.
Per cent. of acres mortgaged,	65.39
Face value of mortgages on record,	$145,665.42
Less 5.21 per cent. for partial payments,	7,589.17
Estimated true value of debt,	138,076.25
Av. debt against each mortgaged acre,	8.78
" " " " mortgagor,	1,517.32
" " " " acre in township,	5.74
" " " " owner in township,	1,022.79

Our next [table deals] with the debt of residents still more largely from a personal point of view. [It distributes] it into divisions according as the borrower was a taker of government land, a purchaser of land from the railroad company, or a purchaser from some other former owner; purchasers of school land are included, for the sake of simplicity, under this last division. [The table] shows the number of owners both with mortgaged and with unmortgaged lands in each of these three classes, and gives the number of acres each class possesses, and the totals of its debts. It also gives the average size of farms, the average debt per man and the average debt per acre for each of these classes. Class "A," composed of those who took their original lands from the government, is divided into two sub-classes according as the farmers have borrowed money on their original homesteads, or still have them free from debt; and those who have their original homes still unencumbered are divided further into those who owe no money whatever upon land, and those who owe money only upon additional lands recently purchased. . . .

These figures are very striking from almost every point of view. First, we observe that half of all the settlers on government land have their lands entirely free from mortgage, while only four have mortgages upon their original homes; in the case of those who have mortgages upon their

REAL ESTATE MORTGAGES OWED BY RESIDENTS, WITH REFERENCE TO THE
MODE OF ACQUISITION OF THE LANDS

A. Settled on Government Land.	Number.	Acres.	Amount of debt.	Average size of farm, acres.	Average debt per man.	Average debt per acre.
a. Original home unmortgaged:						
1. No mortgage on any land,	9	1,680		186.66		
2. Additional lands only mortgaged,	5	1,280	$ 3,950.00	256.00	$ 790.00	$3.09
b. Original home mortgaged,	4	640	3,300.00	160.00	825.00	5.16
B. Settled on Railroad Land.						
a. Lands unmortgaged,	3	720		240.00		
b. Lands mortgaged,	16	3,000	23,400.00	187.50	1,462.50	7.80
C. Purchasers of Land from Individuals.						
a. Lands unmortgaged,	4	440		110.00		
b. Lands mortgaged,	33	5,200	48,769.61	157.57	1,477.87	9.38
	74	12,960	$79,419.61	175.14	$1,073.21	$6.13

additional lands, the average debt per acre is very low, being only $3.09.
Of those who have their original homes mortgaged, two came in among
last of those who took government land; two have very small mortgages;
moreover, the average debt per acre on the property of these is itself
quite low, being $5.16. Then again we notice that the size of the farms
among these settlers averages larger than among either of the other
classes; the homes of those, especially, who have additional lands which
they have mortgaged are much larger than those of any of the others.
Not one of these settlers on government land who has a mortgage to take
care of can be said to be at all seriously embarrassed by it, and some of
them are, despite their mortgages, as well off as any men in the township.

Take up next the settlers on railroad land and what a difference! There
are only three of them without mortgages, as against sixteen holding
mortgaged farms, and the average debt per acre on those lands which
are mortgaged is $7.80, or half again as much as the average debt borne
by those settlers on government land who have their original homes
mortgaged. Following the analogy of class "A," we would expect to find
the mortgaged farms larger than those which are clear, and we shall find
this to be the case in class "C"; but in class "B," the unmortgaged farms
are considerably larger on the average than the mortgaged; this points

to something exceptional in these particular cases, and investigating the cases in detail we find this indication borne out in fact. Of the three purchasers of railroad land who have their lands unmortgaged, two are brothers who had been farmers in Germany, and who, coming to America with considerable property, were able not only to buy and pay for comparatively large farms, but to put considerable money in bank—certainly a very exceptional state of affairs with the ordinary settler on a Nebraska farm. The third case is that of a man who bought railroad land at an early date and farmed it for a number of years, but on the death of his wife drifted away into other employments. Having made the final payments on his land, and having inherited more land in the immediate neighborhood he has now come back with a new wife, once more to try his luck at farming.

When we come to purchasers, we find only four unmortgaged farms, as against thirty-three mortgaged ones. The average size of the farms is very much smaller, being only one hundred and ten acres for the unmortgaged and about one hundred and fifty-seven acres for the mortgaged. The average debt per acre is higher than in either of the other classes; in fact, so much higher that, despite the comparative smallness of the farms, the average debt per farm is higher than elsewhere.

It has already been remarked that none of the settlers on government land are in poor circumstances, while among their ranks the great majority of the most prosperous farmers are to be found. Of the settlers on railroad land, nearly all would be included if they were as a class described as quite heavily mortgaged, but with debts not so great as to make it seem probable that any of them will be unable to extricate themselves with time. The only case here to be ranked among those whose future prospects are doubtful is that of a man whose agricultural experience has been very limited, and as he seems to have almost no capital, and labors under still other disadvantages, it is doubtful how long he will be able to hold out. But now, when we turn from the purchasers of land from the railroad company to class "C," the purchasers from other owners, we find as marked a change in conditions as we noticed in passing from class "A" to class "B." The mortgages are heavier, the well-to-do are comparatively rare, and there are many persons in very poor circumstances. In fact, there are quite a number with whom it seems to be only a question of time, and a short time at that, when they will have to give up their holdings. One is almost tempted to draw the moral that the would-be purchaser, at least the one whose means are not sufficient to pay entirely for his farm and then tide him over all subsequent periods of hard times, had almost better throw his money away than invest it in farming operations in Nebraska, at the current prices of land and under the present agricultural conditions; unless, indeed, he be possessed of unusual energy and ability. . . .

CONCLUSION

We have had before us a class of farmers owning lands of steadily increasing value. Of those who are still residents, about half got their lands either as gifts from the government, or on very easy terms from the Union Pacific Railway Company; the remainder purchased their farms from other owners than the railway company, at prices ranging from seven or eight dollars an acre in earlier times to twenty-five or thirty dollars in late years; in most cases these paid a good part of the purchase money in cash. The farmers of this township have on the average a little over a quarter section of land each, and usually from 125 to 135 acres in a quarter section is plow-land. A large proportion of the farms are mortgaged, and the debts on such as are mortgaged is on the average something over one-third the actual value of the farms. When a tract of land is once encumbered, the tendency is often for the mortgage on it to increase in size as the rise in the value of the security makes a larger loan possible. The mortgages on lands obtained from the government or the railway company are in general lighter than those on lands purchased from individual owners, and the condition of the farmers owning such lands is correspondingly more prosperous. This we find natural to a certain extent, inasmuch as purchasers are very rarely able to pay in full at the time of purchase, and so usually start out encumbered by a mortgage debt; but the frequent increase in the size of mortgages thus incurred, and the corresponding unprosperous condition of those who are to pay them, is indicative of the fact that in very many instances the real burden of a mortgage has been much greater than one would infer from the mere knowledge of its amount. . . .

From our account of the farmers' condition, it is clear that the central fact is the rise in the value of land. For it is this rise that has given the opportunity for the continued increase of mortgage debt; and even a temporary cessation in it has been followed by an increased number of failures among the farmers. We may also infer that in many cases the greater part of the wealth that the farmer of average ability now has must be attributed to this rise in value; for very often the value of the improvements and personal property is covered by the mortgage debt, and this means that the amount of profits which have been realized and invested upon the farm has been very small. Indeed, in many cases the present farmer's equity in his land would be little or nothing were it not for this rise in value, while he would have been unable without it to obtain the means to reach even as advanced a system of cultivation as is in vogue at present. It must be admitted, however, that this conclusion will hold good only for the farmer of average ability. A man of poor personal habits, or one who is shiftless in his management, will dissipate the increment in value of his land as fast as he can make use of it as security for new loans. On the other hand, a skilful, energetic, economical farmer, who knows how to avail himself of every advantage, will probably be able, with average good luck, to pay off in time even a heavy debt incurred in the purchase of his farm. But even with these qualifications, should fortune not favor him he may fail miserably; for he is dependent on credit, and credit, though it furnishes wings to the man fit to use them, so long as the wind of fortune is fair, becomes a dead weight to drag down the less able, or even the competent when fortune fails. If there were space to consider the individual cases of the farmers in Harrison township, we should find a few men whose ability has been such as to enable them thus to overcome the hindrance of heavy debt at the start and become in the end prosperous farmers.

Probably the only other persons besides these exceptionally able ones who have succeeded in making considerable profits and saving any part of them are those farmers who received their land in early times from the government. These, having a clear start, were enabled in most cases to avoid the burden of heavy debt, and consequently, in a year of good crops, they could at once invest their profits permanently on their farms.

It may well seem that these statements in regard to the frequent unprofitableness of farming operations are not in harmony with such facts as that the market price of land is at present increasing rapidly, and that there is now a more eager demand for good agricultural land than has obtained for a number of years; and again that land is now being eagerly sought by renters who are willing to pay a larger proportion of the produce for rent than ever before, and who will in some cases even pay a quite high cash rent. It might be said that in order to occasion such a demand for lands to purchase and to rent, farming must be very profitable, or at least that the chances of high profits in it must be very good, and this would not agree with our preceding inferences. Attention should, however, be directed to one or two influences of importance which, apart from the profitableness of the investment, might create a high demand for land.

In the first place, although the available free government land has been practically exhausted, yet the tradition of cheap farms easily obtainable still lingers in the minds of the people, and so the home-seeker still turns his thoughts toward the West, where prices of land are really low in comparison with those current further east. But the conditions make it necessary for him to resort to new methods of acquiring the desired land. If he has some little capital he will probably try to purchase as large a farm as possible with what means he has at his disposal for the first cash payment; then, giving a mortgage for the balance of the purchase money, he will trust to Providence for the ability to meet the debt when it comes due. If the newcomer has not money enough to purchase land in any way, he will seek for a farm to rent with the hope that he may before long become an owner himself. In these facts we see a prominent reason why the demand for land may have increased without regard to the income produced by it, until its selling price, and as well its rental, have become much higher than the income really warrants. The possibility of such influences having their effect upon the demand for land is made greater by one of the characteristics of investment in farming operations, which may be specially mentioned; this is the slowness with which the true rate of agricultural profits can be estimated, owing to the great variations from year to year in the size of the crops and in the prices at which farm products will sell. . . .

But again, a cause for the increased demand for farming lands may be sought in the deeper relations underlying all industrial society. Farming may be an uncertain means of getting a living, and yet it, or the ideas of it current in the eastern states, may seem to many a laborer so much better than his existing lot, or may actually be such an improvement upon it, that he is only too glad to seek to better himself by means of it; and thus he helps to swell the already over-crowded ranks of agriculturalists, and so raises the price of their primary necessity—the land.

Though the special peculiarities in the character of the income derived from farming operations should by no means be left out of account in considering the status of the farmers, yet a brief mention of these peculiarities must suffice here. In the first place, the irregularity in the amount of the income from year to year has very important effects. Though even the tenant farmer may almost always feel confident that a sufficient supply of food is assured him, no matter how poor the crop, still every farmer is liable to have his year's profits totally wiped out, or even to suffer quite a heavy loss if the season should be very bad; for the margin between the normal net income and the sum of the living expenses and the interest on the investment is often very narrow. Thus while a well-to-do farmer may be able to recuperate in succeeding years from a heavy loss of crops, yet such a blow may be too great for one who is poorer or deeply indebted, and may effect his ruin before he has time to attempt to repair his losses. The effects of bad management in wiping out this margin of profit are very similar to those of bad seasons, and when poor management and poor crops are found in conjunction, there is little hope for the farmer.

It should be remarked, however, that while the crop failure of 1890 ruined many farmers who were already heavily encumbered with debt, still in some cases indirect results of a very different kind can be traced. For many of those farmers whose affairs were in moderately good condition and who had sufficient energy to cause them at once to set to work to recover their lost ground, have really profited by their experience. They have become much more conservative, and are less inclined to enter upon speculative transactions, especially where they would have to make use of credit. Consequently they will soon be in better position to resist heavy losses, should such again befall them.

Next, in regard to direct taxes, it has been seen that these are by no means so high as seriously to affect the farmer's prosperity, being probably in no case above four or five mills on the dollar of true valuation.

Freight rates have played a more important role, especially since of late years it has become necessary to ship large amounts of surplus products to distant markets; and they often absorb a large part of the gross price for which the product sells. Whether the responsibility for this deduction from the farmer's receipts lies with railroad companies which charge excessive rates, or with the conditions which make necessary the shipment of grain for such great distances, must be decided from other evidence than that which we have gathered.

The influence of the use, and more especially of the abuse, of credit will require a more extended treatment, for it is by no means a simple matter and needs to be looked at from several points of view. In the first place, the mere borrowing of money cannot be said to be in itself a harmful thing. Credit has a tendency to multiply as well the opportunities for gain of the man who makes use of it, as to make greater his dangers of loss; but it is only rarely that it can be called the direct cause of either gain or loss. Merely to say that the farmer pays too high interest for his money is in no way an explanation of his financial difficulties; for the rate of interest is adjusted by a competition acting with comparative freedom, and we must go back of it to consider the earning power of the material things in which the borrowed money is invested.

The economic significance of a mortgage debt depends partly on the previous financial conditions of the debtor, perhaps to a still greater extent on what is the corresponding item on the opposite side of his balance-sheet. As to this latter, we must consider whether there stands back of the debt an asset, the liquidation of a loss in the past, or a present personal expenditure. If the money is borrowed for either of the last two purposes, then the debt will be a dead weight, to be provided for from other sources. If the item offsetting it in the account is an asset, then one must consider further whether it has the actual present value of the debt; for in so far as it has not, the debt will be a drag, just as in the cases above. If the asset does actually have a value equal to the debt, then we must examine first whether it is likely to appreciate or depreciate, and second whether it is income-producing or not. If income-producing, then such income must be investigated as to its amount, as to the regularity with which it accrues, and the probability of its permanence.

Applying these principles, we shall be able to see why a mortgage bearing seven per cent interest, that represents in part a payment for high-priced land, in part a new house, and in part losses or expenses in excess of income, may perhaps be more burdensome to the farmer of to-day than a small loan at three per cent a month given by an early settler who had practically no means to obtain funds to begin cultivation or even to make the first payment on cheap land. For the early settler could reasonably expect to make and save both principal and interest out of a single crop, while the variable income of the farmer to-day may often fall so low as to fail to yield sufficient surplus to pay the interest on that part of the debt which is represented by income-producing assets, much less on the remainder of it.

In the region which we are considering, capitalization of all agricultural property is too high (it has been previously maintained that the basis of capitalization is not so much income as a demand arising from other causes), and from this two results follow: first, that the rate of income from land is low compared to that from other investments, and second, that the marginal amount of money that can be borrowed on the land is high in just the proportion that the capitalization is high. Now under these circumstances let a farmer pay the rate of interest which is current in the money markets, and if the debt is large or long-continued, the tendency is for him steadily to lose. It must of course be remembered that agriculture is a highly uncertain occupation, so that a succession of good crops may entirely overcome this normal loss, or a succession of poor ones may greatly increase it.

What we have thus far said of the use of credit has been of such general application as to apply to all borrowers alike, but it will not be necessary to show how borrowing becomes a much greater evil to certain classes of farmers than to others. It is a fact often commented upon that the small *entrepreneur* who is out of debt takes pride in his condition and usually avoids investments or speculations which would make the use of credit necessary to him, while one who has become heavily encumbered becomes callous to the inconveniences caused by his indebtedness, and often does not hesitate to plunge deeper if possible; moreover, the latter will become reckless in his speculations, because if he is successful the gain is his, and if he loses, much of the loss falls on his creditors. Now, as has before been pointed out, an exceptionally energetic man can sometimes attain prosperity even though he starts out with heavy debt incurred for purchase money, and if he meets with good fortune he can gradually free himself from his burden. But under the prevailing conditions, the man of just ordinary ability, who is owing a heavy debt, will be more likely than not to allow it to grow continually larger; and not only will the effect of the debt be seen in making more grievous the ill effects of losses or misfortunes, but when a man's credit is exhausted or badly strained he will often be unable to avail himself of opportunities which he would otherwise have had to make profits, as for instance when he is forced to sell his grain at a low price when, had he been able to wait on the markets, he could have realized a much larger sum.

Perhaps the effect of his debt on a heavily mortgaged man may be summed up by saying that in order to use the money profitably, the borrower must be a man of normal ability; if his qualities are exceptionally good he may profit greatly by his loan; but if they are under the average, or if fortune should go against him, his debt will almost surely operate to increase his troubles. Any man who undertakes farming in Nebraska at the present day requires, in order to be assured of success, at least three things,—first, that he have some little capital, second, that he possess good business qualifications, and third, that he escape any extraordinary misfortunes. If he lack any one of these, or is seriously deficient in it, his success will be much retarded, if not rendered entirely impossible. And though the same statement would probably be true of almost any business enterprise, yet it seems clear from the facts that it applies with especial emphasis to the western agriculturalists of the present time.

Thus far what has been said in discussing the various economic influences at work has been said mainly from the point of view of the unsuccessful farmers. The term unsuccessful must not only be taken to include those who have failed completely owing to causes of a general nature or of nature not clearly personal (for these latter causes have been excluded from our consideration), but it also includes the many who are still struggling for success, though badly embarrassed by debt. In brief, it comprises all those who have to a greater or less extent fallen short of the measure of success which their efforts seemed to deserve. Nor should it be forgotten that to the men classed as successful the same conditions have applied as to the unsuccessful, though not with equal results; for the successful ones are those whose energy or business ability or external advantages have been so great as to enable them to overcome in some degree, at least, all the unfavorable influences.

And now let us see what this measure of success is which the more successful in the township have attained. The largest landowner among them has 480 acres of land, while only four or five, all told, own over 240 acres apiece. Of those who have more than one quarter section of land, the great majority have had some exceptional advantage, such as a capital greater than the average, when they first came to the country, or external help of some kind, as land or money received by inheritance, or they have been men of exceptional thrift. In no case can the improvements be called more than comfortable, and it is rare to find an exceptionally good house without noticing that the outbuildings have to some extent been sacrificed to it, or *vice versa*. In few cases will the income from his farm support the owner after he has retired from active life. To the writer it seems that the condition of the successful farmers more strongly indicates the disadvantages under which they have labored than the condition of the more or less unsuccessful ones. For here we see good business men who have carefully labored for many years, and who come now toward the close of their active careers, feeling fortunate if their farms are unencumbered and their property sufficient to support them in their old age, while they live with their descendants who have taken their places in the active operations of agriculture. It is true these men have had little inherited wealth behind them, but they are among the men who have helped to build up a new country, and who, it would seem, should have as much share in the prosperity of the new territory they have helped to open, as those who cast their lot with the towns and cities. . . .

As compared with the pioneer farmer of twenty years ago, the farmer of to-day requires a much larger capital, and in consequence the cost of production of the grain that he raises is higher. Not only is it found necessary to give the land slightly more cultivating, but also there must be figured into the cost the interest on the investment in the land, which was very small in the early days, but is of considerable importance now. Then the standard of living, by which each family gauges its expenditures, is much higher than formerly, and the enforced economies of the pioneer period cannot be practiced, and indeed ought not to be demanded or expected. The markets are no better to-day than before. In short, if the farmer of to-day expects to achieve the same success as the pioneer achieved, he must, except where good fortune and the possession of unusual personal qualities are combined, have capital in sufficient amount to offset the free land and the low cost of living of the pioneer period.

The Need for a Farmers' Organization

W. A. Peffer

The American farmer of to-day is altogether a different sort of a man from his ancestor of fifty or a hundred years ago. A great many men and women now living remember when farmers were largely manufacturers; that is to say, they made a great many implements for their own use. Every farmer had an assortment of tools with which he made wooden implements, as forks and rakes, handles for his hoes and plows, spokes for his wagon, and various other implements made wholly out of wood. Then the farmer produced flax and hemp and wool and cotton. These fibers were prepared upon the farm; they were spun into yarn, woven into cloth, made into garments, and worn at home. Every farm had upon it a little shop for wood and iron work, and in the dwelling were cards and looms; carpets were woven, bed-clothing of different sorts was prepared; upon every farm geese were kept, their feathers used for supplying the home demand with beds and pillows, the surplus being disposed of at the nearest market town. During the winter season wheat and flour and corn meal were carried in large wagons drawn by teams of six to eight horses a hundred or two hundred miles to market, and traded for farm supplies for the next year—groceries and dry goods. Besides this, mechanics were scattered among the farmers. The farm wagon was in process of building a year or two; the material was found near the shop; the character of the timber to be used was stated in the contract; it had to be procured in a certain season and kept in the drying process a length of time specified, so that when the material was brought together in proper form and the wagon made, both parties to the contract knew where every stick of it came from, and how long it had been in seasoning. During winter time the neighborhood carpenter prepared sashes and blinds and doors and molding and cornices for the next season's building. When the

W. A. Peffer, *The Farmer's Side* (New York: Appleton & Co., 1891), pp. 56–60, 148–161.

frosts of autumn came the shoemaker repaired to the dwellings of the farmers, and there, in a corner set apart to him, he made up shoes for the family during the winter. All these things were done among the farmers, and a large part of the expense was paid with products of the farm. When winter approached the butchering season was at hand; meat for family use during the next year was prepared and preserved in the smoke house. The orchards supplied fruit for cider, for apple butter, and for preserves of different kinds, amply sufficient to supply the wants of the family during the year, with some to spare. Wheat was threshed, a little at a time, just enough to supply the needs of the family for ready money, and not enough to make it necessary to waste one stalk to straw. Everything was saved and put to use.

One of the results of that sort of economy was that comparatively a very small amount of money was required to conduct the business of farming. A hundred dollars average probably was as much as the largest farmers of that day needed in the way of cash to meet the demands of their farm work, paying for hired help, repair of tools, and all other incidental expenses, because so much was paid for in produce.

Coming from that time to the present, we find that everything nearly has been changed. All over the West particularly the farmer thrashes his wheat all at one time, he disposes of it all at one time, and in a great many instances the straw is wasted. He sells his hogs, and buys bacon and pork; he sells his cattle, and buys fresh beef and canned beef or corned beef, as the case may be; he sells his fruit, and buys it back in cans. If he raises flax at all, instead of putting it into yarn and making gowns for his children, as he did fifty years or more ago, he thrashes his flax, sells the seed, and burns the straw. Not more than one farmer in fifty now keeps sheep at all; he relies upon the large sheep farmer for the wool, which is put into cloth or clothing ready for his use. Instead of having clothing made up on the farm in his own house or by a neighbor woman or country tailor a mile away, he either purchases his clothing ready made at the nearest town, or he buys the cloth and has a city tailor make it up for him. Instead of making implements which he uses about the farm—forks, rakes, etc., he goes to town to purchase even a handle for his axe or his mallet; he purchases twine and rope and all sorts of needed material made of fibers; he buys his cloth and his clothing; he buys his canned fruit and preserved fruit; he buys hams and shoulders and mess pork and mess beef; indeed, he buys nearly everything now that he produced at one time himself, and these things all cost money.

Besides all this, and what seems stranger than anything else, whereas in the earlier time the American home was a free home, unincumbered, not one case in a thousand where a home was mortgaged to secure the payment of borrowed money, and whereas but a small amount of money was then needed for actual use in conducting the business of farming, there was always enough of it among the farmers to supply the demand, now, when at least ten times as much is needed, there is little or none to be obtained, nearly half the farms are mortgaged for as much as they are worth, and interest rates are exorbitant.

As to the cause of such wonderful changes in the condition of farmers, nothing more need be said in this place than that the railroad builder, the banker, the money changer, and the manufacturer undermined the farmer. The matter will be further discussed as we proceed. The manufacturer came with his woolen mill, his carding mill, his broom factory, his rope factory, his wooden-ware factory, his cotton factory, his pork-packing establishment, his canning factory and fruit-preserving houses; the little shop on the farm has given place to the large shop in town; the wagon-maker's shop in the neighborhood has given way to the large establishment in the city where men by the thousand work and where a hundred or two hundred wagons are made in a week; the shoemaker's shop has given way to large establishments in the cities where most of the work is done by machines; the old smoke house has given way to the packing house, and the fruit cellars have been displaced by preserving factories. The farmer now is compelled to go to town for nearly everything that he wants; even a hand rake to clean up the door-yard must be purchased at the city store. And what is worse than all, if he needs a little more money than he has about him, he is compelled to go to town to borrow it; but he does not find the money there; in place of it he finds an agent who will "negotiate" a loan for him. The money is in the East, a thousand or three thousand or five thousand miles away. He pays the agent his commission, pays all the expenses of looking through the records and furnishing abstracts, pays for every postage stamp used in the transaction, and finally receives a draft for the amount of money required, minus these expenses. In this way the farmers of the country to-day are maintaining an army of middlemen, loan agents, bankers, and others, who are absolutely worthless for all good purposes in the community, whose services ought to be, and very easily could be, dispensed with, but who, by reason of the changed condition of things, have placed themselves between the farmer and the money owner, and in this way absorb a livelihood out of the substance of the people.

The great thing, the essential matter, that overshadowing all others, and before which everything else pales, is the money power. That must be dealt with and disposed of at all hazards; not that there is to be any destructive method; not that there is to be any anarchistic philosophy about it; not that there is any disposition on the part of farmers or any considerable portion of the working masses to take away from any man his property, or to distribute the existing wealth of the country among the people; not that there is any disposition to repudiate debts, to get rid of honest obligations, to rashly change existing forms or customs, or to indulge in any sort of disloyalty; but simply that the influence of money as a power in society must be neutralized in some way, and there is only one way to do it; that is, to remove from money its interest-bearing function to the extent, at least, of bringing the value of money as a profit-bearing investment to the same level with land and labor and other agencies of production. That is to say, there must be an equalizing as nearly as possible of the profits on money and on profits of other investments. To illustrate: If, as it is generally assumed, upon reasonable ground, the annual net profit on labor and labor's productions generally is about 3 per cent; if that is true—and it is not disputed anywhere—interest on money ought not to be any higher than that. The use of money ought not to be any more profitable than the use of land or the use of machinery, or the use of a railroad, or of any other sort of productive force. This phase of the subject will be treated more fully further along.

The first step necessary in reaching this great consummation of equality in profits is for the persons interested in the movement to organize themselves into a political force. This can not be done at once nor primarily. It must come through the formation of local bodies organized in the first instance for purposes of mutual improvement and benefits socially. This brings men and women into closer social relations with one another in communities. It is one of the best educating agencies ever adopted in any stage of social advancement. The church is organized for religious purposes exclusively; that trains the mind in the direction of religious thought; its methods all appeal to the religious sentiment. But there is not time enough in religious meetings for the people to become well acquainted socially, and there are not enough of auxiliary methods to assist the people materially in developing their social natures; there must be some other arrangement by which this can be done, and the primary object in this kind of association must be social, purely social, having connected with it enough of the religious habit to leaven the whole work with the highest and best motives. Indeed, it is found now that in many of these local bodies, where the proceedings are opened and closed with prayer, that the highest form of devotional feeling is manifested throughout all of the exercises, even though they be largely devoted to what is supposed to be purely social enjoyment. It does really appear that in thousands of this class of meetings the atmosphere is so much tinged with religious feeling that the meetings take the place of religious worship in the churches. It further appears that these meetings to a large extent, and in many instances wholly, take the place of churches in the religious enjoyment of the people. Fashion and the influence of dress have become so much a power that a great many persons of refined natures and of good education find themselves uncomfortable among people in fashionable churches for the reason that they are not able, as they believe, to adorn their persons in costly apparel fitly corresponding with that of their associates; hence they prefer to remain away. But here in these neighborhood assemblies among the farmers, out where the pure air of heaven sweeps over the fields, they meet together upon a plane of perfect equality. They are all neighbors and friends of one grade socially, and they have grown large enough to understand that they need no longer quarrel over differences in matters of religious belief; so they come together in the Grange, in the Alliance meetings, in the Farmers' Mutual Benefit Association, in the assemblies of Knights of Labor, in the anti-monopoly leagues, and in many other bodies where people of the same plane in social life meet and develop their best local advantages.

THE GRANGE

Here, then, is the beginning of the great work that the farmers and their fellow-workers have to accomplish. Fortunately, this has been already largely begun. The Patrons of Husbandry, commonly known as the Grange, began their organization about twenty-four years ago in the city of Washington. The Grange grew rapidly about nine years, then quite as rapidly for a time receded from view; but in the mean time it had accomplished a noble work, much wider in its scope and grander in its proportions than people generally have ever been willing to admit. From the Grange came what is known as the "Granger" railroad legislation, the establishment in our laws of the principle that transportation belongs to the people, that it is a matter for the people themselves to manage in their own way, and that the Congress of the United States, under authority vested in that body by the Constitution, is authorized and empowered to regulate commerce among the several States as well as with foreign nations. That principle, once advocated and urged by the Grange, finally became permanently ingrafted in our laws. Then came the Interstate Commerce Commission; that was another outcome of the Grange movement. Opposition to conspiracies of wealth against the rights of farmers—of labor in general, but of farmers in particular—was among the first and best works of the Grange. The footprints of that first and best organization of farmers ever effected up to that time—are seen plainly in much of the legislation of this country during the last twenty years. Grange influence revived in recent years, and is again growing. It is now one of the most earnest, active, and efficient agencies in the agitation of measures in the interest of agriculture. It lacks but one element of strength, and that will come in due time—namely, the uniting with other bodies of organized farmers in one great political movement to enforce themselves what they have long been trying ineffectually to enforce through their separate party organizations—the dethronement of the money power.

Aside from the political influence of the Grange, it has been a powerful factor in the social development of farmers. Go into a Grange neighborhood any place where the members have maintained their organization during all the troublesome, trying years that followed their first organization, and you find a neighborhood of thrifty, intelligent, well-advanced farmers, their wives and daughters enjoying all of the comforts and conveniences which have been brought into use through the multiplication of inventions for the saving of labor and the production of wealth. Their meetings have been schools in which the best sort of education comes, and now the Grange as a body is one of the most fruitful social institutions in the country. As far as its members see their way clear to a union with their fellow-farmers generally for political purposes they will have accomplished a grand mission, and they will finally come to that.

THE FARMERS' ALLIANCE

The Farmers' Alliance is a body in many respects quite similar to that of the Grange. In both bodies women are equal with men in all of the privileges of the association. They are fast training women in channels of political thought. Many of the best essays and addresses read and delivered in their meetings are prepared by women, and it is beginning to dawn upon the minds of men long incrusted by custom and usage that the women who were chosen in early life as partners and companions— women who first became wives and then mothers and guardians of the best families upon earth, women who have nurtured children and trained them up to useful manhood and womanhood, looked after their interests when the days of childhood were numbered, and never forgot them "even until death"—these same women who of all persons have a fonder attachment, a warmer affection, and a deeper love for their children, in the midst of mature life as well as in childhood, are quite as capable of looking after the interests of men and women when they are grown as while they are prattling infants about the play-grounds of the old homestead. These social bodies of farmers, where men and women are at last made equal in public affairs, even though to a limited degree, are fast, very fast, educating the rural mind to the belief that women are as necessary in public affairs as they are in private affairs. Their influence is constantly growing stronger as the years come and go, and, strange as it may seem to some persons, they are losing none of their womanhood, but are constantly adding graces to lives already beautiful and useful.

The Farmers' Alliance was organized primarily—just as the Grange had been—for social purposes; but yet immediately in connection with its inception was an effort to defeat the absorption of State lands of Texas by speculators. One great object of the association was to save the public lands for the people. It has always been a leading idea among farmers that the public lands ought to be saved for homes for the people. They foresaw what the end would be in case speculators, whether individual or corporate, were allowed to monopolize the land. In time settlers would be required to pay exorbitant prices for what they are entitled to at cost.

The homestead law embodies the true theory of Government disposition of the public lands. They belong to the people, in the right of the people. Whatever they cost in money, if anything, was paid by the money of the people through a system of taxation which was supposed to be just, bearing equally, as far as possible, upon all classes and conditions of the people. It was, as the farmers believed, a stupendous wrong inflicted upon the people of the country generally when lands were given away in immense quantities to corporations. All of that was so much money thrown into the coffers of rich men and wealthy corporations, and taken away from the poor; and now that our public lands are so much curtailed as that there is hardly room enough in fertile areas left to locate a single homestead, a great question comes up of taxing the people to inaugurate a general system of irrigation to reclaim arid lands, and to supply the demand for homes by increasing the productiveness of the public lands which are yet left for the use of the people; and this idea of "land for the landless and homes for the homeless"—once so noisy a party war cry—will again be made part of the platform of a national party which will rise into view within the next year or two.

The Farmers' Alliance is in two bodies now. One was begun in Texas about the year 1875; it is known as the "Southern Alliance." It has absorbed the "Farmers' Union" of Louisiana, the "Agricultural Wheel" of Arkansas, and some other local organizations of farmers in different parts of the Southern States, with Kansas, Missouri, and Kentucky. It has a very large membership in Iowa, Ohio, and New York, and is spreading into all the other States. Thirty-five States now have organized alliances. While the body is strongest in Southern States, if its growth in the Northern and Western States continues to be as rapid the next year or two as it has been in the last two years, it will soon have a large membership in every State in the Union. Its principles, socially and politically, are almost exactly the same as those taught by the Grange—namely, good fellowship and obliteration of sectional prejudices, a nationalizing of the people, a spirit of friendly feeling among the masses, abandonment of old issues, with the discussion of new problems of the present and the future, all based upon the fundamental idea which angels sang to shepherds when the Babe of Bethlehem was born—"peace on earth, good will toward men." The "Southern Alliance," as it is commonly called by outsiders, is the "Farmers' Alliance and Industrial Union"; it is builded upon principles broad and deep as humanity.

NATIONAL FARMERS' ALLIANCE

Then there is another body, known as the "National Farmers' Alliance." It originated about the year 1877 in Illinois. It differs from the Southern Alliance practically only in this, that the Southern Alliance has a "secret work"; it transacts all of its business with closed doors; the members know one another outside as well as inside by means of "grips" and "pass-words," just as Masons and Odd Fellows do. This is true likewise of the Grange. The National Farmers' Alliance, commonly known as the "North-ern Alliance," transacts its business openly, the same as any ordinary public assembly. The objects and aims of both bodies are practically the same—opposition to all private monopolies and the better dispensing of justice among the people. One of the tenets of all these organizations is "equal rights to all, special privileges to none."

FARMERS' MUTUAL BENEFIT ASSOCIATION

There is another rapidly growing body of farmers. It took form in the southern part of Illinois about four years ago. It is known as the Farmers' Mutual Benefit Association, with objects the same as the other bodies before named. It, too, has a secret work, but it differs from the Alliance and the Grange in that it does not admit women to membership; that will doubtless come later, for it seems that no considerable body of men in the discussion of matters which are largely social to begin with can very well get along without the help of women, who have been so serviceable to them in their home life. There is a considerable number of other local bodies of farmers, as the "Farmers' League," the "Farmers' Union," the "Farmers' Protective Association," "Anti-Monopoly League," etc. These are mostly in Ohio and States to the eastward. The difference between the Alliance and other bodies of farmers named is about this: The Alli-ance is more aggressive along political lines than any of the others, and the Alliance has taken more advanced grounds in favor of independent political action. Alliance men and women in very large numbers have come to the conclusion that they have exhausted all of their means for effecting, through the agency of the old political parties, the needed changes in our legislation and customs.

THE KANSAS MOVEMENT

The lesson learned by the movement of Alliance men in Kansas in 1890 has been one of very great profit to the brethren in other parts of the country. It was discovered in Kansas that the party machinery was so completely in the hands of a few men as to make the party's policy sim-ply what was dictated by the little circle of leaders, and it was evident that they were completely wedded to the power which has been absorb-ing the substance of the toilers. Kansas is an agricultural State, one of the most beautiful regions under heaven, with soil rich as any that the sun shines upon, with a climate salubrious, with an atmosphere balmy, with bright skies bending over a landscape delightful in its magnificent proportions, peopled by a rugged yeomanry, industrious, enterprising, sober, intelligent, a body of men and women unsurpassed anywhere in disposition to move forward and upward, men and women who in less than the period of a generation have builded an empire, have produced 50,000,000 bushels of wheat and 250,000,000 bushels of corn in one year, have opened 200,000 farms, have builded 9,000 miles of railroad and 8,000 school-houses; and the farmers of that State came to the conclusion that they were entitled to at least a fair share in the benefits of legislation. They found, however, that it was practically impossible to control the course of political parties, for the reason that the machinery was in the hands of men living in the towns, and connected in one way or another, to a greater or less degree, with railroads and with corporations engaged in the business of lending money for people in the East, deeply immersed in real-estate transactions, and in one way or another interested in matters that were directly and continually and powerfully in opposition to the interests of the farmers. Looking the situation over carefully and deliberately they came to the conclusion that the best way out of their troubles was through an independent political movement; so the Alliance submitted that proposition to their fellow-workers inside and outside of the Alliance, to members of the Grange and of the Farmers' Mutual Benefit Association, to the Knights of Labor, to the Federation of Labor, and to other workers in different departments. The result was the formation of a political party known locally as the People's party, and when the votes were counted after election day it appeared that the party was made up about as follows: Republicans, 45,000 voters; Democrats, 35,000 voters; Union-Labor men, 33,000 voters; Prohibitionists, 2,000 voters; making a total vote of 115,000. The political complexion of the State was changed in six months to the extent of 100,000 votes. At the election in 1888 the Republican majority over all opposition was about 42,000 votes; at the election in 1890 that party fell short of a majority sixty-odd thousand votes. The People's party in Kansas elected one State officer—Attorney-General—five out of the seven members of Congress, 95 of the 125 members of the Lower House of the Legislature (the Senators elected in 1888 holding over to 1892), and secured the election of a United States Senator on the 28th day of January following. . . .

THE CINCINNATI CONFERENCE

The result in Kansas encouraged farmers in other States, and soon a movement was set on foot looking to the organization of an independent political movement covering the whole country. The first step in that direction was the National Union Conference, held at Cincinnati May 19, 1891, composed of nearly 1,500 delegates representing thirty-two States and two Territories.* . . .

* That Cincinnati conference adopted the following declaratory and doctrinal resolutions:
  1. That in view of the great social, industrial, and economical revolution now dawning on the civilized world and the new and living issues confronting the American people, we believe that the time has arrived for a crystallization of the political reform

A national central committee was appointed and arrangements made for a general union of all the industrial forces of the country in a convention in 1892 for the purpose of completing organization and putting a national ticket in the field.

---

forces of our country and the formation of what should be known as the People's Party of the United States of America.

2. That we most heartily indorse the demands of the platforms as adopted at St. Louis, Mo., in 1889, Ocala, Fla., in 1890, and Omaha, Neb., in 1891, by industrial organizations there represented, summarized as follows:

a. The right to make and issue money is a sovereign power to be maintained by the people for the common benefit. Hence we demand the abolition of national banks as banks of issue, and as a substitute for national-bank notes we demand that legal-tender treasury notes be issued in sufficient volume to transact the business of the country on a cash basis without damage or especial advantage to any class or calling, such notes to be legal tender in payment of all debts, public and private, and such notes, when demanded by the people, shall be loaned to them at no more than 2 per cent per annum upon non-perishable products, as indicated in the sub-treasury plan, and also upon real estate, with proper limitation upon the quantity of land and amount of money.

b. We demand the free and unlimited coinage of silver.

c. We demand the passage of laws prohibiting alien ownership of land, and that Congress take prompt action to devise some plan to obtain all lands now owned by alien and foreign syndicates, and that all land held by railroads and other corporations in excess of such as is actually used and needed by them be reclaimed by the Government, and held for actual settlers only.

d. Believing the doctrine of equal rights to all and special privileges to none, we demand that taxation—national, State, or municipal—shall not be used to build up one interest or class at the expense of another.

e. We demand that all revenue—national, State, or county—shall be limited to the necessary expenses of the Government, economically and honestly administered.

f. We demand a just and equitable system of graduated tax on income.

g. We demand the most rigid, honest, and just national control and supervision of the means of public communication and transportation, and if this control and supervision does not remove the abuses now existing we demand the Government ownership of such means of communication and transportation.

h. We demand the election of President, Vice-President, and United States Senators by a direct vote of the people.

The Rise and Doom of the Populist Party

Frank Basil Tracy

The last quarter-century of our national life has been distinct and unique in the absorbed attention which our people have given to the study and discussion of economics. To the gigantic and revolutionary effects of the Civil War, which no man was able even faintly to foresee and which we cannot now adequately comprehend, are we indebted for this condition of the public mind. That Titanic struggle not only obliterated the subjects of political controversy and popular gossip for fifty years, but it overturned all social, political, industrial and economic conditions, bringing to life new conditions, new problems, new policies. The peculiar fruit of that sentimental war has been the removal of sentimental questions from party consideration and the substitution of economic problems, of which the common people of the *ante-bellum* time knew almost nothing. Thus it is that discussions of finance, governmental functions and systems of revenue, which would have cleared the benches of any town-hall previously to 1860, are now heard with attention, intelligence and enthusiasm. Contributory influences have been the false enactments and artificial policies instituted by legislation. It was inevitable, in the nature of things, that a nation's thought, directed so strongly and suddenly along new channels and toward subjects which require for their comprehension the most minute and profound study and trained intelligence, should be often misguided and led into fanaticism, economic blunders and financial fallacies. As the combined result of all these causes we have to-day the so-called People's Party.

That party, in the first year of its national existence, made a record unparalleled in our history, well calculated to cause apprehension among the greater parties. It cast more than a million votes, or nearly as many votes as elected Abraham Lincoln; gave its Presidential candidate twenty-

Frank Basil Tracy, "Rise and Doom of the Populist Party," *The Forum*, XVI (1893–1894), 240–250.

two electoral votes; carried four States and placed eight members in the House; and it has now five members in the Senate. The first definite, immediate steps toward the party's formation were taken about eight years ago, when Farmers' Alliances were organized in all the States of the West. These Alliances were at first purely local and industrial. The members held meetings to discuss crop conditions and the best methods in agriculture and horticulture. The three or four years following were disastrous to the farmers. Their crops failed, they were in want, and had little money, and their produce brought low prices. Distress and discontent came and clamors for assistance arose. Their minds, crammed with unformed socialistic ideas, were inflamed by Alliance orators and by the circulation of books of the Donnelly-Bellamy type. These Alliances determined, independently of one another, that monopolies were grasping the earth, that gigantic conspiracies were forming to enslave them, and that the moneyed classes were united against the masses. The fact that these conclusions were reached simultaneously and independently all over the West does not prove, as the Populists insist, that they are correct; but it does prove that the leaven administered by paternal legislation, after the close of the Civil War, was working throughout all the great social organism of the West. Yet these great uprisings and apprehensions indicated also real and serious grievances and burdens of injustice which bore heavily upon Western farmers. The three main grievances related to transportation, land and money.

The history of the methods of Western railway corporations is a story of rapacity, fraud, extortion, and gigantic plunder. Every reader is doubtless aware of the terms on which the Pacific railways were built. Fifty million dollars were loaned outright by the Government to the constructors of the Union Pacific, and a grant was made to them of land equal in value and extent to an empire. All the valuable land is now sold; but not one cent of that great loan has ever been paid. The mortgage is almost due; yet there is now a scheme before Congress, said to have President Cleveland's sanction, to renew the loan for eighty years and reduce the interest to two per cent. After the road was built, its owners, under the manipulations of the Crédit Mobilier organization, watered the stock to an enormous extent, and out of that deal they secured enormous private fortunes. The road itself tottered near the brink of bankruptcy and was saved only by the protecting arm of the Government, which has sustained it and its owners in their frauds. As no dividends could be paid by reasonable charges on stock so enormously watered, the Union Pacific, aided by the other Pacific railways and by other lines which came later into the field, put in force all over the West rates for freight-carriage, extortionate and unjust beyond any description.

Nothing has done more to injure the region than these freight-rates. The railroads have retarded its growth as much as they first hastened it.

The rates are often four times as large as Eastern rates. For example, let a New York dealer consider a freight-bill of sixty dollars for a car of crockery shipped one hundred and twenty-five miles. That is the Nebraska rate. The extortionate character of the freight-rates has been recognized by all parties, and all have pledged themselves to lower them, but no State west of the Missouri has been able to do so. In the early days, people were so anxious to secure railways that they would grant any sort of concession which the companies asked. There are counties in Iowa and other Western States struggling under heavy loads of bond-taxes, levied twenty-five years ago, to aid railways of which not one foot has been built. Perhaps a little grading would be done, and then the project would be abandoned, the bonds transferred and the county called upon by the "innocent purchaser" to pay the debt incurred by blind credulity. I have known men to sacrifice fortunes, brains and lives in fighting vainly this iniquitous bond-swindle. Railways have often acquired mines and other properties by placing such high freight-rates upon their products that the owner was compelled to sell at the railroad company's own terms. These freight-rates have been especially burdensome to the farmers, who are far from their selling and buying markets, thus robbing them in both directions.

Another fact which has incited the farmer against corporations is the bold and unblushing participation of the railways in politics. At every political convention, their emissaries are present with blandishments and passes and other practical arguments to secure the nomination of their friends. The sessions of these legislatures are disgusting scenes of bribery and debauchery. There is not an attorney of prominence in Western towns who does not carry a pass or has not had the opportunity to do so. The passes, of course, compass the end sought. By these means, the railroads have secured an iron grip upon legislatures and officers, while no redress has been given to the farmer.

The land question, also, is a source of righteous complaint. Much of the land of the West, instead of being held for actual settlers, has been bought up by speculators and Eastern syndicates in large tracts. They have done nothing to improve the land and have simply waited for the inevitable settler who bought cheaply a small "patch" and proceeded to cultivate it. When he had prospered so that he needed more land, he found that his own labor had increased tremendously the value of the adjacent land. The faithfulness of many of the pictures drawn by Mr. Hamlin Garland, in "Under the Lion's Paw," is affirmed, although the remedy proposed, the single tax, would bring worse conditions. Closely connected with the land abuse are the money grievances. As his pecuniary condition grew more serious, the farmer could not make payments on his land. Or he found that, with the ruling prices, he could not sell his produce at a profit. In either case he needed money, to make the payment or maintain himself until prices should rise. When he went to the money-lenders, these men, often dishonest usurers, told him that money was very scarce, that the rate of interest was rapidly rising, *etc.*, so that in the end the farmer paid as much interest a month as the money-lender was paying a year for the same money. In this transaction, the farmer obtained his first glimpse of the idea of "the contraction of the currency at the hands of Eastern money sharks." Disaster always follows the exaction of such exorbitant rates of interest, and want or eviction quickly came. Consequently, when demagogues went among the farmers to utter their calamitous cries, the scales seemed to drop from the farmer's eyes, and he saw gold-bugs, Shylocks, conspiracies and criminal legislation *ad infinitum*. Like a lightning-flash, the idea of political action ran through the Alliances. A few farmers' victories in county compaigns the previous year became a promise of broader conquest, and with one bound the Farmers' Alliance went into politics all over the West.

That campaign of 1890 was the most thrilling ever known in the West. The country school-houses were packed with excited throngs. County, district and State conventions were attended by great crowds of eager, earnest and indignant farmers. The excitement and enthusiasm were contagious, and the Alliance men deserted their former parties by thousands. Putting a gill of fact and grievance into a gallon of falsehood and lurid declamation, these oratorical Alliance quacks doled out an intoxicating mixture. In vain the reports of the meetings were suppressed by the partisan press. In vain the Republican and Democratic leaders sneered at and ridiculed this new gospel, while they talked tariff and War issues to small audiences. The leading Stalwart Republican organ of Nebraska pleasantly referred to the new party members as "hogs." All the ridicule, abuse and evasion aided wonderfully the Alliance cause. Its members shouted that they were being persecuted in their "battle of human rights," and converts came more rapidly. Thus was produced that clamoring brood of Peffers, Simpsons, Kems and McKeighans and the hundred other political rain-makers who proclaimed their virtue on the Western prairies in 1890. Concerned in, but not a part of, the political revolution of that year, the new party presented a strange aspect. The members of the various State Alliances kept up communication during the quiet year of 1891, and gradually, by the steps of the Cincinnati, St. Louis and Omaha conventions, the national party was organized.

For what does this party really and exactly stand? There is much ignorance on this subject, which must be clearly understood in order to determine its strength and forecast its future. The doctrinal basis of Populism is socialism. Without that basis, the castles of Populism could never have been reared so high and so strong. The beliefs of this party are not new. They have often been controverted by argument and by practical tests. But they are especially strong because of their basis, laid by a generation of paternal acts since the War. The three reforms to which this party is pledged relate to the same matters which constituted the real grievances of the farmers: land, transportation and money. The party demands Government ownership of all land not held by actual settlers, Government ownership of all transportation facilities, and Government issue of all money by its fiat alone. The platform declaration on the subject of land is vague, and is a remarkable modification of the communistic ideas first preached by the leaders. With this plank few would quarrel, although the proposed reclamation of lands granted to the railways would be absurd, as nearly all the valuable land has been sold. The Government ownership of railways and other means of transportation is another of their tenets which is undergoing modification. It is still, however, a favorite hobby with thousands and is clearly a scheme of pure socialism. They do not seem to realize that the placing of the seven hundred thousand men now engaged with American railways alone in the hands of any political party, would make that party's dislodgment from power almost impossible and would ultimately lead to a despotism. Nor do they propose a way to secure the ten billion dollars necessary to acquire these railways, except possibly by peculiar and characteristic financial schemes. Indeed, it is marvellous how these men, no matter how ignorant and unlearned, will furnish readily and confidently solutions for all problems of finance—the most intricate, delicate and least understood of all Government concerns.

The chief underlying principle of all Populist financial schemes is fiat money. Free silver, a sub-treasury, *etc.*, are purely incidental. It is the cardinal faith of Populism, without which no man can be saved, that money can be created by the Government, in any desired quantity, out of any substance, with no basis but itself; and that such money will be good and legal tender, the Government stamp, only, being required. Free silver will bring some relief, but nothing permanent so long as "contraction of the currency" is possible. We must increase the volume of our currency; that is the desideratum. The Government, say the Populists, which by Protection rolls wealth into the manufacturer's lap, which constructs great harbors, buildings and defences, which gave us free land, pensions, bounties, railways, and created greenbacks, can do anything to increase our money supply. Nothing can give a clearer idea of the Populist view of money than this illustration given to me lately by one of the ablest Populists in the West: "The money-market is like the pork-market in which John Cudahy lost his millions. Eastern financiers and gold-bugs are attempting to corner the money-market, just as Mr. Cudahy attempted to corner the pork-market. Mr. Cudahy failed because the supply of pork was beyond his estimation. Wall Street is succeeding because the supply of money is limited. We insist that the Government should increase the circulating medium to $50 *per capita* and keep it there. As fast as the plutocrats gather in the money, the Government should issue more money until the money-corner is broken." Assuming that this absurd and ludicrous comparison is correct, one cannot help inquiring where the value of money would go after such a corner were broken. It is quite evident that it would go where Mr. Cudahy's pork went. . . .

It does seem surprising, with John Law only a century removed and the Argentine lesson staring us in the face, that Populist financial notions can exist. It might seem easy to banish all such nonsense by a half-hour's exposition of history and a fifteen-minute lesson from a political economy primer. But these people will accept no political economy as reliable and no history as unbiassed. Their text-books are Bellamy, Donnelly *et id genus omne*. The Populist faith in the "Gover'ment" is supreme. The Government is all-powerful and it ought to be all-willing. When a Populist debtor is approached by a creditor, his reply is actually often in these words: "I can't pay the debt until the Government gives me relief." This intervention or saving grace of the Government is a personal influence to him, a thing of life. What shall minister to a mind diseased like the Populist's? Only constitutional remedies.

The constituent elements of this party give significant hints as to its character. The rank and file are composed of honest, intelligent men, mild in language and demeanor. During the Omaha convention the writer met frequently and conversed with an old friend, a delegate from an Iowa county. He was a "logical" Populist. One could read and analyze the entire movement in that man's record, which has always been socialistic. When I first knew him he was a Granger, then he became successively a Greenbacker, a Prohibitionist and a Populist. He is a man in more than comfortable circumstances, intelligent, honest and a Christian. It was during his early struggle for subsistence that he became inoculated with the socialist virus, and it remains with him. On the day the convention assembled he exclaimed with fervor, "This campaign is opening just like the first Lincoln campaign." Although the adjectives, "honest," "sincere," and "earnest," may be applied to the followers, their antonyms fit the leaders. At least ninety per cent of these candidates and exhorters are destitute of personal or political integrity. They are political vagabonds, slanderers and demagogues. Their records in their former homes are unsavory. All of them keep in the sore spots of their minds the sad memories of conventions in which they were old party candidates to whom came overwhelming disaster.

At one of the first Alliance Congressional conventions in 1890, it was dramatically asserted that one of the candidates was a lawyer. He escaped violence and recovered a portion of his strength by explaining that although he had been a lawyer, he was then disbarred! A Populist convention in 1892 almost nominated for lieutenant-governor a man to whom in former days a jury had been only too kind. Scores of these stump electricians have had lifelong records as mountebanks. General Weaver is an honest man, personally, but he has boxed the compass in politics, always ready warmly to embrace any part of "ism" in the loving ecstasy of political hunger. It has been repeatedly charged that many of these Populist leaders are in the secret employ of the corporations, and the evidence, in some cases, seems conclusive. And so on with almost the entire list. Exceptions may be made of Senators Kyle and Allen, and Mrs. Lease, who knows really little of her themes, but is earnest and honest, and has wonderful hortatory power.

It would be unfair to close this article without recounting the excellent results of the organization of this party in the Western States. Like all third parties, it has done the good work of breaking up old political rings and corrupt administrations, making a cleansing of the old parties imperative. In Kansas it accomplished what would have been an impossibility under previous conditions by electing as a Congressman-at-large an ex-Confederate, thus burying all sectional strife. Barring such circumstances as the Kansas legislative barricades, the State elevator law in Minnesota, and the "State-railway-to-the-gulf" scheme of the Nebraska legislature, the public acts of this party have been very creditable. This is especially true in Nebraska, where the party passed the Australian ballot law and the maximum freight-rate law, an act reducing the extortionate freight-rates. Gigantic forces were at work to accomplish that bill's defeat, but the Populists were assisted by the united Omaha press and the anti-monopolists in the two greater parties. No more glittering baits were ever held out to induce men to swerve from their duty. The law is now suspended by a temporary injunction, issued at the demand of Eastern stockholders, who desire to postpone to a later time this long-deferred act of justice. But the delay will have no permanent effect, except to make good campaign material for the Populists in this year's campaign for the judicial offices. Other meritorious and just laws were passed by this legislature, directed by Populists. In spite of all the great pressure of the corporations, the Populists, by the aid of the Democrats, elected to the Senate an honest man, William Vincent Allen, against the chosen friend of the monopolists, the Republican candidate, the general solicitor of the Union Pacific railway. That election cost Mr. Allen just $74.25. This was probably the smallest sum by which a seat in the present United States Senate was secured. Mr. Allen is a Populist, with a head filled with wrong financial notions; but he is a conservative, pure, incorruptible man, who won renown as an eminent attorney and a just, upright judge, whose acts of kindness and charity are legion.

But the greatest benefit derived from this party's birth has been educational. The whole country has been filled with the desire and spirit of investigation, and questions respecting finance and Governmental functions have been studied by men and women as they are studied nowhere else in the world. Out of this Populist movement are gradually evolving sound arguments to counteract their fallacies, and in this fact lies the very means for accomplishing the party's overthrow.

It would be contrary to all reason, logic and history to presume an extended life for this party. As now constituted, it must fail and fall, because it rests upon error. A significant index to its decay is contained in the remarkable speed with which it is deserting its former tenets and growing in the direction of conservatism and sanity. Fiatism is mild compared with the wild plans of the enforced division of property, the spoliation of millionaires' estates, and the thousand other communistic and anarchistic schemes of the first campaign. The party seems intent on reaching safer ground. Although it would not consider a lawyer as a candidate for Congress in 1890, it elected a lawyer to the United States Senate in 1893. The sub-treasury and Government warehouse schemes have been virtually abandoned. A few weeks ago, Nebraska's most honored Populist in a public address defended the banks. This would have been a treasonable act three years ago. At the present time, the party is growing by the accretions of free-silver Democrats who feel that they have been betrayed by their party and their Executive. Could a Congressional election be held to-day, the Populists would win notable victories. But this growth will be temporary, just as the free-silver frenzy must soon pass away. Parenthetically, let it be understood that Populism will derive no benefit from the Waites, Wolcotts, Stewarts and other monometallists of the silver States. Their creed is purely selfish and is not sincere. This temporary agitation and the perfervid cries of "Western Empire" need alarm no Eastern mind, for their influence is very slight and does not sensibly affect the real Populists. Genuine Populism has its home in Minnesota, the Dakotas, Iowa, Nebraska, Missouri and Kansas. These States contain three times the population of the entire country West of them. What the Populists want is not free silver, *per se*, but more money. And as they have abandoned all their other tenets and staked their existence on fiat, foundationless currency, as a national party the People's Party must fail, just as the Greenback Party failed. Although as Mr. Reed says, humanity is incapable of prolonged virtue, yet the periods of financial heresy are always brief. And with the fiat money heresy dissipated, there will be no tie remaining to unite its elements into a national party.

Whether the party in the various Western States, in its growth toward sanity and reason, will retain strength enough to absorb a majority of the old parties, or whether its members will return to their former parties, are matters of mere conjecture, depending upon local conditions. There are many influences at work to dissolve these State parties as well as the national party. One is the educational impulse given by this movement, which is producing arguments to refute its arguments. Another is the relatively comfortable condition of the Western farmers. Evidences of this dissolution are found in the decay of the Farmers' Alliances, nearly half of them having given up their charters in Nebraska alone. An analysis of last year's election figures will show that, as compared with 1890, the Populists made gains in the towns and lost heavily in the country districts. This farmers' movement cannot long endure when the farmers begin to desert it. Another influence is the recent financial depression, affecting farmers least and "plutocrats" most. The conditions which would tend to prolong the life of the State parties are a continuance of real grievances, and hard times. The same local causes which immediately preceded the uprising would keep it alive. Remedies must be provided for railway and other extortions, and old party leaders will be wise if they continue to remedy real grievances and thus deprive the People's Party of a mission. There is always present a great, overwhelming, unformed anti-monopoly spirit in the West which, when excited to anger, will remedy monopolistic wrongs within, if possible, and, if not, without party lines. But its concern is with local and State affairs only.

So far as the national People's Party is concerned, since Populism is disappearing and its distinctive features are being lost, its dissolution must soon come. The decay of the Western socialistic body, the parent of Populism, will not be so rapid. The deep impressions of thirty years are not so easily removed. There is no doubt, however, that many of the influences now destroying Populism will also affect the greater disease. The Populist movement has itself reacted against the spread of socialism by revealing to many who were regarding socialism favorably the logical end of its doctrines in the foolish schemes of the new party. The face of the nation, too, seems turned away from the enactment and toward the repeal of paternal legislation. And as "looking to Washington" still obtains, let Washington, by careful and wise laws, teach the higher truths of individualism. The American people should congratulate themselves that the discovery has so soon been made and that a movement has begun to analyze and check this Western socialism which revealed its strength and, let us hope, attained its prime in the People's Party.

PART V

THE NEGRO IN AMERICAN LIFE

However contemporaries viewed it, we know now that the aftermath of Reconstruction is to be seen less as the climactic achievement of political freedom for the Negro than as the start of a prolonged and tortuous struggle for the rights of citizenship. Nor can it be said now that the struggle, whatever its point of origin, was merely sectional in scope. The coalition of northern liberals, southern conservatives, and southern radicals—which earlier had provided a dam against anti-Negro fanaticism—crumbled under the weight of both domestic and international pressures, and racism in all its forms came to be a characteristic of every section of the country. In part, this was the result of the very reconciliation between North and South that was hailed everywhere as the final healing of the scars of war; continued agitation on behalf of the Negroes, so it seemed to many, served only to perpetuate the sectional conflict. In part, too, however, the new victimization of the Negro was the result of international pressures. "If the stronger and cleverer race is free to impose its will upon 'new-caught, sullen peoples' on the other side of the globe, why not in South Carolina and Mississippi?" asked the editor of the Atlantic Monthly. Senator Tillman delighted in making crystal-clear the connection between foreign policy and domestic events. "No Republican leader, not even Governor Roosevelt," he declared, "will now dare to wave the bloody shirt and preach a crusade against the South's treatment of the negro. The North has a bloody shirt of its own. Many thousands of them have been made into shrouds for murdered Filipinos, done to death because they were fighting for liberty."

How American policy in the Caribbean affected the Negro's conception of his own status and his own struggle is discussed in the Open Letter to President McKinley, below. For Frederick Douglass, the great Negro leader, the overriding concern was for Negroes, like workingmen, farmers, and women, to speak with one voice—"because the many are more than the few"—against "the practical construction of American life [which] is a convention against us."

Why a Colored Convention?

Frederick Douglass

Charged with the responsibility and duty of doing what we may to advance the interest and promote the general welfare of a people lately enslaved, and who, though now free, still suffer many of the disadvantages and evils derived from their former condition, not the least among which is the low and unjust estimate entertained of their abilities and possibilities as men, and their value as citizens of the Republic; instructed by these people to make such representations and adopt such measures as in our judgment may help to bring about a better understanding and a more friendly feeling between themselves and their white fellow-citizens, recognizing the great fact as we do, that the relations of the American people and those of civilized nations generally depend more upon prevailing ideas, opinions, and long established usages for their qualities of good and evil than upon courts of law or creeds of religion. Allowing the existence of a magnanimous disposition on your part to listen candidly to an honest appeal for fair play, coming from any class of your fellow-citizens, however humble, who may have, or may think they have, rights to assert or wrongs to redress, the members of this National Convention, chosen from all parts of the United States, representing the thoughts, feelings and purposes of colored men generally, would as one means of advancing the cause committed to them most respectfully and earnestly ask your attention and favorable consideration to the matters contained in the present paper.

At the outset we very cordially congratulate you upon the altered condition both of ourselves and our common country. Especially do we congratulate you upon the fact that a great reproach, which for two centuries rested on the good name of your country, has been blotted out; that chattel slavery is no longer the burden of the colored man's complaint, and that we now come to rattle no chains, to clank no fetters, to paint no horrors of the old plantation to shock your sensibilities, to

Frederick Douglass, "Address to the People of the United States," delivered at the Convention of Colored Men, Louisville, Ky., September 24, 1883.

humble your pride, excite your pity, or to kindle your indignation. We rejoice also that one of the results of this stupendous revolution in our national history, the Republic which was before divided and weakened between two hostile and irreconcilable interests, has become united and strong; risen to the possibility of the highest civilization; that this change has that from a low plain of life, which bordered upon barbarism, it has started the American Republic on a new departure, full of promise, although it has also brought you and ourselves face to face with problems novel and difficult, destined to impose upon us responsibilities and duties, which, plainly enough, will tax our highest mental and moral ability for their happy solution.

Born on American soil in common with yourselves, deriving our bodies and our minds from its dust, centuries having passed away since our ancestors were torn from the shores of Africa, we, like yourselves, hold ourselves to be in every sense Americans, and that we may, therefore venture to speak to you in a tone not lower than that which becomes earnest men and American citizens. Having watered your soil with our tears, enriched it with our blood, performed its roughest labor in time of peace, defended it against enemies in time of war, and at all times been loyal and true to its best interests, we deem it no arrogance or presumption to manifest now a common concern with you for its welfare, prosperity, honor and glory.

If the claim thus set up by us be admitted, as we think it ought to be, it may be asked, what propriety or necessity can there be for the Convention, of which we are members? and why are we now addressing you in some sense as suppliants asking for justice and fair play? These questions are not new to us. From the day the call for this Convention went forth this seeming incongruity and contradiction has been brought to our attention. From one quarter or another, sometimes with argument and sometimes without argument, sometimes with seeming pity for our ignorance, and at other times with fierce censure for our depravity, these questions have met us. With apparent surprise, astonishment, and impatience, we have been asked: "What more can the colored people of this country want than they now have, and what more is possible to them?" It is said they were once slaves, they are now free; they were once subjects, they are now sovereigns; they were once outside of all American institutions, they are now inside of all and are a recognized part of the whole American people. Why, then, do they hold Colored National Conventions and thus insist upon keeping up the color line between themselves and their white fellow-countrymen? We do not deny the pertinence and plausibility of these questions, nor do we shrink from a candid answer to the argument which they are supposed to contain. For we do not forget that they are not only put to us by those who have no sympathy with us, but by many who wish us well, and that in any case they deserve an answer. Before, however, we proceed to answer them, we digress here to say that there is only one element associated with them which excites the least bitterness of feeling in us, or that calls for special rebuke, and that is when they fall from the lips and pens of colored men who suffer with us and ought to know better. A few such men, well known to us and the country, happening to be more fortunate in the possession of wealth, education, and position than their humbler brethren, have found it convenient to chime in with the popular cry against our assembling, on the ground that we have no valid reason for this measure or for any other separate from the whites; that we ought to be satisfied with things as they are. With white men who thus object the case is different and less painful. For them there is a chance for charity. Educated as they are and have been for centuries, taught to look upon colored people as a lower order of humanity than themselves, and as having few rights, if any, above domestic animals, regarding them also through the medium of their beneficent religious creeds and just laws—as if law and practice were identical—some allowance can, and perhaps ought to be made when they misapprehend our real situation and deny our wants and assume a virtue they do not possess. But no such excuse or apology can be properly framed for men who are in any way identified with us. What may be erroneous in others implies either baseness or imbecility in them. Such men, it seems to us, are either deficient in self-respect or too mean, servile and cowardly to assert the true dignity of their manhood and that of their race. To admit that there are such men among us is a disagreeable and humiliating confession. But in this respect, as in others, we are not without the consolation of company; we are neither alone nor singular in the production of just such characters. All oppressed people have been thus afflicted.

It is one of the most conspicuous evils of caste and oppression, that they inevitably tend to make cowards and serviles of their victims, men ever ready to bend the knee to pride and power that thrift may follow fawning, willing to betray the cause of the many to serve the ends of the few; men who never hesitate to sell a friend when they think they can thereby purchase an enemy. Specimens of this sort may be found everywhere and at all times. There were Northern men with Southern principles in the time of slavery, and Tories in the revolution for independence. There are betrayers and informers to-day in Ireland, ready to kiss the hand that smites them and strike down the arm reached out to save them. Considering our long subjection to servitude and caste, and the many temptations to which we are exposed to betray our race into the hands of their enemies, the wonder is not that we have so many traitors among us as that we have so few. . . .

Happily for us and for the honor of the Republic, the United States Constitution is just, liberal, and friendly. The amendments to that instrument, adopted in the trying times of reconstruction of the Southern States, are a credit to the courage and statesmanship of the leading men of that crisis. These amendments establish freedom and abolish all unfair and invidious discrimination against citizens on account of race and color, so far as law can do so. In their view, citizens are neither black nor white, and all are equals. With this admission and this merited reproof to trimmers and traitors, we again come to the question, Why are we here in this National Convention? To this we answer, first, because there is a power in numbers and in union; because the many are more than the few; because the voice of a whole people, oppressed by a common injustice, is far more likely to command attention and exert an influence on the public mind than the voice of single individuals and isolated organizations; because, coming together from all parts of the country, the members of a National convention have the means of a more comprehensive knowledge of the general situation, and may, therefore, fairly be presumed to conceive more clearly and express more fully and wisely the policy it may be necessary for them to pursue in the premises. Because conventions of the people are in themselves harmless, and when made the means of setting forth grievances, whether real or fancied, they are the safety-valve of the Republic, a wise and safe substitute for violence, dynamite, and all sorts of revolutionary action against the peace and good order of society. If they are held without sufficient reason, that fact will be made manifest in their proceedings, and people will only smile at their weakness and pass on to their usual business without troubling themselves about the empty noise they are able to make. But if held with good cause, and by wise, sober, and earnest men, that fact will be made apparent and the result will be salutary. That good old maxim, which has come down to us from revolutionary times, that error may be safely tolerated, while truth is left free to combat it, applies here. A bad law is all the sooner repealed by being executed, and error is sooner dispelled by exposure than by silence. So much we have deemed it fit to say of conventions generally, because our resort to this measure has been treated by many as if there were something radically wrong in the very idea of a convention. It has been treated as if it were some ghastly, secret conclave, sitting in darkness to devise strife and mischief. The fact is, the only serious feature in the argument against us is the one which respects color. We are asked not only why hold a convention, but, with emphasis, why hold a *colored* convention? Why keep up this odious distinction between citizens of a common country and thus give countenance to the color line? It is argued that, if colored men hold conventions, based upon color, white men may hold white conventions based upon color, and thus keep open the chasm between one and the other class of citizens, and keep alive a prejudice which we profess to deplore. We state the argument against us fairly and forcibly, and will answer it

candidly and we hope conclusively. By that answer it will be seen that
the force of the object is, after all, more in sound than in substance. No
reasonable man will ever object to white men holding conventions in their
own interests, when they are once in our condition and we in theirs,
when they are oppressed and we the oppressors. In point of fact, however,
white men are already in convention against us in various ways and at
many important points. The practical construction of American life is a
convention against us. Human law may know no distinction among men
in respect of rights, but human practice may. Examples are painfully
abundant. . . .

It is our lot to live among a people whose laws, traditions, and prejudices have been against us for centuries, and from these they are not yet
free. To assume that they are free from these evils simply because they
have changed their laws is to assume what is utterly unreasonable and
contrary to facts. Large bodies move slowly. Individuals may be converted on the instant and change their whole course of life. Nations never.
Time and events are required for the conversion of nations. Not even the
character of a great political organization can be changed by a new platform. It will be the same old snake though in a new skin. Though we have
had war, reconstruction and abolition as a nation, we still linger in the
shadow and blight of an extinct institution. Though the colored man is no
longer subject to be bought and sold, he is still surrounded by an adverse
sentiment which fetters all his movements. In his downward course he
meets with no resistance, but his course upward is resented and resisted
at every step of his progress. If he comes in ignorance, rags and wretched-
ness, he conforms to the popular belief of his character, and in that character he is welcome. But if he shall come as a gentleman, a scholar, and a
statesman, he is hailed as a contradiction to the national faith concerning
his race, and his coming is resented as impudence. In the one case he
may provoke contempt and derision, but in the other he is an affront to
pride, and provokes malice. Let him do what he will, there is at present,
therefore, no escape for him. The color line meets him everywhere, and in
a measure shuts him out from all respectable and profitable trades and
callings. In spite of all your religion and laws he is a rejected man.

He is rejected by trade unions, of every trade, and refused work while
he lives, and burial when he dies, and yet he is asked to forget his color,
and forget that which everybody else remembers. If he offers himself to
a builder as a mechanic, to a client as a lawyer, to a patient as a physician, to a college as a professor, to a firm as a clerk; to a Government Department as an agent, or an officer, he is sternly met on the color line, and
his claim to consideration in some way is disputed on the ground of color.

Not even our churches, whose members profess to follow the despised
Nazarene, whose home, when on earth, was among the lowly and despised, have yet conquered this feeling of color madness, and what is true

of our churches is also true of our courts of law. Neither is free from this all-pervading atmosphere of color hate. The one describes the Deity as impartial, no respector of persons, and the other the Goddess of Justice as blindfolded, with sword by her side and scales in her hand held evenly between high and low, rich and poor, white and black, but both are the images of American imagination, rather than American practices.

Taking advantage of the general disposition in this country to impute crime to color, white men *color* their faces to commit crime and wash off the hated color to escape punishment. In many places where the commission of crime is alleged against one of our color, the ordinary processes of the law are set aside as too slow for the impetuous justice of the infuriated populace. They take the law into their own bloody hands and proceed to whip, stab, shoot, hang, or burn the alleged culprit, without the intervention of courts, counsel, judges, juries, and witnesses. In such cases it is not the business of the accusers to prove guilt, but it is for the accused to prove his innocence, a thing hard for any man to do, even in a court of law, and utterly impossible for him to do in these infernal Lynch courts. A man accused, surprised, frightened and captured by a motley crowd, dragged with a rope around his neck in midnight-darkness to the nearest tree, and told in the coarsest terms of profanity to prepare for death, would be more than human if he did not, in his terror-stricken appearance, more confirm suspicion of guilt than the contrary. Worse still, in the presence of such hell-black outrages, the pulpit is usually dumb, and the press in the neighborhood is silent or openly takes side with the mob. There are occasional cases in which white men are lynched, but one sparrow does not make a summer. Every one knows that what is called Lynch law is peculiarly the law for colored people and for nobody else. If there were no other grievance than this horrible and barbarous Lynch law custom, we should be justified in assembling, as we have now done, to expose and denounce it. But this is not all. Even now, after twenty years of so-called emancipation, we are subject to lawless raids of midnight riders, who, with blackened faces, invade our homes and perpetrate the foulest of crimes upon us and our families. This condition of things is too flagrant and notorious to require specifications or proof. Thus in all the relations of life and death we are met by the color line. We cannot ignore it if we would, and ought not if we could. It hunts us at midnight, it denies us accommodation in hotels and justice in the courts; excludes our children from schools, refuses our sons the chance to learn trades, and compels us to pursue only such labor as will bring the least reward. While we recognize the color line as a hurtful force, a mountain barrier to our progress, wounding our bleeding feet with its flinty rocks at every step, we do not despair. We are a hopeful people. This convention is a proof of our faith in you, in reason, in truth, and justice—our belief that prejudice, with all its malign accompaniments, may yet be removed by peaceful means; that, assisted by time and events and the growing enlightenment of both races, the color line will ultimately become harmless. When this shall come it will then only be used, as it should be, to distinguish one variety of the human family from another. It will cease to have any civil, political, or moral significance, and colored conventions will then be dispensed with as anachronisms, wholly out of place, but not till then. . . .

If liberty, with us, is yet but a name, our citizenship is but a sham, and our suffrage thus far only a cruel mockery, we may yet congratulate ourselves upon the fact that the laws and institutions of the country are sound, just and liberal. There is hope for a people when their laws are righteous whether for the moment they conform to their requirements or not. But until this nation shall make its practice accord with its Constitution and its righteous laws, it will not do to reproach the colored people of this country with keeping up the color line—for that people would prove themselves scarcely worthy of even theoretical freedom, to say nothing of practical freedom, if they settled down in silent, servile, and cowardly submission to their wrongs, from fear of making their color visible. They are bound by every element of manhood to hold conventions in their own name and on their own behalf, to keep their grievances before the people and make every organized protest against the wrongs inflicted upon them within their power. They should scorn the counsels of cowards, and hang their banner on the outer wall. Who would be free, themselves must strike the blow. We do not believe, as we are often told, that the Negro is the ugly child of the national family, and the more he is kept out of sight the better it will be for him. You know that liberty given is never so precious as liberty sought for and fought for. The man outraged is the man to make the outcry. Depend upon it, men will not care much for a people who do not care for themselves. Our meeting here was opposed by some of our members, because it would disturb the peace of the Republican party. The suggestion came from coward lips and misapprehended the character of that party. If the Republican party cannot stand a demand for [justice] and fair play, it ought to go down. We were men before that party was born, and our manhood is more sacred than any party can be. Parties were made for men, not men for parties.

If the six millions of colored people of this country, armed with the Constitution of the United States, with a million votes of their own to lean upon, and millions of white men at their back, whose hearts are responsive to the claims of humanity, have not sufficient spirit and wisdom to organize and combine to defend themselves from outrage, discrimination, and oppression, it will be idle for them to expect that the Republican party or any other political party will organize and combine for them or care what becomes of them. Men may combine to prevent cruelty to animals, for they are dumb and cannot speak for themselves; but we are men and must speak for ourselves, or we shall not be spoken for at all. We have conventions in America for Ireland, but we should have none if Ireland did not speak for herself. It is because she makes a noise and keeps her cause before the people that other people go to her help. It was the sword of Washington and of Lafayette that gave us Independence. In conclusion upon this color objection, we have to say that we meet here in open daylight. There is nothing sinister about us. The eyes of the nation are upon us. Ten thousand newspapers may tell if they choose of whatever is said and done here. They may commend our wisdom or condemn our folly, precisely as we shall be wise or foolish.

We put ourselves before them as honest men, and ask their judgment upon our work.

THE LABOR QUESTION

Not the least important among the subjects to which we invite your earnest attention is the condition of the labor class at the South. Their cause is one with the labor classes all over the world. The labor unions of the country should not throw away this colored element of strength. Everywhere there is dissatisfaction with the present relation of labor and capital, and to-day no subject wears an aspect more threatening to civilization than the respective claims of capital and labor, landlords and tenants. In what we have to say for our laboring class we expect to have and ought to have the sympathy and support of laboring men everywhere and of every color.

It is a great mistake for any class of laborers to isolate itself and thus weaken the bond of brotherhood between those on whom the burden and hardships of labor fell. The fortunate ones of the earth, who are abundant in land and money and know nothing of the anxious care and pinching poverty of the laboring classes, may be indifferent to the appeal for justice at this point, but the laboring classes cannot afford to be indifferent. What labor everywhere wants, what it ought to have, and will some day demand and receive, is an honest day's pay for an honest day's work. As the laborer becomes more intelligent he will develop what capital he already possesses—that is the power to organize and combine for its own protection. Experience demonstrates that there may be a slavery of wages only a little less galling and crushing in its effects than chattel slavery, and that this slavery of wages must go down with the others.

There is nothing more common now than the remark that the physical condition of the freedmen of the South is immeasurably worse than in the time of slavery; that in respect to food, clothing and shelter they are wretched, miserable and destitute; that they are worse masters to themselves than their old masters were to them. To add insult to injury, the reproach of their condition is charged upon themselves. A grandson of John C. Calhoun, an Arkansas land-owner, testifying the other day before the Senate Committee of Labor and Education, says the "Negroes are so indolent that they fail to take advantage of the opportunities offered them to procure the necessities of life; that there is danger of a war of races," etc., etc.

His testimony proclaims him the grandson of the man whose name he bears. The blame which belongs to his own class he shifts from them to the shoulders of labor. It becomes us to test the truth of that assertion by the light of reason, and by appeals to indisputable facts. Of course the land-owners of the South may be expected to view things differently from the landless. The slaveholders always did look at things a little differently from the slaves, and we therefore insist that, in order that the whole truth shall be brought out, the laborer as well as the capitalist shall be called as witnesses before the Senate Committee of Labor and Education. . . .

Let us look candidly at the matter. While we see and hear that the South is more prosperous than it ever was before and rapidly recovering from the waste of war, while we read that it raises more cotton, sugar, rice, tobacco, corn, and other valuable products than it ever produced before, how happens it, we sternly ask, that the houses of its laborers are miserable huts, that their clothes are rags, and their food the coarsest and scantiest? How happens it that the land-owner is becoming richer and the laborer poorer? . . .

This sharp contrast of wealth and poverty, as every thoughtful man knows, can exist only in one way, and from one cause, and that is by one getting more than its proper share of the reward of industry, and the other side getting less, and that in some way labor has been defrauded or otherwise denied of its due proportion, and we think the facts, as well as this philosophy, will support this view in the present case, and do so conclusively. We utterly deny that the colored people of the South are too lazy to work, or that they are indifferent to their physical wants; as already said, they are the workers of that section.

The trouble is not that the colored people of the South are indolent, but that no matter how hard or how persistent may be their industry, they get barely enough for their labor to support life at the very low point at which we find them. We therefore throw off the burden of disgrace and reproach from the laborer where Mr. Calhoun and others of his class would place it, and put in on the land-owner where it belongs. It is the old case over again. The black man does the work and the white man gets the money.

It may be said after all the colored people have themselves to blame for this state of things, because they have not intelligently taken the matter into their own hands and provided a remedy for the evil they suffer.

Some blame may attach at this point. But those who reproach us thus should remember that it is hard for labor, however fortunately and favorably surrounded, to cope with the tremendous power of capital in any contest for higher wages or improved condition. A strike for higher wages is seldom successful, and is often injurious to the strikers; the losses sustained are seldom compensated by the concessions gained. A case in point is the recent strike of the telegraph operators—a more intelligent class can nowhere be found. It was a contest of brains against money, and the want of money compelled intelligence to surrender to wealth. . . .

In contemplating the little progress made by the colored people in the acquisition of property in the South, and their present wretched condition, the circumstances of their emancipation should not be forgotten. Measurement in their case should not begin from the height yet to be attained by them, but from the depths whence they have come.

It should be remembered by our severe judges that freedom came to us not from the sober dictates of wisdom, or from any normal condition of things, not as a matter of choice on the part of the land-owners of the South, nor from moral considerations on the part of the North. It was born of battle and of blood. It came across fields of smoke and fire strewn with wounded, bleeding and dying men. Not from the Heaven of Peace amid the morning stars, but from the hell of war—out of the tempest and whirlwind of warlike passions, mingled with deadly hate and a spirit of revenge; it came, not so much as a boon to us as a blast to the enemy. Those against whom the measure was directed were the land-owners, and they were not angels, but men, and, being men, it was to be expected they would resent the blow. They did resent it, and a part of that resentment unhappily fell upon us.

At first the land-owners drove us out of our old quarters, and told us they did not want us in their fields; that they meant to import German, Irish, and Chinese laborers. But as the passions of the war gradually subsided we were taken back to our old places; but, plainly enough, this change of front was not from choice, but necessity. Feeling themselves somehow or other entitled to our labor without the payment of wages, it was not strange that they should make the hardest bargains for our labor, and get it for as little as possible. For them the contest was easy, their tremendous power and our weakness easily gave them the victory.

Against the voice of Stevens, Sumner, and Wade, and other farseeing statesmen, the Government by whom we were emancipated left us completely in the power of our former owners. They turned us loose to the open sky and left us not a foot of ground from which to get a crust of bread.

It did not do as well by us as Russia did by her serfs, or Pharaoh did by the Hebrews. With freedom Russia gave land and Egypt loaned jewels. . . .

The marvel is not that we are poor in such circumstances, but rather that we were not exterminated. In view of the circumstances, our extermination was confidently predicted. The facts that we still live and have increased in higher ratio than the native white people of the South are proofs of our vitality, and, in some degree, of our industry.

Nor is it to be wondered at that the standard of morals is not higher among us, that respect for the rights of property is not stronger. The power of life and death held over labor which says you shall work for me on my own terms or starve, is a source of crime, as well as poverty.

Weeds do not more naturally spring out of a manure pile than crime out of enforced destitution. Out of the misery of Ireland comes murder, assassination, fire and sword. The Irish are by nature no worse than other people, and no better. If oppression makes a wise man mad it may do the same, or worse, to a people who are not reputed wise. The woe pronounced upon those who keep back wages of the laborer by fraud is self-acting and self-executing and certain as death. The world is full of warnings.

THE ORDER SYSTEM

No more crafty and effective device for defrauding the southern laborers could be adopted than the one that substitutes orders upon shopkeepers for currency in payment of wages. It has the merit of a show of honesty, while it puts the laborer completely at the mercy of the land-owner and the shopkeeper. He is between the upper and the nether millstones, and is hence ground to dust. It gives the shopkeeper a customer who can trade with no other storekeeper, and thus leaves the latter no motive for fair dealing except his own moral sense, which is never too strong. While the laborer holding the orders is tempted by their worthlessness, as a circulating medium, to get rid of them at any sacrifice, and hence is led into extravagance and consequent destitution.

The merchant puts him off with his poorest commodities at highest prices, and can say to him take these or nothing. Worse still. By this means the laborer is brought into debt, and hence is kept always in the power of the land-owner. When this system is not pursued and land is rented to the freedman, he is charged more for the use of an acre of land for a single year than the land would bring in the market if offered for sale. On such a system of fraud and wrong one might well invoke a bolt from heaven—red with uncommon wrath. . . .

EDUCATION

On the subject of equal education and educational facilities, mentioned in the call for this convention, we expect little resistance from any quarter. It is everywhere an accepted truth, that in a country governed by the people, like ours, education of the youth of all classes is vital to its welfare, prosperity, and to its existence.

In the light of this unquestioned proposition, the patriot cannot but view with a shudder the widespread and truly alarming illiteracy as revealed by the census of 1880.

The question as to how this evil is to be remedied is an important one. Certain it is that it will not do to trust to the philanthropy of wealthy individuals or benevolent societies to remove it. The states in which this illiteracy prevails either can not or will not provide adequate systems of education for their own youth. But, however this may be, the fact remains that the whole country is directly interested in the education of every child that lives within its borders. The ignorance of any part of the American people so deeply concerns all the rest that there can be no doubt of the right to pass laws compelling the attendance of every child at school. Believing that such is now required and ought to be enacted, we hereby put ourselves on record in favor of stringent laws to this end.

In the presence of this appalling picture, presented by the last census, we hold it to be the imperative duty of Congress to take hold of this important subject, and, without waiting for the States to adopt liberal school systems within their respective jurisdictions, to enter vigorously upon the work of universal education.

The National Government, with its immense resources, can carry the benefits of a sound common-school education to the door of every poor man from Maine to Texas, and to withhold this boon is to neglect the greatest assurance it has of its own perpetuity. As a part of the American people we unite most emphatically with others who have already spoken on this subject, in urging Congress to lay the foundation of a great national system of aid to education at its next session. . . .

CIVIL RIGHTS

The right of every American citizen to select his own society and invite whom he will to his own parlor and table should be sacredly respected. A man's house is his castle, and he has a right to admit or refuse admission to it as he may please, and defend his house from all intruders even with force, if need be. This right belongs to the humblest not less than the highest, and the exercise of it by any of our citizens toward anybody or class who may presume to intrude, should cause no complaint, for each and all may exercise the same right toward whom he will.

When he quits his home and goes upon the public street, enters a public car or a public house, he has no exclusive right of occupancy. He is only a part of the great public, and while he has the right to walk, ride, and be accommodated with food and shelter in a public conveyance or hotel, he has no exclusive right to say that another citizen, tall or short, black or white, shall not have the same civil treatment with himself. The argument against equal rights at hotels is very improperly put upon the ground that the exercise of such rights, it is insisted, is social equality. But this ground is unreasonable. It is hard to say what social equality is, but it is certain that going into the same street car, hotel, or steamboat cabin does not make any man society for another any more than flying in the same air makes all birds of one feather.

Two men may be seated at the same table at a hotel; one may be a Webster in intellect, and the other a Guiteau in feebleness of mind and morals, and, of course, socially and intellectually, they are as wide apart as are the poles of the moral universe, but their civil rights are the same. The distinction between the two sorts of equality is broad and plain to the understanding of the most limited, and yet, blinded by prejudice, men never cease to confound one with the other, and allow themselves to infringe the civil rights of their fellow-citizens as if those rights were, in some way, in violation of their social rights.

That this denial of rights to us is because of our color, only as color is a badge of condition, is manifest in the fact that no matter how decently dressed or well-behaved a colored man may be, he is denied civil treatment in the ways thus pointed out, unless he comes as a servant. His color, not his character, determines the place he shall hold and the kind of treatment he shall receive. That this is due to a prejudice and has no rational principle under it is seen in the fact that the presence of colored persons in hotels and rail cars is only offensive when they are there as guests and passengers. As servants they are welcome, but as equal citizens they are not. It is also seen in the further fact that nowhere else on the globe, except in the United States, are colored people subject to insult and outrage on account of color. The colored traveler in Europe does not meet it, and we denounce it here as a disgrace to American civilization and American religion and as a violation of the spirit and letter of the Constitution of the United States. From those courts which have solemnly sworn to support the Constitution and that yet treat this provision of it with contempt we appeal to the people, and call upon our friends to remember our civil rights at the ballot-box. On the point of the two equalities we are determined to be understood.

We leave social equality where it should be left, with each individual man and woman. No law can regulate or control it. It is a matter with which governments have nothing whatever to do. Each may choose his own friends and associates without interference or dictation of any.

POLITICAL EQUALITY

Flagrant as have been the outrages committed upon colored citizens in respect to their civil rights, more flagrant, shocking, and scandalous still have been the outrages committed upon our political rights by means of bull-dozing and Kukluxing, Mississippi plans, fraudulent counts, tissue ballots, and the like devices. Three States in which the colored people outnumber the white population are without colored representation and their political voice suppressed. The colored citizens in those States are virtually disfranchised, the Constitution held in utter contempt and its provisions nullified. This has been done in the face of the Republican party and successive Republican administrations.

It was once said by the great O'Connell that the history of Ireland might be traced like a wounded man through a crowd by the blood, and the same may be truly said of the history of the colored voters of the South.

They have marched to the ballot-box in face of gleaming weapons, wounds, and death. They have been abandoned by the Government, and left to the laws of nature. So far as they are concerned, there is no Government or Constitution of the United States.

They are under control of a foul, haggard, and damning conspiracy against reason, law, and constitution. How you can be indifferent, how any leading colored men can allow themselves to be silent in the presence of this state of things, we cannot see. . . .

This is no question of party. It is a question of law and government. It is a question whether men shall be protected by law, or be left to the mercy of cyclones of anarchy and bloodshed. It is whether the Government or the mob shall rule this land; whether the promises solemnly made to us in the Constitution be manfully kept or meanly and flagrantly broken. Upon this vital point we ask the whole people of the United States to take notice that whatever of political power we have shall be exerted for no man of any party who will not, in advance of election, promise to use every power given him by the Government, State or National, to make the black man's path to the ballot-box as straight, smooth and safe as that of any other American citizen.

POLITICAL AMBITION

We are as a people often reproached with ambition for political offices and honors. We are not ashamed of this alleged ambition. Our destitution of such ambition would be our real shame. If the six millions and a half of people whom we represent could develop no aspirants to political office and honor under this Government, their mental indifference, barrenness and stolidity might well enough be taken as proof of their unfitness for American citizenship.

It is no crime to seek or hold office. If it were it would take a larger space than that of Noah's Ark to hold the white criminals.

One of the charges against this convention is that it seeks for the colored people a larger share than they now possess in the offices and emoluments of the Government.

We are now significantly reminded by even one of our own members that we are only twenty years out of slavery, and we ought therefore to be modest in our aspirations. Such leaders should remember that men will not be religious when the devil turns preacher.

The inveterate and persistent office-seeker and office-holder should be modest when he preaches that virtue to others which he does not himself practice. Wolsey could tell Cromwell to fling away ambition properly only when he had flung away his own.

We are far from affirming that there may not be too much zeal among colored men in pursuit of political preferment; but the fault is not wholly theirs. They have young men among them noble and true, who are educated and intelligent—fit to engage in enterprise of "pith and moment"—who find themselves shut out from nearly all the avenues of wealth and respectability, and hence they turn their attention to politics. They do so because they can find nothing else. The best cure for the evil is to throw open other avenues and activities to them.

We shall never cease to be a despised and persecuted class while we are known to be excluded by our color from all important positions under the Government.

While we do not make office, the one thing important, nor the one condition of our alliance with any party, and hold that the welfare, prosperity and happiness of our whole country is the true criterion of political action for ourselves and for all men, we can not disguise from ourselves the fact that our persistent exclusion from office as a class is a great wrong, fraught with injury, and ought to be resented and opposed by all reasonable and effective means in our power.

We hold it to be self-evident that no class or color should be the exclusive rulers of this country. If there is such a ruling class, there must of course be a subject class, and when this condition is once established this Government of the people, by the people, and for the people, will have perished from the earth.

Open Letter
to President McKinley, 1899

We, colored people of Massachusetts in mass meeting assembled to consider our oppressions and the state of the country relative to the same, have resolved to address ourselves to you in an open letter, notwithstanding your extraordinary, your incomprehensible silence on the subject of our wrongs in your annual and other messages to Congress, as in your public utterances to the people at large. We address ourselves to you, sir, not as suppliants, but as of right, as American citizens, whose servant you are, and to whom you are bound to listen, and for whom you are equally bound to speak, and upon occasion to act, as for any other body of your fellow-countrymen in like circumstances. We ask nothing for ourselves at your hands, as chief magistrate of the republic, to which all American citizens are not entitled. We ask for the enjoyment of life, liberty and the pursuit of happiness equally with other men. We ask for the free and full exercise of all the rights of American freemen, guaranteed to us by the Constitution and laws of the Union, which you were solemnly sworn to obey and execute. We ask you for what belongs to us, the high sanction of Constitution and law, and the Democratic genius of our institutions and civilization. These rights are everywhere throughout the South denied to us, violently wrested from us by mobs, by lawless legislatures, and nullifying conventions, combinations, and conspiracies, openly, defiantly, under your eyes, in your constructive and actual presence. And we demand, which is a part of our rights, protection, security in our life, our liberty, and in the pursuit of our individual and social happiness under a government, which we are bound to defend in war, and which is equally bound to furnish us in peace protection, at home and abroad.

We have suffered, sir—God knows how much we have suffered!—since your accession to office, at the hands of a country professing to be Christian, but which is not Christian; from the hate and violence of a people claiming to be civilized, but who are not civilized, and you have seen our sufferings, witnessed from your high place our awful wrongs and miseries, and yet you have at no time and on no occasion opened your

Open Letter to President McKinley from the Colored People of Massachusetts (n.p., n.d.).

lips in our behalf. Why? we ask. Is it because we are black and weak and despised? Are you silent because without any fault of our own we were enslaved and held for more than two centuries in cruel bondage by your forefathers? Is it because we bear the marks of those sad generations of Anglo-Saxon brutality and wickedness, that you do not speak? . . .

The struggle of the Negro to rise out of his ignorance, his poverty and his social degradation . . . to the full stature of his American citizenship, has been met everywhere in the South by the active ill will and determined race hatred and opposition of the white people of that section. Turn where he will, he encounters this cruel and implacable spirit. He dares not speak openly the thoughts which rise in his breast. He has wrongs such as have never in modern times been inflicted on a people, and yet he must be dumb in the midst of a nation which prates loudly of democracy and humanity, boasts itself the champion of oppressed people abroad, while it looks on indifferent, apathetic, at appalling enormities and inequities at home, where the victims are black and the criminals white. The suppression, the terror wrought at the South is so complete, so ever-present, so awful, that no Negro's life or property is safe for a day who ventures to raise his voice to heaven in indignant protest and appeal against the deep damnation and despotism of such a social state. Even teachers and leaders of this poor, oppressed and patient people may not speak, lest their institutions of learning and industry, and their own lives pay for their temerity at the swift hands of savage mobs. But if the peace of Warsaw, the silence of death reign over our people and their leaders at the South, we of Massachusetts are free, and must and shall raise our voice to you and through you to the country, in solemn protest and warning against the fearful sin and peril of such explosive social conditions. We, sir, at this crisis and extremity in the life of our race in the South, and in this crisis and extremity in the life of the republic as well, in the presence of the civilized world, cry to you to pause, if but for an hour, in pursuit of your national policy of "criminal aggression" abroad to consider the "criminal aggression" at home against humanity and American citizenship, which is in the full tide of successful conquest at the South, and the tremendous consequences to our civilization; and the durability of the Union itself, of this universal subversion of the supreme law of the land, of democratic institutions, and of the precious principle of the religion of Jesus in the social and civil life of the Southern people.

With one accord, with an anxiety that wrenched our hearts with cruel hopes and fears, the Colored people of the United States turned to you when Wilmington, N. C. was held for two dreadful days and nights in the clutch of a bloody revolution; when Negroes, guilty of no crime except the color of their skin and a desire to exercise the rights of their American citizenship, were butchered like dogs in the streets of that ill-fated town and when government of the people by the people and for the people perished in your very presence by the hands of violent men during those bitter November days for want of federal aid, which you would not and did not furnish, on the plea that you could not give what was not asked for by a coward and recreant governor. And we well understood at that time, sir, not withstanding your plea of constitutional inability to cope with the rebellion in Wilmington, that where there is a will with constitutional lawyers and rulers there is always a way, and where there is no will there is no way. We well knew that you lacked the will and, therefore, the way to meet that emergency. . . .

And, when you made your Southern tour a little later, and we saw how cunningly you catered to Southern race prejudice and proscription; how you, the one single public man and magistrate of the country, who, by virtue of your exalted office, ought under no circumstances to recognize white men at the Capitol in Montgomery, Ala., and black men afterward in a Negro church; how you preached patience, industry, moderation to your long-suffering black fellow citizens, and patriotism, jingoism and imperialism to your white ones; when we saw all those things, scales of illusion in respect to your object fell from our eyes. We felt that the President of the United States, in order to win the support of the South to his policy of "criminal aggression" in the far East, was ready and willing to shut his eyes, ears and lips to the "criminal aggression" of that section against the Constitution and the laws of the land, wherein they guarantee civil rights and citizenship to the Negro, whose ultimate reduction to a condition of fixed and abject serfdom is the plain purpose of the Southern people and their laws.

When, several months subsequently, you returned to Georgia, the mob spirit, as if to evince its supreme contempt for your presence and the federal executive authority which you represent, boldly broke into a prison shed . . . where were confined helpless Negro prisoners on a charge of incendiarism and brutally murdered five of them. These men were American citizens, entitled to the rights of American citizens, protection and trial by due process of law. . . . They ought to have been sacred charges in the hands of any civilized or semicivilized State and people. But almost in your hearing, before your eyes (and you the chief magistrate of a country loudly boastful of its freedom, Christianity and civilization), they were atrociously murdered. Did you speak? Did you open your lips to express horror of the awful crime and stern condemnation of the incredible villainy and complicity of the constituted authorities of Georgia in the commission of this monstrous outrage, which out-barbarized barbarism and stained through and through with indelible infamy before the world your country's justice, honor and humanity?

Still later, considering the age, the circumstances and the nation in which the deed was done, Georgia committed a crime unmatched for moral depravity and sheer atrocity during the century. A Negro, charged with murder and criminal assault, the first charge he is reported by the newspapers to have admitted, and the second to have denied, was taken one quiet Sunday morning from his captors, and burned to death with indescribable and hellish cruelty in the presence of cheering thousands of the so-called best people of Georgia—men, women and children who had gone forth on a Christian Sabbath to the burning of a human being as to a country festival and holiday of innocent enjoyment and amusement. . . . The death of Hose was quickly followed by that of the Negro preacher, Strickland, guiltless of crime, under circumstances and with a brutality of wickedness almost matching in horror and enormity the torture and murder of the first; and this last was succeeded by a third victim; who was literally lashed to death by the wild, beastlike spirit of a Georgia mob, for daring merely to utter his abhorrence of the Palmetto iniquity and slaughter of helpless prisoners.

Did you speak? Did you utter one word of reprobation, or righteous indignation, either as magistrate or as man? Did you break the shameful silence of shameful months with so much as a whisper of a whisper against the deep damnation of such defiance of all law, human and divine; such revulsion of men into beasts, and relapses of communities into barbarism in the very center of the republic, and amid the sanctuary of the temple of American liberty itself? You did not, sir, but your Attorney-General did, and he only to throw out to the public, to your meek and long-suffering colored fellow citizens, the cold and cautious legal opinion that the case of Hose has no federal aspect. Mr. President, has it any moral or human aspect, seeing that Hose was a member of the Negro race, whom your Supreme Court once declared has no rights in America which white men are bound to respect? Is this infamous dictum of that tribunal still the supreme law of the land? We ask you, sir, since recent events in Arkansas, Mississippi, Alabama, Virginia and Louisiana, as well as in Georgia and the Carolinas, indeed throughout the South, and your own persistent silence, and the persistent silence of every member of your Cabinet on the subject of the wrongs of that race in those States, would appear together to imply as much.

Had, eighteen months ago, the Cuban revolution to throw off the yoke of Spain, or the attempt of Spain to subdue the Cuban rebellion, any federal aspects? We believe that you and the Congress of the United States thought that they had, and therefore used, finally, the armed force of the nation to expel Spain from that island. Why? Was it because "the people of the Island of Cuba are, and of right ought to be free and independent?" You and Congress said as much, and may we fervently pray, sir, in passing that the freedom and independence of that brave people shall not much longer be denied them by our government? But to resume, there was another consideration which, in your judgment, gave to the

Cuban question a federal aspect, which provoked at last the armed interposition of our government in the affairs of that island, and this was "the chronic condition of disturbance in Cuba so injurious and menacing to our interests and tranquillity, as well as shocking to our sentiments of humanity"—wherefore you presently fulfilled "a duty to humanity by ending a situation, the indefinite prolongation of which had become insufferable."

Mr. President, had that "chronic condition of disturbance in Cuba so injurious and menacing to our interests and tranquillity, as well as shocking to our sentiments of humanity," which you wished to terminate and did terminate, a federal aspect, while that not less "chronic condition of disturbance" in the South, which is a thousand times more "injurious and menacing to our interests and tranquillity," as well as far more "shocking to our sentiments of humanity," or ought to be, none whatever? Is it better to be Cuban revolutionists fighting for Cuban independence than American citizens striving to do their simple duty at home? Or is it better only in case those American citizens doing their simple duty at home happen to be Negroes residing in the Southern States?

Are crying national transgressions and injustices more "injurious and menacing" to the Republic, as well as "shocking to its sentiments of humanity," when committed by a foreign state, in foreign territory, against a foreign people, than when they are committed by a portion of our own people against a portion of our own people at home? There were those of our citizens who did not think that the Cuban question possessed any federal aspect, while there were others who thought otherwise; and these, having the will and the power, eventually found a way to suppress a menacing danger to the country and a wrong against humanity at the same time. . . . If, sir, you have the disposition, as we know that you have the power, we are confident that you will be able to find a constitutional way to reach us in our extremity, and our enemies also, who are likewise enemies to great public interests and national tranquillity.

PART VI

EDUCATION FOR
MODERN SOCIETY

That education should have a living connection with the needs of society was no new discovery of the 1890's. The relation between the public school and the maintenance of a democratic society had long been noted. "The common schools are truly republican," wrote John D. Pierce, crusading Western educational leader. "In the public schools all classes are blended together, the rich mingle with the poor, and both are educated in company. Let free schools be established and maintained in perpetuity, and there can be no such thing as a permanent aristocracy in our land. . . ." And at least since the time of Horace Mann advocates had not been wanting to suggest the connection between higher standards of education and higher levels of labor productivity.

What exacerbated the problem for educators during the last quarter of the nineteenth century was that society itself was in such violent flux. New ideas like Darwinism provided one stimulus for change in the content of education. Another was to be found in the special requirements of the immigrant millions. How could the schools provide the institutional framework in which they would find a common experience and learn a common interpretation of the history of their new-found country, without which the unity of the nation itself would be endangered? And pressing, too, upon the schools were the needs of a rapidly developing industry.

To many, the requirements of the age seemed to dictate fundamental changes in the nature of the curriculum. New scientific and technical courses were desired, as well as those courses which would instill a respect for mercantile and industrial occupations at the expense of the professions and liberal arts. To others, these recommendations smacked of an attempt to insinuate castelike notions into the educational system; if the glory of American society was its fluidity, was it desirable, or even possible, to pick out children at an early age and compel them to follow the program that seemed best adapted to their capacities? There were some, finally, who raised more fundamental questions. What kind of human being is required by our system of social institutions, and how may the school contribute to his development?

Professor Charles H. Thurber of the University of Chicago advocated the closest connection between the content of education and the needs of the business community. For Jane Addams, the problem was to infuse education with meaning for immigrant children; and that, she was certain, could not be achieved by training them simply to be machine tenders. Philosopher John Dewey saw the problem in a larger context than that of conflict between special education and general education. The school and the family are the two major institutions through which the child

409

becomes socialized, learns to behave as a member of society. What should the schools teach and how should they be conducted so as to prepare the child to become worker, voter, parent, capable of exercising leadership in carrying out the thousand and one demands imposed on citizens by a democratic society?

The High School as Preparation for Business

Charles H. Thurber

In Walter Besant's novel "Katherine Regina" one of the characters is a young German clerk, a type of the young German who is becoming such a perplexing element in English commercial life. In his conversation with the heroine a good deal of light is thrown upon the difference between the training given in Germany and that given in England for commercial pursuits. The moral is as good for America as it is for England, and I can, I think, do no better in introducing my topic than to quote Dittmer Bock:

"I find the memory of great English merchants, and I find great German houses—Hamburg is the place where you must look now for great merchants. Did you ever hear of the Godefroi brothers?"

Katherine never had.

"They were boys who worked and looked about them. Perhaps they had read history and knew about Whittington and Gresham. And they rose and became rich; they discovered an island, and they established trade with it and planted it; they became rich; they founded the great German colonial empire of the future"—here Dittmer spread his arms—"which will grow and grow until it swallows up your English colonies one after the other. I, too, shall look about the world until I discover another island like Samoa; then I shall go there and begin to trade and to plant."

"It is a great ambition, Dittmer."

"It has been my resolve since I was a child. In order to carry it out I have learned what I could—mathematics, languages, bookkeeping, shorthand, physical geography, commercial and political history, and the present condition of trade over all the world. I know every harbor and its exports and imports, and the principal merchants who carry on its trade."

"That seems a great deal to learn."

Charles H. Thurber, "Is the Present High-School Course a Satisfactory Preparation for Business? If Not, How Should It Be Modified?" *Journal of Proceedings and Addresses, National Educational Association* (Chicago, 1897), pp. 808–818.

"Modern trade wants all this knowledge. There will very soon be no more English merchants, because your young men will not learn the new conditions of trade. In every office there must be clerks who can write and speak foreign languages. Your young men will not learn them. Then we come over—we who have learned them. For my part, I can write and read English, Swedish, Danish, French, Spanish, Italian, Dutch, and German. Do you think we shall be content to stay here as clerks? No, no. Do you think that I have come here to sit down with forty pounds a year? We are cheap, we German clerks. You say so. Mein Gott, you will find us dear! We are learning our trade: we find out all your customers and your correspondents: we learn your profits, and we undersell you. We do not go away. We remain, and presently, instead of an English house, there is a German house in its place, because your young men are so stupid that they will not learn."

At this point Dittmer was quite carried away, and became the American newspaper German.

"I study English commerce—I study how it began and why it is now coming to an end. The English clerk will not learn anything, and expects to be paid like an Amtsrichter at least. In Deutschland we learn, and we are poor at first. Ja wohl, we are poor, but we can wait. It is your high salaries in your army, in your navy, in your church, in your trade, in your administration, which ruin Great Britain. Everywhere the German merchant drives out the English and the American."

This is a very clear statement of the problem. Upon the solution of this problem depends the commercial progress of our country.

It has been characteristic of Anglo-Saxon education, both in England and in the United States, that it has devoted itself almost exclusively to humanistic training, to education which shall make men better, because broader and more cultured citizens. We have developed excellent technical schools, which train men for engineering and architecture; but these are essentially professions. In all our educational literature, however, it is frequently avowed, and always tacitly allowed, that it is beneath the dignity of educators to undertake the task of fitting youth for a specific work in life. It has been often said, and is widely believed, that a college education is a positive damage to one who wishes to pursue a business career. This point of view is very well expressed in letters I have received from prominent Chicago business men upon this question. One writes as follows:

I have known of cases where college training has given its recipients such a pedantic turn of mind as to be an actual hindrance to the broad and liberal policy now so necessary to develop and sustain large enterprises and undertakings.

Another says:

If the young man adopts a commercial career with a view of making it his support and that of those who may be dependent upon him, the years spent at college would be a serious loss to him and, in a measure, even unfit him for the work before him. To gain a practical knowledge of business, it is necessary for the young man to begin at the very bottom, which implies, in most instances, menial tasks. The boy of fifteen or seventeen years of age easily adapts himself to these, but not so the college graduate, who would surely feel a degradation in having assigned to him tasks which usually fall to the lot of the apprentice. . . .

These suggestions from practical business men of high standing bring certain other aspects of the problem before us. In its fundamental character the high-school course of today is essentially the same as the college course, and, therefore, the objections urged against the college course, if they be true, hold good against the high-school course, although to a more limited extent. Is it not true that our whole system of higher education—high school, academy, college, and university—is calculated to turn students aside from commercial pursuits? Is it not shaped from beginning to end rather to encourage professional life? Is it common to find in our higher schools students who are avowedly preparing for business pursuits? We often hear that there is an overcrowding of the professions. Is not the community which supports the present system of education responsible for this overcrowding? In Germany and France it is understood that only the select few will go to the high schools and universities, and the state provides amply to train the others for their appropriate stations in life. There are not only schools of engineering and architecture, forestry, and mining, but also schools for the teaching of all the trades and arts, and schools for giving the training necessary in the broader realms of commerce. In our own country all of these matters have been left to private enterprise. We have a large number of business and commercial colleges, all private schools, generally with short courses. They have frequently produced good bookkeepers and good stenographers, but is there not reason to believe that their courses have been too narrow in their scope, and that these institutions have trained clerks and assistants, rather than leaders and directors of business enterprises? I do not think these schools can fairly be blamed for this, for they have, doubtless, done the best they could; but I do think the communities may be blamed for not providing, at community expense, those fuller and broader courses of study which few can pursue at private expense. There has been rather too much theorizing in every department of the field of education and too little study of the actual facts. In studying a question of this kind, it would seem to be a wise method of procedure to get the views of the business men themselves, who certainly ought to be interested in this question, and who have most intimate knowledge of the facts in the case. To this end, I have undertaken a little study in inductive pedagogy. I prepared and sent out to a large number of business men and bankers, mainly in the city of Chicago, a syllabus, the names having been selected by gentlemen who are acquainted with the commercial life of that city, which I will read to you in part. . . .

I have already received a large number of replies, many of them of the greatest value. . . . A good many of the replies express a decided preference for a college education for all who are able to obtain it, independent of its value in business. Nearly all of them express the belief that it is well for everyone to obtain all the knowledge possible. But the fact is that for 97 per cent. of our population even a high-school education is out of reach. The answers to the first question, "Should a business man have a college education, or is a high-school education sufficient?" are practically uniformly to the effect that a high-school education is sufficient.

In regard to the second question, "Which is of the most value, the amount of knowledge gained in school or the discipline and control of the mind?" there is no difference of opinion, the discipline and control of the mind being considered of first importance.

The replies to the third question, as to the age when it is best to begin the study of business or banking, are largely in favor of beginning before the age of twenty.

In reply to the fourth question, Latin is generally considered of little practical value. One gentleman, however, qualifies this statement in an interesting way. He says: "It would seem to me that these questions cannot be intelligently answered except under certain qualifications. That you may the better understand what I mean, I will say that the writer hereof has been the chief executive for this business for the past twenty-six years, in the important departments known in trade as law, collection, and credit departments, in which a classical education is not only highly advantageous, but most necessary, while in other branches of the same business such education is in no wise necessary, although, of course, it is desirable. The success of a salesman or a buyer of merchandise does not depend upon his general education. The knowledge of Latin in a business man's training is especially advantageous, provided such a man occupies an executive position, where the dictation of the correspondence connected with the business of the firm becomes a part of his duty."

In reply to Question 5, Greek is not considered of any practical value by anyone.

Replying to Questions 6 and 7, the writers differ somewhat, though scarcely anyone assigns a high value to French and German, except in special cases. German is generally considered more important than French.

In reply to Question 8, mathematics is given a very high position by all those answering.

Chemistry and biology are not considered of special importance, though several emphasize the fact that chemistry is undoubtedly of great value in certain special lines. One says: "A reasonable knowledge of biology is of value. A sound and healthy body being admittedly a feature of a successful business career, such knowledge as pertains to the maintenance of health and to physical improvement is desirable."

On Questions 11 and 12, there is a surprising unanimity of opinion. Not one person fails to mark history and English exceedingly high; and, almost uniformly, English is given the first place. Permit me to quote a few opinions:

"History, particularly philosophical history, is valuable to the business man. It has a tendency to broaden his views, teach him the relation between cause and effect, and show him that present ills are simply repetitions. It is also likely to make him conservative and less apt to be carried away by booms and unsound political and business theories." . . .

"A thorough knowledge of English is essential. Clearness and conciseness of expression are more of a desideratum in banking than in any other calling. The aphorism, 'Time is money,' is the watchword of the banker. Every word must be weighed before it is uttered, and each word as spoken must leave no doubt as to its meaning. How can such a result be obtained without a thorough knowledge of the English language and how to speak it?". . .

If a student of business cannot go to college, ought he to study political economy in the high school? The majority of the replies to this question are in the affirmative, but frequently with some qualification. Some are decidedly in the negative. For example: "Emphatically, no. Political economy, as taught in the schools, is full of errors; the text-books in use are those which originated among different conditions from those with which we are now surrounded. I believe it was Carey who said that scientists, sooner or later, all agree, but political economists never, and gives as a reason that, no matter what theories are advocated, they are bound to conflict with the interests of some one. Hence, the truth can never be arrived at. Political economy is to be taken up by the banker in after years as a relaxation study, and perhaps also as a means of cultivating and gratifying controversial tendencies."

"While political economy cannot be said to be a branch of banking, it leads the mind to a consideration of public questions that enables it better to consider many phases of banking not directly connected with such study."

Another answer to the question is: "Not if free-trade text-books are used." And still another: "Not unless he has ambition to become secretary of the treasury." Another reply is: "If a student cannot go to college, he certainly ought to study political economy in the high school, and follow it his entire life, if he continues to be a merchant." . . .

The replies to the next question, "If a student cannot go to college, ought he to study psychology in the high school?" are, as a rule, in the negative. There are several interesting statements which time will not permit me to quote.

In reply to the question concerning ethics, or moral philosophy, I must content myself with quoting one or two answers:

"As honesty and plain dealing are the foundation of the success of the banker, it is to be presumed that these qualities are inherent, and, therefore, do not require any elaboration whatever as to their *raison d'être*. Consequently, a study of psychology, ethics, or moral philosophy, as a part of the banker's training, is not necessary."

"Psychology, ethics, or moral philosophy, can be left until afterwards, and, in my judgment, bring best results when pursued after finishing the high school." . . .

After these criticisms, let us consider what we have left of the model high-school programme. First, and emphatically, English. This is given first place by everyone. In these model programmes, prepared by the Committee of Ten, English has a total of 11 periods out of 80—practically one-eighth of the time. Is this sufficient time to give to the most important study? Latin, on the other hand, has 18 periods, or nearly twice as much as English. The second subject that we have left in these programmes is history, which receives in these programmes a total of 10 periods out of 80, or one-eighth of the total amount of time. Is this an adequate time allowance for this most important subject? The third subject is mathematics, which has a time allowance of 14 periods out of the 80 in the model programme.

These three fundamental studies of the present high-school course are cordially indorsed as desirable and indispensable in the preparation for a business career. Obviously, they should be made very prominent in any course of study specially devised for students of this kind. The other subjects of the curriculum of a high school, as it exists today, are evidently regarded as of indifferent value—serving well, indeed, the purposes of general education, but not specially important for the business life. Shall we consider for a moment, then, what subjects ought to be added to the existing curriculum?

About the value of political economy, when properly taught from suitable text-books, there seems to be no question whatever. All the business men consulted upon this subject agree as to its importance. It would seem, too, as though there was sufficient basis for introducing some elementary study of ethics and moral philosophy. Another subject is geography, which is entirely neglected in our high-school course. This would, of course, take the form of commercial geography. One gentleman writes that French and German should be taught, not alone for the discipline, but also for practical use. The immediate future of the best banking in the United States will call for much closer communication with Germany and France, giving practical advantage to the banker who both speaks and writes these languages. A number favored the addition of bookkeeping and commercial law, though in regard to commercial law another correspondent has grave doubts. . . . Commercial arithmetic is recommended and this comment given: "There is nothing that will help a young man as much during the first years of his banking experience as being able to add or subtract accurately. In Britain a boy can add or subtract as swiftly and accurately the first day he is in a bank as an experienced clerk can in America. My experience is that American boys have to learn after they enter the bank." Another correspondent recommends the addition of the history of commerce, the history of banking, and the history of economics; also the elements of commercial law, maritime law, and of commercial treaties; along with a thorough training in arithmetic. Another addition suggested is that of the study of "personal economy." We now have, in certain institutions, chairs of domestic economy. The gentleman recommending the establishment of a course in personal economy makes the following comments: "It is not disputed anywhere that personal extravagance is a prominent characteristic of the people of this country. Personal economy must always be one of the essentials to success in business. Put it in."

Another careful correspondent makes the following interesting recommendation:

I would suggest that the study of "human nature," if it could only be reduced to a science, be incorporated in a course of study, for there is nothing which so closely constitutes the key which will open the lock of success as the knowledge of human nature. I do not now recall the name of any science which is particularly applicable to this investigation or study, but I wish to emphasize the fact that there is no one qualification which so promptly and unerringly yields success to one's efforts as the knowledge of human nature, and to know how to handle men with whom one comes in contact. If you will pardon me for elaborating a little on this topic, I will say that I have often thought that it is more closely allied to the practice of medicine than to any other science. If one whose duty it is to control and direct the actions of men has a knowledge, first, of the peculiarities possessed by any given man, and a knowledge also of the specific remedy for that peculiarity, that subject at once comes under complete control, without realizing it, and the operator in the first instance can control the results to be obtained. Like the physician, he must know what ails the patient, and he must know, next, the specific remedy for that particular ailment, and, knowing these, such patient in his hands becomes as the clay in the hands of the molder.

By this I mean, not to control his physical movements, but to control his mental conclusions, to make him think as you think and, as a result, to do as you want him to do in any given business transaction. . . . That is what I mean by the knowledge of human nature; not a magnetic or mesmeric influence, but the ability to read one so closely, after a few moments' conversation, as to be able to handle him so delicately as to secure from him whatever may be sought or wanted in any given premises.

Stenography, typewriting, and bookkeeping are very generally recommended.

The last question on the syllabus was: "Do you favor the establishment of so-called 'commercial high schools,' with a course similar to that herewith inclosed?" This course you have before you. . . . There is practical unanimity of opinion in favor of the establishment of such a course. There is also, however, a great deal of adverse comment on the practice of undertaking to teach actual business transaction in school. The course before you would not seem to be open to criticism along this line. Some of the adverse comments ought, perhaps, to be stated, for they will serve as warning beacons in planning a commercial course that will meet the approval of our business men:

"Unless the commercial high school suggested is less theoretical, impractical, and shiftless than those heretofore established, it will prove a waste of time for the student." . . .

"Business methods cannot be successfully taught by men who have never been in business."

The general testimony concerning the commercial high-school course, which you have before you and which was submitted to these gentlemen for their opinion, is, however, most decidedly favorable. Some of the opinions are as follows: . . .

"I would highly favor the establishment of commercial high schools, with such a course as you have outlined, and am very sure that it would elevate the standards of the coming merchant." . . .

"The outline of the proposed curriculum for a proposed commercial high school is adapted in every way for the education of the business man."

"I do favor the establishment of so-called commercial high schools, emphatically. Such an education would, in my opinion, far outweigh the plans proposed for high-school education. . . ."

Certain important questions now arise which demand discussion, but which I shall not have time to discuss. Should a commercial course be for three years or four years? In case a separate commercial course in high schools cannot be provided, should not provision be made for allowing certain commercial subjects as electives, along with the other subjects of the course? In other words, should not the subjects of political economy, history of commerce, commercial geography, history of industries, etc., be introduced, wherever practicable, and even at some expense, into the present high-school course, as equal in value with biology, chemistry, French, German, botany, geology, physiography, and other subjects that might be mentioned and which are now in all high-school courses? Should not great stress be laid in early years on English, history, and mathematics, which seem to be recognized as the subjects of the greatest importance for business life. Only a comparatively small proportion of those who enter upon a high-school course finish it. The early years, which contain the most students, ought also to contain the studies of the most universal helpfulness. Again, the greatest question concerning the high schools of today is, Where are the boys? In a graduating class of forty there will be three boys and thirty-seven girls. Would the boys not be there if the course contained some studies whose practical value they could appreciate? Would not parents be willing to send them, and the boys be eager to go? Therefore, would not the introduction into our high-school curriculum of commercial subjects, such as have been presented this afternoon, tend to attract the boys to the high school, and thus elevate the educational level of the whole community?

In preparing this brief paper, I did not start out with a theory. I have undertaken to get at the facts from the point of view of the business men —citizens of the community who, after all, pay the bills and, therefore, have a right to say what they shall have in their schools. I have presented, in the main, their answers to my inquiries. I can only regard it as a fortunate coincidence that they seem to agree so thoroughly with my own views. I do not consider this question as in any sense inferior to any question now before the educational public. It is a question that affects our whole country as vitally as any educational problem can. The world is changing, things are not as they were; we must adapt our education to the new conditions; we must bring the work of the schools into the closest relation to the life of the people. I cannot close better than to quote substantially the closing remarks in one of the letters I have received:

I cannot refrain from saying that the chief obstacle, in my opinion, to the success of the young man of higher education is that he has instilled into his mind a contempt for the mercantile calling. If educators were to infuse a spirit of commercial ambition into their pupils, and would emphasize the necessity for an education of usefulness by such a course as you are now contemplating, the choice between commerce and the professions would be more evenly distributed, and many a young man who thinks himself too good for anything but a professional life, and, in consequence, spends his years in drudgery and disappointment, would achieve substantial results as a merchant and be, at the same time, a far greater benefit to the community.

The Immigrant in the Primary Schools

Jane Addams

The following paper is given with great diffidence. The writer has never been a teacher, nor even a close observer, in primary schools. She only had unusual opportunities for seeing the children of immigrants during and after the period of their short school life. She submits some of the observations and reflections which have come to her concerning the great mass of those children who never get beyond the primary grades, in the hope that they may prove suggestive to the educators present. The observations are confined to the children of the Italian colony lying directly east of Hull House, in the nineteenth ward of Chicago, although what is said concerning them might be applied, with certain modifications, to the children of Chicago's large Bohemian and Polish colonies.

For the purpose of this paper it will be best to treat of the school as a social institution, within which a certain concentration of social interests takes place, for the purpose of producing certain social results. This is certainly legitimate, if we take Dr. Dewey's statement that "the school selects, and presents in an organized manner, influences and instruments which may expedite and facilitate the socializing of the individual." Certainly, after the child leaves school his experiences consist of his participation in the social life in the various groups of which he is a member, or with which he comes in contact.

Whatever may be our ultimate conception of education, and however much we may differ in definition, as doubtless the members of this convention do widely differ, we shall probably agree that the ultimate aim is to modify the character and conduct of the individual, and to harmonize and adjust his activities; that even the primary school should aim to give the child's own experience a social value; and that this aim too

Jane Addams, "Foreign-Born Children in the Primary Grades," *Journal of Proceedings and Addresses, National Educational Association* (Chicago, 1897), pp. 104–112.

often fails of success in the brief sojourn of the child of the foreign peasant in the public school.

The members of the nineteenth ward Italian colony are largely from south Italy, Calabrian and Sicilian peasants, or Neapolitans, from the workingmen's quarters of that city. They have come to America with a distinct aim of earning money, and finding more room for the energies of themselves and their children. In almost all cases they mean to go back again, simply because their imaginations cannot picture a continuous life away from the old surroundings. Their experiences in Italy have been that of simple, out-door activity, and the ideas they have have come directly to them from their struggle with nature, such a hand-to-hand struggle as takes place when each man gets his living largely through his own cultivation of the soil, with tools simply fashioned by his own hands. The women, as in all primitive life, have had more diversified activities than the men. They have cooked, spun, and knitted, in addition to their almost equal work in the fields. Very few of the peasant men or women can either read or write. They are devoted to their children, strong in their family feeling to remote relationships, and clannish in their community life.

The entire family has been upheaved, and is striving to adjust itself to its new surroundings. The men for the most part work on railroad extensions through the summer, under the direction of a padrone, who finds the work for them, regulates the amount of their wages, and supplies them with food. The first effect of immigration upon the women is that of idleness. They, of course, no longer work in the fields, nor milk the goats, nor pick up fagots. The mother of the family buys all the clothing not only already spun and woven, but made up into garments of a cut and fashion beyond her powers. It is, indeed, the most economical thing for her to do. Her house cleaning and cooking are of the simplest; the bread is usually baked outside of the house, and the macaroni bought prepared for boiling. All of those outdoor and domestic activities, which she would naturally have handed on to her daughters, have slipped away from her. The domestic arts are gone, with all their absorbing interests for the children, their educational value and incentive to activity. A household in a tenement receives almost no raw material. For the hundreds of children who have never seen wheat grow there are dozens who have never seen bread baked. The occasional washings and scrubbings are associated only with discomfort. The child of these families receives constantly many stimuli of most exciting sort from his city street life, but he has little or no opportunity to use his energies in domestic manufacture, or, indeed, constructively, in any direction. No activity is supplied to take the place of that which, in Italy, he would naturally have found in his own home, and no new union is made for him with wholesome life.

Italian parents count upon the fact that their children learn the English language and American customs before they themselves do, and act not only as interpreters of the language about them, but as buffers between them and Chicago, and this results in a certain, almost pathetic dependence of the family upon the child. When a member of the family, therefore, first goes to school, the event is fraught with much significance to all the others. The family has no social life in any structural form, and can supply none to the child. If he receives it in the school, and gives it to his family, the school would thus become the connector with the organized society about them.

It is the children aged six, eight, and ten who go to school, entering, of course, the primary grades. If a boy is twelve or thirteen on his arrival in America, his parents see in him a wage-earning factor, and the girl of the same age is already looking toward her marriage.

Let us take one of these boys, who has learned in his six or eight years to speak his native language, and to feel himself strongly identified with the fortunes of his family.

Whatever interest has come to the minds of his ancestors has come through the use of their hands in the open air; and open air and activity of body have been the inevitable accompaniments of all their experiences. Yet the first thing that the boy must do when he reaches school is to sit still, at least part of the time, and he must learn to listen to what is said to him, with all the perplexity of listening to a foreign tongue. He does not find this very stimulating, and is slow to respond to the more subtle incentives of the schoolroom. The peasant child is perfectly indifferent to showing off and making a good recitation. He leaves all that to his schoolfellows who are more sophisticated and who are equipped with better English. It is not the purpose of this paper to describe the child's life in school, which the audience knows so much better than the writer, but she ventures to assert that if the little Italian lad were supplied, then and there, with tangible and resistance-offering material upon which to exercise his muscle, he would go bravely to work, and he would probably be ready later to use the symbols of letters and numbers to record and describe what he had done; and might even be incited to the exertion of reading to find out what other people had done. Too often the teacher's conception of her duty is to transform him into an American of a somewhat snug and comfortable type, and she insists that the boy's powers must at once be developed in an abstract direction, quite ignoring the fact that his parents have had to do only with tangible things. She has little idea of the development of Italian life. Her outlook is national and not racial, and she fails, therefore, not only in knowledge of, but also in respect for, the child and his parents. She quite honestly estimates the child upon an American basis. The contempt for the experiences and languages of their parents which foreign children sometimes exhibit, and which is most damaging to their moral as well as intellectual life, is doubtless due in part to the overestimation which the school places upon speaking and reading in English. This cutting into his family loyalty takes away one of the most conspicuous and valuable traits of the Italian child.

His parents are not specially concerned in keeping him in school, and will not hold him there against his inclination, until his own interest shall do it for him. Their experience does not point to the good American tradition that it is the educated man who finally succeeds. The richest man on Ewing street can neither read nor write—even Italian. His cunning and acquisitiveness, combined with the credulity and ignorance of his countrymen, have slowly brought about his large fortune.

The child himself may feel the stirring of a vague ambition to go on until he is as the other children are; but he is not popular with his school-fellows, and he sadly feels the lack of dramatic interest. Even the pictures and objects presented to him, as well as the language, are strange.

If we admit that in education it is necessary to begin with the experiences which the child already has, through his spontaneous and social activity, then the city street begins this education for him in a more natural way than does the school.

The south Italian peasant comes from a life of picking olives and oranges, and he easily sends his children out to pick up coal from railroad tracks or wood from buildings which have been burned down. Unfortunately, this process leads by easy transition to petty thieving. It is easy to go from the coal on the railroad track to the coal and wood which stand before the dealer's shop; from the potatoes which have rolled from a rumbling wagon to the vegetables displayed by the grocer. This is apt to be the record of the boy who responds constantly to the stimuli and temptations of the street, although in the beginning his search for bits of food and fuel was prompted by the best of motives. The outlets offered to such a boy by the public school have failed to attract him, and as a truant he accepts this ignoble use of his inherited faculty. For the dynamic force which the boy has within himself, the spirit of adventure and restless activity, many unfortunate outlets are constantly offered.

The school, of course, has to compete with a great deal from the outside in addition to the distractions of the neighborhood. Nothing is more fascinating than that mysterious "down town," whither the boy longs to go to sell papers and black boots; to attend theaters, and, if possible, to stay all night, on the pretense of waiting for the early edition of the great dailies. If a boy is once thoroughly caught in these excitements, nothing can save him from overstimulation, and consequent debility and worthlessness, but a vigorous application of a compulsory-education law, with a truant school; which, indeed, should have forestalled the possibility of his ever thus being caught.

It is a disgrace to us that we allow so many Italian boys thus to waste their health in premature, exciting activity; and their mentality in mere cunning, which later leaves them dissolute and worthless men, with no habits of regular work and a distaste for its dullness.

These boys are not of criminal descent, nor vagrant heritage. On the contrary, their parents have been temperate, laborious, and painstaking, living for many generations on one piece of ground.

Had these boys been made to feel their place in the school community; had they been caught by its fascinations of marching and singing together as a distinct corps; had they felt the charm of manipulating actual material, they might have been spared this erratic development. Mark Crawford, for many years the able superintendent of the Chicago House of Corrections, has said that in looking over the records of that institution he found that of 21,000 boys under seventeen years of age who had been sent there under sentence less than eighty were schoolboys. . . .

Leaving the child who does not stay in school, let us now consider the child who does faithfully remain until he reaches the age of factory work, which is, fortunately, in the most advanced of our factory states, fourteen years. Has anything been done up to this time, has even a beginning been made, to give him a consciousness of his social value? Has the outcome of the processes to which he has been subjected adapted him to deal more effectively and in a more vital manner with his present life?

Industrial history in itself is an interesting thing, and the story of the long struggle of man in his attempts to bring natural forces under human control could be made most dramatic and graphic. The shops and factories all about him contain vivid and striking examples of the high development of the simple tools which his father still uses, and of the lessening expenditure of human energy. He is certainly cut off from nature, but he might be made to see nature as the background and material for the human activity which now surrounds him. Giotto portrayed the applied arts and industries in a series of such marvelous beauty and interest that every boy who passed the Shepherd's Tower longed to take his place in the industrial service of the citizens of Florence. We, on the contrary, have succeeded in keeping our factories, so far as the workers in them are concerned, totally detached from that life which means culture and growth.

No attempt is made to give a boy, who, we know, will certainly have to go into one of them, any insight into their historic significance, or to connect them in any intelligible way with the past and future. He has absolutely no consciousness of his social value, and his activities become inevitably perfectly mechanical. Most of the children who are thus put to work go on in their slavish life without seeing whither it tends, and with no reflections upon it. The brightest ones among them, however, gradually learn that they belong to a class which does the necessary work of life, and that there is another class which tends to absorb the product of that work.

May we not charge it to the public school that it has given to this child no knowledge of the social meaning of his work? Is it not possible that, if the proper estimate of education had been there; if all the children had been taught to use equally and to honor equally both their heads and hands; if they had been made even dimly to apprehend that for an individual to obtain the greatest control of himself for the performance of social service, and to realize within himself the value of the social service which he is performing, is to obtain the fullness of life—the hateful feeling of class distinction could never have grown up in any of them? It would then be of little moment to himself or to others whether the boy finally served the commonwealth in the factory or in the legislature.

But nothing in this larger view of life has reached our peasant's son. He finds himself in the drudgery of a factory, senselessly manipulating unrelated material, using his hands for unknown ends, and his head not at all. Owing to the fact that during his years in school he has used his head mostly, and his hands very little, nothing bewilders him so much as the suggestion that the school was intended as a preparation for his work in life. He would be equally amazed to find that his school was supposed to fill his mind with beautiful images and powers of thought, so that he might be able to do this dull mechanical work, and still live a real life outside of it. . . .

Foreign-born children have all the drudgery of learning to listen to, and read and write an alien tongue; and many never get beyond this first drudgery. I have interrogated dozens of these children who have left school from the third, fourth, and fifth grades, and I have met very few who ever read for pleasure. I have in mind an Italian boy whose arithmetic was connected with real life, while his reading was not. He is the son of a harnessmaker who, although he can neither read nor write, kept his little shop, and slowly made money. The great ambition of his life was that his son Angelo should be enough of a scholar to keep his books and to read him the daily papers; for he had a notion that the latter told you when and how to buy leather to the best advantage. Angelo was kept steadily at school until he was in the fifth grade. He used to come every evening to Hull House for help in his arithmetic, bringing with him slips of paper on which was written the amount of his father's sales during the day. His father himself could not add, but remembered accurately what he had charged for each thing he had disposed of. Before Angelo left school he read fairly well from the Fifth Reader. Five years have passed since then, and, although he keeps the accounts of the shop in which he had a vivid interest from the first, he has almost wholly forgotten how to read. He occasionally picks up a paper and attempts to read it to gratify his father, but he reads it badly and much dislikes the proceeding.

There is one fixed habit, however, which the boy carries away from school with him to the factory. Having the next grade continually before him as an object of attainment results in the feeling that his work is merely provisional, and that its sole use is to get him ready for other things. This tentative attitude takes the last bit of social stimulus out of his factory work, and he pursues it merely as a necessity. His last chance for a realization of social consciousness is gone.

From one point of view the school itself is an epitome of the competitive system, almost of the factory system. Certain standards are held up and worked for; and, even in the school, the child does little work with real joy and spontaneity. The pleasure which comes from creative effort, the thrill of production, is only occasional, and not the sustaining motive which keeps it going. The child in school often contracts the habit of expecting to do his work in certain hours, and to take his pleasure in certain other hours; quite in the same spirit as he later earns his money by ten hours of dull factory work, and spends it in three hours of lurid and unprofitable pleasure in the evening. Both in the school and the factory his work has been dull and growing duller, and his pleasure must constantly grow more stimulating. Only occasionally, in either place, has he had a glimpse of the real joy of doing a thing for its own sake. . . .

If the army of school children who enter the factories every year possessed thoroughly vitalized faculties, they might do much to lighten this incubus of dull factory work which presses so heavily upon so large a number of our fellow-citizens. Has our commercialism been so strong that our schools have become insensibly commercialized, rather than that our industrial life has felt the broadening and illuminating effect of the schools?

The boy in the primary grades has really been used as material to be prepared for the grammar grades. Unconsciously his training, so far as it has been vocational at all, has been in the direction of clerical work. Is it possible that the business men, whom we have so long courted and worshiped in America, have really been dictating the curriculum of our public schools, in spite of the conventions of educators and the suggestions of university professors? The business man has, of course, not said to himself: "I will have the public school train office boys and clerks for me, so that I may have them cheap"; but he has thought, and sometimes said: "Teach the children to write legibly, and to figure accurately and quickly; to acquire habits of punctuality and order; to be prompt to obey, and not question why; and you will fit them to make their way in the world as I have made mine."

Has the workingman been silent as to what he desires for his children, and allowed the business man to decide for him there as he has allowed the politician to manage his municipal affairs? Or has the workingman suffered from our universal optimism, and really believed that his children would never need to go into industrial life at all, but that his sons would all become bankers and merchants?

Certain it is that no sufficient study has been made of the child who enters into industrial life early, and remains there permanently, to give him some set-off to its monotony and dullness; some historic significance of the part he is taking in the life of the commonwealth; some conception of the dignity of labor, which is sometimes mentioned to him, but never demonstrated. We have a curious notion, in spite of all our realism, that it is not possible for the mass of mankind to have interests and experiences of themselves which are worth anything. We transmit to the children of working people our own skepticism regarding the possibility of finding any joy or profit in their work. We practically incite them to get out of it as soon as possible.

I am quite sure that no one can possibly mistake this paper as a plea for trade schools, or as a desire to fit the boy for any given industry. Such a specializing would indeed be stupid when our industrial methods are developing and changing, almost day by day. But it does contend that life, as seen from the standpoint of the handworker, should not be emptied of all social consciousness and value, and that the school could make the boy infinitely more flexible and alive than he is now to the materials and forces of nature which, in spite of all man's activities, are unchangeable.

We do not wish to hold the school responsible for what should be charged up to the industrial system, but we may certainly ask that our schools shall not feed and perpetuate the baser features and motives of that system.

The isolation of the school from life—its failure to make life of more interest, and show it in its larger aspects—the mere equipping of the children with the tools of reading and writing, without giving them an absorbing interest concerning which they wish to read and write, certainly tends to defeat the very purpose of education. . . .

Ethical Principles in Education

John Dewey

It is quite clear that there cannot be two sets of ethical principles, or two forms of ethical theory, one for life in the school, and the other for life outside of the school. As conduct is one, the principles of conduct are one also. The frequent tendency to discuss the morals of the school, as if the latter were an institution by itself, and as if its morale could be stated without reference to the general scientific principles of conduct, appears to me highly unfortunate. Principles are the same. It is the special points of contact and application which vary with different conditions. I shall make no apology, accordingly, for commencing with statements which seem to me of universal validity and scope, and afterwards considering the moral work of the school as a special case of these general principles. . . .

All ethical theory is two faced. It requires to be considered from two different points of view, and stated in two different sets of terms. These are the social and the psychological. We do not have here, however, a division, but simply a distinction. Psychological ethics does not cover part of the field, and then require social ethics to include the territory left untouched. Both cover the entire sphere of conduct. Nor does the distinction mark a compromise, or a fusion, as if at one point the psychological view broke down, and needed to be supplemented by the sociological. Each theory is complete and coherent within itself, so far as its own end or purpose is concerned. But conduct is of such a nature as to require to be stated throughout from two points of view. How this distinction happens to exist may perhaps be guessed by calling to mind that the individual and society are neither opposed to each other nor separated from each other. Society is a society of individuals and the individual is always a social individual. He has no existence by himself. He lives in, for, and by society, just as society has no existence excepting in and through the individuals who constitute it. But we can state one and the

John Dewey, "Ethical Principles Underlying Education," *The Third Yearbook of the National Herbart Society* (Chicago, 1897), pp. 7–26.

same process (as, for example, telling the truth) either from the standpoint of what it effects in society as a whole, or with reference to the particular individual concerned. The latter statement will be psychological; the former, social as to its purport and terms.

If, then, the difference is simply a point of view, we first need to find out what fixes the two points of view. Why are they necessary? Because conduct itself has two aspects. On one side conduct is a form of activity. It is a mode of operation. It is something which somebody does. There is no conduct excepting where there is an agent. From this standpoint conduct is a process having its own form or mode, having, as it were, its own running machinery. That is, it is something which the agent does in a certain way; something which is an outcome of the agent himself, and which effects certain changes within the agent considered as an agent or doer. Now when we ask how conduct is carried on, what sort of a *doing* it is, when, that is to say, we discuss it with reference to an agent from whom it springs, and whose powers it modifies, our discussion is necessarily psychological. Psychology thus fixes for us the *how* of conduct, the way in which it takes place. Consideration from this standpoint is necessary because it is obvious that modifications in results or products must flow from changes in the agent or doer. If we want to get different things done, we must begin with changing the machinery which does them. . . .

But conduct has a *what* as well as a how. There is something done as well as a way in which it is done. There are ends, outcomes, results, as well as ways, means and processes. Now when we consider conduct from this standpoint (with reference, that is to say, to its actual filling, content, or concrete worth) we are considering conduct from a social standpoint—from the place which it occupies, not simply with reference to the person who does it, but with reference to the whole living situation into which it enters. . . .

We may illustrate by reference to business life. A man starts in a business of manfacturing cotton cloth. Now this occupation of his may be considered from two standpoints. The individual who makes the cloth does not originate the demand for it. Society needs the cloth, and thereby furnishes the end or aim to the individual. It needs a certain amount of cloth, and cloth of certain varying qualities and patterns. It is this situation, outside the mere operations of the manufacturer, which fixes the meaning and value of what he does. If it were not for these social needs and demands, the occupation of the manufacturer would be purely formal. He might as well go out into the wilderness and heap up and tear down piles of sand.

But on the other side society must have its needs met, its ends realized, through the activities of some specific individual or group of individuals. The needs will forever go unsatisfied unless somebody takes it as his special business to supply them. So we may consider the manufactory of cotton cloth, not only from the standpoint of the position which it occupies in the larger social whole, but also as a mode of operation which simply as a mode is complete in itself. After the manufacturer has determined the ends which he has to meet (the kinds and amounts of cloth he needs to produce) he has to go to work to consider the cheapest and best modes of producing them, and of getting them to the market. He has to transfer his attention from the ends to the means. He has to see how to make his factory, considered as a mode of activity, the best possible organized agency within itself. No amount of reflection upon how badly society needs cloth will help him here. He has to think out his problem in terms of the number and kind of machines which he will use, the number of men which he will employ, how much he will pay them, how and where he will buy his raw material, and through what instrumentalities he will get his goods to the market. Now while this question is ultimately only a means to the larger social end, yet in order that it may become a true means, and accomplish the work which it has to do, it must become, for the time being, an end in itself. It must be stated, in other words, in terms of the factory as a working agency. . . .

Let us change the scene of discussion to the school. The child who is educated there is a member of society and must be instructed and cared for as such a member. The moral responsibility of the school, and of those who conduct it, is to society. The school is fundamentally an institution erected by society to do a certain specific work—to exercise a certain specific function in maintaining the life and advancing the welfare of society. The educational system which does not recognize this fact as entailing upon it an ethical responsibility is derelict and a defaulter. It is not doing what it is called into existence to do, and what it pretends to do. Hence the necessity of discussing the entire structure and the specific working of the school system from a standpoint of its moral position and moral function.

The above is commonplace. But the idea is ordinarily taken in too limited and rigid a way. The social work of the school is often limited to training for citizenship and citizenship is then interpreted in a narrow sense as meaning capacity to vote intelligently, a disposition to obey laws, etc. But it is futile to contract and cramp the ethical responsibility of the school in this way. The child is one, and he must either live his life as an integral unified being or suffer loss and create friction. To pick out one of the manifold social relations which the child bears, and to define the work of the school with relation to that, is like instituting a vast and complicated system of physical exercise which would have for its object simply the development of the lungs and the power of breathing, independent of other organs and functions. The child is an organic whole, intellectually, socially, and morally, as well as physically. The ethical aim which determines the work of the school must accordingly be interpreted in the most comprehensive and organic spirit. We must take the child as a member of society in the broadest sense and demand whatever is necessary to enable the child to recognize all his social relations and to carry them out.

The child is to be not only a voter and a subject of law; he is also to be a member of a family, himself responsible, in all probability, in turn, for rearing and training of future children, and thus maintaining the continuity of society. He is to be a worker, engaged in some occupation which will be of use to society, and which will maintain his own independence and self-respect. He is to be a member of some particular neighborhood and community, and must contribute to the values of life, add to the decencies and graces of civilization wherever he is. These are bare and formal statements, but if we let our imagination translate them into their concrete details we have a wide and varied scene. For the child properly to take his place with reference to these various functions means training in science, in art, in history; command of the fundamental methods of inquiry and the fundamental tools of intercourse and communication; it means a trained and sound body, skillful eye and hand; habits of industry, perseverance, and, above all, habits of serviceableness. To isolate the formal relationship of citizenship from the whole system of relations with which it is actually interwoven; to suppose that there is any one particular study or mode of treatment which can make the child a good citizen; to suppose, in other words, that a good citizen is anything more than a thoroughly efficient and serviceable member of society, one with all his powers of body and mind under control, is a cramped superstition which it is hoped may soon disappear from educational discussion.

One point more. The society of which the child is to be a member is, in the United States, a democratic and progressive society. The child must be educated for leadership as well as for obedience. He must have power of self-direction and power of directing others, powers of administration, ability to assume positions of responsibility. This necessity of educating for leadership is as great on the industrial as on the political side. The affairs of life are coming more and more under the control of insight and skill in perceiving and effecting combinations.

Moreover, the conditions of life are in continual change. We are in the midst of a tremendous industrial and commercial development. New inventions, new machines, new methods of transportation and intercourse are making over the whole scene of action year by year. It is an absolute impossibility to educate the child for any fixed station in life. So far as education is conducted unconsciously or consciously on this basis, it results in fitting the future citizen for no station in life, but makes him a drone, a hanger-on, or an actual retarding influence in the onward movement. Instead of caring for himself and for others, he becomes one who has himself to be cared for. Here, too, the ethical responsibility of the school on the social side must be interpreted in the broadest and freest spirit; it is equivalent to that training of the child which will give him such possession of himself that he may take charge of himself; may not only adapt himself to the changes which are going on, but have power to shape and direct those changes.

It is necessary to apply this conception of the child's membership in society more specifically to determining the ethical principles of education.

Apart from the thought of participation in social life the school has no end nor aim. As long as we confine ourselves to the school as an isolated institution we have no final directing ethical principles, because we have no object or ideal. But it is said the end of education may be stated in purely individual terms. For example, it is said to be the harmonious development of all the powers of the individual. Here we have no apparent reference to social life or membership, and yet it is argued we have an adequate and thoroughgoing definition of what the goal of education is. But if this definition is taken independently of social relationship we shall find that we have no standard or criterion for telling what is meant by any one of the terms concerned. We do not know what a power is; we do not know what development is; we do not know what harmony is; a power is a power with reference to the use to which it is put, the function it has to serve. There is nothing in the make-up of a human being, taken in an isolated way, which furnishes controlling ends and serves to mark out powers. If we leave out the aim supplied from social life we have nothing but the old "faculty psychology" to fall back upon to tell what is meant by power in general or what the specific powers are. The idea reduces itself to enumerating a lot of faculties like perception, memory, reasoning, etc., and then stating that each one of these powers needs to be developed. But this statement is barren and formal. It reduces training to an empty gymnastic.

Acute powers of observation and memory might be developed by studying Chinese characters; acuteness in reasoning might be got by discussion of the scholastic subtleties of the Middle Ages. The simple fact is that there is no isolated faculty of observation, or memory, or reasoning any more than there is an original faculty of blacksmithing, carpentering, or steam engineering. These faculties simply mean that particular impulses and habits have been coordinated and framed with reference to accomplishing certain definite kinds of work. Precisely the same thing holds of the so-called mental faculties. They are not powers in themselves, but are such only with reference to the ends to which they are put, the services which they have to perform. Hence they cannot be located nor discussed as powers on a theoretical, but only on a practical basis. We need to know the social situations with reference to which the individual will have to use ability to observe, recollect, imagine, and reason before we get any intelligent and concrete basis for telling what a training of mental powers actually means either in its general principles or in its working details.

We get no moral ideals, no moral standards for school life excepting as we so interpret in social terms. To understand what the school is actually doing, to discover defects in its practice, and to form plans for its progress means to have a clear conception of what society requires and of the relation of the school to these requirements. It is high time, however, to apply this general principle so as to give it a somewhat more definite content. What does the general principle signify when we view the existing school system in its light? What defects does this principle point out? What changes does it indicate?

The fundamental conclusion is that the school must be itself made into a vital social institution to a very much greater extent than obtains at present. I am told that there is a swimming school in the city of Chicago where youth are taught to swim without going into the water, being repeatedly drilled in the various movements which are necessary for swimming. When one of the young men so trained was asked what he did when he got into the water, he laconically replied, "Sunk." The story happens to be true; if it were not, it would seem to be a fable made expressly for the purpose of typifying the prevailing status of the school, as judged from the standpoint of its ethical relationship to society. The school cannot be a preparation for social life excepting as it reproduces, within itself, the typical conditions of social life. The school at present is engaged largely upon the futile task of Sisyphus. It is endeavoring to form practically an intellectual habit in children for use in a social life which is, it would almost seem, carefully and purposely kept away from any vital contact with the child who is thus undergoing training. The only way to prepare for social life is to engage in social life. To form habits of social usefulness and serviceableness apart from any direct social need and motive, and apart from any existing social situation, is, to the letter, teaching the child to swim by going through motions outside of the water. The most indispensable condition is left out of account, and the results are correspondingly futile.

The much and commonly lamented separation in the schools between intellectual and moral training, between acquiring information and growth of character, is simply one expression of the failure to conceive and construct the school as a social institution, having social life and value within itself. Excepting in so far as the school is an embryonic yet typical community life, moral training must be partly pathological and partly formal. It is pathological inasmuch as the stress comes to be laid upon correcting wrongdoing instead of upon forming habits of positive service. The teacher is necessarily forced into a position where his concern with the moral life of the pupils takes largely the form of being on the alert for failures to conform to the school rules and routine. These regulations, judged from the standpoint of the development of the child at the time, are more or less conventional and arbitrary. They are rules which have to be made in order that the existing modes of school work may go on; but the lack of inherent necessity in the school is somewhat arbitrary. Any conditions which compel the teacher to take note of failures rather than of healthy growth put the emphasis in the wrong place and result in distortion and perversion. Attending to wrongdoing ought to be an incident rather than the important phase. The child ought to have a positive consciousness of what he is about, and to be able to judge and criticise his respective acts from the standpoint of their reference to the work which he has to do. Only in this way does he have a normal and healthy standard, enabling him properly to appreciate his failures and to estimate them at their right value.

By saying that the moral training of the school is partly formal, I mean that the moral habits which are specially emphasized in the school are habits which are created, as it were, *ad hoc.* Even the habits of promptness, regularity, industry, non-interference with the work of others, faithfulness to tasks imposed, which are specially inculcated in the school, are habits which are morally necessary simply because the school system is what it is, and must be preserved intact. If we grant the inviolability of the school system as it is, these habits represent permanent and necessary moral ideas; but just in so far as the school system is itself isolated and mechanical, the insistence upon these moral habits is more or less unreal, because the ideal to which they relate is not itself necessary. The duties, in other words, are distinctly school duties, not life duties. If we compare this with the well-ordered home, we find that the duties and responsibilities which the child has to recognize and assume there are not such as belong to the family as a specialized and isolated institution, but flow from the very nature of the social life in which the family participates and to which it contributes. The child ought to have exactly the same motives for right doing, and be judged by exactly the same standard in the school, as the adult in the wider social life to which he belongs. Interest in the community welfare, an interest, that is to say, in perceiving whatever makes for social order and progress, and for carrying these principles into execution—is the ultimate ethical habit to which all the special school habits must be related if they are to be animated by the breath of moral life.

We may apply this conception of the school as a social community which reflects and organizes in typical form the fundamental principles of all community life, to both the methods and the subject-matter of instruction.

As to methods, this principle when applied means that the emphasis must be upon construction and giving out, rather than upon absorption and mere learning. We fail to recognize how essentially individualistic the latter methods are, and how unconsciously, yet certainly and effectively, they react into the child's ways of judging and of acting. Imagine forty children all engaged in reading the same books, and in preparing and reciting the same lessons day after day. Suppose that this constitutes by far the larger part of their work, and that they are continually judged from the standpoint of what they are able to take in in a study hour, and to reproduce in a recitation hour. There is next to no opportunity here for any social or moral division of labor. There is no opportunity for each child to work out something specifically his own, which he may contribute to the common stock, while he, in turn, participates in the productions of others. All are set to do exactly the same work and turn out the same results. The social spirit is not cultivated—in fact, in so far as this method gets in its work, it gradually atrophies for lack of use. It is easy to see, from the intellectual side, that one reason why reading aloud in school is as poor as it is is that the real motive for the use of language—the desire to communicate and to learn—is not utilized. The child knows perfectly well that the teacher and all his fellow pupils have exactly the same facts and ideas before them that he has; he is not giving them anything at all new. But it may be questioned whether the moral lack is not as great as the intellectual. The child is born with a natural desire to give out, to do, and that means to serve. When this tendency is not made use of, when conditions are such that other motives are substituted, the reaction against the social spirit is much larger than we have any idea of—especially when the burden of the work, week after week, and year after year, falls upon this side.

But lack of cultivation of the social spirit is not all: Positively individualistic motives and standards are inculcated. Some stimulus must be found to keep the child at his studies. At the best this will be his affection for his teacher, together with a feeling that in doing this he is not violating school rules, and thus is negatively, if not positively, contributing to the good of the school. I have nothing to say against these motives as far as they go, but they are inadequate. The relation between the piece of work to be done and affection for a third person is external, not intrinsic. It is therefore liable to break down whenever the external conditions are changed. Moreover this attachment to a particular person, while in a way social, may become so isolated and exclusive as to be positively selfish in quality. In any case, it is necessary that the child should gradually grow out of this relatively external motive, into an appreciation of the social value of what he has to do for its own sake, and because of its relations to life as a whole, not as pinned down to two or three people.

But unfortunately the motive is not always at this relative best, while it is always mixed with lower motives which are distinctly individualistic. Fear is a motive which is almost sure to enter in—not necessarily physical fear, or of punishment, but fear of losing the approbation of others; fear of failure so extreme and sensitive as to be morbid. On the other side, emulation and rivalry enter in. Just because all are doing the same work, and are judged (both in recitation and in examination, with reference to grading and to promotion) not from the standpoint of their motives or the ends which they are trying to reach, the feeling of superiority is unduly appealed to. The children are judged with reference to their capacity to present the same external set of facts and ideas. As a consequence they must be placed in the hierarchy on the basis of this purely objective standard. The weaker gradually lose their sense of capacity, and accept a position of continuous and persistent inferiority. The effect of this upon both self-respect and respect for work need not be dwelt upon. The stronger grow to glory, not in their strength, but in the fact that they are stronger. The child is prematurely launched into the region of individualistic competition, and this in a direction where competition is least applicable, viz., in intellectual and spiritual matters, whose law is cooperation and participation.

I cannot stop to paint the other side. I can only say that the introduction of every method which appeals to the child's active powers, to his capacities in construction, production, and creation, marks an opportunity to shift the center of ethical gravity from an absorption which is selfish to a service which is social: I shall have occasion later on to speak of these same methods from the psychological side, that is, their relation to the development of the particular powers of the child. I am here speaking of these methods with reference to the relation which they bear to a sense of community life, to a feeling of a division of labor which enables each one to make his own contribution, and to produce results which are to be judged not simply as intellectual results but from the motive of devotion to work, and of usefulness to others.

Manual training is more than manual; it is more than intellectual; in the hands of any good teacher it lends itself easily, and almost as a matter of course, to development of social habits. Ever since the philosophy of Kant it has been a commonplace in the theory of art, that one of its indispensable features is that it be universal, that is, that it should not be the product of any purely personal desire or appetite, or be capable of merely individual appropriation, but should have its value participated in by all who perceive it. . . .

The principle of the school as itself a representative social institution may be applied to the subject-matter of instruction—must be applied if the divorce between information and character is to be overcome.

A casual glance at pedagogical literature will show that we are much in need of an ultimate criterion for the values of studies, and for deciding what is meant by content value and by form value. At present we are apt to have two, three, or even four different standards set up, by which different values—as disciplinary, culture and information values—are measured. There is no conception of any single unifying principle. The point here made is that the extent and way in which a study brings the pupil to consciousness of his social environment, and confers upon him the ability to interpret his own powers from the standpoint of their possibilities in social use, is this ultimate and unified standard.

The distinction of form and content value is becoming familiar, but, so far as I know, no attempt has been made to give it rational basis. I submit the following key to the distinction: A study from a certain point of view serves to introduce the child to a consciousness of the make-up or structure of social life; from another point of view, it serves to introduce him to a knowledge of, and command over, the instrumentalities through which the society carries itself along. The former is the content value; the latter is the form value. Form is thus in no sense a term of depreciation. Form is as necessary as content. Form represents, as it were, the technique, the adjustment of means involved in social action, just as content refers to the realized value or end of social action. What is needed is not a depreciation of form, but a correct placing of it, that is, seeing that since it is related as means to end, it must be kept in subordination to an end, and taught in relation to the end. The distinction is ultimately an ethical one because it relates not to anything found in the study from a purely intellectual or logical point of view, but to the studies considered from the standpoint of the ways in which they develop a consciousness of the nature of social life, in which the child is to live.

I take up the discussion first from the side of content. The contention is that a study is to be considered as bringing the child to realize the social scene of action; that when thus considered it gives a criterion for the selection of material and for the judgment of value. At present, as already suggested, we have three independent values set up: one of culture, another of information, and another of discipline. In reality these refer only to three phases of social interpretation. Information is genuine or educative only in so far as it effects definite images and conceptions of material placed in social life. Discipline is genuine and educative only as it represents a reaction of the information into the individual's own powers so that he can bring them under control for social ends. Culture, if it is to be genuine and educative, and not an external polish or factitious varnish, represents the vital union of information and discipline. It designates the socialization of the individual in his whole outlook upon life and mode of dealing with it.

This abstract point may be illustrated briefly by reference to a few of the school studies. In the first place there is no line of demarkation within facts themselves which classifies them as belonging to science, history, or geography, respectively. The pigeonhole classification which is so prevalent at present (fostered by introducing the pupil at the outset into a number of different studies contained in different text-books) gives an utterly erroneous idea of the relations of studies to each other, and to the intellectual whole to which they all belong. In fact these subjects have all to do with the same ultimate reality, namely, the conscious experience of man. It is only because we have different interests, or different ends, that we sort out the material and label part of it science, part history, part geography, and so on. Each of these subjects represents an arrangement of materials with reference to some one dominant or typical aim or process of the social life.

This social criterion is necessary not only to mark off the studies from each other, but also to grasp the reasons for the study of each and the motives in connection with which it should be presented. How, for example, shall we define geography? What is the unity in the different so-called divisions of geography—as mathematical geography, physical geography, political geography, commercial geography? Are these purely empirical classifications dependent upon the brute fact that we run across a lot of different facts which cannot be connected with one another, or is there some reason why they are all called geography, and is there some intrinsic principle upon which the material is distributed under these various heads? I understand by intrinsic not something which attaches to the objective facts themselves, for the facts do not classify themselves, but something in the interest and attitude of the human mind towards them. This is a large question and it would take an essay longer than this entire paper adequately to answer it. I raise the question partly to indicate the necessity of going back to more fundamental principles if we are to have any real philosophy of education, and partly to afford, in my answer, an illustration of the principle of social interpretation. I should say that geography has to do with all those aspects of social life which are concerned with the interaction of the life of man and nature; or, that it has to do with the world considered as the scene of social interaction. Any fact, then, will be a geographical fact in so far as it bears upon the dependence of man upon his natural environment, or with the changes introduced in this environment through the life of man.

The four forms of geography referred to above represent then four increasing stages of abstraction in discussing the mutual relation of human life and nature. The beginning must be the commercial geography. I mean by this that the essence of any geographical fact is the consciousness of two persons, or two groups of persons, who are at once separated and connected by the physical environment, and that the interest is in seeing how these people are at once kept apart and brought together in their actions by the instrumentality of this physical environment. The ultimate significance of lake, river, mountain, and plain is not physical but social; it is the part which it plays in modifying and functioning human relationship. This evidently involves an extension of the term commercial. It has not to do simply with business, in the narrow sense, but includes whatever relates to human intercourse and intercommunication as affected by natural forms and properties. Political geography represents this same social interaction taken in a static instead of in a dynamic way; takes it, that is, as temporarily crystallized and fixed in certain forms. Physical geography (including under this not simply physiography, but also the study of flora and fauna) represents a further analysis or abstraction. It studies the conditions which determine human action, leaving out of account, temporarily, the ways in which they concretely do this. Mathematical geography simply carries the analysis back to more ultimate and remote conditions, showing that the physical conditions themselves are not ultimate, but depend upon the place which the world occupies in a larger system. Here, in other words, we have traced, step by step, the links which connect the immediate social occupations and interactions of man back to the whole natural system which ultimately conditioned them. Step by step the scene is enlarged and the image of what enters into the make-up of social action is widened and broadened, but at no time ought the chain of connection to be broken.

It is out of the question to take up the studies one by one and show that their meaning is similarly controlled by social consideration. But I cannot forbear a word or two upon history. History is vital or dead to the child according as it is or is not presented from the sociological standpoint. When treated simply as a record of what has passed and gone, it must be mechanical because the past, as the past, is remote. It no longer has existence and simply as past there is no motive for attending to it. The ethical value of history teaching will be measured by the extent to which it is treated as a matter of analysis of existing social relations—that is to say as affording insight into what makes up the structure and working of society.

This relation of history to comprehension of existing social forces is apparent whether we take it from the standpoint of social order or from that of social progress. Existing social structure is exceedingly complex. It is practically impossible for the child to attack it en masse and get any definite mental image of it. But type phases of historical development may be selected which will exhibit, as through a telescope, the essential constituents of the existing order. Greece, for example, represents what art and the growing power of individual expression stands for; Rome exhibits the political elements and determining forces of political life on a tremendous scale. . . .

History is equally available as teaching the methods of social progress. It is commonly stated that history must be studied from the standpoint of cause and effect. The truth of this statement depends upon its interpretation. Social life is so complex and the various parts of it are so organically related to each other and to the natural environment that it is impossible to say this or that thing is cause of some other particular thing. But what the study of history can effect is to reveal the main instruments in the way of discoveries, inventions, new modes of life, etc., which have initiated the great epochs of social advance, and it can present to the child's consciousness type illustrations of the main lines in which social progress has been made most easily and effectively and can set before him what the chief difficulties and obstructions have been. Progress is always rhythmic in its nature, and from the side of growth as well as from that of status or order it is important that the epochs which are typical should be selected. This once more can be done only in so far as it is recognized that social forces in themselves are always the same—that the same kind of influences were at work 100 and 1000 years ago that are now—and treating the particular historical epochs as affording illustration of the way in which the fundamental forces work.

Everything depends then upon history being treated from a social standpoint, as manifesting the agencies which have influenced social development, and the typical institutions in which social life has expressed itself. The culture epoch theory, while working in the right direction, has failed to recognize the importance of treating past periods with relation to the present—that is, as affording insight into the representative factors of its structure; it has treated these periods too much as if they had some meaning or value in themselves. The way in which the biographical method is handled illustrates the same point. It is often treated in such a way as to exclude from the child's consciousness (or at least not sufficiently to emphasize) the social forces and principles involved in the association of the masses of men. It is quite true that the child is interested easily in history from the biographical standpoint; but unless the hero is treated in relation to the community life behind which he both sums up and directs, there is danger that the history will reduce itself to a mere story. When this is done moral instruction reduces itself to drawing certain lessons from the life of the particular personalities concerned, instead of having widened and deepened the child's imaginative consciousness of the social relationships, ideals, and means involved in the world in which he lives.

There is some danger, I presume, in simply presenting the illustrations without more development, but I hope it will be remembered that I am not making these points for their own sake, but with reference to the general principle that when history is taught as a mode of understanding social life it has positive ethical import. What the normal child continuously needs is not so much isolated moral lessons instilling in him the importance of truthfulness and honesty, or the beneficent results that follow from some particular act of patriotism, etc. It is the formation of habits of social imagination and conception. I mean by this it is necessary that the child should be forming the habit of interpreting the special incidents that occur and the particular situations that present themselves in terms of the whole social life. The evils of the present industrial and political situation, on the ethical side, are not due so much to actual perverseness on the part of individuals concerned, nor in mere ignorance of what constitutes the ordinary virtues (such as honesty, industry, purity, etc.) as to inability to appreciate the social environment in which we live. It is tremendously complex and confused. Only a mind trained to grasp social situations, and to reduce them to their simpler and typical elements, can get sufficient hold on the realities of this life to see what sort of action, critical and constructive, it really demands. Most people are left at the mercy of tradition, impulse, or the appeals of those who have special and class interests to serve. In relation to this highly complicated social environment, training for citizenship is formal and nominal unless it develops the power of observation, analysis, and inference with respect to what makes up a social situation and the agencies through which it is modified. Because history rightly taught is the chief instrumentality for accomplishing this, it has an ultimate ethical value.

I have been speaking so far of the school curriculum on the side of its content. I now turn to that of form; understanding by this term, as already explained, a consciousness of the instruments and methods which are necessary to the control of social movements. Studies cannot be classified into form studies and content studies. Every study has both sides. That is to say, it deals both with the actual make-up of society, and is concerned with the tools or machinery by which society maintains itself. Language and literature best illustrate the impossibility of separation. Through the idea contained in language, the continuity of the social structure is effected. From this standpoint the study of literature is a content study. But language is also distinctly a means, a tool. It not simply has social value in itself, but is a social instrument. However, in some studies one side or the other predominates very much, and in this sense we may speak of specifically form studies. As, for example, mathematics.

My illustrative proposition at this point is that mathematics does, or does not, accomplish its full ethical purpose according as it is presented, or not presented, as such a social tool. The prevailing divorce between information and character, between knowledge and social action, stalks upon the scene here. The moment mathematical study is severed from the place which it occupies with reference to use in social life, it becomes unduly abstract, even from the purely intellectual side. It is presented as a matter of technical relations and formulae apart from any end or use. What the study of number suffers from in elementary education is the lack of motivation. Back of this and that and the other particular bad method is the radical mistake of treating number as if it were an end in itself instead of as a means of accomplishing some end. Let the child get a consciousness of what the use of number is, of what it really is for, and half the battle is won. Now this consciousness of the use or reason implies some active end in view which is always implicitly social since it involves the production of something which may be of use to others, and which is often explicitly social.

One of the absurd things in the more advanced study of arithmetic is the extent to which the child is introduced to numerical operations which have no distinctive mathematical principles characterizing them but which represent certain general principles found in business relationships. To train the child in these operations, while paying no attention to the business realities in which they will be of use, and the conditions of social life which make these business activities necessary, is neither arithmetic nor common sense. The child is called upon to do examples in interest, partnership, banking, brokerage, and so on through a long string, and no pains are taken to see that, in connection with the arithmetic, he has any sense of the social realities involved. This part of arithmetic is essentially sociological in its nature. It ought either to be omitted entirely or else taught in connection with a study of the relevant social realities. As we now manage the study it is the old case of learning to swim apart from the water over again, with correspondingly bad results on the practical and ethical side.*

I am afraid one question still haunts the reader. What has all this discussion about geography, history and number, whether from the side of content or that of form, got to do with the underlying principles of education? The very reasons which induce the reader to put this question to himself, even in a half-formed way, illustrate the very point which I am trying to make. Our conceptions of the ethical in education have been too narrow, too formal, and too pathological. We have associated the term ethical with certain special acts which are labeled virtues and set off from the mass of other acts, and still more from the habitual images and motives in the agents performing them. Moral instruction is thus associated with teaching about these particular virtues, or with instilling certain sentiments in regard to them. The ethical has been conceived in too goody-goody a way. But it is not such ethical ideas and motives as these which keep men at work in recognizing and performing their moral duty. Such teaching as this, after all is said and done, is external; it does not reach

---

* With increasing mental maturity, and corresponding specialization which naturally accompanies it, these various instrumentalities may become ends in themselves. That is, the child may, as he ripens into the period of youth, be interested in number relations for their own sake. What was once method may become an activity in itself. The above statement is not directed against this possibility. It is simply aimed at the importance of seeing to it that the preliminary period—that in which the form or means is kept in organic relationship to real ends and values—is adequately lived through.

down into the depths of the character-making agency. Ultimate moral motives and forces are nothing more nor less than social intelligence—the power of observing and comprehending social situations—and social power—trained capacities of control—at work in the service of social interest and aims. There is no fact which throws light upon the constitution of society, there is no power whose training adds to social resourcefulness which is not ethical in its bearing.

I sum up, then, this part of the discussion by asking your attention to the moral trinity of the school. The demand is for social intelligence, social power, and social interests. Our resources are (1) the life of the school as a social institution in itself; (2) methods of learning and of doing work; and (3) the school studies or curriculum. In so far as the school represents, in its own spirit, a genuine community life; in so far as what are called school discipline, government, order, etc., are the expressions of this inherent social spirit; in so far as the methods used are those which appeal to the active and constructive powers, permitting the child to give out, and thus to serve; in so far as the curriculum is so selected and organized as to provide the material for affording the child a consciousness of the world in which he has to play a part, and the relations he has to meet; in so far as these ends are met, the school is organized on an ethical basis. So far as general principles are concerned, all the basic ethical requirements are met. The rest remains between the individual teacher and the individual child. . . .

PART VII

THE OUTWARD
REACH

A foreign policy is one thing; opinions about foreign affairs, quite an-
other. Historians still differ over the degree to which increasing American
involvement in the affairs of the world in the 1880's and 1890's was the
result of conscious policy. There is little disagreement that, toward the
end of the century, this involvement took place in a climate of increasing
expansionist sentiment. That the United States had increased in power
was the result of industrialization, but that it began to cut a wide swathe
in international affairs was due to a sharpening of the temper of both the
American government and the American people. "A new consciousness
seems to have come upon us," the Washington Post wrote on the eve of
the Spanish-American War,

the consciousness of strength—and with it a new appetite, the yearning to show
our strength. . . . Ambition, interest, land hunger, pride, the mere joy of fighting, whatever it may be, we are animated by a new sensation. . . . The taste of
Empire is in the mouth of the people even as the taste of blood in the jungle.
It means an Imperial policy, the Republic, renascent, taking her place with the
armed nations.

The claim of the Washington Post that this was a "new sensation" was
not wholly true; "manifest destiny"—the ideology of expansionism—had
had a great vogue at the time of the acquisition of Texas and California.
But now it was given a new twist. Infused with notions of Anglo-Saxon
superiority and the Darwinian struggle for existence, the doctrine of
"manifest destiny" seemed thoroughly in accord with the most scientific
ideas of the age, and no one did more to popularize it than John Fiske,
the most important contemporary vulgarizer of the ideas of Darwin.
    Not that Fiske's vision of the future was wholly ungenerous. The ex-
pansion of the English-speaking peoples was in the interest of others, as
well as in their own, for it would usher in an era of peace and plenty such
as the world had never seen. The trouble was that by the end of the cen-
tury evidence was accumulating that even when it was accompanied with
the best of will, contact with Asians and Africans did not always have the
expected results. "Civilization cannot be transferred as a whole," Professor
Paul S. Reinsch warned his audience at the Congress of Arts and Science.
"The greatest mischief is wrought by looking upon the natives as so many
individuals, clay to the hand of the potter, to be fashioned with ease into
some resemblance to European or American. It is only as we modify the
structure, principles, and customs of native societies that we can exert
any lasting influence upon individuals." To attempt too much was worse

447

than nothing at all. "... To take a Tagalog and make of him an American is the naive impulse of inexperience. ... Any attempt to deal with natives ... as individuals in the Western sense will, without fail, endanger their independence, their health, and their life."

More to the point was the abundant evidence that good will was an all-too-infrequent accompaniment of colonial expansion. "Tongues thoroughly trained in trick gymnastics stick at vocables like 'equality,' 'brotherhood,' 'the race,' 'humanity,' much more than when only missionaries had firsthand familiarity with Bushmen and Igorrotes," wrote President E. B. Andrews of the University of Nebraska. "Such a generalization as 'man' does well enough in zoölogy, but in practical ethics it finds its position harder and harder to keep. The changed thought promptly sidles over on to political ground. Having radically subordinated certain races to others, we find it easier, if not inevitable to subordinate certain classes."

For some, the idea and practice of expansionism meant betrayal of American principles of self-government. For Mark Twain, it meant man's betrayal to his own worst instincts.

Manifest Destiny

John Fiske

We have seen how desirable it is that self-governing groups of men should be enabled to work together in permanent harmony and on a great scale. In this kind of political integration the work of civilization very largely consists. We have seen how in its most primitive form political society is made up of small self-governing groups that are perpetually at war with one another. Now the process of change which we call civilization means quite a number of things, but there is no doubt that it means primarily the gradual substitution of a state of peace for a state of war. This change is the condition precedent for all the other kinds of improvement that are connoted by such a term as "civilization." Manifestly the development of industry is largely dependent upon the cessation or restriction of warfare; and furthermore, as the industrial phase of civilization slowly supplants the military phase, men's characters undergo, though very slowly, a corresponding change. Men become less inclined to destroy life or to inflict pain; or to use the popular terminology, which happens to coincide precisely with that of the doctrine of evolution, they become less *brutal* and more *humane*. Obviously, then, the primary phase of the process called civilization is the general diminution of warfare. But we have seen that a general diminution of warfare is rendered possible only by the union of small political groups into larger groups that are kept together by community of interests, and that can adjust their mutual relations by legal discussion, without coming to blows. . . . We considered this process of political integration as variously exemplified by communities of Hellenic, of Roman, and of Teutonic race, and we saw how manifold were the difficulties which the process had to encounter. We saw how the Teutons—at least in Switzerland, England, and America—had succeeded best through the retention of local self-government combined with central representation. We saw how the Romans failed of ultimate success because by weakening self-government they weakened that commu-

John Fiske, "Manifest Destiny," *Harper's New Monthly Magazine,* LXX (1894–1895), 578–590.

nity of interest which is essential to the permanence of a great political aggregate. We saw how the Greeks, after passing through their most glorious period in a state of chronic warfare, had begun to achieve considerable success in forming a pacific federation when their independent career was suddenly cut short by the Roman conqueror.

This last example introduces us to a fresh consideration of very great importance. It is not only that every progressive community has had to solve, in one way or another, the problem of securing permanent concert of action without sacrificing local independence of action, but while engaged in this difficult work the community has had to defend itself against the attacks of other communities. In the case just cited of the conquest of Greece by Rome little harm was done, perhaps. But under different circumstances immense damage may have been done in this way, and the nearer we go to the beginnings of civilization, the greater the danger. At the dawn of history we see a few brilliant points of civilization surrounded on every side by a midnight blackness of barbarism. In order that the pacific community may be able to go on doing its work it must be strong enough and warlike enough to overcome its barbaric neighbors, who have no notion whatever of keeping peace. This is another of the seeming paradoxes of the history of civilization, that for a very long time the possibility of peace can be guaranteed only through war. Obviously the permanent peace of the world can be secured only through the gradual concentration of the preponderant military strength into the hands of the most pacific communities. With infinite toil and trouble this point has been slowly gained by mankind through the circumstance that the very same political aggregation of small primitive communities which makes them less disposed to quarrel among themselves tends also to make them more than a match for the less coherent groups of their more barbarous neighbors. The same concert of action which tends toward internal harmony tends also toward external victory, and both ends are promoted by the co-operation of the same sets of causes. But for a long time all the political problems of the civilized world were complicated by the fact that the community had to fight for its life. We seldom stop to reflect upon the imminent danger from outside attacks, whether from surrounding barbarism or from neighboring civilizations of lower type, amid which the rich and high-toned civilizations of Greece and Rome were developed. The greatest work which the Romans performed in the world was to assume the aggressive against menacing barbarism, to subdue it, to tame it, and to enlist its brute force on the side of law and order. This was a murderous work, but it had to be done by some one before you could expect to have great and peaceful civilizations like our own. . . . Such considerations go far toward explaining the military history of the Romans, and it is a history with which, on the whole, we ought to sympathize. In its European relations that history is the history of the moving of the civilized frontier northward and eastward against the disastrous encroachments of barbarous peoples.

This great movement has, on the whole, been steadily kept up, in spite of some apparent fluctuation in the fifth and sixth centuries of the Christian era, and it is still going on to-day. It was a great gain for civilization when the Romans overcame the Keltiberians of Spain, and taught them good manners and the Latin language, and made it for their interest hereafter to fight against barbarians. The third European peninsula was thus won over to the side of law and order. Danger now remained on the north. The Gauls had once sacked the city of Rome; hordes of Teutons had lately menaced the very heart of civilization, but had been overthrown in murderous combat by Caius Marius. Another great Teutonic movement, led by Ariovistus, now threatened to precipitate the whole barbaric force of southeastern Gaul upon the civilized world; and so it occurred to the prescient genius of Cæsar to be beforehand and conquer Gaul, and enlist all its giant barbaric force on the side of civilization. This great work was as thoroughly done as anything that was ever done in human history, and we ought to be thankful to Cæsar for it every day that we live. The frontier to be defended against barbarism was now moved away up to the Rhine, and was very much shortened; but, above all, the Gauls were made to feel themselves to be Romans. Their country became one of the chief strongholds of civilization and of Christianity; and when the frightful shock of barbarism came—the most formidable blow that has ever been directed by barbaric brute force against European civilization—it was in Gaul that it was repelled and that its force was spent.

At the beginning of the fifth century an enormous horde of yellow Mongolians, known as Huns, poured down into Europe, with avowed intent to burn and destroy all the good work which Rome had wrought in the world, and wonderful was the havoc they effected in the course of fifty years. If Attila had carried his point, it has been thought that the work of European civilization might have had to be begun over again. But near Châlons, on the Marne, in the year 451, in one of the most obstinate struggles of which history preserves the record, the career of the "Scourge of God" was arrested, and mainly by the prowess of Gauls and of Visigoths whom the genius of Rome had tamed. That was the last day on which barbarism was able to contend with civilization on equal terms. It was no doubt a critical day for all future history, and for its favorable issue we must largely thank the policy adopted by Cæsar five centuries before. By the end of the eighth century the great power of the Franks had become enlisted in behalf of law and order, and the Roman throne was occupied by a Frank, the ablest man who had appeared in the world since Cæsar's death, and one of the worthiest achievements of Charles the Great was the conquest and conversion of pagan Germany, which threw the frontier against barbarism eastward as far as the Oder, and made it so much the

easier to defend Europe. In the thirteenth century this frontier was permanently carried forward to the Vistula by the Teutonic Knights, who,
under commission from the Emperor Frederick II., overcame the heathen
Russians and Lithuanians; and now it began to be shown how greatly the
military strength of Europe had increased. In this same century Batu, the
grandson of Jinghis Khan, came down into Europe with a horde of more
than a million of Mongols, and tried to repeat the experiment of Attila.
Batu penetrated as far as Silesia, and won a great battle at Liegnitz in
1241, but in spite of his victory he had to desist from the task of conquering Europe. Since the fifth century the physical power of the civilized
world had grown immensely, and the impetus of this barbaric invasion
was mainly spent upon Russia, the growth of which it succeeded in retarding for more than two centuries. Finally, since the sixteenth century
we have seen the Russians, redeemed from their Mongolian oppressors,
and rich in many of the elements of a vigorous national life—we have seen
the Russians resume the aggressive in this conflict of ages, beginning to do
for Central Asia in some sort what the Romans did for Europe. The Aryan
people, after attaining a high stage of civilization in Europe, are at last
beginning to recover their ancient homestead. The frontier against barbarism, which Cæsar left at the Rhine, has been carried eastward to the
Volga, and is now advancing even to the Oxus. The question has sometimes been raised whether it would be possible for European civilization
to be seriously threatened by any future invasion of barbarism or of some
lower type of civilization. By barbarism certainly not; all the nomad
strength of Mongolian Asia would throw itself in vain against the insuper-
able barrier constituted by Russia. But I have heard it quite seriously suggested that if some future Attila or Jinghis were to wield as a unit the
entire military strength of the four hundred millions of Chinese, possessed
with some suddenly conceived idea of conquering the world, even as
Omar and Abderrahman wielded as a unit the newly welded power of
the Saracens in the seventh and eighth centuries, then perhaps a stagger-
ing blow might yet be dealt against European civilization. I will not
waste precious time in considering this imaginary case further than to remark that if the Chinese are ever going to try anything of this sort, they
can not afford to wait very long; for within another century, as we shall
presently see, their very numbers will be surpassed by those of the English race alone. By that time all the elements of military predominance on
the earth, including that of simple numerical superiority, will have been
gathered into the hands not merely of Europeans generally, but more specifically into the hands of the offspring of the Teutonic tribes who conquered Britain in the fifth century. So far as the relations of European
civilization with outside barbarism are concerned to-day, the only serious
question is by what process of modification the barbarous races are to
maintain their foot-hold upon the earth at all. Where once they threat-

ened the very continuance of civilization, they now exist only on sufferance. . . .

Considering my position thus far as sufficiently illustrated, let us go on to contemplate for a moment some of the effects of all this secular turmoil upon the political development of the progressive nations of Europe. I think we may safely lay it down as a large and general rule that all this prodigious warfare required to free the civilized world from peril of barbarian attack served greatly to increase the difficulty of solving the great initial problem of civilization. In the first place, the turbulence thus arising was a serious obstacle to the formation of closely coherent political aggregates, as we see exemplified in the terrible convulsions of the fifth and sixth centuries, and again in the ascendency acquired by the isolating features of feudalism between the time of Charles the Great and the time of Louis VI. of France. In the second place, this perpetual turbulence was a serious obstacle to the preservation of popular liberties. It is a very difficult thing for a free people to maintain its free constitution if it has to keep perpetually fighting for its life. The "one-man power," less fit for carrying on the peaceful pursuits of life, is sure to be brought into the foreground in a state of endless warfare. It is a still more difficult thing for a free people to maintain its free constitution when it undertakes to govern a dependent people despotically, as has been wont to happen when a portion of the barbaric world has been overcome and annexed to the civilized world. Under the weight of these two difficulties combined the free institutions of the ancient Romans succumbed, and their government gradually passed into the hands of a kind of close corporation, more despotic than anything else of the sort that Europe has ever seen. This despotic character, this tendency, if you will pardon the word, toward the *asiaticization* of European life, was continued by inheritance in the Roman Church, the influence of which was beneficent so long as it constituted a wholesome check to the isolating tendencies of feudalism, but began to become noxious the moment these tendencies yielded to the centralizing monarchical tendency in nearly all parts of Europe.

The asiaticizing tendency of Roman political life had become so powerful by the fourth century, and has since been so powerfully propagated through the Church, that we ought to be glad that the Teutons came into the empire as masters rather than as subjects. As the Germanic tribes got possession of the government in one part of Europe after another they brought with them free institutions again. The political ideas of the Goths in Spain, of the Lombards in Italy, and of the Franks and Burgundians in Gaul were as distinctly free as those of the Angles in Britain. But as the outcome of the long and uninterrupted turmoil of the Middle Ages, society throughout the continent of Europe remained predominantly military in type, and this fact greatly increased the tendency toward despotism which was inherited from Rome. After the close of the thirteenth century the whole power of the Church was finally thrown into the scale against the liberties of the people, and as the result of all these forces combined we find that at the time when America was discovered government was hardening into despotism in all the great countries of Europe except England. Even in England the tendency toward despotism had begun to become quite conspicuous after the wholesale slaughter of the great barons in the wars of the Roses. The whole constitutional history of England during the Tudor and Stuart periods is the history of the persistent effort of the English sovereign to free himself from constitutional checks, as his brother sovereigns on the Continent were doing. But how different the result! How enormous the political difference between William III. and Louis XIV., compared with the difference between Henry VIII. and Francis I.! The close of the seventeenth century, which marks the culmination of the asiaticizing tendency in Europe, saw despotism, both political and religious, firmly established in France and Spain and Italy and in half of Germany, while the rest of Germany seemed to have exhausted itself in the attempt to throw off the incubus. But in England this same epoch saw freedom, both political and religious, established on so firm a foundation as never again to be shaken, never again with impunity to be threatened, so long as the language of Locke and Milton and Sidney shall remain a living speech on the lips of men. Now this wonderful difference between the career of popular liberty in England and on the Continent was due, no doubt, to a complicated variety of causes, one or two of which I have already sought to point out. . . . I alluded to the curious combination of circumstances which prevented anything like a severance of interests between the upper and the lower ranks of society; and something was also said about the feebleness of the grasp of imperial Rome upon Britain compared with its grasp upon the continent of Europe. But what I wish now to point out is the enormous advantage of what we may call the *strategic position* of England in the long mediæval struggle between civilization and barbarism. . . . But as the success of Americans in withstanding the unconstitutional pretensions of the crown was greatly favored by the barrier of the ocean, so the success of Englishmen in defying the enemies of their freedom has no doubt been greatly favored by the barrier of the English Channel. . . . But it was not merely in the simple facility of warding off external attack that the insular position of England was so serviceable. This ease in warding off external attack had its most marked effect upon the internal polity of the nation. It never became necessary for the English government to keep up a great standing army. For purposes of external defense a navy was all-sufficient, and there is this practical difference between a permanent army and a permanent navy: both are originally designed for purposes of external defense, but the one can readily be used for purposes of internal oppression, and the other can not readily be so used. Nobody ever heard of a navy putting up an empire at auction sale, and knocking down the throne of the world to a Didius Julianus. When, therefore, a country is effectually screened by water from external attack, it is screened in a way that permits its normal political development to go on internally without those manifold military hinderances that have ordinarily been so obstructive in the history of civilization. Hence we not only see why, after the Norman conquest had operated to increase its unity and its strength, England enjoyed a far greater amount of security and was far more peaceful than any other country in Europe, but we also see why society never assumed the military type in England which it assumed upon the Continent; we see how it was that the bonds of feudalism were far looser here than elsewhere, and therefore how it happened that nowhere else was the condition of the common people so good politically.

We now begin to see, moreover, how thoroughly Professor Stubbs and Mr. Freeman are justified in insisting upon the fact that the political institutions of the Germans of Tacitus have had a more normal and uninterrupted development in England than anywhere else. . . . In England the free government of the primitive Aryans has been to this day uninterruptedly maintained, though everywhere lost or seriously impaired on the continent of Europe, except in remote Scandinavia and impregnable Switzerland. But obviously, if in the conflict of ages between civilization and barbarism England had occupied such an inferior strategic position as that occupied by Hungary or Poland, or even by France or Spain, no such remarkable and quite exceptional result could have been achieved. Having duly fathomed the significance of this strategic position of the English race while confined within the limits of the British Islands, we are now prepared to consider the significance of the stupendous expansion of the English race, which first became possible through the discovery and settlement of North America. . . .

Chronologically the discovery of America coincides precisely with the close of the Middle Ages, and with the opening of the drama of what is called *modern* history. The coincidence is in many ways significant. The close of the Middle Ages, as we have seen, was characterized by the increasing power of the crown in all the great countries of Europe, and by strong symptoms of popular restlessness in view of this increasing power. It was characterized also by the great Protestant outbreak against the despotic pretensions of the Church, which once, in its antagonism to the rival temporal power, had befriended the liberties of the people, but now (since the death of Boniface VIII.) sought to inthrall them with a tyranny far worse than that of irresponsible king or emperor. As we have seen Aryan civilization in Europe struggling for many centuries to prove itself superior to the assaults of outer barbarism, so here we find a decisive struggle beginning between the antagonistic tendencies which had grown up in the midst of this civilization. Having at length won the privilege of living without risk of slaughter and pillage at the hands of Saracens or Mongols, the question now arose whether the Aryans of Europe should go on and apply their intelligence freely to the problem of making life as rich and fruitful as possible in varied material and spiritual achievement, or should fall into the barren and monotonous way of living and thinking which has always distinguished the half-civilized populations of Asia. This, and nothing less than this, I think, was the practical political question really at stake in the sixteenth century between Protestantism and Catholicism. Holland and England entered the lists in behalf of the one solution of this question, while Spain and the Pope defended the other, and the issue was fought out on European soil, as we have seen, with varying success. But the discovery of America now came to open up an enormous region in which whatever seed of civilization should be planted was sure to grow to such enormous dimensions as by-and-by to exert a controlling influence upon all such controversies. It was for Spain, France, and England to contend for the possession of this vast region, and to prove by the result of the struggle which kind of civilization was endowed with the higher and sturdier political life. The race which here should gain the victory was clearly destined hereafter to take the lead in the world, though the rival powers could not in those days fully appreciate this fact. They who founded colonies in America as trading stations or military outposts probably did not foresee that these colonies must by-and-by become imperial states far greater in physical mass than the states which planted them. When the highly civilized community, representing the ripest political ideas of England, was planted in America, removed from the manifold and complicated checks we have just been studying in the history of the Old World, the growth was portentously rapid and steady. There were no Attilas now to stand in the way—only a Philip or a Pontiac. The assaults of barbarism constituted only a petty annoyance as compared with the conflict of ages which had gone on in Europe. There was no occasion for society to assume a military aspect. Principles of self-government were at once put into operation, and no one thought of calling them in question. When the neighboring civilization of inferior type—I allude to the French in Canada—began to become seriously troublesome, it was struck down at a blow. When the mother country, under the guidance of an ignorant king and short-sighted ministers, undertook to act upon the antiquated theory that the new communities were merely groups of trading stations, the political bond of connection was severed; yet the war which ensued was not like the war which had but just now been so gloriously ended by the victory of Wolfe. It was not a struggle between two different peoples, like the French of the old *régime* and the English, each representing antagonistic theories of how political life ought to be conducted; but, like the barons' war of the thirteenth century and the Parliament's war of the seventeenth, it was a struggle sustained by a part of the English people in behalf of principles that time has shown to be equally dear to all. And so the issue only made it apparent to an astonished world that instead of *one,* there were now *two Englands,* prepared to work with might and main toward the political regeneration of mankind.

Let us consider now to what conclusions the rapidity and unabated steadiness of the increase of the English race in America must lead us as we go on to forecast the future. Carlyle somewhere speaks slightingly of the fact that the Americans double their numbers every twenty years, as if to have forty million dollar-hunters in the world were any better than to have twenty million dollar-hunters. The implication that Americans are nothing but dollar-hunters, and are thereby distinguishable from the rest of mankind, would not perhaps bear too elaborate scrutiny. But during the present paper we have been considering the gradual transfer of the preponderance of physical strength from the hands of the war-loving portion of the human race into the hands of the peace-loving portion—into the hands of the dollar-hunters, if you please, but out of the hands of the scalp-hunters. Obviously to double the numbers of a pre-eminently industrious, peaceful, orderly, and free-thinking community is somewhat to increase the weight in the world of the tendencies that go toward making communities free and orderly and peaceful and industrious. . . . I do not know whether the United States could support a population everywhere as dense as that of Belgium, so I will suppose that, with ordinary improvement in cultivation and in the industrial arts, we might support a population half as dense as that of Belgium, and this is no doubt an extremely moderate supposition. Now a very simple operation in arithmetic will show that this means a population of fifteen hundred millions, or more than the population of the whole world at the present date. Another very simple operation in arithmetic will show that if we were to go on doubling our numbers even once in every twenty-five years, we should reach that stupendous figure at about the close of the twentieth century, that is, in the days of our great-great-grandchildren. I do not predict any such result, for there are discernible economic reasons for believing that there will be a diminution in the rate of increase. The rate must nevertheless continue to be very great in the absence of such causes as formerly retarded the growth of population in Europe. Our modern wars are hideous enough, no doubt, but they are short. They are settled with a few heavy blows, and the loss of life and property occasioned by them is but trifling when compared with the awful ruin and desolation wrought by the perpetual and protracted contests of antiquity and of the Middle Ages. Chronic warfare, both private and public, periodic famines, and sweeping pestilences like the Black Death—these were the things which formerly shortened human life and kept down population. In the absence of such causes, and with the abundant capacity of our country for feeding its people, I think it an extremely moderate statement if we say that by the end of the next century the English race in the United States will number at least six or seven hundred millions.

It used to be said that so huge a people as this could not be kept together as a single national aggregate, or, if kept together at all, could only be so by means of a powerful centralized government, like that of ancient Rome under the emperors. I think we are now prepared to see that this is a great mistake. If the Roman Empire could have possessed that political vitality in all its parts which is secured to the United States by the principles of equal representation and of limited State sovereignty, it might well have defied all the shocks which tribally organized barbarism could ever have directed against it. As it was, its strong centralized government did not save it from political disintegration. One of its weakest political features was precisely this, that its strong centralized government was a kind of close corporation, governing a score of provinces in its own interest rather than in the interest of the provincials. In contrast with such a system as that of the Roman Empire the skillfully elaborated American system of federalism appears as one of the most important contributions that the English race has made to the general work of civilization. . . . Stated broadly, so as to acquire somewhat the force of a universal proposition, the principle of federalism is just this: that the people of a state shall have full and entire control of their own domestic affairs, which directly concern them only, and which they will naturally manage with more intelligence and with more zeal than any distant governing body could possibly exercise; but that, as regards matters of common concern between a group of states, a decision shall in every case be reached, not by brutal warfare or by weary diplomacy, but by the systematic legislation of a central government which represents both states and people, and whose decisions can always be enforced, if necessary, by the combined physical power of all the states. . . . obviously the principle of federalism, as thus broadly stated, contains within itself the seeds of permanent peace between nations, and to this glorious end I believe it will come in the fullness of time.

And now we may begin to see distinctly what it was that the American government fought for in the late civil war—a point which at the time was by no means clearly apprehended outside the United States. We used to hear it often said, while that war was going on, that we were fighting not so much for the emancipation of the negro as for the maintenance of our federal union; and I doubt not that to many who were burning to see our country purged of the folly and iniquity of negro slavery this may have seemed like taking a low and materialistic view of the case. From the stand-point of universal history it was nevertheless the correct and proper view. The emancipation of the negro, as an incidental result of the struggle, was no doubt a priceless gain, which was greeted warmly by all right-minded people. But deeper down than this question, far more subtly interwoven with the innermost fibres of our national well-being, far heavier laden, too, with weighty consequences for the future weal of all mankind, was the question whether this great pacific principle of union, joined with independence, should be overthrown by the first deep-seated social difficulty it had to encounter, or should stand as an example of priceless value to other ages and to other lands. The solution was well worth the effort it cost. There have been many useless wars, but this was not one of them, for, more than most wars that have been, it was fought in the direct interest of peace, and the victory so dearly purchased and so humanely used was an earnest of future peace and happiness for the world. . . .

In the United States of America a century hence we shall therefore doubtless have a political aggregation immeasurably surpassing in power and in dimensions any empire that has as yet existed. But we must now consider for a moment the probable future career of the English race in other parts of the world. The colonization of North America by Englishmen had its direct effects upon the eastern as well as upon the western side of the Atlantic. The immense growth of the commercial and naval strength of England between the time of Cromwell and the time of the elder Pitt was intimately connected with the colonization of North America and the establishment of plantations in the West Indies.

These circumstances reacted powerfully upon the material development of England, multiplying manifold the dimensions of her foreign trade, increasing proportionately her commercial marine, and giving her in the eighteenth century the dominion over the seas. Endowed with this maritime supremacy, she has with an unerring instinct proceeded to seize upon the keys of empire in all parts of the world—Gibraltar, Malta, the Isthmus of Suez, Aden, Ceylon, the coasts of Australia, island after island in the Pacific—every station, in short, that commands the pathways of maritime commerce, or guards the approaches to the barbarous countries which she is beginning to regard as in some way her natural heritage. . . . No one can carefully watch what is going on in Africa to-day without recognizing it as the same sort of thing which was going on in North America in the seventeenth century; and it can not fail to bring forth similar results in course of time. Here is a vast country, rich in beautiful scenery, and in resources of timber and minerals, with a salubrious climate and fertile soil, with great navigable rivers and inland lakes, which will not much longer be left in control of tawny lions and long-eared elephants, and negro fetich-worshippers. Already five flourishing English states have been established in the south, besides the settlements on the Gold Coast, and those at Aden commanding the Red Sea. English explorers work their way with infinite hardship through its untravelled wilds, and track the courses of the Congo and the Nile as their forefathers tracked the Potomac and the Hudson. The work of LaSalle and Smith is finding its counterpart in the labors of Baker and Livingstone. Who can doubt that within two or three centuries the African continent will be occupied by a mighty nation of English descent, and covered with populous cities and flourishing farms, with railroads and telegraphs and free schools and other devices of civilization as yet undreamed of? If we look next to Australia we find a country of more than two-thirds the area of the United States, with a temperate climate and immense resources, agricultural and mineral, a country sparsely peopled by a race of irredeemable savages hardly above the level of brutes. Here England within the present century has planted five greatly thriving states. . . . Then there is New Zealand, with its climate of perpetual spring, where the English race is now multiplying faster than anywhere else in the world, unless it be in Texas and Minnesota. And there are in the Pacific Ocean many rich and fertile spots where we shall very soon see the same things going on.

It is not necessary to dwell upon such considerations as these. It is enough to point to the general conclusion that the work which the English race began when it colonized North America is destined to go on until every land on the earth's surface that is not already the seat of an old civilization shall become English in its language, in its religion, in its political habits and traditions, and to a predominant extent in the blood of its people. The day is at hand when four-fifths of the human race will trace its pedigree to English forefathers, as four-fifths of the white people in the United States trace their pedigree to-day. The race thus spread over both hemispheres, and from the rising to the setting sun, will not fail to keep that sovereignty of the sea and that commercial supremacy which it began to acquire when England first stretched its arm across the Atlantic to the shores of Virginia and Massachusetts. The language spoken by these great communities will not be sundered into dialects like the language of the ancient Romans, but perpetual intercommunication and the universal habit of reading and writing will preserve its integrity, and the world's business will be transacted by English-speaking people to so great an extent that whatever language any man may have learned in his infancy, he will find it necessary sooner or later to learn to express his thoughts in English. And in this way it is by no means improbable that, as Jacob Grimm long since predicted, the language of Shakespeare will ultimately become the language of mankind.

In view of these considerations as to the stupendous future of the English race, does it not seem very probable that in due course of time Europe, which has learned some valuable lessons from America already, will find it worth while to adopt the lesson of federalism in order to do away with the chances of useless warfare which remain so long as its different states own no allegiance to any common authority? War, as we have seen, is with barbarous races both a necessity and a favorite occupation; as long as civilization comes in contact with barbarism it remains a too frequent necessity; but as between civilized and Christian nations it is an absurdity. For example, we sympathize keenly with wars such as that which Russia has lately concluded for setting free a kindred race and humbling the worthless barbarian who during four centuries has wrought such incalculable damage to the European world. But a sanguinary struggle for the Rhine frontier, between two civilized Christian nations who have each enough work to do in the world without engaging in such a strife as this, will, I am sure, be by-and-by condemned by the general opinion of mankind. Such questions will have to be settled by discussion in some sort of federal council or parliament if Europe would keep pace with America in the advance toward universal law and order. All will admit that such a state of things is a great desideratum. . . .

We have not quite done away with robbery and murder, but we have at least made private warfare illegal; we have arrayed public opinion against it to such an extent that the police court usually makes short shrift for the misguided man who tries to wreak vengeance on his enemy. Is it too much to hope that by-and-by we may similarly put public warfare under the ban? I think not. Already in America, as we have seen, it has become customary to deal with questions between States just as we would deal with questions between individuals. This we have seen to be the real purport of American federalism. To have established such a system over one great continent is to have made a very good beginning toward establishing it over the world. To establish such a system in Europe will no doubt be difficult, for here we have to deal with an immense complication of prejudices, intensified by linguistic and ethnological differences. Nevertheless the pacific pressure exerted upon Europe by America is becoming so great that it will doubtless before long overcome all these obstacles. I refer to the industrial competition between the Old and the New World, which has become so conspicuous within the last ten years. Agriculturally Minnesota, Nebraska, and Kansas are already formidable competitors with England, France, and Germany; but this is but the beginning. It is but the first spray from the tremendous wave of economic competition that is gathering in the Mississippi Valley. Presently, as with increase of population labor grows cheaper in America, the competition in manufactures also will become as keen as it is now beginning to be in agriculture, as the recent industrial history of New England abundantly proves. Now this economic pressure exerted upon Europe by the United States will very soon become so great that it will be simply impossible for the states of Europe to keep up such military armaments as they are now maintaining. The disparity between the United States, with a standing army of only twenty-five thousand men, and the states of Europe, with their standing armies amounting to two or three millions of men, is something that can not be kept up. The economic competition will become so keen that European armies will have to be disbanded, the swords will have to be turned into ploughshares, and thus the victory of the industrial over the military type of civilization will at last become complete. But to disband the great armies of Europe will necessarily involve the forcing of the great states of Europe into some sort of federal relation, in which congresses will become more frequent, in which the principles of international law will acquire a more definite sanction, and in which the combined physical power of all the states will constitute (as it now does in America) a permanent threat against any state that dares for selfish reasons to break the peace. In some such way as this, I believe, the industrial development of the English race outside of Europe will by-and-by enforce federalism upon Europe. I do not ignore the difficulties that grow out of differences in language, race, and creed; but we have seen how Switzerland has long since triumphantly surmounted such difficulties on a small scale. To surmount them on a great scale will soon be the political problem of Europe, and it is America which has set the example and indicated the method.

Thus we may foresee in general how, by the gradual concentration of physical power into the hands of the most pacific communities, we may finally succeed in rendering warfare illegal all over the globe. As this process goes on, it may, after many more ages of political experience, become apparent that there is really no reason, in the nature of things, why the whole of mankind should not constitute politically one huge federation, each little group managing its local affairs in entire independence, but relegating all questions of international interest to the decision of one central tribunal supported by the public opinion of the entire human race. I believe that the time will come when such a state of things will exist upon the earth, when it will be possible (with our friends of the Paris dinner party) to speak of the United States as stretching from pole to pole, or with Tennyson to celebrate the "parliament of man and the federation of the world." Indeed, only when such a state of things has begun to be realized can civilization, as sharply demarcated from barbarism, be said to have fairly begun. Only then can the world be said to have become truly Christian. Many ages of toil and doubt and perplexity will no doubt pass by before such a desideratum is reached. Meanwhile it is pleasant to feel that the dispassionate contemplation of great masses of historical facts goes far toward confirming our faith in this ultimate triumph of good over evil. Our survey began with pictures of horrid slaughter and desolation; it ends with the picture of a world covered with cheerful homesteads, blessed with a Sabbath of perpetual peace.

King Leopold's Soliloquy

Samuel L. Clemens

[*Throws down pamphlets which he has been reading. Excitedly combs his flowing spread of whiskers with his fingers; pounds the table with his fists; lets off brisk volleys of unsanctified language at brief intervals, repentantly drooping his head, between volleys, and kissing the Louis XI crucifix hanging from his neck, accompanying the kisses with mumbled apologies; presently rises, flushed and perspiring, and walks the floor, gesticulating*]

—— ——!! —— ——!! If I had them by the throat! [*Hastily kisses the crucifix, and mumbles*] In these twenty years I have spent millions to keep the press of the two hemispheres quiet, and still these leaks keep on occurring. I have spent other millions on religion and art, and what do I get for it? Nothing. Not a compliment. These generosities are studiedly ignored, in print. In print I get nothing but slanders—and slanders again—and still slanders, and slanders on top of slanders! Grant them true, what of it? They are slanders all the same, when uttered against a king.

Miscreants—they are telling *everything!* Oh, everything: how I went pilgriming among the Powers in tears, with my mouth full of Bible and my pelt oozing piety at every pore, and implored them to place the vast and rich and populous Congo Free State in trust in my hands as their agent, so that I might root out slavery and stop the slave raids, and lift up those twenty-five millions of gentle and harmless blacks out of darkness into light, the light of our blessed Redeemer, the light that streams from his holy Word, the light that makes glorious our noble civilization—lift them up and dry their tears and fill their bruised hearts with joy and gratitude—lift them up and make them comprehend that they were no longer outcasts and forsaken, but our very brothers in Christ; how America and thirteen great European states wept in sympathy with me, and were persuaded; how their representatives met in convention in Berlin and made

S. L. Clemens, *King Leopold's Soliloquy. A Defense of His Congo Rule*, 2nd ed. (Boston: P. R. Warren Co., 1905), pp. 5–10, 12–20, 23–27, 29–30, 32–34, 40–42.

me Head Foreman and Superintendent of the Congo State, and drafted out my powers and limitations, carefully guarding the persons and liberties and properties of the natives against hurt and harm; forbidding whisky traffic and gun traffic; providing courts of justice; making commerce free and fetterless to the merchants and traders of all nations, and welcoming and safe-guarding all missionaries of all creeds and denominations. They have told how I planned and prepared my establishment and selected my horde of officials—"pals" and "pimps" of mine, "unspeakable Belgians" every one—and hoisted my flag, and "took in" a President of the United States, and got him to be the first to recognize it and salute it. Oh, well, let them blackguard me if they like; it is a deep satisfaction to me to remember that I was a shade too smart for that nation that thinks itself so smart. Yes, I certainly did bunco a Yankee—as those people phrase it. Pirate flag? Let them call it so—perhaps it is. All the same, *they were the first to salute it.*

These meddlesome American missionaries! these frank British consuls! these blabbing Belgian-born traitor officials!—those tiresome parrots are always talking, always telling. They have told how for twenty years I have ruled the Congo State not as a trustee of the Powers, an agent, a subordinate, a foreman, but as a sovereign—sovereign over a fruitful domain four times as large as the German Empire—sovereign absolute, irresponsible, above all law; trampling the Berlin-made Congo charter under foot; barring out all foreign traders but myself; restricting commerce to myself, through concessionaires who are my creatures and confederates; seizing and holding the State as my personal property, the whole of its vast revenues as my private "swag"—mine, solely mine—claiming and holding its millions of people as my private property, my serfs, my slaves; their labor mine, with or without wage; the food they raise not their property but mine; the rubber, the ivory and all the other riches of the land mine—mine solely—and gathered for me by the men, the women and the little children under compulsion of lash and bullet, fire, starvation, mutilation and the halter. . . .

Yes, they go on telling everything, these chatterers! They tell how I levy incredibly burdensome taxes upon the natives—taxes which are a pure theft; taxes which they must satisfy by gathering rubber under hard and constantly harder conditions, and by raising and furnishing food supplies gratis—and it all comes out that, when they fall short of their tasks through hunger, sickness, despair and ceaseless and exhausting labor without rest, and forsake their homes and flee to the woods to escape punishment, my black soldiers, drawn from unfriendly tribes, and instigated and directed by my Belgians, hunt them down and butcher them and burn their villages—reserving some of the girls. They tell it all; how I am wiping a nation of friendless creatures out of existence by every form of murder, for my private pocket's sake, and how every shilling I get costs a rape, a mutilation or a life. But they never say, although they know it, that I have labored in the cause of religion at the same time and all the time, and have sent missionaries there (of a "convenient stripe," as they phrase it), to teach them the error of their ways, and bring them to Him who is all mercy and love, and who is the sleepless guardian and friend of all who suffer. They tell only what is against me, they will not tell what is in my favor. . . .

[*Meditative pause*] Well . . . no matter, I *did* beat the Yankees, anyway! there's comfort in that. [*Reads with mocking smile, the President's Order of Recognition of April 22, 1884*]

". . . the government of the United States announces its sympathy with and approval of the humane and benevolent purposes of (my Congo scheme), and will order the officers of the United States, both on land and sea, to recognize its flag as the flag of friendly government."

Possibly the Yankees would like to take that back, now, but they will find that my agents are not over there in America for nothing. But there is no danger; neither nations nor governments can afford to confess a blunder. [*With a contented smile, begins to read from "Report by Rev. W. M. Morrison, American missionary in the Congo Free State"*]

"I furnish herewith some of the many atrocious incidents which have come under my own personal observation; they reveal the *organized system* of plunder and outrage which has been perpetrated and is now being carried on in that unfortunate country by King Leopold of Belgium. I say King Leopold because he and he *alone* is now responsible, since he is the *absolute sovereign. He styles himself such.* When our government in 1884 laid the foundation of the Congo Free State, by recognizing its flag, little did it know that this concern parading under the guise of philanthropy, was really King Leopold of Belgium, one of the shrewdest, most heartless and most conscienceless rulers that ever sat on a throne. This is apart from his known corrupt morals, which have made his name and his family a byword in two continents. Our government would most certainly not have recognized that flag had it known that it was really King Leopold individually who was asking for recognition; had it known that it was setting up in the heart of Africa an *absolute monarchy*; had it known that, having put down African slavery in our own country at great cost of blood and money, it was *establishing a worse form of slavery right in Africa.*"

[*With evil joy*] Yes, I certainly was a shade too clever for the Yankees. It hurts; it gravels them. They can't get over it! Puts a shame upon them in another way, too, and a graver way; for they never can rid their records of the reproachful fact that their vain Republic, self-appointed Champion and Promoter of the Liberties of the World, is the only democracy in history that has lent its power and influence to the establishing of an *absolute monarchy!*

[*Contemplating, with an unfriendly eye, a stately pile of pamphlets*] Blister the meddlesome missionaries! They write tons of these things. They seem to be always around, always spying, always eye-witnessing the happenings; and everything they see they commit to paper. They are always prowling from place to place; the natives consider them their only friends; they go to them with their sorrows; they show them their scars and their wounds, inflicted by my soldier police; they hold up the stumps of their arms and lament because their hands have been chopped off, as punishment for not bringing in enough rubber, and as proof to be laid before my officers that the required punishment was well and truly carried out. One of these missionaries saw eighty-one of these hands drying over a fire for transmission to my officials—and of course he must go and set it down and print it. They travel and travel, they spy and spy! And nothing is too trivial for them to print. [*Takes up a pamphlet. Reads a passage from Report of a "Journey made in July, August and September, 1903, by Rev. A. E. Scrivener, a British missionary"*]

". . . Soon we began talking, and without any encouragement on my part the natives began the tales I had become so accustomed to. They were living in peace and quietness when the white men came in from the lake with all sorts of requests to do this and that, and they thought it meant slavery. So they attempted to keep the white men out of their country but without avail. The rifles were too much for them. So they submitted and made up their minds to do the best they could under the altered circumstances. First came the command to build houses for the soldiers, and this was done without a murmur. Then they had to feed the soldiers and all the men and women—hangers on— who accompanied them. Then they were told to bring in rubber. This was quite a new thing for them to do. There was rubber in the forest several days away from their home, but that it was worth anything was news to them. A small reward was offered and a rush was made for the rubber. 'What strange white men, to give us cloth and beads for the sap of a wild vine.' They rejoiced in what they thought their good fortune. But soon the reward was reduced until at last they were told to bring in the rubber for nothing. To this they tried to demur; but to their great surprise several were shot by soldiers, and the rest were told, with many curses and blows, to go at once or more would be killed. Terrified, they began to prepare their food for the fortnight's absence from the village which the collection of rubber entailed. The soldier discovered them sitting. 'What, not gone yet?' Bang! bang! bang! and down fell one and another, dead, in the midst of wives and companions. There is a terrible wail and an attempt made to prepare the dead for burial, but this is not allowed. All must go at once to the forest. Without food? Yes, without food. And off the poor wretches had to go without even their tinder boxes to make fires. Many died in the forests of hunger and exposure, and still more from the rifles of the ferocious soldiers in charge of the post. In spite of all their efforts the amount fell off and more and more were killed. I was shown around the place, and the sites of former big chiefs' settlements were pointed out. A careful estimate made the population of, say, seven years ago, to be 2,000 people in and about the post, within a radius of, say a quarter of a mile. All told, they would not muster 200 now, and there is so much sadness and gloom about them that they are fast decreasing." . . .

That is their way; they spy and spy, and run into print with every foolish trifle. And that British consul, Mr. Casement, is just like them. He gets hold of a *diary which had been kept by one of my government officers*, and, although it is a private diary and intended for no eye but its owner's, Mr. Casement is so lacking in delicacy and refinement as to print passages from it. [*Reads a passage from the diary*]

"Each time the corporal goes out to get rubber, cartridges are given him. He must bring back all not used, and for every one used he must bring back a right hand. M. P. told me that sometimes they shot a cartridge at an animal in hunting; they then cut off a hand from a living man. As to the extent to which this is carried on, he informed me that in six months the State on the Mambogo River had used 6,000 cartridges, which means that 6,000 people are killed or mutilated. It means more than 6,000, for the people have told me repeatedly that the soldiers kill the children with the butt of their guns." . . .

It is most amazing, the way that that consul acts—that spy, that busybody. [*Takes up pamphlet "Treatment of Women and Children in the Congo State; what Mr. Casement Saw in 1903"*] Hardly two years ago! *Intruding* that date upon the public was a piece of cold malice. It was intended to weaken the force of my press syndicate's assurances to the public that my severities in the Congo *ceased*, and ceased utterly, *years and years ago*. This man is fond of trifles—revels in them, gloats over them, pets them, fondles them, sets them all down. One doesn't need to drowse through his monotonous report to see that; the mere sub headings of its chapters prove it. [*Reads*]

"Two hundred and forty persons, *men, women and children* compelled to supply government with *one ton* of carefully prepared foodstuffs *per week*, receiving in remuneration, all told, the princely sum of 15s. 10d!"

Very well, it was liberal. It was not much short of a penny a week for each nigger. It suits this consul to belittle it, yet he knows very well that I could have had both the food and the labor for nothing. I can prove it by a thousand instances. [*Reads*]

"Expedition against a village behindhand in its (compulsory) supplies; result, slaughter of sixteen persons; among them three women and a boy of five

years. Ten carried off, to be prisoners till ransomed; among them a child who
died during the march."

But he is careful not to explain that we are *obliged* to resort to ransom
to collect debts where the people have nothing to pay with. Families that
escape to the woods sell some of their members into slavery and thus provide the ransom. He knows that I would stop this if I could find a less
objectionable way to collect their debts. . . .

[*Puts down the Report, takes up a pamphlet, glances along the middle
of it*]

This is where the "death-trap" comes in. Meddlesome missionary spying around—Rev. W. H. Sheppard. Talks with a black raider of mine after
a raid; cozens him into giving away some particulars. The raider remarks:

"I demanded 30 slaves from this side of the stream and 30 from the other
side; 2 points of ivory, 2,500 balls of rubber, 13 goats, 10 fowls and 6 dogs,
some corn chumy, et.

'How did the fight come up?' I asked.

'I sent for all their chiefs, sub-chiefs, men and women, to come on a certain
day, saying that I was going to finish all the palaver. When they entered these
small gates (the walls being made of fences brought from other villages, the
high native ones) I demanded all my pay or I would kill them; so they refused
to pay me, and I ordered the fence to be closed so they couldn't run away;
then we killed them here inside the fence. The panels of the fence fell down
and some escaped.'

'How many did you kill?' I asked.

'We killed plenty, will you see some of them?'

That was just what I wanted.

He said: 'I think we have killed between eighty and ninety, and those in the
other villages I don't know, I did not go out but sent my people.'

He and I walked out on the plain just near the camp. There were three
dead bodies with the flesh carved off from the waist down.

'Why are they carved so, only leaving the bones?' I asked.

'My people ate them,' he answered promptly. He then explained, 'The men
who have young children do not eat people, but all the rest ate them.' On the
left was a big man, shot in the back and without a head. (All these corpses
were nude.)

'Where is the man's head?' I asked.

'Oh, they made a bowl of the forehead to rub up tobacco and diamba in.'

We continued to walk and examine until late in the afternoon, and counted
forty-one bodies. The rest had been eaten up by the people.

On returning to the camp, we crossed a young woman, shot in the back of
the head, one hand was cut away. I asked why, and Mulunba N'Cusa explained that they always cut off the right hand to give to the State on their
return.

'Can you not show me some of the hands?' I asked.

So he conducted us to a framework of sticks, under which was burning a slow fire, and there they were, the right hands—I counted them, eighty-one in all. . . . "

Another detail, as we see!—cannibalism. They report cases of it with a most offensive frequency. My traducers do not forget to remark that, inasmuch as I am absolute and with a word can prevent in the Congo anything I choose to prevent, then whatsoever is done there by my permission is my act, my *personal* act; that *I* do it; that the hand of my agent is as truly *my* hand as if it were attached to my own arm; and so they picture me in my robes of state, with my crown on my head, munching human flesh, saying grace, mumbling thanks to Him from whom all good things come. Dear, dear, when the soft-hearts get hold of a thing like that missionary's contribution they quite lose their tranquility over it. They speak out profanely and reproach Heaven for allowing such a fiend to live. Meaning me. They think it irregular. They go shuddering around, brooding over the reduction of that Congo population from 25,000,0000 to 15,000,000 in the twenty years of my administration; then they burst out and call me "the King with Ten Million Murders on his Soul." They call me a "record." The most of them do not stop with charging merely the 10,000,000 against me. No, they reflect that but for me the population, by natural increase, would now be 30,000,000, so they charge another 5,000,-000 against me and make my total death-harvest 15,000,000. They remark that the man who killed the goose that laid the golden egg was responsible for the eggs she would subsequently have laid if she had been let alone. Oh, yes, they call me a "record." They remark that twice in a generation, in India, the Great Famine destroys 2,000,000 out of a population of 320,000,000, and the whole world holds up its hands in pity and horror; then they fall to wondering where the world would find room for its emotions if I had a chance to trade places with the Great Famine for twenty years! The idea fires their fancy, and they go on and imagine the Famine coming in state at the end of the twenty years and prostrating itself before me, saying: "Teach me, Lord, I perceive that I am but an apprentice." And next they imagine Death coming, with his scythe and hour-glass, and begging me to marry his daughter and reorganize his plant and run the business. For the whole world, you see! By this time their diseased minds are under full steam, and they get down their books and expand their labors, with me for text. They hunt through all biography for my match, working Attila, Torquemada, Ghengis Khan, Ivan the Terrible, and the rest of that crowd for all they are worth, and evilly exulting when they cannot find it. Then they examine the historical earthquakes and cyclones and blizzards and cataclysms and volcanic eruptions: verdict, none of them "in it" with me. At last they do really hit it (as they think), and they close their labors with conceding—reluctantly—

that I have *one* match in history, but only one—the *Flood*. This is intemperate. . . . [*Reads*]

"The crucifying of sixty women!"

How stupid, how tactless! Christendom's goose flesh will rise with horror at the news. "Profanation of the sacred emblem!" That is what Christendom will shout. Yes, Christendom will buzz. It can hear me charged with half a million murders a year for twenty years and keep its composure, but to profane the Symbol is quite another matter. It will regard this as serious. It will wake up and want to look into my record. Buzz? Indeed it will; I seem to hear the distant hum already. . . . It was wrong to crucify the women, clearly wrong, manifestly wrong, I can see it now, myself, and am sorry it happened, sincerely sorry. I believe it would have answered just as well to skin them. . . . [*With a sigh*] But none of us thought of that; one cannot think of everything; and after all it is but human to err.

It will make a stir, it surely will, these crucifixions. Persons will begin to ask again, as now and then in times past, how I can hope to win and keep the respect of the human race if I continue to give up my life to murder and pillage. [*Scornfully*] When have they heard me say I wanted the respect of the human race? Do they confuse me with the common herd? do they forget that I am a king? What king has valued the respect of the human race? I mean deep down in his private heart. If they would reflect, they would know that it is impossible that a king should value the respect of the human race. He stands upon an eminence and looks out over the world and sees multitudes of meek human things worshiping the persons, and submitting to the oppressions and exactions, of a dozen human things who are in no way better or finer than themselves—made on just their own pattern, in fact, and out of the same quality of mud. When it *talks*, it is a race of whales; but a king knows it for a race of tadpoles. Its history gives it away. If men were really *men*, how could a Czar be possible? and how could I be possible? But we *are* possible; we are quite safe; and with God's help we shall continue the business at the old stand. It will be found that the race will put up with us, in its docile immemorial way. It may pull a wry face now and then, and make large talk, but it will stay on its knees all the same.

Making large talk is one of its specialties. It works itself up, and froths at the mouth, and just when you think it is going to throw a brick,—it heaves a poem! Lord, what a race it is! . . .

. . . What is this fragment? [*Reads*]

"But enough of trying to tally off his crimes! His list is interminable, we should never get to the end of it. His awful shadow lies across his Congo Free

State, and under it an unoffending nation of 15,000,000 is withering away and succumbing to their miseries. It is a land of graves; it is *The* Land of Graves; it is the Congo Free Graveyard. It is a majestic thought: that is, this ghastliest episode in all human history is the work of *one man alone*; one solitary man; just a single individual—Leopold, King of the Belgians. He is personally and solely responsible for all the myriad crimes that have blackened the history of the Congo State. He is *sole* master there; he is absolute. He could have prevented the crimes by his mere command; he could stop them today with a word. He withholds the word. For his pocket's sake.

It seems strange to see a king destroying a nation and laying waste a country for mere sordid money's sake, and solely and only for that. Lust of conquest is royal; kings have always exercised that stately vice; we are used to it, by old habit we condone it, perceiving a certain dignity in it; but *lust of money—lust of shillings—lust of nickels—lust of dirty coin,* not for the nation's enrichment but for *the king's alone*—this is new. It distinctly revolts us, we cannot seem to reconcile ourselves to it, we resent it, we despise it, we say it is shabby, unkingly, out of character. Being democrats we ought to jeer and jest, we ought to rejoice to see the purple dragged in the dirt, but—well, account for it as we may, we don't. We see this awful king, this pitiless and blood-drenched king, this money-crazy king towering toward the sky in a world-solitude of sordid crime, unfellowed and apart from the human race, sole butcher for personal gain findable in all his caste, ancient or modern, pagan or Christian, proper and legitimate target for the scorn of the lowest and the highest, and the execrations of all who hold in cold esteem the oppressor and the coward; and—well, it is a mystery, but *we do not wish to look*; for he is a king, and it hurts us, it troubles us, by ancient and inherited instinct it shames us to see a king degraded to this aspect, and we shrink from hearing the particulars of how it happened. *We shudder and turn away* when we come upon them in print."

Why, certainly—*that* is my protection. And you will continue to do it. I know the human race.

PART VIII

INTERPRETATIONS
OF AN AGE

It was not left entirely to a later age to interpret the meaning of the economic and social changes of the late nineteenth century. Even as the events occurred, there were those who tried to understand them, either by assimilating them into accepted categories of analysis or, if these seemed wanting—as increasingly they did—by inventing new categories. No single theory of social change commanded universal assent, yet unity of a sort was provided by both the social reality with which the thinkers tried to deal and the form in which they cast their ideas. Behind even abstract philosophical discussions about the meaning of truth, of value judgments, of the Absolute was an effort to create the tools that could provide both understanding and moral criticism of a turbulent era. But if it was the social problems of the period that provided the content for much of its thought, the idea of evolution provided the form in which that thought was expressed.

Perhaps paradoxically, the idea of evolution proved as easily adapted to the uses of defenders of the social order as it did to its opponents. Herbert Spencer was undoubtedly the preeminent exponent of that version of Social Darwinism which found sanction for the unimpeded activities of the businessman in the theory of the survival of the fittest. His leading American disciple, the famous Yale sociologist William Graham Sumner, was, if anything, an even more rigorous advocate of the principle of noninterference in the operation of the laws of society. Henry George, the great reformer, and Lester F. Ward, scientist and pioneer American sociologist, read Darwin differently. For them, evolution had devised the instruments with which men could direct and improve their future. There was no doubt that environment pressed heavily upon man, but there was equally no doubt that intelligence could alter the shape of that environment. For Henry George, there was, as he said, a social wrong at the bottom of every social problem; for Lester Ward, intelligent use of government—that most powerful tool of society—was the means of correcting the wrong.

George D. Herron, professor of Applied Christianity at Iowa College, agreed with George and Ward that a more just order of society could be achieved only through the use of the power of the state, but for him the increasing use of that power was not evidence of the operation of natural laws but of "the political appearing of Christ." The solution of the social problems that had been created by the development of industry was to be found in infusion of the doctrines of Christian love in all aspects of society. For Herron this was no millennial vision of a second coming of Christ, but a revolutionary doctrine which provided a standard by which *the present world could be judged and at the same time made over.*

The essay with which this section concludes, by William James, by no means represents the most characteristic work of that great philosopher, but it does provide, in James's inimitable style, a refreshing refutation of the essentially antiscientific character of the application of Darwinian ideas to the analysis of social problems. It is, moreover, for all its deceptive simplicity, nothing less than a theory of social change, one which had special attractions to a society in process of transforming itself: ". . . no social community need, by virtue of its purely social forces, evolve fatally in the direction of its own most characteristic aptitudes," James wrote. If this was a warning against the perils of forecast, it was also a license to men to make of their society what they wished.

The Nineteenth Century's Legacy to the Twentieth

William Graham Sumner

Many have invited us to a proud review of the increased inheritance of economic power which the nineteenth century hands down to the twentieth. . . . The new powers and devices, which are just in their infancy, are a legacy at whose ultimate value we can only guess. The outlying parts of the earth are made available and stand open to the use of the next generations. The nineteenth century bequeaths to the twentieth new land and new arts, which are the prime conditions of material welfare. The capital at the disposal of the human race is immensely greater per capita than it ever was before. There are inexhausted improvements all over the globe which the nineteenth century undertook and paid for, the gain of which will come to the twentieth. Science has a mass of acquired knowledge and processes to confide to the coming generation whose power and value in the struggle for existence are beyond imagination. There are acquisitions in the higher branches of pure mathematics, which are fruitless at present but which are certain to prove of inestimable value to sustain the development of the applications of electricity. The population of the globe is far below the number which it could support with the present resources. Consequently men are in demand. The conjuncture favors numbers. While numbers increase, the comfort per capita will increase. Popular education will pay. The life-conditions will improve. The chances for those who inherit nothing will be good provided that they are industrious, prudent, and temperate. The competition of life is so mild that men are hardly conscious of it. So far as we can see ahead there is every reason for even rash optimism in regard to the material or economic welfare of mankind.

William Graham Sumner, "The Bequests of the Nineteenth Century to the Twentieth" (1901) in Albert G. Keller and Maurice R. Davie (eds.), *Essays of W. G. Sumner* (New Haven, Yale University Press, 1934), vol. I, 208–225, 229–231, 234–235.

No one will deny that the enterprises of territorial acquisition on the part of the great states which are now being undertaken or which will be undertaken in the twentieth century are very likely to bring them into collision with each other. . . . The possibilities of disturbance and mischief are very great, and they will so far as they occur traverse the realization of economic welfare which the economic powers and organization promise. It is not, however, the purpose of the present article to dwell upon this outlook of practical international politics, for in that domain one could at best predict and speculate. The prospect that the programme of action will cause war touches upon our subject only so far as it is political. Our present purpose is to notice those elements in the social and political world of to-day which we are handing down together with the above described elements of economic gain, and which are certain to affect the realization of the optimistic prospects above described.

Along with all economic knowledge and industrial effort there must go always decisions of industrial policy. Success in industrial production and success in the selection of wise lines of policy are two very different things. The questions of policy are generally nowadays questions of politics, and here is where the existing conditions contain elements of peril. . . .

These decisions must nowadays be made by the concurrence of large bodies of men because the industrial organization is so large and complex. The decisions of policy affect the relations of parties in the industrial organization, that is to say, they affect rights. The decisions also call into being institutions or provide for ways of using existing institutions by methods which are due to "understandings" or agreements. In the majority of cases these decisions must be made by the legislature and take the form of law. They then affect the interests of the whole population and the rights of individuals and groups. The problem of justice in these cases is a serious one. It is rendered more serious by the speed with which the changes occur, on account of which there is not time to revise and correct one policy before another supersedes it. The coercion of the state to enforce a policy decided upon by the legislature is indispensable. The state is an organization of force. In its origin it was an organization of force for conquest and subjugation, and it produced plunder, slavery, and the exploitation of one group by another. In its highest forms it has become an organization of force to enforce rights and to give efficiency to institutions according to the views and policy which prevail in the community at the time. The co-operation of the state, therefore, with industrial enterprise, to maintain peace and order, to ensure the regular operation of civil institutions, and to guarantee rights is indispensable to industry. This is the connection of economics and politics.

During the nineteenth century the state, as it was inherited from the eighteenth century, has undergone great improvement. The nineteenth

century inherited from the eighteenth vague notions of political beatification. To abolish kings and get a "republic" would, it was expected, bring
universal and endless peace and happiness. Then the idea was to get the
"rights of man" declared and sworn to. Then the result was to come from
universal suffrage in the republic. Then democracy was to be the realizer
of hope and faith. It was thought that a democracy never would be warlike or extravagant in expenditure. Then faith was put in constitutional
government, whether republican or monarchical. Next hope turned to
representative institutions as the key to the right solution. The century
ends with despondency as to each and all of these notions. Now social
democracy and state socialism seem to be the divinities which are to
beatify us. The faith that beatification is possible and that some piece of
political machinery can get it for us seems to be as strong as ever. In the
details of life and practice much has been gained in regard to peace,
security, conditions of welfare, and actual experience in the body politic,
beyond what existed a hundred years ago. The security of life, property,
and honor, for men and women, is greater in all civilized countries than
it was.

Wherever there is a force in human society the problem is to use it and
regulate it; to get the use and prevent the abuse of it. The state is no exception; on the contrary, it is the chief illustration. In all the forms of
the state which ever have existed families, groups, classes, corporations
have struggled with each other to get into their hands the power of the
state. To get control of this power is to win the industrial products
(wealth), after other people have made them, without labor of one's own.
This is the real objection to all class government, and it is just as strong
to-day against the democratic mass or the middle class joint stock company as it ever was against king or aristocracy. The great and standing
abuse of the political organization is the control of it by a clique or faction
so that they can use it to serve their own interests at the expense of everybody else. No state ever has existed which has not been subject to this
abuse, for, in practice, the power of the state must be in the hands of some
group of men. The theory of the state is that this group is to use the
power for the welfare of all. In practice they have always used the power
for their own advantage.

The nineteenth century bequeaths to the twentieth a state organization
which is still infected with this vice under new forms which conform to
the middle class constitutional state with representative institutions,
whether it is monarchical or republican, aristocratic or democratic. In fact,
the immense increase in all facilities of transportation and communication
has made it not only possible but necessary to organize industry in co-
operative combinations which reach over state boundaries and embrace
the whole globe. It is idle to criticise or bewail this fact. The genii whom
we call up will obey, but there are consequences of using genii and he

who uses them must take the consequences. If we use steam and electricity we must get space for their evolutions, and we must adjust our plans to their incidental effects. Organization on a grand scale is a necessary consequence of steam and electricity. The little independent man is forced into a place in a great organization where he may win more but will lose his independence. It is as inevitable as the introduction of machinery and the consequences of machinery. . . .

Populism or social democracy is the abuse of democracy which is parallel to the older abuses of earlier forms of the state. In democracy the power resides in the masses. In social democracy the masses are organized to win materialistic advantages for themselves by the use of their political power. In all our discussions we talk as if political functions ought to be exercised in obedience to some abstract notions of political and societal welfare. In practice they are exercised to serve interests. Debtors *vs.* creditors, tenants *vs.* landlords, shippers *vs.* transporters, wage receivers *vs.* wage givers, passengers *vs.* carriers, *et cetera* are, of course, antagonistic in their interests. Their antagonism is in the industrial organization. They have recourse to political enginery that they try to direct against each other for victory in their economic battles. If a group of us are passengers, let us get passage rates fixed by law. Why then may not the carriers at the next session get a majority and advance their own interests at the expense of passengers? The temperance people took to politics to crush the saloon. The saloon organized politically first for defense, then for aggression, and it became a permanent power in politics. This retaliation or reaction is to be counted upon, and it results in turning politics into a scramble of interests. . . .

Evidently all this tends towards an alternative question. Can the state find anywhere power to repel all the special interests and keep uppermost the one general interest or the welfare of all? Will the state itself degenerate into the instrument of an attack on property, and will it cripple wealth-making or will the wealth-making interest, threatened by the state, rise up to master it, corrupt it, and use it? This is the alternative which the twentieth century must meet. It is the antagonism of democracy and plutocracy. It is the most momentous antagonism which has ever arisen in human society because it is internal; it is in the vitals of society. We have had a foretaste of it in the last two presidential elections in which the voters have shown that they would disregard everything else in order to secure property interests and the public order which is essential to wealth production.

The problem would be far easier to solve if it were not for the easy political optimism which is another of the bequests of the nineteenth century to the twentieth. We are told to "trust the people"; that the people will decide all questions wisely; that the people will protect its institutions and will correct all abuses. Who is "the people" as the term is used in these hard-worn phrases? Where does it stay? How can it be reached? Where does it utter its oracles? How can we test and verify what is asserted about the people? We have been trained in a habit of "wanting to know" on all the other fields. Why may we not demand to be allowed to employ the same processes here? The people is what is called nowadays a "political symbol." It is a mythological product and has no definition. It is an object of reverence and faith like Fate or Destiny. We know that it is not the population. It is a part of the population but an undefined part, a lost part absorbed or immanent somewhere in the total. The word is one of the counters with which party editors, politicians, and half-educated platform orators juggle. Why does not the people do some of the things which we are told that it can do, so that we might believe in it? There are tasks enough undone, which are the people's business. The people is said to rule in a democratic republic. It fills no offices. We see it nowhere. It has reserved to itself the function of selecting legislative bodies from time to time. This is the way in which it rules. The rest of the time it is quiescent. We go into the legislatures, and we see what kind of men the people has selected. We see then how it has performed this function.

The eighteenth-century republicans were sure that if the people elected the legislature, it would select men of brains, character, virtue, independence, and so forth. We have found that this expectation was a delusion as much as the notion that democracies would be unwarlike and frugal. The point now is, however, that it is the legislature which the people elects which has got to meet the assaults of special interests which were described above. The root of all our troubles at present and in the future is in the fact that the people fails of what was assumed about it and attributed to it. If the people is (as the newspapers say it is) angry at the raids of plutocrats on the legislatures, why does not the people elect legislatures which cannot be raided? He who rules is responsible, be it Tsar, Pope, Emperor, Aristocracy, Oligarchy, or Demos. Some people wax very indignant against anybody who, as they say, bribes a legislator. It takes two to perpetrate bribery. The relation between the two may vary through a very wide scale. It is possible that a man may buy a legislature to get what he ought not to have. It is also possible that a legislature many blackmail a man before giving him what he ought to have. There are many grades between these two extremes. The bribee is in any case more base than the briber, for he betrays a public trust. Why does not the people elect legislators who will do their duty and not take bribes at all? The indignant denouncers of bribers stand with their backs to the truth. No one would ever bribe a legislator if he could get what he wanted without it and could not get what he wanted even with it. Of course this is no apology for the briber. It is an attempt to analyze the case in order to see the real elements in it and their relation to each other. Our popular

preachers and teachers will not entertain the possibility that the people
is at fault. In fact, the people is altogether at fault. It has not done its first
duty in the premises, and therefore the whole institution has gone astray.

The current answer which is given with confidence is that the people
is controlled by politicians. It is true, but it is a fatal answer. What shall
be said of an oracle which pleads that somebody deceived it? What shall
be said of a sovereign who says that he was dictated to by somebody?

Democracy is another "political symbol." It is unanalyzed. The term
is used as if it had a single and simple definition. Democracy includes
Jacobinism, Sansculottism, Social Democracy or Populism, Mobocracy,
besides two or three legitimate forms. When it is glorified in orations
and books one kind is meant. When it is in operation another kind is at
work. Before the twentieth century is out, men will know more about
democracy. It answers our present purpose to note only that democracy
is the power of numbers. It assumes that numbers have a right in the
nature of things to rule. Of course that is entirely untrue. There is nobody
who, in the nature of things, ought to rule. The doctrine that the "voice
of the people is the voice of God," is just as silly as the doctrine that the
voice of the autocrat is the voice of God. We have had the fetish man
(king priest) and the fetish book. Now we have the fetish crowd. The
sum of superstition in the world seems to be a constant quantity. The
divine right of a big (or bigger) number to rule is just as false as the
divine right of one to rule. No one has a right to rule. It is all a question
of expediency to get our affairs carried on satisfactorily. Why not have
done with "natural right," and "divine authority," and the rest? We have
got rid of them in metaphysics and theology. Why should a hard-headed
and practical people transfer all this old superstition over into politics?
Why get up a new political mythology and a new apparatus of fictions
and humbugs? Why not look at things as they are; not at words? Democracy is like every other ---ocracy, a dogmatic system; and we are surfeited
with phrases, catchwords, cant, dogmas about democracy which are
false. . . .

It is in the nature of things that a set of conventional falsehoods and
stereotyped dogmas should produce false institutions. You begin by
attributing to numbers an authority which numbers never possess and
cannot exercise, and you end with a legislature which has not the brains
or the integrity to stand a raid by the lobby. You look for some representation of *all* which shall defend all against some. This, as has been shown
above, is the great need in any and every form of the state. You find
agents of all ready to betray all to some. Democracy is jealous of the
power of wealth. It denies the right of wealth to political power and
ostracizes it. What happens? Wealth is power. Everybody knows it. It
is a just social power. In modern society wealth (capital) is the power
which has supplanted rank and which moves the world. Its power in

society is even made subject of exaggeration and denunciation. This surely is recognition of it. Socialism, denouncing property, is only trying to get property (other people's—that of the rich to give it to the poor). All schemes of social amelioration or improvement aim to make poor people richer. It always has been so. Plutocracy has existed in all society in all ages. In truth, it is not as efficient now as in any former age, assertions to the contrary notwithstanding. The jealousy and hostility of democracy to plutocracy are due to the fact that democracy recognizes its adversary.

The economic state of the world at the present time, as described at the beginning of this article, is the cause of the power of democracy. Numbers are now economically demanded. The man is superior, for the time being, to the dinner or the dollar. In other states of things men will be present in greater supply than the demand will employ. Then the dinner will be greater than the man, as it has been many and many a time in the course of human history. During the twentieth century the men will be in demand, and democracy will be strong, but the wealth, denied recognition and legitimate power in politics, will do what we now see it do; it will exert an illicit and corrupting power because its processes will be secret and unavowable. It is amusing to hear "publicity" advocated as a cure when secrecy is a minor symptom only of the disease. Plutocracy is not every form of the power of wealth, much less is the word properly used when, as often occurs, it is used for great wealth and luxury. Plutocracy means properly a form of societal organization in which wealth is the ruling power. Hence a democracy turns into a plutocracy not when it recognizes wealth as a legitimate form of social power in any state but when after trying to exclude it from any power a state of things is produced in which wealth is the real power by secret, illicit, and corrupt operation.

The state of things which results is well known to us, but the current discussion of it is very one-sided. No one appears to admit that democracy can be at fault. What are the facts? Legislative strikes, "hold ups," and special legislation are complementary forms of abuse. The kind of legislature which "the people" elects goes to work to threaten wealth, especially corporate wealth, with hostile legislation or, when asked to pass acts which are needed to organize industry, it makes interested opposition. The men to whom great corporate interests are entrusted have to meet the situation. If they did not attend to the matter before the legislature was elected they would find themselves in calamity a little later. This aspect of the matter is either ignored or denied; but one must have little knowledge of affairs as they go on to dispute the truth of it. The next development is the boss. The money interests would never meddle with legislation if they could help it. It is dangerous. They prefer to deal with a boss who holds no office, who is an individual, who can be held responsible to them but not to the public, who wants only campaign funds. This is a new and very evident corruption of the democracy, for it strengthens the evolution of the boss. When the money interests and the boss have formed their alliance, it is available to enable the plutocrats to get what they ought not to have. The action and reaction of these operations is disastrous to the political system; and this reaction is exactly what forms the chief part of legislative activity to-day. The twentieth century inherits it as a system in full operation whose consequences the next generations must meet and whose remedy they must find. There ought to be a free and pitiless exposition of democracy, as a political system and philosophy, which would show just what it is and is not.

The evolution of democracy has produced a type of person in the nineteenth century which is now to be bequeathed to the twentieth. This is the man-on-the-curbstone. He is now in full control, and his day of glory will be the twentieth century. He is ignorant, noisy, self-sufficient, dogmatic, and impatient of opposition or remonstrance. He is ready to talk at any time about anything, but he prefers to talk of public affairs. He talks a great deal. Often he edits a newspaper. The newspapers bow down to him, flatter him, and treat him as the specimen type of "the people." It is in the name of that venerated "symbol" that he commonly speaks. When he wants to say a thing he says that the people says it. When he wants a thing he says that the people wants it. Taine called him the *cuistre*, for he is well known in France, where he is almost always an editor. He is also in authority in England. He is the typical person who is referred to as the common man, the average citizen, and who is credited with superhuman insight and wisdom. His cleverness is put in especially strong contrast with that of the learned. The doctrine seems to be that if a man who once was humble and ignorant uses all the means mortals have in order to try to find out something, the result is that he knows less than his humble and ignorant comrades who never made any such attempt. The man-on-the-curbstone is not one of the quiet people who go about their own affairs and who, since they make no noise, are neglected. He puts himself in evidence, and seeks opportunity to make demonstrations with badges, with shouts and cries. He responds very promptly to the military appeal. That is exactly in his line. There is no need to know or think much. The affair is one of noise and hurrah, bells and trumpets, flags and drums, speeches and poetry. He is always great on patriotism. He supposes that patriotism is an affair of enthusiasm and brag and bluster. He calls the flag "Old Glory" and wants a law that it shall be raised on all schoolhouses. Such matters as this occupy his mind. He has taken us in hand since the Spanish War and has fixed the destiny of this country. The people who knew better have nearly all thought it policy not to oppose the popular current set by this type of person. The newspapers have taken their cue from him, and our destiny has been settled without any reason or sense, without regard to history or political philosophy. That the press, the pulpit, the universities, the magazines could have so given up their functions and prostrated themselves before this organ of folly, for fear of falling out of sympathy with the man-on-the-curbstone, would have been incredible if we had not lived through it. What is the use of trying to learn anything? What is the use of preaching to young men that they should stick to what they think is true and should act from principle not from popularity? Their parents and teachers do not do it. What is the use of bewailing "commercialism" and the power of money? It is all humbug, if we know that everybody does and will act from gain or policy when the occasion arises. What is the use of talking about making good citizens in our universities when our young men see that what everybody does is to listen for the keynote from the man-on-the-curbstone and then begin to shout it as hard as he can without regard to anything else. All humbug is shameful and disgusting. If commercialism is the code, let us avow it. . . .

The eighteenth century bequeathed to the nineteenth notions of the state of nature, natural rights, social compact, equality of all men, sovereignty of the people, fighting doctrines. The nineteenth century is bequeathing to the twentieth a large assortment of popular or semi-popular notions about economic facts and relations. It is current doctrine in large circles of the ruling classes that the laborer (wage class) is entitled to the whole of the product; that all the wealth which the rich accumulate is taken away from others, especially from the poor; that land is a gratuitous gift of God which never ought to be appropriated by anybody; that God provided a fund (viz. the unearned increment from land) to pay the expenses of the civil organization; that there is some danger from large aggregations of capital; that it is not the man who creates the wealth which he accumulates but the society around him so that this society may justly confiscate it when he dies; that there is some innate tendency in things which is called progress, meaning a tendency all the time to become more and more as men would like to have them. The natural and necessary effect of the increased material comfort of the nineteenth century is to increase discontent. This is perfectly correct in human nature. The contented man is he who never had anything and never had any expectation that he ever could get anything. To get something opens the mind to hope for more and produces discontent. The countries in which the gain has been greatest are those in which the discontent is greatest. A writer who knew Russia said that there was no discontent there except amongst those who expected an order or title on the last royal birthday and did not get it. The social and political philosophy which has been spread abroad in the nineteenth century has nourished a doctrine that if a man wants anything which he has not got it is the fault of somebody else who ought to be found and compelled to give it to him. The age is fond of phrases. It cajoles itself with words. Its literary and rhetorical purveyors treat it as if it would take nothing but honey and pie. The future historian, if he ever reads the newspapers of to-day, will wonder whether the American people of to-day really were so unwilling to listen to reason that it was necessary to feed them all the time with flattery, appeals to national vanity, gratification of their ill-educated prejudices, and reiterated assurances of their greatness, wisdom, and virtue. The real interests of the country and these matters with which popular attention is all the time occupied stand in glaring contrast to each other. It is the combination of all these tendencies which gives significance to the above mentioned economic notions. The United States has its peculiar phases, but other states suffer from the same popular delusions. The rage of disillusion and disappointment will have to be met by the inheriting century.

The bequest of economic and social confusion and contradiction, not to say fallacy, which the dying century leaves to the coming one is a formidable charge of peril and societal burden. . . .

It is very easy to take sides in regard to the antagonisms which have been noted and to say that, of course, the other side is doing wrong and therefore is to blame for all the trouble. Democracy and plutocracy make each other worse by their conflict. That democratic institutions are corrupted to their core by the plutocratic legislation which has been described is obvious. There is nothing left of democracy when politicians squeeze money out of capitalists and corporations with which to win elections and pay it back by jobbing legislation. The most essential interests of everybody who has any property, from the man who has a hundred dollars in the savings bank up to the millionaire, are imperilled by legislative strikes and jobs and crank legislation according to a Henry George or some other half-educated apostle of the millennium, in which everybody is to have everything for nothing by recognizing and securing to him the gifts of God—as if the world bore any evidence that God had made it to be a paradise for everybody without any trouble. Everybody applauds denunciations of plutocracy or of democracy according to his adopted standpoint and pet notions. Everybody dreams of a victory for his pet ideas "in the twentieth century." They will all be disappointed. They will produce great strife and confusion and loss, but the bigger force will prevail over the smaller in 2001 just as surely as it does to-day. Now, what is the greater force—the man or the dollar (we should say the dinner)? There are those who say that the men are, and they wax indignantly eloquent at the idea of putting the dinner above the man.

Now note the facts of experience: (1) the cases of the tariff, the pensions, the socialistic devices, in short, all the cases in which men make friends with the steal when they get into it, prove the power of the dinner over the man, because they show the man repudiating his principles in favor of his interests. (2) All the achievements of the plutocrats which are denounced prove that they are men of transcendent ability, more powerful than thousands of other men put together simply by force of brains. Every disputant who enters the debate affirms these two facts. They are the foundation of the case of all who believe in numbers. Now put them together. Then we have the men of intellectual force, with the force of capital in their hands, and the very arena in which they have shown their power is that of "votes" and of the democratic legislature, where the orators of lunar political economy say that they expect to defeat them. What is the conclusion? That the plutocrats should be allowed to have their own way? Not by any means; but that the lunar politics should be discarded and not allowed to form the platform of attacks on property. Property is the strongest, deepest, most universal interest of mankind. It is the most fundamental condition of the struggle for existence; that is to say, of the welfare of mankind. It does not mean millions of dollars; it means cents. It must be aggregated in large masses under personal control or the work of society cannot go on. It is silly to get into states of excitement about "large aggregations of capital" or the "excessive wealth of individuals." If the legislature were pure and if it restricted itself to its proper business, it would have no trouble at all in regulating any arrogance of wealth whenever it showed itself. The contest of democracy and plutocracy is the contest between the economic power and opportunity mentioned at the outset and the political conditions under which it must be carried on. . . .

The summary of the line of thought in this paper is that while the outlook on the twentieth century from the industrial standpoint is in the highest degree encouraging, the outlook from the political standpoint is of the opposite character. It is essential to the interests of human society that its institutions should be developed harmoniously; its political institutions and methods must be adequate to perform in a healthful manner the functions which they are called on to perform in order to sustain the development of the industrial organization. Such is not now the case, and the consequence is that the nineteenth century bequeaths to the twentieth a great degree of social confusion, both in ideas and in institutions, which is due to the maladjustment between the industrial system and the political system. It is plain that each of these systems has a sphere of legitimate and independent activity. A victory either of democracy over plutocracy or of plutocracy over democracy would be disastrous to civilization. For the present and the immediate future the purification of political institutions is the most urgent task which demands our effort, and it seems that the most effective effort in that direction is to dispel the illusions and popular notions which now prevail in this domain.

Social Problems

Henry George

There come moments in our lives that summon all our powers—when we feel that, casting away illusions, we must decide and act with our utmost intelligence and energy. So in the lives of peoples come periods specially calling for earnestness and intelligence.

We seem to have entered one of these periods. Over and again have nations and civilizations been confronted with problems which, like the riddle of the Sphinx, not to answer was to be destroyed; but never before have problems so vast and intricate been presented. This is not strange. That the closing years of this century must bring up momentous social questions follows from the material and intellectual progress that has marked its course.

Between the development of society and the development of species these is a close analogy. In the lowest forms of animal life there is little difference of parts; both wants and powers are few and simple; movement seems automatic; and instincts are scarcely distinguishable from those of the vegetable. So homogeneous are some of these living things, that if cut in pieces, each piece still lives. But as life rises into higher manifestations, simplicity gives way to complexity, the parts develop into organs having separate functions and reciprocal relations, new wants and powers arise, and a greater and greater degree of intelligence is needed to secure food and avoid danger. Did fish, bird or beast possess no higher intelligence than the polyp, Nature could bring them forth only to die.

This law—that the increasing complexity and delicacy of organization which give higher capacity and increased power are accompanied by increased wants and dangers, and require, therefore, increased intelligence—runs through nature. In the ascending scale of life at last comes man, the most highly and delicately organized of animals. Yet not only do his higher powers require for their use a higher intelligence than exists in other animals, but without higher intelligence he could not live. His

Henry George, *Social Problems* (Chicago and New York: Belfrad, Clark and Co., 1883), pp. 9–21.

skin is too thin; his nails too brittle; he is too poorly adapted for running, climbing, swimming or burrowing. Were he not gifted with intelligence greater than that of any beast, he would perish from cold, starve from inability to get food, or be exterminated by animals better equipped for the struggle in which brute instinct suffices.

In man, however, the intelligence which increases all through nature's rising scale passes at one bound into an intelligence so superior, that the difference seems of kind rather than degree. In him, that narrow and seemingly unconscious intelligence that we call instinct becomes conscious reason, and the godlike power of adaptation and invention makes feeble man nature's king.

But with man the ascending line stops. Animal life assumes no higher form; nor can we affirm that, in all his generations, man, as an animal, has a whit improved. But progression in another line begins. Where the development of species ends, social development commences, and that advance of society that we call civilization so increases human powers, that between savage and civilized man there is a gulf so vast as to suggest the gulf between the highly organized animal and the oyster glued to the rocks. And with every advance upon this line new vistas open. When we try to think what knowledge and power progressive civilization may give to the men of the future, imagination fails.

In this progression which begins with man, as in that which leads up to him, the same law holds. Each advance makes a demand for higher and higher intelligence. With the beginnings of society arises the need for social intelligence—for that consensus of individual intelligence which forms a public opinion, a public conscience, a public will, and is manifested in law, institutions and administration. As society develops, a higher and higher degree of this social intelligence is required, for the relation of individuals to each other becomes more intimate and important, and the increasing complexity of the social organization brings liability to new dangers.

In the rude beginning, each family produces its own food, makes its own clothes, builds its own house, and, when it moves, furnishes its own transportation. Compare with this independence the intricate interdependence of the denizens of a modern city. They may supply themselves with greater certainty, and in much greater variety and abundance, than the savage; but it is by the co-operation of thousands. Even the water they drink, and the artificial light they use, are brought to them by elaborate machinery, requiring the constant labor and watchfulness of many men. They may travel at a speed incredible to the savage; but in doing so resign life and limb to the care of others. A broken rail, a drunken engineer, a careless switchman, may hurl them to eternity. And the power of applying labor to the satisfaction of desire passes, in the same way, beyond the direct control of the individual. The laborer becomes but part of a great machine, which may at any time be paralyzed by causes beyond his power, or even his foresight. Thus does the well-being of each become more and more dependent upon the well-being of all—the individual more and more subordinate to society.

And so come new dangers. The rude society resembles the creatures that though cut into pieces will live; the highly civilized society is like a highly organized animal: a stab in a vital part, the suppression of a single function, is death. A savage village may be burned and its people driven off—but, used to direct recourse to nature, they can maintain themselves. Highly civilized man, however, accustomed to capital, to machinery, to the minute division of labor, becomes helpless when suddenly deprived of these and thrown upon nature. Under the factory system, some sixty persons, with the aid of much costly machinery, co-operate to the making of a pair of shoes. But, of the sixty, not one could make a whole shoe. This is the tendency in all branches of production, even in agriculture. How many farmers of the new generation can use the flail? How many farmers' wives can now make a coat from the wool? Many of our farmers do not even make their own butter or raise their own vegetables! There is an enormous gain in productive power from this division of labor, which assigns to the individual the production of but a few of the things, or even but a small part of one of the things, he needs, and makes each dependent upon others with whom he never comes in contact; but the social organization becomes more sensitive. A primitive village community may pursue the even tenor of its life without feeling disasters which overtake other villages but a few miles off; but in the closely knit civilization to which we have attained, a war, a scarcity, a commercial crisis, in one hemisphere produces powerful effects in the other, while shocks and jars from which a primitive community easily recovers would to a highly civilized community mean wreck. . . .

In a simpler state master and man, neighbor and neighbor, know each other, and there is that touch of the elbow which, in times of danger, enables society to rally. But present tendencies are to the loss of this. In London, dwellers in one house do not know those in the next; the tenants of adjoining rooms are utter strangers to each other. Let civil conflict break or paralyze the authority that preserves order and the vast population would become a terror-stricken mob, without point of rally or principle of cohesion, and your London would be sacked and burned by an army of thieves. London is only the greatest of great cities. What is true of London is true of New York, and in the same measure true of the many cities whose hundreds of thousands are steadily growing toward millions. These vast aggregations of humanity, where he who seeks isolation may find it more truly than in the desert; where wealth and poverty touch and jostle; where one revels and another starves within a few feet of each other, yet separated by as great a gulf as that fixed between Dives in Hell and Lazarus in Abraham's bosom—they are centers and types of our civilization. Let jar or shock dislocate the complex and delicate organization, let the policeman's club be thrown down or wrested from him, and the fountains of the great deep are opened, and quicker than ever before chaos comes again. Strong as it may seem, our civilization is evolving destructive forces. Not desert and forest, but city slums and country roadsides are nursing the barbarians who may be to the new what Hun and Vandal were to the old.

Nor should we forget that in civilized man still lurks the savage. The men who, in past times, oppressed or revolted, who fought to the death in petty quarrels and drunk fury with blood, who burnt cities and rent empires, were men essentially such as those we daily meet. Social progress has accumulated knowledge, softened manners, refined tastes and extended sympathies, but man is yet capable of as blind a rage as, when clothed in skins, he fought wild beasts with a flint. And present tendencies, in some respects at least, threaten to kindle passions that have so often before flamed in destructive fury.

There is in all the past nothing to compare with the rapid changes now going on in the civilized world. It seems as though in the European race, and in the nineteenth century, man was just beginning to live—just grasping his tools and becoming conscious of his powers. The snail's pace of crawling ages has suddenly become the headlong rush of the locomotive, speeding faster and faster. This rapid progress is primarily in industrial methods and material powers. But industrial changes imply social changes and necessitate political changes. Progressive societies outgrow institutions as children outgrow clothes. Social progress always requires greater intelligence in the management of public affairs; but this the more as progress is rapid and change quicker.

And that the rapid changes now going on are bringing up problems that demand most earnest attention may be seen on every hand. Symptoms of danger, premonitions of violence, are appearing all over the civilized world. Creeds are dying, beliefs are changing; the old forces of conservatism are melting away. Political institutions are failing, as clearly in democratic America as in monarchical Europe. There is growing unrest and bitterness among the masses, whatever be the form of government, a blind groping for escape from conditions becoming intolerable. To attribute all this to the teachings of demagogues is like attributing the fever to the quickened pulse. It is the new wine beginning to ferment in old bottles. To put into a sailing-ship the powerful engines of a first-class ocean steamer would be to tear her to pieces with their play. So the new powers rapidly changing all the relations of society must shatter social and political organizations not adapted to meet their strain. . . .

A civilization which tends to concentrate wealth and power in the hands of a fortunate few, and to make of others mere human machines, must inevitably evolve anarchy and bring destruction. But a civilization is possible in which the poorest could have all the comforts and conveniences now enjoyed by the rich; in which prisons and almshouses would be needless, and charitable societies unthought of. Such a civilization only waits for the social intelligence that will adapt means to ends. Powers that might give plenty to all are already in our hands. Though there is poverty and want, there is, yet, seeming embarrassment from the very excess of wealth-producing forces. "Give us but a market," say manufacturers, "and we will supply goods to no end!" "Give us but work!" cry idle men!

The evils that begin to appear spring from the fact that the application of intelligence to social affairs has not kept pace with the application of intelligence to individual needs and material ends. Natural science strides forward, but political science lags. With all our progress in the arts which produce wealth, we have made no progress in securing its equitable distribution. Knowledge has vastly increased; industry and commerce have been revolutionized; but whether free trade or protection is best for a nation we are not yet agreed. We have brought machinery to a pitch of perfection that, fifty years ago, could not have been imagined; but, in the presence of political corruption, we seem as helpless as idiots. The East River bridge is a crowning triumph of mechanical skill; but to get it built a leading citizen of Brooklyn had to carry to New York sixty thousand dollars in a carpet-bag to bribe New York aldermen. The human soul that thought out the great bridge is prisoned in a crazed and broken body that lies bed-fast, and could only watch it grow by peering through a telescope. Nevertheless, the weight of the immense mass is estimated and adjusted for every inch. But the skill of the engineer could not prevent condemned wire being smuggled into the cable.

The progress of civilization requires that more and more intelligence be devoted to social affairs, and this not the intelligence of the few, but that of the many. We cannot safely leave politics to politicians, or political economy to college professors. The people themselves must think, because the people alone can act.

In a "journal of civilization" a professed teacher declares the saving word for society to be that each shall mind his own business. This is the gospel of selfishness, soothing as soft flutes to those who, having fared well themselves, think everybody should be satisfied. But the salvation of society, the hope for the free, full development of humanity, is in the gospel of brotherhood—the gospel of Christ. Social progress makes the well-being of all more and more the business of each; it binds all closer and closer together in bonds from which none can escape. He who observes the law and the proprieties, and cares for his family, yet takes no interest in the general weal, and gives no thought to those who are trodden under foot, save now and then to bestow alms, is not a true

Christian. Nor is he a good citizen. The duty of the citizen is more and harder than this.

The intelligence required for the solving of social problems is not a mere thing of the intellect. It must be animated with the religious sentiment and warm with sympathy for human suffering. It must stretch out beyond self-interest, whether it be the self-interest of the few or the many. It must seek justice. For at the bottom of every social problem we will find a social wrong.

Politico-Social Functions

Lester F. Ward

It is a sign of an approaching crisis in social opinion, when prevailing theories become widely at variance with prevailing practices. While a certain amount of general depravity may be conceded, even to a progressive and apparently prosperous people, it is quite too much to insist that, because they are almost universally running counter to the received philosophy, they must necessarily be pursuing a downward course. They may simply be following social instincts; and when social instincts are found to be powerfully opposed to social tenets, it is time, while deploring the former, to pause, also, and examine the latter.

In one view, all truth is relative. Doctrines that were true for one age cease to be true for a later one; principles which really worked the salvation of the last century cannot be utilized in the present one. The conservative tendencies of society, which perpetuate customs and ceremonies after their usefulness has ceased, preserve also the great social theories by which past ages have been redeemed, and they hand them down to later times, with which they no longer stand in legitimate relationship. Feeling is more powerful than intellect. Society is always moved by the great tide of sentiment long before the voice of reason declares the nature of this motive power. When the tide once fairly sets in one direction, the philosopher knows that there must be a force behind it; but ere he can investigate that force by the slow and cautious methods of science, and announce its true character, long steps will have been taken in the direction of the inevitable. This is a critical period. The interval between action and reason,—between new practice and new theory—is one full of dangers to society. For all the forms of feeling, as well as the particular form called love, are equally blind; and blind sentiment sweeping through new tracks, and encountering old theories and old practices, must inevitably produce innumerable conflicts and perpetually jeopardize the great interests which are at stake.

Lester F. Ward, "Politico-Social Functions" in *The Pennsylvania Monthly* (Philadelphia), Vol. 12, No. 137, May 1881, pp. 321–336.

The second half of the nineteenth century is precisely such a period as that described. Theory and practice are at war. The only social philosophy that exists is one that condemns the bulk of the social action taken. The libraries of the world are filled with arguments against the very course which events are blindly taking. The whole weight of the greatest social writers of the past is massed against the social movement of the age. The works of Adam Smith and Ricardo, of Pitt, Cobden and the two Mills, of Jean Baptiste Say and Michel Chevalier, and of the train of political economists who have followed these leaders, while they abound in discords and contain many conflicting views, are, in the main, hostile to all those schemes of regulation which characterize the action of modern States. The political science of these masters is all there is to be taught in the colleges and universities, and it continues to be so taught. The representatives of science have joined their forces with the ones already named, and, with the added power which science has justly come to wield, stand boldly in the track of current events. There is also an able corps of living writers who are earnestly protesting against the tendencies of the times. The commercial and financial journals are filled with hostile flings at "Government meddling," and "bureaucracy"; the organs of transportation, telegraph, and insurance companies are daily holding up the dangers of "State regulation." The Cobden Club and other "Free Trade" societies are scattering tracts with a liberal hand, in the hope of stemming the tide. Victor Boehmert warns, Augustus Mongredien shouts, and Herbert Spencer thunders. What is the result? Germany answers by purchasing private railroads and enacting a high protective tariff. France answers by decreeing the construction of eleven thousand miles of Government railroad, and offering a bounty to French shipowners. England answers by a compulsory education act, by Government purchase of the telegraph, and by a judicial decision laying claim to the telephone. America answers by an inter-State railroad bill, a national education bill, and a sweeping *plebiscite* in favor of protection to home manufactures. The whole world has caught the contagion, and all nations are adopting measures of positive legislation. . . .

What conclusion is the thoughtful student of social events to deduce from all this? The prevailing school of political economists thinks the world is temporarily mad, but hopes that it will soon return to itself. They declare the entire movement baseless, and believe that all efforts should be directed toward diffusing and reinforcing existing theories, and they insist that there are no grounds on which the events described can be logically defended. In this they are undoubtedly sincere. Reform with them means simply a halt and reversal of prevailing tendencies.

But there is another possible policy, practicable also for those who really desire reform. It is an adage that reforms never go backward. It is always well to inquire whether, underlying a great movement, however perverse it may appear, there may not be a basis of truth concealed by the errors that lie on the surface. In such cases true reform may not consist in open opposition. This may often be fruitful of harm, and usually is fruitless of good.

In the present state of society, the movement above sketched is irresistible. This is sufficiently proved by the powerlessness of the influences allied against it to check it. It behooves all true reformers, therefore, to cease factious opposition, and settle down to the soberer task of studying the causes of the phenomena observed. Society needs less to be told that it is doing wrong than to be shown what it is really doing. If there must be a movement in a given direction, let its true nature be made known. The jars and evils are due, not to the advance itself, but to the clashing of interests which ignorance of their existence and of the whole field swept over renders inevitable. The true need is for enlightenment respecting the causes and consequences of action, by the aid of which alone these conflicts can be avoided and the movement intelligently guided.

In what consists this schism between theory and practice? It is after all a schism between two theories; for all action is based on theory, if it is nothing more than a blind intuition of selfish and momentary benefit. In the present case it is much more. Fundamentally formulated, it is the theory of natural, against that of artificial regulation. The belief in some form or regulation is one deeply implanted in the human mind. A supposed divine regulation of human affairs was the first form in which this belief manifested itself. Then, when government was exercised chiefly by one man or a few men, the belief in the power of these rulers to regulate society was long supreme. It is only since the civilizing agencies of printing and of science have been at work, that this illusion has been dispelled. But in its place the only alternative clearly perceived has been accepted, viz., the idea that nature and the laws of nature are alone competent to regulate the affairs of men. This theory was plausible. It was supported by the spontaneous growth of numerous great industries; it was strengthened by the failures of human regulation in the past, and by the continuance of such failures in the present. It was thought to be in full accord with all the teachings of science which had so greatly contributed to relieve the world of the yoke of despotic regulation. Science taught the uniformity of all of nature's processes. It taught that the universe was controlled by fixed and unchangeable laws which could not be violated with impunity. Progress in nature was due to the secular operation of these laws, which could neither be slackened nor accelerated. Political science followed strictly in the path of physical science. It declared that commerce and industry were controlled by uniform laws of nature which man must interfere with at his peril. The laws of trade must be allowed to take their course. The improvements necessary to further civilization, to be real or substantial, must be spontaneous. Great systems of commercial intercourse, of productive industry, of transportation, intercommunication, finance, and education, would naturally work themselves out, provided the potential qualities necessary for them existed in society. Every attempt on the part of Government to interfere with these great processes of nature only recoiled upon the agent and imperilled the safety of the State. Government must protect—it must not control; it may forbid—it may not command.

Such was the theory which very naturally grew up at a time when it was greatly needed, and emancipated society to such an extent from monarchical and oligarchical rule, that nearly every one of the pretended monarchies of Europe is to-day a virtual democracy. And this is none other than the present prevailing theory of political economists; the one which is embodied in our masterpieces of literature and philosophy, is taught in our colleges, preached in our pulpits, echoed from our rostrums, served up daily by the press, and advocated by many of the most learned men of the time. And now, in these later days of republican institutions, which, as already remarked, it has done much to secure, it finds itself again confronted by an enemy which it cannot distinguish from the old one that it formerly encountered and drove back.

Just here is the great mistake. In so far as artificial regulation in itself is concerned, the modern theory is indeed identical with the original one; but here the parallelism ceases. Government under a real autocrat is the interference by one man with the affairs of millions. Government by popularly chosen representatives is the management by society of its own affairs. This may be true only in theory, but it approaches realization in proportion as representative government approaches perfection.

Now, precisely the conception which vaguely, but not the less obstinately, inspires all the apparently rash tendencies of our times, is that society ought to take its affairs into its own hands, check the abuses of unrestrained competition and combination, and consciously work out certain of the problems of civilization. Against the negative theory that nature must be left to bring about social progress in its own time and way, it holds that nature may be assisted by organized social action, very much as the *vis medicatrix naturae* may be assisted by intelligently directed applications of the healing art. Not, however, that individuals, legislators, or Governments consciously reason out such a scheme. On the contrary, they scarcely know that they are carrying it out, and would in most cases deny it, if openly charged with it. In fact, nearly all classes—even those who are wielding all their influence against it—profess to admit the truth of the prevailing theory. They do not realize, and generally do not know, that they are antagonizing it. They wince under the charges of the theoretical school, and confess or make no response; yet they are not deterred from their work. There is no fixed set of doctrines laid down to govern this movement. Acts advancing it are not defended by argument. It is an impulse without a philosophy; an instinct rather than a conviction. Yet it is deep-seated and ineradicable, and its smouldering fires often burst into view in the form of prejudices and passions. There is a sentiment that something is wrong, and a feeling that something should be done. The opposite school does not share these feelings. It condemns every attempt to *do* anything. "*Laissez faire, laissez passer*," said De Gournay; and with these words was christened the *laissez faire* school of political economists. These writers deride the mistakes of Governments in the past in trying to perform positive functions, and show that such attempts have usually resulted in failures, and often in mischief. All their utterances and teachings imply that it is folly to undertake the control of social events, and wisdom to leave them wholly to the untrammelled influence of what they call natural laws. As above remarked, almost everybody, if separately questioned, would admit this position, so completely has it become part of the education and thought of the present age; and yet, often without perceiving the inconsistency, many entertain a vague but powerful sentiment in favor of mending existing evils, of regulating social events, and of doing something very decisive in many ways.

It is this insidious manner in which these two incompatible theories coexist, often in the same individual, and permeate society, that complicates the problem and creates the urgent need of a clear presentation of their respective claims and a thorough acquaintance with their nature and aims. If man was really, as is often claimed, a rational being, in the sense of always acting upon reasoned-out conclusions, there would be no difficulty. It would then resolve itself into a simple trial of strength between two well-defined parties. But as it is, every house is, as it were, divided against itself. A political speaker may harangue an American audience on the dangers to be apprehended from the centralization of power, from Government interference in private enterprise, from an army of paid office-holders striving to do the business of the country, from attempts of the State to manage lines of transportation and intercommunication, from legislation granting subsidies to rich corporations or taking from the people the right to issue bills of exchange or solicit deposits; and all these sentiments will be applauded. Another speaker may address the same audience the next day, warning them of the dangers of grasping corporations, from industrial, commercial, and financial monopolies, from fraudulent bankruptcies and dishonest failures; and he, too, will receive equally unqualified approbation. The workingman may be excited to the pitch of belligerency by telling him that the clothing he wears, the cutlery and tools he uses, and much of the food he eats, are far dearer than they would be but for a protective tariff which enables certain monopolists to put up the prices of the commodities they manufacture; but the same individual could have been wrought up to the same pitch by informing him that a given increase in the duty on certain articles of foreign importation would enhance his wages a given per cent and that certain persons are trying to reduce these duties still lower, so as to compel him to compete with the pauper labor of Europe. Yet, while in the first of each of these hypothetical cases the appeal is such as would come from the school of *laissez faire* economists, in the second it is, in both cases, that which would come from the school of State regulation.

These examples, however, will help us to obtain a glimpse of the foundation upon which this latter school stands. Science and natural law to the contrary notwithstanding, it remains, and always has remained, a patent fact, that social events, left to themselves, are always attended with glaring evils. There is no necessary harmony beween natural law and human advantage. The laws of trade inevitably result in enormous inequalities in the distribution of wealth. It may, with much truth, be argued that considerable inequality is the better social condition; but the degree and kind of inequality which is actually reached cannot be defended on this ground. The fact is too apparent that all this inequality is not due to the superior intelligence or industry of those who possess most, which, thus limited, many might be disposed to declare just. It is obvious that mere accident of birth or position is sufficient to account for the great bulk of this inequality; that real intelligence, beyond the coarse cunning inspired by avarice, has little or nothing to do with it; that the primary producers—that is, the discoverers and inventors of the laws and appliances by which the production of wealth is accelerated—have generally enjoyed few or none of the advantages of their intellectual efforts, but that these are reaped by men of very moderate abilities beyond a certain business shrewdness and tact; that the immediate creators of wealth—the bone and sinew of labor—are, in nearly all cases, poor, while princely fortunes fall, for the most part, to the class who, far removed from all the objects of production or exchange, busy themselves solely with the medium of exchange or with mere transfers of entries representing the value of commodities produced and exchanged.

Again, natural laws do not prevent monopolies. The theory is that competition will keep down rates and prices; but the fact is that there is so much cooperation attending competition, when neither is under any control, that the former influence is exceedingly limited in its effects. These are chiefly seen in the swallowing up of small industries by larger ones. Competition results in great irregularity and an uncertain state of affairs. Rates and prices frequently fall below the cost of conducting business. This, while it might be continued under national control, where it has no other effect than to alter the distribution of the burden of supporting it, must be of short duration with private individuals or corporations, and soon be followed by failure, involving heavy losses not only to the parties immediately interested, but to the general stock of the world's capital. In short, the uncontrolled operation of natural laws in social affairs involves immense waste of created wealth. . . .

But while this waste and disorder through unrestrained competition constitutes in reality the more serious question for the true economist, monopoly through unrestrained combination is the more vital one for the unphilosophical public. This last, however, is the natural successor of the first. Extreme competition and extreme cooperation are but the crest and trough of the great ocean swell of unregulated social events.

The world today is alarmed—whether justly or not, it matters not—at the prospect of unlimited combination among the vast corporations already in existence. These gigantic enterprises are regarded as threatening to crush out all competition and place every form of product at their mercy. That they have the power to do this, no one can doubt, and their only fear is social revolution. Under the laws they are omnipotent; they dread only the "higher law," and anarchy, which sometimes becomes more tolerable than government by law. Moreover, these immense monopolies are the legitimate product of natural law. They represent the integrated organisms of social evolution. . . .

Lastly, it is not true that all attempts at Government regulation and State management have failed or wrought only mischief. State postal management is admitted by nearly everybody to have proved a success. City corporations now universally undertake the work of extinguishing fires, as being too closely connected with the interests of all to be entrusted to private enterprise. There are still a few who condemn the public school system, such as it exists under State and municipal regulation, but it is generally conceded that the people are considerably better educated than they would have been had education been left entirely to private efforts. These exceptions, if such they may be called, together with some others, apply to the United States with a very weak Government, which is jealously watched by a suspicious democracy, ready to hurl its *personnel* from power for the slightest departure from their prescribed duties. But when we look to the Old World, we see that these so-called encroachments upon individual rights have progressed much further. . . .

But we may go much farther. Of what does government consist? It consists, when rightly understood, simply of a collection of just such cases in which matters of general public interest have been taken out of the hands of individuals and assumed by the central authority. As soon as one such industry becomes permanently established as a proper object of national administration, it drops out of the list of those which it is deemed necessary to defend against Government encroachment. Each one of the body of regulative agencies which constitute the present accepted sphere of normal governmental functions has passed through this stage before settling down into its present place. We see this clearly in the history of finance and the bitter opposition to national banking. We may see it still more plainly where no one ever thinks of looking—in the progress of jurisprudence. It is, comparatively speaking, only recently that in Europe people were obliged to administer their own justice, both civil and criminal; and this is still the prevailing custom among many barbaric peoples and savage tribes.

Government has ever been constantly encroaching upon these supposed private rights, in the interest of the public good; and, though always opposed, it has always been slowly gaining ground. And, whether we like it or not, this process is destined to continue until, one after another, all the important public operations of society shall come more or less directly under the power of State regulation. Contrary to the general belief, this result is not often reached before the time is ripe for it. Such is the aversion to innovation, that the evils of private management usually become well-nigh intolerable before the State is able or willing to step in and relieve them. While, therefore, progress in the direction of enlarging the sphere of Government operation should be very slow and cautious, such is the constitution of society and of the human mind, that there is less danger than is generally supposed that this will take place too rapidly....

The stigma which now attaches to the term "Government regulation," is, therefore, simply that which individuals, seeking to profit by the absence of it, have ingeniously fastened upon it. It applies only so long as there is hope of defeating State interference in the excesses of private competition and combination. As soon as this hope is definitely surrendered these operations become legitimate Government functions, and Government is then abused, if at all, only for not performing them in a wholly infallible manner. . . .

Regarded as the agency of society, it is clear that the acts of Government, theoretically at least, are simply the acts of society through its chosen agents; and Mr. Herbert Spencer has ably shown that even the most despotic forms of Government really reflect the average will and character of the units composing such societies. Opposition to Government regulation is, therefore, in the nature of an attempt to frustrate the will of society as it is constituted to express it; but so long as such opposition is successful, this is itself the proof that the acts opposed do not properly represent the social will as thus constituted, since the only test of this will is the power to enforce it, no matter what the form of Government.

Thus viewed, the entire movement of which we have spoken becomes a social movement, and the conflict must be between individuals and society at large. The question in each case is, then, shall individuals continue to control this industry, or shall society henceforth control it? We have seen that the sphere of social control has been gradually expanding throughout the periods of civilization, sometimes, perhaps, too rapidly, but usually too slowly; and now we find that for more than a century the English school of negative economists has devoted itself to the task of checking this advance. This *laissez faire* school has entrenched itself behind the fortifications of science, and while declaring with truth that social phenomena are, like physical phenomena, uniform and governed by laws, they have accompanied this by the false declaration and *non sequitur* that neither physical nor social phenomena are capable of human control; the fact being that all the practical benefits of science are the result of man's control of natural forces and phenomena which would otherwise have run to waste or operated as enemies to human progress. The opposing positive school of economists simply demand an opportunity to utilize the social forces for human advantage in precisely the same manner as the physical forces have been utilized. It is only through the artificial control of natural phenomena that science is made to minister to human needs; and if social laws are really analogous to physical laws, there is no reason why social science may not receive practical applications such as have been given to physical science. . . .

The Christian State

George D. Herron

. . . A political order that shall associate men in justice is the present search of civilized peoples. The old ways of political thinking and doing have exhausted themselves. Our present systems of human relations are not able to endure the strain that is coming upon them. Political constitutions, now sacred, will be consumed in the fervent heat of the social trial, and present forms of institutions will disappear. While the peoples international are waiting with a marvellous social patience, with no deep or authoritative disposition to any revolution that is not moral, constitutional, and progressive, none expect the existing order to continue. Not since Augustus achieved the Roman unity of a world of splendid misery, has the race so felt the certainty and the dread, the sorrow and the hope, of universal change. The civilization of to-day is the camp of a vast unorganized and undisciplined army, without visible leadership or apparent method, yet consciously preparing for some nearing conflict which shall issue in a new beginning of history.

That civilization is full of trouble and change is not a cause for mere fear and dread, but for faith, sacrifice, and work. Nothing could be more dreadful than to have the present order of things exist without discontent, complaint, and change. The social movement bears only a superficial likeness to any movement of the past, and our possible failure to apprehend its meaning and act with its forces is the only ground it offers for fear. The world-passion of to-day is construction, however destructive some of its manifestations may yet prove. Unorganized and unharmonious as the forces of social change now seem, the peoples will be restrained by their faith in the providence and deliverance of the change, and united in the living sacrifice of their noblest sons upon the altar of their faith. The peoples are not angry, but rather in sorrow and expectancy, because of their inmost conviction that out of their travail and anguish will a better order of society be born. The world is full of discontent; but it is the dis-

George D. Herron, *The Christian State* (New York: Thomas G. Crowell, 1895), pp. 15–21, 24–35, 37–38, 40–42.

content of God with the degradation of his sons and daughters under the tyranny of a material dominion. Society is moving quickly toward revolution; but it is revolution from anarchy to order, from industrial slavery to industrial freedom, from social violence to social peace, from political atheism to the kingdom of God. The revolution is the manifestation of the social self-discovery which man is now making, and comes as the social creation of the world.

Since man first awoke to the consciousness of his being, social progress has been chiefly the development of the self-knowledge and independent powers of the individual. The freedom and equipment of the individual for a fair rivalry with his fellows has been the fundamental thought of modern political philosophy and activity. But we are now seeing that there can be no true individual development except through association; no individual freedom except through social unity. Through experience and suffering, with a knowledge too deep for logic and too high for the understanding of a materialistic philosophy of society, the race is learning that it is not an aggregation of individuals, but one body, one humanity, of which all individuals are members; that it is not natural, but the misapprehension and antagonism of nature, that these members should strive with each other for place and life in the body. We are in the beginnings of an evolution of human life that as truly transcends the self-consciousness of the individual, as the evolved and reasoning man transcends the animal kingdom. Men are no longer simply conscious that they can act as righteous or unrighteous individuals. The self-consciousness of society is the evolution now in process. . . .

Society must henceforth be the end of political science and effort. Men are ceasing to believe, and can no longer be persuaded, that a condition of rivalry, in which they are supposed to act from an enlightened self-interest, is the real ground of social order and progress. The civilization that now builds upon the assumption that men are antagonists, and not members of one social body, is fundamentally anarchical—against the divine course of things. The politics that remains insensible to the waking social consciousness, the politicians who ignore the social conscience and make the holy watchwords of the past the hypocrisy and traffic of the present, will be but fuel for burning in the day of wrath that is coming to consume our trade politics and false social philosophies as stubble. Not individual liberty to compete, and the equilibrium of warring self-interests, but the association of men in a communion of justice, is the work of the politics that would command the patience and win the respect of the people. The vision of brotherhood will not pass away, for it is heavenly. Politics must obey that vision, or the people will try obedience without politics, and a world-tragedy will have to be the school in which the nations shall learn their law and mission.

But revolution, in the historic sense of the word, cannot save civilization, even though revolution lie between us and our social salvation. We need some power sufficient to deliver us from the necessity, to save us the sorrow and waste of revolution. Notwithstanding Carlyle, revolutions go backward as well as forward. Though we sometimes foolishly imagine ourselves separated from the past by great fixed gulfs, the continuity of our one human development cannot be broken. We can only break with the past by getting ourselves out of the universe. The past is, and is to be; and the work of the present is to carry the past, enlarged and sanctified, into the future. There has never been a great revolution, seeming to break with the past and make the earth new for an instant, from which there has not been a terrible recoil. Sooner or later the revolutionized nation, or civilization, has had to return upon its course and connect itself with the good substance of the evil forms from which it revolted. The continuity has had to be taken up again, the broken links reunited. . . .

Not revolution, but divine evolution from the past, is the method of a better future, if we will follow the way of sacrifice and permit God to move his purposes therein. Revolution and separation mean ultimate anarchy and despotism, a last state worse than the first, unless the past is sacredly kept and speedily wrought into the future. The ruined man, the dying system, the decaying order of things, always has within the germ of the living and the new. A new spirit evolves life out of death; a new purpose changes the way of wickedness into the highway of holiness; a new element turns darkness into light. It was a new disclosure of love upon the cross, a new revelation and spirit of life in the Son of man, a new manifestation of sacrifice as universal law, that evolved a living Christendom from an exhausted Roman world. Progress is a divine journey, a sacred pilgrimage, along a holy way of sacrifice, that is leading man into the freedom of God. When the nations have learned through suffering to walk in this way, then God's judgment days will be man's festivals of joy, as God would have them, not times of shame and dread and burning.

It is but just that we sacrifice ourselves in procuring justice for our fellow-dwellers in the present, and for the citizens of a holier future we shall not live to see. We may be misunderstood by our brothers, and they may refuse to move in the way and with the faith we know they ought to move. They may slay us, and trample upon the life we offer in their behalf. We may have to bear the consequences of their sins, and be the bearers of their guilt. But we ought so to suffer for our brothers, and that with joy, while we entreat them to ascend the path that leads to justice and to peace. We are bound to expiate what is evil in the past, and preserve and carry on to our brothers what is good. We ourselves are the products of the past, and the sacrifice of the past is our strength and power now. None of us in the present are righteous, and the future will have to expiate our sins and correct our mistakes. It is unreasonable and unjust that we should seek to separate ourselves from the body of humanity of which we are members; from the divine course and cost of its progress. We can be neither true to the past nor just to the future, neither true nor just to our brothers of the present, save through the sacrifice of our present life in bearing away the sins of the past for the deliverance of the future. We cannot abide in the past—that is death. Nor can we break with the past—that is ultimate suicide. But our faith may, and it must, make future out of the past, through making the present a holy gift and sacrifice to progress—which is the coming of the kingdom of God.

The testimony of history—to which the social movement is listening as has no other world movement—witnesses throughout to sacrifice as the power by which progress has been made. Underneath and within the revolutions and historic adjustments that have appeared to conquer, the structures of civilization are founded and upheld by those who have been faithful witnesses for the right against the wrong, while lifting no hand for the violent overthrow of the organizations of wrong. The almighty forces that are really working out our human destiny are largely unseen in their operation; but their work is clearly manifest in any pure view of the historic retrospect. Not the men who have brought down other lives with the sword, but the men who have laid down their own lives through an unresisting faith in the triumph of right through moral processes, have prepared the way for the advance of man. The world lives upon the lives of love that are given for its redemption and perfection. Christianity more vitally and speedily conquered the world, and that against Roman organizations and legions, in the century of its sacrifice, than in all the succeeding centuries of ecclesiastical alliances with the forces of war and diplomacy. The failure of the faith of Christian institutions in the law and conquering power of sacrifice has been the calamity and sorrow of modern history; the secret of all our social woe and perplexity. The revival of this compromised and decadent faith, the gathering of the forces of sacrifice upon the field of the social conflict, is the present hope and deliverance of the world.

Now, the most significant fact of this present social juncture and crisis of human affairs, when all recognize the inevitability and on-going processes of revolution of some quality, and under some leadership, is the political faith in Jesus Christ that is rising from the waking social consciousness and increasing social purpose of the world. The social and consequent political revival of Christianity is the most significant fact of modern life, and promises a divine and altogether new quality of revolution—revolution by the force of revelation—revolution come down to earth out of heaven. Not merely or mainly in institutions of religion does this awakened and practical faith in the righteousness of Christ appear, but in movements and forces that religious institutions largely ignore or hold in disrepute. Instinctively, the movements for association and social justice are turning to the person of Jesus as the social ideal that can alone satisfy the social aspiration which is the prayer of civilization. The multitudes believe, though they cannot define their belief, that the real Jesus is the one human life perfectly socialized and able to fulfil man's social nature. With a pathetic and almost inarticulate expectancy, they are waiting to be guided into the eternal order of life that Jesus revealed as the natural right and destiny of man upon the earth. Notwithstanding the false habits of religious feeling and doctrine associated with the teachings of Christ, there is everywhere a deepening and intensifying conviction that his mind is the mind that the institutions of the world must receive in order to procure social justice. Christ is to-day the actual leader of the yet unorganized but rapidly developing political thought and effort of Western nations. . . .

The political appearing of Christ is manifest in the increasing social functions of the state, and the socialization of law. There is a growing belief on the part of social reformers of all classes, that a juster order of society can be procured only through the state as the social organ; the state is the only organ through which the people can act collectively in the search for justice; hence all social reform is coming to effect itself through political action. With this turning to the state as the social organ, has risen an increasing faith in Christ as the social lawgiver; the increasing apprehension of his law of sacrifice as the fundamental law of society. It is thus that the various social reformations, without regard to the religious creeds of the reformers, are converging in an almost unconscious movement to translate the Christianity of Christ into political doctrines and institutions. Such necessity has been laid upon the social reforms that they are being divinely compelled to accept the truth of Christ's law of love, by whatever name they may choose to call it, in order to escape their own failure and the social despair of the people.

The political appearing of Christ is thus more than a vision, and no dream, but the accomplished fact with which nations and institutions must begin to reckon, and the distinction and glory of our age. What makes this the most promising as well as critical hour of history, is the fact that all standards of right and wrong are coming to measure themselves by the one standard of Christ's teachings. Popular have far outrun institutional conceptions of justice, and men will no longer be content with any other kind of right than Christ's. The great undercurrents of popular feeling are moving toward Christ, and the deep undertones of social wrong are beginning to articulate political confessions of faith in his power to deliver. Crude and impure as is the faith of the multitudes who are turning to Jesus for social right and political truth, it is yet a faith divinely inspired and full of hope for our nation and the world. Not understanding and hardly knowing the name of him it follows, the world is gone after Christ, and the Pharisees of official religion prevail nothing in keeping the people to the beaten paths. That religious officialism discerns not that it is the Christ of God the peoples are following is not strange, but the perfect continuity of all the divine ways of the past; neither in religion nor in politics do the official classes see the measure and meaning of the great movements that pass before their eyes. The social movement has never been other than the coming of Christ to rule the nations in righteousness, and the social effort of our day is becoming a political manifestation of Christ. . . .

It may be that not until now could the social ideal and law of Christ have a political interpretation and application. It may be that the Spirit in Jesus was greater than his idea, truer than his historical perspective. It is possible that he saw the consummation of the ages nearer than it was really to be; that what we shall be is not appearing as soon as he thought. Of the day of the full consummation, of the hour of the perfect organization of human life in the economy of redemption, the Son of man said he did not know; the time was known only to his Father. Even so, his sacrifice is increasingly apprehended and obeyed as the law of life, and his Spirit is the creative and directive power of the social movement. Without knowing by whom they are conquered, institutions are reluctantly yielding to the advancing Christ. . . .

The discovery of Christ is the reality of our times. The people have found the Christ,—the great peoples collectively as well as men individually,—and are proclaiming their discovery to our economies and institutions. We have found him in the waking social consciousness; in the developing political thought; in the organizations and efforts to reform society; in the moral earnestness and social questioning that make both painful and glorious the upturned faces of great congregations, eager for original inspiration and vital truth; in the social trouble of both rich and poor, each seeking to know if there really be a kingdom of God and a way to realize it upon the earth; in the spiritual life with which our whole nation is quivering, preparing for a great reaping time soon; in his political appearing as Redeemer and Judge of our customs and organizations. Wherever we turn, whether to question or to help, we find the Christ in the need or the faith of men; in the social hope of the organizing social activities of the day.

The Christian who is mainly a religionist has been indefinitely or indifferently telling us of a time when Christ will come to judge the world. But in the hour when we have thought not the Son of man has come, and now sits in actual judgment upon the world, with its civilizations waiting at his judgment seat. The Lord whom the leaders of official religion have sought in their worship and observances, and whom the political rulers have denied, has come to his temple in the movement for social justice. Upon foundations which cannot be moved, his judgment seat has been established by the social aspiration and faith, and his judgments will increase without end. Our eschatology need no longer be concerned with probations in the future, for the judgment day is come. We can no longer remove the judgment to some remote time, for the judgment is in process. It has already come to pass that civilization accepts Christ as its Judge, and that men and movements are submitting themselves to his judgments, without knowing from whence and by whom they are judged. Now is the crisis of this world, and the dominion of self is being broken and his sovereignty cast from our midst before our unseeing eyes. Christ is here, to be both crucified and crowned, in our nation and age, in this room and hour; and all the voices of want and woe, of discontent and social anger, of strike and war, join with the voices of sorrow and judgment, of faith and love, in warning us that we should get ready for the social baptism of the Holy Ghost and fire. Instead of dreaming of some dim and distant millennium, we had best find our divine place and work in the millennium that has begun, and lift up our eyes to behold the King who is here in his abiding kingdom and eternal kingship. This solemn and historic hour of our national destiny has its awful significance, as well as immovable ground of hope, in the fact that Christ is actually ruling and judging our nation, inspiring and leading the reviving political faith of the peole, while the political Sadducees are blindly and foolishly repeating that we have no king but the majority.

Great Men, Great Thoughts, and the Environment

William James

A remarkable parallel, which to my knowledge has never been noticed, obtains between the facts of social evolution and the mental growth of the race, on the one hand, and the zoological evolution, as expounded by Mr. Darwin, on the other.

It will be best to prepare the ground for my thesis by a few very general remarks on the methods of getting at scientific truth. It is a common platitude that a *complete* acquaintance with any one thing, however small, would require a knowledge of the entire universe. Not a sparrow falls to the ground but *some* of the remote conditions of his fall are to found in the milky way, in our federal constitution, or in the early history of Europe. That is to say, alter the milky way, alter the federal constitution, alter the facts of our barbarian ancestry, and the universe would be, *pro tanto*, a different universe from what it is. One fact involved in the difference might be that the particular little street boy who threw the stone which brought down the sparrow might not find himself opposite the sparrow at that particular moment; or, finding himself there, might not be in that particular serene and disengaged mood of mind which expressed itself in throwing the stone. But, true as all this is, it would be very foolish for any one who was inquiring the cause of the sparrow's fall to overlook the boy as too personal, proximate, and so to speak anthropomorphic an agent, and to say that the true cause is the federal constitution, the westward migration of the Celtic race, or the structure of the milky way. If we proceeded on that method, we might say with perfect legitimacy that a friend of ours, who had slipped on the ice upon his door-step and cracked his skull, some months after dining with thirteen at the table, died *because* of that ominous feast. I know, in fact, one such instance; and I might, if I chose, contend with perfect logical

William James, "Great Men, Great Thoughts, and the Environment," *Atlantic Monthly*, XLVI (October, 1880), 441–459.

propriety that the slip on the ice was no real accident. "There *are* no accidents," I might say, "for science. The whole history of the world converged to produce that slip. If anything had been left out, the slip would not have occurred just there and then. To say it would is to deny the relations of cause and effect throughout the universe. The real cause of the death was not the slip, *but the conditions which engendered the slip,* and among them his having sat at a table, six months previous, one among thirteen. *That* is truly the reason why he died within the year." It will soon be seen whose arguments I am, in form, reproducing here. I would fain lay down the truth simply and dogmatically in this paper, without polemics or recrimination. But unfortunately we never fully grasp the import of any true statement until we have a clear notion of what the opposite untrue statement would be. The error is needed to set off the truth, much as a dark background is required for exhibiting the brightness of a picture.

Now the error which I am going to use as a foil to set off what seems to me the truth of my own statements is contained in the statements of the so-called evolutionary philosophy of Mr. Herbert Spencer and his disciples. Our problem is, What are the causes that make communities change from generation to generation,—that make the England of Queen Anne so different from the England of Elizabeth, the Harvard College of to-day so different from that of thirty years ago?

I shall reply to this problem, The difference is due to the accumulated influences of individuals, of their examples, their initiatives, and their decisions. The Spencerian school replies, The changes go on irrespective of persons, and are independent of individual control. They are due to the environment, to the circumstances, the physical geography, the ancestral conditions, the increasing experience of outer relations; to everything, in fact, except the Grants and the Bismarcks, the Joneses and the Smiths.

Now I say that these theorizers are guilty of precisely the same fallacy as he who should ascribe the death of his friend to the dinner with thirteen, or the fall of the sparrow to the milky way. Like the dog in the fable that drops his real bone to snatch at its image, they drop the real causes to snatch at others, which from no possible human point of view are available or attainable. Their fallacy is a practical one. Let us see where it lies. Although I believe in free will myself, I will waive that belief in this discussion, and assume with the Spencerians the universal fatality of human actions. On that assumption I gladly allow that were the *intelligence* investigating the man's or the sparrow's death *omniscient* and *omnipresent,* able to take in the whole of time and space at a single glance, there would not be the slightest objection to the milky way or the fatal feast being invoked among the sought-for causes. Such a divine intelligence would see instantaneously all the infinite lines of convergence towards a given result, and it would, moreover, see *impartially*: it would see the fatal feast to be as much a condition of the sparrow's death as of the man's; it would see the boy with the stone to be as much a condition of the man's fall as of the sparrow's.

The human mind, however, is constituted on an entirely different plan. It has no such power of universal intuition. Its finiteness obliges it to see but two or three things at a time. If it wishes to take wider sweeps it has to use "general ideas," as they are called, and in so doing to drop all concrete truths. Thus, in the present case, if we as men wish to feel the connection between the milky way and the boy and the dinner and the sparrow and the man's death, we can do so only by falling back on the enormous emptiness of what is called an abstract proposition. We must say, All things in the world are fatally predetermined, and hang together in the adamantine fixity of a system of natural law. But in the vagueness of this vast proposition we have lost all the concrete facts and links. And in all practical matters the concrete links are the only things of importance. The human mind is *essentially* partial. It can be efficient at all only by *picking out* what to attend to, and ignoring everything else, —by narrowing its point of view. Otherwise, what little strength it has is dispersed, and it loses its way altogether. Man always wants his curiosity gratified for a particular purpose. If, in the case of the sparrow, the purpose is punishment, it would be idiotic to wander off from the cats, boys, and other possible agencies close by in the street, to survey the early Celts and the milky way. The boy would meanwhile escape. And if, in the case of the unfortunate man, we lose ourselves in contemplation of the thirteen-at-table mystery, and fail to notice the ice on the step and cover it with ashes, some other poor fellow, who never dined out in his life, may slip on it in coming to the door, and fall and break his head, too.

It is, then, a necessity laid upon us as human beings to limit our view. In mathematics we know how this method of ignoring and neglecting quantities lying outside of a certain range has been adopted in the differential calculus. The calculator throws out all the "infinitesimals" of the quantities he is considering. He treats them (under certain rules) as if they did not exist. In themselves they exist perfectly all the while; but they are as if they did not exist for the purposes of his calculations. Just so an astronomer, in dealing with the tidal movements of the ocean, takes no account of the waves made by the wind, or by the pressure of all the steamers which day and night are moving their thousands of tons upon its surface. Just so the marksman, in sighting his rifle, allows for the motion of wind, but not for the equally real motion of the earth and solar system. Just so a business man's punctuality may overlook an error of five minutes, whilst a physicist, measuring the velocity of light, must count each thousandth of a second.

There are, in short, *different cycles* of operation in nature; different departments, so to speak, relatively independent of one another, so that what goes on at any moment in one may be *compatible* with almost any condition of things at the same time in the next. The mold on the biscuits in the store-room of a man-of-war vegetates in absolute indifference to the nationality of the flag, the direction of the voyage, the weather, and the human dramas that may go on on board; and a mycologist may study it in complete abstraction from all these larger details. Only by so studying it, in fact, is there any chance of the mental concentration by which alone he may hope to learn something of its nature. And conversely, the captain who, in manœuvring the vessel through a naval battle, should think it necessary to bring the moldy biscuit into his calculations would very likely lose the battle by reason of the excessive "thoroughness" of his mental nature.

The causes which operate in these incommensurable cycles are connected with one another only *if we take the whole universe into account.* For all lesser points of view it is lawful—nay, more; it is for human wisdom necessary—to regard them as disconnected and irrelevant to one another.

And now this brings us nearer to our special topic. If we look at an animal or a human being distinguished from the rest of his kind by the possession of some extraordinary peculiarity, good or bad, we shall be able to discriminate between the causes which *maintain* it after it is produced. And we shall see, if the peculiarity be one that he was born with, that these two sets of causes belong to two such irrelevant cycles. It was the triumphant originality of Darwin to see this, and to act accordingly. Separating the causes of production under the title of "tendencies to spontaneous variation," and relegating them to a physiological cycle which he forthwith agreed to ignore altogether,* he confined his attention to the causes of preservation, and under the names of natural selection and sexual selection studied them exclusively as functions of the cycle of the environment.

Pre-Darwinian philosophers had also tried to establish the doctrine of descent with modification. But they all committed the blunder of clumping the two cycles of causation into one. What preserves an animal with his peculiarity, if it be a useful one, they saw to be the nature of the environments to which the peculiarity was adjusted. The giraffe with his peculiar neck is preserved by the fact that there are in his environment tall trees whose leaves he can digest. But these philosophers went further, and said that the presence of the trees not only maintained an

---

*Darwin's theory of paragenesis is, it is true, an attempt to account (among other things) for variation. But it occupies its own separate place, and its author no more invokes the environment when he talks of the adhesions of gemmules than he invokes these adhesions when he talks of the relations of the whole animal to the environment. *Divide et imperal*

animal with a long neck to browse upon their branches, but also produced him. . . . Now these changes, of which many more examples might be adduced, are at present distinguished by the special name of *adaptive* changes. Their peculiarity is that that very feature in the environment to which the animal's nature grows adjusted itself *produces* the adjustment. The "inner relation," to use Mr. Spencer's phrase, "corresponds" with its own efficient cause.

Darwin's first achievement was to show the utter insignificance in amount of these changes produced by direct adaptation, the immensely greater mass of changes being produced by internal molecular accidents, of which we know nothing. His next achievement was to define the true problem with which we have to deal when we study the effects of the visible environment on the animal. That problem is simply this: Is the environment more likely to *preserve or to destroy him,* on account of this or that peculiarity with which he may be born? In calling those peculiarities which an animal is born with "spontaneous" variations, Darwin does not for a moment mean to suggest that they are not the fixed outcome of natural law. If the total system of the universe be taken into account, the causes of these variations and the visible environment which preserves or destroys them undoubtedly do, in some remote and roundabout way, hang together. What Darwin means is that, since that environment is a perfectly known thing, and its relations to the organism in the way of destruction or preservation are tangible and distinct, it would utterly confuse our finite understandings and frustrate our hopes of science to mix in with it facts from such a disparate and incommensurable cycle as that in which the variations are produced. This last cycle is that of occurrences before the animal is born. It is the cycle of influences upon ova and embryos; in which lie the causes which tip them and tilt them towards masculinity and femininity, towards strength or weakness, towards health or disease, and towards divergence from the parent type. What are the causes there?

In the first place, they are molecular and invisible; inaccessible, therefore, to direct observation of any kind. Secondly, their operations are *compatible* with any social, political, and physical conditions of environment. The same parents, living in the same environing conditions, may at one birth produce a genius, at the next an idiot or a monster. The visible external conditions are therefore not direct determinants of this cycle; and the more we consider the matter, the more we are forced to believe that two children of the same parents are made to differ from one another by a cause which bears the same remote and infinitesimal proportion to its ultimate effects as the famous pebble on the Rocky Mountain crest, whose angle separates the course of two rain-drops, itself bears to the Gulf of St. Lawrence and to the Pacific Ocean. . . .

And this brings us at last to the heart of our subject. The causes of production of great men lie in a sphere wholly inaccessible to the social philosopher. He must simply accept geniuses as data, just as Darwin accepts his spontaneous variations. For him, as for Darwin, the only problem is, these data being given, How does the environment affect them, and how do they affect the environment? Now I affirm that the relations of the visible environment to the great man is in the main exactly what it is to the "variation" in the Darwinian philosophy. It chiefly adopts or rejects, preserves or destroys, in short *selects* him. And whenever it adopts and preserves the great man, it becomes modified by his influence in an entirely original and peculiar way. He acts as a ferment, and changes its constitution, just as the advent of a new zoological species changes the faunal and floral equilibrium of the region in which it appears. We all recollect Mr. Darwin's famous statement of the influence of cats on the growth of clover in their neighborhood. We all have read of the effects of the European rabbit in New Zealand, and we have many of us taken part in the controversy about the English sparrow here,—whether he kills most canker-worms, or drives away most native birds. Just so the great man, whether he be an importation from without, like Clive in India or Agassiz here, or whether he spring from the soil, like Mahomet or Franklin, brings about a rearrangement, on a large or a small scale, of the preexisting social relations.

The mutations of societies, then, from generation to generation, are in the main due directly or indirectly to the acts or the example of individuals whose genius was so adapted to the receptivities of the moment, or whose accidental position of authority was so critical, that they became ferments, initiators of movement, setters of precedent or fashion, centers of corruption, or destroyers of other persons, whose gifts, had they had free play, would have led society in another direction.

We see this power of individual initiative exemplified on a small scale all about us, and on a large scale in the case of the leaders of history. It is only following the common-sense method of a Lyell, a Darwin, and a Whitney to interpret the unknown by the known, and reckon up cumulatively the only causes of social change we can directly observe. Societies of men are just like individuals in that both at any given moment offer ambiguous potentialities of development. Whether a young man enters business or the ministry may depend on a decision which has to be made before a certain day. He takes the offered place in the counting-house, and is *committed*. Little by little, the habits, the knowledges, of the other career, which once lay so near, cease to be reckoned even among his possibilities. At first, he may sometimes doubt whether the self he murdered in that decisive hour might not have been the better of the two, but with the years such questions themselves expire, and the old alternative *ego*, once so vivid, fades into something less substantial than a dream. It is [not] otherwise with nations. They may be committed by

kings and ministers to peace or war, by generals to victory or defeat, by
prophets to this religion or to that, by various geniuses to fame in art,
science, or industry. A war is a true point of bifurcation of future possibilities. Whether it fail or succeed, its declaration must be the starting-
point of new policies. Just so does a revolution or any great civic precedent, become a deflecting influence, whose operations widen with the
course of time. Communities obey their ideals, and an accidental success
fixes an ideal, as an accidental failure blights it. . . .

The fermentative influence of geniuses *must* be admitted as, at any rate,
one factor in the changes that constitute social evolution. The community
may evolve in many ways. The accidental presence of this or that ferment
decides in which way it *shall* evolve. Why, the very birds of the forest,
the parrot, the mino, have the *power* of human speech, but never develop
it of themselves; some one must be there to teach them. So with us individuals. Rembrandt must teach us to enjoy the struggle of light with
darkness, Wagner to enjoy certain musical effects; Dickens gives a twist
to our sentimentality, Artemus Ward to our humor; Emerson kindles a
new moral light within us. But it is like Columbus's egg. "All can raise the
flowers now, for all have got the seed." But if this be true of the individuals in the community, how can it be false of the community as a
whole? If shown a certain way, a community may take it; if not, it will
never find it. And the ways are to a large extent indeterminate in advance. A nation may obey either of many alternative impulses given by
different men of genius, and still live and be prosperous, just as a man
may enter either of many businesses. Only the prosperities may differ in
their type.

But the indeterminism is not absolute. Not every "man" fits every
"hour." Some incompatibilities there are. A given genius may come either
too early or too late. Peter the Hermit would now be sent to a lunatic
asylum. John Mill in the tenth century would have lived and died unknown. Cromwell and Napoleon need their revolutions, Grant his civil
war. An Ajax gets no fame in the day of telescopic-sighted rifles; and, to
express differently an instance which Spencer uses, what could a Watt
have effected in a tribe which no precursive genius had taught to smelt
iron or to turn a lathe?

Now the important thing to notice is that what makes a certain genius
now incompatible with his surroundings is usually the fact that some previous genius of a different strain has warped the community away from
the sphere of his possible effectiveness. After Voltaire, no Peter the Hermit; after Charles IX. and Louis XIV., no general protestantization of
France; after a Manchester school, a Beaconsfield's success is transient;
after a Philip II., a Castelar makes little headway; and so on. Each bifurcation cuts off certain sides of the field altogether, and limits the future
possible angles of deflection. A community is a living thing, and, in words

which I can do no better than quote from Professor Clifford,* "it is the peculiarity of living things not merely that they change under the influence of surrounding circumstances but that any change which takes place in them is not lost but retained, and, as it were, built into the organism to serve as the foundation for future actions. If you cause any distortion in the growth of a tree and make it crooked, whatever you may do afterwards to make the tree straight the mark of your distortion is there; it is absolutely indelible; it has become part of the tree's nature. . . . Suppose, however, that you take a lump of gold, melt it, and let it cool. . . . No one can tell by examining a piece of gold how often it has been melted and cooled in geologic ages, or even in the last year by the hand of man. Any one who cuts down an oak can tell by the rings in its trunk how many times winter has frozen it into widowhood, and how many times summer has warmed it into life. A living being must always contain within itself the history, not merely of its own existence, but of all its ancestors." . . .

Thus social evolution is a resultant of the interaction of two wholly distinct factors: the individual, deriving his peculiar gifts from the play of physiological and infra-social forces, but bearing all the power of initiative and origination in his hands; and, second, the social environment, with its power of adopting or rejecting both him and his gifts. Both factors are essential to change. The community stagnates without the impulse of the individual. The impulse dies away without the sympathy of the community.

All this seems nothing more than common sense. . . . But there are never wanting minds to whom such views seem personal and contracted, and allied to an anthropomorphism long exploded in other fields of knowledge. "The individual withers, and the world is more and more," to these writers, and in a Buckle, a Draper, and a Taine we all know how much the "world" has come to be almost synonymous with the *climate*. We all know, too, how the controversy has been kept up between the partisans of a "science of history" and those who deny the existence of anything like necessary "laws" where human societies are concerned. Mr. Spencer, at the opening of his Study of Sociology, makes an onslaught on the "great-man theory" of history, from which a few passages may be quoted:—

"The genesis of societies by the action of great men may be comfortably believed so long as, resting in general notions, you do not ask for particulars. But now, if, dissatisfied with vagueness, we demand that our ideas shall be brought into focus and exactly defined, we discover the hypothesis to be utterly incoherent. If, not stopping at the explanation of social progress as due to the great man, we go back a step, and ask, Whence comes the great man? we find that the theory breaks down completely. The question has two conceivable answers: his origin is super-

* Lectures and Essays, vol. i., p. 82.

natural, or it is natural. Is his origin supernatural? Then he is a deputy god, and we have theocracy once removed,—or, rather, not removed at all. . . . Is this an unacceptable solution? Then the origin of the great man is natural; and immediately this is recognized he must be classed with all other phenomena in the society that gave him birth as a product of its antecedents. Along with the whole generation of which he forms a minute part, along with its institutions, language, knowledge, manners, and its multitudinous arts and appliances, he is a *resultant*. . . . You must admit that the genesis of the great man depends on the long series of complex influences which has produced the race in which he appears, and the social state into which that race has slowly grown. . . . Before he can remake his society, his society must make him. All those changes of which he is the proximate initiator have their chief causes in the generations he descended from. If there is to be anything like a real explanation of those changes, it must be sought in that aggregate of conditions out of which both he and they have arisen."*

Now it seems to me that there is something which one might almost call impudent in the attempt which Mr. Spencer makes, in the first sentence of this extract, to pin the reproach of vagueness upon those who believe in the power of initiative of the great man. . . .

The fact is that Mr. Spencer's sociological method is identical with that of one who would invoke the zodiac to account for the fall of the sparrow, and the thirteen at table to explain the gentleman's death. It is of little more scientific value than the Oriental method of replying to whatever question arises by the unimpeachable truism, "God is great." *Not* to fall back on the gods, where a proximate principle may be found, has with us Westerners long since become the sign of an efficient as distinguished from an inefficient intellect.

To believe that the cause of everything is to be found in its antecedents is the starting-point, the initial postulate, not the goal and consummation, of science. If she is simply to lead us out of the labyrinth by the same hole we went in by three or four thousand years ago, it seems hardly worth while to have followed her through the darkness at all. If anything is humanly certain it is that the great man's society, properly so called, does *not* make him before he can remake it. Physiological forces, with which the social, political, geographical, and to a great extent anthropological conditions have just as much and just as little to do as the conditions of the crater of Vesuvius has to do with the flickering of this gas by which I write, are what make him. Surely Mr. Spencer does not hold that the convergence of sociological pressures so impinged on Stratford-upon-Avon about the 26th of April, 1564, that a W. Shakespeare, with all his mental peculiarities, had to be born there,—as the pressure of water outside a certain boat will cause a stream of a certain form to ooze into a particular

* Study of Sociology, pages 33–35.

leak? And does he mean to say that if the aforesaid W. Shakespeare had died of cholera infantum, another mother at Stratford-upon-Avon would needs have engendered a duplicate copy of him, to restore the sociologic equilibrium,—just as the same stream of water will reappear, no matter how often you pass a sponge over the leak, so long as the outside level remains unchanged? Or might the substitute arise at "Stratford-atte-Bowe"? Here, as elsewhere, it is very hard, in the midst of Mr. Spencer's vagueness, to tell what he does mean at all. . . .

Sporadic great men come everywhere. But for a community to get vibrating through and through with intensely active life, many geniuses coming together and in rapid succession are required. This is why great epochs are so rare,—why the sudden bloom of a Greece, an early Rome, a Renaissance, is such a mystery. Blow must follow blow so fast that no cooling can occur in the intervals. Then the mass of the nation grows incandescent, and may continue to glow by pure inertia long after the originators of its internal movement have passed away. We often hear surprise expressed that in these high tides of human affairs not only the people should be filled with stronger life, but that individual geniuses should seem so exceptionally abundant. This mystery is just about as deep as the time-honored conundrum as to why great rivers flow by great towns. It is true that great public fermentations awaken and adopt many geniuses, who in more torpid times would have had no chance to work. But over and above this there must be an exceptional concourse of genius about a time, to make the fermentation begin at all. The unlikeliness of the *concourse* is far greater than the unlikeliness of any particular genius; hence the rarity of these periods and the exceptional aspect which they always wear.

I may be pardoned for taking so present and personal an example. I should like to use our own community as a means of illustrating my point. It seems to me that nothing proves so clearly the fact that no social community *need*, by virtue of its purely social forces, evolve fatally in the direction of its own most characteristic aptitudes. It is a commonplace remark that the intellectual preeminence which Boston so long held over other American cities is slowly passing away. Webster and Choate, Channing and Parker, Howe and Garrison, Prescott and Motley, Thoreau, Hawthorne, and Margaret Fuller, Jackson and Warren, Mann and Agassiz, are gathered to their fathers. Emerson and Holmes, Longfellow and Whittier, have passed their seventieth birthdays, and the new stars which are rising above the horizon are few in number, and hardly of the same order of magnitude with those which have sunk or are sinking to its verge. Meanwhile the "spirit of the people," which seconded so robustly the efforts of these great citizens, is utterly unchanged. There is probably nowhere in the world a more appreciative intelligence, a deeper capacity for enthusiasm, if only the proper object is revealed, or a truer eagerness to live hard and bear a hand in the heavy and heroic work of the world. No positive condition is present which could prevent Boston from becoming, if the means were given, as radiant a focus of human energy as any place of its size in the world. What positive condition is absent? Simply a fortuitous assemblage of great men happening to be born or to migrate there about the same time. Would a Spencerian evolutionist pretend that such an event is *incompatible* with the sociological condition in Boston at the present day? Surely not. With every allowance made for the growth of rival cities in the West, for increased attractiveness of New York as a literary and publishing centre, for the greater exhaustiveness of professional life at the present day, with the impossibility it brings of a professional man being also a man of letters, it still remains perfectly possible to conceive of three or four geniuses in any department being born here, and choosing to stay here and work. Three or four born here might easily attract the rest from outside, and the native temperament would fill in the background. As a matter of fact there is hardly a zoologist to-day in the country, of about the age of forty, who was not made a naturalist by the accidental fact of Agassiz settling in Boston, founding his museum in connection with the Lawrence Scientific School, and preaching with all the force of his magnetic personality the doctrine that to come there and study zoology was the only thing worthy the ambition of an intelligent youth.

It is folly, then to speak of the "laws of history" as of something inevitable, which science has only to discover, and which any one can then foretell and observe, but do nothing to alter or avert. Why, the very laws of physics are conditional, and deal with *ifs*. The physicist don't say, "The water *will* boil anyhow;" he only says it will boil *if* a fire be kindled beneath it. And so the utmost the student of sociology can ever predict is that *if* a genius of a certain sort show the way, society will be sure to follow. It might long ago have been predicted with great confidence that both Italy and Germany would reach a stable unity if some one could but succeed in starting the process. It could not have been predicted, however, that the *modus operandi* in each case would be subordination to a paramount state rather than federation, because no historian could have calculated the freaks of birth and fortune which gave at the same moment such positions of authority to three such peculiar individuals as Napoleon III., Bismarck, and Cavour. . . .

To conclude: The evolutionary view of history, when it denies the vital importance of individual initiative, is, then, an utterly vague and unscientific conception, a lapse from modern scientific determinism into the most ancient Oriental fatalism. The lesson of the analysis that we have made (even on the completely deterministic hypothesis with which we started) forms an appeal of the most stimulating sort to the energy of the individual. Even the dogged resistance of the reactionary conservative to changes which he cannot hope entirely to defeat is justified and shown to be effective. He retards the movement; deflects it a little by the concessions he extracts; gives it a resultant momentum, compounded of his inertia and his adversaries' speed; and keeps up, in short, a constant lateral pressure, which, to be sure, never heads it round about, but brings it up at last at a goal far to the right or left of that to which it would have drifted had he allowed it to drift alone.

I now pass to the last division of my subject, the function of the environment in *mental* evolution. After what has already been said, I may be quite concise. Here, if anywhere, it would seem at first sight as if that school must be right which makes the mind passively plastic, and the outer relations actively productive of the form and order of its conceptions; which, in a word, thinks that all mental progress must result from a series of *adaptive* changes, in the sense already defined. We all know what an immense part of our mental furniture consists of purely remembered, not reasoned, experience. The entire field of habit and association by contiguity belongs here. The entire field of those abstract conceptions which have been taught us with the language into which we were born belongs here also. And, more than this, there is reason to think that the order of "outer relations" experienced by the individual may itself determine the order in which the general characters imbedded therein shall be noticed and extracted by his mind. The pleasures and benefits, moreover, which certain parts of the environment yield, and the pains and hurts which other parts inflict, determine the direction of our interest and our attention, and so decide at which points the accumulation of mental experiences shall begin. It might, accordingly, seem as if there was no room for any other agency than this; as if the distinction we have hitherto found so useful between the agency of "spontaneous variation," as the producer of changed forms, and the environment, as their preserver and destroyer, did not hold in the case of mental progress; as if, in a word, the parallel with Darwinism might no longer obtain, and Spencer might be quite right with his fundamental law of intelligence, which says, "The cohesion between psychical states is proportionate to the frequency with which the relation between the answering external phenomena has been repeated in experience."

But, in spite of all these facts, I have no hesitation whatever in holding firm to the Darwinian distinction even here. I maintain that the facts in question are all drawn from the lower strata of the mind, so to speak,—from the sphere of its least evolved functions, from the region of intelligence which man possesses in common with the brutes. And I can easily show that throughout the whole extent of those mental departments which are highest, which are most characteristically human, Spencer's law is violated at every step; and that, as a matter of fact, the new conceptions, emotions, and active tendencies which evolve are originally *pro-*

duced in the shape of random images, fancies, accidental outbirths of spontaneous variation in the functional activity of the excessively unstable human brain, which the outer environment simply confirms or refutes, adopts or rejects, preserves or destroys,—*selects*, in short, just as it selects morphological and social variations due to molecular accidents of an analogous sort.

It is one of the tritest of truisms that human intelligences of a simple order are very literal. They are slaves of habit, doing what they have been taught without variation; dry, prosaic, and matter of fact in their remarks; devoid of humor, except of the coarse physical kind which rejoices in a practical joke; taking the world for granted; and possessing in their faithfulness and honesty the single gift by which they are sometimes able to warm us into admiration. But even this faithfulness seems to have a sort of inorganic ring, and to remind us more of the immutable properties of a piece of inanimate matter than of the steadfastness of a human will capable of alternative choice. When we descend to the brutes, all these peculiarities are intensified. No reader of Schopenhauer can forget his frequent allusions to the *trockener Ernst* of dogs and horses, nor to their *Ehrlichkeit*. And every noticer of their ways must receive a deep impression of the fatally literal character of the few, simple, and treadmill-like operations of their minds.

But turn to the highest order of minds, and what a change! Instead of thoughts of concrete things patiently following one another in a beaten track of habitual suggestion, we have the most abrupt cross-cuts and transitions from one idea to another, the most rarefied abstractions and discriminations, the most unheard-of combinations of elements, the subtlest associations of analogy; in a word, we seem suddenly introduced into a seething caldron of ideas, where everything is fizzling and bobbing about in a state of bewildering activity, where partnerships can be joined or loosened in an instant, treadmill routine is unknown, and the unexpected seems the only law. According to the idiosyncrasy of the individual, the scintillations will have one character or another. They will be sallies of wit and humor; they will be flashes of poetry and eloquence; they will be constructions of dramatic fiction or of mechanical device, logical or philosophic abstractions, business projects, or scientific hypotheses, with trains of experimental consequences based thereon; they will be musical sounds, or images of plastic beauty or picturesqueness, or visions of moral harmony. But, whatever their differences may be, they will all agree in this,—that their genesis is sudden and, as it were, spontaneous. That is to say, the same premises would not, in the mind of another individual, have engendered just that conclusion; although, when the conclusion is offered to the other individual, he may thoroughly accept and enjoy it, and envy the brilliancy of him to whom it first occurred.

To Professor Jevons is due the great credit of having emphatically

pointed out* how the genius of discovery depends altogether on the number of these random notions and guesses which visit the investigator's
mind. To be fertile in hypotheses is the first requisite, and to be willing to
throw them away the moment experience contradicts them is the next.
The Baconian method of collating tables of instances may be a useful aid
at certain times. But one might as well expect a chemist's note-book to
write down the name of the body analyzed, or a weather table to sum
itself up into a prediction of probabilities, of its own accord, as to hope
that the mere fact of mental confrontation with a certain series of facts
will be sufficient to make *any* brain conceive their law. The conception of
the law is a spontaneous variation in the strictest sense of the term. It
flashes out of one brain, and no other, because the instability of that brain
is such as to tip and upset itself in just that particular direction. But the
important thing to notice is that the good flashes and the bad flashes, the
triumphant hypotheses and the absurd conceits, are on an exact equality
in respect to their origin. Aristotle's Physics and Aristotle's Logic flow
from one spring. The forces that produce the one produce the other.
When walking along the street, thinking of the blue sky or the fine spring
weather, I may either smile at some preposterously grotesque whim
which occurs to me, or I may suddenly catch an intuition of the solution
of a long-unsolved problem, which at that moment was far from my
thoughts. Both notions are shaken out of the same reservoir,—the reservoir
of a brain in which the reproduction of images in the relations of their
outward persistence or frequency has long ceased to be the dominant law.
But to the thought, when it is once engendered, the consecration of agreement with outward persistence and importance may come. The grotesque
conceit perishes in a moment, and is forgotten. The scientific hypothesis
arouses in me a fever of desire for verification. I read, write, experiment,
consult experts. Everything corroborates my notion, which being then
published in a book spreads from review to review and from mouth to
mouth, till at last there is no doubt I am enshrined in the Pantheon of the
great diviners of nature's ways. The environment *preserves* the conception which it was unable to *produce* in any brain less idiosyncratic than
my own. . . .

The plain truth is that the "philosophy" of evolution (as distinguished
from our special information about particular cases of change) is a metaphysic creed, and nothing else. It is a mood of contemplation, an emotional attitude, rather than a system of thought; a mood which is old as
the world, and which no refutation of any one incarnation of it (such as
the Spencerian philosophy) will dispel; the mood of fatalistic pantheism,
with its intuition of the One and All, which was, and is, and ever shall be,
and from whose womb each single thing proceeds. Far be it from us to
speak slightingly here of so hoary and mighty a style of looking on the

* In his Principles of Science, chapters xi., xii., xxvi.

world as this. What we at present call scientific discoveries had nothing to do with bringing it to birth, nor can one easily conceive that they should ever give it its *quietus,* no matter how logically incompatible with its spirit the ultimate phenomenal distinctions which science accumulates should turn out to be. It can laugh at the phenomenal distinctions on which science is based, for it draws its vital breath from a region which—whether above or below—is at least altogether different from that in which science dwells. A critic, however, who cannot disprove the truth of the metaphysic creed, can at least raise his voice in protest against its disguising itself in "scientific" plumes. I think that all who have had the patience to follow me thus far will agree that the Spencerian "philosophy" of social and intellectual progress is an obsolete anachronism, reverting to a pre-Darwinian type of thought, just as the Spencerian philosophy of "force," effacing all the previous phenomenal distinctions between *vis viva,* potential energy, momentum, work, force, mass, etc., which physicists have with so much agony achieved, carries us back to a pre-Galilean age.

Bibliography

POLITICAL HISTORY

If we agree to begin our period in 1877 the book with which to start the political history of the post-Reconstruction period is C. Vann Woodward, *Reunion and Reaction: The Compromise of 1877 and the End of Reconstruction* (1951). Still the most exciting and most general book on the politics of the period is Matthew Josephson, *The Politicos, 1865–1896* (1938), but it must be supplemented by the work of more recent scholarship. Leonard D. White, *The Republican Era, 1869–1901: A Study in Administrative History* (1958), the conclusion of the author's four-volume history of administration, also discusses civil service reform and conflicts between executive and legislative branches of the government. As efforts toward reform bulked so large in the political history of the period, they have, of course, captured the attention of historians as well. Russell B. Nye, *Midwestern Progressive Politics: A Historical Study of Its Origin and Development, 1870–1950* (1951), sees the issues of the day largely as the reformers saw them, as does Eric Goldman, *Rendezvous with Destiny:*

A History of Modern American Reform (1953). More subtle and interpretive is Richard Hofstadter, *The Age of Reform: From Bryan to F.D.R.* (1955). A salutary caution against the latter-day attempt to make the Populists responsible for everything from isolationism to McCarthyism is the article by C. Vann Woodward, "The Populist Heritage and the Intellectual," *The American Scholar* (Winter, 1959–1960). The standard work on the farmers' movement of the 1890's is John D. Hicks, *The Populist Revolt* (reprinted 1955), but it should be read in the light of more recent works: Carl C. Taylor, *The Farmers' Movement, 1620–1920* (1953); Murray S. Stedman, Jr., and Susan W. Stedman, *Discontent at the Polls: A Study of Farmer and Labor Parties, 1827–1948* (1950); and Chester McArthur Destler, *American Radicalism, 1865–1901: Essays and Documents* (1946), for example. In the borderland between politics and economic policy, see Hans Birger Thorelli, *The Federal Antitrust Policy: Origination of an American Tradition* (1955); Lee Benson, *Merchants, Farmers, and Railroads* (1955); and Sidney Fine, *Laissez Faire and the General-Welfare State: A Study of Conflict in American Thought, 1865–1901* (1956).

Useful correctives to some of the grand generalizations based on national political events may be found in some of the local and regional histories. Much the most exciting of these is C. Vann Woodward, *Origins of the New South, 1877–1913* (1951); but also very much to the point are Albert D. Kirwan, *Revolt of the Rednecks: Mississippi Politics, 1876–1925* (1951), and Allen Johnston Going, *Bourbon Democracy in Alabama, 1874–1890* (1951) for the South; and Horace S. Merrill, *Bourbon Democracy of the Middle West, 1865–1896* (1953), and Howard Roberts Lamar, *Dakota Territory, 1861–1889: A Study of Frontier Politics* (1956), for the Middle West.

Among the interesting political biographies are Blair Bolles, *Tyrant from Illinois: Uncle Joe Cannon's Experiment with Personal Power* (1951); Allan Nevins, *Grover Cleveland: A Study in Courage* (1932); C. Vann Woodward, *Tom Watson, Agrarian Rebel* (1938); and Francis B. Simkins, *Pitchfork Ben Tillman, South Carolinian* (1944).

ECONOMIC AND SOCIAL HISTORY

Recent works in the field of economic and social history have been more productive of revaluations of earlier views than have books in political history. An excellent brief synthesis of much of this recent work can be found in Samuel P. Hays, *The Response to Industrialism, 1885–1914* (1957). Fred A. Shannon, *The Farmer's Last Frontier* (1945), is still the most comprehensive economic history of agriculture, but more recent specialized work has resulted in some decisive changes in interpretation. See, for example, Allan G. Bogue, *Money at Interest: The Farm*

Mortgage on the Middle Border (1955), and R. M. Wik, *Steam Power on the American Farm* (1953). Edward C. Kirkland, *Industry Comes of Age: Business, Labor, and Public Policy, 1860–1897* (1961), is the most recent general survey of industrial development during the period and much the most sophisticated book on the subject. An older pioneering effort to weave together the strands of economic, social, and intellectual history is Thomas C. Cochran and William Miller, *The Age of Enterprise: A Social History of Industrial America* (1949). Kirkland and Cochran have also written major works in the field of railroad history: *Men, Cities and Transportation: A Study in New England History, 1820–1900*, 2 vols. (1948), and *Railroad Leaders, 1845–1890: The Business Mind in Action* (1953), respectively. George Rogers Taylor and Irene Neu, in *The American Railroad Network, 1861–1890* (1956), have given us the most complete account of the physical integration of the railway network. Recent reappraisals of the businessman, not all of them entirely convincing, have made the robber baron of an earlier age into an industrial statesman. The best example of the earlier tradition is Matthew Josephson, *The Robber Barons: The Great American Capitalists, 1861–1901* (1934); foremost exponents of the newer view are Allan Nevins, *John D. Rockefeller: The Heroic Age of American Business*, 2 vols. (1940), and its 1953 revision, *Study in Power: John D. Rockefeller, Industrialist and Philanthropist*, 2 vols., and Julius Grodinsky, *Jay Gould: His Business Career, 1867–1892* (1947). There has been a great spate of corporate and industrial histories in recent years; among others the following are notable: Warren C. Scoville, *Revolution in Glassmaking: Entrepreneurship and Technological Change in the American Industry, 1880–1920* (1948); Harold C. Passer, *The Electrical Manufacturers, 1857–1900: A Study in Competition, Entrepreneurship, Technical Change, and Economic Growth* (1953); Oscar E. Anderson, *Refrigeration in America: A History of a New Technology and Its Impact* (1953); and Ralph W. and Muriel E. Hidy, *Pioneering in Big Business, 1882–1911* (1955), the first volume of a general history of the Standard Oil Company. On economic thought, see Edward C. Kirkland, *Dream and Thought in the Business Community, 1860–1900* (1956), and the third volume of Joseph Dorfman's *The Economic Mind in American Civilization, 1865–1918* (1949). An important work is H. J. Habakkuk, *American and British Technology in the Nineteenth Century* (1952). On the subject of business rationalization, see the important article by Leland H. Jenks, "Early Phases of the Management Movement," *Administrative Science Quarterly* (1960), and the work of Alfred D. Chandler, Jr.: "The Beginnings of Big Business in American Industry," *Business History Review* (1959), and *Henry Varnum Poor: Business-Editor, Analyst and Reformer* (1956).

Two early works on the history of the labor movement are still indispensable: John R. Commons *et al.*, *History of Labour in the United*

States, 4 vols. (1918–1935), and Norman J. Ware, *The Labor Movement in the United States, 1860–1895: A Study in Democracy* (1929). The Commons point of view is criticized in Lloyd Ulman, *The Rise of the National Trade Union: The Development and Significance of Its Structure, Governing Institutions, and Economic Policies* (1955). Gerald N. Grob, *Workers and Utopia: A Study of Ideological Conflict in the American Labor Movement, 1865–1900* (1961), is an interesting discussion of the conflict between the Knights of Labor and the American Federation of Labor. A number of recent studies begin to throw long-needed light on the relation between immigration and industrial development. See, for example, Rowland Berthoff, *British Immigrants in Industrial America, 1790–1950* (1953); Charlotte Erickson, *American Industry and the European Immigrant, 1860–1885* (1957); and C. K. Yearley, *Britons in American Labor. A History of the Influence of the United Kingdom Immigrants on American Labor, 1820–1914* (1957).

Slums, urban reform, immigration, and labor disputes are intertwined in the history books as they were in life itself, and a number of recent works lay bare their relation. Arthur Mann, *Yankee Reformers in the Urban Age* (1954), and Ray Ginger, *Altgeld's America: The Lincoln Ideal Versus Changing Realities* (1958), are cases in point. Oscar Handlin, *The Uprooted* (1951), has quickly found its place as one of the most impressive pieces of recent historical writing; it should be read with John Higham, *Strangers in the Land: Patterns of American Nativism, 1860–1925* (1955), an analysis of the dynamics of American nativism. Now thirty years old, Arthur M. Schlesinger's *The Rise of the City 1878–1898* (1933) is still a mine of information. Two excellent works on New York city are James Ford *et al.*, *Slums and Housing with Special Reference to New York City: History, Conditions, Policy*, 2 vols. (1936), and Gordon Atkins, *Health, Housing, and Poverty in New York City, 1865–1898* (1947). More recent and more general is Robert H. Bremner, *From the Depths: The Discovery of Poverty in the United States* (1956).

The increasing importance of the Negro on the contemporary scene has been paralleled by his rediscovery in the histories. Of a large number of books, the three following are indispensable: Rayford W. Logan, *The Negro in American Life and Thought: The Nadir, 1877–1901* (1954); Benjamin Quarles, *Frederick Douglass* (1948); and C. Vann Woodward, *The Strange Career of Jim Crow* (2d ed., 1957).

INTELLECTUAL HISTORY

Perhaps the most useful studies of the impact of evolution on American thought are Richard Hofstadter, *Social Darwinism in American Thought* (rev. ed., 1955); Stow Persons (ed.), *Evolutionary Thought in America* (1950); Philip P. Wiener, *Evolution and the Founders of Pragmatism*

(1949); and Bert James Loewenberg, "Darwinism Comes to America," *Mississippi Valley Historical Review* (1941). The main outlines of the impact of industrialism on religious thought can be found in Henry F. May, *Protestant Churches and Industrial America* (1949), and Charles H. Hopkins, *The Rise of the Social Gospel in American Protestantism, 1865–1915* (1940). Two older works by Merle Curti, *Growth of American Thought* (rev. ed., 1951) and *The Social Ideas of American Educators* (1935), are excellent surveys, but the latter should be supplemented with Richard Hofstadter and Walter P. Metzger, *The Development of Academic Freedom in the United States* (1955). Two books by Morton G. White, *Social Thought in America: The Revolt Against Formalism* (rev. ed., 1957) and (with Lucia White) *The Intellectual Versus the City: From Thomas Jefferson to Frank Lloyd Wright* (1962), contain chapters that are essential for an understanding of the period.

FOREIGN POLICY

The history of American foreign policy between the end of the Civil War and the outbreak of the Spanish-American War has not in recent years been as thoroughly rewritten as have other aspects of our history. Of older works, Albert K. Weinberg, *Manifest Destiny* (1935), and Julius W. Pratt, *Expansionists of 1898: The Acquisition of Hawaii and the Spanish Islands* (1936), deal with problems discussed in the text of this book. Fred H. Harrington, "The Anti-Imperialist Movement in the United States, 1898–1900," *Mississippi Valley Historical Review* (1935), and Merle Curti, *Peace or War: The American Struggle* (1936), deal with opposition to a "larger" policy.

There is, of course, no substitute for going to the sources. The testimony before the United States Industrial Commission, for example, or the articles in the *Arena,* or the reports of the various state labor commissions, or the speeches and articles printed in the *Transactions of the American Society of Mechanical Engineers* contain rich veins of little-used material. A useful guide to these sources can be found in Oscar Handlin *et al., The Harvard Guide to American History* (1954).

FA